Public Law

DIRECTIONS

2nd Edition

ANNE DENNETT

Senior Lecturer, University of Lincoln

D1330154

LND

DEN

OXFORD

UNIVERSITY PRESS

OXFORD
UNIVERSITY PRESS

Great Clarendon Street, Oxford, OX2 6DP,
United Kingdom

Oxford University Press is a department of the University of Oxford.
It furthers the University's objective of excellence in research, scholarship,
and education by publishing worldwide. Oxford is a registered trade mark of
Oxford University Press in the UK and in certain other countries

© Oxford University Press 2021

The moral rights of the author have been asserted

First edition 2019

Impression: 1

All rights reserved. No part of this publication may be reproduced, stored in
a retrieval system, or transmitted, in any form or by any means, without the
prior permission in writing of Oxford University Press, or as expressly permitted
by law, by licence or under terms agreed with the appropriate reprographics
rights organization. Enquiries concerning reproduction outside the scope of the
above should be sent to the Rights Department, Oxford University Press, at the
address above

You must not circulate this work in any other form
and you must impose this same condition on any acquirer

Public sector information reproduced under Open Government Licence v3.0
(http://www.nationalarchives.gov.uk/doc/open-government-licence/open-government-licence.htm)

Published in the United States of America by Oxford University Press
198 Madison Avenue, New York, NY 10016, United States of America

British Library Cataloguing in Publication Data
Data available

Library of Congress Control Number: 2021937977

ISBN 978–0–19–887057–9

Printed in Great Britain by
Bell & Bain Ltd., Glasgow

Links to third party websites are provided by Oxford in good faith and
for information only. Oxford disclaims any responsibility for the materials
contained in any third party website referenced in this work.

To Christopher
and
in memory of my parents

Preface

I remember reading a while ago a comment by Lady Hale when she was giving evidence to the Select Committee on the Constitution in 2019: 'There is a lot more public law about'. This has certainly been true of the last two years.

Public Law changes rapidly but rarely more so than since the first edition of this book was published. Brexit has completed its arduous process; after several delays to exit day, the UK has left the EU, negotiated a future relationship agreement, and completed the transition period, cutting legal and political ties that were almost 50 years old. The statute book has acquired new Brexit-related laws; domestic law has acquired a new category of retained EU law. The calling of an election in December 2019 raised a question mark over the future of the Fixed-term Parliaments Act 2011 and a draft Fixed-term Parliaments Act 2011 (Repeal) Bill was published in December 2020. There have, of course, been a number of significant Supreme Court decisions during this time, notably its strong support for constitutional principle in the *Miller/Cherry* case. And on top of all this, there has been the unique and unforeseen impact of the COVID-19 pandemic, with unprecedented lockdown restrictions, and the development of a new body of coronavirus law in the public arena.

The new edition includes a separate chapter on Brexit, an expanded chapter on the grounds of judicial review, and online resources on coronavirus law. As with the first edition of *Public Law Directions*, I have tried to explain and analyse the law in an accessible way, setting out the essential principles and how they are applied to help understanding of the key framework of a topic, then building in more detail and analysis through features such as close-up focus boxes and examples illustrating the real life relevance of a topic. The reader can then explore links to other sources that appear both in the text and at the end of chapters.

I would like to thank the editorial and production team at Oxford University Press, particularly Emily Cunningham for her much appreciated patience, support, and guidance. I am indebted, as always, to the anonymous reviewers for their helpful and constructive comments and suggestions on the first edition.

The law is stated as at October 2020, except for Chapters 5 and 19 where the law is stated as at January 2021.

Anne Dennett
Lincoln
1st February 2021

New to this edition

- Fully updated to cover the latest developments in public law, including the impact of the *Miller/Cherry* case and its significance for constitutional principles, the response to the coronavirus pandemic, and potential constitutional reform in the future.

- Chapter 4 contains recent developments on devolution, including the *Scottish Continuity Bill case*.

- A new chapter considers the pre- and post-Brexit legal landscape, as well as the process of withdrawing from the EU, and includes discussion of the impact of Brexit on the devolved administrations.

- Analysis of the significant decision in *R (Privacy International) v Investigatory Powers Tribunal* [2019] UKSC 22 in relation to the rule of law and ouster clauses.

- Discusses issues arising from coronavirus legislation particularly the Coronavirus Act 2020 and the use of secondary legislation to implement restrictions.

- A revised chapter on the legislature examines membership, privileges, and standards in the House of Commons and House of Lords.

- Analysis of the *Miller/Cherry* case across a range of topics especially in relation to prerogative powers.

- Recent significant judicial review cases are discussed, including *R (Privacy International) v Investigatory Powers Tribunal* (2019), *R (Palestine Solidarity Campaign Ltd) v Secretary of State for Housing, Communities and Local Government* (2020), *R (Plan B Earth) v Secretary of State for Transport* (2020), *Secretary of State for Work and Pensions v Johnson* (2020), *Elgizouli v Secretary of State for the Home Department* (2020), and *In the matter of an application by Geraldine Finucane for Judicial Review (Northern Ireland)* (2019).

- The chapter on police powers has been updated to include recent cases including *Catt v UK* (2019), *Beghal v UK* (2019), *Gaughran v UK* (2020), *R (Edward Bridges) v Chief Constable of South Wales* (2020), and *R (Jones & Others) v Metropolitan Police Commissioner* (2019).

Late news

Public law continues to move at pace. In December 2020, the government launched an Independent Human Rights Act Review to examine the operation of the Act and whether changes are needed. Its terms of reference require it to consider the relationship between UK courts and the European Court of Human Rights, and how the Act balances the relationship between the judiciary, executive and legislature. The review is due to report later in 2021. See https://www.gov.uk/guidance/independent-human-rights-act-review.

The Supreme Court handed down judgment in the *Plan B Earth* case in December 2020 (*R (Friends of the Earth Ltd and others) v Heathrow Airport Ltd* [2020] UKSC 52; see section 16.3.3.2 of this book). It reversed the Court of Appeal's decision, holding that the Secretary of State had acted rationally and lawfully in relation to the range of climate change issues that he was required to consider when drawing up the government policy statement about the third runway at Heathrow Airport. Citing the three categories of consideration set out by Simon Brown LJ in *R v Somerset County Council, ex p Fewings* [1995] 1 WLR 1037 at 1049, the Supreme Court saw this case as falling within the third category: those matters 'to which the decision-maker may have regard if in his judgment and discretion he thinks it right to do so' [116]. The Supreme Court subdivided this into two types of case, one of which is where a decision-maker turns their mind to a consideration, but decides to give it no weight [120–121]. As long as that decision is not irrational, this is a matter within the decision-maker's discretion and they can lawfully decide to give it no weight [121].

The Court took the view that the Secretary of State did take the Paris Agreement into account and gave weight to it [125, 129] and it was within his discretion to decide that it was not necessary to give it further weight in the government policy statement [126, 129]. The Court also decided that the government's commitment to the Paris Agreement on climate change did not constitute government policy in the sense referred to in section 5(8) Planning Act 2008 because it was not 'a formal written statement of established policy' or at the least, 'clear, unambiguous and devoid of relevant qualification' [106]. The government was still developing how to implement the Paris Agreement commitments domestically.

The Supreme Court's decision in the Shamima Begum case (*R (Begum) v Special Immigration Appeals Commission* [2021] UKSC 7) turned in large part on separation of powers and deference issues on matters involving national security. The Home Secretary had decided to deprive Ms Begum of British citizenship and refused her leave to enter the UK. Upholding the Home Secretary's decisions, the Supreme Court stated that the Court of Appeal had not given the Home Secretary's assessment the respect it deserved [134] and the right to a fair hearing does not automatically prevail over issues of national security and public safety [135].

The Police, Crime, Sentencing and Courts Bill 2021, which was introduced into the House of Commons in March 2021, has proved to be controversial. Amongst many other measures, it aims to make changes to the Public Order Act 1986 by allowing the police to impose a broader range of conditions on assemblies, similar to those which currently apply to processions; giving the police power to impose conditions on both assemblies and processions such as setting noise limits; imposing conditions on one-person protests; and changing the offence of breaching conditions to include where a person knows or *ought to have known* that the condition has been imposed. The Bill itself has provoked protests in the UK. At the time of writing in May 2021, the Bill was currently at Committee stage in the House of Commons. For further information about the Bill, see https://www.gov.uk/government/publications/police-crime-sentencing-and-courts-bill-2021-factsheets/police-crime-sentencing-and-courts-bill-2021-protest-powers-factsheet.

I am grateful to the production team for allowing me to add this late news section.

Guide to using the book

Public Law Directions is enriched with a range of features designed to help support and reinforce your learning. This guided tour shows you how to fully utilise your textbook and get the most out of your study.

Learning objectives

These serve as a helpful signpost to what you can expect to learn by reading the chapter.

> **LEARNING OBJECTIVES**
>
> **By the end of this chapter, you should be able to:**
>
> ● Discuss why Parliament needs to scrutinise the government and t dures it uses to achieve this
>
> ● Evaluate the strengths and weaknesses of those procedures

Close-up focus

We encounter real examples of public law every day, whether we recognise them or not. In each chapter you will find everyday scenarios illustrating how public law applied to real life situations.

> **🔍 CLOSE-UP FOCUS: LAW AND POLICY**
>
> Law evolves from policy, which Parliament is uniquely equipped to decide. L distinguished issues of 'macro-policy', which affect the general public and ar policy-makers, from cases involving the application of policy to individuals, wl resolved by judges with 'no offence to the claims of democratic power' (*R v S State for Education and Employment, ex parte Begbie* [1999] EWCA Civ 2100 [8

Case close-up

Summaries of key cases are clearly highlighted for ease of reference and to develop your understanding.

> **🔍 CASE CLOSE-UP: *COUNCIL OF CIVIL SERVICE UN MINISTER FOR THE CIVIL SERVICE* [1985] AC 374**
>
> Here, Mrs Thatcher, then Prime Minister, exercised the prerogative power of man the Civil Service. Acting under the Civil Service Order in Council 1982, made unde prerogative, which authorised her to give instructions about the conduct and co service of civil servants who are employed at the Crown's pleasure, she decided that c

Diagrams and flowcharts

Numerous diagrams and flowcharts illustrate this book, providing a visual representation of concepts and processes. Use these in conjunction with the text to gain a clear understanding of even the most complex areas.

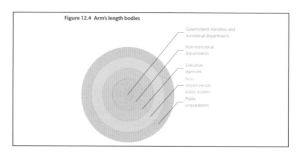

Figure 12.4 Arm's length bodies

Statute boxes

Relevant provisions are set out and clearly explained in the text.

> **📖 STATUTE: THE CONSTITUTIONAL REFORM ACT 2(AND JUDICIAL INDEPENDENCE**
>
> Section 1 upholds the rule of law. Judicial independence is now guaranteed b the first time it has been protected by statute (this provision was added as a r 2004 concordat (agreement) between Lord Woolf and Lord Falconer).

Definition boxes

Key terms are clearly and concisely explained in definition boxes.

> **Definition**
> Devolution is power given on loan by a central authority to subordinate bodies. See section 3.1.3 and Chapter 4

3.1.1.2 Judges and the UK constitution

As the UK lacks a codified constitution with the status of higher law, there is no constitutic court with the power to review and strike down unconstitutional legislation passed by the

Thinking points

Thinking points allow you to pause and reflect on what you are reading. They give you the opportunity to form your own views and provide valuable practice in critical thinking.

 THINKING POINT

What are your impressions of the EVEL procedure?

It is important not to overlook the fact that despite EVEL, *all* legislation st the consent of *all* MPs in the House of Commons. MPs from across the UK opportunities to debate, amend, and vote on legislation for England o

Cross-references

Clearly marked cross-references ensure the book is easy to navigate, pin-pointing particular sections where related themes or cases are covered.

 CROSS REFERENCE
See section 11.1 for more details of how Parliament holds the government to account generally

Opportunities to require ministers to account and e statements to the House, written ministerial statem tions, giving evidence before select committees, and

In 1997 the House of Commons agreed a resolutio clear that ministers who knowingly mislead Parliam March 1997, Vol 292 col 1047). This is now contain inadvertently misleading Parliament can lead to resig

Chapter summaries

The central points and concepts covered in each chapter are condensed into useful summaries. These provide a mechanism for you to reinforce your understanding and can be a helpful revision tool.

 SUMMARY

Parliament scrutinises government through ministerial and Prime Minister's qu bates, and select committees. In his retirement letter in 2014, Sir Robert Roge of the House of Commons, recognised that the House was 'a more effective s the executive . . . than I have ever known it' (old.parliament.uk/documents chief-executive/2014-04-29-RJR-to-Mr-Speaker-(signed).pdf)

End of chapter questions

A selection of questions is provided at the end of each chapter with answer guidance available online. These will help you to recognise any gaps in your understanding.

 Questions

Self-test questions

1. Explain why parliamentary scrutiny of the government is import

2. Outline the three main ways in which scrutiny takes place. Are

The bigger picture

Further information, study suggestions, and additional cases are provided to help you build upon your knowledge of public law and prepare for assessments and examinations.

 THE BIGGER PICTURE

Crichel Down prompted Sir David Maxwell Fyfe, the Home Secretary, to se categories of accountability of ministers for their civil servants. You can fi Constitution Committee, *The Accountability of Civil Servants* [4] Box 1; and July 1954, Vol 530 cols 1285–1287. See also Richard A. Chapman, 'Crichel D ited' (1987) 65(3) Public Administration 339–347.

Further reading

Selected further reading is included at the end of each chapter to provide a springboard for further study. These suggestions help you take your learning further and provide a guide to some of the key academic literature in the field.

Further reading

Books

Horne, A. and Le Sueur, A. (eds), *Parliament: Legislation and A* and Portland, Oregon: Hart Publishing 2016).
Analyses Parliament's two key functions

Guide to the online resources

The online resources that accompany this book provide students with ready-to-use learning resources. The resources are intended to be used alongside the book and are designed to maximise the learning experience.

 www.oup.com/he/dennett2e

Multiple-choice questions

A selection of multiple-choice questions, arranged by chapter, allows you to quickly assess your knowledge of the various topics in public law.

Answers to the self-test questions

Answers to the self-test questions included at the end of each chapter allow you to check that you have correctly understood the key points.

Guidance on answering end-of-chapter exam questions

Advice is given on answering the example exam questions to help you develop essential skills in analysing problems and constructing well-balanced arguments.

Web links

A selection of annotated web links chosen by the author allows you to easily research those topics that are of particular interest to you.

Updates to the law

An indispensable resource providing access to recent cases and developments in the law that have occurred since publication of the book.

Flowcharts

Flowcharts with audio explain key concepts in public law and provide an overview of how topics are linked.

Outline contents

Detailed contents

Table of cases

European Union

INTERNATIONAL

European Court of Human Rights

Other Countries
Canada

South Africa

United States

Table of legislation

PART 1

THE UK CONSTITUTION

This section of the book introduces the idea of constitutions, and more specifically, the essential features of the UK constitution. To help you understand the context of the constitution, its historical development is outlined in Chapter 2, while its specific characteristics are analysed in Chapter 3. Chapter 4 explains how power is allocated in the UK, and its organisation in terms of devolution and regional and local government. Chapter 5 will explain the Brexit process.

1

Introducing constitutions and public law

LEARNING OBJECTIVES

By the end of this chapter, you should be able to:

- Identify and use key terminology
- Evaluate the purpose and characteristics of constitutions and the circumstances in which a constitution is created
- Appreciate that there is more than one way to define a constitution
- Discuss whether the UK has a constitution
- Explain the role and purpose of public law

Introduction

Consider this: the people of a country unexpectedly vote to leave an international organisation that has inextricably linked their laws, trade, and movement of people for more than 40 years; the Prime Minister resigns; the new Prime Minister cannot get Parliament's approval for the withdrawal deal; the third Prime Minister finally secures the UK's exit three and a half years after the vote. Do these events sound familiar? Brexit will resonate in the UK for many years, and it highlights important legal and political questions about the rules that govern how the UK is run—in other words, its constitution.

This chapter introduces you to the idea and importance of constitutions, and in particular to the UK constitution. It is tempting to think of a constitution as something that is abstract, mechanical, and dry, perhaps a dusty volume on a shelf, but it should be remembered that constitutions are living, breathing constructs which are created and operated by human beings. There are both internal and external pressures and drivers for change in all constitutions, and, as we shall see with the UK, they are capable of producing moments of high drama and, occasionally, seismic events.

1.1 Overview of this book

You will no doubt begin reading this book with a number of questions in your mind. What is a constitution? Does the UK have a constitution? If so, what does it look like and where do I find it? How does it affect me? What exactly *is* public law? These are questions that this book will address by introducing you to, and analysing, the operation of the UK constitution and the application of public law.

A constitution is a framework of rules regulating the exercise of power in a particular body or entity. A club or society will have its own constitution and this applies, on a much larger scale of course, to a state whose constitution will normally be in a written document setting out the essential 'rules of operation' for that country; those rules consist of laws, practices, and principles.

The key to understanding the purpose of constitutions is to remember that the elemental force within any state is the power of those who rule the people, whether that ruler is a monarch, a president, or a prime minister. Left unchecked, there is a risk that the power of the ruling body can be misused and can result in autocracy (where a ruler or government has absolute power) or at worst, tyranny. This is why a constitution is needed: to control the power of those who govern. A state's constitution is concerned with how that state is run and organised, and how governmental power is controlled; a constitution allocates and regulates power within the state, identifying the holders of state power, how it is divided between them, the limits on their powers, their relationships with each other, and, importantly, their relationships with the citizens of that state. Thus the key elements of a constitution are:

1. the allocation of power;

2. the control of power;

3. the relationship between governmental institutions, and between individuals and governmental institutions.

The control of power, accountability, and protecting the individual against the state are central themes throughout this book. Part 1 explores where the UK constitution comes from; we look at its historical development and the milestone events in its journey to the twenty-first century. We then analyse the specific characteristics of the UK constitution and, importantly, the sources containing the central rules. We discuss how easily the constitution can change and whether it should be codified. Next, we examine how the UK is structured in terms of the allocation of institutional power, the important topic of devolution, and how regional and local government are organised. We also assess the impact of Brexit. By the end of Part 1, you will have covered and understood essential features of the UK constitution. In Part 2, we examine the important constitutional principles and values which underpin the constitution: Parliamentary sovereignty, the separation of powers, the rule of law (and the emerging 'common law constitution').

Parliamentary sovereignty: the principle that Parliament is the supreme law-making body in the UK, with the power to make or unmake any law (Act of Parliament).

Separation of powers: the concept that the different functions of government should be exercised by separate bodies (the legislature, executive, and judiciary) to prevent a concentration of power in any one body.

The rule of law: the idea that the law is supreme and no government or ruler is above the law, thus placing legal restraints on government, which can only exercise its power in accordance with the law.

In Part 3, we discuss the three main power-holders in the UK: Parliament (the legislature), the government (the executive), and the judiciary. This section also develops the key theme of how central government power is controlled and the importance of democratic accountability, which refers to the UK's operation of representative and responsible government—a system of democratically elected representatives and a government that is accountable to the people's elected representatives.

In Part 4, on the topic of administrative law, we examine the relationship between the citizen and the state and explore how citizens can obtain redress against the state via the courts, tribunals, Ombudsmen, and other procedures. We focus particularly on judicial review, where the courts review the lawfulness of decision-making and actions by public bodies; this is an important process in legal control over government power. We continue the theme of the relationship between the citizen and the state by examining the Human Rights Act 1998 and its impact—here again, the courts review the actions of public authorities to ensure that they are consistent with the rights of individuals—and finally, we analyse Police powers.

Getting started

1.2 What is a constitution?

1.2.1 **Definitions**

A constitution is essentially a rulebook for how a state is run, and its function is to impose order and stability; to allocate power, rights, and responsibility, and control the power of the state. However, we need to look more deeply at the nature of a constitution. A state's constitution sets out the structure and powers of government and the relationship between individuals and the state, and a balanced constitution ensures a balance of power between the institutions of government. The House of Lords Select Committee on the Constitution has described a constitution as:

> the set of laws, rules and practices that create the basic institutions of the state, and its component and related parts, and stipulate the powers of those institutions and the relationship between the different institutions and between those institutions and the individual. (House of Lords Select Committee on the Constitution, *Reviewing the Constitution*, First Report, Session 2001–2, HL 11 [20])

This definition raises some important points. First, a constitution consists not only of laws but also of non-legal rules and political practices (particularly constitutional conventions: see Chapter 3), so that a constitution has both a legal and political function. Second, a constitution not only governs the institutions of government, but actually *creates* those institutions. A constitution is thus a vital foundation or bedrock within a state and possesses a fundamental and overarching nature. It is a constant, stable presence. Moreover, by stipulating the powers of government institutions, and how far those powers extend, a constitution allows us to ascertain when a state institution has exceeded its power. Clearly delineated limits on power are therefore intended to prevent the exercise of arbitrary power by state institutions.

> This is at the heart of an idea known as constitutionalism, which centres on the concept that there should be legal limits on the power of government, and those limits will be contained within a state's constitution.

In the seventeenth century, John Locke espoused the idea of limited government (*Second Treatise of Government*, 1690), arguing that human beings are free and equal, with natural rights, and that legitimate government only exists with their consent in order to provide stability; the government's power, Locke stated, is limited to preserving the public good, and ultimately, a government which exceeds those limits can be replaced by the people. This conveys the idea that there is a higher power than government—the people, according to Locke's treatise—and governmental power is not unlimited. It is essential, therefore, that a constitution sets out rules and principles which govern those who govern the people. Not everyone agrees: Thomas Hobbes argued that human beings would naturally descend to conflict left to their own devices, so a sovereign power such as a monarch with unrestricted authority was needed, and the idea that conflict is at the heart of modern society is echoed by J.A.G. Griffith (see his 'The Political Constitution' in 'Further reading').

▶ CROSS REFERENCE

See section 1.5

1.2.2 'Constitution' has more than one meaning

It is helpful to distinguish between Constitution with a capital 'C' and constitution with a lower case 'c', a distinction made by Anthony King in *The British Constitution* (p 5; in 'Further reading'). A capital 'C' Constitution refers to a codified constitution where a state's most important constitutional rules have been gathered together in one document which has passed through a formal process of adoption (unlike the UK's constitution). King makes the point that a codified constitution will never contain all of a state's constitutional rules, so additional or less important peripheral rules will exist alongside the codified version, and subsequent rules might develop and supplement it. The classic example of the creation of a post-Constitution rule is the US Supreme Court's decision in *Marbury v Madison* 5 US 137 (1803) that it had the power to strike down unconstitutional legislation, even though this was not expressly written into the US Constitution.

A small-'c' constitution, on the other hand, is the entire set of laws, rules, and practices regulating a state's governing institutions. This can refer to an uncodified constitution like the UK's or to the surrounding rules which are not included in a codified constitution. It is therefore clear that the term 'constitution' can have a narrower meaning in the sense of a codified document (King's capital-'C' Constitution), and a wider meaning in the sense of a broader range of laws and rules. It was this broader view of a constitution to which Sir Kenneth Wheare was referring in *Modern Constitutions* (Oxford: Oxford University Press 1951, p 1) when he defined a constitution as 'the whole system of government of a country, the collection of rules which establish and regulate or govern the government'. The distinction between the narrower and wider meaning of 'constitution' is helpfully summarised by Vernon Bogdanor in this way:

> [There are] … two different meanings of the term 'constitution'. The first refers to a written instrument containing the basic and most important rules of government. The second refers to the rules, whether or not written down, which regulate government—and in this sense every society, by definition, has a constitution. (Vernon Bogdanor, *The New British Constitution*, p 10; in 'Further reading').

1.2.3 Constitutions create the system of government in a country

Constitutions create the institutions of government in a country; they establish the order by which a state will be run, sometimes in very spare statements of principle with little extraneous detail and sometimes at length, as in the 444 Articles of the Indian Constitution.

The first step is to create the constitution. Thomas Paine, in his work *The Rights of Man* (1791), wrote:

> A Constitution is a thing antecedent to Government, and a Government is only the creature of a Constitution. The Constitution of a Country is not the act of its Government, but of the People constituting a Government. It is the Body of Elements to which you can refer and quote article by article; and which contains the principles upon which the Government shall be established, the manner in which it shall be organized, the powers it shall have, the Mode of Elections, the Duration of Parliaments, or by what other name such Bodies may be called; the powers which the executive part of the Government shall have; and … every thing that relates to the compleat organization of a civil government, and the principles upon which it shall act, and by which it shall be bound.

Here, Thomas Paine clearly had in mind a written document, one that could be referred to and quoted from and which expressly set out the organisation of government, but the key point is Paine's emphasis that a constitution will *precede* and create the system of government in a state, and this means that government derives its authority from the constitution. Paine's ideas were influential on the drafters of the US Constitution of 1788 and the instrument itself creates, and makes a clear division of power between, the legislative branch (Article I), the presidency (executive branch) (Article II), and the judiciary (Article III). This is a model which has been used subsequently by many other states; see, for example, the Australian Constitution, which sets out the composition and powers of its federal parliament (in Chapter 1), the powers of the executive government (Chapter 2), and the role of the federal courts (Chapter 3). A constitution will create a system of government specific to that particular state, whether it be the 'indivisible, secular, democratic and social Republic' of the French Constitution, or the parliamentary monarchy of Spain, or China's 'socialist state under the people's democratic dictatorship'.

1.2.4 Codified constitutions have special legal status

In states with a codified constitution, there is no higher law than the constitution. It is the benchmark by which all other laws of that state are measured and if those laws infringe provisions of the written constitution they may be declared unconstitutional, usually by a Supreme Court or constitutional court. This cannot happen in the UK because of the absence of a codified constitution and the existence of parliamentary sovereignty, which means that the UK Parliament holds supreme law-making authority. There is no fundamental difference between the laws that form part of the UK's constitutional rules and the UK's ordinary laws. Written constitutions, on the other hand, often expressly stipulate that they are the state's supreme law, and the US Constitution contains a supremacy clause (Article VI Paragraph 2) providing that the Constitution and federal laws made pursuant to it are the supreme law of the land.

CROSS REFERENCE

See Chapters 3 and 6 for more detail

Many written constitutions also set out the rules for how they are to be altered in the future; this can include requiring a supermajority in the legislature (see, for example, Article V of the US Constitution) or by referendum (see Chapter 8 of the Australian Constitution). Protecting a written constitution from the same procedure used for changing ordinary law entrenches it, which means that it is solidly established and in a position of strength, but equally it is more difficult to adapt to changing circumstances.

1.2.5 Each constitution is 'personal' to a state

Constitutions normally reflect a country's political and national values; for example, the constitution of a liberal democracy enshrines and protects human rights and the rule of law, and embodies democratic principles, although some constitutions may profess such principles but fail to follow them in reality (sometimes called a 'façade constitution'). A state's constitution reflects a country's culture and may even set out some of its history. It will record whether it is a monarchy or a republic and will reflect recent transitions, such as changing from an absolute monarchy to a democratic constitutional monarchy, as in the Bhutan Constitution 2008. It may specify the state's national flag, its official language(s), and the prevailing religion and often refers to key values such as the state's sovereignty, independence, and territorial integrity. It may set out the duties of citizens ('Fidelity to the nation and loyalty to the State are fundamental political duties of all citizens' (Irish Constitution 1937 as amended in 2013, Article 9(3)), and the Constitution of Bhutan contains provisions concerning the environment and enshrines that state's unique principle of 'gross national happiness'. However, a codified constitution will usually be entrenched, and by definition more difficult to change, so it is more likely to be a snapshot of the time when it was drafted. It may therefore not be swift to reflect social changes—such as the progress towards civil partnerships and same sex marriages—which are much easier to capture with an uncodified constitution like that of the UK.

1.3 When is a constitution created?

Calvert has stated: 'A constitution may simply develop, or be imposed or adopted. It may regulate state activity in a variety of ways. It always stands to be overthrown; how likely this is depends on how precariously it is in place' (*An Introduction to British Constitutional Law*, Oxford: Blackstone Press 1985, p 15). This suggests that new constitutions can arise either through a process of evolution or as an act of deliberate creation (and they can be replaced). Constitutions are usually adopted as a result of what has been termed 'a constitutional moment'; in other words, there is either a shock event or a sudden break and the need for a fresh start, or a sense that 'the time is right' for a new constitution, with public appetite and the political will for change.

1.3.1 'A constitutional moment'

In one sense, a constitutional moment can involve constitutional turmoil or upheaval. This includes events which have broken the link with a state's continuity and necessitated a fresh start, such as a revolution, a former colony gaining independence, or an armed conflict. Part and parcel of that fresh start will be a reorganisation of the state and state power in the form of a new constitution. Jon Elster has listed the situations that lead to making a constitution:

1. Social and economic crisis
2. Revolution
3. Regime collapse
4. Fear of regime collapse
5. Defeat in war
6. Reconstruction after war
7. The creation of a new state
8. Liberation from colonial rule

(Jon Elster, 'Forces and Mechanisms in the Constitution-Making Process' (1995) 45 Duke Law Journal 364)

There is in each instance 'a political jolt'. Violent events which overturn the old order, such as the American War of Independence of 1775–1783 and the French Revolution in the late eighteenth century, require a new political order. In the aftermath of the English Civil War of the 1640s, the country was briefly governed under a written constitution; after the beheading of the king, Charles I, it was necessary to establish a legal basis for the new regime and therefore the Instrument of Government was drafted in 1653, giving executive power to the new Lord Protector of the Commonwealth (Oliver Cromwell). However, the Instrument was replaced in 1657 by a very short-lived document called the Humble Petition and Advice, and England soon reverted to an unwritten constitution.

Q CLOSE-UP FOCUS: POST-CONFLICT CONSTITUTIONS

A new constitution is a crucial step in the process of rebuilding a state after war or invasion. However, post-war constitutions can carry the risk of failure because the victors may seek to impose a constitution reflecting their own political values on vanquished states. After the Second World War, the United States was instrumental in changing the systems of government in both Germany and Japan into democracies. The United States, as occupying power, chiefly drafted the new Japanese Constitution (having rejected a version drafted by Japanese officials) but although the end result in 1947 was a pacifist Constitution renouncing Japan's sovereign right to war (Article 9), the drafters had taken note of Japan's constitutional identity. With the 1949 West German Constitution (the *Grundgesetz*), care was taken to include German politicians in the drafting process to ensure that its constitutional identity was reflected, while the 1949 East German (GDR) Constitution maintained a degree of continuity with the previous 1919 Weimar Constitution.

However, in Iraq after the 2003 conflict, a transitional constitution known as the Transitional Administrative Law was drafted in 2004 by a body appointed by the United States, setting up an interim government and a framework of milestone dates for the creation of a permanent constitution. The permanent constitution was hurriedly drafted by Iraq's transitional National Assembly in 2005 to meet the tight deadline; the Constitutional Outreach Unit only had eight weeks in which to consult the public, the Constitution Drafting Committee had only one month to work before it was dissolved, and there was increasing US presence in an attempt to speed up the process. Although the permanent constitution was approved by the people in a referendum and adopted in 2006, it was opposed by a number of groups within Iraq, including women's groups and Sunni Arabs, and has been criticised for not allowing sufficient time for the negotiation of the Iraqi federal model and for failing to build alliances and forge an identity in a multi-ethnic, multi-sectarian country.

Nevertheless, the creation of a new constitution for a post-conflict state is a central plank of modern post-conflict reconstruction and nation-building. In peace talks on the Syrian conflict, one of the essential components of the steps towards political transition has been the drafting of a constitution, and a constitutional committee met for the first time in October 2019 to discuss a new constitution for Syria.

For an interesting critique of the creation of the Iraq Constitution, see http://eprints.lse.ac.uk/54927/.

The creation of a new state is a 'constitutional moment'. The break-up of Soviet Russia and the former Yugoslavia into smaller states in the 1990s required those new states to adopt constitutions as a process of establishing their identity and independence. Colonies did the same on becoming independent from colonial rule. Before 1901, Australia consisted of six British colonies with a limited level of self-government whose laws were made by the British Parliament. In order to create a new Australian federal state, a series of constitutional conventions (or conferences) took place, attended by delegates from each colony, producing a draft constitution which was then passed by each of the colonies' parliaments, approved by the people in a referendum, and finally agreed by the British Parliament.

However, constitutions can develop peacefully and calmly, not because of any dramatic event but simply because it is the right time to adopt a written constitution or a new system of government, or to update an existing constitution. Even states with a rigid constitution, such as the United States, can develop new constitutional principles without the constitution being amended. In his theory of constitutional moments, Bruce Ackerman identifies different cycles in the development of constitutional change in America: first, there is 'normal politics', where the people are fairly disengaged from political debate; then there is a signal for 'transformative appeal', where a branch of government, for example the President, makes a proposal for constitutional change which is resisted by another branch of government, for example the courts, producing a set of opposing arguments for the people to make a choice on in a 'critical election'; and finally, the people's choice in that election may show popular support for change (Bruce Ackerman, 'The Storrs Lectures: Discovering the Constitution' (1984) 93 Yale LJ 1013).

▶ CROSS REFERENCE

See the Icelandic experiment in section 1.5.2

1.4 Characteristics of constitutions

Constitutions vary from state to state. They often share the same core elements, and can contain aspirational aims, but their characteristics can differ. Constitutions can be:

- Codified or uncodified
- Flexible or rigid

and they may create a system of government which is:

- Federal or unitary
- Republican or monarchical
- Parliamentary or presidential

1.4.1 Written and unwritten constitutions

As we established in section 1.2.2, a written constitution refers to a formal document specifically codifying the rules for governance of that state. It has special status, almost reverential in some states; there will often be a constitutional court to adjudicate whether an ordinary law is unconstitutional; and it will include rules for the future amendment of the constitution. Where a constitution is unwritten, there is no specific codified document setting out the provisions of the constitution but there is a series of uncodified laws, political practices, and rules found in different sources (some of which may be in written form) which together form a system of governance for a state. Britain, New Zealand, and Israel are the only three democracies in the world with an uncodified constitution, although Israel, created as a new state in 1948, has a series of written Basic Laws which have constitutional status, and are designed to progress towards a future constitution (the controversial 14th Law was passed in July 2018).

1.4.2 **Flexible or rigid**

If a constitution is flexible, it is adaptable and can be easily changed without the need to follow a special procedure protecting provisions in the constitution. The unwritten constitutions of the UK, New Zealand, and Israel, for example, can simply be changed by their respective parliaments, although Singapore has a flexible *written* constitution. However, a rigid and entrenched constitution is more difficult to change; it may contain an 'eternity clause' prohibiting any amendment of particular constitutional principles (see the German Basic Law Article 79), or special procedures for amendment such as a specified majority within the legislature or a referendum (like the US Constitution). The US Constitution (Article V) requires an amendment to be proposed by a two-thirds supermajority vote of both Houses of Congress, and the amendment must then be ratified by three-quarters of the state legislatures. The US Constitution has only been amended 27 times in more than 200 years (and the first ten of those amendments, known as the Bill of Rights, were adopted at the same time in 1791).

Q CLOSE-UP FOCUS: GUN LAWS

A classic example of a constitutional provision which is difficult to change is the Second Amendment to the US Constitution, which gives the right to bear arms: 'A well regulated Militia, being necessary to the security of a free State, the right of the people to keep and bear Arms, shall not be infringed.' This was passed by Congress in 1789 and ratified in 1791, at a time when an armed civilian militia was seen as an important bulwark against an over-powerful federal government with its own standing army. The militias are now long gone but the Second Amendment is regarded as embodying the right of individual citizens to keep guns for their own defence (*District of Columbia v Heller* (2008) 478 F. 3d 370). In the light of mass shootings in America over the years (notably at Columbine High School in Colorado in 1999, Sandy Hook Elementary School in Newtown, Connecticut in 2012, and the Pulse nightclub in Orlando, Florida in 2016), the gun control debate rages on in America, with the powerful gun lobby protective of its constitutional right. State and federal laws, debates in the Senate on gun control (including a vote in 2016 on the introduction of universal background checks and a ban on suspected terrorists on the FBI watch list from purchasing firearms), and a 26-hour sit-in by Democrats in the House of Representatives demanding action on gun control laws in 2016 have been unsuccessful in driving through a change to the Constitution.

By contrast, following the Port Arthur shooting in Tasmania in 1996, where 35 people were killed, Australia swiftly introduced legislation successfully reforming gun control. The difference was that there is no right to bear arms enshrined in the Australian constitution. Six weeks earlier, the Dunblane shooting had taken place in Scotland, with 16 children killed. Following the Cullen Inquiry, the UK Parliament passed strict gun control legislation: the Firearms (Amendment) Act 1997 banned higher calibre handguns and the Firearms (Amendment) (No 2) Act 1997 banned 0.22 calibre single-shot weapons.

However, the Russian constitution was amended on 4 July 2020 following approval by the Russian Parliament and voters in a referendum (one amendment gave President Putin the right to run for two further terms in office), but a lack of popular support—and the impact of coronavirus—disrupted the momentum for constitutional reform in Japan. The Japanese Prime Minister, Shinzo Abe, was unable to fulfil his aim of amending Article 9 of Japan's Constitution by 2020 to allow its armed forces to assist allies under attack as it needed the approval of a two-thirds majority in both houses of its legislature and a majority of the people in a referendum (https://researchbriefings.parliament.uk/ResearchBriefing/Summary/SN07115; https://www.japantimes.co.jp/news/2020/05/03/national/politics-diplomacy/japan-shinzo-abe-amending-constitution-2020/).

Repealing or amending a constitutional provision is only one way of producing change; another is for a state's judiciary to interpret the provision in a different way, though this can be controversial. The scope for varied interpretations can be seen by comparing the majority and minority dissenting judgments in *District of Columbia v Heller*; the majority interpreted Article 2 as protecting the individual's right to own a gun for lawful purposes irrespective of whether they were in a militia, but Justice Stevens, one of the dissenting judges, said that the right applied only to militia service and the Supreme Court was announcing a new constitutional right. Similarly, when the US Supreme Court ruled in *Obergefell v Hodges* 576 US (2015) that same sex marriage was a legal right in all states of the US because of the constitutional right to equal protection of the law in the Fourteenth Amendment, Justice Scalia, in a scathing dissenting judgment, called the majority (5–4) decision a threat to democracy and 'a naked judicial claim to legislative—indeed, super-legislative—power' because the Supreme Court had overridden states' freedom to impose their own laws (by 2015, it was legal in 36 states and banned in 14).

1.4.3 **Federal or unitary**

A constitution will stipulate whether a state is federal or unitary.

> A federal state has a form of government in which power is non-centralised and is dispersed or divided between a central authority and regional centres of power (eg states or provinces).

Power is shared and co-ordinated so that each region has power to manage its internal affairs ('the combination of shared rule and self-rule': Ronald L. Watts, 'Federalism, Federal Political Systems, and Federations' (1998) 1 Annual Review of Political Science 117, 120). It is essential, therefore, in a federal state to enshrine these arrangements in a written constitution. On the other hand, in a unitary state, governing power is centralised and held by a central authority, as has traditionally been the case with the UK (see Chapters 3 and 4).

1.4.4 **Monarchical or republican**

A state's constitution will also reflect the fact that it is a monarchy or a republic (for example, 'Italy is a democratic Republic founded on labour' (Constitution of Italy 1947, Article 1); 'The principle of government is a hereditary and constitutional monarchy' (Constitution of Monaco 1962, Article 2)). Similarly, a constitution will reflect whether that state has a parliamentary or a presidential system of government. In a parliamentary system, the head of government is normally a member of the legislature and the executive is dependent on the legislature so there is no strict separation of powers. In a presidential system of government, the president is directly elected, separate from the legislature, and not usually accountable to it.

Table 1.1 Examples of variations between constitutional characteristics

	Australia	Brazil	Costa Rica	Japan	Nepal	South Africa
Federal	√	√			√	
Unitary			√	√		√
Parliamentary	√			√	√	√
Presidential		√	√			
Monarchy	√			√		
Republic		√*	√		√◊	√

*Despite a 1993 referendum on whether to have a monarchy or remain as a republic
◊Nepal was a monarchy until 2007

The variation in the characteristics of constitutions can be seen in Table 1.1.

1.5 People power

1.5.1 The constituent power

Constitutions need a recognised legal basis to give them their authority and legitimacy, and the fundamental source of authority for a constitution, known as the constituent power, is the people. The US Constitution famously begins:

> We the People of the United States, in Order to form a more perfect Union, establish Justice, ensure domestic Tranquility, provide for the common defence, promote the general Welfare, and secure the Blessings of Liberty to ourselves and our Posterity, do ordain and establish this Constitution for the United States of America.

This has been emulated by numerous constitutions; for example, the 2011 Constitution of South Sudan (Article 3(1)) 'derives its authority from the will of the people and shall be the supreme law of the land'. Moreover, where a constitution can only be amended by referendum, its provisions are fixed until the people approve a change (see, eg, the Tunisian Constitution 2014 Article 3: 'The people are sovereign and the source of authority, which is exercised through the peoples' representatives and by referendum').

Thomas Paine expressed the need for the authority of the people in this way:

> If we trace government to its origin, we discover that governments must have arisen either out of the people or over the people. In those which have arisen out of the people, the individuals themselves, each in his own personal and sovereign right, have entered into a compact with each other to produce a government; and this is the only mode in which governments have a right to arise.

The sequence advocated by Paine is set out in Figure 1.1.

Thus a constitution can be described as 'primarily a social compact, a political declaration that supersedes ordinary legislation by virtue of the fact that the people are superior to Parliament' (Thorvaldur Gylfason, www.democraticaudit.com/?p=8840, 28 October 2014). On this view, the people are seen as the higher law-making authority and their authority is higher than that

Figure 1.1 Thomas Paine's flow of authority

| The people authorise ... | a constitution which creates... | government |

of a legislature. It is for this reason that any ordinary laws passed by the legislature which conflict with a constitution can be overturned because a constitution expresses the higher will of the people.

1.5.2 **The constitution-making process**

The discussion, negotiation, and drafting of a new constitution is carried out by a body known as a constituent assembly. It may be in the form of a constitutional convention, a body elected only for the purpose of drafting the constitution, or it may be a body with existing legislative powers; for example, South Africa's 1996 Constitution was drafted by both Houses of Parliament sitting as a constitutional assembly whereas the Philadelphia Convention responsible for drafting the US Constitution consisted of appointed delegates from 12 American states.

Much of the deliberative process of drafting a constitution has historically been carried out in secret (this was true for the drafting of the US Constitution) so in recent years there has been increasing emphasis on involving the people of a state not only in approving a draft constitution in a referendum, but also in participating in its formation to provide transparency and a sense of ownership. In preparation for the 1996 South African constitution, the constitutional assembly carried out a wide public participation exercise with a successful outreach programme to gather a broad spectrum of public views. Nevertheless, Jon Elster is sceptical about the extent to which such public consultation shapes the final constitution and argues that the most effective constitution process is one where:

> the closed assembly may be supplemented by upstream and downstream public consultations, generating an overall 'hourglass-shaped' procedure' with the narrow middle of the hourglass as the drafting of the constitution in private session, while the 'downstream process of ratification by the citizens, following a national debate, is more important' than preliminary public consultations. (Jon Elster, 'The Optimal Design of a Constituent Assembly', in Hélène Landemore and Jon Elster (eds), *Collective Wisdom: Principles and Mechanisms* (Cambridge University Press 2012, p 169)

The process of ratification, or formal approval of a draft constitution, by the legislative body or by referendum or both, will complete the constitution process.

 CLOSE-UP FOCUS: ICELAND'S CROWDSOURCED CONSTITUTION

Between 2009 and 2013, Iceland carried out an interesting experiment in redrafting its constitution. After the financial crisis of 2008–2009, public protests (known as the 'pots and pans revolution') and the resignation of the government resulted in the desire for a new constitution. Iceland decided to produce what has been called a 'crowdsourced constitution'. First a Constitutional Committee of experts was set up; they organised a National Forum, a gathering of 950 individuals selected at random, who listed what they wanted to see in a new constitution at a meeting which was streamed online. Their ideas were formulated into legal terms by a committee, then a Constitutional Council of 25 citizens drawn from a wide variety of backgrounds and professions (but not including politicians) drafted the Constitution, working in closed sessions but using social media to obtain feedback on their drafts from the population. Feedback included a 'Facebook proposal to entrench a constitutional right to the Internet', which was included in the final draft. The draft was approved by 67 per cent of voters in a non-binding referendum in October 2012 but the Icelandic Parliament (the *Althingi*) failed to progress it further. However, a civic engagement process took place in 2019, including a deliberative poll of citizens in which they discussed constitutional amendments, and the Icelandic Parliament aims to produce a number of constitutional reform bills.

See Hélène Landemore, 'Inclusive Constitution-Making: The Icelandic Experiment' (2015) 23(2) Journal of Political Philosophy 166.

 THINKING POINT

If you were tasked to help draft a constitution, what essential rights, values, and principles would you include? For example, would you include the right to internet access, or the right to paternity leave, or the protection of the environment? Would you use social media and live streaming for more inclusive public participation in drafting your constitution?

1.6 Political and legal constitutions

Constitutions can be 'political' or 'legal', although in practice, many will be a blend of both. The debate here focuses on the critical question: how is government held to account—by the law or by political rules? A legal constitution is typically characterised by a formal, written Constitution with the status of higher law, containing a strong, forceful set of rules which must be followed in the governance of that state; its rules are said to be normative, that is, they are binding and generally observed. The constitution's provisions are entrenched, fixed, and unchangeable until a deliberate act of amendment takes place, and a constitutional or Supreme Court will act as the guardian of the constitution and its provisions.

A political constitution, by contrast, is one where government power is restricted mainly by political processes, which does not contain rules with such strength as a legal constitution, and is therefore more changeable. Gee and Webber describe a political constitution in this way:

> By design, a political constitution leaves it to political actors, operating through the ordinary political process, to prescribe the nature and content of the constitution … A political constitution does not prescribe in any great detail because one of its basic features is its constant liability to the possibility of change effected through the ordinary political process. (Graham Gee and Grégoire C.N. Webber, 'What Is a Political Constitution?' (2010) 30(2) Oxford Journal of Legal Studies 273, 287)

In his seminal article on political constitutions, J.A.G. Griffith argues that political, rather than legal, control of governments is needed and that control of government by laws is 'an unattainable ideal' ('The Political Constitution', p 16). In reality, he argues, a written constitution is a misguided way of trying to resolve conflicts about rights which are a natural part of the activity known as politics. As Britain does not have a written constitution containing superior constitutional laws, it has traditionally had a more political nature, with organically developed checks and balances constraining government power and, at its heart, the sovereignty of the British Parliament. However, it is also true that Britain's constitution is evolving towards a more rule-based legal constitution with the strengthening of judicial review and the protection of human rights. Tom Hickman asserts that the UK constitution is founded on law that is enforceable in the courts and the legal or political constitution debate should be left behind:

> The salient question today is how to marry a legal constitution, founded upon the protection of human rights, with the operation of ordinary politics and political mechanisms of accountability. (Tom R Hickman, 'In Defence of the Legal Constitution' (2005) 55 UTLJ 981, 1022; see also 986–987)

Adam Tomkins acknowledges that Britain now has a constitution comprising legal and political elements but argues that much remains of its political constitution: if a matter is thought inappropriate for Parliament to determine, the alternative is to ask the electorate through a referendum, not the Supreme Court (A. Tomkins, 'What's Left of the Political Constitution?' (2013) 14(12) German Law Journal 2275, 2289).

 THINKING POINT

What is the difference between a legal and a political constitution?

 SUMMARY

- A constitution is a set of rules for how a state is run
- Constitutions exist to impose order and stability; to allocate power, rights, and responsibility and control the power of those who govern
- A constitution consists not only of laws but also of non-legal rules and political practices, and has both a legal and political function
- A constitution not only governs but creates the institutions of government
- In states with a codified constitution, there is no higher law than the constitution
- New constitutions can arise through a process of evolution or as an act of deliberate creation
- Constitutions can be codified or uncodified, flexible or rigid
- All constitutions are subject to debate about their interpretation in courts, legislatures, and the public arena
- Constitutions need a recognised legal basis to give them authority and legitimacy
- Constitutions can be described as 'political' or 'legal', although in practice many are a blend of both

Introducing the UK constitution

1.7 Does Britain have a constitution?

You may be surprised to learn that there are differing views on this fundamental question, and the answer depends on where you start from. One starting point for the debate is the existence—or lack—of a written constitution. Thomas Paine was very clear on whether England (now Britain) had a constitution:

> Wherever it cannot be produced in a visible form, there is none … Can, then, Mr. Burke [an English MP] produce the English constitution? If he cannot, we may fairly conclude that no such thing … exists, or ever did exist … The English government is one of those which arose out of a conquest, and not out of society, and consequently it arose over the people; and though it has been much modified since the time of William the Conqueror, the country has never yet regenerated itself, and is therefore without a constitution. (*Rights of Man*, p 28)

In the 1830s, Alexis de Tocqueville, a French political theorist, also took the view that Britain did not have a constitution because of its unwritten, evolutionary, flexible nature, and because of parliamentary sovereignty: 'In England, the Parliament has an acknowledged right to modify the constitution; as, therefore, the constitution may undergo perpetual changes, it does not in reality exist' (Alexis de Tocqueville, *Democracy in America*, 1835). That view is supported by F.F. Ridley, who argues that there are four characteristics of a constitution and Britain has none of them:

1. A constitution establishes the system of government and is prior to the system of government.

2. A constitution 'involves an authority outside and above the order it establishes' (the constituent power).

3. It is a form of superior law originating from a higher authority than the legislature.

4. It is entrenched and can only be changed by special procedures.

'The term British constitution', says Ridley, 'is near meaningless', and as there is a blurred distinction between constitutional law and ordinary law in Britain, there is nothing to tell us whether something is unconstitutional ('There Is No British Constitution', 342–343, 359; in 'Further reading'). Moreover, Lord Neuberger, former President of the Supreme Court, has said:

> The UK famously has no constitution. Some legal experts argue that it has constitutional documents—including Magna Carta, and certain statutes, the Bill of Rights, the Act of Settlement, and the Act of Union. However … [they] scarcely represent even an attempt at any sort of constitutional set of rules. Furthermore, so long as the UK enjoys parliamentary supremacy, any provision in any of these instruments can be overturned by a simple majority of one in the House of Commons. It may be said with real force that that is scarcely the hallmark of a constitutional provision. ('The Role of Judges in Human Rights Jurisprudence: A Comparison of the Australian and UK Experience', Speech at the Supreme Court of Victoria, Melbourne, 8 August 2014 [8])

Bogdanor expands on the role of parliamentary sovereignty in Britain: 'The British Constitution could thus be summed up in just eight words: "What the Queen in Parliament enacts is law"' (*The New British Constitution*, p 13). In other words, Parliament can change any part of the UK constitution in the same way that it changes ordinary law, simply by passing an Act of Parliament.

You may now be wondering what you are about to embark on studying. It is true that if a 'constitution' is defined in the sense of a written formal document, Britain has no constitution. But if we use Kenneth Wheare's wider definition of a constitution (see section 1.2.2), Britain *does* have a collection of rules which regulate and govern the institutions of government, and this is the basis on which Barendt argues that the UK has a constitution (Eric Barendt, 'Is There a United Kingdom Constitution?'; in 'Further reading'). First, we have a constitution in the sense of a power map with constitutional rules describing the lines of power and the relations between government institutions, and between government institutions and the people (rather like an organogram); Barendt calls this a constitution 'in the descriptive sense' (see also Anthony King, *The Hamlyn Lectures: Does the United Kingdom Still Have a Constitution?* (London: Sweet & Maxwell 2001, p 101). But Barendt also points out that there is more to a constitution than a codified text and that Britain has more than a descriptive constitution because it has laws 'of a constitutional character' which would be included in a codified constitution if there was one. In this sense, the constitution is a unique product of history and political and legal development (we find out in Chapter 2 how the UK constitution evolved). The Supreme Court endorses this view:

> [a]lthough the United Kingdom does not have a single document entitled 'The Constitution', it nevertheless possesses a Constitution, established over the course of our history by common law, statutes, conventions and practice. Since it has not been codified, it has developed pragmatically, and remains sufficiently flexible to be capable of further development … it includes numerous principles of law, which are enforceable by the courts in the same way as other legal principles. (*R (Miller) v The Prime Minister; Cherry and others v Advocate General for Scotland* [2019] UKSC 41 [39])

 THINKING POINTS

Do you think Britain has a constitution? Which set of arguments above do you find more convincing?

1.8 Understanding the UK constitution

The UK constitution is a survivor, chiefly because of its flexible nature. While its most fundamental principles have remained stable for many years, the UK constitution is nevertheless adaptable and can be easily changed. It has modernised rapidly in the past 20 years and it can justifiably be seen as organic and dynamic, with a forward-looking energy. However, it breaks the mould of the normal constitutional development that we saw earlier in the chapter. The UK constitution has evolved over centuries rather than being consciously created by and for the people. It has developed a wide range of constitutional rules which can be found in various forms such as certain Acts of Parliament (statutes), specific case law developed by the courts, and unwritten rules of political practice (known as constitutional conventions). It is uncodified, which means that while many of the UK's constitutional rules are in written form, they have not been collated in a single document; as a result, there is no neatly packaged constitution that you can buy in a bookshop or access online. Even if you are not yet familiar with the UK constitution, you might already have identified a key issue emerging from the fact that it is not consolidated in a single document: where do we find the rules? That is the key question that this book explores.

❯ CROSS REFERENCE

For more on this, see Chapters 2 and 3

1.8.1 **The key players and essential terminology**

It is essential at this stage to be able to define and understand the terminology to which we will be referring and it is also important to distinguish clearly between the UK's three arms of state and their different functions. In any state, there will be law-makers, law-enforcers, policy-makers, and arbiters of disputes, and thus a functional state needs the following: officials to make its laws (the legislative function); officials to carry out the day-to-day running of the state and implementing policy and law (the executive function); and officials to decide legal disputes (the judicial function). In the UK, there are three institutions (known as arms or branches of state) between whom power is divided:

- Parliament (the legislature);
- the government (the executive);
- the judiciary (the judicial body).

A basic but very important point is to avoid confusing 'Parliament' and 'the government'. It should also be remembered that there is not always a distinct division in power between institutions in the UK; for example, Parliament has the supreme law-making function but government ministers can be given law-making powers by Parliament, and judges create common law.

The monarch: is also referred to as 'the sovereign' and is the head of state; the Queen is a constitutional monarch whose powers are defined by the constitution

The Crown: refers to the monarch, or in its more technical sense the functions of government and state administration; the legislative, executive, and judicial functions in the UK are carried out in the name of the Crown

The legislature: the law-making body in a state

Parliament: the UK's supreme law-making body, divided into two chambers (the House of Commons and the House of Lords). In the United Kingdom, legislation is made by the Queen in Parliament, consisting of the House of Commons, the House of Lords, and the monarch. 'Parliament' derives from the French *parler*, meaning 'to talk'; hence Parliament is the central debating forum where new laws are discussed and created

The executive: the bodies concerned with creating and implementing policy and implementing law; in many cases these are government departments headed by ministers, who form the Cabinet

Government: the word 'government' derives from *gubernare*, the Latin word for steering a ship or regulating. The political party that wins a general election becomes the new government, whose role is to carry out the day-to-day administration of the state—that is, an executive function

The judiciary: the judges, whose function is to apply and interpret the law and decide legal disputes in court

1.8.2 The UK constitution in action

As one of the first steps to understanding the UK constitution, it helps to develop a sense of how it operates, and to recognise that you will have seen, or been involved in, events that show the constitution in action. It affects us more than you might think. Take, for example, the 2016 Brexit referendum which began a dramatic reshaping of the UK constitution and raised some novel constitutional questions. What were the rules for leaving the EU? Who triggered the leaving mechanism under Article 50 of the Treaty of the European Union: the government or Parliament? (See Chapter 5.) And the coronavirus outbreak in 2020 required the government to introduce unprecedented peacetime restrictions of public freedom in order to control the spread of the virus. How can the limits of those powers be tested? Public law, to which we now turn, provides the answers to these questions.

1.9 The role, scope, and importance of public law

Public law, which includes constitutional and administrative law, is a fundamentally important part of UK law because it places legal limits on the power of the state, and protects citizens against breaches of those laws by state bodies. Constitutional law is the law about government. It defines and regulates the structure and powers of government, the distribution of power between government institutions, their functions, and the relationship between individuals and the state. We can see the scope of constitutional law in John Laws' definition of a constitution:

> What is a constitution? It is that set of legal rules which governs the relationship in a state between the ruler and the ruled. All constitutional questions are about the laws which identify the ruler, define the nature and extent of their power, and set the conditions for its exercise.
> (John Laws, 'The Constitution: Morals and Rights' (1996) (Winter) Public Law 622)

These are the essential laws which would be found in a written constitution and, because it relates to the institutions which make, implement, and interpret the UK's laws, UK constitutional law also underpins the legal system.

 CROSS REFERENCE

See Chapters 15–16 for judicial review

Administrative law concerns public administration and regulates the power of public bodies, particularly through judicial review, where the courts determine whether a public body has exercised its power beyond its legal limits.

THINKING POINT

Summarise your understanding of the purpose of public law.

1.9.1 Public law and private law

Private law regulates the relationships between individuals, companies, or other private entities; for example, disputes concerning contract, tort, divorce, wills, and succession are matters of private law (although some areas such as cases involving children can raise both private and public law issues). Public law, on the other hand, regulates the public face of the state and has a strong impact on citizens' rights and relationships with public bodies, enabling individuals to challenge in court the actions of government departments and agencies, local councils, the police, the armed forces, health authorities, and other bodies in areas such as immigration and asylum, human rights, prisoners' rights, planning and housing, schools and universities, state benefits and welfare, and freedom of information. Lawyers practising in the public law arena will act in a broad range of cases where individuals are challenging the actions of the government and other public bodies, from challenges to the government's policy of culling badgers to eradicate TB in cattle (*R (Badger Trust) v Secretary of State for the Environment, Food and Rural Affairs* [2012] EWHC 1904 (Admin)) to the lawfulness of the Prime Minister's advice to the Queen to prorogue (suspend) Parliament (*R (Miller) v The Prime Minister; Cherry v Advocate General for Scotland* [2019] UKSC 41).

1.9.2 **The limits on public law**

While public law regulates governmental power, there are also *limits* on what it can control— such as decisions made by the government in certain politically sensitive areas. The courts have acknowledged that they cannot 'enter the forbidden areas, including decisions affecting foreign policy' (*R (Abbasi) v Secretary of State for Foreign and Commonwealth Affairs & Secretary of State for the Home Department* [2002] EWCA Civ 1598, [2003] UKHRR 76 [106]) and in the case of *R (Gentle) v Prime Minister* [2008] UKHL 20, Lord Bingham referred to 'the restraint traditionally shown by the courts in ruling on what has been called high policy—peace and war, the making of treaties, the conduct of foreign relations' ([8]). Similarly, in *R (Campaign for Nuclear Disarmament) v Prime Minister* [2002] EWHC 2777 (Admin), the claimants unsuccessfully asked the court to declare that the UK's Prime Minister would be in breach of international law if he deployed British armed forces to Iraq without United Nations authorisation, and in his judgment, Simon Brown LJ stated: 'The court will ... decline to embark upon the determination of an issue if to do so would be damaging to the public interest in the field of international relations, national security or defence' ([47]; see also *R (Miller) v Secretary of State for Exiting the European Union* [2017] UKSC 5 [47, 49, 240] ('*Miller 1*')). Thus, the UK courts acknowledge that there are certain issues on which it would not be appropriate for them to make a decision because of wider political and geopolitical considerations.

> **CROSS REFERENCE**
> To find out more about the courts' approach to cases involving high policy, see section 7.4, section 12.3.1.2, and section 16.6.1.

1.9.3 **Studying public law**

As the final point, if you have studied or are studying contract law or tort, for example, you will be familiar with applying black letter law (ie a clear set of legal principles). With public law, you will notice a difference. While public law does contain many legal rules, it also interweaves them with the specific constitutional principles set out in Part 2 of this book. This is part of the nature of public law. While this is not a book about politics, which concerns the activities of those who exercise government power, public law and politics are intrinsically linked and your study of the subject will be enhanced by an interest in current affairs. It helps your understanding of key principles to see their real life application, and it is good practice to cultivate the habit of reading quality newspapers, either as hard copy or online. A study of the constitution and public law also has historical roots and context, and Chapter 2 of this book provides a survey of the milestone events of which you need to be aware in order to understand and appreciate the subject.

Questions

Self-test questions

1. What is a constitution? What is the purpose of a constitution?

2. Summarise the narrower and wider meanings of 'constitution'.

3. What is meant by 'entrenched'?

4. What is 'a constitutional moment'?

5. What is a 'constituent power' and why is it important?

6. What is a 'constituent assembly'?

7. In the context of the UK constitution, explain what each of the following terms means:

    (a) the Crown

    (b) the legislature

    (c) the executive

    (d) the judiciary

8. What is the difference between Parliament and the government?

Exam question

'Britain does not have a constitution'. Discuss.

Further reading

Books

Bogdanor, V. *The New British Constitution* (Oxford and Portland, Oregon: Hart Publishing 2009).
For thought-provoking and incisive insights into the workings of the modern constitution

King, A. *The British Constitution* (Oxford: Oxford University Press 2007).
An accessible dissection of the early twenty-first-century constitution in Britain

Journal articles

Barendt, E. 'Is There a United Kingdom Constitution?' (1997) 17(1) Oxford Journal of Legal Studies 137.
Addresses arguments that there is no UK constitution

Eleftheriadis, P. 'In Defence of Constitutional Law' (2018) 81(1) MLR 154.
This review article explores more sophisticated constitutional theory

Elster, J. 'Forces and Mechanisms in the Constitution-Making Process' (1995) 45 Duke Law Journal 364.

Helps understanding of how constitutions are made

Griffith, J.A.G. 'The Political Constitution' (1979) 42 MLR 1.
A classic, authoritative analysis of the political nature of the UK constitution

Matsui, S. 'Fundamental Human Rights and "Traditional Japanese Values": Constitutional Amendment and Vision of the Japanese Society' (2018) 13(1) Asian Journal of Comparative Law 59.
A case study of the route towards constitutional change

Ridley, F.F. 'There Is No British Constitution: A Dangerous Case of the Emperor's Clothes' (1988) 41(3) Parliamentary Affairs 340.
A good counterbalance to Barendt's views, arguing against the existence of a UK constitution

Tomkins, A. 'In Defence of the Political Constitution' (2002) 22(1) Oxford Journal of Legal Studies 157.
An analysis of the relationship between law and politics within public law and the constitution

Other sources

The Constitution Unit: www.ucl.ac.uk/constitution-unit/whatis/uk-constitution.

Provides a brief summary of what a constitution is, and the website contains many useful links to research and information across the constitutional spectrum

US Constitution: www.whitehouse.gov/1600/constitution.

Use this link to access the US Constitution and accompanying commentary

Online resources

www.oup.com/he/dennett2e

This chapter is accompanied by a selection of online resources to help you with this topic, including:

- Multiple-choice questions
- Answers to the self-test questions
- Guidance on answering the exam question

2

How the UK constitution has developed

☐ **LEARNING OBJECTIVES**

By the end of this chapter, you should be able to:

● Evaluate the significance of major contributing events in the development of the UK constitution

● Understand the evolutionary nature of change in the British constitution

● Identify events that produce constitutional change

● Appreciate the flexible and adaptable nature of the UK constitution

Introduction

You might be tempted to skip this chapter and dismiss it as 'just history' but it is worth bearing in mind that, as the historian A.J.P. Taylor reminds us, 'events now long in the past were once in the future' (A.J.P. Taylor, *War by Timetable: How the First World War Began* (London: Macdonald & Co 1969). Awareness of how the UK constitution has developed over the centuries provides a deeper understanding of its current arrangements. In two significant cases in 2017, the UK Supreme Court returned to the roots of the UK constitution to decide contemporary issues, illustrating the broad span and relevance of its evolution. In *R (Miller) v Secretary of State for Exiting the European Union* [2017] UKSC 5, the Court assessed the historical development of key constitutional principles to determine whether Parliament or the government had the legal power to trigger the UK's withdrawal from the EU, and in *Belhaj v Straw* [2017] UKSC 3, a case on rendition (the forcible abduction of individuals for detention and interrogation with the risk of torture), Lord Mance referred to an 800-year-old provision in Magna Carta, considered as the founding instrument of the UK constitution:

> English law recognises the existence of fundamental rights, some long-standing, others more recently developed. Among the most long-standing and fundamental are those represented in Magna Carta 1225, article 29, which reads: 'No free-man shall be taken, or imprisoned, or dispossessed, of his … Liberties … or be outlawed, or exiled, or in any way destroyed; nor will we condemn him, nor will we commit him to prison, excepting by the legal judgment of his peers, or by the laws of the land. To none will we sell, to none will we deny, to none will we delay right or justice.' ([98])

The purpose of this chapter is to provide historical background and context to the constitution's journey to the present day, highlighting the main themes and milestone events to help you understand the features of the constitution for the next chapter. What follows can only be a brief overview of significant developments, but each one was a step on the path to the modern constitution. Table 2.1 provides a timeline to refer back to as you work through the book.

2.1 The historical narrative

The key to understanding the evolution of the British constitution is to imagine it being shaped by a dynamic ebb and flow of power between the key players—the monarch, Parliament, the Church, governments, judges—to determine the issue of where supreme power and authority would ultimately settle and reside. While it is too simplistic to see the development of the constitution only as a series of power struggles, the conflicts that have principally shaped it over the centuries have been about the fundamental question: who has sovereignty? The king? Parliament? The people? Dominic Grieve QC has summarised the backdrop of historical development as:

> embodying the Common Law; its confirmation through Magna Carta and its numerous reissues in the Middle Ages; the outcome of the conflict of authority between King and Parliament in the 17th century in the Petition of Right; the abolition of Star Chamber and the prohibition of torture; Habeas Corpus and the Bill of Rights of 1689, Lord Mansfield's ruling on slavery in Somerset's case and the Commentaries of William Blackstone. This national narrative has been so powerful that it has acted as an almost mythic restraint on successive British governments trying to curb freedoms. (Dominic Grieve, 'Why Human Rights Should Matter to Conservatives' (2015) 86(1) Political Quarterly 62, 63)

This forms the basis of our discussion to follow, which shows that the constitution is fluid and changing, despite the received view that it has evolved slowly and peacefully since 1066 without invasion or violent revolution. Those changes have often been a reaction either to grievances on the part of sections of the community or to events (Harold Macmillan, the British Prime Minister from 1957 to 1963, is reputed to have described the greatest challenge for a government as 'Events, dear boy, events'). Despite fluctuations in power, and changes in Britain's territorial composition and external alliances, there has always been a sense that the constitution is based on the collective memory of ancient laws and principles that fundamentally protect us and cannot be changed. In fact, it can be argued that the constitution has acquired the ability to appear outwardly stable and constant while in reality being in a continual state of churn and readjustment. Walter Bagehot described it in this way:

> [A]n ancient and ever-altering constitution is like an old man who still wears with attached fondness clothes in the fashion of his youth: what you see of him is the same; what you do not see is wholly altered. (Walter Bagehot, *The English Constitution*, Oxford: Oxford University Press 2009, p 5)

2.1.1 Pre-1066: the ancient constitution?

Magna Carta, or the Great Charter, is commonly regarded as the foundation stone for the British constitution but it did not emerge from a vacuum. It had its roots in Anglo-Saxon traditions where kings issued charters granting liberties or privileges. In Saxon England, law was Germanic in origin, consisting of tribal community law known as the 'folkright' which the king could override by granting special privileges. Saxon kings had a Witan or Witenagemot (literally a meeting of wise men), a council of bishops, noblemen and officials who assembled to discuss important

Table 2.1 A timeline of milestone events

Year	Event
1066	The Norman invasion
1215	Magna Carta sealed by King John
1217	The Charter of the Forest
1265	The first Parliament
1297	Magna Carta and the Charter of the Forest issued as a statute
1534	Act of Supremacy establishes the monarch as Head of the Church of England
1536	Laws in Wales Acts unite England and Wales
1628	Petition of Right
1642	The English Civil War begins
1649	Charles I beheaded
1653–1658	England governed as a protectorate
1660	Restoration of the monarchy
1668	The Glorious Revolution
1689	The Bill of Rights signals a new constitutional settlement
1701	Act of Settlement
1707	Act of Union with Scotland
1800	Act of Union with Ireland
1832	Representation of the People Act begins a series of electoral reforms
1911	The Parliament Act reduces the powers of the House of Lords
1914–1918	The First World War
1922	Ireland leaves the Union
1928	Representation of the People Act gives women the vote
1939–1945	The Second World War
1945–1948	The beginnings of the welfare state
1950	Britain signs the European Convention on Human Rights
1973	Britain joins the Common Market, which later became the European Union
1997	Labour government's constitutional reform programme begins, including the Human Rights Act 1998, the devolution Acts, the Constitutional Reform Act 2005
2016	Brexit referendum
2020	Britain leaves the European Union

matters, and to deliberate and advise on laws, taxes, and administration. Kings such as Aethelberht and Alfred introduced written law codes, made with their council, to consolidate or change legal customs and set out basic rights, penalties for crimes, and in some cases, limits on the king's power. These are the tap roots of what was later referred to as 'the ancient constitution'.

The milestone events

 THINKING POINT

As you read, consider how royal power begins to separate.

2.2 1066–1603: rebalancing royal power

The Norman invasion in 1066 heralded an era of powerful kings but the defining characteristic of the next 600 years was the concerted attempts by members of the aristocracy and Parliament to restrict royal power. This tug-of-war over power helped to shape some of the constitution's most enduring features.

The Norman invasion, led by William the Conqueror in 1066, introduced lasting changes to governance and law in England, and Norman French pervaded the English legal system for several centuries. The Normans were best known for the Domesday Book, their supremely efficient audit of landholding throughout the country, and they developed feudalism, a top-down pyramid of landholding where the king granted land to his barons (tenants in chief) in return for fealty (an oath of loyal and faithful service), money, and the provision of knights for military service. William swore an oath to maintain Saxon laws to keep continuity and one notable feature continued: the king ruled with advice from a council of senior noblemen, royal officials and the Church in what was now called the Curia Regis (the King's Court). The origins of Parliament, government ministers, the higher law courts, and the Privy Council (a body of advisors to the Queen) can be found here. Originally, the Curia Regis carried out all state business—it was Parliament, government, and law court rolled into one—but over time it divided into an inner council of the king's officials and the Great Council, to which the king periodically summoned his tenants in chief and the clergy to advise on law-making and judicial functions; eventually the judicial functions of the Curia Regis would split away to form the early courts of law.

 CLOSE-UP FOCUS: THE DEVELOPMENT OF JUDICIAL POWER

An assortment of medieval local courts existed, such as lords' courts, hundred courts, and shire courts, but the king himself, as the fount of justice, decided higher level legal disputes. Initially the king moved with his court (the Curia Regis) round the country;

for litigants, the royal court was where the king happened to be. Henry I introduced itin-erant justices, state officials who travelled to preside over courts in the counties—although 'courts' at that time were mainly concerned with government and administration—but his grandson, Henry II, reformed the justice system. By the Assize of Clarendon 1166 and the Assize of Northampton in 1176 (an Assize was a meeting of the King's Council), Henry introduced a centralised judicial system, ordering the country to be divided into six circuits, each with a set of royal judges (justices in eyre) who travelled round the Assize courts, conducting government administration and hearing legal disputes on the king's behalf. In 1178, Henry appointed five judges to sit at a permanent royal court at Westminster (called the 'Bench') to hear disputes between the king's subjects; difficult cases were reserved for the king and his council. The law that was developed centrally at Westminster was applied by the itinerant judges throughout the country, becoming the 'common law' of England. By the mid-thirteenth century, the high courts were taking shape. The Court of King's Bench, Court of Common Pleas, Court of Exchequer and Court of Chancery all developed from the Curia Regis and continued until 1875. Circuit judges still exist, and Assize courts only disappeared in 1971.

For more detail of the development of the court system, see Sir John Baker, *An Introduction to English Legal History* (5th edn, Oxford: OUP 2019) or S.F.C. Milsom, *Historical Foundations of the Common Law* (2nd edn, London: Butterworths 1981).

⏵ **CROSS REFERENCE**

See section 3.2.3

In some ways, this was an age of personal rule by kings, who exercised power known as the royal prerogative.

In reality, however, monarchs were not all powerful. They could not make laws without the assent of their council of advisors, and when kings needed money, usually to pursue foreign policy such as fighting wars, they needed the consent of their council to impose taxes. At times this was ignored, with disastrous consequences, and royal power would fluctuate until the late seventeenth century. Nevertheless, kings continued to maintain a council of advisors which came to be known as the King's Council. The King in Council made law, raised taxes, and dis-pensed justice, and although the king could choose to ignore its members, his council could act as a brake on royal power. An early example of this is Henry I's Coronation Charter, or Charter of Liberties, drawn up in 1100 with the advice and counsel of the 'barons of England', in which the king promised concessions to his noblemen, and which served as a model for Magna Carta (see the Charter at www.bl.uk/collection-items/coronation-charter-of-henry-i).

THINKING POINT

Where do power and authority seem to reside at this stage?

2.2.1 **Magna Carta**

Magna Carta began as a political expedient but has become an iconic symbol of freedom and liberty. It came about as a result of the grievances of rebel barons under King John, an unpop-ular and extravagant king. Among a plethora of issues, he exploited his feudal rights to gener-ate income, imposing excessive and arbitrary taxes and demanding large sums of money from members of the nobility when they wanted to marry or claim an inheritance. In 1215, he demanded an unprecedented level of *scutage* from his barons (scutage was 'shield money', a tax that knights could pay instead of providing military service). In protest, rebel barons renounced their oaths of allegiance to the king and armed conflict erupted. In June 1215 at Runnymede in Surrey, the king was presented with a set of written demands drawn up by the barons, the Church, and merchants, which focused chiefly on protection from oppressive royal rule and restoring the ancient freedoms in Henry I's Coronation Charter to all free men. The king was forced to attach his seal to the charter which became known as Magna Carta.

CLOSE-UP FOCUS: MAGNA CARTA (1215) AND THE CHARTER OF THE FOREST (1217)

Although the reasons for Magna Carta were political, its lasting significance lies in affirming that the king did not have absolute power. The king's behaviour had highlighted an ambiguity: was 'law' the law of the land or the king's wishes? Glanvill, a twelfth-century lawyer and Henry II's Chief Justiciar (chief minister), wrote that the king's will was law but by 1215 the barons believed that the king was breaking the *law of the land*, and the law needed defining in writing. Magna Carta therefore made it clear that the king was subject to the law and to an element of control by his subjects. Key provisions of the 1215 version were:

- No tax was to be payable without the consent of the kingdom. [Clause 12—this was omitted in later versions]
- Noblemen and clergy were to be summoned to a fixed place to provide consent to taxation. [Clause 14—also omitted in later versions but one of the fundamental features of Parliament]
- There was to be no punishment without the lawful judgment of one's peers or the law of the land, and justice should not be delayed or denied. [Clauses 39 and 40—these were renumbered as Clause 29 in later versions]
- There are a number of references in the Charter to the 'law of the land' [eg Clauses 39 and 55], supporting the barons' view that the law was not simply the king's wishes but existed separately with a force of its own

Four copies of the 1215 Magna Carta still survive. For a full version of Magna Carta, see www.bl.uk/magna-carta/articles/magna-carta-english-translation.

The Charter of the Forest 1217 was significant in controlling royal law, and it related specifically to 'forest law'. The forest consisted of large swathes of land designated by Norman kings as royal hunting grounds; significantly extended over time, they included the whole of the county of Essex. The forest was strictly controlled by arbitrary royal laws, separate from the common law, and stringent punishments were imposed on those who breached them, including death, castration, and mutilation. The Charter of the Forest repeated a provision in Magna Carta that the forest area was to be reduced; it also abolished the death penalty, reduced other punishments, and provided rights for free men living in the forest. Some laws in the Charter of the Forest remained in force until 1971, and it created rights that still operate today in the New Forest in Hampshire.

For more background detail on Magna Carta, see Anthony Arlidge and Igor Judge, *Magna Carta Uncovered* (Oxford and Portland, Oregon: Hart Publishing 2014).

For a critical focus, see Andrew Blick, *Beyond Magna Carta* (Oxford and Portland, Oregon: Hart Publishing 2015), and Lord Sumption, 'Magna Carta Then and Now', Address to the Friends of the British Library, 9 March 2015.

❱ CROSS REFERENCE
See Chapter 8

Less than three months after Magna Carta was sealed, the Pope declared at the king's request that it was void, but in 1216 King John died, and Magna Carta was revised, reduced and reissued in 1216, 1217, and 1225. In 1297, Magna Carta and the Charter of the Forest were confirmed as a statute which was read to the people twice a year, thus increasing its significance; in 1369, Parliament passed a statute declaring that any law infringing Magna Carta was void. However, most of Magna Carta's provisions were repealed between 1863 and 1947, and today only three clauses are still in force, the best known of which is Clause 29.

2.3 The beginnings of Parliament

 THINKING POINT

The modern Parliament sits at Westminster and consists of two chambers: the House of Commons and the House of Lords. Law is made by the 'Queen in Parliament'. Note how these features develop in the section that follows.

The term 'parliament' was in use by 1236 to describe an assembly for debate, which at that time included the King's Council; the seeds of the first Parliament were sown by discontent with King John's son Henry III, a weak king who imposed extortionate taxes and had fought disastrous wars. A group of barons led by Simon de Montfort, the king's brother-in-law, attempted to restrict his authority by drawing up radical new rules in the Provisions of Oxford in 1258, requiring the king to govern under the supervision of a Council which would be monitored by a Parliament, meeting three times a year. The king agreed in return for financial support, then went back on his pledge; civil war followed in which de Montfort took the king prisoner and ruled England in the king's name. De Montfort held two parliaments: the first in 1264, when he ordered four knights elected by each county to attend, and the second in January 1265 at Westminster (by then England's capital). The second one was significant because for the first time, representatives from the wider community or the 'commons' (two citizens and two burgesses from each city and town) were also summoned to attend to join the noblemen and bishops.

De Montfort was killed in 1265 at the Battle of Evesham but his legacy of Parliament lived on. It was very different from today's Parliament, meeting once or twice a year, often with considerable gaps in between. The king had the power to summon, suspend, and dissolve it, and there was no true democracy yet, but de Montfort's idea of elected representatives from the shires and the towns continued.

 EXAMPLE

There is an early reference to the Commons in the 1275 Statute of Westminster (still on the statute books for its provision on free elections), which was expressed to be 'the Act of King Edward at his first Parliament' made 'by his Council and by the assent of Archbishops, Bishops, Earls, Barons, and the *Commonalty* of the Realm'.

Early Parliaments were mainly concerned with raising money through taxation; Magna Carta established that the king could not impose taxes directly and Parliament was needed to grant the king finance (known as 'supply'), setting in train the essential pairing of taxation and representation which remains today. As the need for taxation grew, so did the need for a wider cross-section of representatives of taxpayers. In the 1295 Model Parliament, Edward I set the standard by requiring the regular attendance of elected representatives from the Commons in the cities, towns, and counties on the basis of 'what concerns all should be approved by all', and this had become a permanent arrangement by 1327.

In the 1340s, the Commons was extended to merchants and gentry and in 1341, Parliament divided into two Houses, with elected knights, burgesses, and citizens in the House of Commons, and the nobility and clergy in the House of Lords. Military campaigns in the fourteenth century meant a greater need for taxation, providing Parliament with more leverage to impose conditions on the king, particularly on new laws. In law-making, the king was now consulting the representatives of the people in Parliament to ascertain the opinion of the country, and as the membership broadened, it provided a more representative view of what the people would tolerate and what they would not. By the 1440s, Fortescue (a Chief Justice of the King's Bench who wrote *In Praise of the Laws of England*) was stating: 'A King of England cannot, at his pleasure, make any alterations in the laws of the land.' He made it plain that the king needed the consent of his subjects to change the law and the people were to be governed by laws made with their consent. The monarch and Parliament were becoming closely linked, and law was being made with the consent of the 'three estates of the realm': the king, the Lords, and the Commons.

By the 1500s, though its meetings were intermittent and it could be dominated by the monarch, Parliament was becoming stronger. Henry VIII needed Parliament's co-operation to enable him to break from the Catholic Church in Rome and establish the Church of England, with himself as its head, so that he could marry Anne Boleyn. Parliament passed the Act of Supremacy 1534, establishing the king and successive monarchs as the Supreme Head of the Church of England and linking the Church and State. Parliament also passed the Laws in Wales Acts 1536–1542, uniting England and Wales, extending English law into Wales to make one legal system, and allowing Welsh MPs to sit in Parliament in Westminster.

THINKING POINT

Who holds law-making authority at this point? Has your answer changed?

In the meantime, government power was developing in the form of the King's Council or Royal Council; its members consisted of bishops, the Lord Chancellor, the Treasurer, noblemen, lawyers, and judges, though the king was still the dominant figure. By the fifteenth and sixteenth centuries, the Council was concerned with public administration, but still advised the monarch and had a judicial role with power to summon and punish individuals. Specialist committees and departments began to form to deal with specific areas such as tax and home affairs, and they were the forerunners of modern government departments. An inner circle of influential, trusted advisors also evolved, known by Tudor times as the Privy Council, a key element of government and a powerful body administering affairs of state.

2.4 1603–1688: the turbulent journey to a constitutional settlement

> James I and his sons staunchly exercised the royal prerogative, which conflicted with supporters of parliamentary government and the rule of law. This led to increasing tensions between the king and Parliament which would ultimately change the balance of power and reshape the constitution.

James I was the first of the Stuart kings and came to the throne in 1603, after the death of Elizabeth I. He was also James VI of Scotland but although England and Scotland now shared a monarch, they continued to have separate Parliaments for another hundred years. Best known for narrowly escaping assassination at the hands of Guy Fawkes in the 1605 Gunpowder Plot, James fervently believed in the divine right of kings (the idea that the king was only answerable to God and not to any authority on earth) and asserting royal power (the royal prerogative); he thought that the king was above the law, accountable to no one, and could make and unmake law as he pleased. Unversed in the workings of the English Parliament, he believed that he could summon and suspend Parliament as he wished and intervene in its business, and he expected Parliament to be compliant and respectful. He was wrong. Parliament refused to vote him additional monies; he began to sell political and judicial offices to raise funds, and subsequently dissolved Parliament from 1614 to 1622.

 THINKING POINT

Do you think this was consistent with the developments outlined in section 2.3?

The tensions between James I and one of his judges, Sir Edward Coke (Chief Justice of the Court of Common Pleas until the king dismissed him in 1616), forged legal principles which still endure. In a series of cases (the *Case of Prohibitions* (1607), the *Case of Proclamations* (1611), and *Dr Bonham's Case* (1610)), Coke set clear limits on the king's power, stating that the king was subject to the law and that judges, not the king, exercised the judicial function. Coke's celebration of Magna Carta as the source of rights and freedoms in English law in his works, *The Institutes of the Laws of England*, elevated it to become greater than the sum of its parts and a metaphor for freedom and liberty. The liberties expressed in Magna Carta were exported into North American law and early state constitutions in the 1600s, and later into the US Constitution and Bill of Rights.

⟩ CROSS REFERENCE
See section 12.3.1.2

2.4.1 **Civil War**

> The causes of constitutional change or strife over the centuries were often religion, royal power, or events abroad. With the English Civil War, all three elements came into play.

Charles I became king in 1625 when his father, James I, died. Like James, Charles believed in absolute monarchy and the divine right of kings with no limits on his power, and that he had the royal power to rule without Parliament. An assertive king meeting an increasingly assertive Parliament was bound to end in trouble. There were repeated clashes between Charles and Parliament over money; in 1626, in an attempt to address significant shortfalls in finances to wage war against France, Charles imposed forced loans on wealthier members of society. A total of 76 men refused to pay; five were imprisoned without charge and applied for writs of *habeas corpus*. In the subsequent *Five Knights Case (Darnel's case* (1627) 3 St Tr 1), the court held that the king had a discretionary power to imprison them for reasons of state necessity and did not have to show the reasons on the warrant. This allowed the king and the state a lawful, but very broad, discretion. The *Five Knights Case* spurred Parliament into presenting the Petition of Right 1628 to Charles. One of its chief architects was Sir Edward Coke, by this time a Member of Parliament, and the Petition set out liberties based on Magna Carta and limits on the king's prerogative powers, especially taxation without Parliament's consent and imprisonment without trial. The king was forced to agree to it.

Habeas corpus is an action allowing the lawfulness of a person's detention to be challenged in court

 THINKING POINT

Who were the judges supporting in the *Five Knights Case*? Be aware of how the tensions over authority are building here with Parliament asserting itself—and the law—against the king.

However, in 1629 Charles dissolved Parliament, which did not sit again until 1640, and in the interim he ruled England personally. This added to his difficulties as he could not raise taxes without Parliament's consent but could not obtain Parliament's consent if it was not sitting. The king needed money to build up the navy, so he tried to extend the payment of 'ship money'. This was a tax which had been imposed for many years by the Crown on ports and coastal towns to provide ships and equipment for naval defence. After consulting his judges, the king gradually extended the ship money tax to inland towns throughout the country. John Hampden from Buckinghamshire (a nephew of one of the Five Knights) refused to pay. In *R v Hampden* (the *Ship Money Case* (1637) 3 St. Tr. 825), the court held that the demand to pay ship money was lawful, but the case highlighted the king's autocratic rule. In 1642, Charles overreached himself further when, unbidden, he entered Parliament with an armed guard and demanded the arrest of five MPs. The scene was set for conflict between the Royalists (the king's supporters) and Parliamentarians.

The First Civil War was fought from 1642 to 1646 and ended with Charles's defeat and surrender. Had it stopped there, constitutional history might have taken a different turn, but Charles incited a Second Civil War in 1648. He was tried by the House of Lords, found guilty of treason, and beheaded on 30 January 1649. The monarchy and House of Lords were abolished and from 1653 to 1658 England became a republic ruled by Oliver Cromwell, the Lord Protector, who introduced a short-lived written constitution known as the Instrument of Government that was in place from 1653 to 1657.

In 1660, the monarchy in England was restored and Charles I's son, Charles II, became king, promising to rule with Parliament and unpicking many of the reforms of Cromwell's Protectorate. In particular, the Instrument of Government was abolished as treasonable and the House of Lords and Privy Council were reinstated.

2.4.2 **The Glorious Revolution**

> The Glorious Revolution culminated in the 'constitutional settlement' denoting the transition from personal rule by the monarch to parliamentary government. The era of the King-in-Parliament had arrived, where Parliament and the monarch shared law-making power.

When Charles II died in 1685 without any legitimate children, his brother James became king (James II). James had earlier converted to Catholicism at a time when Protestants in Britain feared a Catholic conspiracy to overthrow the church and the state. Their fears were compounded when, as king, James built up a considerable standing army and suspended Parliament in 1685 after a clash over the appointment of Catholic army officers; once again, England was ruled directly by the monarch. James also believed that he was above the law and used his royal power to allow Catholics to hold public office by suspending a law passed by Parliament known as the Test Act 1673 (which required anyone taking public office to take a religious oath or test). The key question was: could the king suspend laws made by Parliament? This was tested in the case of *Godden v Hales*.

🔍 CASE CLOSE-UP: *GODDEN v HALES* (1686) 11 ST TR 1166

Colonel Hales had taken office without swearing the required religious oath of loyalty to Protestantism. Effectively bringing a test case, Hales told his coachman, Godden, to inform on him, and Hales was convicted and punished. On appeal, Hales argued that the king had personally suspended the requirement for an oath. The court held that the king *did* have the right to suspend the Test Acts because the kings of England were sovereign, the laws of England were the king's laws, therefore the king retained an ancient prerogative power to dispense with any laws as he thought necessary. That power came not from the people, but was the 'ancient remains of the sovereign power and prerogative of the kings of England'.

In 1687 James issued a Declaration of Indulgence, which promoted Catholicism and religious freedom by suspending the Penal Laws which required worship in the Church of England; he also dissolved Parliament. The following year, his second wife gave birth to a son, the new Catholic heir to the throne and the last straw for a group of influential Protestants who invited James' Protestant daughter, Mary, and her husband, William of Orange—a Dutch Protestant—to seize the throne. William duly 'invaded' England, landing unchallenged at Brixham in Devon, and when James eventually fled, Parliament treated it as an abdication. These events are known as the Glorious Revolution, so called because it was achieved with limited bloodshed in England, although there was considerably more loss of life in subsequent fighting in Ireland and Scotland.

🔍 CLOSE-UP FOCUS: THE BILL OF RIGHTS 1689

When William and Mary were offered the throne, Parliament read out to them a Declaration of Rights which was subsequently passed as the Bill of Rights 1689. It established constitutional monarchy by limiting the power of the monarch and strengthening the powers of Parliament in a rebalancing known as the 'constitutional settlement'. It provided that:

- it was illegal for the monarch to suspend or dispense with laws;
- there was no right of taxation without Parliament's consent;
- the monarch could not raise or keep a standing army in peacetime without Parliament's consent;
- there should be free elections of Members of Parliament;
- there should be freedom of speech within Parliament;
- Parliament should be summoned frequently.

In short, it settled the constitutional see-sawing of power and established the King-in-Parliament who made law with Parliament's consent. Parliament was now imposing *its* terms on the monarchy and at this point, although Parliament was still not a democratically elected body, the notion of parliamentary sovereignty begins.

See www.legislation.gov.uk/aep/WillandMarSess2/1/2/introduction.

> **CROSS REFERENCE**
> See Chapter 6

💬 THINKING POINT

Who had supreme authority after the Bill of Rights 1689?

2.5 1689–1800: consolidation and expansion

This was the age of Britain's upward trajectory as a prosperous world power: the age of global trade and empire-building, of natural rights and the enlightenment, but also of the slave trade and Britain's loss of America in 1783 after the War of Independence.

When Princess Anne, the heir to the throne, lost her only surviving child in 1700, Parliament wished to settle once and for all the issue of the succession. It therefore passed the Act of Settlement 1701, providing that there could not be a Catholic monarch and that the succession would pass through Electress Sophia of Hanover, a granddaughter of James I, as the nearest Protestant relative. However, the English Parliament did not consult the Scots about this and Scotland was unhappy with the line of succession, threatening to put its own monarch in place; to resolve the crisis, the English Parliament passed a statute (the Alien Act 1705) introducing an embargo on trade with Scotland which would be suspended if Scotland accepted the Hanoverian succession and negotiated a union with England (union between England and Scotland had been broached on and off since 1689). The Scottish economy was not strong and Scotland wanted access to the lucrative colonial trade offered by England's burgeoning Empire, so union prevailed; a treaty was signed in 1706 and was ratified by the Act of Union with Scotland 1707, creating the United Kingdom of Great Britain 'for ever after'.

❱ CROSS REFERENCE

See section 13.2.1

The Act of Settlement 1701 also provided that judges could not easily be dismissed and effectively had job security. Until the seventeenth century, judges could be dismissed at the king's pleasure and put on trial by Parliament for misconduct; this was known as 'impeachment' and applied to holders of public office under the Crown (the judges from the *Ship Money case* were impeached for 'treasons and misdemeanours' for setting themselves above Parliament in their decision). But it was perhaps no coincidence that judges, once securely appointed, turned their attention in a number of important eighteenth-century cases, notably *Entick v Carrington* (1765) 19 St Tr 1030, to the limits on the power of government ministers, establishing that they were bound by the law and curbing any notion of undefined arbitrary power. There was also greater recognition of the right to liberty, notably in *Somersett v Steuart* (1772) 20 St Tr 1 where the court held that the common law did not recognise the right to enforce ownership of a slave.

Meanwhile, government was developing. In the early 1700s, an early Cabinet of ministers began to form and in 1721 the role of Prime Minister emerged, albeit hazily, when Robert Walpole was created First Lord of the Treasury. This was a response to practicalities. George I, the first Hanoverian king, spoke little English and was often abroad. As monarch, he was head of the executive and it was sensible that a competent, influential minister should be responsible for the day-to-day administration of state business, although it took until the end of the century before the office of Prime Minister was firmly established. In the last 20 years of the eighteenth century, defined political parties developed and would come to dominate Parliament (the Whigs and Tories had first emerged in the 1600s as political divisions), and although there had been a Treasury since the Norman Conquest, government departments began to form, with a Colonial Office in 1768 and the Home Office and Foreign Office in 1782.

❱ CROSS REFERENCE

For modern government, see Chapter 12

As the eighteenth century drew to a close, the French revolution (1789–1799) unleashed thoughts of freedom and fighting tyranny. It inspired Thomas Paine to publish *The Rights of Man* in 1791; his encouragement of republicanism and wider participation in electing representatives inspired political rights campaigns well into the next century. War broke out between Britain and France in 1793, and in 1796 there was a real possibility of invasion by Napoleon Bonaparte, using Ireland as a base from which to attack England. That fear of invasion and the instability in Ireland caused by a rebellion in 1798 were the catalysts for promoting union with Ireland, and the Act of Union with Ireland 1800 created the United Kingdom of Great Britain and Ireland 'for ever after'.

 THINKING POINT

Compare the reasons for union (a) with Scotland and (b) with Ireland.

2.6 1800–1914: prosperity and reform

> During the nineteenth century Britain became a dominant world power, and the growth of the urban working class as a result of the Industrial Revolution generated a period of electoral and social reform, and an increase in local government and public administration.

This began as an era where the French Revolution was fresh in the minds of British politicians. There was a mutual fear between the rulers and the governed: government feared revolution, and the people feared tyranny and rule without law. From the early 1800s, the impetus for electoral reform took hold, with pressure for the vote to be extended to working-class men. Instead of barons seeking to change the law, it was now the people in a tug-of-war of power with the government.

The right to vote had been based on property qualifications for centuries and in 1780, fewer than 2 per cent of people could vote; in 1820 it was still only around 5 per cent, though some constituencies—known as 'rotten boroughs'—could return MPs to Parliament with only a handful of voters (the most commonly cited example is Old Sarum, with seven voters and two MPs). One of the catalysts for change was the Peterloo massacre. In 1819, at St Peter's Fields in Manchester, 60,000 peaceful protestors were campaigning for universal suffrage at a mass meeting. Local magistrates ordered that the meeting should be broken up by force and soldiers were sent in to arrest the leading speaker, Henry Hunt; the troops charged the crowd on horseback with swords and clubs. Fifteen people were killed and many hundreds injured. A collection of six statutes, known as the Six Acts 1819, was subsequently enacted to suppress and regulate public meetings, introduce search powers and punish seditious writing, but the drive for the vote continued.

In 1832, the Representation of the People Act (popularly known as the Great Reform Act) increased the electorate to around 18 per cent of adult males by redistributing seats and lowering the property qualification needed to vote. The Chartist movement campaigned during the 1830s and 1840s to extend the vote to the working class, drawing up a Charter in 1838 setting out proposed voting reforms and presenting petitions to the House of Commons in 1839 and 1842, supported by more than one million and three million signatures respectively. Eventually, the Representation of the People Acts in 1867 and 1884 tripled the electorate in England and Wales, enabling more men (but still not women) to consent to law-making through their elected representatives in Parliament.

Parliamentary sovereignty became stronger during the nineteenth century, in an era which recognised that law could achieve social reform, as acknowledgement of the need to protect society's vulnerable and less privileged emerged. The slave trade was ended by the Abolition of the Slave Trade Act 1807, and the Abolition of Slavery Act 1833 provided for the gradual abolition of slavery in British territories. Laws to improve public health and working conditions were introduced, particularly in relation to child labour; for example, the Factory Act 1833 prohibited employing children younger than nine years old in woollen mills, and the Factory Act 1847 ensured a ten-hour working day for women and young people. These measures needed enforcement at national or local level so a new network of administrators, inspectors, and regulators was created; as a consequence, a system of public administration was born, and as public bodies increased, the executive grew stronger. At the beginning of the twentieth century, the Liberal government initiated the welfare state by introducing old age pensions; the question of how they would be

⟩ CROSS REFERENCE

To find out more about the Parliament Act, see section 10.4

financed resulted in a constitutional crisis which was ultimately resolved by the Parliament Act 1911. The Act enabled the House of Commons to become the dominant chamber of Parliament.

2.7 1914–1945: global conflict

> Within the space of just over 30 years in the twentieth century, unprecedented global conflict in the two world wars etched inevitable and lasting change on Britain.

In large part due to the work undertaken by women as part of the war effort in the First World War (1914–1918), the Representation of the People Act 1918 gave the vote to women over the age of 30 who met a property qualification, and to all men over 21, although it was only with the Representation of the People (Equal Franchise) Act 1928 that women over 21 were given the same voting rights as men.

After the First World War, the rise of nationalism and self-determination in Britain's colonies started the fragmentation of its Empire. The Easter Rising in Dublin in 1916 and rebellion in Ireland led to the Anglo-Irish Treaty 1921, which partitioned Ireland into Northern Ireland—which remained part of the UK—and the Irish Free State. In 1922, the Irish Free State became an independent dominion and left Britain, despite the 'for ever after' clause in the Act of Union with Ireland. Britain now became the United Kingdom of Great Britain and Northern Ireland. In 1937, the Irish Free State became known as Eire.

In 1942, in the middle of the Second World War (1939–1945), William Beveridge, a Liberal politician, produced the Beveridge Report, proposing a welfare state with a national health service, a social security system funded by national insurance, free education, and strategies for full employment. In July 1945, just before the war ended and as fighting still continued in the Far East, a General Election was held. Winston Churchill, the wartime Prime Minister, was confident of victory, but, not for the first time—or the last—the British people delivered a surprise result, voting the Labour party into power. As the war brought Britain to the edge of bankruptcy, the people wanted change and an end to wartime austerity (the economist John Maynard Keynes was sent to America and negotiated a loan totalling $3.75 billion—Britain made the last repayment of this in 2006). Change was going to happen.

2.8 1945–1997: rebuilding Britain's changing role in the world

> After the Second World War, a radical programme of reconstruction took place in Britain. Between 1945 and 1948, statutes were introduced creating the welfare state, in addition to a programme of nationalisation and town planning. Beyond Britain, there was a new international focus on human rights.

The Family Allowances Act 1945, National Insurance Act 1946, and National Health Service Act 1946 set up the framework of the welfare state, and led to increased expansion of the administrative state and stronger government. A more complex state required more detailed legislation and as a result saw a significant increase in delegated legislation made by ministers under powers conferred by Parliament. As power was conferred on a growing number of administrative bodies, there was greater need for regulation through public law to ensure accountability, and the state's increased impact on individuals' lives required avenues for redress via the administrative justice system, particularly through judicial review, where the courts review the lawfulness of actions by public bodies.

⟩ CROSS REFERENCE
See section 11.4

⟩ CROSS REFERENCE
See Chapters 14, 15, and 16

With post-war recovery, Britain's global power waned and it struggled to find its place in a re-ordered world (in Dean Acheson's memorable words, 'Great Britain has lost an empire and not yet found a role'). India and Pakistan became independent in 1947. Southern Ireland (Eire) became the Republic of Ireland and left the Commonwealth in 1949. The 1960s and 1970s saw many of Britain's colonies in Africa and the Caribbean become independent, and Britain needed to look outside its Empire for trade and alliances.

In 1950, the European Convention on Human Rights was created, setting out a code of human rights and fundamental freedoms to promote peace and democracy in post-war Europe. Britain was a founder signatory. One of the periodic seismic shifts in Britain's constitutional history followed in 1972 when Britain signed the Brussels Treaty, becoming a member of the European Economic Community trading bloc (the Common Market), enabling it to trade freely with other member states. The European Communities Act 1972 gave effect to European law within the UK, which meant that the UK was now inextricably bound by the rules and laws of what later became the European Union.

2.9 1997–present day: constitutional reform

> This has been an era of profound social change and a search for British identity in a multi-cultural, multi-faith society, and a more interconnected world. The UK has also seen a period of intense and far-reaching constitutional change.

Promising national renewal, decentralised power, and real rights for citizens in its election manifesto, the Labour government that came to power in 1997 introduced a programme of significant and sweeping constitutional changes resulting in an unprecedented flurry of reforming statutes between 1998 and 2005, although Turpin and Tomkins observe that 'It is difficult to discern an overall constitutional vision that binds the reforms together' (*British Government and the Constitution: Text and Materials*, 6th edn, Cambridge: Cambridge University Press 2007, p 24). Rather than the evolving, often reactive change that we have seen so far, the Labour reforms set out to introduce deliberate, forward-looking changes to government, institutions and the law, including:

- the Human Rights Act 1998, incorporating the European Convention on Human Rights into UK law and giving a stronger role to judges as guardians of human rights, with the power to review decisions of public authorities for human rights compliance;

⟩ CROSS REFERENCE
See Chapter 17

- devolution of power to Scotland, Wales and Northern Ireland in 1998, resulting in decentralised government;

❱ CROSS REFERENCE
See Chapter 10

- removal of the right of hereditary peers to sit in the House of Lords (House of Lords Act 1999);

- more transparent and open government introduced by the Freedom of Information Act 2000;

❱ CROSS REFERENCE
See Chapters 7 and 13

- reform of the office of Lord Chancellor and the creation of a new Supreme Court to replace the Appellate Committee of the House of Lords (Constitutional Reform Act 2005).

Definition

Devolution means the delegation of power by a central body to a subordinate body. See Chapter 4.

❱ CROSS REFERENCE
See Chapter 10

In 2009, the Freedom of Information Act helped bring to light the MPs' expenses scandal, which resulted in parliamentary reforms to restore public confidence in the political system; the Parliamentary Standards Act 2009 created a new independent body to regulate MPs' expenses. In 2011, the Fixed-term Parliaments Act removed the Prime Minister's discretion over when to call an election, and in a referendum, the public was offered the opportunity to change the voting system in general elections (the result was decisively in favour of keeping the current system). Increasing use of referendums on key constitutional issues has placed more emphasis on decision-making by the people, resulting in less predictability. In the Scottish independence referendum of 2014, Scotland voted against leaving the UK, but the decision to leave the EU in the Brexit referendum in June 2016 shook the foundations of the UK's constitutional arrangements of the past 45 years, leaving the UK rocking on its heels. The UK left the EU on 31 January 2020 but the Brexit process has reinvigorated the Scottish independence debate. At present it remains to be seen whether the UK will fragment once more into separate states, but the likelihood is that, whatever happens, the UK has probably seen it all before.

❱ CROSS REFERENCE
For detail on Brexit, see
Chapter 5

 SUMMARY

- The question posed at the beginning of this chapter was: where would sovereignty settle? The answer is that supreme authority settled in the King/Queen in Parliament, while political power resides with the executive

- There was never an overarching plan for the development of Britain's constitution and no one knows the final destination

- The UK constitution is never static and is constantly changing, yet—at least until recently—it has retained the appearance of stability and constancy

- The UK constitution has the flexibility to change and forge, through trial and error, crucially important constitutional principles which can stand the test of time

? Questions

Self-test questions

1. What was (a) a Witan; (b) the Curia Regis?

2. What important principle is Magna Carta best known for?

3. What was Simon de Montfort's legacy?

4. Why was it important for the monarch to require Parliament's consent when making laws and imposing taxation?

5. What was the constitutional settlement achieved by the Bill of Rights 1689?

6. Explain the significance of extending the right to vote to all adults.

Exam question

'Until 1997, it could reasonably be said that our Constitution, by which I mean our system of government, was what has been called a historic Constitution. What I mean by that is not merely that it is very old, though it certainly is that, but that it was unplanned; the product of evolution rather than, as it were, human thinking. It just evolved, in a way that so many British institutions have been evolved, and it was very difficult to actually discover what it was.' (Vernon Bogdanor, Gresham Lecture 16 June 2009, available at https://www.gresham.ac.uk/lectures-and-events/the-new-british-constitution)

To what extent do you agree with this statement?

Further reading

Books

Allison, J.W.F. *The English Historical Constitution: Continuity, Change and European Effects* (Cambridge: Cambridge University Press 2007).
A more advanced text which analyses the formation of the constitution from a critical, historical perspective

Arlidge, A. and Judge, I. *Magna Carta Uncovered* (Oxford and Portland, Oregon: Hart Publishing 2014).
An immersive account of the background and context of Magna Carta and its influence on subsequent constitutional developments

Blick, A. *Beyond Magna Carta: A Constitution for the United Kingdom* (Oxford and Portland, Oregon: Hart Publishing 2015).
A detailed critique of Magna Carta and its legacy on the constitutional narrative

Sedley, S. *Lions under the Throne: Essays on the History of English Public Law* (Cambridge: Cambridge University Press 2015).
A lively, very readable tour through key historical events which provides a wealth of detail for the topics outlined in this chapter

Other sources

Baroness Hale, 'Magna Carta: Did She Die in Vain', Gray's Inn, 19 October 2015 (www.supremecourt.uk/docs/speech-151019.pdf).
An accessible discussion of the constitutional importance and resonance of Magna Carta on its 800th anniversary

Lord Sumption, 'Magna Carta Then and Now', Address to the Friends of the British Library, 9 March 2015 (www.supremecourt.uk/docs/speech-150309.pdf).
Another 800th anniversary speech with a critical focus on the lawyer's view of Magna Carta versus the historian's view, written by a former Justice of the Supreme Court who is also an eminent historian

Mostyn, J., 'Magna Carta and Access to Justice in Family Proceedings', National Access to Justice and Pro Bono Conference, Sydney 18–19 June 2015 (www.judiciary.uk/wp-content/uploads/2015/06/mostyn-speech-najpbc-sydney-18-june-15.pdf).
An accessibly written critique of Magna Carta

؛ Online resources

www.oup.com/he/dennett2e

This chapter is accompanied by a selection of online resources to help you with this topic, including:

- Multiple-choice questions
- Answers to the self-test questions
- Guidance on answering the exam question

3 The features and sources of the UK constitution

☐ LEARNING OBJECTIVES

By the end of this chapter, you should be able to:

- Identify and discuss the features of the UK constitution
- Appreciate the flexibility of the UK constitution
- Assess the operation of the sources of the UK constitution
- Discuss the nature and operation of constitutional conventions
- Evaluate the arguments for and against a written constitution

Introduction

Constitutions are normally a higher form of law, often made by and for the people, and most are codified, whereas the UK constitution is uncodified and still predominantly a political constitution. If you had to draft a constitution for the UK, how would you go about it? Where would you find the existing rules so that you could codify them; would you only include broad principles or provide for every eventuality; how easy would it be to change its provisions; or would you decide it works well as it is and let it be? These are issues that this chapter addresses.

The UK constitution has evolved largely through a process of action and reaction to events rather than by deliberate design, more as a meandering ancient highway than a purpose-built motorway, and in doing so, it has accumulated a rich variety of rules in scattered sources. It is a constitution that is still based to a large extent on custom and political practice, and J.A.G. Griffith encapsulated its practical operation when he observed: 'Our constitution in the UK is "no more and no less than what happens". Everything that happens is constitutional. And if nothing happened that would be constitutional also' ('The Political Constitution' (1979) 42 MLR 1, 19).

This chapter explains the characteristics of the UK constitution and introduces you to important concepts, such as parliamentary sovereignty, and constitutional reforms, such as devolution, to pave the way for the substantive discussions in later chapters. It goes on to explain the sources of the UK constitution and where we find its essential rules, focusing particularly on constitutional conventions. We finish by discussing whether the constitution should be codified, but first, we turn to the UK constitution's specific characteristics.

3.1 The features of the UK constitution

> **The main features of the UK constitution**
>
> It is:
>
> - uncodified;
> - flexible;
> - traditionally unitary but now debatably a union state;
> - monarchical;
> - parliamentary;
> - based on a bedrock of important constitutional doctrines and principles: parliamentary sovereignty, the rule of law, separation of powers; the courts are also basing some decisions on bedrock principles of the common law (see Chapter 9).

⟫ CROSS REFERENCE

For the characteristics of constitutions generally, see Chapter 1

3.1.1 **Uncodified**

> I love the British Constitution being unwritten or still largely unwritten. It means that we historians can do it rather than the lawyers. (Lord Hennessy, *The Educational Indispensability of Political History: British Prime Ministers since 1945*, The Sir John Cass Foundation Lecture, 23 October 2013)

It is more accurate to describe the UK constitution as uncodified rather than unwritten. While there is no single document that specifically embodies the UK constitution, many of its laws, practices, and non-legal rules *are* in written form (particularly statutes, law reports, and ministerial codes). The UK is one of only three democracies in the world without a written constitution; the others are New Zealand and Israel, and New Zealand's constitution, like the UK's, is scattered among sources that include 45 Acts of Parliament, 12 treaties, nine common law sources, and eight conventions (see Matthew Palmer, 'What Is New Zealand's Constitution and Who Interprets It?' (2006) 17 PLR 133. In 2016, Sir Geoffrey Palmer, a former prime minister of New Zealand, published proposals for a written constitution. Observing that New Zealanders think little about their constitution because they cannot find it, he stated:

> The current New Zealand Constitution consists of a hodge-podge of rules, some legally binding, others not. It is formed by a jumble of statutes, some New Zealand ones and some very old English ones; a plethora of obscure conventions, letters patent and manuals, and a raft of decisions of the courts … no attempt has been made to bring the sum of the parts together. (https://constitution-unit.com/2016/08/18/new-zealand-needs-a-new-written-constitution/)

Much the same can be said of the UK constitution. Imagine the UK's power structure as a pyramid; at the apex, supreme authority vested originally in the monarch, then in Parliament, so there has been no vacancy at the top for a written constitution. The fact that a codified constitution has never gained traction in the UK (apart from the 1653 Instrument of Government) is often said to be because of the UK's political continuity, with no revolution for 300 years, no invasion since 1066, and no sudden break to overthrow the old system of government; however, there *have* been upheavals of sufficient weight and force to have given rise to one. But the move to a codified constitution needs political will at government and parliamentary level and it needs to capture the imagination of the people to gain popular support—the constitutional moment. Those transitions have not happened in the UK—yet—although proposals to move to a codified constitution are gathering pace (see section 3.4).

3.1.1.1 A partially codified constitution?

It may no longer even be accurate to describe the UK constitution as wholly uncodified. It is certainly the case that some rules within the UK constitution have been gathered together in documentary form; we can find codified rules for operating the constitution in the *Cabinet Manual*, *Ministerial Code*, and *Civil Service Code* (though they do not have legal status), and a category of constitutional statutes has been recognised (see 3.2.1), including the devolution Acts which set out the rules for how devolution operates for each institution. It can be argued that these documents and statutes set out at least some of the instructions and normative rules for running the UK.

> **Definition**
> Devolution is power given on loan by a central authority to subordinate bodies. See section 3.1.3 and Chapter 4

3.1.1.2 Judges and the UK constitution

As the UK lacks a codified constitution with the status of higher law, there is no constitutional court with the power to review and strike down unconstitutional legislation passed by the UK Parliament because there is no overriding constitution against which to measure it. However, the courts *can* decide on the validity of laws made by the devolved legislatures in Scotland, Wales, and Northern Ireland, who must not create law beyond the power that they have been given by the UK Parliament (see Chapter 4).

 THINKING POINT

In 2016, China initiated a national campaign to encourage citizens to copy out the Chinese constitution over 100 days to promote education and awareness (there were media reports that one couple spent their honeymoon doing this). Would an exercise encouraging UK citizens to copy out the UK constitution be possible?

3.1.2 Flexible

The UK constitution is described as flexible because it is adaptable and can be easily altered. There is no special parliamentary procedure required to pass statutes that change the constitution, except that bills of 'first class constitutional importance' are considered by a committee of the entire House of Commons (though in 2011 the House of Lords Constitution

Committee recommended a special process for legislation proposing constitutional change: see *The Process of Constitutional Change* report in 'Further reading'). Thus the UK constitution is changed in the same way as ordinary law, in contrast to the rigid American constitution which has provisions that are protected by special procedures from change or removal, and are therefore entrenched to elevate them above ordinary law. However, while an entrenched constitution stands the test of time and enshrines constitutional rights, it can become outdated, whereas a flexible uncodified constitution like Britain's is more adaptable to change, particularly in social and cultural attitudes. For example, by passing the Marriage (Same Sex Couples) Act 2013, Parliament allowed same sex marriage: section 1(1) simply stated, 'Marriage of same sex couples is lawful'.

» CROSS REFERENCE

Refer to section 1.4.2 for the procedure needed to change the American constitution

At the heart of the UK is a sovereign Parliament instead of an entrenched constitution with supreme status, and it is parliament's sovereignty and significant *legal* discretion that help to generate the constitution's flexibility; an Act of Parliament can introduce constitutional changes which can later be reversed or altered. However, the UK constitution contains a large degree of *political* discretion which also allows it to be flexible and responsive to new issues, rather than being hidebound by hard and fast rules. Lord Bingham has observed:

> It would no doubt be possible, in theory at least, to devise a constitution in which all political contingencies would be the subject of predetermined mechanistic rules to be applied as and when the particular contingency arose. But such an approach would not be consistent with ordinary constitutional practice in Britain. There are of course certain fixed rules, such as those governing the maximum duration of parliaments or the period for which the House of Lords may delay the passage of legislation. But matters of potentially great importance are left to the judgment either of political leaders ... or ... the crown ... Where constitutional arrangements retain scope for the exercise of political judgment they permit a flexible response to differing and unpredictable events in a way which the application of strict rules would preclude. (*Robinson v Secretary of State for Northern Ireland* [2002] UKHL 32 [12])

Three important points can be drawn from this. Having constitutional rules that deal with every possible eventuality would not be consistent with how Britain operates its adaptable constitution (in reality, it is not possible for any form of constitution to predict every contingency). Second, the UK's constitutional rules that allow for political judgment produce flexibility in responding to unforeseen events. Finally, and importantly, there are fixed rules within the constitution that do not easily change, otherwise the constitution would be *too* fluid and uncertain. Those fixed points are the essential scaffolding of the constitution: the institutions of government (the monarchy, Parliament, the executive, the judiciary); their fundamental rules of operation; and key constitutional principles such as the rule of law and respect for fundamental rights.

In a flexible constitution, however, we have to trust government and Parliament not to initiate arbitrary change, and Lord Carswell expressed the view in the important case of *Jackson v AG* that 'An unwritten constitution, even more than a written one, is a living organism and develops with changing times, but it is still a delicate plant and is capable of being damaged by over-rigorous treatment, which may have incalculable results' (*Jackson v AG* [2006] 1 AC 262, 323).

This sounds a note of caution against introducing change for change's sake, or change that does not pay heed to the constitutional niceties, and this can be an issue in a flexible constitution. Sir John Baker, for example, has warned against 'incessant tinkering and experimentation' (see J.W.F. Allison, 'History in the Law of the Constitution' (2007) 28(3) Journal of Legal History 263 at 264).

EXAMPLE

A controversial proposal for change came with Tony Blair's announcement in 2003 that he intended to abolish the office of Lord Chancellor (it had been in existence since at least the fourteenth century), which he badged as a government reshuffle. The proposal caused something of a constitutional crisis.

The Lord Chancellor, as Speaker of the House of Lords, a Cabinet minister, and head of the judiciary, played a significant role in the constitution, but there was very little consultation about the reform plan—especially with the Lord Chancellor at the time, Lord Irvine. The response of Oliver Letwin, the shadow Home Secretary, was: 'To remake constitutions on the hoof, on the basis of personnel changes within the Cabinet, is the height of irresponsibility. To announce it in a press release at 5.45pm on a Thursday evening is nothing short of a disgrace' (*The Guardian*, 'Blair's Reforming Reshuffle', 13 June 2003). It was conceded that legislation was needed to implement the change (though this was not needed if it had gone ahead as a ministerial reshuffle) and a consultation and scrutiny of the legislative proposals by Parliamentary Select Committees then took place. Ultimately, Blair revised the plan, and the ensuing Constitutional Reform Act 2005 reformed the office of Lord Chancellor but did not abolish it.

Commenting critically on the Constitutional Reform Act 2005, Lord Woolf (the Lord Chief Justice at the time) believed that the government had not appreciated the 'pivotal role' of the Lord Chancellor. He also cautioned that 'little attention has been paid to [the] cumulative effect' of changes to the constitution in separate Acts of Parliament and 'whether as part of the process of change we are paying sufficient attention to retaining or replacing the checks upon which, in the past, the delicate balance of our constitution has depended'. See Lord Woolf, 'The Rule of Law and a Change in the Constitution' (2004) 63(2) CLJ 317, pp 319 and 320.

For background details on Tony Blair's proposals, see https://constitution-unit.com/2013/06/20/john-crook-the-abolition-of-the-lord-chancellor/. For a critical view of the proposals, see Sir John Baker, 'The Unwritten Constitution of the United Kingdom' pp 5 and 10, in 'Further reading'.

⟩ **CROSS REFERENCE**
For more on this, see Chapters 7 and 13

 THINKING POINT

Which branch of state was proposing this constitutional change? Which branch eventually needed to approve the revised proposal?

While the UK constitution is characteristically flexible, in practice some changes can lock themselves in and become semi-entrenched, which means that they are more difficult—though not impossible—to change or remove. This issue has arisen with devolution, UK membership of the European Union, and the Human Rights Act.

⟩ **CROSS REFERENCE**
For further details on this debate, see Chapter 6

3.1.3 **Unitary**

Whether a state is unitary or federal relates to the way in which power is organised within it. Federal countries like the USA have a non-centralised political system where authority is shared between central and regional government, and regional government has powers which central government cannot override; their written constitutions set out rules to prevent one level of government from interfering in the functions of the other. The UK has traditionally been a unitary state with a centralised form of government where the central government manages the UK (subject to devolution) and the UK Parliament has ultimate legislative authority; there is no institution in the UK with equal authority to Parliament.

▶ CROSS REFERENCE

See also section 1.4.3

As the holder of central law-making authority, the UK Parliament can delegate power to subordinate bodies, and this is what it has done with devolution. Devolved systems of government divide regional and central government, but allow the central government ultimate power to make decisions for the whole country. We examine this in more detail in Chapter 4, but in 1998 the UK Parliament passed three statutes (the 'devolution Acts') which began a cascade of devolved power to the component units of the UK, creating new devolved bodies in Scotland, Wales, and Northern Ireland and delegating varying law-making and executive powers to them:

- The Scotland Act 1998 created the Scottish Parliament and the Scotland Acts 2012 and 2016 increased Scotland's devolved powers.
- The Government of Wales Act 1998 and Government of Wales Act 2006 created the Welsh Assembly, and Wales' devolved powers were increased by the Wales Act 2017.
- The Northern Ireland Act 1998 created the Northern Ireland Assembly.

There is one notable omission: England does not have its own Parliament, so devolution is unevenly distributed.

It may be argued that, as long as the central UK Parliament retains ultimate legal sovereignty, the UK remains a unitary state, despite devolution—what Parliament creates, it can take away—but post-devolution it has been argued that the UK has changed from a unitary state to a union state, a state comprising four nations (Neil Walker, 'Beyond the Unitary Conception of the United Kingdom Constitution?' (2000) (Autumn) Public Law 384–404), or even a quasi-federal state. This will be explored in section 4.6.

3.1.4 **Monarchical**

The UK's hereditary monarch is Head of State, Commander-in-Chief of the Armed Forces, and Supreme Governor of the Church of England. The UK has a constitutional monarchy, introduced by the Bill of Rights 1689, where constitutional rules imposed by Parliament limit the powers of the Crown; Bogdanor has described a constitutional monarch as 'a sovereign who reigns but does not rule' (Vernon Bogdanor, 'The Monarchy and the Constitution' (1996) 49(3) Parliamentary Affairs 407). A thousand years ago, legislative, executive, and judicial power vested in the king, and vestiges of that power structure remain: the monarch is no longer involved with executive decision-making but retains formal authority; many executive functions are carried out in the name of the Queen, and the monarch still has a formal role in making law. In the modern UK, the Queen's formal roles within Parliament and government include:

- granting royal assent to legislation;
- summoning Parliament;
- appointing a new prime minister;
- approving Orders in Council made by the Privy Council (see Chapter 11);
- holding regular meetings with her prime minister.

However, these roles are governed by constitutional conventions and in practice, involve decision-making by government.

If the monarch is unable to carry out his or her official duties, the Regency Act 1937 provides that the person next in line of succession will be appointed as Regent if the monarch is under the age of 18 on acceding to the throne or becomes incapacitated by mental or physical illness (sections 1 and 2). For short-term illness or absences from the UK, Counsellors of State are appointed by Letters Patent to act in the monarch's place (normally the sovereign's spouse and the next four people in the line of succession over the age of 21 (section 6)).

3.1.5 **Parliamentary**

The UK has developed a parliamentary democracy which has come to be known as the 'Westminster system of parliamentary government'; in this system, which is common throughout the world, the executive and legislative arms of state are not clearly separated. In the UK, the Prime Minister and government ministers are members of both the executive and Parliament, and as a result the government, particularly the Cabinet, tends to dominate Parliament, although the government of the day must retain the confidence of the House of Commons; without that, it cannot function. The UK is a liberal democracy, applying the principle of representative government (where (almost) all adults have the right to vote for members of a representative institution—the House of Commons) and the principle of responsible government (where the government is answerable to Parliament for how it conducts itself).

❯ CROSS REFERENCE
See Chapters 10 and 12

SUMMARY OF FEATURES OF THE UK CONSTITUTION

- The UK constitution is uncodified, but many of its sources are written, and it is arguably becoming partly codified
- It is flexible and can be changed quickly and easily, but change needs to be managed responsibly
- The UK is traditionally a unitary state, though devolution has challenged that status
- The constitution is monarchical and parliamentary

3.1.6 **The bedrock of important constitutional principles**

Here we need to flag up the fundamental constitutional principles that underpin the UK constitution, though they are examined in depth in Part 2 of the book. These principles are:

- Parliamentary sovereignty
- The rule of law
- The separation of powers

They can seem rather abstract and metaphysical in comparison with black letter law but they are vital for understanding how the constitution works. Parliamentary sovereignty provides the flexible legal core of the constitution, and the rule of law and the separation of powers exist as protective mechanisms. The Supreme Court in *Miller/Cherry* referred to the courts' 'responsibility of upholding the values and principles of our constitution and making them effective' (*R (Miller) v The Prime Minister; Cherry and others v Advocate General for Scotland* [2019] UKSC 41 [39]).

3.1.6.1 **Parliamentary sovereignty**

Parliamentary sovereignty describes the overriding legal authority of Parliament to create law and it is the most important underpinning principle of the UK constitution. Baroness Hale has made a fundamental point that is key to appreciating its nature:

> [The UK constitution] is different from most other constitutions in that … its governing principle is that sovereign power is not distributed between the three branches of government but resides solely in Parliament (or strictly the Queen in Parliament). Parliament can make or unmake any law. (Sultan Azlan Shah Lecture, 2016)

CROSS REFERENCE

We explore this topic further in Chapter 6

So Parliament's sovereign law-making power lies at the heart of the UK constitution and it flows from this that Parliament has the legal authority to change the constitution.

3.1.6.2 **Rule of law**

The rule of law is the concept that no governing body or individual is above the law. The universally binding nature of law is essentially a protective principle against oppressive, arbitrary government, an idea that Magna Carta came to embody (see Chapter 2). In the absence of a codified constitution, an independent judiciary upholding the rule of law is crucially important for protecting the rights and freedoms of the people. As Lord Woolf has pointed out:

> Constitutions have to evolve to meet the needs of their citizens. A virtue of our being one of the three developed nations that does not have a written constitution, is that our constitution has always been capable of evolving as the needs of society change. The evolution can be incremental in a way which would be difficult if we had a written constitution. But flexibility comes at a price. We have never had the protection that a written constitution can provide for institutions that have a fundamental role to play in society. One of those institutions is a legal system that is effective, efficient and independent. A democratic society, pledged to the rule of law, would be deeply flawed without such a legal system. (Lord Woolf, 'The Rule of Law and a Change in the Constitution' (2004) 63(2) CLJ 317, p 318)

CROSS REFERENCE

For details of the rule of law, see Chapter 8

Respect for the rule of law is therefore an essential part of the UK constitution's toolkit of controlling mechanisms.

3.1.6.3 **Separation of powers**

Power within a state is divided into the legislative, executive, and judicial branches, and the separation of powers doctrine holds that those powers should each be allocated to clearly separate bodies to protect the citizens of a state against oppressive, tyrannical rule. However, in the UK, the separation of power between the branches of state has not always been strict and there have been overlaps—for example, government ministers are drawn from Parliament so are part of the legislature and executive—therefore a system of controls known as 'checks and balances' has developed to enable one branch of state to scrutinise or regulate another and restrain excesses of power.

CROSS REFERENCE

For details on separation of powers, see Chapter 7

3.2 The sources of the UK constitution

If there is no single codified document, where do we find the rules of the UK constitution? The answer is that they are scattered between various sources, much like the New Zealand constitution. The laws, rules, and practices of the UK constitution can be found in the sources in Table 3.1.

Table 3.1 Sources of the UK constitution

Source	Written or unwritten
Statutes	Written
Judicial decisions	Written
Constitutional conventions	Traditionally unwritten but now partly codified
International treaties	Written
The royal prerogative	Unwritten
The law and custom of Parliament	A mix of written and unwritten
Works of authoritative writers	Written

The sources in Table 3.1 reflect the evolutionary and practice-based elements of the UK constitution, in addition to the formal, written legal rules which act as its normative, restraining influence. It is this combination of written and unwritten, legal and non-legal sources that gives the constitution its sense of hidden, mysterious rules that are difficult to pin down.

3.2.1 Constitutional statutes

In the UK, statutes make the most significant changes to the constitution but many ordinary UK statutes do not contain constitutional rules. Our focus here is on the constitutional statutes which collectively form the backbone of the UK's constitutional laws. They have existed for as long as there has been a Parliament—but what exactly is a constitutional statute?

Until recently, there was no distinction between statutes that affected the constitution and ordinary statutes. They were passed in the same way by a simple majority in Parliament and had equal status in terms of superiority, as shown by Dicey's well-known observation that there was no difference between the Act of Union with Scotland and the Dentists Act 1878. However, in 2002 Laws LJ suggested in the case of *Thoburn v Sunderland City Council* [2002] EWHC 195 (Admin), [2003] QB 151 that the common law recognises a category of constitutional statutes, which he defined in this way:

> We should recognise a hierarchy of Acts of Parliament: as it were 'ordinary' statutes and 'constitutional' statutes. The two categories must be distinguished on a principled basis. In my opinion a constitutional statute is one which (a) conditions the legal relationship between citizen and State in some general, overarching manner, or (b) enlarges or diminishes the scope of what we would now regard as fundamental constitutional rights. ([62])

This means that a statute will be classed as constitutional if (a) it affects the legal relationship between the citizen and the state in a key way, or (b) it changes fundamental rights; in other words, if it affects rights that would be contained in a written constitution. The distinction made by Laws LJ is an important one because he went on to state that constitutional statutes cannot be *impliedly* repealed by an ordinary statute and may only be repealed expressly and unambiguously in a later statute (which would also be constitutional eg the European Communities Act 1972, a constitutional statute, has been expressly repealed by section 1 of the European Union (Withdrawal) Act 2018, also a constitutional statute). Laws LJ believed that this hierarchy of statutes provided most of the benefits of a written constitution, giving special protection to

> Where a statute conflicts with an earlier one but does not expressly repeal it, the later statute is treated as impliedly repealing the earlier one. See section 6.2.2.2

fundamental rights. However, while it gives a level of protection to constitutional statutes, it still does not entrench them or make them impossible to change or repeal. Lord Hope has also pointed out that constitutional statutes must be interpreted like any other statute, though their purpose can be taken into account (*Imperial Tobacco Ltd v The Lord Advocate* [2012] UKSC 61 [15]; see also *Robinson v Secretary of State for Northern Ireland* [11] (Lord Bingham)).

 EXAMPLES OF CONSTITUTIONAL STATUTES:

- Magna Carta 1297
- Petition of Right 1628
- Bill of Rights 1689
- Act of Settlement 1701
- Acts of Union (Scotland 1707 and Ireland 1800)
- European Communities Act 1972
- Parliament Acts 1911 and 1949
- Scotland Act 1998, Northern Ireland Act 1998, Government of Wales Act 2006
- Human Rights Act 1998
- European Union (Withdrawal) Act 2018

 THINKING POINT

Using Chapter 2 to help, briefly summarise the importance of each of the above statutes.

Laws LJ's distinction (made *obiter* but generally accepted; see for example *R (Miller) v Secretary of State for Exiting the European Union* [2017] UKSC 5 [67] ('*Miller I*')) has raised a number of issues. The first is how we really distinguish between an ordinary statute and a constitutional statute; it is generally agreed that there is no easy way to do this and the issue has provoked some debate. The government's view is that it is 'impossible to provide a watertight definition of significant constitutional legislation' (see Government Response to the House of Lords Constitution Committee Report, *The Process of Constitutional Change* September 2011 Cm 8181, para 20). David Feldman disagrees with Laws LJ's definition on the basis that linking constitutional statutes to fundamental rights is (a) too narrow because some clearly constitutional legislation relates not to rights, but to institutions and their powers and functions; and (b) too wide because most statutes relate to the relationship between citizens and the state in some way. Feldman suggests that constitutional statutes set out the structure of the state, its institutions, and their functions, powers, and responsibilities; statutes conferring individual rights are only included if they relate to the powers or functions of institutions. Feldman also points to another issue—only some provisions in a statute might be of a constitutional nature, which raises the question: does that make the *whole* statute constitutional? (See David Feldman, 'The Nature and Significance of "Constitutional" Legislation' (2013) 129 LQR 343.)

THE BIGGER PICTURE: DEFINING CONSTITUTIONAL STATUTES

To explore this issue further, look at the following sources:

- In evidence to the House of Lords Constitution Committee, Sir John Baker proposed eight measures that would be classed as 'constitutional', such as altering the structure and composition of Parliament; for the full list, see the Committee's Report, *The Process of Constitution Change* (pp 9–10, para 11), available at: www.publications.parliament.uk/pa/ld201012/ldselect/ldconst/177/177.pdf.

- Andrew Blick, David Howarth, and Nat le Roux suggest giving power to a committee of each House of Parliament to decide whether a Bill contains provisions of constitutional significance. See 'Distinguishing Constitutional Legislation: A Modest Proposal', Constitution Society (2014) at: https://consoc.org.uk/wp-content/uploads/2014/08/COSJ2237_Constitutional_Legislation_WEB.pdf. Appendix B contains a helpful list of constitutional statutes.

- Farrah Ahmed and Adam Perry ('Constitutional Statutes' (2017) 37(2) Oxford Journal of Legal Studies 461) analyse in detail what defines a constitutional statute.

The notion of constitutional statutes raises a third issue: is there a hierarchy of constitutional statutes? And what happens where two constitutional statutes or principles conflict? This point was considered in the *HS2 case (R (HS2 Action Alliance Ltd) v Secretary of State for Transport* [2014] UKSC 3). Here, the Supreme Court raised the question of whether the European Communities Act 1972 impliedly repealed the Bill of Rights 1689—in the event, they did not have to decide it—but Lords Neuberger and Mance suggested that the answer to the question was 'no':

> It is … certainly arguable (and it is for United Kingdom law and courts to determine) that there may be fundamental principles, whether contained in … constitutional instruments or recognised at common law, of which Parliament when it enacted the European Communities Act 1972 did not either contemplate or authorise the abrogation. ([207])

This raises the possibility that some constitutional rules are so important that they cannot be removed by a later constitutional statute and suggests that there *is* a hierarchy of constitutional laws and principles. (For comment on the *HS2 case*, see M. Elliott, 'Reflections on the HS2 Case: A Hierarchy of Domestic Constitutional Norms and the Qualified Primacy of EU Law' UK Const L Blog (23 January 2014) (available at https://ukconstitutionallaw.org).)

EXAMPLE: HOW CONSTITUTIONAL CHANGE WORKS IN PRACTICE

This example of a constitutional change introduced by statute illustrates how the constitution adapts to new issues.

Succession to the Crown Act 2013

For centuries, succession to the Crown was governed by the 'male preference primogeniture rule', which meant that younger male children had preference over their older sisters as heir to the throne. At the Commonwealth Heads of Government Meeting in Perth in 2011, the Prime Minster announced a proposal to make the royal succession gender neutral. Since the Queen is also Head of State of 15 other Commonwealth countries, they needed to approve the change in the law and co-ordinate changes in their own laws. The Succession to the Crown Act 2013 was fast-tracked through Parliament before Prince George was born to the Duke and Duchess of Cambridge, and it changed the law by allowing the Crown to pass to heirs to the throne born after 28 October 2011 in order of birth and regardless of gender. It also removed the bar on future monarchs marrying Roman Catholics but kept the disqualification preventing a Catholic becoming monarch. The Act came into force on 26 March 2015 to allow the other 15 states time to make the necessary changes to their law and constitutions.

3.2.2 Judicial decisions

The common law was hugely influential in developing and shaping constitutional principles in the seventeenth and eighteenth centuries, recognising and affirming fundamental rights and freedoms, and was regarded by Coke and Blackstone as the pre-eminent source of law at that time. Today, however, common law has been overtaken by statute in relation to the creation of constitutional rules, but decisions by the courts make a vital contribution to constitutional issues, both in their interpretation of statutes and, increasingly, in the clarification of constitutional law. There is no hard and fast rule defining what a constitutional case is—they need to be picked out from the 'ordinary' decisions of the courts—but the examples of the judiciary's constitutional role given by Professor Andrew Le Sueur in evidence to the Political and Constitutional Reform Committee help us classify constitutional decisions. They include:

- decisions about 'the respective powers of different institutions within the constitution, for example between the UK Parliament and the UK government';
- legal questions about the exercise of powers by the devolved bodies in Scotland, Wales, and Northern Ireland;
- protection of rights under the Human Rights Act 1998;
- judicial review of actions of the executive.

For more details, see House of Commons Political and Constitutional Reform Committee, 'Constitutional Role of the Judiciary if There Were a Codified Constitution', 14th Report of Session 2013–14, HC 802, p 6.

Throughout this book, you will find examples of judicial decisions that are a source of constitutional law; as a general guide, those decisions often set out a principle that might be included in a written constitution (see Table 3.2 for illustrative examples).

THE BIGGER PICTURE: JUDGES AS GUARDIANS OF THE UK CONSTITUTION

In recent years, UK judges have been developing a more 'quasi-constitutional' role, particularly because of the increase in judicial review and the operation of the Human Rights Act. Lady Hale, former President of the Supreme Court, has expressed the view that judges have become 'guardians of the UK constitution' because they now have the power to decide whether laws made by the devolved institutions are valid; they have a supervisory role over the executive through judicial review to ensure that it acts within its lawful powers; and the courts protect the rights of individuals against the state under the Human Rights Act (see the Sultan Azlan Lecture). This quasi-constitutional role is particularly evident in the *Miller* cases (*Miller I* [2017] UKSC 5; *R (Miller) v The Prime Minister; Cherry v Advocate General for Scotland* [2019] UKSC 41). We explore the changing role of judges in Chapters 9 and 13 but you might wish to read the following sources:

- Jo Murkens and Roger Masterman, *The New Constitutional Role of the Judiciary* (2014) LSE Law Policy Briefing Series, 2, The London School of Economics and Political Science, London

- Lord Neuberger, 'The UK Constitutional Settlement and the Role of the UK Supreme Court' (2014) (www.supremecourt.uk/docs/speech-141010.pdf) especially paras 24–29

- House of Commons Political and Constitutional Reform Committee, *Constitutional Role of the Judiciary if There Were a Codified Constitution*, 14th Report of Session 2013–14, HC 802

Table 3.2 Judicial decisions and constitutional principles

Case	Constitutional principle
Pickin v BRB [1974] AC 765: the claimant alleged that Parliament had been misled in passing a private Bill. The court held that it had no power to examine what happened during the legislative process; this was a matter for Parliament.	**Judges apply the law made by Parliament**
Cheney v Conn [1968] 1 All ER 779: it was alleged that parts of the Finance Act were invalid because they authorised taxes which were used to make nuclear weapons, contrary to international law. Held: what a statute says is the law in the UK.	**Judges do not have the power to strike down an Act of Parliament**
R v Secretary of State for the Home Department, ex parte Fire Brigades Union [1995] 2 AC 513: A minister acted unlawfully where he ignored a duty to consider when to introduce a compensation scheme under a statute.	**Ministers are bound by the law enacted by Parliament**

3.2.3 The royal prerogative

The royal prerogative is classed as a source of the constitution because it is an unwritten source of executive (government) legal power; for example, the power to make treaties, issue passports, and deploy the armed forces. Prerogative power is recognised by the common law but does not derive from an Act of Parliament. It stems from the historic powers of the monarch, but as royal power diminished and responsible and representative government developed, many of the monarch's prerogative powers came to be exercised by government ministers (the Crown as executive) rather than the monarch personally, although those powers are still exercised in the name of the monarch. Prerogative power therefore refers to the remaining rights and powers of the Crown (monarch and ministers) which they can exercise without the need for Parliament's authority or approval. Dicey described the royal prerogative as 'the residue of discretionary or arbitrary authority, which at any given time is legally left in the hands of the Crown' (A.V. Dicey, *Introduction to the Study of the Law of the Constitution*, 10th edn (London: Macmillan 1959), p 424). Blackstone defined it as *special* powers: 'that special pre-eminence which the King hath, over and above all other persons, and out of the ordinary course of common law, in right of his regal dignity' (Sir William Blackstone, *Commentaries on the Laws of England* (1765)), but Dicey saw it as *every* act which the Crown can lawfully do without the authority of an Act of Parliament.

There is no definitive list of prerogative powers and it is unclear whether some still exist; the right to pressgang (impress) men into the Royal Navy and dig for saltpetre, which is used to make gunpowder, are certainly no longer exercised. As prerogative powers are residual, they cannot be extended nor new powers created; as Diplock LJ said, 'It is 350 years and a civil war too late for the Queen's courts to broaden the prerogative' (*BBC v Johns* [1965] Ch 32, 79). Where a prerogative power is subsequently incorporated into a statute, it becomes a *statutory* power eg the Fixed-term Parliaments Act 2011.

Prerogative powers fall into two categories:

- Prerogative powers exercised by the Queen.
- Prerogative executive powers which are exercised by government ministers.

3.2.3.1 Prerogative powers exercised by the Queen

These comprise:

- the Queen's constitutional prerogatives ('the personal discretionary powers which remain in the Sovereign's hands');
- the legal prerogatives of the Crown, which 'the Queen possesses as the embodiment of the Crown'.

(See Select Committee on Public Administration, *Taming the Prerogative: Strengthening Ministerial Accountability to Parliament*, 4th report of Session 2003–04, HC 422 [5, 7])

The Queen's constitutional prerogatives include:

- Royal assent: This is a formality signifying the monarch's consent to new law and was last refused in 1707 (see section 11.2.3). Note also Queen's consent: where a Bill affects the monarchy's interests (the prerogative, hereditary revenues, or personal property or interests), the Queen must consent to the Bill being debated in Parliament otherwise the Bill cannot proceed, but refusal would only be exercised on the advice of ministers. Prince's consent applies similarly to the Prince of Wales.

- Appointment of the Prime Minister and other ministers: By convention, this power must be exercised in favour of the leader of the party commanding a majority in the House of Commons. The Queen does not actively choose the Prime Minister.

- Patronage (the granting of honours): The Prime Minister and others make nominations for most honours in the Queen's name but the Queen still personally awards the Order of the Garter, the Order of the Thistle, the Order of Merit, and the Royal Victoria Order.

- The summoning and prorogation (suspension) of Parliament: On the prerogative power to prorogue Parliament, see the discussion of *Miller/Cherry* in section 12.3. The dissolution of Parliament, which brings a current Parliament to an end before an election, was a prerogative power of the Crown exercised by the monarch on the Prime Minister's advice but this is now governed by the Fixed-term Parliaments Act 2011 which removed the Prime Minister's discretion on when to call a general election.

The legal prerogatives of the Crown include 'the principle that the Crown can do no wrong, and that the Crown is not bound by statute save by express words or necessary implication' (House of Commons Public Administration Select Committee, *Taming the Prerogative: Strengthening Ministerial Accountability to Parliament*, 4th Report of Session 2003–04, HC 422). It also includes ancient rights vested in the monarch personally, including ownership of all unmarked swans in open water and 'royal fish' (sturgeons, dolphins, porpoises, and whales) in the waters around the UK. The Crown has the rights to gold and silver across the UK under the royal prerogative (known as 'Mines Royal'), and owns just over half of the seashore below the high-water mark and most of the territorial seabed, including the oil and gas within it. See further www.thecrownestate.co.uk.

3.2.3.2 **Prerogative executive powers**

Prerogative executive powers are exercised by government ministers on behalf of the Crown and are examined in section 12.3.

The prerogative remains an important source of discretionary government power, enabling government to function efficiently. Its exercise can be judicially reviewed by the courts (see section 12.3.1.2) and it is regulated by constitutional conventions, to which we now turn.

3.2.4 **Constitutional conventions**

Constitutional conventions are a *political* source of the constitution and they can be difficult to envisage at first. They should not be confused with conventions in the sense of a treaty (like the European Convention on Human Rights), or a constitutional convention in the sense of a committee or body which drafts a new constitution for a state. We are examining here conventions in the sense of customs or traditional practice, but there is more to them than that. Constitutional conventions are non-legal rules of political practice, often unwritten. They are not laws, but they are binding on—and, importantly, are regarded as binding by—the people who operate the constitution. They are considered in more detail in section 3.3.

3.2.5 **The law and custom of Parliament**

This refers to Parliament's unique internal rules and procedures that regulate the conduct of its members and its proceedings, and no outside body such as the courts can interfere in Parliament's self-regulation. The law and custom of Parliament includes parliamentary privilege (the special rights and immunities of Members of Parliament and the privileges of the two Houses of Parliament) and it can be found in statutes (for example, the Bill of Rights 1689), judicial decisions, resolutions of Parliament, and parliamentary practices.

▶ CROSS REFERENCE
For more detail, see section 10.5

3.2.6 **International treaties**

Treaties are a more oblique source of the constitution. The UK does not exist in isolation from the rest of the world and, as a state, it has legal rights and obligations under international law, particularly flowing from its membership of international organisations such as the United Nations, NATO, and until recently, the European Union. To give its international relations a legal basis, the UK enters into treaties, which are legally binding international agreements made between states. In this respect, it is helpful to understand two theories about the relationship between domestic law and international law: dualism and monism.

> **Dualism**   regards international law and a state's domestic law as two separate, distinct legal systems; therefore a dualist state such as the UK needs to consciously and expressly adopt an international law rule as part of its domestic law before it can be effectively enforced in its courts. In the UK, a treaty is not part of English law until it has been incorporated by an Act of Parliament; only then can rights and obligations under the treaty be enforced in the UK courts. The reason for this is that making treaties is an executive power; if treaties automatically created enforceable legal rights and duties in the UK, the executive would be creating law without the sovereign Parliament, so the UK's dualist approach goes hand in hand with parliamentary sovereignty (see *Tin Council case (JH Rayner (Mincing Lane) Ltd v Department of Trade and Industry* [1990] 2 AC 418) at pp 476–477 and 500; see also discussions in *Miller I* especially [54–58]).
>
> **Monism,**   on the other hand, views international and national law systems as having equal effect, both regulating the conduct of individuals in a state, so treaties are automatically incorporated into a monist state's national law, creating rights and duties directly for the inhabitants.
>
> To discover which approach a particular state adopts, look at its constitution. For example, Article 25 of the German Constitution (the Basic Law) adopts a monist approach as it states that 'the general rules of public international law form part of the Federal law. They take precedence over the laws and directly create rights and duties for the inhabitants of the Federal territory.' By contrast, with the UK, we look at what happens in practice.

Parliamentary sovereignty is at the heart of the relationship between UK law and international law. An Act of Parliament is needed as a bridge between an international treaty and the UK's domestic law before the treaty can have an effect within the UK. The UK courts presume when interpreting statutes that Parliament does not intend to make laws that breach its international obligations (see *Salomon v Commissioners of Customs and Excise* [1967] 2 QB 116 at 143–144; *Garland v British Rail Engineering* [1983] 2 AC 751 at 771), but Diplock LJ also made it clear in *Salomon* that 'the sovereign power of the Queen in Parliament extends to breaking treaties'. Thus where a UK statute and international law conflict, the courts respect the sovereignty of Parliament and the statute prevails (see, eg, *Collco Dealings Ltd v IRC* [1962] AC 1; *Mortensen v Peters* (1906) 8 F (J) 93).

For 50 years, the major exception to the principles above was European Union law. On 1 January 1973, the UK became a member of the Common Market (now the European Union), having signed the Treaty of Brussels 1972. The UK Parliament passed the European Communities Act 1972 (the ECA) to give domestic effect to obligations under the treaty and allowed directly applicable EU law (treaties and regulations) to take effect as part of UK national law without the need for further legislation by Parliament; this enabled EU law to be a direct source of UK law, and because EU law was legally *superior* to UK law, it allowed EU law to prevail where the two conflicted. This was an unprecedented constitutional arrangement but it needed an Act of Parliament to open the door to EU law initially.

⟫ CROSS REFERENCE

See Chapter 5 for more detail

Following the Brexit referendum, the European Union (Withdrawal) Act 2018 repealed the European Communities Act 1972 from exit day (31 January 2020) so that EU law is no longer a new source of UK law though it retained effect until 31 December 2020.

3.2.7 **Authoritative works**

In the absence of a codified set of constitutional rules, it is instructive for judges, lawyers, ministers, and civil servants to turn to the written works of authoritative commentators on the constitution for guidance, although they are not a *legal* source of the constitution. Notable examples include: Coke's *Institutes of the Laws of England*, Blackstone's *Commentaries on the Laws of England*, A.V. Dicey's *Introduction to the Study of the Law of the Constitution*, and Erskine May's *A Treatise upon the Law, Privileges, Proceedings and Usage of Parliament*.

 SUMMARY

- The uncodified UK constitution consists of a variety of laws, principles, and practices which together form a framework to ensure accountability, control, and efficient functioning
- The sources are scattered and have not been gathered together in one document; they are partly written, partly unwritten; some are legal, some political

3.3 Constitutional conventions

Constitutional conventions are rules of political custom and practice; they are not laws so are not made by Parliament and are not enforced by the courts, but their importance should not be underestimated. They generate an understanding of behaviour and are binding on the key players in the constitution (the Queen, the Prime Minister, ministers, Members of Parliament, civil servants) and for this reason, Dicey called them 'rules of political morality'. They are essentially the way in which things *must* be done within the practical operation of the constitution (what Griffith meant by 'what happens'), enabling it to work efficiently and flexibly. They operate in the background and are largely invisible to the public, and have been likened to the oil in a car engine or, in this case, the oil in the political machinery of the state. Importantly, they produce not only flexibility, but the stability which holds the essential scaffolding of the constitution in place. This is because they can:

- introduce changes, such as creating a new role or practice and governing how it subsequently works (for example, the office of Prime Minister arose through practice that gradually became accepted, though it took a long time);
- regulate how institutions within the constitution work, particularly the workings of Parliament (for example, many unwritten conventions govern the relationship between the government and Parliament); and
- control and limit discretionary power, particularly of the monarch, the Cabinet, and the Prime Minister.

Key point Constitutional conventions regulate the exercise of the royal prerogative. For example, by constitutional convention the Queen acts on the advice of her ministers when exercising her powers and may only act without ministerial advice in times of grave constitutional crisis. See www.ucl.ac.uk/constitution-unit/sites/constitution-unit/files/170.pdf. In this way, political rules constrain the exercise of power. So the power to order the prorogation of Parliament is a prerogative power exercised by the Crown (the Queen acting on the advice of the Prime Minister) and constitutional convention obliges the Queen to accept that advice. See *Miller/Cherry* [30].

Table 3.3 Examples of constitutional conventions

The Queen must give royal assent to Bills that have properly passed through the legislative process	The Prime Minister sits in the House of Commons rather than the House of Lords
The Sewel convention: the UK Parliament will not legislate on devolved matters without the devolved legislatures' consent	The Salisbury convention: the House of Lords will not oppose Bills that are promised in the government's election manifesto
Collective ministerial responsibility: ministers are required to support all government decisions in public, and a government losing a vote of confidence must resign	The House of Lords respects the primacy of the House of Commons on financial matters

For specific examples of conventions, see Table 3.3 and note how those examples regulate conduct.

3.3.1 **The creation of conventions**

Conventions can come into existence either through political agreement or by a political act or habit which becomes accepted as obligatory. Sir Ivor Jennings set out three questions for the creation of a convention:

- what are the precedents;
- do the actors in the precedents believe they are bound by a rule;
- is there a reason for the rule? (Sir Ivor Jennings, *The Law and the Constitution* (5th edn, University of London Press 1959) at 136)

This means: look at what the relevant individuals have been doing; did they believe they *had* to do it; is there a good reason for doing it? It is the last two points that validate and establish a new rule of practice. Equally, unsatisfactory or unworkable conventions can change, and old or unused ones can disappear; for example, a convention had emerged around 1945 that Prime Ministers did not appear before Select Committees in Parliament, but this changed in 2002 when Tony Blair, then Prime Minister, agreed to appear before the Liaison Committee to account for the government's annual report; all subsequent PMs have since done so. Tony Wright MP, who had proposed this change, shed some light on the background:

> I was told that Prime Ministers did not do that sort of thing and did not come to the House of Commons to appear before Select Committees. Of course, that was wrong, as Prime Ministers used to do so. The subsequent convention has developed only since the war. Indeed, it really began only because when the new Select Committee system started after 1979, Mrs. Thatcher did not want to appear before the Defence Committee in the Westland inquiry. If one scratches a convention, one will always find expediency. (Tony Wright, HC Deb 14 May 2002, Vol 385 col 685)

 THINKING POINT

Look at the sequence here: a suggestion for change, followed by agreement, then subsequent conformity to the practice. Do you think the public noticed this change to the constitution?

CLOSE-UP FOCUS: THE FORMATION OF A CONSTITUTIONAL CONVENTION?

There has been much debate over whether a War Powers Convention has come into existence since 2003.

Authorising the deployment of UK armed forces in armed conflict abroad

The decision to go to war was an ancient prerogative power of the monarch; since the nineteenth century, it has been exercised by the Prime Minister as a decision which the government is best suited to make, involving, as it does, issues of international relations and diplomacy, military strategy, and economic and political considerations. As a prerogative power, deploying British troops abroad has traditionally not required parliamentary approval. However, a month before the Iraq war in 2003, Tony Blair sought Parliament's approval for military action to disarm Iraq of weapons of mass destruction (the vote was 412 to 149 in favour: HC Deb 18 March 2003, cols 760–911). The issue then arose: did that vote set a precedent and would future prime ministers need to ask Parliament to approve military action?

In 2011, the *Cabinet Manual* firmed up the new practice by stating that the government acknowledged that a constitutional convention had developed to give Parliament the opportunity, before troops were committed, to debate the decision, except in emergency situations (see the *Cabinet Manual* 2011, para 5.38). However, there was no parliamentary debate or vote before the UK engaged in military action in Libya in 2011 to protect the Libyan population against human rights abuses by Colonel Gaddafi. Instead, the debate took place *after* military action had begun, although the vote was resoundingly in favour.

In 2013, then Prime Minister David Cameron strengthened the convention by asking Parliament for approval to carry out military intervention in Syria after the Assad government's use of chemical weapons against its people. Parliament voted against intervening by 285 to 272; David Cameron heeded the vote and did not take military action. In 2015, he called a debate on whether the UK should join American-led airstrikes against Islamic State militants in Syria. After ten hours of impassioned debate (during which Hilary Benn's speech was applauded—a rare occurrence in the House of Commons), it was passed by 397 to 223 votes, and airstrikes commenced within hours of the vote.

However, after an alleged chemical weapons attack in 2018, the UK joined airstrikes against the Syrian government without Parliament's prior approval. Jeremy Corbyn, the Labour leader, said that the convention was broken and a War Powers Act was needed, but the Prime Minister claimed that the convention did not apply to every overseas mission in advance. There is at best ambiguity about the convention; at worst, its existence is in doubt.

For a more in-depth view of this issue, see:

- G. Phillipson, '"Historic" Commons' Syria vote: The Constitutional Significance (Part I)' UK Const L Blog (19 September 2013) (available at https://ukconstitutionallaw.org)
- House of Commons Political and Constitutional Reform Committee, 'Parliament's Role in Conflict Decisions: A Way Forward', 12th Report of Session 2013–14, HC 892
- House of Commons Library Briefing Paper 7166, 'Parliamentary Approval for Military Action', Claire Mills, 8 May 2018
- V. Fikfak and H.J. Hooper, 'Whither the War Powers Convention? What Next for Parliamentary Control of Armed Conflict after Syria?', UK Const L Blog (20 Apr 2018) (available at https://ukconstitutionallaw.org/)

THINKING POINT

Is it possible to pinpoint whether a new convention has formed here? Which is more help-ful: examining actual practice or recording the convention in writing? Who seems to be defining the convention?

3.3.2 **Why constitutional conventions are obeyed**

Conventions are obeyed because of the undesirable consequences of breaching them. Breach of a constitutional convention carries political, rather than legal, consequences ranging from political disapproval to a constitutional crisis. The Supreme Court of Canada pointed out in *Reference re Amendment of the Constitution of Canada* [1981] 1 SCR 753 that conventions embody constitutional principles and values, and protect the constitution; this means that some conventions can be more important than laws, because breaching a convention means doing something *unconstitutional* (though not necessarily unlawful). For example, the convention that the House of Lords respects the primacy of the elected House of Commons on financial matters protects the principle of democracy. However, a breach of this convention in 1910 led to the passing of the Parliament Act 1911 (see section 10.4), and in 2015, the House of Lords delayed government plans to reform tax credit, leading to accusations of a breach of convention and a constitutional crisis, as well as a threat from David Cameron to limit the Lords' powers, before the government revised its plans to reduce the impact of the cuts. (See section 11.4.2.2 and R.B. Taylor, 'The House of Lords and Constitutional Conventions: The Case for Legislative Reform' UK Const L Blog (16 Nov 2015) (available at https://ukconstitutionallaw.org/.)

THINKING POINT

What would be the consequences if any example in Table 3.3 was not followed? What might be the result if the Queen refused to give her assent to a Bill?

3.3.3 **Conventions and the courts**

As they are not legal rules, conventions are not enforced by the courts. Munro states that 'the validity of conventions cannot be the subject of proceedings in a court of law' ('Laws and Conventions Distinguished' (1975) 91 LQR 218) and we see this principle operating in *Madzimbamuto v Lardner-Burke* [1969] 1 AC 645. There was a convention that the UK Parliament would not make laws for Southern Rhodesia (a former colony) without its agreement, but after Southern Rhodesia unilaterally declared independence from the UK in 1965, the UK breached the convention by passing a law affecting Southern Rhodesia without its consent. The court held that the convention had no legal effect and did not limit Parliament's legal power, and raised the possibility that the unlawful declaration of independence had suspended the operation of the convention anyway.

However, the courts can, and do, recognise that a convention exists. For example, in *AG v Jonathan Cape* [1976] QB 752, the court recognised not only that the convention of collective ministerial responsibility existed, but also that it was sometimes ignored in practice, although this did not make it an enforceable law; it remained a rule of political practice. This was emphasised by the majority judgment of the Supreme Court in *Miller I*; while not underestimating the importance of constitutional conventions, 'some of which play a fundamental role in the operation of our constitution' ([151]), the court made it clear that:

> Judges … are neither the parents nor the guardians of political conventions; they are merely observers. As such, they can recognise the operation of a political convention in the context of deciding a legal question … but they cannot give legal rulings on its operation or scope, because those matters are determined within the political world. ([146])

However, Tom Mullen has criticised this view as painting a sharper division than the approach taken in *AG v Jonathan Cape*, where the convention was more intricately integrated into the judgment (see 'The Brexit Case and Constitutional Conventions' (2017) 21(3) Edinburgh Law Review 442).

 THE BIGGER PICTURE

For argument on the distinction between laws and conventions, see:

- N.W. Barber, 'Laws and Constitutional Conventions' (2009) 125 Law Quarterly Review 294
- Joseph Jaconelli, 'Do Constitutional Conventions Bind?' (2005) 64 Cambridge Law Journal 149
- Colin Munro, 'Laws and Conventions Distinguished' (1975) 91 LQR 218

3.3.4 **Codifying conventions**

The issue of whether constitutional conventions should be gathered together and codified in statute has been the subject of debate for many years. The main arguments in favour of statutory codification are:

- gaining certainty, clarity, and transparency
- conventions would change their nature and become legally binding rules subject to enforcement by the courts, with legal consequences for breaching them

Against this, it can be argued that:

- conventions would lose their flexibility and informality
- they are difficult to codify
- disputes about breaches of conventions would draw judges into deciding political issues

The Joint Committee on Conventions considered the issue of codifying conventions in 2006 and took the view that conventions, 'by their very nature, are unenforceable' and that codifying them was 'a contradiction in terms', adding that a 'contested convention is not a convention at all'. The Committee made it very clear that the courts have no role in adjudicating on possible breaches of parliamentary convention (see Joint Committee on Conventions, 'Conventions of the UK Parliament' 1st Report, Session 2005–06, HL Paper 265-I, HC 1212-I, [279, 282, and 285]).

In practice, there has been some codification of conventions in non-statutory form. In 2010, the then Prime Minister, Gordon Brown, asked Cabinet Secretary Sir Gus O'Donnell to draft the *Cabinet Manual*, which set out for the first time the laws, conventions, and rules on the operation of government, but while this is authoritative and makes conventions more formal, it does not transform them into laws (see Andrew Blick, 'The Cabinet Manual and the Codification of Conventions' (2014) 67(1) Parliam Aff 191).

3.4 Codifying the UK constitution

3.4.1 **Progressing towards a written constitution for the UK?**

In some ways the process has already begun. Over the past 25 years, there has been an unprecedented constitutional revolution which has introduced far-reaching and fast-moving changes, producing a constitution that is much more complex and has less fluid structures. As we have seen in 3.1.1.1, some rules within the UK constitution have already been partially codified, such as executive rules of operation and statutory codification of the legal rules for the operation of devolution.

The debate on whether the UK should have a written constitution goes back a long way but in 2007, the Governance of Britain Green Paper hinted at a written constitution in the future; Gordon Brown, then Prime Minister, announced a national consultation to draft a Bill of Rights and establish a written constitution in time for the 800th anniversary of Magna Carta in 2015, but a written constitution did not materialise. In 2010, the House of Commons Political and Constitutional Reform Committee focused on the feasibility of codification and began its 'Mapping the Path towards Codifying—or Not Codifying—the UK Constitution' inquiry; in 2014, the Committee published its report on options for a codified constitution for the UK (see House of Commons Political and Constitutional Reform Committee, *A New Magna Carta?* 2nd Report, Session 2014–15, HC 463), and even ran a public competition for the best written preamble for a constitution. (For the findings of its consultation on the options for a codified constitution, see House of Commons Political and Constitutional Reform Committee, *Consultation on A New Magna Carta?* 7th Report, Session 2014–15, HC 599.)

But constitutional reform is in the air. In 2019, a number of election manifestos supported a codified UK constitution, and the Conservative party manifesto committed to a post-Brexit programme of constitutional reform, including creating a Constitution, Democracy and Rights Commission to examine aspects of the constitution such as the relationship between the government, Parliament and the courts, the Royal Prerogative, and updating the Human Rights Act (see The Johnson government's constitutional reform agenda: prospects and challenges, 28 February 2020, The Constitution Unit at https://constitution-unit.com/2020/02/28/the-johnson-governments-constitutional-reform-agenda-prospects-and-challenges/#more-9146).

3.4.2 **Arguments for and against codifying the UK constitution**

There is a wealth of material on the arguments about codifying the constitution, and Part I of the Political and Constitutional Reform Committee's *A New Magna Carta?* report sets out a very helpful summary of the main arguments for and against a written constitution (www.publications.parliament.uk/pa/cm201415/cmselect/cmpolcon/463/463.pdf). Some key issues are set out below, but first, here is a point to consider.

CLOSE-UP FOCUS: THE BREXIT QUESTION

Article 50 of the Treaty on European Union allows a member state to withdraw from the European Union 'in accordance with its own constitutional requirements'. After the Brexit vote, it soon became apparent that the UK's constitutional requirements were not clear on this, but the issue was resolved through interplay between different arms of state. Initially, the government argued that *its* role was to negotiate Britain's withdrawal from the European Union and trigger the withdrawal process under Article 50. In the absence of a codified constitution, it fell to the judiciary to determine the legal question of the division of power between the government and Parliament on this issue. The Supreme Court held in *Miller I* that Parliament's authority was needed because citizens' rights were being removed. Two points are worth noting:

- even a codified constitution might not have covered EU withdrawal if it had not been considered at the time of drafting;

- how would the issue have been resolved if individuals had not made the challenge in court?

Further reading

Sionaidh Douglas-Scott, 'Brexit and the British Constitution: An Update on Sionaidh Douglas-Scott "Brexit, Article 50 and the Contested British Constitution"' (2016) 79(6) MLR 1019–1040 at www.modernlawreview.co.uk/brexit-british-constitution/

 THINKING POINT

Is this a good example of the UK constitution being flexible and responding to new problems, or do you think it shows that a codified constitution is needed?

3.4.2.1 The arguments in favour of codifying the UK constitution

The Political and Constitutional Reform Committee's *A New Magna Carta?* report, referred to previously, described the UK constitution as a 'sprawling mass of common law, Acts of Parliament, and European treaty obligations, surrounded by a number of important but sometimes uncertain unwritten conventions', expressing concern that it 'has become too easy for governments to implement political and constitutional reforms to suit their own political convenience' (see p 19). It is sometimes argued that drafting a constitution for the UK would be too difficult but in 2010 Richard Gordon QC produced a blueprint for a codified constitution (R.J.F. Gordon, *Repairing British Politics: A Blueprint for Constitutional Change* (London: Bloomsbury 2010)), and as part of the Political and Constitutional Reform Committee's inquiry Professor Robert Blackburn proposed three options for reform, advocating a 'building block' approach towards a fully written constitution, which he believes will materialise in time:

1. A Constitutional Code (a non-legal, authoritative guide setting out existing rules and principles on how government operates).

2. A Constitutional Consolidation Act (a statute codifying existing constitutional laws and constitutional conventions).

3. A written constitution (see *A New Magna Carta*, p 29).

❱ CROSS REFERENCE

See section 1.3.1 on
constitutional moments and
see Chapter 5 for the impact
of Brexit on this debate

Even pre-Brexit, the Political and Constitutional Reform Committee discerned some support for the view that a constitutional moment was approaching (see House of Commons Political and Constitutional Reform Committee, *Consultation on A New Magna Carta?* 7th Report, Session 2014–15, HC 599, paras 40–44) and Brexit has moved this debate higher up the agenda.

Other arguments in favour of codifying the constitution include criticism of the existing constitution and the benefits of clarity, transparency, and accessibility. It can be argued that the current constitution is unclear to the public, an anachronism and not suitable for the twenty-first century. A written constitution would be accessible and tangible. It would express national values and identity, allowing a sense of public ownership. It would entrench and protect fundamental rights and powers, and could educate people on the ground rules of the state, enabling them to be aware of the rules governing the Prime Minister, government ministers, and MPs. More technical benefits of codification would include clearly delineated limits on governmental powers and a clear line between constitutional laws and ordinary laws. The bigger argument is that a written constitution with the status of higher law could replace parliamentary sovereignty with the sovereignty of the people, as it would require popular approval to come into force.

 THINKING POINT

Read the suggested pocket constitution at:

www.parliament.uk/documents/commons-committees/political-and-constitutional-reform/The-UK-Constitution.pdf. What are your impressions? Does this seem a workable blueprint?

3.4.2.2 The arguments against codifying the UK constitution

The current UK constitution has its merits: it is pragmatic and responsive, and every so often it rolls up its sleeves to cope in a practical way with a new political crisis by creating, changing, or dismantling a specific law or rule. Beatson has described reforming an unwritten constitution as like pulling a loose thread on a pullover ('Reforming an Unwritten Constitution', p 51, in 'Further reading'), while Bogdanor and Vogenauer point out some of the difficulties involved in producing a written constitution for the UK, not least: what it should include and what to leave out (bearing in mind that it is more difficult to codify a fully functioning constitution than to make a fresh start); distinguishing between the constitution as it is and as it ought to be; and 'identifying what the constitution in fact is, since much of it is composed of conventions whose content and scope is at times unclear' (Vernon Bogdanor and Stefan Vogenauer, 'Enacting a British Constitution: Some Problems' (2008) Public Law 38, 44). Sir Stephen Laws, a former First Parliamentary Counsel, has cautioned of the risks in changing from a political to a legal constitution, an issue that can be overlooked; he argues that the UK has become adept at managing a political constitution, and politics and law have different purposes: politics is about change, while a legal, written constitution is about preserving and protecting. This highlights that the political aspect of the UK constitution provides its dynamism and forward-moving drive. Then there is the issue of parliamentary sovereignty. Having both a written constitution and a sovereign Parliament would be difficult, if not incompatible, because Parliament's ability to enact and change any law it wishes would be compromised by a higher law constitution. However, it is possible for a written constitution to protect Parliament's position;

the Instrument of Government of 1653 did this, and the constitution of the Netherlands, for example, does not allow the courts to review the constitutionality of legislation.

Arguments against codifying the constitution often include maintaining the status quo on the basis that if it works as it is, why change it (the 'if it ain't broke, why fix it?' argument). Practical objections can also be raised: there is a lack of popular demand for change, and capturing the UK constitution in written form would be difficult, particularly in the light of its current state of flux post-Brexit. There are more technical objections, too: the UK constitution's distinctive traditional flexibility would be lost, and Griffith has argued that written constitutions transfer political questions to the judges, so a written UK constitution would politicise the judiciary, who are unelected but would be required to adjudicate on whether legislation passed by democratically elected representatives was constitutional. Again, in pragmatic terms, a written constitution would not necessarily close down the debate; new issues would arise and amendments would be needed otherwise the constitution would become outdated, and peripheral rules and interpretations of the constitution would develop and exist alongside it.

 THE BIGGER PICTURE

For views in support of a codified constitution, see:

- Lord Hailsham, Elective Dictatorship, The Richard Dimbleby Lecture (London: BBC, 1976), p 4

- Stephen Hockman QC, Vernon Bogdanor et al, 'Towards a Codified Constitution' (2010) 7(1) Justice Journal 74

- House of Commons Political and Constitutional Reform Committee *A New Magna Carta?* 7th Report, Session 2014–15, HC 599

- Andrew Blick and Brice Dickson, 'Why Does the United Kingdom Now Need a Written Constitution?' (2020) 71 Northern Ireland Legal Quarterly 59

For views against a codified constitution, see:

- N.W. Barber, 'Against a Written Constitution' (2008) (Spring) Public Law 11

- Sir Stephen Laws (http://blogs.lse.ac.uk/constitutionuk/2014/09/15/-there-are-substantial-and-unacceptable-risks-in-moving-to-a-legal-constitution-from-our-current-political-one/)

- House of Commons Political and Constitutional Reform Committee, *A New Magna Carta?* 7th Report of the Political and Constitutional Reform Committee, Session 2014–15, HC 599

For both sides, see:

- Do we need a written constitution? 8 January 2020, The Constitution Unit at https://constitution-unit.com

- https://www.prospectmagazine.co.uk/magazine/does-britain-need-constitution-debate-sionaidh-douglas-scott-adam-tomkins

 THINKING POINT

Can you think of other arguments for or against codification?

Questions

Self-test questions

1. What are the main features of the UK constitution?

2. What makes the UK constitution flexible?

3. What are the benefits of a flexible constitution? What are the risks?

4. Summarise the sources of the UK constitution.

5. How did Laws LJ define constitutional statutes in the *Thoburn case*?

6. Explain what constitutional conventions are and how they operate.

7. What is dualism and what is its significance?

8. Outline three arguments for codifying the UK constitution.

9. Outline three arguments against codifying the UK constitution.

Exam questions

1. 'Constitutional conventions are unnecessary and the UK constitution can function well without them.' Discuss.

2. Critically discuss the case for codifying the UK constitution.

Further reading

Books

Bogdanor, V. *The New British Constitution* (Oxford and Portland, Oregon: Hart Publishing 2009).
See chapter 9 for thoughts on a written constitution

Elliott, M., Williams, J., and Young, A.L. (eds) *The UK Constitution after Miller: Brexit and Beyond* (Oxford: Hart Publishing 2018).
A critical assessment of the constitutional significance of the *Miller* decision.

Jowell, J. and O'Cinneide, C. (eds) *The Changing Constitution* (9th edn, Oxford: Oxford University Press 2019).
See Jeff King's discussion about a written constitution in chapter 15

Journal articles

Baker, Sir John. 'The Unwritten Constitution of the United Kingdom' (2013) 15 (1) Ecclesiastical Law Journal 4.

A thought-provoking critique of change in the UK's constitution with argument on how best to codify the constitution

Beatson, J. 'Reforming an Unwritten Constitution' (2010) 126 Law Quarterly Review 48.
A clear assessment of the current constitution, post-1997 reforms, and the need to rebalance the legislature and executive

Blackburn, R. 'Enacting a Written Constitution for the United Kingdom' (2015) 36(1) Statute Law Rev 1.
Argues in favour of a written constitution and provides a helpful overview of the UK constitution

Hazell, R. 'The Continuing Dynamism of Constitutional Reform' (2007) 60(1) Parliam Aff 3.
A useful summary of recent reforms in the UK constitution

Marshall, G. 'What Are Constitutional Conventions?' (1985) 38(1) Parliam Aff 33.
An in-depth discussion written by an authority on constitutional conventions

Other sources

Blick, Andrew, 'Entrenchment in the United Kingdom: A Written Constitution by Default?' (2017) The Constitution Society https://consoc.org.uk/publications/entrenchment-written-constitution/.
Argues for entrenchment of elements of the constitution

House of Lords Select Committee on the Constitution, *The Process of Constitutional Change*, 15th Report of Session 2010–12, HL Paper 177.
This in-depth examination helps a deeper understanding of how change in the UK constitution happens

See also the Government Response at: www.gov.uk/government/uploads/system/uploads/attachment_data/file/238144/8181.pdf.

For the oral and written evidence presented to the Committee, see: www.parliament.uk/documents/lords-committees/constitution/CRP/CRPOralandwritten.pdf.

Lady Hale, 'The United Kingdom Constitution on the Move', speech at The Canadian Institute for Advanced Legal Studies' Cambridge Lectures 2017 (see www.supremecourt.uk/docs/speech-170707.pdf).
Discusses recent changes in the UK constitution and concludes that a written constitution is unlikely to be adopted yet

Lord Neuberger, 'The UK Constitutional Settlement and the Role of the UK Supreme Court', speech at Legal Wales Conference, 2014 (see www.supremecourt.uk/docs/speech-141010.pdf).
A survey of many issues covered in this chapter, written by a former President of the Supreme Court, including an even-handed assessment of arguments for and against a written constitution

Craig, R. 'Miller Supreme Court Case Summary', UK Const L Blog (26 Jan 2016) (available at https://ukconstitutionallaw.org/).

A useful commentary on the *Miller I case* to keep to hand for a range of *Miller*-related issues

Jonathan Sumption, The Reith Lectures 2019: Law and the Decline of Politics, 18 June 2019 Lecture 5: Shifting the Foundations, available at www.bbc.co.uk/radio4.

Reflects on whether a written constitution is needed

⁏ Online resources

www.oup.com/he/dennett2e

This chapter is accompanied by a selection of online resources to help you with this topic, including:

- Multiple-choice questions
- Answers to the self-test questions
- Guidance on answering the exam question

How the UK is organised

Introduction

The 4th of June 2017 was a significant day for reasons which many people will be unaware of, except for voters in certain areas of England: it was because of the election of metro mayors, who represent a facet of the profound changes currently taking place in the organisation of the UK: the shift of power from the centre.

This chapter begins with an overview of the UK's 'power map' (see section 1.7) and the institutional arrangement of power; a written constitution would, of course, outline how power is allocated. The chapter then discusses the organisation of government in the UK from the devolved to the local level, with a particular focus on devolution, one of the most important and dynamic changes to have taken place in the modern UK constitution. We examine the devolution arrangements in each of the three nations, followed by discussion of a number of issues that devolution raises, notably the implications for parliamentary sovereignty, the role of the courts, issues of representation in the House of Commons, and whether the post-devolution UK remains a unitary state.

In the context of our discussion in this chapter, it is important to be able to distinguish between the terms United Kingdom, Great Britain, and British Isles, and this is explained in Table 4.1. The United Kingdom is a sovereign state composed of four component countries or nations (England, Wales, Scotland, and Northern Ireland). England is the largest both geographically and in

Table 4.1 Distinguishing the UK, Great Britain, and the British Isles

The **United Kingdom** is a sovereign state consisting of four countries: England, Wales, Scotland, and Northern Ireland. It does not include the Channel Islands or the Isle of Man (they are **Crown dependencies**, which means that, though the Queen is their Head of State, they are self-governing with their own legislature, administration, courts, and legal systems).

Great Britain consists of England, Wales, and Scotland and their respective islands—but not Northern Ireland.

The British Isles is a geographical term referring to the entire group of around 6,000 islands. It therefore comprises England, Wales, Scotland, Northern Ireland, the Republic of Ireland, the Channel Islands, the Isle of Man, and all other islands.

See www.ordnancesurvey.co.uk/blog/2011/08/whats-the-difference-between-uk-britain-and-british-isles/

terms of population, with more than 54 million people (84 per cent of the UK's population); Wales has a population of just over 3 million, while Scotland has 5.3 million and Northern Ireland 1.8 million.

4.1 The allocation of power in the UK

Power in the UK is divided into three branches or arms of state: legislature (law-makers), executive (government and administration), and judiciary (courts and judges). Lord Mustill's classic summary of the institutions of Parliament, the government, and the judiciary is a helpful introduction to understanding their functional balance:

▶ CROSS REFERENCE
See further Chapter 7

> It is a feature of the peculiarly British conception of the separation of powers that Parliament, the executive and the courts have each their distinct and largely exclusive domain. Parliament has a legally unchallengeable right to make whatever laws it thinks fit. The executive carries on the administration of the country in accordance with the powers conferred on it by law. The courts interpret the laws, and see that they are obeyed. (*R v Secretary of State for the Home Department ex parte Fire Brigades Union* [1995] 2 AC 513, 567)

These are the fundamentals. However, this statement was made before devolution and it describes the simpler, centralised arrangement of the various institutions within the UK. As we are about to see, in the past 20 years, there has been a significant flow of power from the centre to lower levels (decentralisation). This is referred to as the UK's territorial constitution, reflecting the regional, or territorial, dispersal of power. Since 1998, there has been an additional, devolved layer in the structure of government in the UK, but when you are reading this chapter it is helpful to remember that, overall, there is still a top-down structure:

- **At central level:** the Crown, the UK Parliament in Westminster (the UK legislature), the central UK government (the executive); in terms of the judiciary, although Scotland and Northern Ireland have their own judicial systems, the Supreme Court is the highest court of appeal for the UK.

- **At devolved level:** the devolved administrations in Scotland, Wales, and Northern Ireland.

- **At regional and local level:** local authorities (for example, county councils and London metropolitan boroughs), with increasing movement of devolved power to the English regions through local councils.

4.1.1 Power at central level

The Crown 'The Crown' has two meanings: the monarch and the executive, or 'the Crown as monarch' and 'the Crown as executive', as Lord Templeman has referred to them (*M v Home Office* [1994] 1 AC 377, 395). The monarch retains a role in law-making (the Queen in Parliament), justice in the UK is administered in the name of the Crown, and the executive retains its title of 'the Crown'. Janet McLean explains that 'the Crown theoretically represents a unity of the different branches of Government, being the Queen in Parliament, the Queen's advisors, and the Queen's judges' ('The Crown in Contract and Administrative Law' (2004) 129 Ox J Legal Studies 129, 135).

The UK Parliament The Westminster Parliament, as the UK's sovereign law-making body, is the only Parliament or assembly in the UK that does not owe its original existence to statute (the Parliament of Great Britain and Ireland was created by the Acts of Union but they were passed by the preceding Parliament). Parliament has the power to make primary legislation; Acts of Parliament are the highest form of law in the UK and cannot be judicially reviewed by the courts. Parliament has the legal authority to create new bodies or institutions and to designate their powers, as it has done with devolution; by the same token, it has legal authority to change or abolish what it creates.

Central government The key roles of central government in the UK (sometimes referred to as 'Whitehall') are to formulate and implement policy, allocate public spending, and carry out day-to-day management and administration of the country. The heart of power in government is the Prime Minister, who is responsible for the organisation of the government and is supported by the Cabinet, which consists chiefly of senior government ministers.

> **CROSS REFERENCE**
> Don't worry if you do not fully grasp the more abstract meaning of the Crown at first; it is a question that has vexed academics and lawyers for centuries and we return to the idea in Chapter 12

> **CROSS REFERENCE**
> For more detail on Parliament, see Chapters 10–11

> **CROSS REFERENCE**
> See Chapter 12 for more detail

4.1.2 Decentralising power

Before devolution, the government's administrative power was centralised—imagine it as the hub of a wheel—and it extended to the whole of the UK, but devolution has made significant changes to the constitution and has brought a substantial rebalancing of power in the UK. The pre-devolution position was summarised by Lord Rodger:

> Until devolution took effect . . . the central government of the United Kingdom was carried on by a single executive and a single Parliament. The executive was responsible for, and could determine, all areas of policy for the entire United Kingdom. Similarly, Parliament could legislate to give effect to the chosen policy in all parts of the United Kingdom. (*Martin v Most* [2010] UKSC 10 [68])

Since devolution's introduction, the power of central government no longer extends to the growing areas of domestic policy that have been devolved to Scotland, Wales, and Northern Ireland. The UK government's remit therefore now covers England and the whole of the UK on non-devolved matters including the conduct of foreign affairs, defence, national security, and oversight of the Civil Service and government agencies. Modern central government is thus decentralised and multi-layered.

It is important to remember that the systems of government at devolved, regional, and local levels are all created by the UK Parliament in Westminster. Because they derive their powers through statutes, devolved and local bodies must act within the powers they have been given by Parliament; the courts have the power to judicially review any acts that are *ultra vires* (outside

Figure 4.1 The decentralisation of power

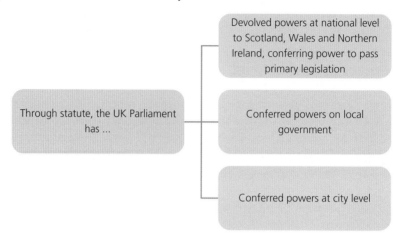

their powers) and judges can review both primary and secondary legislation made by the devolved administrations. Figure 4.1 shows the conferral of statutory power from the UK Parliament to devolved and local bodies.

Since devolution was introduced in 1998, the UK Parliament *voluntarily* has not normally made laws on devolved matters without a devolved legislature's consent (see section 4.3); thus the UK Parliament now makes law for England, and for the UK as a whole on non-devolved matters. However, the key point to understand is that, although the UK Parliament has transferred a growing range of powers to the devolved administrations, it retains ultimate legal authority over them (though practicalities are a different matter).

4.2 Devolution in the UK

This is one of the most fundamental constitutional reforms of recent years, percolating deeply through the constitutional layers of the UK, though there is at times an inescapable suspicion that devolution has had more significant consequences than originally intended. (See Vernon Bogdanor's 2009 Gresham lecture for an interesting anecdote about Tony Blair's comments on 'all this devolution stuff', at www.gresham.ac.uk/lectures-and-events/the-new-british-constitution#jAKQ6JpXltcysy5q.99?) Devolution has brought a fundamental renegotiation of power within the UK, but without a masterplan or blueprint, it has evolved incrementally in a piecemeal and haphazard fashion. We begin by examining the overall scheme of devolution.

> **🔍 CLOSE-UP FOCUS: THE JOURNEY TO DEVOLUTION**
>
> The idea of devolution in Britain has been discussed since the nineteenth century, coming particularly to the fore with the issue of Home Rule for Ireland between the 1880s and 1914. As a compromise measure, central government set up the Scottish Office in 1885 and the Welsh Office in 1964 to exercise governmental functions over domestic issues relating solely to those countries (the Northern Ireland Office was created in 1972 for

different reasons). In 1973, the Royal Commission on the Constitution published the Kilbrandon Report, in which the majority recommended devolution for Scotland and Wales, but it failed to get popular support in referendums in 1979; in Scotland, 52 per cent of those who voted were in favour of devolution but it reflected only 33 per cent of the electorate (40 per cent was required for a valid result), and only 20 per cent of the Welsh public supported a devolved Welsh Assembly.

Given the growing threat to seats coming from nationalist parties from the 1960s onwards (the Scottish Nationalist Party in Scotland and Plaid Cymru in Wales), the Labour party promised in its 1997 election manifesto to decentralise power from Westminster and introduce devolution to Scotland and Wales, although devolution in each region was driven by different reasons. The Labour party believed that devolution was the answer to Scottish dissatisfaction with government by Westminster, and if Scotland was to get devolution, Wales should also have a degree of self-government. Northern Ireland's special circumstances set it on a different path to devolution. There had been a Parliament in Northern Ireland from 1920 (under the Government of Ireland Act 1920) and a short-lived assembly in 1973/4, but in 1998 Tony Blair brokered the Belfast Agreement (known as the Good Friday Agreement), which brought an end to the 'Troubles'—the 30 years of sectarian violence between Loyalists, who wanted Northern Ireland to remain in the UK, and the Irish Republican Army (IRA), who wanted it to be part of Ireland. The Good Friday Agreement set the framework for the new Northern Ireland Assembly and promoted power-sharing between political factions.

In the first flush of the new Labour government's constitutional reforms, referendums were held in Scotland and Wales in 1997, and in Northern Ireland in 1998, as the preliminary step to devolution. In Scotland, 74 per cent of those who voted supported a Scottish Parliament; in Wales, devolution proposals scraped through with the narrowest majority of 50.3 per cent in favour of a Welsh Assembly on a turnout of only 50 per cent; in Northern Ireland, 71 per cent backed a Northern Ireland Assembly.

 THINKING POINT

Why do you think referendums took place on devolution?

In 1998, the UK Parliament passed three devolution Acts creating devolved institutions in Scotland, Wales, and Northern Ireland and transferring to them varying degrees of legislative and executive powers, known as devolved powers:

- Scotland Act 1998 (and subsequently, the Scotland Acts 2012 and 2016);
- Government of Wales Act 1998, Government of Wales Act 2006 (which repealed most of the 1998 Act), Wales Acts 2014 and 2017;
- Northern Ireland Act 1998.

The question of exactly which powers were (and continue to be) devolved is negotiated and agreed politically between the different nations. However, devolution was not delivered to each administration in a uniform, symmetrical way, and devolution has followed a different path for each one. The UK Parliament still has the authority to make law for Scotland, Wales, and Northern Ireland on *any* matter (but see section 4.3) and it has not devolved a number of key areas affecting the UK as a whole as part of its statehood. These are known as 'reserved matters' or 'reserved powers'; only the UK Parliament can make law on them, and the UK government has sole responsibility for administering them.

Reserved matters include:

- broadcasting;
- the constitution;
- defence and national security;
- employment and social security (except Northern Ireland);
- energy (with specific exceptions);
- foreign affairs;
- immigration and nationality;
- tax (but Scotland and Wales have power to vary income tax).

Another point to note is that the UK Parliament did not make the devolved bodies sovereign. As each of the three devolved administrations was created by an Act of Parliament, they must act within the powers that the UK Parliament has delegated to them. In particular, they cannot make laws which they do not have the power to make; if they do, the courts have the power to hold those laws invalid.

Beyond the legislation, the practicalities of devolution are governed by the Memorandum of Understanding, an informal structure of non-legally binding agreements, guidance notes on devolution, concordats, and conventions between the UK government and the devolved administrations which is regularly revised and sets out the principles and practice of intergovernmental relations under the devolution settlement, such as on international relations, and dispute avoidance. The UK government also gives funding to Scotland, Wales, and Northern Ireland, and the amount granted varies according to the Barnett formula (created in 1978 by Joel Barnett, the Chief Secretary to the Treasury at the time, this started life as a temporary measure and is an example of a political convention). The Treasury uses the Barnett formula to allocate funding based on the population and devolved powers of each nation, and adjusts the amount according to changes in public spending in England on comparable services such as health. The formula has been criticised as it has resulted in a lack of parity among the different nations of the UK, but so far no substitute has taken its place. (For more details on the Barnett formula, see http://researchbriefings.files.parliament.uk/documents/CBP-7386/CBP-7386.pdf.)

 SUMMARY

The essence of devolution is helpfully summarised by Lord Hope:

Devolution is an exercise of its law-making power by the United Kingdom Parliament at Westminster. It is a process of delegation by which, among other things, a power to legislate in areas that have not been reserved to the United Kingdom Parliament may be exercised by the devolved legislatures. (*AXA General Insurance Ltd v Lord Advocate (Scotland)* [2011] UKSC 46, [2012] 1 AC 868 [45])

4.2.1 **Devolution in Scotland**

The UK Parliament created the Scottish Parliament in the Scotland Act 1998 in six words:

STATUTE

Section 1(1) Scotland Act 1998: 'There shall be a Scottish Parliament.'

The Scottish Parliament sits in Edinburgh and consists of 129 Members of the Scottish Parliament (MSPs); 73 are constituency MSPs and 56 are regional MSPs. By section 44, the Act also created the Scottish Executive, led by a First Minister and consisting of Scottish Ministers appointed from among the members of the Parliament (section 47), reflecting the Westminster system. The Scottish Parliament has very wide law-making powers, known as transferred competences, and it operates under a 'reserved powers' model of devolution. This means that it can make primary legislation (Acts of the Scottish Parliament) on any matter that is not specifically reserved to the UK Parliament; its powers are therefore said to be defined negatively.

STATUTE: SCOTLAND ACT 1998—THE KEY LAW-MAKING PROVISIONS

Section 28(1): Subject to section 29, the Parliament may make laws, to be known as Acts of the Scottish Parliament.

Section 28(2) provides for Acts of the Scottish Parliament to receive royal assent.

Section 29(1): An Act of the Scottish Parliament is not law so far as any provision of the Act is outside the legislative competence of the Parliament. (This makes it clear that legislation passed by the Scottish Parliament is not valid law if it falls outside its law-making power.)

Schedule 5 sets out the list of reserved powers; the Scottish Parliament can make law on all other areas, including agriculture, forestry and fisheries, health, education, housing, and the environment. It was also given powers to make secondary legislation.

Under section 28(7), the UK Parliament retains the right to legislate on all matters in Scotland, but in 1998 Lord Sewel, the Minister for the Scotland Office who was responsible for piloting the Scotland Act through Parliament, stated:

> as happened in Northern Ireland earlier in the century, we would expect a convention to be established that Westminster would not normally legislate with regard to devolved matters in Scotland without the consent of the Scottish parliament. (HL Deb 21 Jul 1998, Vol 592 col 791)

This is known as the Sewel convention and while not legally binding, it is a significant rule of political practice (we examine it further in section 4.3).

The range of devolved powers to Scotland has not remained static. The Scotland Act 2012 made a number of amendments to the Scotland Act 1998, including renaming the Scottish executive as the Scottish government and devolving certain financial powers to the Scottish

Parliament, specifically the power to set a new Scottish rate of income tax from April 2016 (by varying the UK basic rate of income tax by up to 3 pence in the pound).

Devolution can drive the impetus for more devolution and, ultimately, complete independence. This is what prompted the 'once in a lifetime' Scottish independence referendum in 2014. After long discussion, the Edinburgh Agreement, setting out the terms for the referendum, was signed in 2012 by David Cameron, on behalf of the UK government, and representatives of the Scottish government. As constitutional matters are reserved to the Westminster Parliament, the Scottish Parliament then had to be given competence to make legislation enabling the independence referendum to take place. This was done by an Order in Council under section 30 Scotland Act 1998. However, David Cameron pointed out at the time: 'One thing is clear: that if independence goes ahead, it's the end of devolution. All those who want to see not only the status quo but further devolution from the United Kingdom to Scotland must vote to stay within the United Kingdom.' In 2014, two days before the Scottish independence referendum, David Cameron, Nick Clegg, and Ed Miliband signed 'The Vow', promising that in the event of a 'No' vote, 'extensive new powers' would be delivered for the Scottish Parliament. This opened up the prospect of 'devo max', the maximum range of devolved powers, or at least 'devo more'. In the event, the referendum result was 55.3 per cent against independence and the UK government charged Lord Smith of Kelvin with the task of developing proposals for further devolution. In November 2014 the Smith Commission Report recommended strengthening the devolution settlement, in particular the further devolution of taxation and welfare matters.

> **Definition** An Order in Council is made by the Queen on the Privy Council's advice

The Scotland Act 2016 was the result of the Smith Commission's recommendations and it has made the Scottish Parliament the most powerful of the three devolved administrations in terms of self-government.

 STATUTE

Section 1 of the Scotland Act 2016 added a new section 63A to the Scotland Act 1998, emphasising the permanence of the Scottish Parliament and Scottish government. Note the referendum provision in subsection (3).

Section 63A Scotland Act 1998

(1) The Scottish Parliament and the Scottish Government are a permanent part of the United Kingdom's constitutional arrangements.

(2) The purpose of this section is . . . to signify the commitment of the Parliament and Government of the United Kingdom to the Scottish Parliament and the Scottish Government.

(3) In view of that commitment it is declared that the Scottish Parliament and the Scottish Government are not to be abolished except on the basis of a decision of the people of Scotland voting in a referendum.

The Scotland Act 2016 also put the Sewel convention in statutory form though this did not make it legally binding (see section 2: 'it is recognised that the Parliament of the United Kingdom will not normally legislate with regard to devolved matters without the consent of the Scottish Parliament'). It granted new devolved powers, to be transferred by 2018, including: tax (notably setting rates and thresholds of income tax, setting air passenger duty, receiving some VAT revenues); welfare; equal opportunities; licensing onshore oil and gas extraction; and greater powers over setting speed limits and legislating on road signs. However, the Economic Affairs Committee warned: 'The UK Government is relinquishing full receipt, and almost full control, of £11 billion of income tax revenues in Scotland. No comparable central government has ever done this' (House of Lords Select Committee on Economic Affairs, *A Fracturing Union? The Implications of Financial Devolution to Scotland*, 1st Report of Session 2015–16, HL Paper 55 [9]).

Following the Brexit vote, Nicola Sturgeon, the Scottish First Minister, announced plans for a second referendum ('Indyref2'). Theresa May, then UK Prime Minister, responded that the time was not right; the results of the June 2017 general election diminished the prospect of Indyref2, but, reinvigorated by Brexit, the Scottish government published a draft independence referendum Bill in 2021.

 SUMMARY

Under Scotland's reserved powers model, everything is devolved unless a matter is specifically reserved to the UK Parliament in Schedule 5 to the Scotland Act 1998 (as amended by the 2012 and 2016 Acts). Stronger devolved powers have been granted to Scotland incrementally to make it the most powerful of the devolved administrations.

4.2.2 Devolution in Wales

The Government of Wales Act 1998 created the National Assembly for Wales. On 6 May 2020, the Welsh Assembly was renamed Senedd Cymru-Welsh Parliament. It sits in Cardiff Bay and currently consists of 60 elected Members of the Senedd (MS) led by a First Minister. Of the Senedd Members, 40 represent constituencies and 20 represent the five regions (four for each region). The original Assembly was created as an executive government, a single corporate body exercising both executive and legislative functions, but it was initially only given power to make secondary legislation with the authority of the UK Parliament on specific areas previously exercised by the Welsh Office. It was not given power to make primary legislation or change taxes.

However, a gradual process of strengthening the Assembly's legislative powers began. Following the recommendations of the Richard Commission in 2004, the Government of Wales Act 2006 progressed devolution in Wales:

- It created a separate legislature (the National Assembly for Wales) and a separate executive (the Welsh Assembly Government) headed by a First Minister.
- It gave the Assembly competence (power) to make law in the specified subjects set out in Schedule 7 to the Government of Wales Act 2006, but the Welsh Assembly could not act outside those areas. Wales therefore operated under a 'conferred powers' model, unlike the Scottish Parliament.

- As a transitional measure, the 2006 Act allowed the Assembly to request permission from the UK government to make primary legislation known as 'Assembly Measures' within specified fields (sections 93–101), but more importantly, the Act also provided that the Welsh Assembly would have the power to make primary legislation if two thirds of Assembly Members passed a resolution requesting primary law-making powers be devolved to Wales, and the Welsh electorate supported it in a referendum.

- In 2010 the Assembly voted unanimously in favour of holding a referendum on gaining primary law-making powers and in March 2011, 63.5 per cent of Welsh voters, on a turnout of 35.6 per cent, approved the proposal.

- Thus, the Assembly gained the power to make primary legislation (Acts of the Assembly) in its specified subjects of competence. The power to make secondary legislation was transferred to Welsh ministers.

In 2011, the Silk Commission on Devolution in Wales was set up to examine the devolution settlement in Wales, and it made two reports: one in 2012 on financial powers, and a second in 2014 setting out 61 recommendations for strengthening Welsh devolution, particularly on legislative powers and moving to a reserved powers model. The 2012 report resulted in the Wales Act 2014, which renamed the Welsh Assembly Government as the Welsh Government and devolved power to make primary legislation to impose taxes and extend the borrowing powers of the Welsh government. However, it provided that the power to set Welsh rates of income tax would first need to be approved by a referendum of the Welsh people (this requirement was removed by the Wales Act 2017).

In 2015, following the St David's Day agreement, David Cameron announced a new devolution model for Wales and after a controversial journey through the legislative process, the Wales Act 2017 gave Wales a reserved powers model similar to Scotland's.

 STATUTE

The Wales Act 2017 provides that the Welsh Assembly is a permanent part of the UK's constitutional framework and recognises the Sewel convention (see sections 1 and 2). It also allows the Assembly to make law on any matter not reserved to the UK Parliament, although there are almost 200 reserved areas, and some powers that were previously within the Assembly's competence are now reserved (section 3 and Schedules 1 and 2 Wales Act 2017). Powers over Welsh rates of income tax, energy, transport, the Assembly's own elections, and changing the number of its ministers have now been devolved, with most of the changes coming into force in 2018.

However, one further question remains for Wales. England and Wales have shared a legal system for centuries but stronger devolved powers and the move to a reserved powers model will inevitably result in increasing differences between English law and Welsh law. At some point, the question of whether there should be two separate jurisdictions may need to be considered. The Wales Act 2017 did not include a provision creating a separate legal jurisdiction for Wales and this has been a criticism of the Act, although it recognises that the law that applies in Wales includes a distinct body of Welsh law. (This was a question considered by Lord Thomas, the Lord Chief Justice, in his 2016 Report; see http://data.parliament.uk/writtenevidence/committeeevidence.svc/evidencedocument/justice-committee/lord-chief-justice-annual-report-2016/oral/43679.html, Qs 25 and 26; see also Lord Lloyd-Jones, 'Codification of Welsh Law' (speech delivered at the Association of London Welsh Lawyers, 8 March 2018).) The Commission on Justice in Wales recommended that the law applicable in Wales should be formally identified as the law of Wales (*Justice in Wales for the People of Wales,* October 2019 pp 57–59, 486–489).

 SUMMARY

Wales has moved from an executive government to a reserved powers model where everything is devolved except matters specifically reserved to the UK Parliament (the Government of Wales Act 2006 as amended by the 2014 and 2017 Wales Acts).

 THINKING POINT

What is your impression of the pattern of devolution in Wales? How would you describe the process that has taken place? Note the pattern of change: recommendations by Commissions, followed by political agreement, then legislation.

4.2.3 Devolution in Northern Ireland

Northern Ireland was the first part of the UK to have devolved government with the Parliament of Northern Ireland from 1921 to 1972 but devolution was suspended in the early years of the 'Troubles'. The Northern Ireland devolution settlement is the result of the Good Friday Agreement (the Belfast Agreement), a treaty made in April 1998 between the UK and Ireland about the governance of Northern Ireland. This has given unique features to devolution in Northern Ireland, whose power-sharing model between the Unionists and Nationalists reflects its emergence from conflict. The Good Friday Agreement was based on three strands:

- Strand One—setting up the Northern Ireland Assembly to build relationships and co-operation within Northern Ireland.
- Strand Two—developing co-operation between Northern Ireland and Ireland by setting up a North/South Ministerial Council.
- Strand Three—promoting co-operation between Britain and Ireland (the East/West relationship) by setting up a British–Irish Council.

The Northern Ireland Act 1998 created the Northern Ireland Executive and the Northern Ireland Assembly in Belfast, with 108 Members of the Legislative Assembly (MLAs) representing 18 constituencies, though powers were only transferred in December 1999. (The number of MLAs was reduced to 90 in 2016.)

 STATUTE

Only the Northern Ireland Act refers to the possibility of future independence; section 1 provides that Northern Ireland will remain part of the UK unless the majority of the people of Northern Ireland vote to leave in a referendum (a similar provision was included in a mirror amendment to the Irish Constitution). This provision was included to assure Unionists that Northern Ireland would not leave the United Kingdom without it reflecting the wishes of the people (the 'principle of consent').

The Northern Ireland Assembly has power to make law on any matter (known as 'transferred matters') *unless* it is an excepted or reserved matter (section 4 Northern Ireland Act 1998). Excepted matters (listed in Schedule 2) are issues of national importance to the UK as a whole and include the constitution, defence, international relations, and national security; only the UK Parliament can legislate on them. Reserved matters (in Schedule 3) are areas on which the UK Parliament continues to legislate but some of which the Secretary of State may decide to devolve to the Northern Ireland Assembly; they include firearms and explosives, financial services, and import and export controls.

The Northern Ireland Executive is run on a power-sharing basis between the Unionists and Nationalists. The First Minister and the Deputy First Minister have equal status and must act jointly. Assembly votes on important matters or legislation can only be passed with 'cross-community support', which means either:

1. a majority of the members voting plus a majority of Unionists and a majority of Nationalists (parallel consent); or

2. a majority of 60 per cent of the members voting plus 40 per cent of the designated Nationalists voting and 40 per cent of the designated Unionists voting (weighted majority) (see Northern Ireland Act section 4(5)).

The Northern Ireland Act 2009 devolved powers over policing, prisons, and criminal law, and following the cross-party Stormont House agreement in 2014, the Corporation Tax (Northern Ireland) Act 2015 devolved new powers to the Assembly to set its own rate of corporation tax from April 2018.

STATUTE: NORTHERN IRELAND ACT 1998: KEY LAW-MAKING PROVISIONS

Section 5(1): [T]he Assembly may make laws, to be known as Acts.

Section 5(2): A Bill shall become an Act when it has been passed by the Assembly and has received Royal Assent.

Section 6(1): A provision of an Act is not law if it is outside the legislative competence of the Assembly.

The Northern Ireland Assembly, however, has been suspended several times: direct rule from Westminster was imposed in 2000 for three months because of a lack of progress on the decommissioning of IRA weapons (see Northern Ireland Act 2000), and from 2002 to 2007 until devolved power was restored under the Northern Ireland (St Andrews Agreement) Act 2006. In 2017, the power-sharing coalition between the Unionists and Nationalists collapsed after the Deputy First Minister resigned over issues concerning a green energy scheme, and Northern Ireland was run by civil servants until devolved government was restored in January 2020. The Northern Ireland (Executive Formation etc) Act 2019 had required the UK government to report regularly on progress before the UK and Irish governments and five main political parties in Northern Ireland agreed to the *New Decade, New Approach* deal to restore devolved government.

SUMMARY

The Northern Ireland Assembly may legislate on any matter which is not excepted or reserved. It may legislate on reserved matters with the consent of the Secretary of State.

4.3 Devolution and the sovereignty of the UK Parliament

Under the devolution settlements, Westminster remains the sovereign Parliament. It has *delegated* powers to three subordinate legislatures which do not have parliamentary sovereignty, and the sovereignty of the UK Parliament is preserved by the devolution Acts:

STATUTE

- **Section 28(7) Scotland Act 1998:** This section does not affect the power of the Parliament of the United Kingdom to make laws for Scotland.
- **Section 107(5) Government of Wales Act 2006:** This Part does not affect the power of the Parliament of the United Kingdom to make laws for Wales.
- **Section 5(6) Northern Ireland Act 1998:** This section does not affect the power of the Parliament of the United Kingdom to make laws for Northern Ireland.

This was reinforced by Lord Hope in *AXA General Insurance Ltd v Lord Advocate (Scotland)* [2011] UKSC 46:

> The United Kingdom Parliament has vested in the Scottish Parliament the authority to make laws that are within its devolved competence. It is nevertheless a body to which decision making powers have been delegated . . . Sovereignty remains with the United Kingdom Parliament. The Scottish Parliament's power to legislate is not unconstrained. It cannot make or unmake any law it wishes. [46]

The Memorandum of Understanding between the UK government and the devolved bodies clearly states that the Westminster Parliament retains authority to legislate on any matter whether or not it is devolved:

> It is ultimately for Parliament to decide what use to make of that power. However, the UK Government will proceed in accordance with the convention that the UK Parliament would not normally legislate with regard to devolved matters except with the agreement of the devolved

legislature. The devolved administrations will be responsible for seeking such agreement as may be required for this purpose on an approach from the UK Government. (*Memorandum of Understanding and Supplementary Agreements Between the United Kingdom Government, the Scottish Ministers, the Welsh Ministers, and the Northern Ireland Executive Committee,* 2013 version [14])

However, we encountered in section 4.2.1 the Sewel convention, a self-imposed limitation, by which the UK Parliament will not *normally* legislate on devolved matters without the consent of the devolved administrations; this means that even though Westminster could theoretically make whatever law it wished, it would not normally do so without getting permission from the devolved legislatures, which requires a Legislative Consent Motion.

 EXAMPLES

The UK Parliament legislated on a devolved matter with the devolved administration's consent with the Anti-Terrorism, Crime and Security Act 2001, which extended to Scotland even though criminal law was devolved; the Scottish Parliament consented in view of the UK-wide terrorist threat. The three devolved legislatures also consented to the Coronavirus Act 2020 (health is a devolved matter).

In practice, the Sewel convention has become the central pivot for the operation of devolution. It is now recognised in two devolution Acts (section 28(8) Scotland Act 1998 and section 107(6) Government of Wales Act 2006; it is not expressed in the Northern Ireland Act but does apply to Northern Ireland), but the majority in *R (Miller) v Secretary of State for Exiting the European Union* [2017] UKSC 5 ('*Miller I*') pointed out in clear terms that the language used does not turn it into a legal rule—it remains a political rule:

the UK Parliament is not seeking to convert the Sewel Convention into a rule which can be interpreted, let alone enforced, by the courts; rather, it is recognising the convention for what it is, namely a political convention, and is effectively declaring that it is a permanent feature of the relevant devolution settlement. That follows from the nature of the content, and is acknowledged by the words ('it is recognised' and 'will not normally'), of the relevant subsection. We would have expected UK Parliament to have used other words if it were seeking to convert a convention into a legal rule justiciable by the courts. (*Miller I* [2017] UKSC 5 [148]; see also [149])

The majority went on to acknowledge the convention's 'important role in facilitating harmonious relationships between the UK Parliament and the devolved legislatures', but emphasised that its operation was not a matter for the judiciary (see [151]).

However, Brexit has highlighted the limits of the convention.

- In the *Miller I* case, the Supreme Court decided that the devolved assemblies did not have a legal veto on the UK's withdrawal from the EU ([150]); there was no legal obligation on the UK Parliament to consult on legislation giving effect to Brexit because the devolution Acts did not require the UK to remain a member of the EU, and relations with the EU were a reserved matter.

- The UK Parliament passed the EU (Withdrawal) Act 2018 without the Scottish Parliament's consent. The Secretary of State for Scotland said that the devolution settlements provided that where there was disagreement, the UK Parliament may be required to legislate without the consent of devolved legislatures (HC Hansard 14 June 2018, Vol 642 col 1122).

- None of the devolved legislatures consented to the EU (Withdrawal Agreement) Act 2020. Having sought, but failed to get, consent, the UK government asserted that Brexit was not normal circumstances (see questions-statements.parliament.uk/written-statements/detail/2020-01-23/HCWS60; Nicola McEwen, 'The Sewel convention and Brexit' 7 April 2020, The Constitution Unit).

If the UK Parliament legislates on a devolved matter without consent, the legislation is *lawful* because Parliament retains legal sovereignty; the convention 'operates as a political restriction on the activity of the UK Parliament' (*Miller I* [145]).

The Memorandum of Understanding also suggests an element of give and take, and mutual awareness of the delicate balance of power in the devolution arrangements. It expressly states that the UK Parliament retains 'the absolute right to debate, enquire into or make representations about devolved matters' but 'it is a consequence of Parliament's decision to devolve certain matters that Parliament itself will in future be more restricted in its field of operation' (see para 15, 2013 version). Equally, the devolved legislatures can debate non-devolved matters, but should 'bear in mind the responsibility of the UK Parliament in these matters' (para 16).

CROSS REFERENCE
We pick this discussion up again in section 6.3.1.4

 SUMMARY

The devolution settlements mean that legally, the UK Parliament retains parliamentary sovereignty, but in practice it has increasingly reduced power to make laws for Scotland, Northern Ireland, and Wales. The practical reality is that the longer devolution operates, the more conventions and practices develop as protective foundations, making devolution more entrenched.

4.4 The courts and devolution

The key point to note here is that the primary legislation of the devolved legislatures can be challenged in the courts if it was made outside their legal competence. The Supreme Court has what is known as devolution jurisdiction, which means that under the devolution Acts it reviews whether law made by the devolved bodies is outside the legislative competence granted to them by the UK Parliament, and decides on its legal validity. (The devolution Acts initially gave devolution jurisdiction to the Judicial Committee of the Privy Council; the Constitutional Reform Act 2005 then transferred devolution jurisdiction to the new Supreme Court when it was created in 2009.) Law made by devolved bodies will be outside legislative competence—and not valid law—particularly if:

- it relates to reserved matters;
- it was contrary to EU law (pre-Brexit) and as a temporary measure post-Brexit, if it is contrary to retained EU law (section 12 European Union (Withdrawal) Act 2018);
- it conflicts with the European Convention on Human Rights (ECHR).

CROSS REFERENCE
See section 5.3.3

There is no doubt that devolution has given the Supreme Court a clear constitutional role and its decisions are shaping devolution law, especially that in the *Miller I* case. This is especially important in relation to the interpretation of the devolution Acts and the extent of the devolved bodies' powers. Effectively, the court is determining the division of power between the UK's central institutions and the devolved bodies, and where the boundaries lie.

The Supreme Court's devolution jurisdiction works like this:

- Questions on 'devolution issues' can be referred to the Court under a special procedure set out under the devolution Acts. Devolution issues are questions relating to the legislative or executive powers and functions of the devolved bodies, such as whether an Act was within their competence (see Schedule 6 para 1 Scotland Act 1998; Schedule 9 Government of Wales Act 2006; Schedule 10 Northern Ireland Act 1998; see also Supreme Court Practice Direction 10).

- The Court can also be asked to scrutinise a Bill of one of the devolved legislatures before it becomes law to ascertain whether it is within their competence (see section 33 Scotland Act 1998; section 112 Government of Wales Act 2006; section 11 Northern Ireland Act 1998). This type of question can be referred to the Supreme Court by a law officer of the UK or of a devolved legislature. (This is similar to the power of abstract review in countries with a written constitution, where a proposed law is referred to the courts to determine whether it is constitutional.)

- Issues concerning devolution can also arrive at the court via the normal appeal process from lower courts' devolution appeals.

The analysis that follows examines the courts' approach to interpreting the devolution Acts and reviewing legislation from the devolved administrations, including legislation that might encroach on reserved matters or breach human rights.

4.4.1 Interpreting the devolution Acts

 CASE CLOSE-UP: *ROBINSON v SECRETARY OF STATE FOR NORTHERN IRELAND* [2002] UKHL 32

This early devolution case involved a challenge to whether the election of the First Minister and Deputy First Minister by the Northern Ireland Assembly was legal as it took place later than the six-week time limit after devolved government had been restored as set out in the Northern Ireland Act. The House of Lords held that the election was valid even though it was outside the specified time. Lords Bingham, Hoffmann, and Millett took the view that the Northern Ireland Act was effectively a constitution and should be interpreted 'generously and purposively', not too literally or strictly ([11, 30–31]). The court chose the approach that was more consistent with the purpose of the Act, which was to implement the Belfast Agreement and promote its values; deciding that the election was invalid could have caused political deadlock. The minority disagreed on the basis that the Northern Ireland Act should not be interpreted differently from any other statute. The *Robinson* approach of viewing devolution Acts as constitutions has not been followed—certainly not for Scotland and Wales—but the political context of Northern Ireland made this a special case.

Lord Hope has subsequently echoed that a devolution Act 'must be interpreted like any other statute', but stated that the court should have regard to the Act's purpose (*Welsh Byelaws case*, *Local Government Byelaws (Wales) Bill 2012—Reference by the Attorney General for England and Wales* [2012] UKSC 53 [80] and *Imperial Tobacco Limited v The Lord Advocate* [2012] UKSC 61 [15]). Furthermore, Lord Neuberger pointed out in the *Welsh Byelaws case* that each devolution Act is different and the courts must 'be wary of assuming that they have precisely the same effect' ([50]).

The court in *AXA General Insurance Ltd v HM Advocate* expressed that greater weight should be given to decisions of the Scottish Parliament as a democratically elected legislature; it was not at the same level as local government. Lord Hope pointed out that there were limits on the courts' ability to scrutinise Acts of the Scottish Parliament ([49]), an idea which elevates the Parliament to a special status as a legislature. (In this case, the Supreme Court held that an Act of the Scottish Parliament (the Damages (Asbestos-related Conditions) (Scotland) Act 2009) had not breached property rights of insurance companies under Article 1 Protocol 1 to the European Convention on Human Rights.)

4.4.2 **Reviewing legislation from the devolved administrations**

Statutes do not normally tell courts how to interpret them, but under section 101 Scotland Act 1998 and section 154(2) Government of Wales Act 2006 the courts must first read a provision 'as narrowly as is required for it to be within competence, if . . . possible'. If the court finds that a provision in an Act was made outside competence, it can also suspend its invalidation to allow the devolved legislature time to put it right, rather than automatically invalidating it (eg section 102 Scotland Act 1998).

Q | **CASE CLOSE-UP: *THE CHRISTIAN INSTITUTE AND OTHERS v THE LORD ADVOCATE (SCOTLAND)* [2016] UKSC 51**

This was applied in *The Christian Institute and Others v The Lord Advocate (Scotland)* [2016] UKSC 51, where the Children and Young People (Scotland) Act 2014, which assigned a named person to every child and young person in Scotland to give advice and support, was challenged as being outside the Scottish Parliament's competence. The Supreme Court held that the Act was invalid because it was incompatible with the right to privacy and family life under Article 8 ECHR, but the court considered allowing the Scottish Parliament opportunity to correct the defects.

Reviewing legislation from the devolved legislatures centres on the interpretation of relevant Acts and Bills. In the *Imperial Tobacco case*, Imperial Tobacco argued that certain provisions in the Tobacco and Primary Medical Services (Scotland) Act 2012 were outside the competence of the Scottish Parliament because they related to consumers and product safety, which were reserved matters under the Scotland Act. The Supreme Court decided that the purpose of those provisions was to discourage tobacco sales and did not concern consumer protection; therefore the Act was valid. Three Welsh Assembly Bills had been referred by 2015:

- In the *Welsh Byelaws case*, the UK Attorney General referred the question of whether the National Assembly of Wales had competence to pass certain clauses in the Local Government Byelaws (Wales) Bill, the first Bill passed by the Assembly under its stronger law-making powers under the Government of Wales Act 2006. The Supreme Court upheld the Bill.
- In *Agricultural Sector (Wales) Bill—Reference by the Attorney General for England and Wales* [2014] UKSC 43, the Agricultural Sector (Wales) Bill was challenged by the UK government on the ground that it related to employment, a reserved matter, so went beyond the Assembly's competence. The Court upheld the Bill on the basis that it related to agriculture, a devolved matter.

- In *Recovery of Medical Costs for Asbestos Diseases (Wales) Bill* [2015] UKSC 3, [2015] 1 AC 1016, a Bill from the Welsh Assembly required employers and insurers to pay for NHS treatment for asbestos-related diseases caused by employers' breach of duty. The Counsel General for Wales (a law officer) referred the Bill to the Supreme Court to ascertain that it was within the scope of competence and that it related to the NHS (a devolved matter). In a decision that was less deferential to a democratically elected legislature than *AXA*, the Supreme Court held by a majority that the Bill was outside the competence of the Assembly because it did not relate to devolved matters.

(For comment, see A. Tomkins, 'Confusion and Retreat: The Supreme Court on Devolution', UK Const L Blog (19 Feb 2015) (available at https://ukconstitutionallaw.org/).)

In 2018, the UK government referred the Scottish Continuity Bill to the Supreme Court for a ruling on whether it was within the devolved legislative powers of the Scottish Parliament—the first time that legislation from the Scottish Parliament had been referred (*The UK Withdrawal from the European Union (Legal Continuity) (Scotland) Bill—A Reference by the Attorney General and the Advocate General for Scotland* [2018] UKSC 64). (The Welsh Continuity Bill was also referred but this was later withdrawn.) The Bill provided for existing EU law relating to devolved matters such as agriculture to continue post-Brexit. The Supreme Court found that specific provisions—though not the whole Bill—were beyond the Scottish Parliament's competence. Section 17 of the Bill provided that certain UK secondary legislation would not have effect in Scotland without Scottish ministers' consent, so could prevent legislation enacted by the UK Parliament from coming into force. The Scottish Parliament did not have the power to do this as it would modify section 28(7) Scotland Act 1998, which makes it clear that the UK Parliament continues to have power to make laws for Scotland.

 SUMMARY

Devolution is being overseen, not by a codified constitution, but by Acts of the UK Parliament which are interpreted and applied by the courts. This shows the UK constitution evolving and adapting flexibly to a new arrangement.

4.5 The West Lothian question

Scotland, Wales, and Northern Ireland still return MPs to the House of Commons in Westminster to represent their constituencies, and issues have arisen on their voting rights in Westminster. A 1977 proposal by James Callaghan, the Prime Minister, for a devolved assembly in Scotland prompted Tam Dalyell, then the Labour MP for West Lothian, to ask what has become known as the West Lothian question:

> For how long will English constituencies and English Honourable members tolerate . . . at least 119 Honourable Members from Scotland, Wales and Northern Ireland exercising an important, and probably often decisive, effect on English politics while they themselves have no say in the same matters in Scotland, Wales and Northern Ireland? (Tam Dalyell MP, HC Deb, Vol 939 col 122–123 (14 November 1977))

The West Lothian question became particularly pertinent after the introduction of devolution. By asking why Scottish, Welsh, and Northern Ireland MPs at Westminster can debate and vote on laws only affecting England, while English MPs have no say in devolved issues in Scotland, Wales, and Northern Ireland, the question reflects the broader issue of the asymmetrical nature of devolution (known as the English question). For example, both health and education are devolved matters but in 2003, without the support of Scottish and Welsh MPs, the Labour government would have lost the vote to set up foundation hospitals in England (around 60 English Labour MPs either rebelled or abstained) and in 2004, Scottish Labour MPs voted in favour of introducing university tuition fees in England under the Higher Education Bill although Scotland had abolished them.

Various proposals have been suggested in response to the West Lothian question, including:

- English votes for English laws (EVEL) (see Chapter 11 for details);
- setting up an English Parliament (although Peter Hain, then the Secretary of State for Wales, warned in 2007 that replacing the composite UK with multiple countries would risk the 'Balkanisation' of Britain, reducing the countries' collective importance on the world stage);
- English regional assemblies (see section 4.8);
- reducing the number of MPs from Scotland, Wales, and Northern Ireland in the House of Commons;
- stopping asking the question (Lord Irvine).

After the 2014 Scottish independence referendum, David Cameron committed himself to a 'devolution revolution' across Britain, including votes on English issues by English MPs at Westminster. In 2013, the McKay Commission suggested adopting a constitutional convention that decisions in the UK Parliament which affect only England (or England and Wales) should normally be taken only with the consent of a majority of MPs for English or English and Welsh constituencies, but in October 2015, the House of Commons changed its Standing Orders (its parliamentary procedures) to introduce the English votes for English laws process. In outline, this is how it works:

- During the legislative process, the Speaker decides whether in his opinion a Government Bill or part of a Bill relates to England (or England and Wales).
- If so, the Bill is given a Speaker's Certificate.
- An 'England only' Bill will only be considered by MPs representing English constituencies (or English and Welsh MPs for an England and Wales Bill) before being considered by all MPs.

> **CROSS REFERENCE**
For details of the EVEL procedure, see Chapter 11

However, in 2016, the Public Administration and Constitutional Affairs Committee expressed 'significant doubts' that changing Standing Orders was the right solution and stated that this 'may be unlikely to survive the election of a government that cannot command a double majority of both English and UK MPs' (House of Commons Public Administration and Constitutional Affairs Committee, *The Future of the Union, Part one: English Votes for English Laws*, 5th Report of 2015–16, HC 523 [72]). The Constitution Committee found that, while EVEL went some way to addressing the West Lothian question, it did not fully mirror the power of devolved administrations to drive a legislative agenda and that the EVEL procedure was attempting to utilise the *central* Westminster Parliament to express a separate voice for England and Wales (House of Lords Select Committee on the Constitution, *English Votes for English Laws*, 6th Report of Session 2016–17, HL Paper 61).

4.6 A unitary or federal state?

The UK is traditionally a unitary state where ultimate authority is centralised (see Chapter 3), but devolution is a way of decentralising power. You may be about to spot the issue that arises here: by decentralising power, has the UK ceased to be a unitary state and become a federal state? The answer is no, at least not yet. Federal systems of government share power between regional and central government, whereas devolved systems of government allow the central government ultimate power to make decisions for the whole country. As long as the Westminster Parliament retains sovereignty over the devolved administrations and, at least in theory, could revoke their powers, the system is not federal. Furthermore, the component parts of the UK do not have an even distribution of power because England does not have its own Parliament. The Royal Commission on the Constitution 1973 (the Kilbrandon Commission) concluded that England would not fit into a fully federal system because of its disproportionate size. However, Bogdanor argues that the UK now has a quasi-federal system, with the Westminster Parliament 'transformed into a Parliament for England [and] a federal Parliament for Scotland and Northern Ireland' and also now for Wales (*The New British Constitution*, Oxford: Hart 2009, p 114). He also argues that devolution has gone beyond mere delegation of power but has divided the power to legislate for each of the three nations between Westminster and each devolved legislature (see p 115). With the more recent devolution Acts, even reserved matters are starting to be shared between Westminster and Scotland.

It can be argued that while the UK Parliament retains legal sovereignty, the UK is a unitary state, but there is now more focus on the UK as a 'union state' rather than a unitary state. Aileen McHarg argues that while it is formally unitary, constitutional practice suggests that the UK is better viewed as a union state ('The Future of the United Kingdom's Territorial Constitution: Can the Union Survive?' 2016, available at https://ssrn.com/abstract=2771614), and this view is supported by Professor Adam Tomkins (House of Lords Select Committee on the Constitution, *The Union and Devolution*, 10th Report of Session 2015–16, HL Paper 149, Written ev; see para 31 of the Report for an imaginative range of descriptive labels for the UK). See also the Bingham Centre Devolution Review, discussed presently, and Peter Leyland, 'The Multifaceted Constitutional Dynamics of UK Devolution' (2011) 9(1) International Journal of Constitutional Law 251.

☐ THE BIGGER PICTURE: MOVING TOWARDS A FEDERAL STATE?

There are concerns that post-Brexit Britain could separate into its component countries, and in response the Constitution Reform Group (a group of cross-party politicians) drafted an Act of Union bill in 2016, proposing a federal UK to maintain the union in which power flows from the bottom up rather than top down, so the four nations would decide what the centre could do (see http://www.constitutionreformgroup.co.uk/).

The Bingham Centre Devolution Review has highlighted that the informal way in which the UK government does things is no longer appropriate in a state with devolution and that 'Moving towards a more federal, codified constitutional arrangement for the UK would therefore establish "permanent" devolution on the basis of more clearly defined principles and rules'. (See 'A Constitutional Crossroads: Ways Forward for the United Kingdom', May 2015, at: www.biicl.org/documents/595_a_constitutional_crossroads.pdf at p 49 [6].) See also the House of Lords Select Committee on the Constitution, *The Union and Devolution* [268–275] for a discussion on whether federalism would suit the UK.

THINKING POINT

Do you think that devolution strengthens or weakens the argument for a written constitution for the UK?

 SUMMARY

The UK can now be described as a decentralised unitary state with an asymmetric model of devolution, or arguably as a union state. Scotland, Wales, and Northern Ireland each have a different form of devolved power and England has no devolved Parliament. Devolution is now seen as a permanent change to the constitution.

❱ **CROSS REFERENCE**
For discussion of devolution and Brexit, see Chapter 5

Where next for devolution? In one sense, it has become more complex and deeply embedded with increasingly shared powers, but the Constitution Committee has observed that there has been 'no guiding strategy or framework of principles to ensure that devolution develops in a coherent or consistent manner and in ways which do not harm the Union' (House of Lords Constitution Committee, *The Union and Devolution* [99]). At times, devolution has creaked at the seams with the impact of Brexit, and the four nations' policies on coronavirus, especially on easing lockdown, have differed despite some intergovernmental co-operation. There has also been confusion about when the UK government's announcements only applied to England (Scottish Affairs Committee, *Coronavirus and Scotland: Interim Report on Intergovernmental Working*, First Report of Session 2019–21, HC 314 [42]). See 'Five key questions about coronavirus and devolution', 31 May 2020, The Constitution Unit; Nicola McEwen et al, 'Intergovernmental Relations in the UK: Time for a Radical Overhaul?' (2020) 91(3) The Political Quarterly 632.

4.7 Regional government in England

Although England is alone in not having a devolved Parliament, there have been attempts to provide elements of English regional government. In 1999, eight indirectly elected regional development agencies (known as regional assemblies) were established to improve economic development (they were abolished between 2008 and 2010). However, a government White Paper (*Your Region, Your Choice: Revitalising the English Regions*, Cm 5511, May 2002) recommended *elected* regional assemblies for England. By 2004, the Labour government had introduced plans for elected regional assemblies in the north of England, but a referendum in the north-east in 2004 decisively rejected the idea by four to one and it was shelved. (For further details, see House of Commons Justice Committee, *Devolution: A Decade On*, 5th Report, Session 2008–09, HC 529–I, paras 202–221.)

In 2009, David Cameron made an election speech promising to 'tear down' big government, beginning the road to the implementation of devolution to *local* government in England, and this is now effectively creating a regional layer of government which we examine in section 4.8.2.

4.8 Local government

Local government dates back to the Saxon era. Town councils or corporations have existed since the creation of boroughs (fortified towns) by Henry II in the twelfth century, and until the nineteenth century, Justices of the Peace carried out local administration in addition to their judicial function. It has long been recognised that government is needed at local level to deal with community issues, and this is the level of government with the most immediate impact on individuals; it enables local decision-making, local democracy, and local accountability. The rationale for local government has been explained in this way:

> The debate about the balance of power between central and local government can appear rather abstract. However, we are convinced that the balance of power matters . . . because at its heart is the challenge of improving the lives of local people and local communities, and determining where the decisions that affect them directly should be made. (House of Commons Communities and Local Government Committee, *The Balance of Power: Central and Local Government*, 6th Report of Session 2008–09 HC 33-I, [1])

However, the picture of local government has become increasingly complex and anyone who believes that the UK constitution is slow to change need only look at the shifting sands of local government over the past 50 years to be convinced otherwise. What follows below shows a pattern of continual reorganisation and reform of local government, with increasing emphasis on rebalancing power from central to local government, known as 'localism', and greater emphasis on what the Lyons Report 2007 called 'place-shaping', the idea of more strategic local government (see Communities and Local Government Committee, *The Balance of Power: Central and Local Government*, Report, [18]).

The first key point is that all levels of local government are created by statute and thus are given their powers by Parliament in Westminster. In England and Wales, the first elected county councils and the London County Council were created by the Local Government Act 1888; this was followed by the Local Government Act 1894, which created elected urban and rural district councils and parish councils. There were also county boroughs, metropolitan boroughs, and London boroughs. From 1965, London was run by the Greater London Council (GLC).

A major reorganisation of local government took place with the Local Government Act 1972, which came into force on 1 April 1974 and swept away existing local government areas, introducing a simpler framework. It established a two-tier local government structure for England and Wales, with county councils as the upper tier and district councils as the lower tier, and it created six new metropolitan counties (West Midlands, Greater Manchester, Merseyside, Tyne and Wear, West Yorkshire, and South Yorkshire). Similar changes were introduced in Scotland (Northern Ireland's two-tier system had been replaced in 1973 by a single-tier district council system). However, in 1986 both the metropolitan counties and the GLC were abolished under the Local Government Act 1985 (the 1983 Conservative manifesto had called the GLC 'a wasteful and unnecessary tier of government'). In the 1990s, a review carried out by the Local Government Commission for England recommended that many shire counties (though not all) should change from the two-tier structure to one tier of unitary authorities; between 1996 and 1998, 46 new unitary authorities were created, with a further nine set up between 2007 and 2009. The two-tier systems in Scotland and Wales were replaced in 1996. However, reform did not stop there, and Table 4.2 summarises some of the further developments.

Table 4.2 Local government reforms 1999–2011

Act	Reform
Greater London Authority Act 1999	Created the Greater London Authority
Local Government Act 2000	To update and streamline decision-making in local government, this Act replaced the old committee system of decision-making in councils with three options, focusing on a new executive cabinet system. Each local authority had to choose one 'governance arrangement': an elected mayor and cabinet executive (a cabinet of 2–10 councillors); a leader elected by the council and cabinet executive (the most popular choice); or an elected mayor with a council manager appointed by the council.
Local Government and Public Involvement in Health Act 2007	This substantial Act, 246 sections long, made extensive amendments to earlier statutes, including changes to the executive arrangements outlined above (abolishing the mayor and council manager arrangement). It allowed the Secretary of State to invite proposals from local councils to become unitary authorities.
Local Government Act 2010	Prevented the implementation of proposals by councils to become unitary authorities under the above Act.
Localism Act 2011	To enable more decentralisation of power, this Act gave local authorities greater flexibility and a 'general power of competence', provided for referendums for directly elected mayors, and gave greater rights to communities, including the right to bid for community assets such as pubs and shops; it also made reforms for a more democratic planning system. Allowed councils to go back to the committee system of decision-making.

THINKING POINT

How would you assess the pattern of the legislation in Table 4.2?

For further details of the English administrative structure, see: www.ons.gov.uk/methodology/geography/ukgeographies/administrativegeography/england.

4.8.1 Structure and powers of local government

There are currently 408 local councils in the UK, of which 343 are in England (see www.lgiu.org). They deal with a range of issues, including housing, adult social care, public health, environmental protection, highways, and road traffic management, and have the power to make byelaws, a form of secondary legislation, under powers given to them by the UK Parliament. Local government is partly funded by government grant (£25 billion in 2016–17; see www.nao.org.uk) and partly by locally generated income, especially through council tax. Within central government, the Ministry for Housing, Communities and Local Government is responsible for regional and local government in England, while the Local Government Boundary Commission for England decides the number of councillors and the boundaries of electoral areas for each local authority in England. Most decisions are taken by elected councillors, being debated and voted on at public meetings, while paid employees carry out the day-to-day running of local councils, each of which has a chief executive, directors of service areas, and council officers.

At present, the picture of local government is a varied one. It can consist of one layer of local government, known as a single-tier structure, or two layers, known as the two-tier structure. London has its own arrangement.

4.8.1.1 **Two-tier structure**

Some parts of England retain the two-tier structure of county council and district councils, dividing responsibility for local services between them. In England, there are 26 county councils covering, as their name suggests, the whole of a county, which is then divided into several districts, each with its own council; there are 192 district councils.

District, borough, or city councils deal with:

- Council tax
- Housing
- Parks
- Planning applications
- Recycling
- Rubbish collection
- Street cleaning

County councils deal with:

- Education
- Fire and public safety
- Highways and transport
- Libraries
- Planning
- Social care
- Trading standards

(Source: https://www.gov.uk)

There are also around 9,000 town and parish councils in some parts of England, dealing with issues including planning applications, local amenities such as playing fields, and the issuing of fixed penalty fines for offences such as dropping litter and spraying graffiti. In Scotland and Wales, they are known as Community Councils; none exist in Northern Ireland.

4.8.1.2 **Single-tier structure**

Some areas (often large towns or cities) have a single tier of local government known as a unitary authority, which provides all local government services in their area. There are now 125 unitary authorities in England, of which there are essentially three types: unitary authorities in the shires, London boroughs, and metropolitan boroughs. Scotland, Wales, and Northern Ireland have single-tier councils providing all local government services.

Single-tier authorities

England

- 55 unitary authorities in shire areas
- 32 London boroughs
- 36 metropolitan boroughs
- City of London Corporation
- The Council of the Isles of Scilly (unitary)

Wales

22 unitary authorities

Scotland

32 unitary authorities

Northern Ireland

11 unitary authorities

(Source: http://www.lgiu.org)

4.8.1.3 The Greater London Assembly

In London, the Greater London Assembly (GLA) was set up in 2000. It was created by the Greater London Authority Act 1999, following a referendum in 1998 supporting an elected London Mayor and Assembly; the Greater London Authority Act 2007 increased the powers devolved to the GLA and the Mayor. The GLA builds on the idea of strategic regional governance. It has a directly elected mayor with an executive function whose term of office lasts four years. The Mayor has control over a wide range of areas, including arts, policing, business, environmental issues, housing, planning and regeneration, and transport. The Mayor sets an annual budget for, among others, the GLA, the London Fire and Emergency Planning Authority, the Metropolitan Police, and Transport for London, and more funding and devolved powers were given to the Mayor under the London Devolution Agreement 2017. The Mayor is held to account by the London Assembly (but for a critical view of the GLA's scrutiny role, see the House of Commons Communities and Local Government Committee, *Post-Legislative Scrutiny of the Greater London Authority Act 2007 and the London Assembly*, 4th Report of Session 2013–14, HC 213).

4.8.1.4 Elected mayors

Elected mayors chosen directly by people outside London were first introduced by the Local Government Act 2000, which enabled people to vote in a local referendum on their local authority's governance model (though not many referendums were in favour). Since 2007, local authorities in England have been able to introduce an elected mayor without a referendum (under the Local Government and Public Involvement in Health Act 2007).

4.8.1.5 Police and Crime Commissioners

Key changes in the local oversight of policing took place in 2012. The Police Reform and Social Responsibility Act 2011 introduced elected Police and Crime Commissioners (PCCs) to hold the police to account in their local communities in England and Wales (policing is devolved in Scotland and Northern Ireland). The PCCs replaced the former police authorities, set up in 1964 to hold local police to account. The first PCCs were elected in 2012 and elections take place every four years, although the turnout for the 2012 elections was only 15 per cent. In total, 40 police force areas in England and Wales have a PCC, but in Greater Manchester and London the mayor carries out PCC responsibilities. Under the 2011 Act, the PCC's role includes securing an efficient and effective police force for their area and holding the Chief Constable to account (section 1); to issue police and crime plans (sections 5 and 7), and to set the force budget. The PCC also has the power to appoint, suspend, and dismiss Chief Constables (section 38; see on this *R (Rhodes) v Police and Crime Commissioner for Lincolnshire* [2013] EWHC 1009 (Admin)). (See www.apccs.police.uk.)

The reasons for introducing PCCs included promoting local democracy and making police scrutiny more visible. However, by virtue of being elected, PCCs are democratically accountable, and the Police Reform and Social Responsibility Act 2011 section 28 introduced a Police and Crime Panel for each police force area with responsibility for supporting and scrutinising PCC activities and holding PCCs to account. They have been in place since 2012. Complaints about PCCs can be referred to the Independent Office for Police Conduct.

4.8.2 Devolution to local government

Recent reforms have been at the heart of the 'devolution revolution' in England by placing more emphasis on the regional level, with a shift towards devolution for local authorities (largely for economic reasons). First, the Local Democracy, Economic Development and Construction Act 2009 introduced the idea of combined authorities, where two or more local councils (except in London) can combine to form a legal body for more 'effective and convenient local government'. The aim of the Act was primarily to allow collaborative decision-making on economic regeneration and development (and also transport) across wider areas, and to allow some functions to be transferred from central to local government. Combined authorities can exercise a broader range of powers, including on health and social care, and local authorities who wish to become combined authorities need to obtain approval from central government; the Secretary of State for Housing, Communities and Local Government confers powers on the combined authority through a statutory instrument (secondary legislation). The Greater Manchester Combined Authority was the first combined authority to be set up in 2011.

Driving the 'city devolution' programme, the Cities and Local Government Devolution Act 2016 enabled devolution agreements to be made between central government and combined authorities, enabling funding and new powers over transport, planning, and skills to be transferred to the local level and allowing retention of business rates. Section 2 of the Act allows combined authorities to have a directly elected mayor (these are known as 'metro mayors') with powers over housing, transport, planning, and policing; central government can devolve powers separately to the mayor under a 'mayoral devolution deal'. By 2019, ten combined authorities had been created, all but two of which have a directly elected mayor. The first six metro mayors of combined authority areas were elected in May 2017. (For more detail on combined authorities, see: www.local.gov.uk/.) A Devolution White Paper for 'unleashing regional potential in England' was announced in the Queen's Speech in 2019, but publication of an English Devolution and Local Recovery White Paper, aimed at expanding regional devolution, was postponed until 2021.

CASE CLOSE-UP: *R (DERBYSHIRE CC) v BARNSLEY, DONCASTER, ROTHERHAM AND SHEFFIELD COMBINED AUTHORITY* **[2016] EWHC 3355 (ADMIN)**

The first legal challenge relating to combined authorities was brought by Derbyshire County Council. In 2016, the Sheffield City Region Combined Authority (SCRCA) proposed extending its geographical area to include two new local councils, Chesterfield Borough and Bassetlaw District. Derbyshire County Council opposed Chesterfield's inclusion in the SCRCA's area and requested a judicial review of the proposal. The High Court decided that there had not been sufficient consultation about Chesterfield becoming part of the SCRCA.

The phrase 'combination creep' has now been coined to describe the ability of combined authorities to extend outside county boundaries.

 SUMMARY

Local government has been significantly reformed since the 1970s and continues to be so. Recent reforms denote an outflow of power from the centre to the local level of government, primarily for reasons of economic growth and development and local accountability.

The final point may come as no surprise as you catch your breath after this chapter. The UK's constitution has recently been referred to by some commentators as an 'unsettled constitution', not only in relation to the topics we have covered here, but also more broadly. However, you can probably now go some way to appreciating the force of that description in the light of changes brought about by devolution and local government. (See Neil Walker, 'Our Constitutional Unsettlement' (2014) (July) Public Law 529.)

? **Questions**

Self-test questions

1. Explain the difference between the United Kingdom and Great Britain.

2. Which central institution delegates powers to devolved and local government?

3. Which parts of the UK does the Westminster Parliament legislate for after devolution?

4. Define (a) 'devolution' and (b) reserved matters.

5. Describe Scotland's model of devolution.

6. How have Wales' devolved powers developed since 1998?

7. What is the unique feature contained in the Northern Ireland Act 1998?

8. What is the Supreme Court's devolution jurisdiction?

9. What is the West Lothian question?

10. Define (a) a combined authority and (b) a metro mayor.

Exam question

'The devolution arrangements for Scotland, Wales and Northern Ireland could easily be removed by the Westminster Parliament.' Discuss.

 Further reading

Books

Jowell, J., and O'Cinneide, C. (eds) *The Changing Constitution* (9th edn, Oxford: Oxford University Press 2019).
See chapters 9–11 for an in-depth analysis of devolution

Journal articles

Bogdanor, V. 'Our New Constitution' (2004) 120 Law Quarterly Review 242.
An overview of how devolution fits into the bigger picture

Brazier, R. 'The Constitution of the United Kingdom' (1999) 58 (1) Cambridge Law Journal 96.
A classic assessment of devolution in its infancy

Hadfield, B. 'Devolution, Westminster and the English Question' (2005) (Summer) Public Law 286.
Examines the options for answering the English question in the House of Commons

Norton, P. (Lord Norton of Louth), 'Governing Alone' (2003) 56(4) Parliamentary Affairs 543.
Commentary on the fragmentation of the Westminster model of government

Other sources

The *Cabinet Manual* 2011.
A very helpful and readable point of reference

https://constitution-unit.com/2017/06/19/evel-wont-worry-the-new-government-but-the-west-lothian-question-may-well-do/.
A post-2017 election assessment of the West Lothian question

Hazell, R. 'The English Question' January 2006, The Constitution Unit, available at: www.ucl.ac.uk/constitution-unit/research/research-archive/nations-regions-archive/english-question.
A thorough assessment of how to correct the asymmetry of devolution

https://ukhumanrightsblog.com/2017/01/26/defying-convention-supreme-court-puts-sewel-on-the-sidelines/.
Post-*Miller* analysis of the status of the Sewel convention

Lord Reed, 'Scotland's Devolved Settlement and the Role of the Courts', The Inaugural Dover House Lecture, London, 27 February 2019 at: https://www.supreme-court.uk/docs/speech-190227.pdf.
Helpful discussion of devolution case law

; Online resources

www.oup.com/he/dennett2e

This chapter is accompanied by a selection of online resources to help you with this topic, including:

- Multiple-choice questions
- Answers to the self-test questions
- Guidance on answering the exam question

5 Brexit

Introduction

The most significant shake-up of the UK constitution in a generation began in 2016 with the Brexit referendum when a narrow majority of the public voted in favour of leaving the European Union. It then fell to the UK government to negotiate the UK's withdrawal from an organisation of which it had been a member for over 40 years. Unravelling the political and legal ties that bound the UK to the EU proved to be difficult and complex.

5.1 The pre-Brexit landscape

5.1.1 The development of the EU

The EU began as the European Coal and Steel Community, a trading bloc of six states which in 1952 created a common market for free trade in coal and steel products. The underlying idea—a response to World War II—was that countries that co-operate in producing coal and steel cannot fight each other because one of them cannot manufacture arms without the

Table 5.1 Development of the EU

1951	Treaty of Paris: came into force on 23 July 1952 and established the European Coal and Steel Community, creating a common market for free trade in coal and steel products; was valid for 50 years and expired in 2002
1957	Treaty of Rome: established the European Economic Community (EEC), a trading bloc enabling the free movement of people, goods, and services across borders; the Euratom Treaty was also signed, creating the European Atomic Energy community; there were now three separate European Communities
1972	Treaty of Brussels: treaty of accession enabling the UK to join the EEC
1986	Single European Act: provided for changes needed for the single market
1992	Maastricht Treaty on European Union: created a European Union based on three pillars (the European Communities, Common Foreign and Security Policy, and co-operation in justice and home affairs); strengthened economic and political union
1997	Treaty of Amsterdam: amended and consolidated the EU and EC treaties
2001	Treaty of Nice: reformed EU institutions to help efficient functioning after an increase in member states
2007	Treaty of Lisbon (Treaty on the Functioning of the European Union (TFEU)): aimed to increase democracy, transparency, and efficiency; modernised EU institutions

others knowing. The trading bloc grew with the creation of the European Economic Community (EEC) in 1957, and closer union was established in 1992 when the European Union (EU) was created. The EU's development is summarised in Table 5.1; note the role of treaties in its creation and continued development.

The EU has created its own unique framework of institutions as outlined in Table 5.2. The European Council and Council of the EU should not be confused with the Council of Europe, an organisation distinct from the EU, created in 1949 to promote democracy and the rule of law and protect human rights, and now with a much wider membership (47 states) than the EU (27 states).

For more information, see: http://europa.eu/european-union/about-eu/institutions-bodies_en and http://www.europarl.europa.eu.

From early on, the view of the European Court of Justice (ECJ; now the Court of Justice of the European Union) was clear: by joining the EU, every member state transferred legal sovereignty to the EU on matters over which it has competence. The court developed its own interpretation of the organisation as 'a new legal order' (see *Van Gend en Loos v Nederlandse Tariefcommissie* [1963] ECR 1) where 'the member states have limited their sovereign rights, albeit within limited fields, and have thus created a body of law which binds both their nationals and themselves' (*Costa v ENEL Case 6/64*, [1964] ECR 585, 593). Furthermore, in the eyes of the ECJ, where there was a conflict, European law prevailed over national law:

> . . . in accordance with the principle of the precedence of Community law . . . the provisions of the Treaty . . . render automatically inapplicable any conflicting provisions of . . . national law (*Amministrazione delle Finanze dello Stato v. Simmenthal SpA* [1978] ECR 629 [17])

Table 5.2 The European Union institutions

European Council	Defines and drives EU policies; membership consists of heads of state or government of the member states, the President of the European Commission, and European Council President
European Commission	The powerhouse and main administrative body of the EU; promotes EU interests, ensures EU law is properly implemented, proposes new laws, implements policies and the EU budget; membership consists of Commissioners (one from each member state)
Council of the EU	Chief decision-maker of the EU; represents interests of member states, shares legislating power with the European Parliament, adopts EU laws and co-ordinates EU policies; government ministers from each member state attend and each member state holds the presidency for six months at a time
European Parliament	Democratically elected law-making body; Members of the European Parliament (MEPs) represent EU citizens; co-legislates with the Council of the EU and shares power over the budget with the Council, supervises EU institutions
Court of Justice of the EU (formerly the European Court of Justice)	Interprets EU law to ensure uniform application in member states (rules on requests for preliminary rulings from national courts), hears cases against national governments for failing to comply with EU law (infringement proceedings), and direct actions by individuals and companies against EU institutions
Court of Auditors	Independent auditor, checks collection and use of EU budget

These cases established the principle of the primacy of EU law.

The sources of EU law are:

Primary legislation

- **EU treaties:** the two main treaties are the Treaty on the Functioning of the European Union (originally the Treaty of Rome 1957 establishing the EEC) and the Treaty on European Union (originally known as the Maastricht Treaty 1992); both were amended by the Treaty of Lisbon. The treaty provisions are the basis of EU law; they are **directly applicable** in all member states which means that they take effect without further legislation by national parliaments. They are also **directly effective**, so they create rights that are immediately enforceable by individuals as long as they are clear and unconditional. Those rights can be enforced vertically against the state (see *Van Gend en Loos v Nederlandse Tariefcommissie*) or horizontally between individuals (see *Defrenne v Sabena No. 2* Case 43/75, [1976] ECR 455).

> **The principle of direct effect** enables individuals and companies to enforce EU law rights in national courts thus ensuring the effective application of EU law in member states. The principle was articulated by the ECJ in *Van Gend en Loos*—not set out in an EU treaty—but the court set out conditions for direct effect to apply: the obligations must be clear and precise, unconditional and not requiring additional law, and must confer a specific right on which an individual can base a claim.

> **Indirect effect** requires national courts to interpret domestic law consistently with directives.
>
> **EU law has vertical direct effect** if an individual can enforce it directly against a member state. It has **horizontal direct effect** if an individual can enforce it directly against another individual.

Secondary legislation

- **Regulations:** are directly applicable and binding in their entirety so take effect in all member states without further legislation by national parliaments; they are directly effective vertically and horizontally where they are sufficiently precise.

- **Directives:** set out aims which are binding on member states, but states must pass their own laws to give effect to them within a specified time. Directives are not directly enforceable between individuals but individuals can sue their state for loss where the state has failed to implement a directive *(Francovich v Italy* (Joined Cases C-6/90 and C-9/90) [1991] ECR I-5357; see below).

- **Decisions:** by the Council or Commission are binding on states, individuals or companies to whom they are addressed.

- **Decisions of the Court of Justice of the EU:** are binding on national courts regarding interpretation of EU law.

EU law can be enforced and given effect in various ways:

- **The *Francovich* principle** gives individuals the right to claim damages (known as *Francovich* damages) against a member state for breaches of EU law as long as the rule of EU law was intended to confer rights on individuals, the breach was sufficiently serious, and there was a direct causal link between the breach of the obligation and the damage sustained by the injured party (see the discussion in *Nuclear Decommissioning Authority v EnergySolutions EU Ltd* [2017] UKSC 34). This is an important principle of state liability.

- **Validity challenges** can be brought before the CJEU by individuals or companies to challenge the legality of acts of EU institutions. The CJEU may declare an EU law invalid if, for example, the EU did not have legal power to act in that area, or it infringes the Treaties.

- **References to the CJEU** allow the court to give guidance on how EU law should be interpreted which ensures that EU law is applied uniformly in national courts throughout member states. Where an issue concerning the interpretation of EU law is raised in a national court, the court may submit the question(s) about its interpretation or validity and ask the CJEU for a preliminary ruling.

For information on EU law and law-making, see: europa.eu/european-union/law_en.

5.1.2 Britain's membership of the EU

Britain had wanted to join the EEC—often referred to as the Common Market—since 1961 but it was not until 1972 that it successfully negotiated membership and signed the Treaty of Brussels. This was a treaty of accession, allowing Britain to accede (or become a party) to the 1957 Treaty of Rome. On 1 January 1973, the UK formally became a member of the EEC, joining a supranational organisation with a superior legal order whose law had primacy over the national law of its member states.

An Act of Parliament was needed to give domestic effect to the provisions of the Treaty of Brussels, and the UK Parliament passed the European Communities Act 1972 (the ECA).

In doing so, Parliament opened the door to an unprecedented constitutional arrangement. The ECA provided that all rights and obligations created from time to time under the treaties were, without further legal enactment, to be given legal effect in the UK (section 2(1)). This meant that directly applicable European laws (Treaties and Regulations) were to take effect as part of UK national law without the need for Parliament to pass further statutes to enable this, and they would be given effect by the UK courts. So Parliament was allowing EU law to take effect as part of UK domestic law without further reference to Parliament. This enabled EU law to be a source of UK law, and because EU law was legally *superior* to UK law, it allowed EU law to prevail where the two conflicted.

》 CROSS REFERENCE

This had a significant effect on the sovereignty of Parliament. See Chapter 6

It took a long time for the full implications of the overriding effect of EU law to be felt in the UK courts, although Lord Denning warned in 1974:

> . . . when we come to matters with a European element, the Treaty is like an incoming tide . . . It cannot be held back, Parliament has decreed that the Treaty is . . . to be part of our law. It is equal in force to any statute. (*Bulmer Ltd. v Bollinger SA* [1974] Ch. 401, 418; see also *Blackburn v AG* [1971] 1 WLR 1037; and Anthony King, *The British Constitution*, Chapter 5)

As a result of the ECA, UK domestic law now had EU law content, and the ECA created 'a new constitutional process for making law in the United Kingdom' *(R (Miller) v Secretary of State for Exiting the European Union* [2017] UKSC 5, [2018] AC 61 [62] ('*Miller I*')). The Supreme Court in *Miller I* pointed out that:

> In one sense . . . it can be said that the 1972 Act is the source of EU law, in that, without that Act, EU law would have no domestic status. But in a more fundamental sense . . . where EU law applies in the United Kingdom, it is the EU institutions which are the relevant source of that law. ([61])

Section 2(4) ECA required the UK courts to interpret UK statutes to ensure that they were consistent with European law, establishing 'a rule of construction for later statutes, so that any such statute has to be read . . . as compatible with rights accorded by European law' (Sir John Laws, 'Law and Democracy' (1995) PL 72, 89). Courts in the UK therefore read section 2(4) into subsequent legislation where there was no express rejection of European law, which made the 1972 Act semi-entrenched. Lord Denning said in 1980:

> Community law is now part of our law, and whenever there is any inconsistency, Community law has priority. It is not supplanting English law. It is part of our law which overrides any other part which is inconsistent with it. (*Macarthys Ltd v Smith (No 2)* [1981] 1 QB 180, 200)

However, Lord Denning stated that if Parliament deliberately and expressly legislated contrary to EU law, it would be the duty of the courts to follow the statute (*Macarthys Ltd v Smith* [1979] ICR 785, 789) although the decision in *R v Secretary of State for Transport, ex parte Factortame (No 2)* [1991] 1 AC 603 later made it clear that where a UK statute conflicted with directly applicable EU law, the UK courts had to disapply the statute (see Chapter 6).

The third significant innovation introduced by the ECA was the requirement that the UK courts must follow legal principles laid down by the ECJ in cases involving the meaning or effect of the treaties or the validity, meaning or effect of any EU instrument (section 3(1)).

For 40 years, the status, effect, and repealability of the ECA 1972 was the subject of academic debate (see Chapter 6) but the Supreme Court in *Miller I* pointed out that the status of EU law was only brought about by the ECA 1972 and would only last until it was repealed.

> In our view, then, although the 1972 Act gives effect to EU law, it is not itself the originating source of that law. It is . . . the 'conduit pipe' by which EU law is introduced into UK domestic

law. So long as the 1972 Act remains in force, its effect is to constitute EU law an independent and overriding source of domestic law. (*Miller I* [65])

Because those changes were contained in an Act of Parliament, they were repealable. Brexit has proved this to be the case.

 THE BIGGER PICTURE

For more on the 'conduit pipe' debate, see:

- Professor John Finnis, 'Brexit and the Balance of our Constitution', Sir Thomas More lecture, Lincoln's Inn, 1 December 2016, https://judicialpowerproject.org.uk/john-finnis-brexit-and-the-balance-of-our-constitution/
- P. O'Brien, 'All for Want of a Metaphor: Miller and the Nature of EU Law', UK Const L Blog (30 January 2017), at https://ukconstitutionallaw.org/

5.2 The Brexit process

Table 5.3 summarises the key events in the Brexit process. Three defining features were the fluctuations in control over the process between government and Parliament, the eleventh hour nature of steps taken, and the speed and ease with which some Brexit-related legislation was passed, in marked contrast to the May government's struggles to steer the initial withdrawal agreement through Parliament. The European Union (Withdrawal) (No 2) Act 2019 passed through all its Commons stages in one day. The European Union (Withdrawal Agreement) Act 2020 (100 pages long) was subject to 11 days' scrutiny and passed unamended (Lisa James and Meg Russell, 'Has parliament just got boring? Five conclusions from the passage of the EU Withdrawal Agreement Act', 30 January 2020, The Constitution Unit). (There is, perhaps, a fourth feature which is the similarity between the titles of the statutes and care needs to be taken in distinguishing them.)

Table 5.3 Key events in the Brexit process

March 2017	**European Union (Notification of Withdrawal) Act 2017** passed
26 June 2018	**European Union (Withdrawal) Act 2018** receives royal assent
November 2018	Prime Minister (Theresa May) negotiates withdrawal agreement and non-legally binding political declaration with the EU
2019	
15 January	Withdrawal agreement rejected by MPs by 230 votes with 202 in favour of the deal and 432 against
12–14 March	MPs reject withdrawal agreement for a second time by 149 votes, vote against leaving the EU without a deal, and vote (by 413 to 202) for an extension to Article 50 to 30 June

Continued

Table 5.3 Key events in the Brexit process *(Cont.)*

22 March	European Council offers a delay until 22 May if withdrawal deal approved or 12 April if rejected
29 March	MPs reject withdrawal agreement for a third time by 286 votes to 344
8 April	**European Union (Withdrawal) Act 2019** passed requiring the Prime Minister to request an extension to Article 50 to avoid a no-deal exit. The Act was later repealed by section 36 European Union (Withdrawal Agreement) Act 2020
11 April	European Council agrees extension to 31 October 2019
24 May	Theresa May announces her resignation as Prime Minister, stepping down on 7 June
24 July	Boris Johnson becomes Prime Minister after being elected leader of the Conservative party
9 September	**European Union (Withdrawal) (No 2) Act 2019** (the Benn Act) passed to avoid a no-deal Brexit by requiring Prime Minister to request a three month extension of exit date until 31 January 2020. The Act was later repealed by section 36 European Union (Withdrawal Agreement) Act 2020
24 September	Supreme Court determines that the prorogation of Parliament was unlawful (*Miller/Cherry*)
17 October	Withdrawal agreement agreed between UK and EU
12 December	Conservative party wins general election with a majority of 80 seats
2020	
23 January	**European Union (Withdrawal Agreement) Act 2020** passed to implement withdrawal agreement negotiated by the UK government
24 January	Prime Minister signs the revised withdrawal agreement
29 January	Withdrawal agreement approved by EU Parliament
31 January	UK leaves the EU at 11pm and the transition period begins
24 December	An agreement on the future trade relationship is reached (the EU–UK Trade and Cooperation Agreement)
30 December	EU–UK Trade and Cooperation Agreement signed. **European Union (Future Relationship) Act 2020** passed to implement the Trade and Cooperation Agreement and supplementary EU–UK agreements
31 December	Transition period ends at 11pm

See the Brexit timeline at https://commonslibrary.parliament.uk/research-briefings/cbp-7960/

In January 2013, David Cameron, then Prime Minister, promised an 'in-out' referendum on EU membership by the end of 2017 if the Conservative party won the next election. Accordingly, the European Union Referendum Act 2015 was passed, allowing a referendum to be held the following year and on 23 June 2016, the UK electorate voted by 51.9 per cent to 48.1 per cent to leave the EU. The result of the referendum was not legally binding but the government undertook to implement the result.

CLOSE-UP FOCUS: THE BREXIT REFERENDUM—A DAY IN THE LIFE OF THE UK CONSTITUTION

By 6am on the morning of 24 June, the day after the referendum took place, it became clear that the majority had voted in favour of leaving the UK and so began a day which has been described as the most dramatic in the modern history of British politics.

The referendum produced an unexpected result which caused shock in the UK, and throughout the EU and the wider world. At 8.15am on 24 June, David Cameron, the Prime Minister, announced his resignation, saying that he would hand over to a new Prime Minister by October, starting the process of a Conservative party leadership election. (In the event, there was a swifter transition and Theresa May became the new Conservative party leader and Prime Minister on 11 July 2016.) Mr Cameron stated that the will of the British people, as manifested by the referendum, must be respected and was an instruction that must be delivered.

Regional variations in the vote were clear from the outset. The majority in England and Wales voted to leave the EU (53.4 per cent in England and 52.5 per cent in Wales) while the majority in Scotland and Northern Ireland favoured remaining in the EU (62 per cent in Scotland and 55.8 per cent in Northern Ireland). Shortly after David Cameron's announcement, Nicola Sturgeon, the Scottish First Minister, declared that the outcome of the EU referendum did not reflect Scotland's wishes, Scotland wished to remain in the EU, and a second referendum on Scottish independence was likely. This raised immediate concerns about the future break-up of the UK.

The events of 24 June raised questions of constitutional relevance:

- What are the constitutional rules on referendums? Could Parliament overrule the result? Could a second EU referendum be held?
- What are the rules for leaving the EU? Who triggers the leaving mechanism under Article 50 of the Treaty on European Union: the government or Parliament? Could the UK revoke its withdrawal notice?

It soon became apparent that the UK found itself in uncharted waters. No member state has ever left the EU (although Greenland voted to leave in 1982, it was a self-governing but dependent territory of Denmark and therefore not itself a member state) and legal questions arose about the process of triggering the leaving mechanisms. Article 50 of the Treaty on European Union provides that:

1. Any member state may decide to withdraw from the EU 'in accordance with its own constitutional requirements'.

2. The state must notify the European Council of its intention and the EU will negotiate and conclude a withdrawal agreement with that state.

3. The Treaties will cease to apply to the state from the date when the withdrawal agreement enters into force or, failing that, two years after the withdrawal notification unless the European Council unanimously decides to extend this period.

On 2 October 2016, Theresa May, the Prime Minister, stated that it was for the *government*, not Parliament, to start the withdrawal process and she would give notice under Article 50 before the end of March 2017 (the government has a prerogative power to make and withdraw from treaties). However, Gina Miller challenged this in the English courts on the basis that triggering withdrawal would lead to changing the ECA 1972 and only Parliament can change the law. In the *Miller I* case, the Supreme Court agreed, holding that withdrawing from the EU would change domestic law by removing rights that had been incorporated into UK law and Parliament should start the process. Consequently, in March 2017, Parliament passed the European Union (Notification of Withdrawal) Act 2017, authorising the Prime Minister to notify the UK's intention to withdraw from the EU under Article 50(2) of the Treaty on European Union. On 29 March 2017, the government began the UK's formal withdrawal process and on 30 March, a White Paper set out the legislative proposals for withdrawal (*Legislating for the United Kingdom's withdrawal from the European Union*, Department for Exiting the European Union, Cm 9446, March 2017).

In June 2018, Parliament passed the constitutionally significant European Union (Withdrawal) Act 2018. This Act had been introduced to Parliament on 13 July 2017 as the European Union (Withdrawal) Bill (also known as the Great Repeal Bill), which as originally drafted had been criticised as undermining legal certainty and failing to give sufficient clarity and guidance to the courts on interpreting retained EU law, and being constitutionally unacceptable (see House of Lords Constitution Committee *European Union (Withdrawal) Bill*, 9th Report of Session 2017–19, HL Paper 69, p 5).

 STATUTE

The EU (Withdrawal) Act (later amended by the European Union (Withdrawal Agreement) Act 2020):

- expressly repealed the European Communities Act 1972 on exit day (section 1). Exit day was originally specified in the Act as 29 March 2019 at 11pm (section 20(1)) but was subsequently extended several times;

- created a new category of law known as 'retained EU law' by converting EU law into UK domestic law (sections 2–4);

- gave ministers powers to make secondary legislation to allow corrections to be made to laws once the UK had left the EU.

Significantly, section 13 of the Act required Parliament's approval of any withdrawal agreement reached by the government with the EU. The agreement had to be approved by the House of Commons (in what was known as the meaningful vote), taken note of by the House of Lords, and an Act of Parliament had to be passed providing for its implementation.

After months of negotiation by UK and EU officials, a draft withdrawal agreement and a non-legally binding political declaration on the future relationship between the UK and the EU were eventually published on 14 November 2018. The withdrawal agreement set out the terms of the UK's exit from the EU, with a transition period from exit day on 29 March 2019 until the end of 2020 to allow discussions on a permanent UK/EU arrangement. On exit day, the UK would cease to be a member state of the EU but during the transition period, it would remain in the EU customs union and single market, contribute to the EU budget, and be bound by EU law. The agreement contained a controversial provision known as the Irish backstop; it provided for an open border between Northern Ireland and the island of Ireland if the UK and EU were unable to agree on their future relationship. (Although the Cabinet signed off the agreement, several ministers, including Dominic Raab, then Brexit Secretary, resigned the following day in protest at what it proposed.) The withdrawal agreement then needed to be approved by Parliament but on 15 January 2019, it was overwhelmingly defeated in the House of Commons by 230 votes, the largest ever government defeat. This prompted Jeremy Corbyn, then Labour party leader, to table a vote of no confidence in the government but the government won by 19 votes on 16 January.

There was little consensus in Parliament about the way forward. Possible options included leaving the EU with no deal, extending Article 50 and attempting a renegotiated deal (though the EU repeatedly made it clear that the withdrawal agreement was not open for renegotiation), a second vote in the Commons on the withdrawal agreement, or cancel Brexit altogether. In 2018, Members of the Scottish Parliament and others opposed to Brexit had asked the Scottish courts to declare whether the UK could unilaterally withdraw notice of its intention to leave the EU. The Inner House of the Court of Session referred the question to the CJEU (*Wightman v Secretary of State for Exiting the European Union* [2018] CSIH 62). In December 2018, the CJEU ruled that a member state could unilaterally revoke notification of withdrawal under Article 50 (*Wightman v Secretary of State for Exiting the European Union* (Case C–621/18) [2018] 3 WLR 1965). This meant that the UK could cancel Brexit without the permission of the other EU members but the government made it clear that this would not happen. Nevertheless, an e-petition calling for notification of withdrawal to be revoked gathered over six million signatures and was debated in the Commons on 1 April 2019.

During March 2019, the withdrawal agreement was overwhelmingly rejected twice more by MPs in the House of Commons and they also voted against leaving the EU without a deal. As a result, Mrs May had to request an extension to the original exit date of 29 March 2019 to avoid leaving the EU without a deal approved by Parliament. Parliament then asserted control over the Brexit process when Oliver Letwin MP successfully proposed taking control of Commons business for one day through business motions (the Letwin amendment) to enable votes to be held to find agreement on alternatives to the government's withdrawal deal (though none of the eight options found a majority in the Commons vote on 27 March). The Letwin amendment was used again to allow Yvette Cooper MP to introduce a private members' Bill which would enable the Commons to require the Prime Minister to request an extension to Article 50 and prevent a no-deal exit on 12 April when the first extension expired. It was fast-tracked through the Commons in one day on 4 April, passing by a majority of one vote, and coming into force as the European Union (Withdrawal) Act 2019 on 8 April. Mrs May requested a further extension and on 10 April, the European Council agreed an extension to 31 October though the UK could leave earlier if a withdrawal agreement was agreed by Parliament. As it was still a member of the EU, the UK had to take part in European elections on 23 May. Mrs May announced her resignation as Prime Minister the following day and was replaced by Boris Johnson in July 2019. Mr Johnson's policy was for the UK to leave the EU on 31 October with or without a deal.

On 28 August 2019, seven weeks before the UK was due to leave the EU and on the Prime Minister's advice to the Queen, an Order in Council was made proroguing Parliament for five weeks until 14 October. The government maintained that this was to enable delivery of its new legislative programme but it raised concerns that, by suspending its operation, prorogation would prevent Parliament from legislating and scrutinising government action at a crucial juncture of the Brexit process. As a result, challenges were brought in the Scottish and English courts to the lawfulness of the Prime Minister's advice to the Queen to prorogue Parliament on the

> **CROSS REFERENCE**
> Proroguing is a prerogative power exercised by the government and ends the current session of Parliament

basis that its real reason was 'to stymie Parliamentary scrutiny of Government action' (*Cherry and others v Advocate General for Scotland* [2019] CSIH 49 [51]).

> **CASE CLOSE-UP: *R (MILLER) v THE PRIME MINISTER; CHERRY AND OTHERS v ADVOCATE GENERAL FOR SCOTLAND* [2019] UKSC 41**
>
> In *Cherry v Advocate General for Scotland* [2019] CSIH 49, the Scottish Inner House of the Court of Session held that the Prime Minister's decision to prorogue Parliament was unlawful because its purpose was to 'reduce the time available for parliamentary scrutiny of Brexit at a time when such scrutiny would appear to be a matter of considerable importance', and it would allow the government to pursue a no-deal Brexit without parliamentary interference before exit day (*Cherry* [53]).
>
> On appeal, the Supreme Court ruled that that the prorogation was unlawful because it conflicted with the principles of parliamentary sovereignty and parliamentary accountability; against the backdrop of the fundamental change to the UK constitution posed by Brexit, the Prime Minister had to be ready to face the House of Commons (*R (Miller) v The Prime Minister; Cherry and others v Advocate General for Scotland* [2019] UKSC 41 [57]).

» CROSS REFERENCE

For more details on *Miller/ Cherry* see Chapter 12

In early September 2019, Hilary Benn MP proposed a Bill to delay Brexit. The Bill passed through its Commons stages on 4 September and through the House of Lords on 5 and 6 September, receiving royal assent on 9 September. The resulting European Union (Withdrawal) (No 2) Act 2019 (known as the Benn Act) required the Prime Minister to request from the European Council an extension of three months to 31 January 2020 using the letter set out in the Act, unless the House of Commons approved either a withdrawal agreement or a no-deal exit by 19 October. However, this meant that Brexit could be delayed until after the 31 October deadline which the Prime Minister was very reluctant to do: 'I'd rather be dead in a ditch' was how he memorably described his view on this (*Cherry* [2019] CSIH 49 [89] (Lord Brodie)). Nevertheless, the extension was duly agreed.

By 17 October 2019, the government had found a way through the impasse by negotiating a revised withdrawal agreement with the EU (see https://commonslibrary.parliament.uk/research-briefings/cbp-8713/). Pledging to 'get Brexit done', the Prime Minister went on to win a general election on 12 December 2019 with a much increased majority which made it easier to get government legislation through the Commons. On 23 January 2020, the European Union (Withdrawal Agreement) Act 2020 received royal assent and gave effect to the revised withdrawal agreement in UK law. At 11pm on 31 January 2020, the UK left the European Union and the transition period began.

And yet the story did not end there. In September 2020, the UK government introduced a UK Internal Market Bill designed to preserve free trade across the UK after the end of the transition period, ensuring the free movement of goods, services and recognition of professional qualifications within the UK and avoiding the UK home nations making divergent regulations which could act as barriers to trade. However, the Bill as originally drafted contained clauses that were inconsistent with the withdrawal agreement agreed with the EU: it gave ministers the power in specified circumstances to disapply provisions on customs declarations and EU state aid rules agreed in the Northern Ireland Protocol (an important part of the withdrawal agreement providing that Northern Ireland would continue to follow some EU rules post-transition to keep an open border between Ireland and Northern Ireland) and to disapply the principle of direct effect enshrined in Article 4 of the withdrawal agreement (see section 5.3.1 below). This led to concerns that the UK government could unilaterally change the withdrawal agreement (an international treaty) and thereby breach international law. This was compounded when the UK Northern Ireland Secretary acknowledged that the Bill did break international law 'in a very specific and limited way' (HC Hansard 8 September 2020, Vol 679 col 509). The European Commission President warned of legal proceedings if the UK used domestic law to override parts of the withdrawal agreement but the provisions conflicting with the agreement were removed from the Bill which became law on 17 December 2020 as the United Kingdom Internal Market Act 2020.

> The Internal Market Act also raised issues on devolution and the rule of law. The Act could allow the UK Parliament to restrict the legislative powers of the devolved bodies (see section 5.3.3 below) and the issue of passing legislation that could breach international law was the subject of a debate on the rule of law in the House of Lords (House of Lords Hansard, 10 September 2020, Vol 805 cols 918–922).

Negotiating a future relationship between the UK and the EU proved fraught and it was only on Christmas Eve 2020—just a week before the end of the transition period—that an agreement was reached. The Trade and Cooperation Agreement was approved by the UK Parliament and the European Union (Future Relationship) Act 2020 was passed—in one day—to give it effect.

5.3 The post-Brexit landscape

5.3.1 Understanding the Brexit legislation

There were three milestones in the Brexit process which triggered the need for legislation: exit day; the conclusion of the 2019 withdrawal agreement and arrangements for the transition period; and the end of the transition period and the 2020 agreement on the UK–EU relationship.

Exit day (31 January 2020) Legislation was required to prepare for and give effect to exit day when the UK left the EU as a member state. The EU (Withdrawal) Act 2018 is the fundamental Brexit Act that made provision for the UK's withdrawal from the EU on exit day, but it was passed before a withdrawal agreement had been made so it was subsequently amended by the European Union (Withdrawal Agreement) Act 2020 once a withdrawal agreement was in place.

The conclusion of the 2019 withdrawal agreement and arrangements for the transition period The withdrawal agreement reached in October 2019 set out the arrangements for the UK's withdrawal from the EU. Under the terms of the agreement, the UK entered a transition, or implementation, period when it left the EU until 31 December 2020. During this time, the UK followed EU law and remained in the single market and customs union while negotiations took place on the future UK–EU relationship, particularly on trade. As the withdrawal agreement is an international treaty, Parliament needed to pass an Act to give it legal effect domestically in the UK so the EU (Withdrawal Agreement) Act 2020 implemented the agreement and amended the EU (Withdrawal) Act 2018 to reflect its terms. This included extending some provisions until the end of the transition period on 31 December 2020, instead of exit day (the transition period is called the implementation period in the Act; 'IP completion day' means 31 December 2020 (section 39)).

STATUTE

The effect of the EU (Withdrawal) Act 2018 (EUWA) as amended by the EU (Withdrawal Agreement) Act 2020 (WAA) was that:

- The European Communities Act 1972 was repealed on exit day, but continued to have effect until the end of the transition period on 31 December 2020; see section 1A EUWA 2018 which 'saved' the ECA for the transition period. This enabled most EU law to continue to apply in the UK during the transition period as agreed in the withdrawal agreement. Existing EU-derived UK legislation continued to operate during the transition period (section 1B EUWA 2018).

- EU law no longer has supremacy over UK law passed after the end of the transition period on 31 December 2020 (section 5(1) as amended), but it does continue to apply after that date to the interpretation, disapplication, or quashing of any law passed *before* it (section 5(2)).

- For a smooth transition and to avoid gaps in the law, existing EU law was converted into UK domestic law at the end of the transition period, creating a new body of retained EU law (see section 5.3.2 of this chapter).

- Ministers were given powers to make secondary legislation to correct deficiencies in retained EU law once the UK had left the EU, for example, redundant references to the EU (section 8). Additional powers were given to correct the statute book during the transition period.

The EU (Withdrawal Agreement) Act 2020 implemented withdrawal agreement provisions that would apply from the end of the transition period, such as citizens' rights, the UK–EU financial settlement, and the specific arrangements on customs and movement of goods enshrined in the Northern Ireland Protocol; created powers to make secondary legislation to enable the withdrawal agreement to be implemented into UK law; repealed section 13 EUWA 2018, removing the requirement for the government to report back to Parliament on negotiations with the UK–EU future relationship (section 31); recognised the sovereignty of the UK Parliament (section 38); and put into effect the important provisions in Article 4 of the withdrawal agreement.

Article 4 of the withdrawal agreement required the provisions of the withdrawal agreement and the EU law that applied under it to have the same legal effects of direct effect and direct applicability as they had in the EU member states. This meant that:

- rights and obligations in the withdrawal agreement and EU law applying under it would automatically become part UK domestic law without requiring further legislation;

- rights and obligations in the withdrawal agreement would be legally enforceable directly in the UK courts subject to certain conditions;
- provisions of EU law applied in the withdrawal agreement would have supremacy over UK domestic law and UK legislation that is inconsistent with the withdrawal agreement would be disapplied;
- provisions of the agreement referring to EU law should be interpreted and applied in the UK using the principles of EU law, in conformity with (ie following) pre-31 December 2020 CJEU case law, and having regard to relevant CJEU case law handed down after this date.

The 2020 Act therefore inserted new section 7A in EUWA to give effect to the direct effect and supremacy provisions in Article 4, and making the rights and obligations referred to in Article 4 available in domestic law without requiring further legislation.

Under Article 131 of the withdrawal agreement, the CJEU retained its jurisdiction in the UK until the end of the transition period. After that date, the CJEU only has jurisdiction in circumstances specified by the withdrawal agreement.

The end of the transition period (31 December 2020) and the 2020 agreement on the UK–EU relationship At 11pm on 31 December 2020, the UK left the EU single market and customs union and EU law no longer applied to the UK. The European Union (Future Relationship) Act 2020 was fast-tracked, passing all its stages on 30 December 2020, and gave effect to the future relationship agreements which had just been concluded (the Trade and Cooperation Agreement, covering matters such as trade in goods and services, fisheries, and aviation and road transport, and agreements on UK–EU security of classified information and UK–Euratom nuclear co-operation). The rules in the Trade and Cooperation Agreement took effect provisionally from 1 January 2021 as they still required the European Parliament's consent.

Inevitably, numerous issues arise from Brexit, specifically its impact on the constitution. It raises the ultimate question of whether Brexit has been a sufficiently compelling constitutional moment as to trigger the move to a codified constitution for the UK. Vernon Bogdanor argues that it has ('Brexit Means Britain Needs a Constitution', 8 October 2019 at https://foreignpolicy.com/2019/10/08/brexit-means-britain-needs-a-constitution/).

 THINKING POINT

Do you think that Brexit has strengthened the argument for a codified constitution for the UK?

John Bercow, the former Speaker of the House of Commons, raised the possibility of at least codifying and entrenching the House of Commons' role in relation to the executive (The Sixth Annual Bingham Centre Lecture, 'Process of Discovery: What Brexit has taught us (so far) about Parliament, Politics and the UK Constitution', 12 September 2019, Middle Temple, London (available at https://binghamcentre.biicl.org/newsitems/25/weekly-update)). See also Mark Elliott, 'The United Kingdom's Constitution and Brexit: A "Constitutional Moment"?' (2020) Horitsu Jiho 15–22 (available at https://ssrn.com/abstract=3609965). However, we examine below two other issues: the new category of retained EU law and the impact of Brexit on devolution.

5.3.2 Retained EU law

If all EU-related UK law had simply disappeared overnight after Brexit and the transition arrangements, the result would have been chaotic so in order to maintain continuity and a 'functioning statute book', the EUWA 2018 (as amended by the WAA 2020) converted into UK domestic law all existing direct EU law and EU-related domestic law in force at the end of the transition period. This created a new body of retained EU law. Initially, the EUWA converted EU law as it stood immediately before exit day on 31 January 2020, but section 25 of the WAA extended the point of conversion to the end of the transition period.

Retained EU law provisions

Retained EU law is mainly anything which, on or after 31 December 2020, 'continues to be, or forms part of, domestic law by virtue of section 2, 3 or 4' EUWA 2018 (section 6(7) EUWA as amended).

- Section 2: all 'EU-derived domestic legislation' continues in force after the end of the transition period, as it had effect in domestic law immediately before 31 December 2020; this refers to secondary legislation made under section 2(2) ECA 1972 eg to implement EU directives into UK law (section 1B(7) EUWA). Without this preserving section, repealing the ECA 1972 would have revoked the secondary legislation made under it.

- Section 3 converted 'direct EU legislation' into domestic law after the end of the transition period, as it operated immediately before the end of the transition period; this refers to EU regulations, EU decisions and EU tertiary legislation (tertiary legislation means measures that supplement the rules in regulations, directives or decisions).

- Section 4 allowed 'rights, powers, liabilities, obligations, restrictions, remedies and procedures' to continue in operation that were recognised and available in UK law at the end of the transition period because of section 2(1) ECA 1972. This includes some directly effective rights under the EU treaties, and carries those rights over into domestic law even though the underpinning treaties no longer apply.

Section 7 sets out the categories of retained EU law: retained direct principal EU legislation (mainly EU regulations), retained direct minor EU legislation (mainly EU decisions and EU tertiary legislation), and retained EU law by virtue of section 4, and how each one should be modified.

Exceptions to sections 2 to 4 are set out in section 5 and Schedule 1 EUWA. The principle of supremacy of EU law does not apply to legislation enacted after the transition period where it is inconsistent with retained EU law (section 5(1)). The EU Charter of Fundamental Rights is not part of domestic law after the end of the transition period (section 5(4)). There is no right in domestic law to *Francovich* damages after the transition period (Schedule 1).

Once preserved or converted, retained EU law will not automatically change to reflect future changes in EU law so it will be a 'frozen' version of the relevant EU law as it operated immediately before the end of the transition period. As a result, there will be increasing differences between retained EU law in the UK and EU law within the EU. And, of course,

Table 5.4 Interpreting retained EU law

Key: Changes made by the WAA 2020 appear in blue

'IP completion day' means the end of the transition period on 31 December 2020

Section 6 EUWA 2018 sets out the rules for interpreting retained EU law.

Section 6(1): when interpreting retained EU law, the UK courts are not bound by any decisions made on or after IP completion day by the CJEU and they can no longer refer any matter to the CJEU.

They may 'have regard to anything done on or after IP completion day by the European Court or the EU' (section 6(2)).

Questions about the validity, meaning or effect of retained EU law (if it is unmodified after IP completion day) are to be decided in accordance with retained case law and retained general principles of EU law (section 6(3)).

'Retained case law' means retained domestic case law and retained EU case law (section 6(7)).

Section 6(4) allowed the Supreme Court and the Scottish High Court of Justiciary to depart from EU case law, but originally required lower UK courts to follow retained EU case law when interpreting EU retained law. However, section 26(1) WAA amended this to allow government ministers to use secondary legislation before the end of the transition period to enable other UK courts and tribunals to depart from EU case law. Before making those regulations, the minister had to consult senior members of the judiciary (section 6(4)(ba); 6(5A)–(5D)).

The rules in section 6 are subject to relevant separation agreement law* (section 6(6A)).

*Separation agreement law refers to the withdrawal agreement, the EEA EFTA Separation Agreement with Norway, Iceland, and Liechtenstein, and the Swiss Citizens' Rights Agreement.

it can be amended either by the UK Parliament or by ministers through secondary legislation, as appropriate.

Table 5.4 sets out how retained EU law is to be interpreted.

5.3.2.1 Changing and correcting retained EU law

Because of the tight timescale for withdrawal, the EUWA 2018 made provision for future changes to retained EU law and for correcting deficiencies in retained law arising from the UK leaving the EU. Section 7 sets out three categories of retained EU law and how each one is to be changed; for example by Act of Parliament or by using Henry VIII powers which allow primary legislation to be amended or repealed by secondary legislation made by government ministers. The Constitution Committee took the view that choosing which EU laws to keep should be done by primary legislation after debate in Parliament (see House of Lords Select Committee on the Constitution, *The 'Great Repeal Bill' and delegated powers*, 9th Report of Session 2016–17, HL Paper 123). Under section 8 (as amended), government ministers were given powers to make secondary legislation as appropriate to prevent or remedy a deficiency in retained EU law, for example, redundant references to the UK's membership of the EU or to relationships with EU bodies. The correcting power in section 8 lasts for two years from the end of the transition period to allow time for deficiencies to come to light.

Giving evidence to the Constitution Committee in 2019, Lord Reed (then Deputy President of the Supreme Court) saw the complexity of post-Brexit law as a major challenge, with three different types of EU-related law and different rules applying to each one:

- retained EU law, created by the EUWA 2018 (as amended by the WAA 2020);
- 'withdrawal agreement law' consisting of the withdrawal agreement and areas of EU law to which it gave continued force; and
- ordinary EU law which may still apply as foreign law eg a contract governed by an EU contract directive.

Lord Reed concluded—rightly—that 'We will have a colossal body of law for lawyers to get their teeth into' (Select Committee on the Constitution, Uncorrected oral evidence: President and Deputy President of the Supreme Court, 20 March 2019, Q15).

5.3.3 The impact of Brexit on devolved administrations

As the UK has left one Union, there are concerns over another. A majority of the voters in Scotland and Northern Ireland supported remaining in the EU, driving the Scottish government's desire to hold a further independence referendum. Devolution came about during the UK's membership of the EU, and Brexit has removed that foundational element. The European Union Committee has referred to the EU as 'part of the glue holding the United Kingdom together since 1997' (House of Lords European Union Committee *Brexit: devolution*, 4th Report of Session 2017–19, HL Paper 9 [36]) and raised concerns that Brexit could risk making 'the complex overlapping competences within the UK' increasingly unstable ([37]). According to the Committee, 'the impact of UK withdrawal from the EU on the UK's devolution settlements is one of the most technically complex and politically contentious elements of the Brexit debate' (page 3 [1]), and the Committee saw Brexit as presenting fundamental constitutional challenges to the UK.

Northern Ireland posed a unique difficulty for the UK government in negotiations with the EU because of its land border with Ireland and the need to honour the Good Friday Agreement. Special arrangements therefore had to be agreed in the Protocol on Ireland/Northern Ireland (which was part of the 2019 withdrawal agreement) to avoid a hard border with visible checks and controls on the border with Ireland. Northern Ireland therefore remains subject to certain EU rules relating to goods and customs, with checks and controls on goods entering Northern Ireland from the rest of the UK. Article 18 of the Protocol also set out a democratic consent mechanism to allow the Northern Ireland Assembly, by the end of October 2024, to give its consent to the continued operation of the Protocol. If consent is withheld, the Protocol ceases to have effect two years later.

Brexit affects devolved powers, and devolved policy areas such as agriculture and fisheries which had been governed by EU law pre-Brexit, have been repatriated (brought home). However, this has the potential to result in inconsistent policies or standards, or regulatory divergence, in those areas between the four nations across the UK so, since 2017, there have been discussions between the UK government and devolved administrations to develop UK-wide common frameworks. These are agreed common approaches on various policy areas and are designed to co-ordinate specific policies. In some areas, legislation has given effect to the common approach, for example, the Fisheries Act 2020 on fisheries management.

The Brexit process has shown the limits on the competences of the devolved administrations. The consent of the devolved legislatures was not a legal requirement before legislation was passed authorising the UK's withdrawal from the EU (see *Miller I* [150]). The Scottish Parliament could not legislate to require Scottish ministers' consent before secondary legislation made by UK government ministers on certain matters of retained EU law had legal effect in Scotland (*The UK Withdrawal from the European Union (Legal Continuity) (Scotland) Bill—A Reference by the Attorney General and the Advocate General for Scotland* [2018] UKSC 64). Brexit legislation also flagged up the limits of the Sewel convention: the UK Parliament passed the EU (Withdrawal) Act 2018 without the Scottish Parliament's consent, and none of the devolved legislatures consented to the EU (Withdrawal Agreement) Act 2020. The UK Internal Market Act 2020 was passed without the legislative consent of the Scottish and Welsh governments as they regarded it as encroaching on their legislative space and undermining the devolution settlement because the Act could allow the UK Parliament to override future legislation passed by the devolved legislatures (see section 5.2 above). The Welsh government, supported by the Scottish government, announced its intention to seek judicial review of the scope of the Act's provisions (Welsh Counsel General, Written Statement: Possible Legal challenge to the UK Internal Market Bill, 16 December 2020, https://gov.wales/written-statement-possible-legal-challenge-uk-internal-market-bill). Formal proceedings were commenced in January 2021.

Finally, under the devolution Acts, the devolved legislatures did not have competence to legislate contrary to EU law. At the end of the transition period, this requirement was removed from each of the devolution statutes by section 12 EUWA 2018 and replaced with provisions that the devolved legislatures cannot legislate contrary to restrictions specified by a minister in regulations (secondary legislation); a minister can specify areas in which the devolved legislatures may not change retained EU law. As the explanatory notes to the Act put it, this can act as a temporary 'freeze' on devolved competence in relation to retained EU law so that decisions can be taken on where common policy approaches are needed. These 'freezing powers' were intended as a time-limited arrangement to allow common frameworks to be put into place, and the power to make such regulations expires two years after exit day.

❭ CROSS REFERENCE
See Chapter 4

 SUMMARY

- It is clear that Brexit has not turned the clock back but has turned it forward to a new more complex landscape.
- There were undoubted, but voluntary, restrictions on the UK Parliament's legal sovereignty during the UK's membership of the EU until the repeal of the ECA 1972.
- The Brexit process proved long and arduous, giving rise to the two constitutionally significant *Miller* cases.
- New important constitutional statutes have been introduced to implement the withdrawal and transition process.

- On exit day (31 January 2020), the UK ceased to be an EU member state.
- During the transition period, the UK followed EU law because of the withdrawal agreement provisions, not because of its membership of the EU which had ended.
- A new category of UK domestic law known as retained EU law has been created.
- Brexit has had a marked impact on devolution and has highlighted potential cracks in its structure.

? Questions

Self-test questions

1. What did the 1957 Treaty of Rome establish?

2. What is the role of the Court of Justice of the EU?

3. What is the principle of direct effect?

4. How did the primacy of EU law affect parliamentary sovereignty in the UK?

5. What did the Benn Act provide?

6. Which statute did the EU (Withdrawal) Act 2018 repeal and what was the effect of this?

7. What was the purpose behind creating retained EU law?

8. How could the UK Internal Market Act 2020 affect devolved legislative powers?

Exam question

Select three key provisions of the European Union (Withdrawal) Act 2018 and critically evaluate their legal effect and impact.

Further reading

Books

Bogdanor, V. *Beyond Brexit: Towards a British Constitution* (London: I.B. Tauris 2019).
Discusses the constitutional implications of leaving the EU and whether Brexit is a constitutional moment

Elliott, M., Williams, J., and Young, A.L. (eds), *The UK Constitution After Miller: Brexit and Beyond* (Oxford: Hart Publishing 2018).

A collection of essays on different aspects of the *Miller I* case. See in particular chapters 1 and 5. Chapter 10 is also helpful for parliamentary sovereignty

Jowell, J. and O'Cinneide, C (eds), *The Changing Constitution* (9th edn, Oxford: Oxford University Press 2019).
See Paul Craig's discussion of Brexit and the UK constitution in chapter 4

Journal articles

Bradley, K. 'Agreeing to Disagree: The European Union and the United Kingdom after Brexit' (2020) 16(3) European Constitutional Law Review 379.
Reflections on the withdrawal agreement

Craig, P. 'Brexit: A Drama in Six Acts' (2016) 41(4) European Law Review 447.

Craig, P. 'Brexit, A Drama: The Interregnum' (2017) (36) Yearbook of European Law 3.

Craig, P. 'Brexit a drama: the endgame - Part I' (2020) 45(2) European Law Review 163.
This series of articles provides an in-depth narrative and analysis of the legal issues flowing from Brexit

Craig, P. 'Constitutional principle, the rule of law and political reality: the European Union (Withdrawal) Act 2018' (2019) 82(2) MLR 319.
An appraisal of the 2018 Act, including the status and interpretation of retained EU law, and executive powers to make regulations (though pre-EU (Withdrawal Agreement) Act 2020)

Elliott, M. and Tierney, S. 'Political pragmatism and constitutional principle: the European Union (Withdrawal) Act 2018' (2019) (Jan) Public Law 37.
Examines the constitutional implications of the 2018 Act

Feldman, D. 'Pulling a Trigger or Starting a Journey? Brexit in the Supreme Court' (2017) 76(2) CLJ 217.
Case comment on *Miller I* including the devolution issues in the case

Gordon, M. 'The UK's Sovereignty Situation: Brexit, Bewilderment and Beyond' (2016) 27(3) King's Law Journal 333.
Discusses notions of sovereignty in the light of Brexit

Young, A. 'R. (Miller) v Secretary of State for Exiting the European Union: thriller or vanilla?' (2017) 42(2) European Law Review 280.
Case comment on *Miller I*

Other sources

House of Commons Library Briefing paper, *Constitutional implications of the Withdrawal Agreement legislation*, Number 08805, Graeme Cowie, Sylvia de Mars, Richard Kelly, and David Torrance (20 February 2020) at https://commonslibrary. parliament.uk/research-briefings/cbp-8805/.
An admirably clear and detailed guide to the withdrawal agreement and European Union (Withdrawal Agreement) Act 2020

Online resources

www.oup.com/he/dennett2e

This chapter is accompanied by a selection of online resources to help you with this topic, including:

- Multiple-choice questions
- Answers to the self-test questions
- Guidance on answering the exam question

PART 2

IMPORTANT CONSTITUTIONAL PRINCIPLES AND VALUES

The three principles of parliamentary sovereignty, separation of powers, and the rule of law form the defining foundations of the UK constitution and have significant impact in public law decisions in the courts. Parliamentary sovereignty concerns Parliament's legislative authority. The separation of powers ensures that power is not concentrated in one body, while the rule of law affirms the supremacy of law. Both the separation of powers and the rule of law aim to prevent the arbitrary or oppressive exercise of power and are elements of constitutionalism, the idea that there should be legal and political limits on the powers of government. Chapter 9 discusses the courts' protection of constitutional principles, and tensions between parliamentary sovereignty and the rule of law.

6 Parliamentary sovereignty

LEARNING OBJECTIVES

By the end of this chapter, you should be able to:

- Appreciate the constitutional significance of parliamentary sovereignty
- Discuss the classic view of parliamentary sovereignty
- Identify and explain areas where the classic view operates
- Evaluate the practical operation of limits on parliamentary sovereignty
- Appraise different theoretical viewpoints on parliamentary sovereignty

Introduction

Could the UK Parliament pass an Act abolishing itself? What would happen if an Act of Parliament crossed a constitutional red line, for example, denying access to the courts or allowing terrorist suspects to be tortured? Could judges refuse to recognise it as supreme law? These are some of the issues raised by parliamentary sovereignty. If you have read earlier chapters, you will have noticed the significance of parliamentary sovereignty in the UK constitution, and we now examine this central concept in more depth. The key to understanding this topic is to be aware of the two sides of the coin of parliamentary sovereignty: first, the traditional view; second, the realistic view of how it operates in practice. This chapter explains the classic theory and importance of parliamentary sovereignty, with particular reference to Dicey, then goes on to examine modern inroads on the doctrine. It is important to note that we are looking here at *legal* sovereignty, that is, the authority to create and change law, which rests with Parliament.

6.1 The meaning and significance of parliamentary sovereignty

'[T]he principle of Parliamentary sovereignty: that laws enacted by the Crown in Parliament are the supreme form of law in our legal system, with which everyone, including the Government, must comply' (*R (Miller) v The Prime Minister; Cherry and others v Advocate General for Scotland* [2019] UKSC 41 [41]).

Lord Bingham described parliamentary sovereignty as 'the bedrock of the British constitution' (*Jackson v Attorney General* [2005] UKHL 56, [2006] 1 AC 262 [9]), and it defines the UK constitution. However, as Professor Bradley has pointed out, the term 'Parliamentary sovereignty' has a number of meanings which can get confused (see House of Commons European Scrutiny Committee, *The EU Bill and Parliamentary Sovereignty*, 10th Report of Session 2010–11, HC 633-II, Written evidence from Professor Anthony Bradley [6]); it is normally defined as the 'legislative supremacy of Parliament', and this is the sense in which the term is used in this chapter. Since the constitutional settlement brought about by the Bill of Rights 1689 (see Chapter 2), the UK Parliament has had unchallenged authority to create primary law (Acts of Parliament), and this is reflected in a definition by Dominic Grieve, a former Attorney General 'What we are really referring to when we speak of Parliamentary supremacy is no more and no less than the present Parliament's right to make or repeal any law, and the inability to prevent a future Parliament from doing the same' (Dominic Grieve QC MP, 'Parliament and the Judiciary', speech to BPP Law School, 25 October 2012). Parliament's legislative supremacy means, therefore, that there is no competing body with equal or greater law-making power and there are no legal limits on Parliament's legislative competence (though in practice, Parliament's powers are not unlimited).

Parliament makes law by simple majority and Acts of Parliament express the will of Parliament, particularly the House of Commons as a democratically elected chamber representing the electorate. Acts of Parliament are a superior form of law which can change:

- older Acts of Parliament;
- the common law (though note the discussion in section 6.4.2 on judicial debate about the limits of Parliament's power on this);
- the royal prerogative;
- the constitution;
- Parliament's composition and procedures.

They can abolish old Parliaments and create a new Parliament (the Acts of Union), and, with the exception of pre-Brexit EU law (see *R v Secretary of State for Transport, ex parte Factortame (No 2)* [1991] 1 AC 603, 658–659 (Lord Bridge)), statutes can conflict with international law and be applied by the courts (*Mortensen v Peters* (1906) 8 F (J) 93).

6.2 The traditional view of parliamentary sovereignty

The classic description of parliamentary sovereignty was expressed by A.V. Dicey:

> The principle of Parliamentary Sovereignty means neither more nor less than this, namely, that Parliament . . . has, under the English constitution, the right to make or unmake any law whatever; and, further, that no person or body is recognised by the law of England as having a right to override or set aside the legislation of Parliament. (Professor A.V. Dicey, *An Introduction to the Study of the Law of the Constitution*, 1885)

This notion of legislative supremacy is very strong. It conveys the idea that Parliament has unlimited authority to make law which no one can override, that all statutes are repealable, and that Parliament's law-making power is unrestricted so that entrenchment of Acts of Parliament passed by a previous Parliament is legally impossible. The traditional view of Parliament's legislative supremacy has been staunchly supported, from Sir Edward Coke in the seventeenth century ('Of the power and jurisdiction of the Parliament, for making of laws in proceeding by Bill, it is so transcendent and absolute, as it cannot be confined either for causes or persons within any bounds' (4 *Inst* 36)), to its endorsement in *R (Miller) v Secretary of State for Exiting the European Union* [2016] EWHC 2768 (Admin) ('*Miller I*')

> It is common ground that the most fundamental rule of UK constitutional law is that the Crown in Parliament is sovereign and that legislation enacted by the Crown with the consent of both Houses of Parliament is supreme . . . Parliament can, by enactment of primary legislation, change the law of the land in any way it chooses. There is no superior form of law than primary legislation, save only where Parliament has itself made provision to allow that to happen. (*Miller I* [20])

> **Definition**
> The Crown in Parliament refers to the legislative authority of the House of Commons, the House of Lords, and the Queen

> Dicey's traditional view can be broken down into three elements:
>
> 1. Parliament can make or unmake any law (those laws will then be obeyed by the courts; Dicey called this the 'positive side' of parliamentary sovereignty).
> 2. If each Parliament can make any law, no Parliament can bind its successors (an individual Parliament cannot pass laws which restrict future Parliaments).
> 3. No one has the legal authority to override or set aside an Act of Parliament (Dicey called this the 'negative side' of parliamentary sovereignty).

'A Parliament' runs from the election of a new Parliament to the date when it is suspended before the next election (usually five years)

6.2.1 Parliament has the right to make or unmake any law

This means that Parliament has legal authority (or competence) to make any law it chooses and has a free hand to change or repeal existing statutes created by earlier parliaments. Furthermore, there is no written constitution against which to measure its laws. It can:

Repeal means revoking or removing a statute (or sections of a statute) so that it no longer has legal force

- **Change the constitution:** For example, the Parliament Act 1911 provided for elections every five years (previously seven) and removed the House of Lords' right of veto over public Bills from the House of Commons except for Bills extending the life of a Parliament. Parliament's authority to change the constitution shows it as a constitutive as well as a legislative power.

- **Legislate retrospectively:** In *Burmah Oil v Lord Advocate* [1965] AC 75, it was held that the Crown had to compensate owners of property which had been destroyed by British troops in the Second World War except during battle. Soon afterwards, Parliament passed the War Damage Act 1965, which abolished the rights to compensation acquired *before* the Act was passed, and effectively reversed the *Burmah Oil* decision.

- **Legislate beyond UK territory (extraterritorially):** Parliament can create laws that extend to acts committed abroad. Jennings' classic example is that Parliament could pass a law making it an offence to smoke on the streets of Paris (an offender would be punished on their return to the UK). Other UK statutes with extraterritorial effect include section 72 Sexual Offences Act 2003 (sexual offences against children committed abroad by UK nationals and residents), section 59 Terrorism Act 2000 (inciting an act of terrorism abroad), and section 6 Bribery Act 2010 (bribing foreign public officials).

6.2.2 No Parliament may be bound by a predecessor or bind a successor

There are two strands to this idea, as shown in Figure 6.1. The first strand is backward-looking in that each Parliament is free to make laws and repeal earlier statutes without being restricted by laws made by earlier parliaments. The second strand is forward-looking in that each Parliament cannot legislate in a way that limits future parliaments by passing an Act which states, for example, that it cannot be repealed, or dictates how it must be amended or repealed in the future, such as by requiring a referendum or a super-majority.

In the UK constitution, therefore, legislation cannot be entrenched (protected from future change); all statutes are repealable, though see section 6.3.2.3 for academic argument on this.

6.2.2.1 Express repeal

For an example of express repeal, see section 1 Terrorism Prevention and Investigation Measures Act 2011

Normally, an Act of Parliament will clearly state which statutes, or specific sections of earlier statutes, it is repealing. This is known as express repeal. The Law Commission also periodically recommends out-of-date laws for repeal, the legislative equivalent of clearing out the attic. The Statute Law (Repeals) Act 2013, for example, repealed a number of obsolete statutes, including one from around 1322 (the schedules of this Act are interesting reading in themselves; for background detail, see www.lawcom.gov.uk/project/statute-law-repeals-19th-report/).

Figure 6.1 Making law is a forward-moving process

| Earlier parliaments cannot restrict future Parliaments | Each parliament is free to make new laws and repeal old laws |

6.2.2.2 **The doctrine of implied repeal**

Occasionally, however, a statute may conflict with an earlier statute but does not expressly repeal it. This causes difficulties for the courts, who cannot apply two conflicting statutes; they therefore adopt the doctrine of implied repeal to deal with this.

> In general, the rule is that the courts will apply the provisions from the most recent statute if they contradict the earlier statute. As we will see presently, there is an exception for a category of statutes deemed to be 'constitutional statutes'.

At first glance, this looks as though the courts are ignoring an Act of Parliament (the earlier Act), but the doctrine of implied repeal upholds Dicey's principle that no Parliament is restricted by the laws passed by earlier parliaments and a Parliament is free to move away from earlier statutes. The cases of *Vauxhall Estates v Liverpool Corporation* [1932] 1 KB 733 and *Ellen Street Estates v Minister of Health* [1934] 1 KB 590 illustrate this. They involved the application of two statutes on assessing compensation for land that was compulsorily purchased to clear slums for redevelopment: section 2 Acquisition of Land (Assessment of Compensation) Act 1919 and section 46 Housing Act 1925. Section 7(1) of the 1919 Act provided that if other Acts were inconsistent with it, they had no effect—but provisions in the Housing Act 1925 *were* inconsistent with it. In *Vauxhall Estates,* Avory J stated:

> no Act of Parliament can effectively provide that no future Act shall interfere with its provisions . . . [I]f they are inconsistent . . . the earlier Act is impliedly repealed by the later. (*Vauxhall Estates v Liverpool Corporation,* 743–744)

Thus, the inconsistent provisions of the 1919 Act were impliedly repealed by the 1925 Act, which meant that the Parliament of 1919 was unable to protect its statute in the way it intended, and subsequent parliaments were free to enact inconsistent provisions. The intention of the later Parliament prevails.

 THINKING POINT

Was the 1919 Parliament sovereign?

However, the case of *Thoburn v Sunderland City Council* [2002] EWHC 195 (Admin) modified the doctrine of implied repeal: while ordinary statutes may be impliedly repealed, constitutional statutes may not, and they can only be expressly repealed by unambiguous words in the later statute as evidence of the legislature's actual intention, which implied repeal does not provide. Known as the 'metric martyrs case', *Thoburn* concerned traders who sold goods in pounds and ounces. The Weights and Measures Act 1985 allowed goods to be sold in both pounds and ounces and metric weight, but it was amended by secondary legislation, the Weights and Measures Regulations 1994 (implementing an EU Metrication Directive by virtue of section 2(2) European Communities Act 1972), requiring goods to be sold by metric weight only. Mr Thoburn argued that section 1 of the Weights and Measures Act, as the later statute, impliedly repealed section 2(2) of the European Communities Act 1972 to the extent that it allowed inconsistent laws to be produced, but Laws LJ stated:

> The common law has in recent years allowed, or rather created, exceptions to the doctrine of implied repeal: a doctrine which was always the common law's own creature. There are now

⯮ CROSS REFERENCE

See section 3.2.1 for constitutional statutes

classes or types of legislative provision which cannot be repealed by mere implication [60] . . . Ordinary statutes may be impliedly repealed. Constitutional statutes may not. [63]

Laws LJ classified the European Communities Act 1972 as a constitutional statute; therefore it prevailed, even though it was the earlier statute.

The courts have also stressed that there is now a strong presumption *against* implied repeal in the light of high standards of parliamentary draftsmanship, especially where a 'weighty enactment' is concerned (see *BH v Lord Advocate* [2012] UKSC 24 [30]).

6.2.3 No person or body has the right to override or set aside the legislation of Parliament

In the UK, the courts cannot question the validity of an Act of Parliament that has passed through the correct legislative process and received royal assent, or strike down an Act for being invalid. Sir Robert Megarry VC in *Manuel v AG* [1983] Ch 77 stated: 'the duty of the court is to obey and apply every Act of Parliament, and . . . the court cannot hold any such Act to be *ultra vires*'; once an Act is recognised as an Act of Parliament, 'no English court can refuse to obey it or question its validity' (p 86). This is the Enrolled Bill rule, as expressed by Lord Campbell:

> All that a Court of Justice can do is to look to the Parliamentary roll: if from that it should appear that a bill has passed both Houses and received the Royal assent, no Court of Justice can inquire into the mode in which it was introduced into Parliament, nor into what was done previous to its introduction, or what passed in Parliament during its progress in its various stages. (*Edinburgh & Dalkeith Railway Co v Wauchope* (1842) 8 Cl & Fin 710, 725)

🔍 CASE CLOSE-UP: THE ENROLLED BILL RULE

This rule was applied in *British Railways Board v Pickin* [1974] 1 All ER 609, where Mr Pickin challenged the British Railways Act 1968 on the grounds that it had not been properly passed because certain matters had been fraudulently concealed from Parliament. The court made it clear that it had no authority to investigate those allegations; its function was to construe and apply Acts of Parliament, not how Parliament performs its functions. The court cannot go behind the Act.

In the *HS2 case* (*R (HS2 Action Alliance Limited) v Secretary of State for Transport and another* [2014] UKSC 3), the government intended to obtain consent for the HS2 high speed rail link through introducing two hybrid Bills in Parliament but it was argued that Parliament's legislative process for hybrid Bills would contravene an EU Directive (the Environmental Impact Assessment Directive) which required public participation in environmental decision-making procedures. The Supreme Court referred to the constitutional principle that it was not open to judges to scrutinise parliamentary procedure (see Lord Reed [78] and Lords Neuberger and Mance [203–208]) and raised the issue of whether EU law overrode Article 9 Bill of Rights 1689. Article 9 prevents the questioning in any court of debates or proceedings in Parliament, thus enshrining the constitutional principles of parliamentary sovereignty and the separation of powers. In the event, the Supreme Court did not have to pursue the issue as it found that parliamentary procedures satisfied conditions in the Directive.

A hybrid Bill shares characteristics of public and private Bills and follows a specific legislative process

SUMMARY

Parliament has broad legislative power but cannot make unchangeable statutes, and a current Parliament can reverse laws made by a previous Parliament. Nobody but Parliament can override Acts of Parliament. The Enrolled Bill rule requires that, if a Bill has passed through the House of Commons and House of Lords and received royal assent, the courts will not enquire into what happened before or during the legislative process.

6.2.4 The rule of recognition

We have established what parliamentary sovereignty is and the extent of Parliament's legislative authority, but there is a more fundamental question to be considered now: where does the rule about Parliament's legislative authority come from? It cannot derive from a statute because Parliament would be giving itself the power it needed to make that Act in the first place. As Wade has argued: 'Legislation owes its authority to the rule: the rule does not owe its authority to legislation' (H.W.R. Wade, 'The Basis of Legal Sovereignty' (1955) CLJ 172, 188). For example, David Cameron proposed a new sovereignty law in 2016 confirming that the UK Parliament had given powers to the EU, and it is sovereign because it has the right to withdraw them (www.bbc.co.uk/news/uk-politics-eu-referendum-35342010). Had it become law, this would only have confirmed what we already know as the common law position and would not *create* parliamentary sovereignty. The answer is that parliamentary sovereignty derives from judges' recognition of Parliament as sovereign and having legislative supremacy. This is known as the 'rule of recognition'.

CLOSE-UP FOCUS: THE RULE OF RECOGNITION

Every legal system has a basic rule identifying what constitutes valid law within that system. Hart called it 'the ultimate rule of recognition'; Hans Kelsen called it the *grundnorm*; Salmond called it the 'ultimate legal principle'. The UK's rule of recognition is that the courts recognise a statute as valid law because it is passed by Parliament; Parliament is the sovereign law-maker so what the statute says is the law. Parliament's authority rests on acceptance of its sovereignty by the courts. This means that if judges regard Parliament as the sovereign law-maker, it *is* the sovereign law-maker. However, academic and judicial opinion differs on whether parliamentary sovereignty was actually *created* by judges as a common law rule (in which case it could be taken away by them).

Craig explains the rule of recognition:

> This is the top rule of the system, to which the validity of all other rules can ultimately be traced. Its validity is said to be based on social fact, in the sense that the content of the rule . . . is the result of acceptance by the key players in the system, which includes courts, Parliament, and senior members of the bureaucracy. The rule of recognition is dynamic not static. It can change, but not *per se* through the passage of an Act of Parliament, or judicial decision. These may be the catalyst for a reformulation of the rule of recognition, but it will only become clear whether this has occurred after the effluxion of time, during which it will become apparent whether the other players have accepted the change initially suggested

by a court or Parliament itself. (Paul Craig, 'Constitutionalising Constitutional Law: HS2' (2014) (July) Public Law 373, 391)

Lord Steyn has stated unambiguously that 'the supremacy of Parliament is . . . a construct of the common law. The judges created this principle' (*Jackson v AG* [102]), but this view raises the prospect that ultimate control over parliamentary sovereignty rests with the judiciary. See also T.R.S. Allan, 'Parliamentary Sovereignty: Law, Politics, and Revolution' (1997) 113 LQR 443.

Wade points out that the rule that the courts recognise Acts of Parliament as valid law is one rule that Parliament cannot change because it is not in a statute; it has a historical source and can only be changed by constitutional revolution or an evolution in the opinion of the courts. He described judicial obedience as the ultimate political fact, as opposed to a legal rule, arguing: 'The rule of recognition is itself a political fact which the judges themselves are able to change when they are confronted with a new situation which so demands' (H.W.R. Wade, 'Sovereignty—Revolution or Evolution?' (1996) 112 LQR 568, 574).

However, Lord Bingham has persuasively commented:

[T]he principle of parliamentary sovereignty has been recognised as fundamental in this country not because the judges invented it but because it has for centuries been accepted as such by judges and others officially concerned in the operation of our constitutional system. The judges did not by themselves establish the principle and they cannot, by themselves, change it. (*The Rule of Law* (2011), p 167; see 'Further reading'; see also Professor Tomkins, House of Commons European Scrutiny Committee, *The EU Bill and Parliamentary Sovereignty*, Tenth Report of Session 2010–11, HC 633-II, Ev. 4–6 [22–30, 32])

This view gives the impression of a deeply engrained custom embedded in the fabric of the constitution.

For practical reasons why the UK courts accept parliamentary sovereignty, see Dawn Oliver, 'Parliamentary Sovereignty: A Pragmatic or Principled Doctrine?' 3 May 2012 (https://ukconstitutionallaw.org/2012/05/03/dawn-oliver-parliamentary-sovereignty-a-pragmatic-or-principled-doctrine/).

For a clear summary of views on parliamentary sovereignty, see European Scrutiny Committee, *The EU Bill and Parliamentary Sovereignty*, HC 633-I [22–28].

6.3 Parliamentary sovereignty in reality

Dicey presented a picture of an all-powerful Parliament but in practice, parliamentary sovereignty is not absolute, and there have been a number of inroads into Dicey's traditional view. Lord Hope has expressed the view that the 'question whether the principle of the sovereignty of the United Kingdom Parliament is absolute or may be subject to limitation in exceptional circumstances is still under discussion' (*AXA General Insurance Ltd v Lord Advocate* [2011] UKSC 46, [2012] 1 AC 868 [50]). Parliamentary sovereignty is not written in stone and can change over time. Internally, the balance of power within Parliament has changed over the centuries, with the active involvement of the monarch until the seventeenth century, a powerful House of Lords until the Parliament Acts of 1911 and 1949, and over the past century a pre-eminent House of Commons. Parliamentary sovereignty has developed in accordance with changing allegiances and political demands. Dicey believed that parliamentary sovereignty was absolute but by 1915, even he doubted that it was as strong as he had portrayed it 30 years earlier. It is recognised today that, although parliamentary sovereignty remains a central principle of the UK constitution, Parliament can choose to limit it. The *Cabinet Manual* summarises the current position:

> In the exercise of its legislative powers, Parliament is sovereign. In practice, however, Parliament has chosen to be constrained in various ways—through its Acts, and by elements of European and other international law. (*Cabinet Manual*, p 3 para 9)

Parliament has, from time to time, given up some of its legislative competence in certain areas, and important questions have arisen over possible limits on the Diceyan view of parliamentary sovereignty:

- In reality, can the UK Parliament create entrenched, unchangeable statutes?
- Can Parliament redefine its own powers? Can it specify the way in which a statute is to be changed or repealed in the future? Would any statute not following that procedure be invalid?
- Are there practical limitations on parliamentary sovereignty?

6.3.1 Can Parliament create entrenched statutes?

This question has arisen chiefly in respect of statutes delivering constitutional reform or far-reaching change. Parliament has passed statutes which have limited its powers to a greater or lesser degree and the issue has arisen to what extent those statutes are repealable. They are as follows:

1. Statutes granting independence to colonies.
2. Acts of Union.
3. European Communities Act 1972.
4. Devolution Acts.
5. Human Rights Act 1998.

6.3.1.1 Grants of independence to British colonies

In the 1930s, the UK gave greater powers to its dominions (Canada, Australia, New Zealand, South Africa, the Irish Free State, and Newfoundland). The Statute of Westminster 1931 gave legislative power to the parliaments of the dominions and under section 4, no UK Act of Parliament would extend to a dominion unless the Act expressly stated that the dominion had requested and consented to it. In *Manuel v AG*, the UK courts *almost* had the opportunity to decide whether the UK Parliament can give up its sovereign legislative power. Here, the Canada Act 1982 was passed by the UK Parliament at the request of the Canadian Parliament, and it brought into effect the Constitution Act 1982, which ended the UK's role in amending the Canadian constitution. Chiefs of the Canadian First Nations (who enjoyed recognised hunting rights under the constitution) argued that the Canada Act was inconsistent with the Statute of Westminster and therefore invalid, because the UK Parliament did not have power to enact the Canada Act without their consent, but the Court of Appeal decided that it was not for the court to question whether consent had *actually* been given: section 4 of the Statute of Westminster only required an Act to expressly *declare* that a dominion had requested and consented to an Act, so a literal interpretation of the statute avoided trickier constitutional questions.

> **Definition**
>
> A dominion is a self-governing colony

When the UK began to grant freedom to its former colonies, Parliament completely surrendered its authority over those territories to the parliaments of the new states. Under the Zimbabwe Act 1979, for example, the UK Parliament can no longer make law for Zimbabwe and is no longer responsible for its government. In theory, Parliament could repeal the statute and revoke independence, but this is extremely unlikely to happen (even Dicey recognised this: see *An Introduction to the Study of the Law of the Constitution*, 8th edn, 1915). Lord Denning's dictum in *Blackburn v AG* captures the dilemma:

> We have all been brought up to believe that, in legal theory, one Parliament cannot bind another and that no Act is irreversible. But legal theory does not always march alongside political reality. Take the Statute of Westminster 1931, which takes away the power of Parliament to legislate for the Dominions. Can any one imagine that Parliament could or would reverse that Statute? Take the Acts which have granted independence to the Dominions and territories overseas. Can anyone imagine that Parliament could or would reverse those laws and take away their independence? Most clearly not. Freedom once given cannot be taken away. *Legal theory must give way to practical politics.* (*Blackburn v AG* [1971] 1 WLR 1037, 1040, emphasis added; see also *British Coal and The King* [1935] AC 500)

6.3.1.2 The Acts of Union

The Act of Union with Scotland 1707 extinguished the separate parliaments of Scotland and England and Wales, and created the Parliament of Great Britain; the Act of Union with Ireland 1800 created the Parliament of Great Britain and Ireland. Both Acts created a Union that was expressed to be 'for ever after'. Did the parliaments of 1707 and 1800 create laws that future parliaments could never change? It would, after all, be difficult for Parliament to repeal the very statutes that created it in its new form. However, Ireland left the Union in 1922, so (a) the 'for ever' clause in the Acts was not binding and (b) subsequent parliaments were free to pass the Government of Ireland Act 1920, dividing Northern Ireland from the south, and the Ireland Act 1949, by which the Republic of Ireland left the Commonwealth.

 CROSS REFERENCE

See sections 2.5 and 2.7

> **THINKING POINT**
>
> The Northern Ireland Act 1998 provides that Northern Ireland remains in the Union unless the majority of the electorate decides to leave. Could that provision be repealed by a future UK Parliament?

In relation to Scotland, it can be argued that the Act of Union is a founding instrument and therefore cannot be repealed. However, section 37 Scotland Act 1998 states that the Acts of Union have effect subject to the Scotland Act, and Brazier has argued that the Act of Union is qualified by the Scotland Act 1998 (see Rodney Brazier, 'The Constitution of the United Kingdom' (1999) 58 CLJ 96). The Scottish courts have also asserted that there is nothing in the Acts of Union which state that Parliament has absolute sovereignty. In *MacCormick v Lord Advocate*

[1953] SC 396 (a case involving a challenge to the right of the Queen to use the title Elizabeth II in Scotland because Elizabeth I had been Queen of England), Lord Cooper said that 'the principle of unlimited sovereignty of Parliament is a distinctively English principle which has no counterpart in Scottish constitutional law' (p 411).

THINKING POINT

What would happen to the Act of Union in the event of Scottish independence?

6.3.1.3 **The European Communities Act 1972**

The traditional UK position of a Parliament which is sovereign, has no competing law-makers, and is free to make or unmake any law was challenged by the UK's membership of the EU. When the UK became a member of the European Economic Community (EEC) on 1 January 1973, it joined an organisation whose law had primacy over the national law of its member states. The European Communities Act 1972 (ECA) allowed European law to take effect as part of UK domestic law without further reference to Parliament. As it was legally superior to English law, European law would prevail in the event of a conflict between the two. This raised the question: was law made by the UK Parliament still supreme? The full effect on Parliament's sovereignty was not altogether clear at the outset. By joining the EEC, did Parliament intend to retain its sovereignty or yield it to the EEC? The ECA was not explicit about the effect on parliamentary sovereignty and it raised a further issue: was the 1972 Act repealable or entrenched? By passing the ECA, did the Parliament of 1972 bind its successors, and what would the UK courts decide where a UK statute conflicted with European law?

The ECA contained three provisions enabling European law to have primacy in the UK:

- Section 2(1) effectively provided that directly applicable European laws were to be given effect by the UK courts as if they were UK Acts of Parliament, and there was no need for Parliament to pass a further law to give them effect.

- Section 2(4) required the UK courts to interpret UK Acts of Parliament (present and future) so that they were consistent with European law.

- Section 3(1) required the UK courts to follow legal principles laid down by the European Court of Justice.

The effect on Dicey's first rule: These provisions suggest that the UK Parliament was giving up or transferring some of its sovereign law-making powers to the EU in return for the benefits of membership (see *Stoke-on-Trent City Council v B&Q plc* [1991] 2 WLR 42 [2] (Hoffmann J)). Parliament did not specify that it could not enact laws which conflicted with European law, but that is the combined effect of sections 2(1) and 2(4). As Lord Hope has stated, 's 2(1) . . . concedes the last word in this matter to the courts. The doctrine of the supremacy of Community law restricts the absolute authority of Parliament to legislate as it wants in this area' (*Jackson v AG* [105]). Thus, while in theory Parliament could make a law inconsistent with European law, it usually would not, because if it was challenged in court, the judges would measure it against European law as the ECA required them to do. Membership of the EU therefore challenged Dicey's principle that Parliament can make or unmake any law whatsoever, although if Parliament deliberately and expressly legislated contrary to EU law, Lord Denning stated pre-*Factortame* that it would be the duty of the courts to follow the statute (*Macarthys Ltd v Smith* [1979] ICR 785, 789).

The effect on Dicey's second and third rules: Section 2(4)'s requirement for the courts to construe words in UK statutes to ensure consistency with European law was often sufficient to avoid conflict (see, for example, *Garland v BR Engineering* [1983] 2 AC 751 and *Pickstone v Freemans plc* [1989] AC 66). However, the *Factortame* case (*R v Secretary of State for Transport, ex parte Factortame (No 2)* [1991] 1 AC 603) made it clear that when a UK statute clearly conflicted with European law and there was no scope for interpretation, the courts had to do what Dicey would have believed unthinkable and disapply the statute.

Q   **CASE CLOSE-UP:** *R v SECRETARY OF STATE FOR TRANSPORT, EX PARTE FACTORTAME* (NO 2) [1991] 1 AC 603

The *Factortame cases* involved a dispute about fishing quotas which began a sequence of litigation.

The UK Parliament passed the Merchant Shipping Act 1988 to protect the UK's fishing fleet against Spanish vessels which were registering in the UK and catching part of the UK's fishing quota. The Act introduced a register of British fishing vessels and imposed a British nationality requirement for registration as British vessels, but this was challenged on the basis that the 1988 Act was discriminatory and inconsistent with European law. The court at first instance suspended the operation of the 1988 Act but the House of Lords held that the courts could not disapply statutes under the traditional view of parliamentary sovereignty. The House of Lords referred questions on interpretation of European law to the ECJ, which ruled that the UK courts had to disregard the incompatible provisions of the Act. Where a UK statute conflicted with directly enforceable European law, European law prevailed and the UK courts had to 'disapply'—or suspend—the incompatible UK legislation. It is important to note that the Merchant Shipping Act was not made void (see *Fleming v Customs and Excise Commissioners* [2008] 1 WLR 195 [24]), though the statute was subsequently amended.

Lord Bridge observed that 'whatever limitation of its sovereignty Parliament accepted when it enacted the European Communities Act 1972 was entirely voluntary . . . there is nothing in any way novel in according supremacy to rules of Community law in those areas to which they apply' (*Factortame (No 2)* 658–659).

The *Factortame* case produced much debate about the constitutional changes made by the UK's membership of the EU to parliamentary sovereignty and the rule of recognition. See, for example:

T.R.S. Allan, 'Parliamentary Sovereignty: Law, Politics and Revolution' (1997) 113 LQR 443

N.W. Barber, 'The Afterlife of Parliamentary Sovereignty' (2011) 9(1) Int J Const Law 144

P.P. Craig, 'Sovereignty of the United Kingdom Parliament after Factortame' (1991) 11(1) Yearbook of European Law 221

Factortame made it clear that parliamentary sovereignty had been limited, although while it gave the impression of the UK courts being able to set aside an Act of Parliament, the courts were giving effect to Parliament's intention in the ECA that legislation should accord with EU law and EU law should prevail for as long as the UK was a member.

THINKING POINT

Consider how implied repeal might have applied in *Factortame*. Two statutes conflicted but it was the *earlier* Act that prevailed. What do you think the reason was? Did the Parliament of 1972 limit the law that the Parliament of 1988 could make?

In the light of *Factortame*, Wade argued that the Parliament of 1972 'succeeded in binding the Parliament of 1988, something that was supposed to be constitutionally impossible' ('Sovereignty—Revolution or Evolution' (1996) 112 LQR 568, 572). He took the view that the ECA was entrenched and that Parliament had created an unprecedented situation by permanently restricting its sovereignty with section 2 ECA; a revolution had taken place in the rule of recognition. On the other hand, Laws LJ believed that the courts had 'found their way through the impasse seemingly created by two supremacies, the supremacy of European law and the supremacy of Parliament' (*Thoburn* [60]) and that Parliament's sovereignty was preserved (though by 2014 the Supreme Court was questioning the overriding supremacy of European law within the UK constitution (*R (HS2 Action Alliance Limited) v Secretary of State for Transport* [2014] UKSC 3)).

The European Union Act 2011 attempted to redress the perceived imbalance in parliamentary sovereignty by providing in section 18 that directly applicable or directly effective EU law was only recognised as law in the UK because of the ECA—though this was simply a reminder of parliamentary sovereignty.

The Brexit referendum in 2016 disentangled the sovereignty question although as Michael Gordon points out, parliamentary sovereignty is 'not a doctrine which can be restored by Brexit, for it had never been lost' (Michael Gordon, 'Parliamentary Sovereignty and the Political Constitution(s): From Griffith to Brexit' (2019) 30(1) King's Law Journal 125, 141). In a strong endorsement of parliamentary sovereignty, the Supreme Court in *Miller I* laid the ECA entrenchment debate to rest, stating: 'this unprecedented state of affairs will only last so long as Parliament wishes: the 1972 Act can be repealed like any other statute', and affirmed that the fundamental rule of recognition had not been changed by the 1972 Act and would not be changed by its repeal (*R (Miller) v Secretary of State for Exiting the European Union* [2017] UKSC 5 [60]). EU law had 'automatic and overriding effect' only while the 1972 Act remained in force, reflecting the fact that 'Parliament was and remains sovereign' ([61]). Parliament subsequently asserted its sovereignty in the European Union (Withdrawal) Act 2018 by expressly repealing the ECA 1972 on exit day (section 1).

> **CROSS REFERENCE**
> See Chapter 5 for details on Brexit

THINKING POINT

With the repeal of the ECA, whose view of parliamentary sovereignty has prevailed: Dicey's or Wade's?

6.3.1.4 Devolution

Section 4.3 considers the effect of devolution on parliamentary sovereignty. The devolved administrations are created by statute and hence are subordinate to the Westminster Parliament, but devolution is becoming increasingly complex and more tightly woven into the fabric of the UK constitution. The Scotland Act 2016's introduction of a provision making the Scottish Parliament and Scottish government 'permanent' now raises the question whether future parliaments are bound by it (see Chris Himsworth, 'Legislating for Permanence and a Statutory Footing' (2016) 20(3) Edinburgh Law Review 361; House of Lords Select Committee on the Constitution, *Proposals for the Devolution of Further Powers to Scotland*, 10th Report of Session 2014–15 HL Paper 145 [60]). The *Miller I* judgments emphasised that the devolution arrangements lie within no stronger a construct than Acts of Parliament, which are ultimately repealable but while Parliament has the legal power to repeal the devolution Acts, the political implications are another matter. Bogdanor believes that the UK Parliament has no effective sovereignty over Scotland and argues that the UK is quasi-federal because it would be very difficult politically for the UK Parliament to take away the powers that have been devolved to Scotland, Wales, and Northern Ireland (see Bogdanor, 'Our New Constitution' (2004) 120 LQR 242). Furthermore, devolution was set up after referendums in the three nations showing popular support. Referendums would be required before devolved power was taken away, and although the UK Parliament would not be legally bound by the result it would feel bound by the mandate of the people, as it did with the Brexit referendum; it would therefore be very difficult for the UK Parliament to dismantle devolution in the face of the people's support for it. Thus a popular mandate can entrench devolution. Yet, the supremacy of the Westminster Parliament can be seen in its power to suspend the Northern Ireland Assembly from October 2002 to 2007, and to pass the EU (Withdrawal) Act 2018 without the Scottish Parliament's consent and the EU (Withdrawal Agreement) Act 2020 without any of the devolved legislatures' consent.

CROSS REFERENCE

See section 4.3

6.3.1.5 **The Human Rights Act 1998**

The Human Rights Act incorporates the European Convention on Human Rights (ECHR) into UK law, which allows rights in the Convention to be enforced in the UK courts. However, the Human Rights Act carefully preserves parliamentary sovereignty by *not* allowing the courts to strike down any statute that is incompatible with a Convention right. Any inconsistent statute continues in force until it is amended by Parliament (or by a government minister under delegated powers). At most, the higher courts can issue a declaration of incompatibility, which serves as a warning flag to Parliament that an Act contains provisions infringing human rights, though in reality Parliament takes note of a declaration of incompatibility by the courts and amends or repeals the offending statute. An example is the declaration of incompatibility made in *A & Others v Secretary of State for Home Department* [2004] UKHL 56 in relation to section 23 of the Anti-terrorism, Crime and Security Act 2001, which allowed the indefinite detention of foreign terrorist suspects without trial; this decision prompted a change in the law with the Prevention of Terrorism Act 2005. The Human Rights Act is expressly repealable; whether it *should* be repealed is another issue. (See Janet L. Hiebert 'The Human Rights Act: Ambiguity about Parliamentary Sovereignty' (2013) 14(12) German Law Journal 2253.)

CROSS REFERENCE

For further details on the Human Rights Act, see Chapter 17

 THINKING POINT

Look back over section 6.3.1. Can you see how, in each case, any limitations on Parliament's powers have been of its own making? It follows that a future Parliament can remove those limitations by a new Act.

THE BIGGER PICTURE

Mark Elliott rationalises these limits on Parliament's sovereignty by arguing that the UK's constitution is not one-dimensional, consisting only of parliamentary sovereignty, but multi-dimensional. See https://publiclawforeveryone.com/2014/04/16/parliamentary-sovereignty-in-a-multidimensional-constitution-some-preliminary-thoughts/.

6.3.2 Can Parliament redefine itself?

This question raises (1) the 'reconstitution or redefinition' argument where Parliament legislates to change its substantive composition and powers and (2) the 'manner and form' argument where legislation seeks to change how existing powers are used by altering the manner and form of the future legislative process, though the two are not always clearly distinguished. Whether such legislation is binding on future Parliaments has been the subject of academic debate which centres on two competing ideas: continuing and self-embracing parliamentary sovereignty.

6.3.2.1 Continuing and self-embracing sovereignty

Continuing parliamentary sovereignty is the orthodox, traditional view that Parliament cannot redefine itself permanently; any statute attempting to do so could be repealed by a future Parliament. Self-embracing parliamentary sovereignty (also known as the 'new view') means that Parliament can redefine itself because each Parliament is sovereign and whatever it enacts is law—as long as the Act giving effect to those changes was validly passed.

The foremost example of a 'redefining' statute is the Parliament Act 1911, which reduced the legislative powers of the House of Lords by removing its power to reject money bills and replacing its veto over most public bills with the power to delay them for two years. Lord Steyn has stated that Parliament may redistribute its legislative power in different ways (*Jackson v AG* [81]) and the Parliament Act 1911 'created a new method of ascertaining the declared will of Parliament. It restated the manner and form in which laws may be made in respect of . . . "delayed Bills"' (*Jackson* [75]). Lord Hope noted that, while it is not helpful to describe the 1911 Act as redefining Parliament because no Parliament can bind its successors, in practice the 1911 Act did redefine it by limiting the power of the House of Lords to legislate and changing the balance of power between the Commons and the Lords (*Jackson* [113]). It should be remembered, however, that the 1911 Act was created to reduce friction between the two Houses of Parliament and did not change the legislative process for most statutes. For comment on *Jackson*, see Vernon Bogdanor, 'Imprisoned by a Doctrine: The Modern Defence of Parliamentary Sovereignty' (2012) 32 (1) Oxf J Leg Stud 179, 187.

6.3.2.2 Are future parliaments bound to follow specified legislative procedures?

The cases of *AG for New South Wales v Trethowan* [1932] AC 526 and *Harris v Minister of the Interior* [1952] 1 TLR 1245 suggested that the subsequent statute *should* follow the procedure set down in the earlier statute. In *Trethowan*, it was held that the NSW Parliament had to comply with the Colonial Laws Validity Act 1865, passed by the UK Parliament; this authorised colonial legislatures to change their constitutions, but amendments had to be made in the 'manner and form' required by any Act of Parliament. In *Harris*, the South African Supreme

Court held that the provisions of the South Africa Act 1909 were entrenched (the Act was passed by the UK to create the South African Parliament, and required a two-thirds majority of both houses of the South African Parliament to remove voting rights of specified voters) but these decisions involved governing Acts passed by the UK giving legislative powers to subordinate Parliaments, and do not directly help on whether the UK Parliament may bind itself. (For comment on *Trethowan* and *Harris*, see H.W.R. Wade, 'The Basis of Legal Sovereignty' (1955) 13(2) CLJ 172.)

However, in *Ellen Street Estates* Maugham LJ was quite clear (*obiter*) about the position in the UK:

> The legislature cannot, according to our constitution, bind itself as to the form of subsequent legislation, and it is impossible for Parliament to enact that in a subsequent statute dealing with the same subject-matter there can be no implied repeal. If in a subsequent Act Parliament chooses to make it plain that the earlier statute is being to some extent repealed, effect must be given to that intention just because it is the will of the Legislature (p 597).

Laws LJ in *Thoburn* was equally clear when discussing the ECA 1972:

> Parliament cannot bind its successors by stipulating against repeal, wholly or partly, of the 1972 Act. It cannot stipulate as to the manner and form of any subsequent legislation. It cannot stipulate against implied repeal any more than it can stipulate against express repeal. ([59])

 THINKING POINT

The Scotland Act 2016 stipulates that the Scottish Parliament and Scottish government are not to be abolished except on the basis of a decision of the people of Scotland voting in a referendum. Would a statute ignoring the referendum requirement be invalid?

6.3.2.3 **Sovereignty vs supremacy**

If Parliament lacks the power to bind itself, it cannot be omnipotent and supreme, and if a Parliament can pass laws that bind or limit future parliaments, those parliaments cannot be sovereign. This returns us to the definition of parliamentary sovereignty: does it mean supremacy or, more narrowly, unlimited and unchallengeable legislative authority?

 THE BIGGER PICTURE: SOVEREIGNTY VS SUPREMACY

Jennings took the view that, in calling Parliament sovereign, Dicey had been referring to Parliament as a supreme power, but a true sovereign cannot be limited by its own acts. He believed that a legally sovereign Parliament could place legal limitations on itself, and argued that 'legal sovereignty' is a legal concept meaning that each Parliament has 'for the time being power to make laws of any kind in the manner required by the law' (Sir Ivor Jennings, *The Law and the Constitution* (5th edn, London: University of London Press 1959), p 153). The courts will recognise a law if it has been made in the proper form, so if Parliament passes an Act changing the legislative procedure (eg all constitutional statutes must be passed with a two thirds majority in the House of Commons and House of Lords), that becomes the manner required by the law. All relevant statutes must then comply or be invalid. Jennings therefore believed that Parliament's power to change the law includes the power to change the law affecting itself.

Wade disagreed. While Jennings viewed parliamentary sovereignty as a legal doctrine, Wade pointed out that there is only one limit to Parliament's sovereignty: 'it cannot detract from its own continuing sovereignty' ('The Basis of Legal Sovereignty', p 174). He argued that 'no Act of Parliament can be void but any Act of Parliament is repealable' (p 186) and saw Parliament as continuously sovereign in the eyes of the courts, so it could not bind its successors. (See Michael Gordon, 'The Conceptual Foundations of Parliamentary Sovereignty: Reconsidering Jennings and Wade' (2009) (July) Public Law 519.) Laws LJ has stated: 'Being sovereign, [Parliament] cannot abandon its sovereignty' (*Thoburn* [59]), and Jeffrey Goldsworthy believes that Parliament cannot lawfully change or limit its powers because ultimately acceptance of that change depends on whether the courts recognise and apply it, that is, the rule of recognition (see https://ukconstitutionallaw. org/2012/03/09/jeffrey-goldsworthy-parliamentary-sovereigntys-premature-obituary/).

6.3.3 Practical limitations

In practice, Parliament can develop constitutional conventions which, though not laws, effectively place self-imposed limits on its legislative powers; the prime example of this is the Sewel convention which acts as a voluntary cap on Parliament's power to legislate on devolved matters. In addition, political common sense and the influence of popular opinion impose practical limits on the laws that Parliament enacts. It could not, as Dicey pointed out, realistically enact a statute that demanded all blue-eyed babies be put to death, and the reaction of the people (and media) to a provision that clearly subverted the rule of law would need to be reckoned with (see P.P. Craig, 'Dicey: Unitary, Self-Correcting Democracy and Public Law' (1990) 106 LQR 105). The increasing use of referendums on constitutional matters has also raised issues. The outcome of a referendum is normally advisory, not legally binding, but in reality Parliament follows the result—as with Brexit—thus yielding ultimate decision-making to the people. (See House of Commons Public Administration and Constitutional Affairs Committee, *Lessons Learned from the EU Referendum*, 12th Report of Session 2016–17, HC 496 [7–14, 20–26].)

THINKING POINT

Do you think that referendums undermine or strengthen parliamentary sovereignty?

6.4 Modern views of parliamentary sovereignty in the courts

The case of *Jackson v AG* is one of the most significant cases on parliamentary sovereignty and encapsulates modern views on the subject.

CASE CLOSE-UP: *JACKSON v AG* **[2005] UKHL 56, [2006] 1 AC 262**

❯ **CROSS REFERENCE**

See section 10.4

This case involved a challenge to the validity of the Hunting Act 2004. The Act had been passed by invoking the Parliament Acts and had not been approved by the House of Lords. The claimants argued that the Hunting Act 2004 was not valid because the Parliament Act 1949 was not valid. This was because it had been passed by invoking the Parliament Act 1911, which meant that an Act altering the powers of the House of Lords had been passed without its assent. However, the court held that the 1911 Act had successfully redefined the powers of Parliament, removing the requirement for the Lords' assent to Bills in specified circumstances; therefore the 1949 Act had been validly passed, and so was the Hunting Act 2004.

The case highlighted differences of opinion within the House of Lords Appellate Committee on the strength of parliamentary sovereignty. Lord Bingham was clearly of the view that parliamentary sovereignty retained its classic force, observing that Parliament was 'unconstrained by any entrenched or codified constitution. It could make or unmake any law it wished. Statutes, formally enacted as Acts of Parliament, properly interpreted, enjoyed the highest legal authority' ([9]). Two members of the court steered markedly away from the classic view. Lord Steyn stated: 'The classic account given by Dicey of the doctrine of the supremacy of Parliament, pure and absolute as it was, can now be seen to be out of place in the modern United Kingdom. Nevertheless, the supremacy of Parliament is still the general principle of our constitution' ([102]).

Lord Hope took the view that:

> Our constitution is dominated by the sovereignty of Parliament. But Parliamentary sovereignty is no longer, if it ever was, absolute . . . It is no longer right to say that its freedom to legislate admits of no qualification whatever. Step by step, gradually but surely, the English principle of the absolute legislative sovereignty of Parliament which Dicey derived from Coke and Blackstone is being qualified. ([104])

However, Lord Hope added that these qualifications were mainly 'the product of measures enacted by Parliament' ([105]). Lady Hale expressed similar views on Parliament's limitation of its own powers by the European Communities Act 1972 for the duration of UK membership of the EU and the Human Rights Act 1998, adding that 'the constraints upon what Parliament can do are political and diplomatic rather than constitutional' ([159]).

By contrast, the Supreme Court was strongly protective of parliamentary sovereignty in the *Miller I* and *Miller/Cherry* cases, underscoring it as a fundamental principle of the UK constitution (*Miller I* [43, 183]; *Miller/Cherry* [41]). In *Miller/Cherry*, the court also highlighted a new angle of parliamentary sovereignty: Parliament must not be prevented by the government from exercising its legislative powers ([42]).

6.4.1 **The courts' interpretation of statutes**

The basic principle, as stated by Lord Hope, is that 'A sovereign Parliament is, according to the traditional view, immune from judicial scrutiny because it is protected by the principle of sovereignty' (*AXA General Insurance Ltd v Lord Advocate* [49]). Therefore it is not the role of judges to change, overturn, or question the validity of Acts of Parliament. Parliament can, of course, give specific interpretive duties to the courts in a statute; the ECA 1972 empowered the courts to interpret domestic law so far as possible consistently with EU law, and the HRA requires the courts to interpret statutes so as to be compatible with the rights in the European Convention on Human Rights. Both statutes were designed to ensure consistency between Acts of Parliament and the UK's international obligations under the EU treaties and the ECHR.

However, there is an argument that the courts can put limitations on statutes through their interpretation of them (though Dominic Grieve insists that 'the courts do no such thing': BPP speech, 25 October 2012). Laws LJ has observed that 'the construction of statutes is hardly ever a value-free exercise' (*A & Others v SSHD* [2004] EWCA Civ 1123, [2005] 1 WLR 414 [233]). In *Anisminic Ltd v Foreign Compensation Commission* [1969] 2 AC 147, for example, section 4(4) Foreign Compensation Act 1950 provided that decisions by the Foreign Compensation Commission 'shall not be called in question in any court of law', but the House of Lords interpreted it as meaning that the court *could* examine whether the Commission's decision was a nullity. Lord Reid manoeuvred neatly by stating:

> It is a well established principle that a provision ousting the ordinary jurisdiction of the court must be construed strictly—meaning, I think, that, if such a provision is reasonably capable of having two meanings, that meaning shall be taken which preserves the ordinary jurisdiction of the court. (p 170)

Similarly in *R (Privacy International) v Investigatory Powers Tribunal* [2019] UKSC 22, section 67(8) Regulation of Investigatory Powers Act 2000 excluded decisions of the Investigatory Powers Tribunal from appeal or challenge in court, but a Supreme Court majority strictly construed it and held that the wording was not clear enough to show that Parliament intended to exclude judicial review challenges based on an error of law ([107, 111]). See Chapters 9 and 15 for further discussion of this case.

6.4.2 The controlling common law

At a time when judges wielded significant power, Coke CJ in *Dr Bonham's Case* (1610) suggested that 'When an Act of Parliament is against common right and reason, or repugnant, or impossible to be performed, the common law will control it, and adjudge such Act to be void'. This has come to be known as 'the controlling common law' and some modern judges have reflected similar thoughts, giving rise to 'common law constitutionalism' as a challenger to parliamentary sovereignty, whereby the courts uphold fundamental common law values to the extent of being prepared to invalidate statutes that do not respect them. While the UK was a member of the EU, the courts could disapply UK statutes where they were inconsistent with EU law, but in doing this they were complying with the will of Parliament in the ECA 1972 to give primacy to EU law. We saw in section 6.2.2.2 that the doctrine of implied repeal requires the courts to apply the later statute where two statutes conflict, to avoid uncertainty in the application of law and uphold parliamentary sovereignty. However, in any other circumstances, if the courts decided not to apply a statute they would be in direct conflict with Parliament, which could provoke a constitutional crisis, and Goldsworthy takes the view that the judges would not have constitutional authority to disobey an Act of Parliament (see https://ukconstitutional-law.org/2012/03/09/).

Nevertheless, judges have sometimes expressed the possibility of limits on parliamentary sovereignty and of no longer recognising a statute as supreme law if Parliament crossed a constitutional red line, such as taking away the power of courts to judicially review actions of government ministers. Some members of the court in *Jackson v AG* suggested that if Parliament strayed beyond acceptable limits, the courts might be prepared not to apply the offending statute. Lord Steyn reasoned that as parliamentary sovereignty was created by the judges, the judges can change or remove it:

> If that is so, it is not unthinkable that circumstances could arise where the courts may have to qualify a principle established on a different hypothesis of constitutionalism. In exceptional circumstances involving an attempt to abolish judicial review or the ordinary role of the courts, the . . . Supreme Court may have to consider whether this is a constitutional fundamental which even a sovereign Parliament acting at the behest of a complaisant House of Commons cannot abolish. ([102])

▶ CROSS REFERENCE

For further details, see section 9.2.1

Lord Hope observed that as enforcers of the rule of law, 'the courts have a part to play in defining the limits of Parliament's legislative sovereignty' ([107]), while Lady Hale stated more overtly that the courts might even reject a statute that tried to remove the right to judicial review of governmental action ([159]).

 THINKING POINT

If this view is correct, which body would be at the top of the hierarchy in the UK constitution?

This view should not be overstated, however, as such clauses are likely to be voted down or removed as a Bill passes through the legislative process in Parliament; for example, in 2004 a proposed ouster clause in the Asylum and Immigration (Treatment of Claimants) Bill was withdrawn after criticism by the House of Commons Constitutional Affairs Committee, constitutional lawyers, and a former Lord Chancellor, and warnings by judges that the clause conflicted with the rule of law and was unlikely to be effective (see Lord Woolf, *The Rule of Law and a Change in the Constitution*, Squire Centenary Lecture, Cambridge, 3 March 2004). In effect, Parliament would be enacting something regarded as unconstitutional, but Lord Reid defined what 'unconstitutional' means in relation to the UK Parliament:

Definition

An ouster clause removes the courts' power of judicial review of a tribunal's decision

---

> It is often said that it would be unconstitutional for the United Kingdom Parliament to do certain things, meaning that the moral, political and other reasons against doing them are so strong that most people would regard it as highly improper if Parliament did these things. But that does not mean that it is beyond the power of Parliament to do such things. If Parliament chose to do any of them the Courts could not hold the Act of Parliament invalid. (*Madzimbamuto v Lardner-Burke* [1969] 1 AC 645, 723)

This comes back to the point that there is no written constitution against which to measure Parliament's authority, that parliamentary sovereignty is at the heart of the UK constitution, and it remains a powerful concept.

SUMMARY

- Parliamentary sovereignty is a cornerstone of the UK constitution. Parliament's legislative supremacy means that it has unchallenged authority to create law but one Parliament cannot bind another

- The courts' acceptance of Parliament's sovereignty is crucial to its sovereign authority

- Parliament has chosen to impose limits on its law-making powers through, for example, devolution and membership of the EU until the ECA 1972 was repealed

- There are differing views on whether Parliament can entrench changes to its powers. Parliament can impose changes which operate for as long as they are accepted by future parliaments, until there is the political will and consensus for change

- Some judges have expressed the possibility of limits on parliamentary sovereignty

? Questions

Self-test questions

1. What does parliamentary sovereignty mean?

2. Outline Dicey's description of parliamentary sovereignty.

3. Explain the idea that no Parliament may bind a successor.

4. How does the doctrine of implied repeal operate?

5. Do UK judges have the authority to set aside an Act of Parliament?

6. What is the rule of recognition?

7. Can Parliament create entrenched statutes?

8. Are the devolution Acts repealable?

9. What is meant by (a) continuing and (b) self-embracing sovereignty?

Exam question

The classic account given by Dicey of the doctrine of the supremacy of Parliament, pure and absolute as it was, can now be seen to be out of place in the modern United Kingdom. (*Jackson v Attorney General* [2005] UKHL 56, [102] (Lord Steyn))

To what extent is this an accurate description of parliamentary sovereignty in the modern UK constitution?

Further reading

Books

Bingham, T. *The Rule of Law* (London: Penguin Books 2011).
See chapter 12 for a clear, accessible discussion of parliamentary sovereignty

Goldsworthy, J. *The Sovereignty of Parliament: History and Philosophy* (Oxford: Clarendon Press 1999).
An authoritative assessment of parliamentary sovereignty

Gordon, M.J. *Parliamentary Sovereignty in the UK Constitution: Process, Politics and Democracy* (Oxford: Hart 2015).
Examines current challenges to parliamentary sovereignty

Jowell, J. and O'Cinneide, C. (eds) *The Changing Constitution* (9th edn, Oxford: Oxford University Press 2019).
See Mark Elliott's discussion of parliamentary sovereignty in chapter 2

Journal articles

Allan, T.R.S. 'Parliamentary Sovereignty: Law, Politics, and Revolution' (1997) 113 LQR 443.
An opposing view to Wade

Barber, N.W. 'Sovereignty Re-examined: The Courts, Parliament and Statutes' (2000) 20(1) Oxf J Leg Stud 131.
Turns sovereignty on its head and opens up the possibility of more than one source of legal power and different judicial reactions to statute

Elliott, M. 'United Kingdom: Parliamentary Sovereignty under Pressure' (2004) 2(3) Int J Const Law 545.
Surveys the pressures and effects of the ECA, the HRA, and devolution on parliamentary sovereignty

Ekins, R. 'Legislative Freedom in the United Kingdom' (2017) 133 (Oct) Law Quarterly Review 582.
Puts forward a refreshing argument that Parliament's legislative wings are unclipped

Ewing, K. 'Brexit and Parliamentary Sovereignty' (2017) 80(4) MLR 711.
A thorough analysis of various facets of parliamentary sovereignty in the light of Brexit

Jowell, J. 'Parliamentary Sovereignty under the New Constitutional Hypothesis' (2006) (Autumn) Public Law 562.
Examines parliamentary sovereignty in the light of the decision in *Jackson*

Wade, H.W.R. 'The Basis of Legal Sovereignty' (1955) 13(2) CLJ 172.
The seminal article on parliamentary sovereignty. See also Wade, H.W.R. 'Sovereignty—Revolution or Evolution?' (1996) 112 LQR 568

Other sources

House of Commons European Scrutiny Committee, *The EU Bill and Parliamentary Sovereignty*, 10th Report of Session 2010–11 HC 633-I.

Very clearly stated principles on parliamentary sovereignty, particularly at paras 9–28.

For contemporary academic views on parliamentary sovereignty, see House of Commons European Scrutiny Committee, *The EU Bill and Parliamentary Sovereignty: Written and Oral Evidence* HC 633-II (7 December 2010).

⨟ Online resources

www.oup.com/he/dennett2e

This chapter is accompanied by a selection of online resources to help you with this topic, including:

- Multiple-choice questions
- Answers to the self-test questions
- Guidance on answering the exam question

7 Separation of powers

☐ **LEARNING OBJECTIVES**

By the end of this chapter, you should be able to:

● Explain the nature and purpose of the separation of powers principle

● Discuss how partial separation of powers operates in the UK constitution

● Appraise the significance of checks and balances

● Evaluate the relationship between the three arms of state in the UK and identify areas where the boundaries are less clear

● Assess the reforms introduced by the Constitutional Reform Act 2005

Introduction

If you had been convicted of a crime and were appealing against your conviction, how would you feel if one of the judges hearing your appeal was also a government minister, or was also a member of the legislature which had passed the statute under which you had been convicted? This is what separation of powers is about: the distribution and division of power within the constitution, and the constitutional relationship and interaction between the three arms of state (the legislature, executive, and judiciary). In this chapter, we look at what this important constitutional principle means, and how far the UK constitution respects the separation of powers doctrine. We focus on the division of power and the delicate balance between the three arms of state in the modern UK constitution, the need for control and accountability (checks and balances), and the impact of the Constitutional Reform Act 2005.

7.1 The meaning and significance of separation of powers

The separation of powers is a doctrine requiring that executive, legislative, and judicial powers within a state should be clearly divided and allocated to separate institutions; the aim is to prevent the concentration of power in any one branch and reduce the potential for arbitrary or oppressive exercise of power (reflecting Lord Acton's well-known notion that 'power tends to corrupt, and absolute power corrupts absolutely'). Imagine the arms of state as three spheres; each has its own lawful arena with defined roles and functions to achieve balanced, well-defined power in a constitution. Although the degree of separation between the three branches varies between states, codified constitutions will regulate those spheres of power by allocating specific roles and functions to each branch (see, for example, the US Constitution) and will allow checks or controls to operate between them to ensure accountability.

7.1.1 Separation of powers theories

The concept that the three branches of governmental power within a state should be exercised separately to prevent a concentration of power is not a new one. In the seventeenth century, John Locke identified three types of power in a state: legislative, executive (internal affairs/law enforcement), and federative (international affairs) (*Two Treatises of Government*, 1690). Locke advocated a separate legislative authority because if law-makers also have the power to execute those laws, they may exempt themselves from the laws they make and use the law to their own private advantage. The founder of modern ideas on separation of powers was Baron Montesquieu, a French lawyer and political philosopher. After observing the English constitution, Montesquieu saw separation of powers in terms of protecting liberty and believed that state powers, including judicial power, should be distributed between the three arms of state (the tripartite model):

> When the legislative and executive powers are united in the same person, or in the same body of magistrates, there can be no liberty . . . there is no liberty if the power of judging be not separated from the legislative and executive powers . . . there would be an end of everything, were the same man or the same body . . . to exercise those three powers. (*The Spirit of the Laws*, 1748)

7.1.2 Pure and partial separation of powers

Pure separation of powers aims to prevent tyranny by strictly dividing power between the three branches; each has its own self-contained functions and membership, with no exertion of power or control by the others. This requires:

- institutional separation (the three institutions are separate);
- functional separation (each institution has separate functions);
- separation of personnel (each institution has different membership).

However, over-restricting state institutions in this way is not practical in a complex modern democratic state, so under partial separation of powers the branches have more freedom to overlap and interact, and Professor Bradley has noted that 'The interaction of judiciary, executive and legislature is a fundamental aspect of any constitution founded on democracy and the rule of law' (House of Lords Select Committee on the Constitution, *Relations between the Executive, the Judiciary and Parliament*, 6th Report of Session 2006–07, HL Paper 151, p 69 [2]). This allows the exercise of a degree of control between the branches through checks and balances, and although a state may have separate institutions, their functions or membership may overlap. (For further discussion of pure and partial separation of powers, see Barendt, 'Separation of Powers and Constitutional Government' in 'Further reading'.)

7.2 The operation of separation of powers in the UK

The classic model of the separation of powers is shown in Table 7.1.

In reality, the UK does not conform to this. Barber sees the essence of the separation of powers doctrine not as 'liberty, as many writers have assumed, but efficiency' ('Prelude to the Separation of Powers' 59, 'in 'Further reading'). This is particularly important in the UK with its system of mixed government, and rather than strict separation of powers the UK constitution adheres to partial separation, with an intermingling of powers and some significant overlaps. It operates a *balance* of powers to ensure efficiency, mutual respect, and harmonious relations between the arms of state—though tensions do exist from time to time where one branch appears to encroach on another's 'territory'.

We see from Figure 7.1 that separation of powers in the UK is weakest between the legislature and executive (this is common in parliamentary systems), and strongest and most distinct between the judiciary and the other two branches. (It should also be remembered that separation

Table 7.1 The classic model of the separation of powers

Legislature	Executive	Judiciary
• Law-makers	• Make and implement policy • Implement law	• Interpret and apply law

Figure 7.1 Separation of powers in the UK

Parliament

Executive

Judiciary

of powers applies in the devolved administrations which have been granted both legislative and executive powers by the UK Parliament.) Over the past 20 years, the dynamics between Parliament, the judiciary, and the executive have changed. The Human Rights Act 1998 has produced a more active judiciary while the Constitutional Reform Act 2005 has brought stronger separation between the judiciary and the executive, making the judiciary more autonomous, though tensions have sometimes flared between them (this is explored in Chapter 13). For an excellent mapping of the changing relationships between the three branches, see House of Lords Select Committee on the Constitution, *Relations between the Executive, the Judiciary and Parliament*, 6th Report of Session 2006–07, HL Paper 151.

7.2.1 The division of power in the UK

Lord Templeman succinctly summarised the essential functions of the three arms of state in the UK as: 'Parliament makes the law, the executive carry the law into effect and the judiciary enforce the law' (*M v Home Office* [1994] 1 AC 377, 395). Lord Mustill, meanwhile, said:

> It is a feature of the peculiarly British conception of the separation of powers that Parliament, the executive and the courts each have their distinct and largely exclusive domain. Parliament has a legally unchallengeable right to make whatever laws it thinks right. The executive carries on the administration of the country in accordance with the powers conferred on it by law. The courts interpret the laws, and see that they are obeyed. (*R v Secretary of State for the Home Department ex p Fire Brigades Union* [1995] 2 AC 513, 567)

However, while their functions are largely separate in broad terms, there is a sophisticated interplay at work between the three branches of UK government, which Lord Mustill went on to describe:

> This requires the courts on occasion to step into the territory which belongs to the executive, not only to verify that the powers asserted accord with the substantive law created by Parliament, but also, that the manner in which they are exercised conforms with the standards of fairness which Parliament must have intended. Concurrently with this judicial function Parliament has its own special means of ensuring that the executive, in the exercise of delegated functions, performs in a way which Parliament finds appropriate. (*Ex p Fire Brigades Union*, 567)

It can be seen from Lord Mustill's description that the balance of power is weighted towards Parliament: it has legislative supremacy, the judges are subordinate to Parliament, and both Parliament and the judiciary hold the executive to account. Parliament has greater authority than the executive and judiciary, so the UK institutions do not have equal weight. Lord Neuberger has identified that:

> in a parliamentary democracy without a constitution, I think that it is fair to say that there is a pecking order. First, there is the legislature who can always overrule court decisions; second come the judiciary, who have to give effect to statutes and respect to parliament, but are otherwise free to develop and enforce the law; and third comes the executive, who must comply with the law as laid down by the legislature and judiciary. (Lord Neuberger, 'The Role of Judges in Human Rights Jurisprudence: A Comparison of the Australian and UK Experience', Conference at the Supreme Court of Victoria, Melbourne, 8 August 2014, para 9)

 THINKING POINT

Consider this 'pecking order' and Lord Mustill's description. Why do you think the executive is subject to more control by the other two institutions?

Table 7.2 Areas of overlap in the UK constitution

The Prime Minister and government ministers are members of the executive and also members of Parliament (the legislature)

Government ministers can be given power by Parliament to make delegated legislation so have a law-making function

Judges have a law-making function through the creation of common law

The Attorney General is the chief law officer of the Crown and a member of the government, a role that can lead to conflicts of interest (see section 12.1.3)

Some executive procedures are judicial in nature, eg planning appeals

Judges can head public inquiries ordered by the government, eg the Grenfell Tower Inquiry

Before the Constitutional Reform Act 2005:

- the Lord Chancellor was a member of all three branches
- the UK's highest court of appeal (the Appellate Committee of the House of Lords) was in Parliament
- the most senior judges (the Law Lords) were also members of the legislature
- judges were appointed by the executive

THINKING POINT

Try to identify whether each of the above is an overlap between institutions, functions, or personnel (see 7.1.2).

Because of the way in which the UK's governmental institutions have evolved from the legislative, executive, and judicial powers of the monarch (see Chapter 2), their functions, powers, or personnel have not always been clearly divided, with the result that there is still some degree of overlap (see Table 7.2)—although historically there was even less separation than there is now. Parliament was also a court (the High Court of Parliament) and the House of Lords carried out a judicial function for centuries, while even in the nineteenth century, judges could be MPs and members of the executive.

7.2.2 The need for checks and balances

In the light of the lack of strict separation of powers just outlined, it is essential that mechanisms exist to regulate the relations between the three arms of state; these controls are known as 'checks and balances' and they ensure accountability. However, they are not expressly articulated in the UK's uncodified constitution, and Lord Mustill observed that 'much sensitivity is required of the parliamentarian, administrator and judge if the delicate balance of the unwritten rules evolved . . . in recent years is not to be disturbed' (*Fire Brigades Union case*, 567). This is an important point to appreciate: tacit understanding and mutual respect operates between the three branches to ensure that dividing lines are not crossed and there is no undue interference or encroachment which could cause conflict. Thus Bennion has noted that 'The unwritten constitution is a subtler, more organic, and more flexible framework. Instead of a broad (and

Figure 7.2 Direction of control over the executive

 **THINKING POINT**

Note the absence of control arrows flowing out from the executive, then note the discussion in section 7.3.

crude) separation of powers it operates by ensuring the independence of operation of certain organs of the state where it really matters' (Francis Bennion, 'Separation of Powers in Written and Unwritten Constitutions' (2006) 15 Com L 17, 22).

Similarly, Lord Hope describes how 'the delicate balance between the various institutions whose sound and lasting quality Dicey . . . likened to the work of bees when constructing a honeycomb is maintained to a large degree by the mutual respect which each institution has for the other' (*Jackson v Attorney General* [2005] UKHL 56, [2006] 1 AC 262 [125]).

In practice, the greatest potential for excessive power lies with the executive through action that might be arbitrary, unfair, or unlawful. The other two branches subject it to parliamentary and judicial control and accountability (this 'pincer movement' is shown in Figure 7.2) and we turn next to examine the relationships between each of the three arms of state.

 **SUMMARY**

The UK operates on a partial model of separation of powers which produces balance and efficiency but requires mutual respect and understanding. Checks and balances are important to ensure control and accountability between the branches of state.

7.3 The weakest separation: the legislature and executive

▶ CROSS REFERENCE
See Chapters 10–12 for details on Parliament and the executive

The legislature/executive division is the area of weakest separation and greatest overlap in the UK constitution. Bagehot referred to the 'efficient secret' of the 'almost complete fusion of legislative and executive power' because under the Westminster system, government ministers are drawn from within Parliament; the majority of ministers are members of the House of Commons, so are also elected MPs representing their constituencies. Ministers in both chambers of

Parliament are involved in the law-making process *and* the administrative process. However, Bagehot's reference to fusion is misleading because although the personnel may overlap, their functions as members of the executive differ from their functions within the legislature. Moreover, the House of Commons Disqualification Act 1975 imposes safeguards by:

- disqualifying judges, civil servants, members of the armed forces and police, and other prescribed office holders from membership of the House of Commons (section 1);
- providing that no more than 95 government ministers are to be members of the House of Commons (section 2).

There are also control mechanisms at work. Parliament exercises control over the executive in two ways:

1. It passes primary legislation which is legally binding on the executive, and where ministers are given statutory powers to make secondary (or delegated) legislation, they must act within the limits of the power conferred on them by Parliament. If not, their actions and decisions can be judicially reviewed by the courts.

2. Parliament holds the government to account. One of the most important aims of the separation of powers principle is to control or prevent excessive executive power, and parliamentary scrutiny through select committees and ministerial questions ensures that individual ministers and the government as a whole are accountable for their actions and decisions—although this is less effective with a weak Parliament and a powerful executive. See Chapter 11 for more details on holding the executive to account.

The executive does not exert control over Parliament in a checks-and-balances sense. However, in reality, if a party wins an election with a commanding majority, it will dominate the House of Commons due to the lack of separation between legislature and executive. This means that the government can be fairly assured of success in passing legislation because of the sheer numbers supporting its Bills (we explore this further in Chapter 11), and this creates a tension in the control model illustrated in Figure 7.2.

⫸ CROSS REFERENCE

See Chapter 13 for more detail on the judiciary

7.4 The judiciary

⫸ CROSS REFERENCE

These are also key requirements of the rule of law. See Chapter 8

The strongest separation of power in the UK is between the judiciary and the legislature/executive (see *DPP of Jamaica v Mollison* [2003] UKPC 6, [2003] 2 AC 411 [13]). This ensures: an independent judiciary free from external influence from Parliament and government; a legally accountable executive; unhindered access to the courts; and fair hearings. These features are crucial in a liberal democracy like the UK, and the Constitutional Reform Act 2005 did much to strengthen and widen the separation between the judiciary and the other two arms of government. The judiciary is unelected and is not directly accountable either to Parliament or the executive, but the 2016 *Guide to Judicial Conduct* required that 'the relationship between the judiciary and the other arms should be one of mutual respect, each recognising the proper role of the others' (*Guide to Judicial Conduct*, March 2013, amended July 2016, para 2.1). Lord Bingham also forcefully pointed out that:

> It is of course true that the judges in this country are not elected and are not answerable to Parliament. It is also of course true . . . that Parliament, the executive and the courts have different functions. But the function of independent judges charged to interpret and apply the law is universally recognised as a cardinal feature of the modern democratic state, a cornerstone of the rule of law itself. The Attorney General . . . is wrong to stigmatise judicial

decision-making as in some way undemocratic. (*A v Secretary of State for the Home Department* [2005] 2 AC 68 [42])

The judiciary's role is:

1. to interpret, apply and enforce the law in legal disputes;

2. to uphold the rule of law;

3. the High Court has an inherent supervisory role which enables it to carry out judicial review of executive action.

A key point to note is that in the absence of a codified constitution, it can also fall to the judges to decide where decision-making power lies between the three branches, as expressed by Lord Hoffmann in the *Pro-life Alliance case*:

> In a society based upon the rule of law and the separation of powers, it is necessary to decide which branch of government has in any particular instance the decision-making power and what the legal limits of that power are. That is a question of law and must therefore be decided by the courts. (*R (Pro-life Alliance) v BBC* [2003] UKHL 23, [2004] 1 AC 185 [75])

CASE CLOSE-UPS: *R (MILLER) v SECRETARY OF STATE FOR EXITING THE EUROPEAN UNION* **[2017] UKSC 5 ('MILLER I') AND** *R (MILLER) v THE PRIME MINISTER; CHERRY AND OTHERS v ADVOCATE GENERAL FOR SCOTLAND* **[2019] UKSC 41**

In the *Miller I* case, the Supreme Court had to identify where the division of responsibility lay between Parliament and the government in relation to triggering the UK's withdrawal from the EU. The government argued that it had the prerogative power to withdraw from treaties; the applicants argued that because legal rights under EU law would no longer apply, giving notice to withdraw would change the law, which is a matter for Parliament, not the government. The court agreed with the applicants and decided that an Act of Parliament was needed to authorise ministers to begin the withdrawal process (*Miller I* [34–36], [99–101]). (See N. Barber, T. Hickman, and J. King, 'Pulling the Article 50 "Trigger": Parliament's Indispensable Role', UK Const L Blog, 27 Jun 2016, available at https://ukconstitutionallaw.org/.)

In *Miller/Cherry*, an important case on separation of powers, the Supreme Court had to determine the legal limits of the prerogative power of prorogation, and held that the Prime Minister's decision to prorogue Parliament was unlawful because it trespassed on Parliament's ability to carry out its constitutional functions of legislating and holding the government to account (*R (Miller) v The Prime Minister; Cherry and others v Advocate General for Scotland* [2019] UKSC 41 [37–51]). It was, said the court, 'their particular responsibility to determine the legal limits of the powers conferred on each branch of government, and to decide whether any exercise of power has transgressed those limits' [39].

7.4.1 The judiciary and Parliament

There is no parliamentary control over the judicial process; the only way in which Parliament can exert supremacy over the courts is through statute, or in order to remove a senior judge from office because of misconduct (this has only happened once, in 1830; see section 13.4.2).

However, while Parliament will not interfere in judicial decision-making, it *can* pass statutes that override judicial decisions (see, eg, *Burmah Oil v Lord Advocate* [1965] AC 75 and the War Damage Act 1965 in Chapter 6). Emphasising that the judiciary is an independent arm of government, Lord Neuberger observes:

> In a country which has no constitution and does have parliamentary sovereignty, the Judges traditionally enjoy a relatively limited function as against the legislature. They cannot quash any statutes enacted by the legislature. Judges also know that any decision they take which a majority of the legislature does not like can be overturned by a simple majority in Parliament. (Lord Neuberger, 'The Role of Judges in Human Rights Jurisprudence', para 9)

In short, Parliament can change the common law but judges cannot change Acts of Parliament, thus respecting parliamentary sovereignty.

Equally, the courts do not interfere in parliamentary processes and Table 7.3 summarises the courts' relationship with Parliament.

It is fair to say that judges can exert subtle influence on the legislative process, either through dicta in cases calling for a change in the law—which, it must be emphasised, are *not* binding on Parliament but which can start the debate rolling (for example, dicta in the Court of Appeal in *Al Rawi v Security Service* [2010] EWCA Civ 482 led to the passing of the Justice and Security Act 2013, which governs how sensitive material can be disclosed in court)—and through Select Committee consultation with the judiciary on proposed Bills within carefully defined limits (see section 13.5.1 and Lord Woolf, 'The Rule of Law and a Change in Constitution', Squire

Table 7.3 The courts' relationship with Parliament

The courts clearly see Parliament as maker of law and judges as interpreters of law. Traditionally, in the words of Lord Diplock, 'it cannot be too strongly emphasised that the British constitution, though largely unwritten, is firmly based upon the separation of powers; Parliament makes the laws, the judiciary interpret them' (*Duport Steels v Sirs* [1980] 1 WLR 142, 157).

The courts do not enquire into the legislative process (*Pickin v BRB* [1974] AC 765), although they can examine what was said in parliamentary debates to resolve ambiguities in legislation (*Pepper v Hart* [1993] 1 All ER 42). In the *HS2 case* (*R (HS2 Action Alliance Limited) v Secretary of State for Transport* [2014] UKSC 3, [2014] 1 WLR 324), the Supreme Court interpreted the EU's Environmental Impact Assessment Directive 2011/92/EU so as not to require the court to scrutinise the legislative process in Parliament, thus upholding the separation of powers as a constitutional principle.

Judges respect parliamentary sovereignty as a central plank of the constitution (though see Chapter 9, where the views expressed by some members of the judiciary are a potentially radical deviation from this).

Because of their subordinate role to Parliament, judges have never had the power to judicially review primary legislation made by the UK Parliament or strike down an Act of Parliament and declare it void. They accept statutes as valid because they are made by Parliament (*Cheney v Conn* [1968] 1 All ER 779), though some judges have referred to the theoretical power to invalidate statutes that do not respect fundamental common law values (*Dr Bonham's Case* (1610); *Jackson v AG* [2005] UKHL 56; see section 6.4.2).

However, they can judicially review secondary legislation and the actions of the executive to ensure that they act within the law, and judges can review both primary and secondary legislation made by the devolved administrations.

Centenary Lecture, Cambridge, 3 March 2004). However, the dividing line between the territory of Parliament and the judiciary is not always clear-cut, as we will see in the next section.

7.4.1.1 The dividing line between legislation and judicial law-making

In the eighteenth century, Blackstone put forward the view that judges do not make law; they declare what the law is. However, this is regarded as outdated and it is accepted that the common law is judge-made law. Lord Nicholls has described the common law as 'a living system of law, reacting to new events and new ideas', adding that '[c]ontinuing but limited development of the common law . . . is an integral part of the constitutional function of the judiciary' (*National Westminster Bank plc v Spectrum Plus Limited* [2005] UKHL 41, [2005] 2 AC 680 [32]). However, it is important to be clear that creating common law is not assuming a legislative role and usurping Parliament; it is a judicial function. Parliament is the legislator because it (or at least the House of Commons) is a democratically elected institution representing public opinion, and judges have to exercise care not to cross the boundary between developing the law and legislating, though in *Woolwich Building Society v Inland Revenue Commissioners* [1993] AC 70, Lord Goff confessed: 'I feel bound . . . to say that, although I am well aware of the existence of the boundary, I am never quite sure where to find it. Its position seems to vary from case to case' (p 173).

When deciding cases, the courts must be mindful of the dividing line between issues that are suitable for decision by judges and those more appropriate for the elected legislature. Lord Scarman suggested that 'the objective of judges is the formulation of principles; policy is the prerogative of Parliament' (*McLoughlin v O'Brian* [1983] 1 AC 410) but this division is not always clear. As a general rule, social, economic, or other policy issues and allocation of resources are Parliament's province. This is because the parliamentary process is better equipped to debate and decide these issues and take into account wider competing interests in society. The courts can only take account of the interests of the parties in a case before them, which gives a much narrower focus on an issue. (See Lord Sumption, 'The Limits of Law', 27th Sultan Azlan Shah Lecture, Kuala Lumpur, 20 November 2013.) Lord Bingham has stated:

> The degree of respect to be shown to the considered judgment of a democratic assembly will vary according to the subject matter and the circumstances . . . The democratic process is liable to be subverted if, on a question of moral and political judgment, opponents of the [Hunting] Act achieve through the courts what they could not achieve in Parliament. (*R (Countryside Alliance) v Attorney General* [2008] 1 AC 719 [45])

Locating the boundary can prove particularly problematic in cases involving a moral, ethical, or religious dimension, and the need for mutual respect and understanding of respective constitutional positions is illustrated in the 'right to die' cases below.

 CASE CLOSE-UPS: FINDING THE DIVIDING LINE BETWEEN PARLIAMENT AND THE COURTS

You need to be aware that section 2 Suicide Act 1961 prohibits assisting another person to commit suicide.

R (Pretty) v DPP [2001] UKHL 61, [2002] 1 AC 800

Diane Pretty, who had motor neurone disease, asked the Director of Public Prosecutions (DPP) for an assurance that her husband would not be prosecuted if he assisted her

CROSS REFERENCE

The cases below also raised significant human rights issues. See Chapter 18 suicide. The DPP refused and Mrs Pretty challenged his refusal in the courts. On the issue of whose decision it was to decriminalise assisted suicide, Lord Bingham said that the court's duty was to resolve issues of law; it was not a legislative body or 'a moral or ethical arbiter' ([2]). Lord Steyn said it was a matter for democratic debate and decision-making by the legislature ([57]) and was for Parliament to 'strike the balance between the interests of the community and the rights of individuals' ([62]). Lord Hope stated that a change in the law making assisted suicide acceptable was a matter for Parliament because of competing moral arguments and a lack of consensus in public opinion in favour of assisted suicide ([96]).

R (Purdy) v DPP [2009] UKHL 45, [2010] 1 AC 345

Debbie Purdy suffered from multiple sclerosis and her husband was willing to help her travel to Switzerland to end her life, but could have faced prosecution in England for assisting her suicide. Ms Purdy sought judicial review of the DPP's refusal to publicise the criteria used to decide when to prosecute. The House of Lords made it clear that only Parliament, not the DPP, could authorise suspension of a law. Again, the court emphasised that it was not its function to change the law to decriminalise assisted suicide and any changes were a matter for Parliament. 'We do not venture into that arena, nor would it be right for us to do so. Our function as judges is to say what the law is and, if it is uncertain, to do what we can to clarify it' (Lord Hope [26]).

In *R (Nicklinson) v Ministry of Justice* **[2014] UKSC 38, [2015] AC 657**, there was a clear sense of the judges feeling their way carefully forward in a difficult case. Three men who were severely paralysed wanted to be allowed to end their lives with assistance (one had died by the time of the Supreme Court hearing) but were unsuccessful in challenging the law and the DPP's policy on assisted suicide. The court had to consider 'the limits of the courts' deference to Parliament's judgment' on criminalising assisting suicide (Lord Neuberger [78]) and it was 'not easy to identify in any sort of precise way the location of the boundary between the area where it is legitimate for the courts to step in and rule that a statutory provision, which is not irrational, infringes the [European Convention on Human Rights] and the area where it is not' ([101]). Five members of the Supreme Court held that the court had the authority to consider whether section 2 infringed Article 8 ECHR but three took the view that it was so controversial that Parliament should consider it first. Four members of the court decided that the question of whether the law on assisted suicide was incompatible with the ECHR was a matter for Parliament. Lord Sumption, for example, believed that it was 'an inherently legislative issue for Parliament, as the representative body in our constitution, to decide' and that it would lack 'constitutional legitimacy' if judges imposed their personal views on such matters (see [230–234]).

Lord Neuberger and Lord Sumption disagreed as to whether the Supreme Court was constitutionally and institutionally well placed to decide on assisted suicide. Lord Neuberger stated that judges may be better placed to take difficult or unpopular decisions:

> Although judges are not directly accountable to the electorate, there are occasions when their relative freedom from pressures of the moment enables them to take a more detached view. As Lord Brown said in the Countryside Alliance case at para 158, '[s]ometimes the majority misuses its powers. Not least this may occur when what are perceived as moral issues are involved' ([104]).

Lord Neuberger acknowledged, however, that the legislature has the final say, but since the *Nicklinson* decision Parliament has rejected three private members' bills seeking to change the law on assisted dying; another Bill was introduced in the House of Lords in January 2020.

For a clear discussion of separation of powers issues, *see R (Newby) v Secretary of State for Justice* [2019] EWHC 3118 (Admin) [38–43]. For further reading in this area, see:

> The Rt Hon Lord Dyson, Master of the Rolls, 'Are the Judges Too Powerful?' Presidential Address, Bentham Association, 12 March 2014
> W Friedmann, 'Limits of Judicial Lawmaking and Prospective Overruling' (1966) 29(6) MLR 593 (see p 595 on the division of power between legislators, administrators, and the courts)
> Lord Reid, 'The Judge as Lawmaker' (1972) 12 J Socy Pub Tchrs L 22
> Jonathan Sumption QC, 'Judicial and Political Decision-Making: The Uncertain Boundary', F.A. Mann Lecture 2011
> Jonathan Sumption, The Reith Lectures 2019, 'Law and the Decline of Politics', Lecture 2: 'In Praise of Politics', 28 May 2019, available at www.bbc.co.uk/radio4

Sumption argues that the increased constitutional role of judges has brought them into the arena of legislative and ministerial policy so that 'law is now the continuation of politics by other means'; reviewing the merits of policy decisions for which ministers are answerable to Parliament 'confers vast discretionary powers' on judges who are not constitutionally accountable and undermines the chief advantage of the political process: accommodating the varied interests and opinions of citizens (Reith Lecture 2, 2019).

 SUMMARY

There is strong separation and mutual respect between the judiciary and Parliament, but it is not always easy to find a clear dividing line between issues for Parliament and issues which the courts are competent to decide. In the absence of a codified constitution, it is a matter of determining who has 'institutional authority' to decide.

7.4.2 The judiciary and the executive

In *M v Home Office*, where the court found the Home Secretary in contempt of court, Nolan LJ in the Court of Appeal expressed the principle that 'The proper constitutional relationship of the executive with the courts is that the courts will respect all acts of the executive within its lawful province, and that the executive will respect all decisions of the courts as to what its lawful province is' (*M v Home Office* [1992] QB 270, 314–15). The executive must not interfere in the judicial process or influence judicial decisions—as Lord Steyn has noted, a 'cosy relationship between Ministers and Law Lords would be a worrying development' ('Democracy, the Rule of Law and the Role of Judges' (2006) EHRLR at 248)—nor, by convention, should government ministers publicly criticise judges (though this sometimes happens—see Chapter 13 and for a discussion of the *Sweeney case* in June 2006 involving criticism by the executive of the judiciary, see House of Lords Select Committee on the Constitution, *Relations between the Executive, the Judiciary and Parliament*, 6th Report of Session 2006–07, HL Paper 151, pp 18–21).

> ❱ CROSS REFERENCE
>
> See discussion of this case in section 8.3.1

In a democratic society, an independent judiciary is a bulwark against an over-powerful state (see *Yukos Capital S.A.R.L v OJSC Rosneft Oil Company* [2012] EWCA Civ 855 [21, 90] for comments on the Russian courts' subservience to matters of state interest). In the UK constitution, the judiciary plays a crucial role in ensuring the accountability of the executive, so it is vital that judges are independent from the executive to safeguard the rights and freedoms of individuals and uphold the rule of law. The most important ways in which the judiciary keeps a check on the executive are:

1. through judicial review—an important process of judicial scrutiny of executive actions;

2. under the Human Rights Act—judges measure executive decisions and actions against the ECHR to ensure compatibility with human rights.

The independence of the UK's judiciary is guaranteed by section 3 Constitutional Reform Act 2005; section 3(5) provides that the executive must not seek to influence judicial decisions through special access to the judiciary. The Lord Chancellor 'must ensure that the judiciary are free to act without undue pressure from the executive, that the executive respects the outcome of court judgments, and that the legal system is adequately resourced' (Constitution Committee, *The Office of Lord Chancellor* 6th Report of Session 2014–15, HL Paper 75 [142]).

7.4.2.1 Judicial deference

Judges need to find the legal dividing line in cases involving policy-based issues (this is particularly important in judicial review cases) and will respect decisions of the executive on politically sensitive issues. 'Judicial deference' describes recognition by the courts that in certain cases, they should not step into the decision-maker's territory (the courts can defer to Parliament or the executive, though Lord Sumption has criticised the term's 'overtones of cringing abstention in the face of superior status' (see *R (Lord Carlile of Berriew QC) v Secretary of State for the Home Department* [2014] UKSC 60, [2015] AC 945 [22])). Also known as 'judicial restraint', deference demonstrates the self-regulating aspect of the separation of powers in practice; the courts place self-imposed limits on their jurisdiction to determine certain issues, as Lord Hoffmann has pointed out:

> [T]he courts often have to decide the limits of their own decision-making power . . . But it does not mean that their allocation of decision-making power to the other branches of government is a matter of courtesy or deference . . . when a court decides that a decision is within the proper competence of the legislature or executive, it is not showing deference. It is deciding the law. (*Pro-life Alliance case*, [76])

We consider now examples of judicial 'deference' to the executive which shows Bennion's idea of independent operation of state organs 'where it really matters'.

 CASE CLOSE-UPS: JUDICIAL DEFERENCE

There are areas of executive power—especially national security, foreign policy, the decision to go to war, and resource allocation in the welfare state—where judges will not intervene when issues of a highly political nature arise. It is a question of deciding who has 'institutional legitimacy' (which institution is best equipped) to make a decision. In these cases, the executive is the primary decision-maker and Laws LJ describes below the courts' approach although deciding how much weight to give to the primary decision-maker's view 'can be elusive and problematic' (*R (Al Rawi) v Secretary of State for Foreign and Commonwealth Affairs* [2006] EWCA Civ 1279, [2008] QB 289 [146]):

The elected government has a special responsibility in . . . strategic fields of policy, such as the conduct of foreign relations and matters of national security. It arises in part from considerations of competence, in part from the constitutional imperative of electoral accountability . . . The court's role is to see that the government strictly complies with all formal requirements, and rationally considers the matters it has to confront. Here, because of the subject matter, the law accords to the executive an especially broad margin of discretion . . . But it is the court's duty to decide where lies the legal edge between the executive and judicial functions. (*Al Rawi* [147–148])

 THINKING POINT

What does 'electoral accountability' mean and why is it important here?

National security

Secretary of State for the Home Department v Rehman [2001] UKHL 47, [2003] 1 AC 153

The Home Secretary ordered Mr Rehman to be deported from the UK on grounds of national security. Lord Hoffmann said deciding whether something was in the interests of national security was a matter for the executive, not judges ([50, 53]), because the executive has access to special information and expertise in these matters; decisions such as this can have 'serious potential results for the community' so they need to be made by democratically elected individuals ([62]). 'This does not mean that the whole decision on whether deportation would be in the interests of national security is surrendered to the Home Secretary . . . it is important neither to blur nor to exaggerate the area of responsibility entrusted to the executive' ([54]).

See also *A v Secretary of State for the Home Department* [2005] 2 AC 68: 'It is the function of political and not judicial bodies to resolve political questions. Conversely, the greater the legal content of any issue, the greater the potential role of the court, because . . . it is the function of the courts and not of political bodies to resolve legal questions' ([29] (Lord Bingham)).

Foreign policy

R (Al-Haq) v Secretary of State for Foreign and Commonwealth Affairs [2009] EWHC 1910 (Admin)

The claimants applied for (a) a declaration that the UK government's response to Israel's military action in Gaza in 2008/9 had breached the UK's international obligations, and (b) an order requiring the UK to denounce and respond to Israel's actions. Pill LJ stated: 'Constitutionally, the conduct of foreign affairs is exclusively within the sphere of the executive . . . While there may, exceptionally, be situations in which the court will intervene in foreign policy issues, this case is far from being one of them' ([46]). This was because the object of the claim was effectively to tell the UK government to condemn Israel and dictate what foreign policy it should follow. It concerned matters of policy involving international relations, and therefore could not be considered by the courts.

See also *R (Abbasi) v Secretary of State for Foreign and Commonwealth Affairs and Secretary of State for the Home Department* [2002] EWCA Civ 1598, [2003] UKHRR 76.

R (Lord Carlile of Berriew QC) v Secretary of State for the Home Department [2014] UKSC 60, [2015] AC 945

The claimants (members of the House of Lords and the Commons) wanted to meet an Iranian politician at Westminster to discuss human rights and democracy issues in Iran. She lived in France but had been excluded from the UK since 1997 because of her involvement with an Iranian political group that had previously been banned as a terrorist organisation. The claimants asked the Home Secretary to lift the exclusion but, following advice from the Foreign Office, the Home Secretary refused because of possible reprisals by Iran which might put British economic and diplomatic interests, and British nationals, at risk. The claimants argued that the Home Secretary's decision was unlawful and contravened the right to freedom of expression under the European Convention on Human Rights. The Supreme Court held that it would not interfere with the Home Secretary's decision because it was based on an assessment of matters of international relations and national interests which fell within the executive's area of competence and expertise. They were not matters which the court had sufficient evidence or knowledge to judge (see [22–28] and [68]).

> Judges should always be vigilant and fearless in carrying out their duty to ensure that individuals' legal rights are not infringed by the executive. But judges must also bear in mind that any decision of the executive has to be accorded respect—in general because the executive is the primary decision-maker, and in particular where the decision is based on an assessment which the executive is peculiarly well equipped to make and the judiciary is not. ([57] (Lord Neuberger))

Going to war

The courts have traditionally shown restraint in ruling on the executive's decision to go to war because they recognise the limitations on their competence to judge the issues involved. See *R (Gentle) v The Prime Minister* [2008] UKHL 20, [2008] AC 1356; *R v Jones (Margaret)* [2007] 1 AC 13 [30], [65–67].

Making treaties

The courts have repeatedly emphasised that making treaties is a political matter for the executive, not the courts. See *Blackburn v AG* [1971] 2 All ER 1380; *R v Secretary of State for Foreign and Commonwealth Affairs ex parte Rees-Mogg* [1994] QB 552; *R (Wheeler) v Office of the Prime Minister* [2008] EWHC 1409 (Admin), [2008] All ER (D) 333 (Jun).

For further reading, see:

Jeffrey Jowell, 'Judicial Deference: Servility, Civility or Institutional Capacity?' (2003) (Winter) Public Law 592

Lord Steyn, 'Deference: A Tangled Story' (2005) (Summer) Public Law 346

However, in *Miller/Cherry*, although the High Court had regarded the prorogation of Parliament as a political issue and not a matter for the court to determine, the Supreme Court disagreed and decided that it had a legitimate role in deciding the matter ([31–34]). The government had argued that the courts should respect the separation of powers and not enter the political arena ([28]) but, while acknowledging that it could not decide political questions, the court stated that by ensuring that the Prime Minister was not using the power of prorogation unlawfully so as to prevent Parliament from carrying out its constitutional functions, the court was promoting separation of powers ([34]; see also [33, 36, 47]); and the fact that the Prime Minister is accountable to Parliament did not exclude the courts from deciding the issue.

7.5 The Constitutional Reform Act 2005

Before 2005, there were three separation-of-powers issues involving the judiciary:

1. the Lord Chancellor was involved in all three arms of government;
2. the highest court of appeal (the Appellate Committee of the House of Lords) was in Parliament, and its judges were members of the judiciary and the legislature;
3. the executive appointed judges.

The Lord Chancellor: The Lord Chancellor was Speaker of the House of Lords, headed the Lord Chancellor's Department and was a senior member of the Cabinet, was head of the judiciary in England and Wales, and could sit as a judge in the Appellate Committee of the House of Lords and the Judicial Committee of the Privy Council. Walter Bagehot criticised the office of the Lord Chancellor as 'a heap of anomalies' (*The English Constitution*, 1867). Lord Woolf, however, has pointed out the positive aspects of the arrangement. The Lord Chancellor was a conduit between the judiciary and executive and could 'act as a lightning conductor at times of high tension between the executive and the judiciary' (Lord Woolf, 'The Rule of Law and a Change in Constitution', Squire Centenary Lecture, Cambridge, 3 March 2004). Embedding the head of the judiciary in government ensured dialogue that brought benefits to the justice system:

> He can explain to his colleagues in the Cabinet the proper significance of a decision which they regard as being distasteful in consequence of an application for judicial review. He can, as a member of the Government, ensure that the courts are properly resourced. On the other hand, on behalf of the Government, he can explain to the judiciary the realities of the political situation and the constraints on the resources which they must inevitably accept. (Harry Woolf, 'Judicial Review—the Tensions between the Executive and the Judiciary' (1998) 114 LQR 579, 582)

See also Johan Steyn, 'The Weakest and Least Dangerous Department of Government' (1997) (Spring) Public Law 84; Lord Lester of Herne Hill, House of Lords, Hansard 17 Feb 1999, Vol 597 col 711.

The Appellate Committee of the House of Lords: For historical reasons, the House of Lords was both a chamber of Parliament and the highest court of appeal. The Appellate Jurisdiction Act 1876 created Lords of Appeal in Ordinary (known as Law Lords) to hear appeals but although they were judges, the Law Lords were also members of the legislative chamber of the House of Lords, so had the right to speak in the House and vote on legislation. They could provide independent expert legal knowledge and act as a check on clauses in Bills, though a convention developed where they would not speak on controversial matters, and if a Law Lord spoke against a measure in debate they were precluded from sitting as a judge in subsequent relevant cases.

> Note the role of constitutional conventions in limiting powers of the arms of government here.

The appointment of judges by the executive: Before the Constitutional Reform Act, judges were appointed by the Lord Chancellor, normally after consulting senior judges about suitable candidates. Judicial appointments to the Court of Appeal and the House of Lords (as it was then) were made by the Prime Minister on the Lord Chancellor's advice.

In 2003, Tony Blair announced that he was abolishing the office of Lord Chancellor; there was some support for this proposal but, in the face of opposition, it was thinned down to reforming

▶ CROSS REFERENCE
See section 3.1.2 for more
details on this

the office. It coincided with judicial criticism of members of the legislature/executive who also sat as judges (*McGonnell v UK* [2000] ECHR 62; *Davidson v The Scottish Ministers* [2004] UKHL 34), although Lord Irvine, a former Lord Chancellor, did not sit as a judge in most cases and his successor, Lord Falconer, did not sit as a judge at all. In 2004 the government and judiciary entered into an agreement called a concordat, a constitutionally significant document which set out the arrangements for dividing the Lord Chancellor's judicial and administrative roles, guaranteed the continued independence of the judiciary, and governed the future relationship between the judges and the executive.

> The Constitutional Reform Act 2005 made three important changes:
>
> - It reformed the office of Lord Chancellor (see Table 7.4).
> - It created a new Supreme Court to replace the Appellate Committee of the House of Lords, separating the judicial face of the House of Lords from the legislative chamber.
> - It created the Judicial Appointments Commission.

The Act also embodied two fundamental constitutional principles: the independence of the judiciary (section 3) and the rule of law (section 1). A recent research project found that judicial independence has become stronger since 2005. The judiciary is 'institutionally more independent of the executive, and of the legislature'; it has 'greater autonomy and responsibility for running the judicial system and the courts; and there are now multiple guardians of judicial independence as a value, instead of the single Lord Chancellor' (Robert Hazell, 'Judicial Independence and Accountability in the UK Have Both Emerged Stronger as a Result of the Constitutional Reform Act 2005' (2015) (April) Public Law 198, 201).

While the Lord Chancellor need no longer be a qualified lawyer, the Constitution Committee has concluded that 'a legal or constitutional background is a distinct advantage' and recommended that either the Permanent Secretary at the Ministry of Justice should be legally qualified, or the department's top legal advisor should be appointed at permanent secretary level (Constitution Committee, *The Office of Lord Chancellor* [153]).

The Supreme Court: The Supreme Court came into operation in 2009 (section 23) and is situated in the old Middlesex Guildhall in Parliament Square, so is also physically separate from Parliament. It has the same powers as the Appellate Committee of the House of Lords (unlike Supreme Courts in other states, it does *not* have the constitutional power to strike down Acts of Parliament). The Law Lords became known as Justices of the Supreme Court; the first Justices are still members of the legislative chamber of the House of Lords, but cannot sit and vote in the House until retirement. Subsequently appointed Justices are not members of the House of Lords (section 137 Constitutional Reform Act 2005 disqualifies all senior serving judges from sitting and voting in the House of Lords).

The Judicial Appointments Commission: This is an independent body which selects candidates on merit through open competition, and makes recommendations for judicial appointment to the Secretary of State for Justice/Lord Chancellor. This reform was designed to increase openness and transparency and visibly reduce the role of the executive in judicial appointments.

For more details on the Act, see House of Lords Select Committee on the Constitution, *Relations between the Executive, the Judiciary and Parliament*, 6th Report of Session 2006–07, HL Paper 151, Appendix 3, Paper by Professor Kate Malleson, 'The Effect of the Constitutional Reform Act 2005 on the Relationship between the Judiciary, the Executive and Parliament'.

Table 7.4 How the Constitutional Reform Act 2005 changed the office of Lord Chancellor

Judicial role	No longer the head of the judiciary; that role is now carried out by the Lord Chief Justice. S/he no longer sits as a judge so need not be a lawyer.	Section 7 Section 2(1) Section 17 sets out the Lord Chancellor's oath to respect the rule of law and defend judicial independence
Executive role	The Lord Chancellor retains a position as a member of the executive as a senior Cabinet minister and is now also the Secretary of State for Justice heading the Ministry of Justice. Now acts on recommendations of Judicial Appointments Commission to appoint judges.	Section 61
Legislative role	No longer Speaker of House of Lords. Not now a member of the House of Lords but is a member of the House of Commons so retains a role in the legislature.	Section 18 introduced an elected Speaker of the House of Lords

SUMMARY

- The UK operates partial separation with some overlaps. There is no pressing need for absolute separation of powers in the UK because it would be impractical in a constitution which is efficient at managing co-operation, mutual understanding, and balance between the institutions

- There is weak separation between Parliament and the executive; Parliament exerts control over the government through the principle of accountable government but a strong government can dominate Parliament

- The courts respect decisions of the democratically accountable executive on questions of political judgment which the courts are not as well equipped to decide

- Since 2005, the UK constitution has moved towards a stricter separation of powers in relation to the judiciary; the most important division is seen in a judiciary that is distinct from the other two arms of state

Lord Woolf summed up the separation of powers in the UK in 2004:

we have benefited from a tradition of mutual respect, restraint and co-operation between the three arms of Government. Of course there have been times of tension, but with good sense and good will on all sides they have been successfully managed. This was made easier not because of the separation of powers, but because of the absence of the separation of powers. ('The Rule of Law and a Change in the Constitution')

Questions

Self-test questions

1. What is meant by the separation of powers?

2. What is the purpose of separation of powers?

3. Explain (a) pure and (b) partial separation of powers. Which model does the UK operate?

4. Overall, how is power divided in the UK?

5. What are 'checks and balances' and why are they important?

6. Which branch is subject to most control by the others?

7. What did Bagehot mean by the 'almost complete fusion of legislative and executive power' in the UK?

8. How did Nolan LJ describe the relationship between the executive and the judiciary?

9. Why is it important to have an independent judiciary?

10. Which three important reforms did the Constitutional Reform Act 2005 introduce?

Exam question

'The separation of powers has no relevance in the UK constitution.' Discuss.

Further reading

Books

Tomkins, A. *Public Law* (Oxford: Clarendon Press 2003).
A clear, detailed survey of pre-CRA separation of powers in chapter 2

Wheatle, S. *Principled Reasoning in Human Rights Adjudication* (Oxford and Port-land, Oregon: Hart Publishing 2017).
Read chapter 4 for a detailed analysis of the application of separation of powers in the UK

Journal articles

Barber, N.W. 'Prelude to the Separation of Powers' (2001) 60(1) Cambridge Law Journal 59.
A thought-provoking evaluation of separation of powers

Barendt, E. 'Separation of Powers and Constitutional Government' (1995) (Winter) Public Law 599.
A classic discussion and an essential read on pure and partial separation

Bruff, H.H. 'The President and Congress: Separation of Powers in the United States of America' (2014) 35(2) Adelaide Law Review 205.
For a comparative angle, offers an assessment of separation of powers in the USA and the stretching of powers by presidents, and a particularly interesting section on targeted killing

Masterman, R. and Wheatle, S. 'Unpacking Separation of Powers: Judicial Independence, Sovereignty and Conceptual Flexibility in the UK Constitution' (2017) (July) Public Law 469.
See this article for more advanced arguments on the role of separation of powers in judicial decision-making

Other sources

House of Commons Library Standard Note, *The Separation of Powers*, Richard Benwell and Oonagh Gay, 15 August 2011 SN/PC/06053.
A helpful explanation of separation-of-powers principles and operation

Online resources

www.oup.com/he/dennett2e

This chapter is accompanied by a selection of online resources to help you with this topic, including:

- Multiple-choice questions
- Answers to the self-test questions
- Guidance on answering the exam question

8 Rule of law

□ **LEARNING OBJECTIVES**

By the end of this chapter, you should be able to:

● Discuss the purpose of the rule of law

● Evaluate different meanings of the rule of law

● Distinguish between formal and substantive theories on the rule of law

● Assess the practical application of the rule of law in the UK

Introduction

What would happen if Parliament decided to abolish elections? Or it enacted a law discriminating against members of your religion, or passed legislation removing the right of appeal to the courts? What could you do if government officials seized your property without legal authority? These scenarios all raise rule of law issues.

The rule of law can seem rather abstract at first, but it is a crucially important constitutional principle and is part of the UK constitution's armoury of protective, controlling mechanisms, particularly through its application by the courts. The Constitution Committee has affirmed that 'The maintenance of the rule of law is as vital now as it has ever been' (House of Lords Select Committee on the Constitution, *The Office of Lord Chancellor*, 6th Report of Session 2014–15, HL Paper 75 [159]), and it has had greater emphasis in the higher courts in recent years. This chapter introduces you to the different meanings of the rule of law and its key theories, demonstrates its practical operation through case law and other examples, and shows its close links to the judiciary and judicial review.

》 CROSS REFERENCE

See Chapters 13 and 15–16

While there is great variation in theories about the rule of law, its central idea is simple: no one is higher than the law, and the law binds everyone, including state officials. Adhering to the rule of law therefore helps to secure legally controlled and accountable government, and maintains good law-making and a fair justice system; modern views on the rule of law also regard law as a source and protector of the rights and freedoms of citizens. The key to unlocking the concept is to think of law as the dominant force in a constitution, and to focus on the importance of the practical application of the rule of law in everyday life.

8.1 What is the rule of law?

Anthony Lester has written: '"The rule of law" is a weighty and ponderous phrase, much quoted by politicians and judges but much misused, sometimes it is just meaningless verbiage' ('Five Ideas to Fight For' (2016) 3 EHRLR 231, 241). It is true that the rule of law is a phrase that is not often defined (eg section 1 of the Constitutional Reform Act 2005 refers to the existing constitutional principle of the rule of law but does not define it), and it is capable of multiple definitions because theorists disagree on its precise content, but it is still possible to distil central meanings.

The rule of law is a constitutional value or principle which measures good governance, fair law-making, and applying law in a just way. It is a powerful guiding principle but is not itself a law, and it is not written down in a tangible source (which can make it seem slippery to grasp initially), but it is a cherished ideal, both in the UK constitution and universally:

> Although the rule of law is a single value, it includes many different principles, each of which contributes to the rule of law overall. These principles cover a range of matters that have practical implications for all of us, every day, like access to justice, independent and impartial courts, legal aid, transparency in executive decision-making, fair and rational decision-making, and government accountability. (Swee Leng Harris and Alexia Staker, *The Rule of Law in Parliament: A Review of the 2015–16 Session*, Bingham Centre for the Rule of Law, p 3)

> Lord Bingham's definition of the rule of law is: 'all persons and authorities within the state, whether public or private, should be bound by and entitled to the benefit of laws publicly made, taking effect (generally) in the future and publicly administered in the courts' (Tom Bingham, *The Rule of Law*, p 8, in 'Further reading').

The rule of law sets standards for making and enforcing law, and protecting fundamental rights and principles; it acts as a protecting mechanism by preventing state officials from acting unfairly, unlawfully, arbitrarily, or oppressively. These are key concepts in judicial review. The rule of law is also regarded as an external measure for what a state does; if the rule of law breaks down in a state, it will fail to function in an internationally acceptable way. There is a strong perception that the 'good guys' respect rule of law and the bad ones do not, and states which, for example, imprison political opponents without trial, or discriminate against individuals on the basis of their race, gender, or religion, are condemned for not respecting the rule of law. The rule of law is therefore multi-faceted but its essence lies in four words: the law is supreme. It binds everyone: as Lord Steyn observes, 'nobody is above the law and nobody is outside the law' ('Democracy, the Rule of Law and the Role of Judges', 246; see 'Further reading').

> **CROSS REFERENCE**
>
> You will find a strong synergy between rule of law and judicial review (see Chapters 15–16)

Definitions of the rule of law can set out a variable set of requirements, but we can break them down into core, middle, and wide meanings, as shown in Figure 8.1. In a paper written for the Constitution Committee, Professor Paul Craig described the core meaning of the rule of law as 'lawful authority', the middle meaning as 'guiding conduct', and the wider meaning as 'justice and accountable government' (House of Lords Select Committee on the Constitution, *Relations between the Executive, the Judiciary and Parliament*, 6th Report of Session 2006–07, HL Paper 151, Appendix 5). The core meaning can stand alone but each further layer adds more substance and greater weight to the rule of law.

Figure 8.1 The rule of law's three meanings

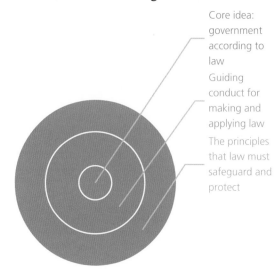

Core idea: government according to law

Guiding conduct for making and applying law

The principles that law must safeguard and protect

8.1.1 The core meaning of the rule of law

The core meaning is that the law binds everyone. Lord Reed has stated that 'At the heart of the concept of the rule of law is the idea that society is governed by law' (*R (UNISON) v Lord Chancellor* [2017] UKSC 51 [68]). It means that:

1. *Everyone* is bound by the law.

2. This includes those in government, who must obey the law.

3. Any action taken by the government must be authorised by law, that is, government needs lawful authority to act.

Points 2 and 3 are known as 'government according to law', which means that the law acts as both a restraint on government *and* as the source of its authority, as shown in Figure 8.2. This is the narrowest view of what the rule of law means, but it does not specify criteria for good law and so offers little protection against unfair or unjust laws, or interference with rights.

8.1.2 The middle meaning of the rule of law

The middle definition builds on the core meaning by setting out guiding standards for making and enforcing law. It specifies that laws should be in a certain form—for example, they should be clear and accessible—and follow a fair process of creation and implementation (see section 8.2.1).

Figure 8.2 Government according to law

The law controls government

The law also gives government its authority to act

8.1.3 **The wide meaning of the rule of law**

On top of the core and middle meanings, the wide meaning also requires that the law should offer benefits and protection of fundamental rights and values, such as democracy, human rights, equality, and justice, which Jeffrey Jowell summarises as 'legality, certainty, equality and access to justice and rights' (*The Changing Constitution*, 9th edn (Oxford: Oxford University Press 2019), 14). These requirements can also be seen in current global perspectives on the rule of law, which indicate that it has moved to an internationally expected standard of governance.

 THINKING POINT

Although the definitions given below vary to some extent, try to identify their common requirements.

 THE BIGGER PICTURE: GLOBAL VIEWS ON THE RULE OF LAW

The Universal Declaration of Human Rights

The Preamble of the Universal Declaration of Human Rights 1948 states: 'it is essential, if man is not to be compelled to have recourse . . . to rebellion against tyranny and oppression, that human rights should be protected by the rule of law.'

World Justice Project

The World Justice Project has compiled a Rule of Law Index measuring adherence to the rule of law in 128 states, and sets out four universal principles in its definition of the rule of law:

1. **Accountability** The government as well as private actors are accountable under the law.

2. **Just Laws** The laws are clear, publicised, and stable; are applied evenly; and protect fundamental rights, including the security of persons and contract, property, and human rights.

3. **Open Government** The processes by which the laws are enacted, administered, and enforced are accessible, fair, and efficient.

4. **Accessible and Impartial Dispute Resolution** Justice is delivered timely by competent, ethical, and independent representatives and neutrals who are accessible, have adequate resources, and reflect the makeup of the communities they serve. (See World Justice Project, *Rule of Law Index*, 2020 p 10–11 at https://worldjustice-project.org.)

The eight factors measured by the project also help to clarify the requirements of the rule of law: constraints on government powers; absence of corruption; open government; fundamental rights; order and security; regulatory enforcement; access to civil justice; and effective criminal justice.

The United Nations

In 2004, the Secretary-General of the United Nations described the rule of law as:

> [A] principle of governance in which all persons, institutions and entities, public and private, including the State itself, are accountable to laws that are publicly promulgated [published], equally enforced and independently adjudicated, and which are consistent with international human rights norms and standards. It requires, as well, measures to ensure adherence to the principles of supremacy of law, equality before the law, accountability to the law, fairness in the application of the law, separation of powers, participation in decision-making, legal certainty, avoidance of arbitrariness and procedural and legal transparency.

> (Report of the Secretary-General, The Rule of Law and Transitional Justice in Conflict and Post-Conflict Societies (S/2004/616) 3 August 2004)

Note the separation of powers as one of the rule of law requirements

In 2012, the United Nations General Assembly reaffirmed member states' commitment to the rule of law and recognised the importance of universal respect for human rights; fair, stable and predictable legal frameworks; good governance; an independent judicial system; the right of equal access to justice; and equal rights and equal protection of the law without any discrimination. (See United Nations General Assembly Declaration of the High-level Meeting of the General Assembly on the Rule of Law at the National and International Levels, A/RES/67/1, 30 November 2012.)

For more on the UN's work on rule of law, see www.un.org/ruleoflaw/.

See also the UN's Rule of Law Indicators for building the rule of law in countries after conflict (peacekeeping.un.org/en/building-rule-of-law-and-security-institutions).

8.1.4 What is the purpose of the rule of law?

 THINKING POINT

Consider the views set out below. What is the common thread between them?

Aristotle (c. 350 BC) expressed the idea that rule by law was preferable to rule by individuals, and that those who govern are guardians of the law (*Politics* Book 3, XVI).

Bracton, a thirteenth-century English judge, recognised that the king was subject to the law ('the king must not be under man, but under God and under the law' (*On the Laws and Customs of England*)).

Fortescue wrote in the fifteenth century that a 'King of England can not, at his pleasure, make any alterations in the laws of the land'; his people were to be ruled by the laws that *they* desired (*In Praise of the Laws of England*).

John Locke, the English philosopher, famously asserted that 'wherever law ends, tyranny begins' and that if state officials exceed the power given to them by the law and act without authority, they can be challenged, just like anyone else, for invading the rights of another (*Second Treatise on Government*, chapter XVII s 202 (1690)).

John Adams, the second US President, wrote that the United States was 'a government of laws and not of men' (Novanglus Essays, No 7, 1775).

The people and those who rule a country are governed by the law. The core purpose of the rule of law is to keep in check the people who govern, prevent the abuse of power, and require that all government action must be authorised by law. An early example of the idea that rulers were subject to the law is Magna Carta in 1215; King John's barons made it clear that the law was not simply the king's wishes, but a stronger and higher force which bound the king. It is preferable to be governed by the law than by the random whims and wishes of individuals in positions of power, which can be arbitrary, unpredictable, subjective, and unfair. Even though it is made by human beings, law is neutral, objective, and based on reason because of the processes it must go through in its creation. Blackstone wrote that a law 'is a rule: not a transient sudden order from a superior to or concerning a particular person; but something permanent, uniform, and universal' (*Commentaries*, Introduction, Section II), and this idea can clearly be seen in the decision of *Entick v Carrington*, one of the founding cases of the modern constitution.

▶ CROSS REFERENCE

For details of Magna Carta, see Chapter 2

> ### 🔍 CASE CLOSE-UP: *ENTICK v CARRINGTON* (1765) 19 ST TR 1030
>
> The Secretary of State (a government minister) granted a warrant for Entick's arrest for seditious writings. The king's messengers broke into Entick's house, carried out a four-hour search, and seized hundreds of his books and papers. Entick sued for trespass. The Secretary of State argued that his power to seize goods was lawful and necessary to government (state necessity) but the court held that there was no law authorising what the minister had done, nor did the law recognise the argument of state necessity; there was no law of state distinct from the common law. The court therefore judged the warrant to be illegal and void.
>
> The key principle here, which still resonates today, is that government ministers require the authority of the law to act, and government interference with an individual's property must be justified by law. The case shows that rule of law is not purely an abstract concept but has practical application; the law protects individuals against unlawful interference by the state, and helped John Entick challenge oppressive governmental action.

Discretionary government power needs legal limits, and the idea of law constraining government power can clearly be seen in the *Miller/Cherry* case (*R (Miller) v The Prime Minister; Cherry v Advocate General for Scotland* [2019] UKSC 41) where the Prime Minister was held to have acted outside the legal limits of the prerogative power to prorogue Parliament.

8.2 Rule of law theories

Knowledge of key theories underpins understanding and appreciation of the application of rule of law in practice, and outlined in what follows are the views of Dicey, Joseph Raz, and Lord Bingham on the rule of law. Theories on the rule of law can be divided into two categories, formal and substantive; however, at the heart of each theory is the core idea that the law is supreme and controls government:

- Formal theories set out the form and procedures that good law-making and the application of law should follow (also called the 'thin definition').

- Substantive theories tell us the content that good law should have (also called the 'thick definition').

8.2.1 Formal theories on the rule of law

Formal theories focus on the form and procedure for making and applying law and require that due process is observed, but do not set out the substantive content of laws; they are content-neutral. To illustrate how this works, we examine the formal theories of Dicey and Raz.

Dicey's definition of the rule of law

Dicey set out his principles on the rule of law in 1885 (*Introduction to the Study of Law and Constitution*) and they are still relevant today. Dicey suggested three views of the rule of law based on the supremacy of law and the idea that no man is above the law ('Englishmen are ruled by the law, and by the law alone'). It is useful to know in advance that Dicey did not trust wide governmental power.

1. '[N]o man is punishable or can be lawfully made to suffer in body or goods except for a distinct breach of law established in the ordinary legal manner before the ordinary Courts of the land. In this sense the rule of law is contrasted with every system of government based on the exercise by persons in authority of wide, arbitrary, or discretionary powers of constraint.'

Here, Dicey was referring to two things: (a) people can only be punished for a breach of an established law proved in court; and (b) regular law excludes arbitrary power, prerogative, or wide discretionary government powers. It follows from this that government power should be clearly specified and predictable, and must be authorised and controlled by law.

2. '[E]very man, whatever be his rank or condition, is subject to the ordinary law of the realm and amenable to the jurisdiction of the ordinary tribunals.'

This means that everyone is equally bound by the law of the land administered by the ordinary courts. For Dicey this contrasted with continental practice, such as French administrative law (*droit administratif*), where disputes involving the government or its officials were dealt with by special bodies outside the civil courts, which he did not approve of.

3. '[T]he general principles of the constitution (as for example the right to personal liberty, or the right of public meeting) are with us the result of judicial decisions determining the rights of private persons in particular cases brought before the Courts; whereas under many foreign constitutions the security (such as it is) given to the rights of individuals results, or appears to result, from the general principles of the constitution.'

In the UK, rights and freedoms are the result of the common law, not a written constitution or code of rights; therefore the UK's unwritten constitution is the result of the ordinary law of the land and is 'pervaded by the rule of law'. (While this was true at the time that Dicey was writing, rights and freedoms are now also protected by statutes such as the Equality Act 2010 and Human Rights Act 1998.)

Summary of Dicey's views

- People should only be punished for a breach of the law proved in court after a fair trial.
- Government power needs legal limits and should not be arbitrary or based on wide discretion.

- Everyone is equally subject to the law.
- In the UK, rights and freedoms originate from the courts and common law, not from a constitutional code.

Note that Dicey does not prescribe the content of good law.

For criticisms of Dicey's views, see Jowell, *The Changing Constitution* (2019), chapter 1.

Joseph Raz, *The Rule of Law and Its Virtue*

Raz defined the rule of law as:

a political ideal which a legal system may lack or may possess to a greater or lesser degree . . . the rule of law is just one of the virtues which a legal system may possess and by which it is to be judged. It is not to be confused with democracy, justice, equality (before the law or otherwise), human rights of any kind or respect for persons or for the dignity of man (*The Authority of Law* (1979), 211; 'The Rule of Law and Its Virtue' (1977) 93 LQR 195).

Raz argued that the rule of law requires (a) that people should be ruled by the law and obey it, and (b) if the law is to be obeyed, it must be capable of guiding people's behaviour (*The Authority of Law,* 213). He put forward eight characteristics (or postulates) that a legal system should have to give effective guidance (pages 214–18):

1. All laws should be prospective [regulating future conduct and not making past conduct retrospectively unlawful], open [published], and clear.

2. Laws should be relatively stable [not changing frequently].

3. The making of particular laws should be guided by open, stable, clear, and general rules.

4. The independence of the judiciary must be guaranteed.

5. The principles of natural justice must be observed [a fair hearing by an impartial tribunal].

6. The courts should have review powers over the implementation of the other principles.

7. The courts should be easily accessible.

8. The discretion of the crime-preventing agencies should not be allowed to pervert the law [the police and other bodies must apply the law, not their own discretion].

Summary of Raz's views

- The rule of law requires law to comply with minimum standards, rules, and procedure but does not require rights-based content.

- Raz saw the rule of law as a political yardstick to measure a legal system so that it gives people effective guidance.

However, because Raz is only concerned with the form and procedure that law should follow, not its content, morally objectionable laws and oppressive regimes can satisfy his conditions. Steyn notes: 'History has shown that majority rule and strict adherence to legality is no guarantee against tyranny. Hitler came to power by democratic vote' ('Democracy, the Rule of Law and the Role of Judges', 245), while Anthony Lester, an eminent human rights lawyer, also recognised that:

To dictators the rule of law means blind obedience to the law even if the law is arbitrary—a law is a law is a law. According to the Nazi judges, the Nuremberg Decrees stripping German

Legal positivism is the view that law is a set of rules created by a legitimate authority and its moral content is irrelevant

Jews of their rights as citizens had to be obeyed because they were 'the law'. The same was said of South Africa's apartheid law and of the slave laws in the United States. That mind set is known as 'legal positivism'—a way of thinking that does not ask if the law is fair or reasonable but simply whether it is 'the law'. (Anthony Lester, 'Five Ideas to Fight For' (2016) 3 EHRLR 231, 241)

Raz acknowledged the possibility of immoral laws being passed in a valid form, and a government that obeys them acting in accordance with the law:

A non-democratic legal system, based on the denial of human rights, on extensive poverty, on racial segregation, sexual inequalities, and religious persecution may, in principle, conform to the requirements of the rule of law better than any of the legal systems of the more enlightened Western democracies. (*The Authority of Law: Essays on Law and Morality* (Oxford: Clarendon Press 1979), p 211)

The law, argues Raz, may 'institute slavery without violating the rule of law' (p 221). However, that depends on how we define the rule of law. Bingham argues that a state introducing slavery *would* be violating the rule of law (*The Rule of Law*, 2011, p 67). To be truly effective and protective, therefore, the rule of law needs to require something more to ensure fairness, equality, and justice. This is where substantive theories (see section 8.2.2) add the wider, or thicker, layer of the content and protective value of good law.

THE BIGGER PICTURE

Lon Fuller argued in The *Morality of Law* (New Haven: Yale University Press 1964) that laws should be based on moral standards for fairness. He set out eight formal principles (desiderata) to achieve this 'internal morality'. Laws should be: general, published, prospective, intelligible, consistent [not contradicting each other], practicable [not ordering people to do something impossible], stable, and congruent [applied in accordance with the purpose of the law-makers, eg procedural requirements for fair decision-making 'promote congruence between the actions of decision-makers and the law which should govern their actions' (*Osborn v Parole Board* [2013] UKSC 61, [2014] AC 1115 [71] (Lord Reed)). However, Fuller omitted key elements such as an independent judiciary and access to justice.

SUMMARY

Formal theories set important standards and directions for law-making and operating the justice system, but are neutral on content of laws. The formal (thin) meaning of the rule of law requires that:

1. Laws must be in a specified form: clear, accessible, understandable, published (so that people know what the law is and what will happen if they break it), general (not produced ad hoc but of general application), stable (not changing often), prospective (not retrospectively making an act unlawful).

2. Laws must be applied and enforced by fair procedures: no punishment except for a breach of the law; a fair hearing by impartial, accessible courts; and an independent judiciary. These fair procedures are important in practice. See, for example, *R (Roberts) v Parole Board* [2005] UKHL 45, [2005] 2 AC 738.

8.2.2 **Substantive theories on the rule of law**

Substantive theories on the rule of law are rights-based, and convey the idea that good law should also protect rights and values (the 'thick definition'). These ideas have their origins in natural law.

> Natural law refers to a set of rules said to be derived from nature and reason, which have an inherent moral content and are superior to manmade laws. John Locke in the seventeenth century and Rousseau in the eighteenth century regarded natural law as a source of democratic rights, liberties, and basic freedoms that protected individuals, and their views influenced the US Constitution.

The modern, substantive view of the rule of law is encapsulated by Lord Bingham's widely respected contribution to contemporary rule of law debate in the Sir David Williams lecture in Cambridge in 2006 (see 'The Rule of Law' (2007) 66 CLJ 67; Tom Bingham, *The Rule of Law* (2011)). Lord Bingham's eight principles of the rule of law are summarised as follows:

1. The law must be accessible, intelligible, clear and predictable [this helps individuals know in advance what conduct is unlawful].

2. Legal questions should be resolved by applying the law, not discretion [this ensures that legal rules, not personal preference, are applied].

3. The law should apply equally to all, except where objective differences justify different treatment [eg children under ten do not have criminal responsibility].

4. Ministers and public officers must exercise their powers in good faith, fairly, for the purpose for which they were given, without exceeding the limits of their powers, and not unreasonably.

5. The law must adequately protect fundamental human rights.

6. Means must be provided for resolving civil disputes without prohibitive cost or inordinate delay [rights which cannot be enforced in court have little value].

7. The state should provide fair adjudicative procedures [the right to a fair trial, both criminal and civil].

8. The state should comply with its international law obligations.

For an interesting debate on principle 8, see G. Letsas, 'The Rule of All Law: A Reply to Finnis, Ekins and Verdirame', UK Const L Blog, 26 Nov 2015 (available at https://ukconstitutionallaw.org/).

> **THINKING POINT**
>
> Consider the facts of *Congreve v Home Office* [1976] QB 629. Which of Lord Bingham's principles of the rule of law did the court uphold?
>
> The Home Secretary had a statutory power to revoke television licences. Using that power, he revoked the validly issued television licences of people who had surrendered their old licence and bought a new one before an increase in the licence fee. It was held that the Home Secretary could not lawfully revoke their licences without good reasons to justify this. The court set aside his revocation because he had misused the power given to him by Parliament and was using it to raise money which Parliament had not authorised.

An excellent example of the law protecting the rights of individuals is *A & Others v SSHD* [2004] UKHL 56, [2005] 2 AC 68; here, the courts were applying the Human Rights Act 1998. The Anti-Terrorism, Crime and Security Act 2001 allowed the detention of terrorist suspects indefinitely without trial but *only* applied to foreign nationals, which was discriminatory. The court delivered a powerful reminder that even in the fight against terrorism, equality, non-discrimination, and freedom from arbitrary detention must still be respected ([57–58] (Lord Bingham)). The right to liberty is a fundamental right belonging to everyone in the UK, irrespective of nationality ([106] (Lord Hope)) and indefinite imprisonment without charge or trial is 'anathema in any country which observes the rule of law' ([74] (Lord Nicholls)).

❯ CROSS REFERENCE

See also Chapter 17

THE BIGGER PICTURE

In 1959, the International Commission of Jurists held a conference to define the rule of law and produced the Delhi Declaration, which focused strongly on the content and substance of law, recognising the rule of law as 'a dynamic concept' which should be used to protect and advance citizens' civil and political rights and to create the social, economic, and other conditions to help people achieve 'their legitimate aspirations and dignity' (see www.icj.org/rule-of-law-in-a-free-society-a-report-on-the-international-congress-of-jurists-new-delhi-india-january-5-10-1959/).

In 2016, the Council of Europe's Venice Commission on Democracy through Law adopted a Rule of Law Checklist which includes detailed benchmarks for measuring a state's adherence to the rule of law: legality, legal certainty, prevention of abuse of powers, equality before the law, and non-discrimination and access to justice (see www.venice.coe.int).

SUMMARY

Substantive theories on the rule of law require not only that the law should bind government and satisfy standards of form and fair procedures, but also that it should protect fundamental rights. Lord Neuberger summarises the rule of law as requiring not only that laws are applied by and to everyone (which is rule *by* law), but also that laws must:

- be freely accessible (available and understandable);

- 'satisfy certain requirements: they must enforce law and order in an effective way while ensuring due process, they must accord citizens their fundamental rights against the state, and they must regulate relationships between citizens in a just way.'

- be enforceable: otherwise the fundamental rights above 'might as well not exist' (Lord Neuberger, *Justice in an Age of Austerity*, Justice–Tom Sargant Memorial Lecture, 15 October 2013, p 1).

8.3 The practical application of the rule of law in the UK constitution

The Bingham Centre Rule of Law Report reflects that:

> The rule of law lies at the heart of the UK's system of government. It has been recognised in Parliament as a 'fundamental British value'—a value which must be protected just as carefully and resolutely as other values that form the basis of our society, such as democracy, individual liberty, and respect for diversity. The UK is also recognised internationally for its commitment to the rule of law, and the benefits that has brought.

> (Swee Leng Harris and Alexia Staker, *The Rule of Law in Parliament: A Review of the 2015–16 Session*, Bingham Centre for the Rule of Law, p 2)

In the UK, there are four main elements to the application of rule of law in practice: an accountable executive; an independent judiciary; open access to the courts and justice system; and respect for human rights.

 THINKING POINT

The exercise that follows helps you to gauge your understanding of the rule of law so far and to think about how it applies in the UK. Suppose that the government plans to reduce the cost of the justice system by introducing a scheme in which *all* civil claims for less than £500 can no longer be heard in the courts. The government intends to introduce a draft Bill into Parliament to give effect to the scheme. It would need to be approved by Parliament to become law, then would have to be enforced by the courts.

Carefully read sections 8.3.1–8.3.3 on how each of the three arms of state applies the rule of law. Would a statute removing the right of access to the courts breach any rule of law requirements? Could it be passed and enforced? Are there points at which someone can act as a 'constitutional backstop' and authoritatively say, 'You can't do that'?

8.3.1 **The executive**

The Constitution Committee has pointed out that because the UK government often has a majority in the House of Commons, it can normally successfully drive changes in the law through Parliament and, through the Parliament Acts, can pass legislation without the consent of the House of Lords, so it is important that the government understands and respects the 'wider conception of the rule of law' as a constitutional constraint on its power (House of Lords Select Committee on the Constitution, *The Office of Lord Chancellor* [24]). Commitment to, and observance of, the rule of law is therefore critically important for good government, especially with increases in government power. Table 8.1 sets out how this happens in practice. Consider whether any factor could prevent the UK government from promoting the draft Bill in our scenario.

CROSS REFERENCE
See Chapters 10–11

Table 8.1 Executive key points

Government ministers have an overarching duty to comply with the law (see the *Ministerial Code* 2019, para 1.3).

Section 17(1) of the Constitutional Reform Act 2005 requires the Lord Chancellor, a government minister, to take an oath to respect the rule of law (the Constitution Committee recommended that the oath should be amended to 'respect and uphold the rule of law', given the Lord Chancellor's role in ensuring that the government acts in accordance with the rule of law (Constitution Committee, *The Office of Lord Chancellor* [145])).

The government's law officers (the Attorney General and the Solicitor General) also have an important role in upholding the rule of law.

When a Bill starts its life, it has significant input from lawyers: it is drafted by Parliamentary Counsel on instructions from the relevant government department, particularly its lawyers, and departmental legal advisors prepare a legal issues memorandum setting out, for example, the Bill's compatibility with the European Convention on Human Rights. (See the Cabinet Office, 'Guide to Making Legislation' (July 2017) para 3.8 and section 3 generally.)

▶ CROSS REFERENCE

See Chapters 11–12

In addition to being politically accountable to Parliament, government ministers are legally accountable in the courts if they act outside the scope of their lawful powers or contrary to constitutional principles.

🔍 CASE CLOSE-UP: AN ACCOUNTABLE EXECUTIVE

M v Home Office [1994] 1 AC 377

This case is a powerful judicial reminder that government ministers are not above the law. The issue was whether a government minister could overrule the decision of a court. An asylum seeker from Zaire failed in his application to be allowed to stay in the UK, was notified that he would be returned to Zaire, and on the same day started new judicial review proceedings. A judge ordered that his removal be delayed pending the outcome of his case (and understood the Crown's barrister to give an undertaking to that effect) but Home Office officials went ahead with his deportation. The judge issued an order that he be returned to the UK but the Home Secretary cancelled arrangements to return him. The court held that the Home Secretary was in contempt of court. Lord Templeman reasoned that if there was no power to enforce the law against a minister, it would mean that the executive obeyed the law as a matter of grace (ie when it felt like it) and not by necessity, which would 'reverse the result of the Civil War'.

8.3.2 Parliament

▶ CROSS REFERENCE

See Chapter 11 for details of the legislative process

In practice, Parliament has a role in upholding the rule of law when scrutinising draft legislation and through holding the government to account to ensure that it governs in accordance with the rule of law. Would any step in Table 8.2 prevent the scenario Bill from becoming law?

Table 8.2 Parliament key points

During the legislative process, Bills are debated in both chambers in Parliament, allowing for amendment, and controversial, unfair, or objectionable clauses can be voted down. There is also scrutiny in Public Bill committees.

Legislative scrutiny by parliamentary select committees provides a valuable filter in identifying and discussing Bills which potentially threaten the rule of law (see Constitution Committee, *The Office of Lord Chancellor* [83, 150]).

The House of Lords Select Committee on the Constitution examines all Public Bills for constitutional implications and wider constitutional issues. In doing this, it applies rule of law principles in a practical way, including checking that retrospective legislation is avoided unless there is a compelling reason, ensuring legal certainty, and defining delegated power to ministers as narrowly as possible. The UCL Constitution Unit has collated the standards applied by the Committee in the *Constitutional Standards of the House of Lords Select Committee on the Constitution* report of 2014 (see www.ucl.ac.uk/constitution-unit). See also Robert Hazell, 'Who Is the Guardian of Legal Values in the Legislative Process: Parliament or the Executive?' (2004) (Autumn) Public Law 495.

> Public Bills are bills promoted by the government

The Office of the Parliamentary Counsel promotes laws which are necessary, clear, coherent, effective, and accessible.

CLOSE-UP FOCUS: THE ROLE OF SELECT COMMITTEES IN SCRUTINISING BILLS

The Immigration Bill 2015

The Immigration Bill 2015 (enacted as the Immigration Act 2016) proposed that people appealing against deportation on human rights grounds must leave the UK before being able to appeal; they would only be able to remain in the UK during the appeal process if they would suffer 'serious and irreversible harm'. This was intended to implement government policy to tackle illegal immigration by making it harder to live and work illegally in the UK. These 'deport first, appeal later' powers caused concern because the appeal process can be prolonged and so could amount to a denial of justice. Schedule 7 of the Bill also allowed a minister to override judicial decisions about immigration bail conditions.

The Select Committee identified rule of law concerns about the Bill's length and complexity—168 pages, 65 clauses, and 12 schedules; the provision giving a member of the government the authority to override judicial decisions; clauses with retrospective effect; and human rights issues, stating that it was 'a general requirement of the rule of law that the lawfulness of executive decisions should be capable of being tested either by way of an effective right of appeal or by way of judicial review' (House of Lords Select Committee on the Constitution, *Immigration Bill*, 7th Report of Session 2015–16, HL Paper 75 [44]; see also [18–38]; Bingham Centre for the Rule of Law Briefing Note, *The Rule of Law in Parliament in 2015–16*, January 2017 (available at www.biicl.org)).

8.3.2.1 **The rule of law and parliamentary sovereignty**

Dicey believed that the English constitution (as he called it) was founded on the twin principles of parliamentary sovereignty and the rule of law, but at first sight, that view appears to be contradictory. If Parliament is sovereign, how can it be bound by the rule of law; if the law is supreme, how can Parliament also be supreme? Dicey saw parliamentary sovereignty as the stronger principle, but Trevor Allan rationalises the contradiction by arguing that parliamentary sovereignty refers to its legislative supremacy, and it can be assumed to intend, when legislating, to preserve underlying constitutional principles, which is compatible with the rule of law (see T.R.S. Allan, *The Sovereignty of Law*, p 194, in 'Further reading'). Lord Steyn has stated that 'unless there is the clearest provision to the contrary, Parliament must be presumed not to legislate contrary to the rule of law' (*R v Secretary of State for the Home Department, ex p Pierson* [1998] AC 539, 591). Tom Bingham, however, states that Parliament may, if it wishes, legislate contrary to the rule of law, and expresses concern that this could ultimately lead to conflict between Parliament and the judges (see *The Rule of Law*, chapter 12).

> **CROSS REFERENCE**

For more discussion on this, see Chapter 9

8.3.3 **The judiciary**

The judiciary has a vitally important role in upholding the rule of law, especially as a check on executive power. An independent judiciary 'is universally recognised as a cardinal feature of the modern democratic state, a cornerstone of the rule of law itself' (*A & Others v SSHD* [2004] UKHL 56 [42] (Lord Bingham)). This is particularly relevant in judicial review, where the rule of law demonstrably springs into action, enabling individuals to challenge in court the lawfulness of actions of the executive, including not only the government but public bodies more widely. The dramatic increase in judicial review cases over the last 40 years has led to increased prominence for the rule of law.

Q   CASE CLOSE-UP: THE IMPORTANCE OF AN INDEPENDENT JUDICIARY

Director of Public Prosecutions of Jamaica v Mollison **[2003] UKPC 6, [2003] 2 AC 411**

In Jamaica, the Governor-General, a member of the executive, was allowed to decide the length of sentences of detention which had been imposed by the Jamaican courts for murder. The issue was whether it was compatible with the Jamaican constitution. Lord Bingham held that the separation between the exercise of judicial powers on the one hand and legislative and executive powers on the other is total and based on the rule of law, and detention during the Governor-General's pleasure was incompatible with 'the constitutional principle that judicial functions (such as sentencing) must be exercised by the judiciary and not by the executive' ([13]).

See also *R (Anderson) v Secretary of State for the Home Department* [2002] 3 WLR 1800.

Note the separation of powers issues arising in this case

In the UK, there were concerns that the Constitutional Reform Act 2005 might adversely affect the rule of law by removing the Lord Chancellor as an important channel of communication between the judiciary and the executive, but there is still significant dialogue and interaction between the two branches. The Lord Chancellor holds discussions with senior members of the judiciary, and regular meetings with the Lord Chief Justice and President of the Supreme Court, and senior members of the judiciary may be invited to attend select committees to express certain concerns—within strictly specified limits—about draft Bills or policy, providing an important communication link between the judiciary and Parliament. Moreover, the Lord Chancellor's duty under the 2005 Act to respect the rule of law includes upholding judicial independence which has been strengthened by the Act.

CROSS REFERENCE
See Chapter 13 for details

Access to justice is a particularly important aspect of the rule of law and Lord Neuberger has identified its components as:

> First, a competent and impartial judiciary; secondly, accessible courts; thirdly, properly administered courts; fourthly, a competent and honest legal profession; fifthly, an effective procedure for getting a case before the court; sixthly, an effective legal process; seventhly effective execution; eighthly, affordable justice. (Lord Neuberger, *Justice in an Age of Austerity*, p 11)

The following cases illustrate the significance of the requirement for right of access to the courts.

 CASE CLOSE-UPS: THE RIGHT OF ACCESS TO THE COURTS

R (UNISON) v Lord Chancellor [2017] UKSC 51

In this significant case, the Supreme Court upheld an action by UNISON (a trade union) which claimed that the introduction of fees for cases in employment tribunals was invalid because it interfered with the right of access to justice. Lord Reed stated that 'The constitutional right of access to the courts is inherent in the rule of law' and noted that the importance of the rule of law is not always understood—the administration of justice is not merely a public service, but access to the courts maintains the rule of law ([66, 67]).

Lord Reed explained the importance of the principle of unhindered access to the courts as a key component of the rule of law:

> Parliament exists primarily in order to make laws for society in this country. Democratic procedures exist primarily in order to ensure that the Parliament which makes those laws includes Members of Parliament who are chosen by the people of this country and are accountable to them. Courts exist in order to ensure that the laws made by Parliament, and the common law created by the courts themselves, are applied and enforced. That role includes ensuring that the executive branch of government carries out its functions in accordance with the law. In order for the courts to perform that role, people must in principle have unimpeded access to them. Without such access, laws are liable to become a dead letter, the work done by Parliament may be rendered nugatory, and the democratic election of Members of Parliament may become a meaningless charade. That is why the courts do not merely provide a public service like any other. ([68])

R v Secretary of State for the Home Department ex parte Anufrijeva [2003] UKHL 36

The House of Lords held (by 4 to 1) that it was unlawful to withdraw income support from an asylum seeker before the decision had been notified to the individual, who needed notice of the decision to be able to challenge it in the courts if they wished. The right of access to justice was applied as a fundamental constitutional principle, and Lord Steyn said that in 'our system of law surprise is regarded as the enemy of justice. Fairness is the guiding principle of our public law' ([30]), adding that the rule of law required fundamental principles to be upheld 'even in unprepossessing cases' ([36]).

See also:

Raymond v Honey [1983] 1 AC 1 (it was a denial of access to justice for a prison governor to refuse a prisoner access to his lawyer).

Ferguson v Attorney General of Trinidad and Tobago [2016] UKPC 2, 40 BHRC 715: Trinidad and Tobago introduced a statute providing that criminal prosecutions could not take place more than ten years after an alleged crime, but after only two weeks in force it was retrospectively repealed by a new statute. This was challenged as unconstitutional by individuals who would have benefited from the limitation period but the Privy Council disagreed because, if they were convicted, they would have undergone a fair trial and the protection of due process of law.

In the absence of a statutory definition of the rule of law, it falls to the judges to determine its content and limits (*R (Privacy International) v Investigatory Powers Tribunal* [2019] UKSC 22 [121] (Lord Carnwath)). For example, in *Privacy International*, the Supreme Court analysed at length the requirements of the rule of law in relation to an ouster clause purporting to exclude the High Court from reviewing a decision of a tribunal (see sections 9.3.2 and 15.2). However, judges may sometimes disagree about what the rule of law requires in the case before them and this is exemplified by the case of *R (Evans) v Attorney General* [2015] UKSC 21 (for discussion on *Evans*, see section 9.3.1). Some judges see the rule of law as dominant over parliamentary sovereignty, raising the possibility that the courts might not enforce a statute that infringed the rule of law (the 'nuclear option').

 THE BIGGER PICTURE: THE 'NUCLEAR OPTION'

Lord Hope has said that 'The rule of law enforced by the courts is the ultimate controlling factor on which our constitution is based' (*Jackson v Attorney General* [2005] UKHL 56 [107]), and that 'Parliamentary sovereignty is an empty principle if legislation is passed which is so absurd or so unacceptable that the populace at large refused to recognise it as law' ([120]).

▶ CROSS REFERENCE

We explore this further in Chapter 9

Considering the possible response to legislation attempting to abolish judicial review or reduce the courts' role, Lord Hope has asserted that 'the rule of law requires that judges must retain the power to insist that legislation of that extreme kind is not law which the courts will recognise' (*AXA General Insurance v Lord Advocate* [2011] UKSC 46 [51]). This has echoes of *Dr Bonham's case* (see section 6.4.2), and it endorses Lord Woolf's view that, 'if Parliament did the unthinkable', the courts would be required to place limits on parliamentary sovereignty to uphold the rule of law (Lord Woolf, 'Droit Public—English Style' (1995) (Spring) Public Law 57, 69). This is because the UK's parliamentary democracy is based on the rule of law; both Parliament and the courts derive their authority from the rule of law and are both subject to it, so cannot repudiate it ('Droit Public—English Style', 68). Lord Woolf's argument is that if Parliament ignored the rule of law, it would fall to the courts to protect it, casting the courts as the constitutional backstop. However, Lord Woolf also points out that this situation is avoided in practice because of the separation of powers and mutual respect of the division of roles between Parliament and the courts; they are, he states, partners in upholding the rule of law.

THINKING POINT

How might the judiciary protect individuals if the draft Bill in our scenario became law?

8.4 Final thoughts on the rule of law

Adherence to the rule of law is relative, and, while the UK respects the rule of law, there are areas in which it sometimes falls short of the ideals, as illustrated in the examples that follow.

 THINKING POINT

Is the law always clear and understandable? Consider this example cited by the Plain English campaign:

Income Tax (Construction Industry Scheme) Regulations 2005 Schedule 1.

Para 12(1): The revocation by these Regulations of a provision previously revoked subject to savings does not affect the continued operation of those savings.

12(2): The revocation by these Regulations of a saving on the previous revocation of a provision does not affect the operation of the saving in so far as it is not specifically reproduced in these Regulations but remains capable of having effect.

(See www.plainenglish.co.uk/campaigning/examples/legal-jargon.html.)

The Office of Parliamentary Counsel is mindful of the issue of the complexity of legislation: see 'When Laws Become Too Complex', 16 April 2013, available at www.gov.uk/government/publications/when-laws-become-too-complex.

1. **Statutes can give the executive wide-ranging powers**

The High Court in *Miller I* stated that the 'subordination of the Crown (ie the executive government) to law is the foundation of the rule of law in the United Kingdom' (*R (Miller) v Secretary of State for Exiting the European Union* [2016] EWHC 2768 (Admin) [26]) but the rule of law can be undermined by broadly drafted laws that allow the executive potentially excessive power, especially the power to change primary legislation made by Parliament. The Civil Contingencies Act 2004, for example, gives government ministers the power to repeal, amend, or suspend primary legislation in an emergency—including constitutional statutes, with the exception of the Human Rights Act (see section 22(3) and the safeguards in section 23); and section 75 Banking Act 2009 gives the Treasury the power to disapply or modify the effect of any law without parliamentary approval. The legislative arrangements for Brexit in the European Union (Withdrawal) Act 2018 make significant use of delegated legislation by government ministers to bring about many of the changes in the law needed as the UK transitions. While this is aimed at promoting efficient transitional arrangements, there are concerns that it gives too much power to the executive (see section 11.4.2.4; and the Bingham

Centre's 'Briefing Paper on Parliament and the Rule of Law in the Context of Brexit' at www.biicl.org).

The Coronavirus Act 2020 also gives wide delegated powers to ministers. While the government needs sufficiently strong powers to ensure swift, effective responses to the COVID-19 pandemic, the Act has been criticised as having 'potentially significant constitutional and civil liberties implications in relation to powers of detention and quarantine, restrictions on free assembly and the conduct of criminal trials' and many of the delegated powers are only subject to limited parliamentary scrutiny (House of Lords Select Committee on the Constitution *Coronavirus Bill* 4th Report of Session 2019–21, HL Paper 44 [3]). Those broad delegated powers 'would not be acceptable save for the exceptional circumstances' ([11]) and the Committee emphasised that parliamentary scrutiny and legal accountability were crucial restraints. In England the initial lockdown enforcement measures were contained in secondary legislation (the Health Protection (Coronavirus, Restrictions) (England) Regulations 2020) which came into force as a matter of urgency on 26 March and were only approved by Parliament on 4 May; waves of fresh regulations as restrictions eased and tightened have raised issues about legal certainty for the public. See section 11.4.2.1; https://ukconstitutionallaw.org/2020/03/24/stephen-tierney-and-jeff-king-the-coronavirus-bill/; https://commonslibrary.parliament.uk/research-briefings/cbp-8875/; and Daniel Greenberg, 'Dangerous Trends in Modern Legislation' (2015) (January) Public Law 96.

Another example of broad executive power concerns laws allowing state officials to enter premises: there are around 900 separate powers of entry for officials under primary and secondary legislation (www.gov.uk/guidance/powers-of-entry), and associated powers allow them to conduct searches and take other action. The Finance Act 1976 gave the power to enter premises by day or night, if necessary by force, and seize anything whatsoever reasonably believed to be evidence of a tax fraud offence (see *R v Inland Revenue Commissioners ex parte Rossminster Ltd* [1980] AC 952). To address this issue, the Home Secretary introduced a new code of practice in 2014 to ensure greater consistency and clarity on powers of entry; it was approved by Parliament and came into force in April 2015.

2.   Equality before the law and accessible courts

Everyone should have access to the courts, but reductions in legal aid can leave people unable to enforce their legal rights, and so deny justice. The Ministry of Justice estimates that 25 per cent of the population in England and Wales are financially eligible for free or contributory civil legal aid, compared with 80 per cent in 1950 (see Lucy Logan Green and James Sandbach, *Justice in Free Fall: A Report on the Decline of Civil Legal Aid in England and Wales*, LAG, December 2015). However, in 2013, the Lord Chancellor used statutory powers to put forward draft regulations proposing a 12-month residence test for legal aid, under which people who failed the residence test would no longer qualify for civil legal aid for any type of claim, subject to limited exceptions. Just before the draft Legal Aid, Sentencing and Punishment of Offenders Act (Amendment of Schedule 1) Order 2014 was laid before Parliament, the Public Law Project challenged the residence test's lawfulness in the courts. The Supreme Court held that it was unlawful because it was *ultra vires* (that is, outside the Lord Chancellor's statutory powers); by excluding a group of people based on personal circumstances, he was trying to do something that Parliament had not contemplated when it gave him those powers (*R (The Public Law*

Project) v Lord Chancellor [2016] UKSC 39 [23]; see also *R (Howard League for Penal Reform) v Lord Chancellor* [2017] EWCA Civ 244).

3. Operation of judicial deference

There are some areas of executive decision-making where the judiciary is reluctant to interfere (see section 7.4.2.1) and this can curtail the impact of the rule of law; an example is a prosecutor's decision whether to investigate or prosecute an alleged crime. There was certainly a more nuanced approach to the rule of law in *R (Corner House Research) v Director of the Serious Fraud Office* [2008] UKHL 60, [2008] 3 WLR 568, where the Serious Fraud Office (SFO) began a criminal investigation into alleged bribes paid by BAE to Saudi Arabian officials on a contract for military aircraft (the Al-Yamamah contract). Saudi Arabia told Britain that if the investigation went ahead, it would suspend intelligence co-operation, which could have put UK lives at risk due to the threat of terrorist attack. The Attorney General carried out a 'Shawcross exercise', which allows the Attorney to sound out ministers and invite them to provide any relevant information to help him decide whether it is in the public interest to prosecute in a case. The Prime Minister was concerned about the national security implications, and after much discussion with the Attorney General, the Director of the SFO decided to discontinue the investigation. The court had to decide whether the Director had acted outside the lawful limits of the power given to him by Parliament when deciding that the public interest in protecting British citizens outweighed the public interest in pursuing the investigation (see Lord Bingham [38]). The House of Lords held that the Director's decision had been made in the public interest and was therefore lawful. The court was reluctant to encroach on decision-making by independent prosecutors, and the Director's decision had not offended the rule of law (see [30–41]).

 SUMMARY

The rule of law is a constitutional value or principle. Its core idea is that the law is supreme and binds everyone equally, including those who govern a country. Although broader definitions are phrased in various ways, common features are that the rule of law:

- controls and limits the power of government to ensure good governance and accountability;
- ensures fair, stable legal systems, and law-making that conforms to required standards;
- upholds an independent judiciary and equal access to the courts and justice;
- defends and protects fundamental rights.

The rule of law is a protective, guiding principle that controls government and authorises government officials only to do what the law allows them. It is an internal and external measure for good governance. It ensures that law is made and applied clearly and fairly, and requires the law to protect fundamental rights and values.

The rule of law is not always perfectly applied but it is a powerful, pervasive guide for the legislature, executive, and judiciary. It is ultimately protected by judges, and judicial review is central to maintaining the rule of law.

Questions

Self-test questions

1. What is the core idea of the rule of law?

2. What are: (a) the middle and (b) the wide meanings of the rule of law?

3. What is the purpose of the rule of law principle?

4. Explain the decision in *Entick v Carrington*.

5. Summarise Dicey's three principles on the rule of law.

6. What do formal theories on the rule of law describe?

7. Is Lord Bingham's view of the rule of law formal or substantive?

8. What aspect of the rule of law did the court uphold in *M v Home Office*?

9. Why is the right of access to the courts important?

Exam question

Critically examine the importance of the rule of law in the UK, providing examples of its application to support your answer.

Further reading

Books

Allan, T.R.S. *The Sovereignty of Law: Freedom, Constitution, and Common Law* (Oxford: Oxford University Press 2013).
See in particular chapters 3 and 5

Bingham, T. *The Rule of Law* (London: Penguin Books 2011).
Essential reading on the rule of law

Jowell, J. 'The Rule of Law', in Jeffrey Jowell and Colm O'Cinneide (eds) *The Changing Constitution* (9th edn, Oxford: Oxford University Press 2019).
Clear discussion of the rule of law with particular reference to Dicey

Tamanaha, B.Z. *On the Rule of Law: History, Politics, Theory* (Cambridge: Cambridge University Press 2004).
A readable examination of the rule of law from roots to theories

Journal articles

Bedner, A. 'An Elementary Approach to the Rule of Law' (2010) 2(1) HJRL 48.
A detailed survey of literature on the definition of the rule of law

Lord Bingham, 'The Rule of Law' (2007) 66 CLJ 67.
Lord Bingham's seminal lecture on the rule of law

Craig, P. 'Formal and Substantive Conceptions of the Rule of Law: An Analytical Framework' (1997) (Autumn) Public Law 467.
An important analysis of formal and substantive views on the rule of law

Endicott, T.A.O. 'The Impossibility of the Rule of Law' (1999) 19(1) Oxf J Leg Stud 1.
Examines how states can fall short of attaining the ideal of the rule of law

Laws, J. 'The Constitution: Morals and Rights' (1996) (Winter) Public Law 622.
Discussion of what makes a good constitution and the rights it should contain

Lord Steyn, 'Democracy, the Rule of Law and the Role of Judges' (2006) 3 European Human Rights Law Review 243.
A helpful all-round assessment of the rule of law

Other sources

Bogdanor, V. 'The Sovereignty of Parliament or the Rule of Law?' Magna Carta lecture 15 June 2006.
A clearly defined argument on the tension between parliamentary sovereignty and rule of law (also helpful for Chapter 9)

Lord Justice Gross, 'How Can Judges Strengthen The Rule Of Law?' Argentina, October 2018 https://www.judiciary.uk/announcements/speech-by-lord-justice-gross-how-can-judges-strengthen-the-rule-of-law/.
Discusses the importance of the rule of law in the justice system

Lord Woolf, The Lord Chief Justice of England and Wales, *The Rule of Law and a Change in the Constitution*, Squire Centenary Lecture, Cambridge University, 3 March 2004.
An accessible discussion, especially on the role of the Lord Chancellor and judicial independence

Linklaters Report, *In Defence of the Rule of Law*, at www.linklaters.com/en/insights/thought-leadership/rule-of-law/the-rule-of-law.
Wide-ranging suggestions for improving the rule of law post-Brexit

Online resources

www.oup.com/he/dennett2e

This chapter is accompanied by a selection of online resources to help you with this topic, including:

- Multiple-choice questions
- Answers to the self-test questions
- Guidance on answering the exam question

9 Constitutional rights and principles

□ **LEARNING OBJECTIVES**

By the end of this chapter, you should be able to:

● Explain how the judiciary's role in protecting fundamental rights and principles connects to the rule of law

● Evaluate the issues in case law concerning the rule of law and parliamentary sovereignty

● Appreciate the tensions that can exist between parliamentary sovereignty, separation of powers, and the rule of law

● Be aware of differences in judicial and academic opinion in this area

Introduction

There is something interesting happening in the courts, particularly the UK Supreme Court; in this chapter, we explore contemporary judicial thinking on the constitution at a deeper level, in the form of the courts' application of common law constitutional rights and principles. This is a controversial area where judges uphold the rule of law to restrict not only government power, but occasionally the meaning of statutes in order to protect the fundamental rights, principles, and values that permeate the UK constitution. This can create tensions between parliamentary sovereignty, separation of powers, and rule of law. The courts' increasing emphasis on constitutional rights and principles-based reasoning is strengthening the normative foundations of the constitutional order and moving the UK closer to being a legal constitution.

This chapter is designed to give you a more in-depth understanding of the application of constitutional principles by the courts, showing a more nuanced view of the operation of the constitution and highlighting the dynamic nature of public law. The chapter explains the concept of common law constitutional rights and common law constitutionalism, and introduces you to the important principle of legality; understanding the application of this principle by the courts helps to connect parliamentary sovereignty, separation of powers, and rule of law, and will help you understand elements of the judicial review process. We examine the relationship

Figure 9.1 Summary of parliamentary sovereignty, separation of powers, and the rule of law

Parliamentary sovereignty remains a cornerstone of the UK constitution. It is not an absolute idea of an all-powerful Parliament, but means that the UK Parliament has legislative supremacy. It is the role of judges to interpret and apply statutes but they cannot strike down an Act of Parliament for being invalid, or change the words or meaning of a statute.

The separation of powers requires that each of the three arms of state has its own functions, but in the UK, rather than rigid separation, there is interaction, ensuring accountability of the executive through parliamentary control and Judicial Review by the courts. Within the triangle of state institutions, the balance of power is still weighted towards Parliament.

The rule of law is respected by all three arms of state and ensures that the law binds everyone, especially those in government. The courts are the ultimate guardians of the rule of law and ensure that procedures are followed fairly and the substantive principles, rights, and values that it protects are upheld.

between parliamentary sovereignty and the rule of law, focusing in particular on the *Evans* and *Privacy International* cases, and the issues that can sometimes arise in cases where the courts uphold common law constitutional rights.

9.1 Background: constitutional principles

The three bedrock constitutional principles are parliamentary sovereignty, separation of powers, and the rule of law, and their application can have significant impact in the operation of public law in the courts (see Figure 9.1 for a recap and Chapters 6–8).

 THINKING POINT

Do you think there is a dominant principle?

We can progress the ideas in Figure 9.1 to raise some controversial issues:

- If Parliament enacted a statute that ignores or overrides fundamental constitutional principles such as the right of access to the courts, could judges change the meaning of words in the statute or declare it invalid?

- What happens if the judiciary gives more weight to the rule of law than to parliamentary sovereignty? These are issues that we address in this chapter, but first we explore the doctrine of common law constitutional rights.

9.2 The doctrine of common law constitutional rights

⟩ CROSS REFERENCE

For more on Convention rights, see Chapters 17–18

Here, we open up a new layer which underlies the constitution: common law constitutional (or fundamental) rights. In the UK, certain fundamental rights exist within the common law; they are not found in statutes or a written constitution, and operate alongside the rights enshrined in the European Convention on Human Rights. In the past decade, there has been an expansion in the constitutional role of the judiciary through a notable trend where the courts give greater emphasis to their role as guardians of the rule of law and apply common law fundamental rights, values and principles when they are interpreting statutes and reviewing executive actions. This can be seen, for example, in *Osborn v Parole Board* [2013] UKSC 61 (see Lord Reed at paras 55–62) and *Kennedy v Charity Commission* [2014] UKSC 20. Elliott identifies this as 'part of a new stream of constitutional jurisprudence emerging from the Supreme Court' ('Common-Law Constitutionalism and Proportionality in the Supreme Court: Kennedy v The Charity Commission', Public Law for Everyone blog, 31 March 2014, https://publiclawforeveryone.com/2014/03/31/common-law-constitutionalism-and-proportionality-in-the-supreme-court-kennedy-v-the-charity-commission/). The *Miller/Cherry* case demonstrates how the constitutional principles of parliamentary sovereignty and parliamentary accountability restricted the Prime Minister's exercise of the prerogative power to prorogue Parliament (*R (Miller) v The Prime Minister; Cherry and others v Advocate General for Scotland* [2019] UKSC 41, [2019] 3 WLR 589). The Supreme Court described the courts' responsibility 'of upholding the values and principles of our constitution and making them effective' ([39]) and added that 'the legal principles of the constitution are not confined to statutory rules, but include constitutional principles developed by the common law' to protect individual rights and regulate the conduct of public bodies and the relationships between them [40].

Lord Toulson has described the common law as 'the soil in which our courts work and have nurtured the rights which have come to be regarded as part of the essential framework of the law' ('Fundamental Rights and the Common Law', Keynote address at the Fundamental Rights Conference: A Public Law Perspective, LSE, 10 October 2015), while Lord Cooke has observed that 'some rights are inherent and fundamental to democratic civilised society' (*R v Secretary of State for the Home Department, ex parte Daly* [2001] UKHL 26 [30]). The courts presume that government ministers and Parliament—within the limits of parliamentary sovereignty—will act in conformity with those fundamental rights.

Consequently, common law rights and principles can operate as a constitutional constraint. It should be pointed out, however, that this notion of 'common law constitutionalism' has been criticised and its legitimacy is controversial among some academic commentators

9.2.1 What are common law constitutional rights and values?

There is no definitive list of common law constitutional rights and values and they are unwritten, but they are essentially the rights and values protected by the rule of law that have evolved as rules of 'fair play' and justice (see Chapter 8; and *Miller/Cherry* [40]). They include:

- Justice
- Legality (see section 9.2.2)
- Fundamental rights such as liberty, freedom of expression, and equality

- Accountable government (a government that is politically answerable to the democratically elected representatives of the people and legally to the courts)

- Democracy (respect for democratic principles and representative government, though see *Moohan v The Lord Advocate* [2014] UKSC 67 [33–38 and 56] on the right of convicted prisoners to vote in the Scottish independence referendum).

These common law rights are not simply plucked out of thin air by judges but have evolved and been applied in cases over a long period of time (though new rights can emerge). However, the unwritten nature of this can make it unclear whether a particular right or principle exists. In *Elgizouli v Secretary of State for the Home Department* [2020] UKSC 10, four Justices of the Supreme Court thought there was no common law principle deeming it unlawful to facilitate the trial of an individual abroad where there was a risk of being executed ([4]); Lord Kerr concluded that there was ([142]). Lord Reed argued that it was more apt to describe the right to life in this sense as a value to which the courts attach great significance ([175]).

To help you understand how constitutional rights and values are applied by the courts, the principles of justice are used as an illustration in Table 9.1.

Lord Hoffmann's widely cited statement in the case of *Simms* is the classic embodiment of the doctrine of common law constitutional rights. The case concerned two prisoners serving life sentences for murder, who had unsuccessfully appealed against their convictions and wanted to speak to journalists so that the safety of their convictions could be investigated and publicised in the media to help their cases to be reopened; however, the Home Secretary's policy was generally not to allow interviews with journalists in prisons, so the prison governors refused to allow the interviews unless the journalists undertook not to publish anything, which they refused to do. The case therefore raised issues of the prisoners' rights of freedom of speech and access to justice. The House of Lords held that the blanket ban on interviews was unlawful. Lord Hoffmann said:

> Parliamentary sovereignty means that Parliament can, if it chooses, legislate contrary to fundamental principles of human rights … The constraints upon its exercise by Parliament are ultimately political, not legal. But the principle of legality means that Parliament must squarely confront what it is doing and accept the political cost. Fundamental rights cannot be overridden by general or ambiguous words. This is because there is too great a risk that the full implications of their unqualified meaning may have passed unnoticed in the democratic process. In the absence of express language or necessary implication to the contrary, the courts therefore presume that even the most general words were intended to be subject to the basic rights of the individual. In this way the courts of the United Kingdom, though acknowledging the sovereignty of Parliament, apply principles of constitutionality little different from those which exist in countries where the power of the legislature is expressly limited by a constitutional document. (*R v Secretary of State for the Home Department ex parte Simms* [2000] 2 AC 115, at p 131)

The important points in Lord Hoffmann's statement are:

- Parliament is sovereign and can make laws which override fundamental rights, but it must do so in clear language, not in general or ambiguous words.

- While Parliament can legally pass such legislation, there may be a political price to pay (for example, would people re-elect MPs who had passed such an Act?).

- Generalised or ambiguous words in a statute will be interpreted by the courts in a limited way as the courts are responsible for defending fundamental rights.

Table 9.1 Principles of justice include the following

- **The right of unimpeded access to the courts** In *R v SSHD ex parte Anufrijeva* [2003] UKHL 36, Lord Steyn affirmed the right of access to justice as 'a fundamental and constitutional principle of our legal system' ([26]). Laws LJ in *R (The Children's Rights Alliance for England) v Secretary of State for Justice* [2013] EWCA Civ 34 said that 'The common law recognises access to the Queen's courts as a constitutional right' ([29]), describing it as 'a duty, owed by the State, not to place obstacles in the way of access to justice' that 'is inherent in the rule of law' ([38]). In *R v Lord Chancellor ex parte Witham* [1998] QB 575, secondary legislation removing exemptions from court fees for people on income support was held to be invalid because it denied individuals the constitutional right of access to the courts. Laws J observed that common law constitutional rights can only be overridden by specific provisions in an Act of Parliament, and Parliament had not given the Lord Chancellor the power to deprive individuals of the constitutional right of access to the courts; this right acted as an implied limit on the Lord Chancellor's powers (see *Witham* pp 580, 586). See also *Raymond v Honey* [1981] UKHL 8, [1982] AC 1; *Bremer Vulkan Schiffbau und Maschinenfabrik v South India Shipping Corpn Ltd* [1981] AC 909; *R (UNISON) v Lord Chancellor* [2017] UKSC 51.

- **Open justice** Hearings in court should be in public, not in secret, to ensure transparency and public confidence that justice is being done in the courts, and Lord Judge CJ has observed that the principle of open justice brings together democratic accountability, freedom of expression, and the rule of law (see *R (Binyam Mohamed) v Secretary of State for Foreign and Commonwealth Affairs* [2010] EWCA Civ 65 [39]). In *Al Rawi v The Security Service* [2011] UKSC 34, six former detainees at Guantanamo Bay claimed damages in tort from the respondents (who included MI5, MI6, and two government departments). The respondents wished to disclose certain evidence to the court in 'closed material proceedings' but not to disclose it to the claimants and their lawyers because of its sensitivity. The Supreme Court held that, unless a statute allowed it, the common law would not permit ordinary civil claims to be conducted in private and in the absence of a party and their legal advisors, and the majority strongly affirmed the fundamental common law principles that all parties to a case see all the evidence and that trials should be conducted in public ([10–17, 47–48] (Lord Dyson)). See also *Bank Mellat v Her Majesty's Treasury (No 1)* [2013] UKSC 38; *A v BBC* [2014] UKSC 25, [2014] 2 WLR 1243; Lord Neuberger of Abbotsbury MR, *Open Justice Unbound?* Judicial Studies Board annual lecture 2011, 16 March 2011.

- **Access to legal advice and the right to legal professional privilege** In *R (Daly) v Secretary of State for the Home Department* [2001] UKHL 26, [2001] 2 AC 532, a policy that prisoners were not allowed to be present while their cells were being searched by prison officers was held to be unlawful, because searches could include examination of correspondence between prisoners and their solicitors. The policy therefore infringed the common law right to confidential privileged legal correspondence. See also *R v SSHD ex parte Anderson* [1984] QB 778; *R v Secretary of State for the Home Department, ex parte Leech* [1994] QB 198.

> Legal professional privilege means that correspondence between solicitors and clients is confidential

- **Procedural fairness** The common law principle of procedural fairness requires ministers and public bodies to act fairly in following procedures, making decisions and allowing fair hearings. For example, it was held in *Osborn v Parole Board* [2013] UKSC 61, a leading case on procedural fairness, that the Parole Board should hold an oral hearing whenever fairness to the prisoner requires one. *R v SSHD ex parte Doody* [1994] 1 AC 531 held that a prisoner should be provided with material which the Home Secretary would consider when fixing his life sentence to enable the prisoner to make effective arguments about the length of his sentence (see also *R v SSHD, ex parte Venables* [1997] 3 WLR 23). *Anufrijeva* (above) held that individuals have the right to know of a decision before their rights can be adversely affected. Procedural fairness is an important ground for judicial review (see Chapter 16).

THINKING POINT

Is Lord Hoffmann putting constraints on Parliament's legislative authority here?

- Although they acknowledge parliamentary sovereignty, the courts are protecting constitutional principles and values, just as if the UK had a written constitution setting them out, but it is important to understand that Lord Hoffmann's view only applies where an Act of Parliament overrides the rule of law or fundamental rights using general or ambiguous words. The courts must apply words in a statute that are clear, and they have no power to strike down an Act of Parliament.

THE BIGGER PICTURE: COMMON LAW CONSTITUTIONALISM

'Constitutionalism' is the idea that there should be legal and political limits on the power of government; common law constitutionalism refers to the idea of a constitution based on unassailable common law principles. By upholding the rights of the individual in the way described by Lord Hoffmann, the courts are applying the rule of law and using the common law as a controlling mechanism to protect constitutional rights and principles. This, however, raises the question of whether the rule of law means control by common law.

The concept of 'common law constitutionalism' supports the courts' use of the common law as a legal control on governmental power (see Lady Hale, 'UK Constitutionalism on the March?' Keynote address to the Constitutional and Administrative Law Bar Association Conference, 12 July 2014; T.R.S. Allan, *The Sovereignty of Law*, Oxford: Oxford University Press, 2013, chapters 3 and 8). An example of this is the *UNISON case (R (UNISON) v Lord Chancellor* [2017] UKSC 51), where the Supreme Court decided that the government's imposition of fees in employment tribunal cases was illegal because it prevented access to justice, a fundamental common law principle. Lord Reed stated that the court must consider not only the text of the relevant statutory provision, 'but also the constitutional principles which underlie the text, and the principles of statutory interpretation which give effect to those principles' ([65]). Here is the doctrine of common law constitutional rights in operation.

In a critical analysis of the *UNISON case*, Sir Stephen Laws has argued that by setting aside the Fees Order because it had the *effect* of preventing access to justice, the Supreme Court was applying a retrospective success test, and by asking whether the Fees Order could be justified as a necessary intrusion on the right of access to justice, it was also determining a policy question that was not for a court to decide; public expenditure decisions on services are complex matters for political rather than judicial resolution. Sir Stephen argues for a better understanding between the arms of state about their constitutional roles in this respect and cautions that the courts and Parliament should not compete with each other to find different solutions to the same problem (*Second-Guessing Policy Choices: The Rule of Law after the Supreme Court's UNISON Judgment*, Policy Exchange, 14 March 2018, p 37).

Opponents of common law constitutionalism argue that there is a risk of unelected judges over-asserting their power and usurping parliamentary sovereignty (see Jeffrey Goldsworthy, 'Losing Faith in Democracy: Why Judicial Supremacy Is Rising and What to Do about It', Launch of Policy Exchange Judicial Power Project, 9 March 2015; see also Richard Ekins, 'Judicial Supremacy and the Rule of Law' (2003) 119 LQR 127). In short, common law constitutionalism can raise separation of powers issues, and tensions can arise between upholding the rule of law and parliamentary sovereignty. If judicial power expands, then Parliament's authority diminishes.

CROSS REFERENCE

See section 6.4.2 on the controlling common law

9.2.2 The principle of legality

Lord Hoffmann refers in *Simms* to 'the principle of legality'. This is an important, long-standing principle of statutory construction that where a statute overrides common law rights and principles, it will be interpreted by the courts in a limited way unless the words are very clear (*United States v Fisher* (1805) 6 US (2 Cranch) 358; *Viscountess Rhondda's Claim* [1922] 2 AC 339). Lord Steyn explains it in this way: 'Unless there is the clearest provision to the contrary, Parliament must be presumed not to legislate contrary to the rule of law. And the rule of law enforces minimum standards of fairness, both substantive and procedural' (*R v Secretary of State for the Home Department, ex p Pierson* [1997] UKHL 37, [1998] AC 539, 591). Lord Reed has defined the principle of legality as meaning 'not only that Parliament cannot itself override fundamental rights or the rule of law by general or ambiguous words, but also that it cannot confer on another body, by general or ambiguous words, the power to do so' (*AXA General Insurance Ltd v HM Advocate* [2011] UKSC 46, [2012] 1 AC 868 [152]; see also *Pham v SSHD* [2015] UKSC 19 [118] (Lord Reed)), so when a statute gives powers to ministers or public bodies, the courts presume that Parliament intended them to act in conformity with common law principles.

The principle of legality is important because it protects common law procedural safeguards and fundamental rights, and shows the practical operation of the rule of law in the courts; some judges see this as common law 'supplementing statutes on the basis of the principle of legality' (*Pierson*, 588 (Lord Steyn)).

However, it must be emphasised that the principle of legality does not override parliamentary sovereignty, which still predominates. Lady Hale has stated: 'The courts will … decline to hold that Parliament has interfered with fundamental rights unless it has made its intentions crystal clear' (*Jackson v Attorney General* [2005] UKHL 56 [159]). This is because clear language denotes that the provision has been carefully considered by Parliament; words which are unclear, or that do not specifically spell out their scope or effect, suggest that the implications for rights may not have been thought through. Thus, Parliament *can* override fundamental rights by statute if it does so expressly in crystal clear language, and it is free to amend or repeal any statute that the courts have interpreted in a restrictive way. As Lord Steyn points out:

> Parliament does not legislate in a vacuum. Parliament legislates for a European liberal democracy founded on the principles and traditions of the common law. And the courts may approach legislation on this initial assumption. But this assumption only has prima facie force. It

can be displaced by a clear and specific provision to the contrary. (*R v Home Secretary, ex parte Pierson* [1998] AC 539, 587; see also Lord Browne-Wilkinson at 576).

Alison Young and Paul Craig regard the principle of legality as not only a tool of statutory interpretation, but a constitutional principle which the court applied to the prerogative power to prorogue in *Miller/Cherry*, a discretionary power not based on statute (A. Young, 'Prorogation, Politics and the Principle of Legality', UK Const L Blog (13 September 2019) (available at https://ukconstitutionallaw.org/); Paul Craig, 'The Supreme Court, Prorogation and Constitutional Principle' (2020) (April) Public Law 248).

SUMMARY

- The principle of legality means that the courts presume that Parliament did not intend to override or interfere with fundamental rights or principles when it creates law, unless it has made it crystal clear.

- Where Parliament grants powers in a statute to members of the executive or other public bodies, the courts also presume that Parliament intended those powers to be exercised in accordance with common law principles.

- However, the courts need to balance protecting fundamental rights and principles with recognising that Parliament has the final word. Parliament can curtail rights by clear statutory language. At most, the courts can interpret a statute in a restricted way if it overrides or interferes with constitutional rights or principles in words that are not crystal clear.

9.3 Parliamentary sovereignty and the rule of law

Dicey saw the constitution as based on the principles of parliamentary sovereignty and the rule of law, with parliamentary sovereignty as the dominant principle (see Chapter 8). But what would happen if the rule of law prevailed over parliamentary sovereignty in the courts (see Figure 9.2)? Is it possible to respect both the sovereignty of the legislature and the rule of law?

Masterman and Murkens refer to 'the tension between the legal controls imposed by the rule of law and the theoretically limitless legal powers wielded by Parliament' ('Skirting Supremacy and Subordination', 812, in 'Further reading'), and the *Evans case* discussed presently demonstrates these tensions. Lord Steyn points out that 'until recently it was confidently assumed that parliamentary supremacy ultimately always trumps the rule of law' ('Democracy, the Rule of Law and the Role of Judges', 248, in 'Further reading') and 'the rule of law could never prevail against an express enactment of Parliament' (249). Dicta in *Jackson v AG* loosened the ties of parliamentary sovereignty (see Chapter 6) and in *Moohan v The Lord Advocate* [2014] UKSC 67, Lord Hodge suggested that in the—admittedly unlikely—event that Parliament passed a law curtailing the right to vote, 'the common law, informed by principles of democracy and the rule of law and international norms, would be able to declare such legislation unlawful' [35]. However, this would fly in the face of parliamentary sovereignty, and there is the possibility that if judges become too assertive, 'Parliament may clip their wings' (H.W.R. Wade and C.F. Forsyth,

Figure 9.2 The balance between parliamentary sovereignty and rule of law

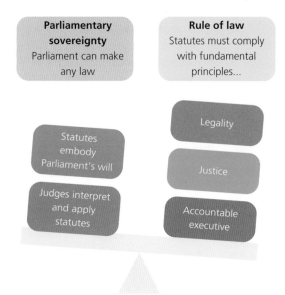

Administrative Law, 10th edn (Oxford: Oxford University Press 2009) p 26). The Supreme Court in *Miller I* made it clear that the judiciary's role is to uphold the rule of law by impartially identifying and applying the law, but not to apply or develop common law inconsistently with Acts of Parliament (*R (Miller) v Secretary of State for Exiting the European Union* [2017] UKSC 5 [42]). It therefore depends on how 'upholding the rule of law' is defined.

9.3.1 The *Evans case* (the 'black spider memo case')

The tension between rule of law and parliamentary sovereignty was one of the central issues in the *Evans case*. This was a significant constitutional decision which highlights that the balance between the principles of parliamentary sovereignty, separation of powers, and the rule of law is a delicate one, and giving too much emphasis to one can disrupt that balance.

> **🔍 CASE CLOSE-UP: *R (EVANS) v ATTORNEY GENERAL* [2015] UKSC 21, [2015] AC 1787**
>
> A *Guardian* newspaper journalist, Rob Evans, used the Freedom of Information Act 2000 to request the disclosure of letters written by Prince Charles to government ministers in 2004–2005 on policy issues, including environmental matters. The correspondence was known as the 'black-spider memos' because of Prince Charles's handwriting style and the black ink used. The relevant government departments refused to release the letters on the grounds of public interest (Part II of the Freedom of Information Act 2000 allows certain exemptions from disclosure). This was the subsequent sequence of events:
>
> • Mr Evans complained to the Information Commissioner, who upheld the departments' refusal to disclose the letters.

The Freedom of Information Act 2000 was created to ensure more transparent and accountable government by allowing public access to information held by public authorities

- He appealed to the Upper Tribunal, a judicial body with the same status as the High Court, which determined that many of the letters should be disclosed because the public right to know about Prince Charles' influence on ministers was greater than the public interest in keeping the letters confidential.

- The Attorney General then issued a certificate overriding the Upper Tribunal's decision and stating that the government departments had been entitled to refuse disclosure because the letters were private and confidential and protected by constitutional conventions; they were part of Prince Charles' preparation for kingship and disclosure might damage perceptions of his political neutrality and undermine his ability to serve as king. Section 53 of the Freedom of Information Act allows members of the government to issue a certificate overriding an order for disclosure where there are reasonable grounds for their opinion that non-disclosure would not be unlawful; this is known as an 'executive-override power' or the 'ministerial veto power'.

> Note the constitutional conventions arising in this case

- So Mr Evans brought judicial review proceedings, claiming that the Attorney General's certificate was invalid. His claim failed in the High Court, but succeeded in the Court of Appeal.

- The Attorney General appealed to the Supreme Court.

The Supreme Court held by a majority that the letters were not exempt from disclosure, but there was a marked difference of opinion in the four judgments. The central issue in the case was the meaning of section 53 but the theme is: who has the last word—Parliament, the executive, or the courts?

Parliamentary sovereignty and the rule of law

The reason for the differences in judicial opinion was the different weight given by members of the court to the principles of parliamentary sovereignty and the rule of law.

At one end of the scale, Lord Neuberger, Lord Kerr, and Lord Reed gave greater weight to the rule of law and applied a weak view of parliamentary sovereignty, interpreting section 53(2) very restrictively as requiring exceptional circumstances for overriding a disclosure order, to ensure compliance with fundamental principles (even though section 53(2) did not expressly refer to 'exceptional circumstances').

Lord Neuberger took the view that the Attorney General had interpreted section 53 as meaning that members of the executive could override a judicial decision because they disagreed with it, and said that when the courts interpret an Act, 'they should bear in mind established constitutional principles' ([92]). Applying a clear separation of powers between the judiciary and executive, he stated:

> A statutory provision which entitles a member of the executive … to overrule a decision of the judiciary merely because he does not agree with it would not merely be unique in the laws of the United Kingdom. It would cut across two constitutional principles which are also fundamental components of the rule of law … subject to being overruled by a higher court or (given Parliamentary supremacy) a statute, it is a basic principle that a decision of a court is binding as between the parties, and cannot be ignored or set aside by anyone, including (indeed it may fairly be said, least of all) the executive ([51–52]).

Furthermore, in the UK, decisions of the executive are reviewable by the courts, not the other way round. Lord Neuberger concluded that the words of section 53 needed to be crystal clear that fundamental constitutional principles were not being applied, and they were not clear ([58, 90]).

Lord Mance and Lady Hale concluded that section 53 had a wider meaning than the one given by Lord Neuberger, but the Attorney General had not shown reasonable grounds for disagreeing with the Upper Tribunal.

Lord Hughes (dissenting in part) stated that Parliament, in section 53, had given an override power to the executive where there were reasonable grounds for disagreeing with the Information Commissioner or a court, and the Attorney General had given reasonable reasons for deciding that non-disclosure was in the public interest. Lord Hughes said that the rule of law is 'of the first importance', but 'it is an integral part of the rule of law that courts give effect to Parliamentary intention' ([154]). He also pointed out that the rule of law does not mean that courts must always prevail. The issue was 'a matter of the plain words of the statute' ([155]) and Parliament had made its intention plain. If it had wanted to limit the power as argued by Lord Neuberger, Parliament would have said so.

At the opposite end of the scale from Lord Neuberger, Lord Wilson (dissenting) upheld a strong view of parliamentary sovereignty. He forcefully criticised the Court of Appeal (and the majority decision) for rewriting section 53 rather than interpreting it, stating that among the most precious constitutional principles is 'parliamentary sovereignty, emblematic of our democracy' ([168]). He concluded that section 53 allowed the Attorney General to override the Tribunal where he disagreed on matters of public interest (which lie within the government's sphere of expertise) ([171]). To avoid 'executive encroachment', Parliament had written safeguards into the Act, and the certificate could be challenged by judicial review ([172]).

 THINKING POINT

Which of the four approaches in *Evans* do you find most persuasive? Look back at each judgment and think about who had the final word on section 53: Parliament, the executive, or the courts?

 THE BIGGER PICTURE: A CRITICAL VIEW OF THE EVANS CASE

The *Evans* case has shone a bright light on differences of opinion, academic and judicial, about the balance between parliamentary sovereignty and the rule of law, and especially the use of constitutional principles in the interpretation of statutes. For commentary, see:

T.R.S. Allan, 'The Rule of Law, Parliamentary Sovereignty, and a Ministerial Veto over Judicial Decisions' (2015) 74(3) Cambridge Law Journal 385. Allan takes the view that the majority correctly applied the rule of law to limit parliamentary sovereignty.

Mark Elliott, 'A Tangled Constitutional Web: The Black-Spider Memos and the British Constitution's Relational Architecture' (2015) (October) Public Law 539. Elliott describes Lord Neuberger's approach as 'radical interpretive surgery pursuant to the principle of legality', and observes that judges are obliged to interpret statutes, not treat them as 'an essentially blank canvas on which to project constitutional values' which can overwhelm them; he argues that Lord Neuberger's interpretation of section 53 may have crossed the dividing line between 'bold statutory construction' and 'a soft form of judicial strike-down'.

Richard Ekins and Christopher Forsyth, 'Judging the Public Interest: The Rule of Law vs. The Rule of Courts', Policy Exchange (https://policyexchange.org.uk/). Ekins and Forsyth argue that the majority judgments in *Evans* are contrary to separation of powers and the rule of law and the quashing of executive power granted by Parliament demonstrates 'judicial over-reach'.

See also:

T.R.S. Allan, 'Law, Democracy, and Constitutionalism: Reflections on Evans v Attorney General' (2016) 75(1) Cambridge Law Journal 38

Robert Craig, 'Black Spiders Weaving Webs: The Constitutional Implications of Executive Veto of Tribunal Determinations' (2016) 79(1) MLR 166

T. Fairclough, 'What's New about the Rule of Law? A Reply to Michal Hain', UK Const L Blog (18 Sept. 2017) (available at https://ukconstitutionallaw.org/)

9.3.2 The *Privacy International case*

The judgments in *R (Privacy International) v Investigatory Powers Tribunal* [2019] UKSC 22 also illustrate the spectrum of judicial thinking on the rule of law and parliamentary sovereignty. Members of the court disagreed on precise aspects of what the rule of law required in this case. It concerned the effect of an ouster clause in section 67(8) Regulation of Investigatory Powers Act 2000 which excluded decisions of the Investigatory Powers Tribunal from appeal or challenge in any court, and the issue turned on the requirements of the rule of law. The majority (4:3) of the Supreme Court interpreted the wording in section 67(8) as not explicit enough to exclude the High Court's jurisdiction over judicial review challenges based on an error of law. Lord Carnwath, for the majority, saw this not as a matter of ordinary statutory interpretation to discern Parliament's intention but of applying the strong common law presumption against excluding judicial review except by 'the most clear and explicit words' [37, 107]; if Parliament had not made its intention sufficiently clear, it was not for the court to stretch the words used beyond their natural meaning [111].

In arriving at his conclusion, Lord Carnwath strongly upheld the rule of law, stating that it is for the courts to determine the content and limits of the rule of law and no ouster clause can exclude certain fundamental requirements of the rule of law from the supervision of the courts [122–123]. He referred to a balance between parliamentary sovereignty and the rule of law [130] and a 'more flexible approach to the relationship between the legislature and the courts' where it is ultimately for the courts, not Parliament, 'to determine the limits set by the rule of law' to ouster clauses [131; see also 144]. He regarded this as 'an essential counterpart' to Parliament's law-making power; it respected the constitutional roles of Parliament as law-maker, and the courts as guardians and interpreters of that law [132].

Lord Sumption and Lord Reed (dissenting) decided that section 67(8) excluded the High Court's jurisdiction in this case. They agreed that a right of access *to* a judicial body to review the lawfulness of executive acts is an essential part of the rule of law, but the rule of law did not require a right of appeal or judicial review *from* such a body [182]. Lord Sumption stated:

> The rule of law applies as much to the courts as it does to anyone else, and under our constitution, that requires that effect must be given to Parliamentary legislation. In the absence of a written constitution capable of serving as a higher source of law, the status of Parliamentary legislation as the ultimate source of law is the foundation of democracy in the United Kingdom. The alternative would be to treat the courts as being entitled on their own initiative to create a higher source of law than statute, namely their own decisions ([209])

Lord Wilson (dissenting) took a strong view of parliamentary sovereignty, warning that, in ascertaining the presumed intention of Parliament, the courts cannot strain the meaning of statutory words too far [214] and he decided that section 67(8) clearly excluded judicial review of all the IPT's decisions.

While the majority positioned the courts firmly as gatekeepers of the rule of law, Lord Wilson made a telling observation: Lord Carnwath's view that it was for the courts to determine the extent to which an ouster clause should be upheld, based on the rule of law, did not identify 'any robust criterion' to enable a court's decision in a case to be predicted [237]. Lord Sumption also pointed out the dangers of the more radical view where the rule of law is the foundation of the constitution (see *R (Jackson) v Attorney General* [2006] 1 AC 262 [102] (Lord Steyn); [104–108] (Lord Hope)); it would limit the sovereignty of Parliament 'in the name of a higher law, ascertained and applied by the court', and Parliament would not be able to legislate contrary to the rule of law [208].

9.4 Parliamentary sovereignty and the separation of powers

The *Evans case* highlights the importance of maintaining the dividing line between judicial interpretation and Parliament's role as legislator, and particularly divisions on the issue of who has the last word. However, on one view, the relationship between Parliament and the courts is interactive and based on a constitutional dialogue. Lord Steyn observed in *Pierson* that 'Ultimately, common law and statute law coalesce in one legal system' (p 589). Some commentators have suggested a view of sovereignty which is shared between Parliament and the judiciary—known as 'bi-polar sovereignty'—where Parliament has legislative sovereignty and the courts have enforcement sovereignty based on their interpretative function of statutes (see S. Sedley, 'Human Rights: A Twenty-First Century Agenda' (1995) (January) Public Law 386; C.J.S. Knight, 'Bi-polar Sovereignty Restated' (2009) 68(2) Cambridge Law Journal 361; C.J.S. Knight, 'Striking Down Legislation under Bi-polar Sovereignty' (2011) (January) Public Law 90). Laws LJ saw the symbiotic nature of the rule of law's requirement of an impartial, authoritative judicial interpreter of law as affirming parliamentary sovereignty by ensuring that Parliament's statutes are effective (*R (Cart) v The Upper Tribunal* [2009] EWHC 3052 (Admin) [36–39]). Sedley refers to the 'unique interpenetration of the legislative and judicial powers, for what an Act of Parliament means is what the courts decide it means' (S. Sedley, 'This Beats Me', (1998) (2 April) 20(7) London Review of Books 3), and this echoes the words of Hart: 'A supreme tribunal has the last word in saying what the law is and, when it has said it, the statement that the court was "wrong" has no consequences within the system: no one's rights or duties are thereby altered' (H.L.A. Hart, *The Concept of Law*, 2nd edn, Oxford: Oxford University Press, 1994, p 141).

However, there are equally strong views in support of traditional parliamentary sovereignty. Forsyth cautions against seeing a statute as 'an empty vessel' into which judges can pour a meaning, and emphasises the critical importance of judicial obedience to parliamentary supremacy; in other words, a statute means what Parliament intended. For the judges to deprive Parliament of its supremacy, he argues, 'would amount to a group of unelected officials taking over the ultimate decision-making authority in our constitutional order. No misty eyed rhetoric about the wisdom or the method of the common law can conceal the fact that this would be a coup, a seizure of power' (Professor Christopher Forsyth, 'Who Is the Ultimate Guardian of the Constitution? In Reply to Sir John Laws' [7, 11], in 'Further reading'). Lord Wilberforce cautioned that where legislation impairs the rights of citizens, the courts should resolve any doubt in interpretation in their favour, but 'it is no part of their duty, or power, to restrict or impede the working of legislation, even of unpopular legislation; to do so would be to weaken rather than to advance the democratic process' (*R v Inland Revenue Commissioners ex p Rossminster Ltd* [1980] AC 952, 998). Ensuring the separation of powers thus involves self-regulation by the judges so as not to encroach on Parliament's legislative role, and respect on Parliament's part for constitutional rights and principles.

 SUMMARY

- The courts uphold and apply the rule of law by protecting and enforcing constitutional principles, rights and values in their interpretation of statutes and through the judicial review process

- But the UK Parliament can override fundamental rights in a statute by crystal clear wording because parliamentary sovereignty is still the cornerstone of the UK constitution

- There is a delicate balance between the constitutional principles of parliamentary sovereignty, separation of powers, and rule of law

? | # Questions

Self-test questions

1. What is meant by 'constitutional rights and values'?

2. Summarise the key points made by Lord Hoffmann in the *Simms* case.

3. What is common law constitutionalism?

4. What is the principle of legality? Why is it important?

5. Summarise the different approaches in the judgments in the *Evans* case.

6. What issues can arise where judges give greater weight to the rule of law and constitutional principles when interpreting statutes?

7. What is bi-polar sovereignty?

Exam question

'The *Evans* case clearly shows that the judiciary, not Parliament, has ultimate decision-making authority on legislation in the UK constitution.' Critically discuss whether this is an accurate view, or whether Parliament is still sovereign.

 Further reading

Books

Elliott, M. and Hughes, K. (eds) *Common Law Constitutional Rights* (Oxford: Hart Publishing 2020).
Examines developing judicial reasoning based on common law constitutional rights

Journal articles

Allan, T.R.S. 'Questions of Legality and Legitimacy: Form and Substance in British Constitutionalism' (2011) 9(1) International Journal of Constitutional Law 155.
This more advanced article argues that the UK has a common law constitution in which parliamentary sovereignty is implicitly limited by the principle of legality

Elliott, M. 'Beyond the European Convention: Human Rights and the Common Law' (2015) 68(1) Current Legal Problems 85.
Examines the resurgence of common law rights and values in the Supreme Court; this is a useful article to return to when you have studied the Human Rights Act and judicial review

Lakin, S. 'Debunking the Idea of Parliamentary Sovereignty: The Controlling Factor of Legality in the British Constitution' (2008) 28 (4) Oxf J Leg Stud 709.
Argues that the UK constitution operates on the basis of the principle of legality, not parliamentary sovereignty

Masterman, R. and Murkens, J.E.K. 'Skirting Supremacy and Subordination: The Constitutional Authority of the United Kingdom Supreme Court' (2013) (Oct) Public Law 800.
A challenging but enlightening article which helps an understanding of the role of the Supreme Court in applying constitutional rights and upholding the rule of law

Masterman, R. and Wheatle, S. 'A Common Law Resurgence in Rights Protection?' (2015) 1 EHRLR 57.
Examines protection of common law rights by the Supreme Court; again, an article to re-read after study of the Human Rights Act

Poole, T. 'Back to the Future? Unearthing the Theory of Common Law Constitutionalism' (2003) 23(3) Oxford Journal of Legal Studies 435.
Explains and analyses the theory of common law constitutionalism (also helpful for study of judicial review)

Sales, P. 'Rights and Fundamental Rights in English Law' (2016) 75(1) Cambridge Law Journal 86.
Written by a member of the judiciary, this article is helpful for its discussion of the principle of legality and rule of law

Lord Steyn, 'Democracy, the Rule of Law and the Role of Judges' (2006) 3 European Human Rights Law Review 243.
Revisit this accessible discussion cited in Chapter 8 on the rule of law for greater appreciation of constitutional values and principles

Other sources

Forsyth, C. 'Who Is the Ultimate Guardian of the Constitution? In Reply to Sir John Laws', Debating Judicial Power: Papers from the ALBA Summer Conference, 13 December 2016 (http://judicialpowerproject.org.uk/wp-content/uploads/2016/12/Forsyth-reply-to-Laws2.pdf).
A concise, trenchant critique of judicial assertiveness

Masterman, R. and Wheatle, S. 'Miller/Cherry and Constitutional Principle', UK Const L Blog (14 October 2019) (available at https://ukconstitutionallaw.org/).
A discussion of the Supreme Court's approach in *Miller/Cherry* and *Privacy International*

; Online resources

http://www.oup.com/he/dennett2e

This chapter is accompanied by a selection of online resources to help you with this topic, including:

- Multiple-choice questions
- Answers to the self-test questions
- Guidance on answering the exam question

PART 3

THE ALLOCATION OF POWER IN THE UK: THE THREE ARMS OF STATE

This section examines the allocation of powers and functions, and the interaction, between the three arms of state: the legislature, the executive, and the judiciary. We begin with the legislature, Parliament. Chapter 10 assesses the role and membership of Parliament's two component chambers, the House of Commons and the House of Lords; the operation of parliamentary privilege; and accountability of members; Chapter 11 focuses on Parliament's primary functions of making law and scrutinising government action.

10 The Legislature: membership, privileges, and standards

☐ LEARNING OBJECTIVES

By the end of this chapter, you should be able to:

- Assess the functions of, and relationship between, the House of Commons and the House of Lords
- Discuss issues surrounding the democratic process and representation
- Evaluate reforms of the Lords and whether more reform is necessary
- Analyse the operation of the Parliament Acts 1911 and 1949
- Evaluate the significance and operation of parliamentary privilege and comity between Parliament and the courts

---

Introduction

There is a long-established societal need to organise assemblies to debate important matters such as public finances, good governance, and law-making, evidenced by the Saxon Witan and the Tynwald, the Parliament of the Isle of Man, which was established by the Vikings and has continued uninterrupted for more than a thousand years. Modern legislative assemblies around the world still have the same function.

≫ CROSS REFERENCE

For the historical development of Parliament, see Chapter 2

Parliament in Westminster is the UK's legislature, although Scotland, Wales, and Northern Ireland each have their own legislative bodies with the power to make law on devolved matters (see Chapter 4). The discussion in this chapter focuses on the UK Parliament, the democratically elected, sovereign law-maker whose essential functions are to make primary legislation (Acts of Parliament) and hold the government to account. Parliament is bicameral (composed of two chambers, these being the House of Commons and the House of Lords), but only the House of Commons has elected members and is politically accountable to the electorate.

Since devolution was introduced, the UK Parliament normally makes law for the whole of the UK on non-devolved matters and for England. In this chapter, we examine issues concerning the membership of the House of Commons and the House of Lords, the impact of the Parliament Acts 1911 and 1949, the operation of parliamentary privilege, and members' accountability for conduct.

See the online resources for a glossary of parliamentary terminology

10.1 The role and functions of Parliament

'Parliament is at the heart of our system of governance. It is sovereign. It determines the law and holds the executive to account. Its legitimacy in the eyes of British citizens, and its natural authority depends on the representative, democratic chamber of the Commons and its exclusive role in the raising of taxation and the granting of "supply"—the public's money—to the executive.' (House of Commons Select Committee on Modernisation of the House of Commons, *Revitalising the Chamber: The Role of the Back Bench Member*, First Report of Session 2006–07, HC 337, para 1).

The UK Parliament's functions are summarised by the *Cabinet Manual*:

> controlling national expenditure and taxation; making law; scrutinising executive action; being the source from which the Government is drawn; and debating the issues of the day. All areas of the UK are represented in the House of Commons, which provides a forum for MPs to speak and correspond on behalf of their constituents, where they can seek redress if necessary. (*Cabinet Manual* (2011) p 3, para 7)

It is important to remember the distinction between Parliament and government: Parliament makes law and controls government. The government initiates ideas for new law, and formulates and implements policy.

10.1.1 Controlling national expenditure and taxation

Only the House of Commons has the power to authorise taxes and vote for the supply of money to the government, providing the finances it needs to run the UK. The Commons has asserted 'financial privilege' since the seventeenth century. The Chancellor of the Exchequer delivers the annual Budget Statement to the Commons, detailing the government's financial plans for expenditure and raising revenue. The Statement is debated; Budget Resolutions are agreed; and the Budget's taxation and spending requirements are converted into a Finance Bill which goes through the parliamentary legislative process. Money Bills (Bills of 'aids' (Finance Bills concerning taxation) and Bills of 'supplies' (Consolidated Fund Bills which authorise government spending)) can only be introduced in the House of Commons, and may not be amended by the Lords (Parliament Act 1911 section 1). See House of Lords Constitution Committee, *Money Bills and Commons Financial Privileges*, 10th Report of Session 2010–11, HL Paper 97.

10.1.2 Being the source from which the Government is drawn

The UK's system of parliamentary government means that the government must work through Parliament (see Figure 10.1). The government is created through the House of Commons: the largest political party in the Commons normally forms the government, and most members of the government are drawn from the Commons. The Commons also sustains the government, which needs the consent, support and continued confidence of the House to govern, and a government which cannot command the confidence of the House of Commons must resign (see the Fixed-term Parliaments Act 2011). In this way, Parliament exerts control over the government.

> ▶ CROSS REFERENCE
>
> See Chapter 12

Figure 10.1   The relationship between Parliament and the government

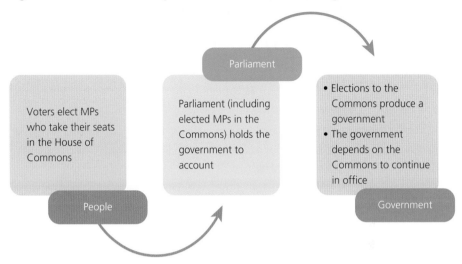

10.1.3   Making law and scrutinising executive action

Both chambers have a law-making role, particularly in scrutinising and assenting to government-driven legislation. The House of Lords' legislative powers have reduced over the past century but it is still an important revising and scrutinising chamber. Its scrutiny, revision and improvement of legislation, often initiated by the government, is vital given the pressure on the Commons' legislative timetable. It can delay controversial Bills and frequently reminds the democratic chamber of the impact of legislation on human rights and the rule of law. Bills can also be introduced in the Lords, with some exceptions.

Both chambers scrutinise government actions and hold government to account but the government is primarily accountable to the House of Commons as the democratic body. Nevertheless, the House of Lords' scrutiny and questioning of government activity is important in a Parliamentary system where the Commons is dominated by the government and there is no codified constitution to act as a normative benchmark.

> **CROSS REFERENCE**
> See Chapter 11 for Parliament's law-making and scrutiny functions

10.1.4   The relationship between the two Houses

The House of Commons is the pre-eminent chamber and dominates Parliament although the Commons in turn is often dominated by the government of the day. Bagehot recognised even in the nineteenth century that the House of Lords' secondary position to the Commons made it the revising chamber to the Common's 'suggesting chamber' but until 1911, the House of Lords had the same legislative powers as the House of Commons and could veto Bills. Their powers were radically limited by the Parliament Acts 1911 and 1949 which asserted the dominance and primacy of the Commons and effectively limited the Lords to a weaker revise-and-scrutinise role with no power over finance (see section 10.4 below).

As the House of Lords is subordinate to the democratically elected House of Commons, it should not challenge its legitimacy or block its democratic will—the Commons has its say and has its way. While it respects the primacy of the Commons, the Lords has a key constitutional role as a safeguard against the concentration of power in a House of Commons dominated by the government and through its veto on the Commons extending its life. The fact that the

House of Lords is unelected means it can take an objective view of issues without the pressure of re-election and the party pressure of the Commons, and its role in the legislative process enables it to exercise 'the most direct influence over the government, promoting and defending the interests of the public' (*Report of the Leader's Group on Working Practices* [70]). Lord Simon of Glaisdale asserted that the Lords is 'effectively the only place in which the legislature can curb the power of the executive' (HL Deb 19 May 1993, Vol 545 col 1804). As an Opposition MP, Theresa May praised the Lords as 'a thorn in the Government's side', and warned against losing its independence as a check on the executive's power (HC Hansard 7 Feb 2007, Vol 456 col 846).

A number of constitutional conventions regulate the relationship between the two Houses and protect the Commons' primacy, including:

- The Salisbury Convention: the House of Lords will not vote down a Bill promised in the government's election manifesto. This means it is given a second reading and no 'wrecking amendments' are imposed on it. This preserves the government's democratic mandate.

- The House of Lords does not normally object to secondary legislation: the Lords *can* veto secondary legislation but rarely do so because it means rejecting secondary legislation outright (known as a fatal motion as it 'kills off' the instrument).

- The Lords considers government business in reasonable time: this prevents unreasonable delays, especially in the legislative process.

- The Lords observes the financial privilege of the House of Commons.

In 2006, a Joint Committee considered codifying the conventions on the relationship between the two Houses of Parliament relating to legislation (Joint Committee on Conventions, *Conventions of the UK Parliament*, Report of Session 2005–06, HL Paper 265, HC 1212). Lord Peyton in the Lords strongly objected to the Committee's appointment:

> I fear, and the Government must hope, that the committee's study of the conventions will somehow help them on a further step down the road to the reduction of your Lordships' House to the status of a laundry. I do not say that a laundry is not needed to tidy up the legislation which comes before us in such bulk, but the idea that we should simply wash and tidy up and iron the laundry and then deliver it again to its source seems unacceptable. (HL Hansard 22 May 2006, Vol 682 col 583)

In the event, the Committee decided against codification.

We turn now to examine each chamber in more detail.

10.2 The House of Commons

Bagehot said that the House of Commons was elective, expressive, teaching, informing, legislative: this means it can sustain and dismiss governments, expresses the views of the people, teaches the nation what it does not know, informs the people about grievances, and makes law. The House of Commons consists of Members of Parliament (MPs) who are democratically elected by the public to represent their interests in Parliament (see Table 10.1 for more details). As at September 2020, there are 650 MPs (see https://members.parliament.uk/parties/Commons).

Table 10.1 Who's who in the House of Commons

The Speaker	The Speaker of the House of Commons is an MP who is the chief officer of the House, presiding over, controlling, and chairing debates, with the power and authority to censure or suspend MPs. The Speaker is elected to office by fellow MPs but must then be politically impartial. This requires them to resign from their party but they retain constituency duties and responsibilities. In a general election, other parties will usually not oppose the 'Speaker seeking re-election' in their constituency to avoid a campaign on party politics
Backbench MPs	Most MPs in the Commons are backbenchers; a backbencher is any MP who is neither a government minister nor a member of the Shadow Cabinet. Their name derives from the fact that they sit on the benches in the Commons chamber behind members of the government and Shadow Cabinet on the front benches (the opposing banks of green leather benches in the House of Commons encourages adversarial debate). See the online resources for more detail about backbenchers and see Chapter 5 for how MPs took control of the parliamentary agenda over Brexit
Whips	Whips (named after the whippers-in who keep packs of hunting hounds in line) keep party discipline in both the Commons and the Lords. In the Commons, each political party appoints its own Whips, with a Chief Whip in larger parties; they have responsibility for organising the business of the House, acting as an important channel of communication between backbench MPs and party leaders, and ensuring that as many MPs as possible vote according to their party line
Her Majesty's Official Opposition	'The opposition' can refer to the official opposition party, or all political parties which are not in government. Her Majesty's Official (or Loyal) Opposition is usually the second largest party in the House of Commons, and has recognised constitutional status; the Leader of the Opposition receives an official salary and is appointed to the Privy Council (there is also a leader of the Opposition in the Lords)

10.2.1 The Opposition

Edward Stanley described the duty of the Opposition as 'very simple . . . to oppose everything, and propose nothing' (House of Commons, 4 June 1841), but an effective opposition in the Commons is an essential feature of a democracy. The Opposition's role is to scrutinise and criticise the government and present itself to the electorate as a government-in-waiting. Sir Ivor Jennings observed:

> The Opposition is at once the alternative to the Government and a focus for the discontent of the people. Its function is almost as important as that of the Government. If there be no Opposition there is no democracy. 'Her Majesty's Opposition' is no idle phrase. Her Majesty needs an Opposition as well as a Government. (*Cabinet Government*, 3rd edn, Cambridge: Cambridge University Press, 1959, p 16)

The Opposition's Leader appoints a Shadow Cabinet comprising MPs from Her Majesty's Opposition; Shadow Cabinet ministers mirror or 'shadow' corresponding ministerial positions in the real Cabinet, and are usually the Opposition party's spokesperson on affairs arising in that subject area (eg the Shadow Foreign Secretary in August 2020 was Labour MP Lisa Nandy). In this way, they can hold their counterparts in the government to account. Effective, critical opposition can pressure the government to defend, moderate, and explain its actions, and by questioning and challenging government policy, the Opposition can help to improve and promote government efficiency. For more details, see Grégoire Webber, 'Loyal Opposition and the Political Constitution' (2017) 37(2) Oxford Journal of Legal Studies 357–382.

Ensuring that the voices of citizens are heard is a key part of the Commons' work as the democratically elected chamber of Parliament where MPs can raise national and constituency issues in debates in both the Commons chamber and since 1999, in Westminster Hall, the Commons' secondary chamber. MPs correspond with ministers and others on behalf of their constituents to raise grievances, acting as an important conduit for constituency issues and helping to inform government about voters' concerns. The voices of citizens can also be brought to Parliament's attention through e-petitions. The Petitions Committee considers e-petitions which have attracted more than 100,000 signatures and decides which to recommend for debate in Westminster Hall (eg the 'Do not prorogue Parliament' petition attracted 1,725,630 signatures and was debated in Parliament on 9 September 2019; see https://petition.parliament.uk/).

10.2.2 **Membership**

Local constituency parties select candidates for election to the Commons. To stand as a candidate, individuals must be aged 18 or over and be a British, Irish, or an eligible Commonwealth citizen (see Table 10.2 for disqualifications from standing).

10.2.3 **How representative is the House of Commons?**

'To elect, and to reject, is the prerogative of a free people.' Thomas Paine (Letter III, The National Intelligencer, 29 November 1802)

'If you cannot get rid of the people who govern you, you do not live in a democratic system.' Tony Benn (HC Hansard 22 Mar 2001, Vol 365 col 510)

> The word 'democracy' derives from the Greek *demos* and *kratos*, which means rule by the people (Winston Churchill told the House of Commons in 1947 that it had been said that democracy was the worst form of government, except all the other forms that had been tried).

Table 10.2 Individuals who are disqualified from standing for election to the House of Commons

- Judges, civil servants, and members of the armed forces and the police (section 1(1) House of Commons Disqualification Act 1975; this ensures separation of powers)

- Members of the House of Lords

- Persons currently subject to a bankruptcy restrictions order or debt relief restrictions order

- Persons convicted or reported guilty of corrupt or illegal practices in relation to an election (section 160(4) Representation of the People Act 1983)

- Prisoners sentenced to more than one year's imprisonment (section 1 Representation of the People Act 1981)

For further details, see: www.electoralcommission.org.uk

The UK is a parliamentary democracy. The people elect MPs as their democratically accountable representatives in the Commons and this connection to the people through representation gives legitimacy to their law-making authority. At each general election, the electorate decides the composition of the Commons and the political party of government; and what the electorate gives, it can take away by choosing fresh representatives at the next election. However, the UK's electoral system can produce a House of Commons which is not truly representative of the majority, where a party with a minority share of the national vote routinely gains a majority of seats. A number of issues arise: are all votes of equal value; does everyone have equal voting rights; and is the voting system representative?

10.2.3.1 One vote, one value

The UK is divided into 650 parliamentary constituencies:

- England 533;
- Scotland 59;
- Wales 40;
- Northern Ireland 18 (see www.parliament.uk/about/how/elections-and-voting/constituencies/).

Each constituency returns one MP to represent it in the House of Commons. Equality of voter numbers between constituencies ensures that people are fairly represented in Parliament, with a similar ratio of voters per MP: the aim is 'one person, one vote, one value'. However, constituencies can vary from below 22,000 voters to more than 110,000. The four national Boundary Commissions periodically review constituency boundaries in the UK, applying the Rules for Redistribution set out under the Parliamentary Constituencies Act 1986 (as amended). However, there are political tensions in redrawing the constituency map: constituencies may disappear which could change the outcome of general elections; the government of the day can be accused of seeking to gain an electoral advantage from resizing ('gerrymandering'); fewer constituencies mean greater workload for MPs; and existing MPs must compete for seats. In order to lower House of Commons expenses following the MPs' expenses scandal in 2009 (see section 10.6.3), the Parliamentary Voting System and Constituencies Act 2011 provided that the number of constituencies should be reduced from 650 to 600. The Boundary Commissions submitted recommendations for a reduced set of constituencies to the government in 2018 (see https://boundarycommissionforengland.independent.gov.uk/2018-review/) but in 2020, the government introduced the Parliamentary Constituencies Bill which removed the requirement to implement the recommendations of the 2018 review and set the number of constituencies at 650 because of increased post-Brexit workload for MPs. The next review is due in 2023.

10.2.3.2 The franchise and restrictions on voting

The franchise means the right to vote; the UK enjoys universal adult suffrage to enable wide participation in elections, but not everyone has the right to vote. For elections to the UK Parliament, voters must be 18, a British, Irish or a qualifying Commonwealth citizen, and resident at an address in the UK, or a UK citizen living abroad who has been registered to vote in the UK in the past 15 years (Representation of the People Act 1983 (as amended in 2000); www.electoralcommission.org.uk). Those eligible to vote must be registered on the Electoral Register, but in 2019 the Electoral Commission found that 9.4 million people eligible to vote in the UK were not correctly registered (www.electoralcommission.org.uk, 26 September 2019); the result is that they are disenfranchised. Registration is lower in urban and socially deprived areas and higher in affluent areas, and the Electoral Reform Society has observed that 'Unrepresentative electoral registers will lead to unrepresentative constituencies' (www.electoral-reform.org.uk/

campaigns/upgrading-our-democracy/voter-registration/). This contributes to an unrepresentative House of Commons. For further details on voter registration, see the online resources.

Individuals cannot vote in elections to the UK Parliament if they are:

- not British, Irish, or qualifying Commonwealth citizens (section 1(1) Representation of the People Act 1983);

- convicted criminals serving a prison sentence (section 3 Representation of the People Act 1983), but remand prisoners and civil prisoners (people imprisoned for not obeying court orders such as not paying fines or maintenance) can vote if they are on the electoral register;

- offenders detained for mental health reasons (section 3A Representation of the People Act 1983);

- persons found guilty within the previous five years of corrupt or illegal electoral practices (section 160(4) Representation of the People Act 1983);

- members of the House of Lords (because they can voice their opinions directly in the UK Parliament) although they can vote in elections to local authorities and devolved legislatures.

The Queen, though not legally disqualified from voting, does not do so in order to maintain political neutrality.

 THINKING POINT

In Scotland and Wales, 16 and 17-year-olds can vote in elections for the Scottish and Welsh Parliaments. Do you think the voting age should be lowered to 16 in England and Northern Ireland? See https://yougov.co.uk/news/2018/05/23/public-support-right-vote-16-more-reducing-voting-/.

An area of the franchise that has provoked controversy—and a 12-year conflict between the UK Parliament and the European Court of Human Rights—is the issue of prisoners' votes.

 CLOSE-UP FOCUS: PRISONERS AND THE VOTE

Hirst v UK (No 2) [2005] ECHR 681

John Hirst, a prisoner serving a life sentence for manslaughter, brought a challenge in the European Court of Human Rights (ECtHR) to the blanket ban on prisoners voting under section 3 Representation of the People Act 1983. The Court held that the automatic, indiscriminate ban in section 3 breached the right to free elections under Article 3 Protocol 1 of the European Convention on Human Rights. The UK was given until 22 November 2012 to change its law but did not comply. Successive UK governments took the view that it was for the sovereign Parliament to change the law:

- In 2009, the Council of Europe reprimanded the UK and urged progress (Interim Resolution ECtHR [2009] ECHR 2260).

- In a House of Commons debate in 2011, a motion to keep the ban was carried by 234 votes to 22.

- The then Attorney General, Dominic Grieve QC, affirmed that the UK was under a legal duty to implement the judgment (Justice Committee, *The Work of the Attorney General*, 24 October 2012, HC 644, Ev Q.24) but the Prime Minister, David Cameron, was adamant that prisoners were not getting the vote under his government.

- In 2012, Chris Grayling, then Lord Chancellor, introduced the Voting Eligibility (Prisoners) Draft Bill to the House of Commons, putting forward three options: (a) a ban for all prisoners sentenced to four years or more; (b) a ban for all prisoners sentenced to six months or more; (c) a ban for all prisoners. He stated that while the government was under a legal obligation to implement the judgment, Parliament was sovereign so could vote against it, and many MPs were concerned that the ECtHR could overrule Parliament's will.

- A Joint Committee report on the Bill in 2013 recommended that the government should introduce legislation to allow all prisoners serving sentences of 12 months or less to vote in all UK parliamentary, local, and European elections, but the law was not changed (Joint Committee on the Draft Voting Eligibility (Prisoners) Bill, *Draft Voting Eligibility (Prisoners) Bill Report*, Session 2013–14, HL Paper 103, HC 924).

- Subsequent cases in the ECtHR affirmed the breach of Article 3 Protocol 1 though did not award compensation (see *Greens v UK* (App No 60041/08) [2010] ECHR 1826; *Firth and Others v UK* (App No 47784/09) [2014] All ER (D) 57 (Aug); *McHugh and Others v UK* [2015] ECHR 155).

- In 2017, David Lidington, then Justice Secretary, announced that the government intended to change prison rules to allow offenders on short sentences to vote while released on a temporary licence (www.gov.uk/government/speeches/secretary-of-states-oral-statement-on-sentencing). This did not change the law—so did not require parliamentary approval—but the proposal was accepted by the Council of Europe in December 2017.

Further reading

Easton, S. 'Electing the Electorate: The Problem of Prisoner Disenfranchisement' (2006) 69(3) Modern Law Review 443

Lardy, H. 'Prisoner Disenfranchisement: Constitutional Rights and Wrongs' (2002) (Autumn) Public Law 524

Factsheet: www.echr.coe.int/Documents/FS_Prisoners_vote_ENG.pdf

http://researchbriefings.parliament.uk/ResearchBriefing/Summary/SN01764

 THINKING POINT

Think about parliamentary sovereignty here. The UK is under an obligation to comply with the court's judgments but only Parliament can change UK law. Was the European Court of Human Rights 'dictating' to the UK Parliament what laws it should pass?

10.2.3.3 **The voting system**

The 'first past the post system' is used in general elections to the UK Parliament whereby the candidate who wins most votes in a constituency becomes the MP, but there is no requirement to achieve more than 50 per cent of the vote, and in 2015, 331 of 650 MPs won their seat with less than half of the vote in their constituencies (www.bbc.co.uk/news/uk-england-39847512). Labour won the 2001 election with 41 per cent of the vote, but because only 59 per cent turned out to vote, it equated to support from 24 per cent of the entire electorate. (See http://research-briefings.files.parliament.uk/documents/CBP-7529/CBP-7529.pdf.) The number of seats won by a party in the Commons frequently does not reflect its share of the national vote; compare the percentages of votes cast and the percentages of seats gained in Table 10.3. In the 2005 general election, for example, Labour's 'winning' share of the vote was 36 per cent, the lowest on record for a government mandate.

The first past the post system is easy to understand, establishes a strong constituency link between MPs and electors, and normally produces decisive results with a majority party which can form a government, although it produced hung Parliaments in 2010 and 2017, where no party achieved an overall majority of 326 or more seats in the House of Commons. However, it encourages safe seats (constituencies where a political party is almost guaranteed to win) and tactical voting, which means voting for a candidate with a better chance of winning than one's genuine choice (see Jess Garland, Michela Palese, and Ian Simpson, Electoral Reform Society Report, *Voters Left Voiceless: The 2019 General Election*, March 2020).

Alternatives to first past the post include proportional representation (PR) which is more representative of the national vote because seats are allocated in proportion to the number of votes cast overall for political parties, not on a constituency basis; however, it can be more complex and produces less decisive results. An e-petition calling for adoption of PR gathered more than 100,000 signatures and was debated in Parliament on 30 October 2017 but the government had no plans to change the voting system in general elections (HC Deb 30 October 2017,

Table 10.3 2019 General Election

Party	Percentage of total votes cast	Number of seats won in the House of Commons	Percentage of seats gained in the House of Commons
Conservatives	43.6%	365	56%
Labour	32.2%	203	31.2%
Lib Dem	11.5%	11	1.7%
SNP (Scottish National Party)	3.9%	48	7.4%
DUP (Democratic Unionist Party)	0.8%	8	1.2%
Green Party	2.7%	1	0.2%
Turnout was 67.3%			

https://www.bbc.co.uk/news/election/2019/results

Vol 630 cols 238WH–286WH). Alternative vote (AV) is a preferential voting system where candidates are marked as 1st, 2nd, 3rd preference, and so on. If no candidate receives 50 per cent of the vote initially, the preferences are redistributed until one candidate has a majority. A referendum was held on 5 May 2011 on whether the public wished to adopt the Alternative vote system (see the Parliamentary Voting System and Constituencies Act 2011); the result was a decisive 'no', with 68 per cent against and 32 per cent in favour.

Alternative voting systems already used in the UK

- Additional member system (Scottish Parliament, Welsh Parliament, and London Assembly)
- Single transferable vote (Northern Ireland Assembly)
- Supplementary vote system (London Mayor and Police and Crime Commissioner elections)

See www.parliament.uk/about/how/elections-and-voting/voting-systems/.

In its 2019 election manifesto, the government announced proposals for electoral reform including voter identification and updated constituency boundaries, but committed to keeping the first past the post system. See 'The government's electoral reform agenda: an assessment', 12 February 2020, The Constitution Unit (https://constitution-unit.com/2020/02/12/the-governments-electoral-reform-agenda-an-assessment/).

10.3 The House of Lords

Upper chambers are typically smaller than the lower chamber and are often elected, either directly or indirectly, or with a mixed elected/appointed membership. They act as a check and control on the lower chamber and normally have a different basis of representation; for example, the US Senate, the upper house of Congress, represents the states in the federation, whereas the House of Representatives, the lower house, represents the people. The UK's House of Lords diverges from the standard form: it is an unelected upper chamber and unusually for a second chamber, there are more members in the Lords than MPs in the House of Commons.

Until 2009, the House of Lords had a judicial function; the Appellate Committee of the House of Lords was the highest court of appeal in the UK. The Constitutional Reform Act 2005 transferred this function to the new Supreme Court (Schedule 18 repealed the Appellate Jurisdiction Acts 1876–1947; section 23 created the Supreme Court).

⟩ CROSS REFERENCE

For further details on the Constitutional Reform Act 2005, see Chapters 7 and 13

10.3.1 **Membership**

Membership of the House of Lords largely relies on patronage and the executive has the power to create peers (see Table 10.4 for who's who in the House of Lords). Its members have a variety of backgrounds with wide-ranging expertise, and are appointed by the Queen on the Prime Minister's advice. They can be nominated by political parties, the public, or by themselves. The House of Lords Appointments Commission, an independent advisory body, was set up in 2000

Table 10.4 Who's who in the House of Lords

685 Life peers	The Life Peerages Act 1958 provided for the monarch to appoint individuals as life peers; their titles cannot be inherited. Life peers bring diverse professional experience and specialist knowledge to the Lords in areas such as politics, medicine, and law
87 Excepted hereditary peers	Have an inherited title which traditionally gave them the right to sit and vote in the House of Lords but the House of Lords Act 1999 removed the right of most hereditary peers to sit in the Lords; only 92 seats are available to hereditaries eligible to sit in the House of Lords
26 Lords Spiritual (Bishops of the Church of England)	The Archbishops of Canterbury and York; the Bishops of London, Durham, and Winchester; and 21 other diocesan bishops of the Church of England. The Lords Spiritual (Women) Act 2015 was passed to fast-track female bishops into the House of Lords; section 1 provides that until 2025, a woman will take priority over a male bishop when a vacancy arises. The Lords Spiritual represent only the Church of England, and it has been argued that other religious faiths and Christian denominations should be reflected in the House of Lords (see *Living with Difference: Community, Diversity and the Common Good*, Report of the Commission on Religion and Belief in British Public Life, para 3.24; Royal Commission on the Reform of the House of Lords, *A House for the Future* (2000) Cm 4534, pp 150–159)
The Lord Speaker	Presides over business in the House of Lords from a seat known as the Woolsack, and is elected by members of the House of Lords for five years. On appointment, s/he becomes independent from political parties. Until the Constitutional Reform Act 2005, the Lord Chancellor presided over debates in the House of Lords. In 2006, Baroness Hayman became the first elected Lord Speaker
Black Rod	Responsible for organisation of, and maintaining order in, the House of Lords. At the State Opening of Parliament each year, Black Rod, as the monarch's representative in the House of Lords, traditionally knocks on the door of the House of Commons chamber to summon MPs to attend the House of Lords for the Queen's Speech. The door is slammed shut, signifying the House of Commons' independence, and s/he must knock three times before being allowed in. In 2017, Sarah Clarke was appointed as The Lady Usher of the Black Rod, the first female holder of the office in 650 years
The Clerk of the Parliaments	The most senior official in the House of Lords, head of the permanent administration, and advisor on House procedure

Membership figures current at October 2020 Source: https://members.parliament.uk/parties/Lords

to recommend non-party-political life peers and check all life peer nominations for propriety. It also ensures a diversity balance for appointed members, and 'People's peers' were appointed on their advice from 2001, yet in 2019, while the age of members ranged from 34 to 94, the average age was 70 and only 27 per cent of members were female (https://lordslibrary.parliament.uk/research-briefings/lln-2019-0161/).

In October 2020, there were 798 eligible members (those eligible to take part in the work of the House of Lords who are not disqualified or on leave of absence). Disqualifications from sitting and voting in the House of Lords include holding judicial office (section 137 Constitutional Reform Act 2005); being declared bankrupt under the Insolvency Act 1986 (disqualification lasts for the period of bankruptcy); and being convicted of treason (the Forfeiture Act 1870 requires disqualification from sitting or voting as a member of the House of Lords until they have served their term of imprisonment or received a pardon).

10.3.2 Reforming membership of the House of Lords

'Lords reform is like opening the lid of Pandora's box' (Lord Strathclyde, HL Hansard 11 October 2010, Vol 721 col 338).

'I am kind of a bit undecided on some aspects of it myself' (Tony Blair, Prime Minister's Press Conference, 12 May 2005).

Reform of the House of Lords has been a thorny problem for many years. Until the reforms to its membership in the House of Lords Act 1999, all members sat in the House of Lords either by right of birth through an inherited title (hereditary peers) or by appointment of the Crown, and its composition of unelected nobility and bishops had continued largely unchanged from its medieval origins as an elite chamber of 'elders and betters'. The Life Peerages Act 1958 opened up membership beyond the aristocracy and the Church, but still relied on patronage, and the House had long been criticised as being undemocratic and unrepresentative of the UK population. Membership was mainly for life and the Conservative party had a permanent majority regardless of who won the election; in 1997, for example, there were 157 Labour peers, 322 crossbenchers, and 495 Conservatives. Change was slow; it was only with the Peerage Act 1963 that women inheriting a title could sit and vote in the House of Lords. The Act also allowed hereditary titles to be disclaimed (this enabled Tony Benn to renounce his inherited title of Viscount Stansgate and sit in the House of Commons).

> **CROSS REFERENCE**
> See Chapter 2 for a summary of the historical development of the House of Lords

A crossbench peer is independent of any political party and sits on the benches that cross the chamber of the House of Lords.

The Parliament Act 1911 envisaged the future replacement of the House of Lords' hereditary basis with an elected second chamber, heralding a process of reform that is still not complete 100 years later. Various proposals for change were unsuccessfully suggested over the years; the Bryce Conference 1917–1918 reported on the composition and powers of the Lords but its proposals were never implemented; the 1948 Conference of Party Leaders failed to agree on revised powers for the Lords; and the Parliament (No 2) Bill 1968 proposed phasing out hereditary peers and reducing powers but never got through the Commons and was abandoned by the government. (For more details, see Joint Committee on House of Lords Reform, *House of Lords Reform: First Report*, Session 2002–03, HL Paper 17, HC 171, Appendix 1.)

By the 1990s, the House of Lords consisted of approximately 1,200 members (see Table 10.5).

10.3.2.1 The House of Lords Act 1999

In four parliamentary sessions from 1975 to 1979, the House of Lords inflicted 240 defeats on the Labour government, compared with 241 on the Conservative government between 1979 and 1997. This disproportionate number was a key driver for House of Lords reform by the 1997 Labour government. At the 1997 General Election, the Labour party manifesto promised a more democratic and representative House of Lords by ending the right of hereditaries to sit and vote in the Lords and replacing it with an elected second chamber. The House of Lords Act 1999 provided that:

Table 10.5 Pre- and post-1999 membership of the House of Lords

	Pre-1999		Post-1999
Lords spiritual	Bishops and archbishops of the Church of England	Appointed	Remains the same
Lords temporal	Hereditary peers (members of the aristocracy who inherited the right to sit in the House of Lords)	Inherited until 1999	No one is now a member of the House of Lords by virtue of a hereditary peerage.
Lords temporal	Law Lords (Lords of Appeal in Ordinary created by the Appellate Jurisdiction Act 1876)	Appointed	In 2009, as a result of the Constitutional Reform Act 2005, the Law Lords became Justices of the Supreme Court and cannot sit and vote in the House of Lords (section 137). They can return as members of the Lords on retirement from the Supreme Court, but new Justices of the Supreme Court do not have seats in the House of Lords.
Lords temporal	Life peers	Appointed	Remains the same

- No one is now a member of the House of Lords by virtue of a hereditary peerage (section 1).
- The Earl Marshal, the Lord Great Chamberlain, and 90 hereditary peers are excepted and remain as members for life or until the law is changed (section 2).

The Act removed over 600 hereditary peers, but the government agreed to let 92 hereditaries remain until the second stage of reform in order to get support for the Bill; this was called the Weatherill amendment. To choose which hereditaries remained, 75 were elected by the hereditary peers in their political party or crossbench grouping; the other 15 were elected by the whole House to act as various office-holders. Vacancies due to death, retirement, or exclusion are filled by holding a by-election.

The House of Lords Act 1999, while reforming the membership of the Lords and envisaged as the first step to more sweeping reform, did not change its powers. The elusive second stage of Lords reform has still not happened and remains unfinished business. It has been characterised by a lack of consensus and deadlock, except for agreement that the size of the House should be reduced. The issue is that reform seeks to deliver a second chamber that is democratic and accountable, but also one that is secondary to the Commons and does not threaten its supremacy.

> The complexities involved in further reform can be seen in the timeline in the online resources.

10.3.2.2 **An elected House of Lords?**

Should the House of Lords be democratically elected? When introducing his House of Lords Reform Bill in 2012, Nick Clegg said: 'we are only one of only two countries in the world—the other being Lesotho—with an upper parliamentary chamber that is totally unelected and instead selects its members by birthright and patronage' (HC Deb 9 July 2012, Vol 548 col 24). Of 77 bicameral Chambers globally, 61 are elected (Lord Ashdown, HL Hansard 21 June 2011, Vol 728 col 1198). While appointed members can provide an independent, expert element, it is broadly agreed that 'those who make the laws of the land should be elected by those who must obey those laws' (Charles Kennedy, 'Lords Reform: We'll Defeat the Rebels', *The Guardian*, 9 July 2012, www.theguardian.com/commentisfree/2012/jul/09/lords-reform-beat-rebels). This ensures that law-makers are accountable to the electorate and provides democratic legitimacy. Yet the Wakeham Commission recognised in 2000 that a wholly elected House of Lords would challenge the democratic authority of the Commons (Royal Commission on the Reform of the House of Lords, Cm 4534). It would have equal status to the Commons and be in competition with it, increasing the possibility of power struggles between the two chambers, perhaps demanding the right of veto over legislation. If elected in the same way, it could produce a mirror image of the Commons, losing the constitutional safeguard provided by its current diversity. A change in composition can affect the behaviour of the Lords: ironically, after hereditaries were removed, the Labour governments suffered 458 legislative defeats in a more assertive Lords between 1999 and 2010 (www.parliament.uk/about/faqs/house-of-lords-faqs/lords-govtdefeats/).

Lord Steel has argued that the Lords does not need to be elected, at least with its current powers:

> We must distinguish between power and influence—this House has no power, since any revision we make can be undone by the other place, but we have influence. That is why it is perfectly acceptable to have a House that is dealing with influence and not power that is not necessarily elected. (HL Hansard 21 June 2011, Vol 728 col 1200)

Lord Norton has argued that an elected second chamber would divide accountability; electors would not know which of the two bodies to hold to account for outcomes of public policy. At present, the appointed House of Lords is 'a complementary, not a competing, second Chamber', which does not challenge the core accountability of the House of Commons (HL Hansard 3 February 2017, Vol 778 col 1432–1433).

The 2012 House of Lords Draft Reform Bill's attempt to introduce a mainly elected second chamber was criticised. Eleanor Laing MP said 'there is no reasonable question to which 450 extra elected politicians is the answer' (Today programme, BBC R4, 27 June 2012). Wayne David, then Shadow Constitutional Affairs Minister, criticised the Bill for not setting out a 'stable, coherent long-term relationship between the two Houses' (www.theguardian.com/politics/2012/may/09/labour-lords-reform-bill-timetable). The Bill was also criticised for ignoring reform of the Lords' powers. Clause 2 provided that the Bill did not affect the powers of either House of Parliament, or the conventions governing the relationship between them (reference to conventions was later omitted). Lord Hennessy warned that to reform its composition without reforming its powers 'is almost certainly fatal—it is certainly undesirable' (Joint Committee on the Draft House of Lords Reform Bill, *Draft House of Lords Reform Bill*, Report, Session 2010–12 HL Paper 284–II, HC 1313–II, Ev p 4). MPs feared that a democratically elected second chamber would be less deferential to the Commons, revealing the heart of the deadlock: an unelected Lords is not democratically legitimate, but an assertive elected second chamber would be in a stronger position to wreck bills and frustrate the democratic will of the House of Commons. As Lord Strathclyde has asked: 'Is the House too strong or too weak? Is the aim to enable us to defeat all Governments more, with "more legitimacy" . . . or what?' (HL Hansard 7 Feb 2007, Vol 689 col 714).

THINKING POINT

Given its current functions, does the House of Lords need to be democratically elected?

10.3.3 Reducing the size of the House of Lords

The House of Lords is one of the largest legislative chambers in the world (second only, it is often pointed out, to China's National People's Congress). Between 1997 and 2016, 652 life peers were appointed to the Lords, including 374 nominated by Tony Blair and 245 by David Cameron, whose 2016 resignation honours list was controversial (https://commonslibrary.parliament.uk/research-briefings/sn05867/; https://lordslibrary.parliament.uk/research-briefings/lln-2016-0007/; see also Meg Russell, https://constitution-unit.com/2020/07/31/boris-johnsons-36-new-peerages-make-the-need-to-constrain-prime-ministerial-appointments-to-the-house-of-lords-clearer-than-ever/). Peers can now retire or resign from the House (House of Lords Reform Act 2014 section 1(1)) and be expelled for non-attendance or serious misconduct; peers who do not attend for a whole session cease to be members of the House at the beginning of the following session (House of Lords Reform Act 2014 section 2). Bishops leave the House when they retire on reaching the age of 70, although the Archbishops of Canterbury and York are, by convention, given a life peerage on retirement. From 2014–19, 101 peers retired and six left through non-attendance (https://lordslibrary.parliament.uk/research-briefings/lln-2019-0161/).

In 2017, the Burns Committee recommended reducing the size of the House of Lords to 600 members, to be achieved by a 'two out, one in' principle, and all new members to serve a non-renewable fixed term of 15 years (*Report of the Lord Speaker's Committee on the Size of the House of Lords*, 31 October 2017). The proposals were supported by the House of Commons Public Administration and Constitutional Affairs Committee (*A smaller House of Lords: The report of the Lord Speaker's committee on the size of the House* Thirteenth Report of Session 2017–19 HC 662) but the government responded that reform was not then a priority.

10.3.4 The ultimate reform?

Around 60 per cent of legislative assemblies around the world are unicameral with a single chamber, for example, New Zealand, Sweden, and Denmark (see https://data.ipu.org). Should Parliament be unicameral? There have long been advocates of abolishing the House of Lords; Oliver Cromwell temporarily achieved it in 1649. More recently, the Lords' repeated attempts to give the House of Commons a 'meaningful vote' on the final Brexit deal fuelled public support for abolishing the Lords. On 18 June 2018, the Commons debated an e-petition signed by more than 170,000 people asking for a referendum on the abolition of the House of Lords; Paul Scully MP believed that its popularity had been encouraged by the Lords' consideration of the EU Withdrawal Bill (now the EU (Withdrawal) Act 2018) and by concern that the Lords might be 'overstepping the mark' (HC Hansard 18 June 2018, Vol 643 col 1WH). However, the government's view was that it was not the right time for a referendum.

THINKING POINT

See the online resources for an exercise in evaluating the arguments for and against retaining the second chamber.

SUMMARY

- The Lords is subordinate to the democratically elected House of Commons but complements it as an important revising and scrutinising chamber and as a check on the powerful Commons

- The composition of the House of Lords has been reformed to an extent, but further reform has proved elusive

10.4 The Parliament Acts 1911 and 1949

The Parliament Act 1911 redefined and reduced the Lords' legislative powers over public bills, creating a way of resolving disputes between the Commons and the Lords and any future stalemate over a Bill. The Act also stated in its preamble that it regulated the relationship between both Houses of Parliament and restricted the existing powers of the House of Lords until further reform could take place.

CLOSE-UP FOCUS: THE PARLIAMENT ACTS 1911 AND 1949

The Parliament Act 1911

In the early years of the twentieth century, the Liberal government had a programme for radical social reform to help those in poverty, but its legislative proposals had been subject to the veto of the House of Lords. In 1909, David Lloyd George, the Liberal Chancellor of the Exchequer, introduced the 'people's budget' to provide funding for the new old age pensions introduced the previous year. He proposed increasing income tax and death duties, a supertax on the wealthy, and a new land tax which would have significant impact on the landowners among the Conservative majority in the House of Lords. At that time there was already a constitutional convention that peers would not block financial measures originating in the Commons, but peers successfully rejected the budget proposals in the Finance Bill 1909 by 350 votes to 75, provoking a constitutional crisis which would ultimately reduce their legislative powers.

In 1910, the Liberal Prime Minister, Herbert Asquith, called a general election and the government introduced the Parliament Bill; it asserted the House of Commons' predominance over finance and legislation by removing most of the Lords' legislative veto power. The government also drew up a list of 249 candidates for Liberal peerages and threatened to flood the Lords with Liberal peers to support the Bill. To avoid a permanent Liberal majority in the House of Lords, Conservative peers agreed the Bill. On 10 August 1911, the Parliament Act was passed by 131 votes to 114 in the Lords (see *R (Jackson) v AG* [2005] UKHL 56 [9–20, 142–156]).

The 1911 Act removed the Lords' power of veto on all public Bills introduced in the Commons except those extending the life of Parliament beyond five years:

- It removed the House of Lords' veto over money Bills which raise money through taxation. If the Commons passes a money Bill, and the Lords do not pass it without amendment within one month, it can be presented for royal assent (section 1). This enshrined the constitutional convention of Commons' authority over finance.

- It restricted the Lords to a two-year delaying power (a suspensory veto) over public Bills introduced in the House of Commons (except money Bills and Bills to extend a Parliament beyond five years). The Lords could delay a Bill over three parliamentary sessions but it could be passed without the Lords' consent if two years had elapsed between second reading in the Commons in the first session, and being passed in the Commons in the third session (section 2). So a Bill rejected by the Lords could receive royal assent after two years.

- It reduced the maximum life of a Parliament from seven years to five by amending the Septennial Act 1715 (now repealed by the Fixed-term Parliaments Act 2011 Schedule para 2).

The House of Lords kept its power of veto over the following:

- Bills extending a Parliament beyond five years (now governed by the Fixed-term Parliaments Act 2011);

- Bills sent to the Lords less than a month before the end of a session;

- Bills introduced in the Lords—the Parliament Act only applies to public Bills starting in the Commons (Commons Bills);

- Private Bills.

See www.parliament.uk/about/how/laws/parliamentacts/.

Parliament Act 1949

The Labour government's plans to nationalise the iron and steel industries in the 1940s faced rejection in a Conservative-dominated House of Lords so the Parliament Act 1949 was passed, reducing the Lords' delaying powers to one year. A Bill passed by the Commons in two successive sessions (with at least one year between second reading in the Commons in session one and third reading in the Commons in the following session) can be presented for royal assent (see Table 10.6).

It is still the general rule that all Bills have to be passed by both the House of Commons and the House of Lords; the House of Lords always participates in the legislative process and is not 'bypassed' under the Parliament Acts.

Table 10.6 Parliament Acts procedure

Session 1	Bill passed by House of Commons and sent to House of Lords
	Bill rejected by the Lords
Session 2	The identical Bill is passed again by the Commons and sent to House of Lords at least one month before the end of the second session
	Bill rejected again by the Lords. One year (13 months) must have elapsed between the date of second reading in the Commons in the first session, and being passed in the Commons in the second session. Presented for royal assent

However, the Parliament Act 1949 was passed by invoking the Parliament Act 1911, so the House of Commons reduced the powers of the Lords without its consent. Some scholars and lawyers have taken the view that the 1949 Act was invalid because it was passed by invoking the 1911 Parliament Act—the Act it was amending—and was not made by the sovereign Parliament of Commons, Lords, and royal assent (see H.W.R. Wade, 'The Basis of Legal Sovereignty' (1955) CLJ 172, 193–194; Lord Donaldson (HL Hansard 19 January 2001, Vol 620 col 1308–1309)). This was put to the test in *R (Jackson) v AG* [2005] UKHL 56, [2006] 1 AC 262, where the claimants argued that:

- the validity of the Hunting Act 2004 rested on the validity of the Parliament Act 1949;
- the 1949 Act was invalidly enacted because it could not amend the 1911 Act without the Lords' consent;
- legislation made under the 1911 Act is delegated, not primary, since it depends for its validity on a prior Act; the Commons was a delegated body trying to enlarge its power.

The court disagreed with the claimants, pointing out that the 1949 Act was validly enacted primary legislation that followed a different legislative procedure. Lord Bingham stated that the 1911 Act provided that laws passed by invoking the Parliament Act are called 'Acts of Parliament' and it created a new way of making primary legislation ([24]; and see Lord Steyn [75]). The Act could not be interpreted as delegating power to the Commons ([25]). There was nothing in the 1911 Act to preclude use of the procedure laid down by the Act to amend the Act itself ([36]; see also Lord Steyn [94–96]). The 1949 Act was therefore validly enacted.

The court considered whether the Parliament Acts could be used by the House of Commons to reform the House of Lords. Lord Bingham disagreed with the Court of Appeal's *obiter* view that the consent of the House of Lords would be needed to enact fundamental constitutional reform ([31]). Constitutional reform was not one of the exceptions to the 1911 Parliament Act ([62] (Lord Nicholls); [158] (Baroness Hale)) but Lord Steyn was 'deeply troubled' at the prospect of the Act being invoked to abolish the House of Lords ([101]).

Lord Pannick has observed that the Parliament Acts regulate the relationship between both Houses when one is elected and the other is not, and would not apply if the upper chamber was wholly or mainly elected. He suggested that if the government wished to ensure that the Parliament Acts apply to a reformed House, they should make statutory provision (Written Ev Joint Committee, *Draft House of Lords Reform Bill*, First Report Session 2010–12, HL Paper 284–II, HC 1313–II, pp 426–430; see also David Pannick, '"Securing political success by repetition" (F.E. Smith): Can the Parliament Act 1911 be Used by the House of Commons to Insist on

Reform of the House of Lords?' (2012) (April) Public Law 230; House of Lords Select Committee on the Constitution, *Constitutional Aspects of the Challenge to the Hunting Act 2004*, 7th report of session 2005–06, HL Paper 141).

 THINKING POINT

On debating the Hunting Bill in the Lords, Earl Ferrers said: 'The Government are saying to your Lordships, "If you do not agree with this, we will Parliament Act it". What a funny kind of democracy that is . . . What a shocking way to treat people who happen to hold a view contrary to that held by the Government' (HL Deb 12 October 2004, Vol 665 col 181). Do you agree with this view of the Parliament Acts?

 SUMMARY

Members of the House of Lords can still criticise, question, and delay public Bills approved by the Commons but cannot veto them, and can only delay a Bill for one year over two parliamentary sessions. After that, it can be passed in the next parliamentary session without the consent of the House of Lords under section 2 of the Parliament Act 1911, as amended by the Parliament Act 1949.

10.5 Parliamentary privilege

'Parliamentary privilege is the sum of certain rights enjoyed by each House collectively . . . and by Members of each House individually, without which they could not discharge their functions, and which exceed those possessed by other bodies or individuals.' (Sir David Natzler and Mark Hutton (eds), *Erskine May's Treatise on The Law, Privileges, Proceedings and Usage of Parliament*, 25th edn (London: LexisNexis Butterworths 2019), para 12.1)

Parliamentary privilege is a powerful collection of rights and immunities which protects the sovereign Parliament's internal affairs from external interference, enabling it to conduct its business 'without fear or favour, let or hindrance' (Joint Committee on Parliamentary Privilege *Parliamentary Privilege—First Report*, Session 1998–99, HL 43-I/HC 214-I [23]). Both Houses of Parliament enjoy similar privileges, Parliamentary privilege is part of the law and custom of Parliament, deriving from its historical development (see Chapter 2). It is uncodified—the Joint Committee on Parliamentary Privilege 1999 unsuccessfully recommended a Parliamentary Privileges Act—but the rules can be found in statutes, judicial decisions, resolutions of Parliament, and Erskine May's authoritative text *Parliamentary Practice*. Traditionally, the Speaker of the House of Commons still claims the Commons' 'ancient and undoubted rights and privileges' from the monarch at the beginning of each Parliament. For detailed historical background, see Joint Committee, *Parliamentary Privilege*, 1999.

There are two strands to parliamentary privilege:

1. The narrower statutory protection in Article 9 of the Bill of Rights 1689;

2. The wider, pre-1689 common law privilege of 'exclusive cognisance', which means Parliament's right to exercise sole jurisdiction over its own proceedings.

The central plank of the discussion that follows is the relationship between Parliament and the courts; at the heart of parliamentary privilege lies the separation of powers, where 'the courts and Parliament are both astute to recognise their respective constitutional roles' (*Prebble v Television New Zealand Ltd* [1995] 1 AC 321, 332D (Lord Browne-Wilkinson); see also *Office of Government Commerce v Information Commissioner* [2008] EWHC 774 (Admin), [2010] QB 98 [46–50] (Stanley Burnton J)). Parliament does not trespass on the courts' jurisdiction, and the courts do not trespass on Parliament's privileges, demonstrating the mutual respect, understandings, and carefully calibrated dividing lines needed for the operation of the UK's unwritten constitution. Matters within the bounds of parliamentary privilege are beyond the jurisdiction of the courts, although the courts can interpret what is and is not a privileged matter (see section 10.5.2). This enables Parliament to conduct its core business effectively without fear of outside interference, and as the absolute judge of its own privileges, Parliament is largely self-regulating and self-policing.

The key parliamentary rights and privileges examined in what follows are:

- freedom of speech in Parliament;
- the right of each House to control its own affairs (exclusive cognisance), including:
  - the power to discipline members for misconduct
  - the power to punish members and non-members for contempt of Parliament.

Other privileges include freedom from arrest in civil cases and the protection of official papers published by order of either House. Members also enjoy freedom from service of court documents within the precincts of Parliament, and freedom from obstruction when going to and leaving Parliament. Privilege extends to parliamentary officials in carrying out their duties, and to witnesses in parliamentary committees, but privileges can change or be abolished; for example, the House of Commons' right to decide disputed elections was transferred to the courts in 1868. New privileges can now only be created by Act of Parliament, and privileges should only ever exist to protect Parliament's core functions.

10.5.1 **Freedom of speech**

Members of the Commons and Lords need to be able to debate and speak freely in Parliament, without fear of being sued or prosecuted for what they say, especially when legislating and deliberating as part of Parliament's collective decision-making process. Freedom of speech in Parliament is one of the most important privileges; it is an ancient right, first claimed by the Commons under Elizabeth I, which provides blanket protection against the questioning of parliamentary proceedings by the courts, giving MPs absolute legal immunity against criminal or civil actions for anything said or done in parliamentary proceedings—even if said maliciously. It is protected by Article 9 of the Bill of Rights 1689 which provides 'that the freedom of speech and debates or proceedings in Parliament ought not to be impeached or questioned in any court or place out of Parliament'.

However, Article 9's phrasing is obscure and ambiguous (see *Toussaint v Attorney General of Saint Vincent and the Grenadines* [2007] 1 WLR 2825 [10] (Lord Mance) and generally [11–18]; *Pepper v Hart* [1993] AC 593, 638 (Lord Browne-Wilkinson)). The 1999 Joint Committee suggested that 'impeach' means 'hinder, challenge and censure' ([36]) and interpreted 'place out of Parliament' as any tribunal having power to examine witnesses on oath ([96]). The meaning of the pivotal phrase 'proceedings in Parliament' has caused most debate. There is no precise definition and the Committee recommended that the phrase needed to be clarified. It defined 'proceedings in Parliament' as 'all words spoken and acts done in the course of, or for the purposes of, or necessarily incidental to, transacting the business of either House of Parliament or of a committee' [129]; ie 'activities which are recognisably part of the formal collegiate activities of Parliament' (Joint Committee, *Parliamentary Privilege*, 1999 [103]). (See also Erskine May's definition quoted in *R v Chaytor* [2010] UKSC 52 [28].)

The scope of proceedings in Parliament can be seen in Table 10.7.

Table 10.7 The scope of proceedings in Parliament

Proceedings in Parliament include:	Not proceedings in Parliament, therefore not protected:
Speeches, debates, parliamentary questions and answers, votes, proceedings on bills, presenting committee reports	Members repeating their words outside Parliament or confirming a statement by reference (*Buchanan v Jennings* [2005] 1 AC 115), unless repeating them is in the public interest and the two occasions are very closely connected (*Makudi v Triesman* [2014] EWCA Civ 179)
Preparing for debates, such as giving written notice of a motion or question	Press statements published prior to parliamentary debates. Casual conversations between members even during a debate
Proceedings in committees and sub-committees formally appointed by either House, even if a committee is sitting outside Parliament. Non-members participating in parliamentary proceedings, eg witnesses before select committees	Proceedings of committees not appointed by either House, such as backbench and party committees
Statements and documents produced for parliamentary proceedings, eg draft statements submitted by witnesses to parliamentary inquiries	Acts/words unconnected with a matter in Parliament, eg posting defamatory letters in the precincts of Parliament (*Rivlin v Bilainkin* [1953] 1 QB 485)
Officials of either House carrying out its orders	Proceedings of All Party Parliamentary Groups
The work of the Parliamentary Commissioner for Standards and the House of Lords Commissioner for Standards	The registers of members' interests are not 'proceedings in Parliament' (*Rost v Edwards* [1990] 2 QB 460 but see Joint Committee 2013 [233])

Table 10.7 The scope of proceedings in Parliament *(Cont.)*

Proceedings in Parliament include:	Not proceedings in Parliament, therefore not protected:
Official internal House or committee papers directly related to parliamentary proceedings, and communications arising directly out of parliamentary proceedings, eg providing further information	Words repeated in a publication not authorised by Parliament. Newspapers enjoy qualified privilege for fair and accurate reports of parliamentary proceedings made without malice. This includes parliamentary sketches (*Cook v Alexander* [1974] QB 279) and media interviews (*Church of Scientology v Johnson-Smith* [1972] 1 QB 522)
Activities outside the Houses and committees if connected to the core business of Parliament	Many constituency activities of MPs are not protected by parliamentary privilege

The dividing line between what is and what is not a proceeding in Parliament is sometimes difficult to assess, even for Parliament itself. In the *Strauss case* (1958), an MP, George Strauss, wrote a letter to a minister that was strongly critical of the London Electricity Board, and was alleged to be defamatory. The House of Commons resolved that the letter did not relate to any matter before the House so was not a proceeding in Parliament and was not covered by parliamentary privilege (although the Committee of Privileges had decided it *was* protected). The Freedom of Information Act revised guidance endorses this view, stating that correspondence from MPs and members of the House of Lords is not covered by parliamentary privilege unless it relates to current or potential proceedings of the relevant House or of a parliamentary committee (Patricia Barratt, 'The New Guidance on Parliamentary Privilege Exemption' (2013) 9(4) FOI 6; https://ico.org.uk/media/for-organisations/documents/1161/section_34_parliamentary_privilege.pdf; S.A. de Smith, 'Privilege and Communications to MPs' (1953) 16(3) MLR 379–381).

Q CLOSE-UP FOCUS: FREEDOM OF SPEECH IN PARLIAMENT

- Members of both Houses of Parliament have absolute privilege (complete protection from being sued) in defamation actions for what they say in proceedings in Parliament. The Defamation Act 1996 section 13 allowed MPs to waive (set aside) parliamentary privilege so they could use their words in Parliament in a defamation case, but this was repealed by the Deregulation Act 2015 (Schedule 23 paragraph 44). See *Hamilton v Al Fayed* [2001] 1 AC 395; *Yeo v Times Newspapers Ltd* [2015] EWHC 3375 (QB).

- Members can choose what to debate in Parliament even if a matter is subject to an injunction. In 2009, Paul Farrelly MP tabled a written parliamentary question concerning a super-injunction obtained by Trafigura, an oil trading company. Super-injunctions prevent publication of confidential information *and* prevent disclosure that the injunction exists. The injunction had been served on *The Guardian* to prevent publication of a report about toxic waste dumping, but *The*

Guardian would also breach the injunction if it published Paul Farrelly's parliamentary question. The injunction was therefore amended so as not to prohibit the media reporting of parliamentary proceedings. In 2011, John Hemming MP named the footballer Ryan Giggs in the House of Commons as the claimant in a court case, even though Giggs' identity was protected by an injunction. (See *CTB v News Group Newspapers Ltd (No 3)* [2011] EWHC 1334 (QB); and *Super-Injunctions, Anonymised Injunctions and Open Justice*, Report of the Committee on Super-Injunctions, 20 May 2011 [5.1–5.6].) In *ABC v Telegraph Media Group Ltd* [2018] EWCA Civ 2329, the court granted an interim injunction to prevent the claimants' identities being published but Lord Hain named the main claimant in the House of Lords. While lawful, this means that an MP is overruling a judge in deciding to reveal a name.

- The Joint Committee on Privacy and Injunctions considered that it is not constitutionally possible for court orders, including injunctions, to apply to Parliament because of Article 9 of the Bill of Rights; therefore it is not a contempt of court to reveal injunction information in parliamentary proceedings (*Privacy and Injunctions*, Session 2010–12, HL Paper 273, HC 1443 [214–215]). But careful consideration of the province of the courts is needed. The Committee emphasised the constitutional principle of comity between Parliament and courts where 'each takes care not to intrude on the other's territory, or to undermine the other' ([216]).

- Parliament has a self-imposed *sub judice* rule which prevents references to active cases before the courts except when the House is considering legislation or the Speaker decides the rule should not apply (see [216–219]). It is important that Parliament does not reach decisions on matters within the courts' domain 'to avoid . . . setting itself up as an alternative forum in which a case might be tried' (Select Committee on Procedure, *The Sub Judice Rule of the House of Commons*, 1st Report Session 2004–05, HC 125 [13]).

- Members can be protected from prosecution under the Official Secrets Acts for their words in Parliament. In the Duncan Sandys case (1938–1939), an MP was informed of the possibility of prosecution because of the sensitive contents of his draft written parliamentary question about national defence. The Commons decided it was part of the business of the House, and was therefore privileged.

- MPs and peers are protected from prosecution for 'speech crimes' such as inciting terrorism or incitement to racial or religious hatred in relation to words in proceedings in Parliament (although this has not been tested).

Parliament's freedom of speech immunity has the potential to leave a claimant without a legal remedy, but it was held to be a proportionate restriction on the right of access to a court in *A v UK* (2003) 36 EHRR 51; it pursued the legitimate aims of protecting free speech in Parliament and maintaining the separation of powers between the legislature and the judiciary ([77, 83–89]). The European Court of Human Rights observed that Parliament is essential for political debate in a democracy, and very weighty reasons are needed to justify interfering with its exercise of freedom of expression ([79]).

Further reading

Green Paper, *Parliamentary Privilege*, 2012 (Cm 8318) April 2012 [163–175]

https://www.lrb.co.uk/v33/n12/stephen-sedley/the-goodwin-and-giggs-show

10.5.2 Parliament's control of its affairs (exclusive cognisance)

Exclusive cognisance refers to the right of each House of Parliament to regulate its own proceedings and have sole jurisdiction over its own internal affairs without outside interference. This protects its independence and includes the right of each House to:

- determine its own internal procedures, such as deciding what to debate, creating and applying its own procedural rules, controlling its composition (eg whether a member is disqualified);
- decide whether there has been a breach of its rules and procedures;
- discipline its members for misconduct;
- punish members or non-members for contempt of Parliament (interfering with the proper conduct of parliamentary business).

The courts accept Parliament's exclusive cognisance—although where there is uncertainty in a case, the courts can determine how far it extends (*R v Chaytor* [16] (Lord Phillips)). They do not question or intervene in Parliament's internal proceedings, particularly in the law-making process (*BRB v Pickin* [1974]), and will not determine alleged breaches of parliamentary procedure. In *Bradlaugh v Gossett* (1884) 12 QBD 271, Charles Bradlaugh, an atheist, was elected as an MP but the House of Commons resolved that he could not swear the oath of allegiance, even though this was required by the Parliamentary Oaths Act 1866, and he was prevented from entering the House; the court held that this decision fell within the sole jurisdiction of the House and it could not interfere. Coleridge LCJ observed that 'What is said or done within the walls of Parliament cannot be inquired into in a court of law' (p 275). The courts are thus protecting Parliament's rights and immunities.

The courts can, of course, refer to parliamentary materials (records of debates, what ministers said when promoting Bills) to help with statutory construction if an Act is ambiguous, obscure, or leads to absurdity (*Pepper v Hart* [1993] AC 593), or to prove what was done or said in Parliament as a matter of historical record (*Prebble v Television New Zealand Ltd* [1995] 1 AC 321); however, this is not interference in parliamentary proceedings, and the courts must certainly not pass judgment on the quality or merits of debates (*R (Conway) v Secretary of State for Justice* [2017] EWHC 640 (Admin) [19–20]).

10.5.2.1 Exclusive cognisance and the rule of law

Parliament's exclusive right to regulate its own affairs excludes the jurisdiction of the courts; this means exemption from certain laws, and therefore from the rule of law (see Joint Committee on Parliamentary Privilege, *Parliamentary Privilege*, Report of Session 2013–14, HL Paper 30, HC 100 [18–20]). This tension requires carefully delineated and acknowledged separation between 'the areas where the ordinary law of the land prevails, enforceable by the courts, and the no-go areas where the courts must step back and the special rights and immunities of parliamentary privilege prevail' (Joint Committee, *Parliamentary Privilege*, 1999 [24]). Parliament's privileges and exclusive cognisance should therefore be limited to what is necessary for its effective functioning and core work (see Joint Committee, *Parliamentary Privilege*, 2013 [20–24]).

 EXAMPLE

Parliament can pass laws that do not apply to it. In *R v Graham-Campbell, ex p Herbert* [1935] 1 KB 594, the court held that selling alcohol without a licence in the precincts of the House of Commons related to the internal affairs of the House and the court could not interfere; if the Licensing Acts applied to Parliament, it would take away its right to regulate its own internal procedure.

10.5.3 Freedom from civil arrest

MPs are protected from civil arrest while Parliament is in session to ensure their availability, but this now only applies to arrest for civil contempt of court (disobeying a court order imposing a civil obligation). It had more relevance when debtors could be arrested and imprisoned but this was abolished in 1870, and it provides no effective protection today (but see *Stourton v Stourton* [1963] P 302). It does *not* provide immunity from arrest for criminal offences.

The privilege of freedom from arrest is claimed from the sovereign. In January 1642, Charles I entered the House of Commons with armed soldiers, sat in the Speaker's chair, and demanded that the Speaker, William Lenthall, point out five MPs whom the king accused of treason. The Speaker refused, saying: 'I have neither eyes to see nor tongue to speak in this place but as this house is pleased to direct me whose servant I am here.' The MPs had fled earlier. 'I see the birds have flown', the king replied, and left the Chamber.

10.5.4 Parliamentary publications

Contents of official authorised reports and papers printed by order of Parliament are protected by parliamentary privilege under the Parliamentary Papers Act 1840. This reversed the confrontational decision in *Stockdale v Hansard* (1839) 9 Ad&El 1 that a House of Commons resolution that official publications had absolute privilege was not law and had no legal effect.

10.5.5 Are MPs exempt from the criminal law?

The Joint Committee on Parliamentary Privilege stated in its 1999 report that the precincts of the House are not a haven from the law. However, in 2008, the question arose whether the police had breached parliamentary privilege by searching an MP's office and seizing documents.

On 27 November 2008, the Metropolitan Police arrested Damian Green MP, then the Shadow Immigration Minister, at his constituency home on suspicion of conspiring to commit misconduct in public office and related offences. When the police searched his office in the House of Commons, MPs were outraged. On 3 December 2008, the Speaker, Michael Martin, who was responsible for controlling access to the precincts of the House, was criticised after explaining to the Commons that he had not authorised the search, nor had he been told that the police did not have a search warrant (the Serjeant at Arms had given written consent). The Committee on Issue of Privilege later concluded that the Speaker should have taken more responsibility for exercising his authority (House of Commons Committee on Issue of Privilege, *Police Searches on the Parliamentary Estate*, HC 62, 22 March 2010 [176]).

On 8 December 2008, the Speaker issued a Protocol for future police searches: a warrant would always be required for searching a Member's office or parliamentary papers, including electronic records, and any warrant would be referred to the Speaker for their personal decision. The Protocol also made it clear that 'A criminal offence committed within the precincts is no different from an offence committed outside and is a matter for the courts. It is long established that a Member may be arrested within the precincts' (see Committee on Issue of Privilege, *Police Searches on the Parliamentary Estate* [145]).

MPs or peers can be prosecuted for criminal offences unconnected with parliamentary business. As the Speaker reminded MPs in his statement of 3 December, parliamentary privilege has 'never prevented the operation of the criminal law' (HC Deb 3 December 2008, Vol 485 col 3); see also *Wellesley v Duke of Beaufort* (1831) 2 Russ & M 639, where Brougham LC stated that parliamentary privilege did not extend to criminal matters and never protects from punishment (pp 665, 673). In 2013, for example, Chris Huhne, an MP and Cabinet minister, was prosecuted and imprisoned for eight months for perverting the course of justice, having asked his wife to accept his speeding points to avoid losing his licence. He resigned from the Cabinet after being charged, and as an MP after pleading guilty. However, the leading case in this area is *R v Chaytor*.

Three Labour MPs (Elliot Morley, David Chaytor, and Jim Devine) and a Tory peer, Lord Hanningfield, were charged with false accounting over their expenses claims. They claimed that criminal proceedings could not be brought against them because that would infringe parliamentary privilege. A nine-member Supreme Court held that:

- submitting claims for allowances and expenses was administrative and not part of the core business of Parliament; it was not part of the proceedings in Parliament under Article 9 of the Bill of Rights 1689 ([47, 48, 62]) nor within the exclusive cognisance of the two Houses ([89, 91–92]);

- parliamentary privilege did not prevent the defendants being prosecuted in the criminal courts for ordinary crimes unconnected with carrying out the business of

> Parliament. Lord Phillips noted that Parliament had never challenged the application of criminal law in its precincts ([80]), and it allowed the police to investigate breaches of criminal law in Parliament ([83]).
>
> However, in 2016, Lord Hanningfield was acquitted at a second trial for submitting false expenses after the House of Lords made written submissions to the court on whether parliamentary privilege might apply to aspects of the trial, including what amounted to 'parliamentary work'. The submissions were careful to state that this did not mean that the trial should not proceed. The Crown did not offer evidence and the judge confirmed that it was not for the court to determine whether Lord Hanningfield was carrying out parliamentary work (https://old.parliament.uk/business/news/2016/july/hanningfield-statement/).

After the *Chaytor case*, the government published a Green Paper (*Parliamentary Privilege* (Cm 8318) 26 April 2012) inviting views on the scope and operation of parliamentary privilege, particularly whether it should prevent prosecution for criminal offences and whether proceedings in Parliament should be defined in legislation, but the draft Parliamentary Privilege Bill included in the Green Paper did not become law.

10.5.6 Disciplinary and penal powers

Parliament has the exclusive right to judge for itself whether a breach of privilege or contempt has occurred. It is not for the courts to decide. The House of Commons refers issues concerning privileges and contempt to the Committee of Privileges; in the Lords, privileges are considered by the Committee for Privileges and Conduct, which oversees the conduct of members.

> **Breach of privilege**   means abuse of or interference with the privileges of Parliament; a breach of privilege is a contempt of Parliament.
>
> **Contempt**   means 'any act or omission which obstructs or impedes either House of Parliament in the performance of its functions', or any Member or officer of the House in discharging their duty (Erskine May, *Parliamentary Practice*, para 15.2). This includes, for example, misleading the House, disorderly conduct, refusing to give evidence to a committee of the House, and bribing or threatening an MP. It extends to non-members.

10.5.6.1 The right to punish for contempt

The two Houses of Parliament have an inherent power to punish breaches of privilege or contempt, stemming from their historic roots as the High Court of Parliament. The procedure for alleging contempt in the House of Commons is:

- An MP refers the allegation to the Speaker in writing.
- The Speaker decides if the criteria are satisfied.
- The issue is then referred to the Committee of Privileges.
- The Committee considers and reports to the House.
- The House debates the report and decides on any penalty.

Punishments for contempt are normally:

- censure (a reprimand) by the Speaker;

- suspension;
- expulsion from the House.

Imprisonment for contempt was last used in 1880 (see *Sheriff of Middlesex Case* (1840) 11 Ad.&E. 273) and a fine for contempt has not been imposed since 1666. (For further details, see Joint Committee, *Parliamentary Privilege*, 1999 [262–324].)

10.5.7 **Reform of parliamentary privilege?**

In 2002, the Committee on Standards in Public Life, led by Sir Nigel Wicks, examined self-regulation by Parliament (8th Report of the Committee on Standards in Public Life, *Standards of Conduct in the House of Commons* (Cm 5663) 2002). In evidence to the Committee, Robin Cook MP stated that parliamentary privilege was a necessary part of Parliament's sovereignty (Ev [19]), and many Parliamentarians were strongly protective of its privileges and self-regulation, expressing concern about intervention by the courts and the dangers of 'judicial tanks on the parliamentary lawn'. The Committee concluded that standards of conduct in the House of Commons were generally high, and recommended a self-regulatory system with an element of independent adjudication ([9.6]). See Rhoda James and Richard Kirkham, 'Slow Progress in Parliament: The Eighth Report of the Committee on Standards in Public Life' (2003) 66 MLR 906.

The 2013 Joint Committee recommended against comprehensive codification of parliamentary privilege (Joint Committee, *Parliamentary Privilege* [47]; and see Andrew Blick, 'Should a UK Constitutional Convention Consider the Clarification and Codification of Parliamentary Privilege?' at http://blogs.lse.ac.uk/constitutionuk/tag/parliamentary-privilege/).

 SUMMARY

- Parliament needs parliamentary privilege to conduct its core business effectively, independently, and without fear of outside interference, and to protect everything said or done in the transaction of parliamentary business.

- Article 9 Bill of Rights 1689 protects the freedom of speech that is necessary for full and uninhibited debate in Parliament.

- Parliament is self-regulating and, as a sovereign body, operates outside the jurisdiction of the courts except for the criminal law. Observing the boundary between their respective provinces is important and depends on mutual respect and uncodified rules.

10.6 Accountability and conduct

10.6.1 **Pre-election**

Candidates' activities in campaigns for election to the House of Commons are regulated by law to ensure free and fair conduct, and the Representation of the People Act (RPA) 1983 sets out a number of electoral offences; where electoral law has been breached, elections can be challenged in the courts. In *Watkins v Woolas* [2010] EWHC 2702 (QB), Phil Woolas was elected as

Labour MP for Oldham East and Saddleworth by 103 votes but Elwyn Watkins, the Liberal Democrat candidate, claimed that Mr Woolas had made untrue claims about him in election leaflets. Under section 106 RPA 1983, it is an offence to publish a false statement of fact about a candidate's personal character or conduct to prevent them being elected. A special Election Court (consisting of two High Court judges) found Mr Woolas guilty of an illegal practice and declared the election void under section 159 RPA 1983. The High Court: (a) held that decisions of the Election Court could be judicially reviewed, emphasising that it was consistent with the constitutional principles of the separation of powers and the rule of law that the courts could determine the meaning of the law enacted by Parliament ([52]); and (b) upheld much of the Election Court's decision (*R (Woolas) v Parliamentary Election Court* [2010] EWHC 3169 (Admin)). The election was re-run and Mr Woolas was barred from standing for elected office for three years.

 THINKING POINT

Should a court be able to overturn the effect of a democratic election?

10.6.2 Post-election accountability: the power of recall

MPs can lose their seat under the Recall of MPs Act 2015 where they have been convicted of an offence and received a custodial sentence (including a suspended sentence), barred from the House of Commons for ten sitting days or 14 calendar days, or convicted of providing false or misleading information for allowance claims under the Parliamentary Standards Act 2009. The Speaker of the House of Commons notifies the Petition Officer who opens a recall petition for constituents to sign. If successful, the MP loses their seat in the House of Commons and a by-election is called. The first successful recall was in 2019 in relation to Fiona Onasanya, former MP for Peterborough, after her conviction and three-month prison sentence for perverting the course of justice.

10.6.3 Standards of conduct in Parliament

Each House has its own standards of conduct and disciplinary powers which require members not to abuse their privileged position, as shown in Table 10.8.

 CLOSE-UP FOCUS: THE EXPENSES SCANDAL OF 2009

MPs can claim expenses to reimburse them for the additional costs of performing their parliamentary functions, such as office and staffing, accommodation, and travel.

In 2008, following freedom of information requests, the Information Tribunal ordered the Commons to disclose details of 14 MPs' expenses claims. The Commons unsuccessfully challenged the ruling in the High Court (*Corporate Officer of the House of Commons v The Information Commissioner* [2008] EWHC 1084 (Admin)). In 2009, the *Daily Telegraph* published a stream of disclosures detailing numerous MPs' claims, including second home allowances and headline-grabbing claims for the costs of clearing a moat and installing a £1,645 duck house. There was widespread public anger at the extent of the claims, funded by public money, and the cumulative effect of the disclosures damaged Parliament's reputation, presenting a picture of an institution whose self-regulation on expenses lacked control, rigour, and transparency.

Between May and July 2009, the Prime Minister publicly apologised for the scandal, Michael Martin stood down as Speaker over his handling of it, and the Parliamentary Standards Act 2009 was passed to end Parliament's self-regulation of allowances. The Act created the Independent Parliamentary Standards Authority to independently administer and control MPs' salaries and expenses, and established a Commissioner for Parliamentary Investigations to investigate alleged breaches of the rules. An inquiry into MPs' expenses was carried out by the Committee on Standards in Public Life which made 60 recommendations (see 12th Report of the Committee on Standards in Public Life, *MPs' Expenses and Allowances: Supporting Parliament, Safeguarding the Taxpayer* (Cm 7724), November 2009, pp 13–21).

For background detail, see:
http://www.telegraph.co.uk/news/newstopics/mps-expenses/6499657/MPs-expenses-scandal-a-timeline.html.
G. Little and D. Stopforth, 'The Legislative Origins of the MPs' Expenses Scandal' (2013) 76(1) Modern Law Review 83–108.
See also The Independent Parliamentary Standards Authority v The Information Commissioner [2015] EWCA Civ 388.

Table 10.8 Standards of conduct

Standards of conduct in the House of Commons	Standards of conduct in the House of Lords
As a result of the Nolan Report's recommendations (*First Report of the Committee on Standards in Public Life* (Cm 2850) 1 May 1995 pp 3–14), the House of Commons established: • an independent Parliamentary Commissioner for Standards to investigate complaints about MPs; • a Select Committee on Standards and Privileges (replaced in 2013 by the Committee on Standards and the Committee of Privileges). The Committee on Standards oversees the work of the Parliamentary Commissioner for Standards, monitors the Register of Members' Interests, and recommends modifications to the Code of Conduct; • a Code of Conduct, incorporating the seven principles of public life (the 'Nolan principles'). The House of Commons *Code of Conduct* (2019, HC 1882) requires that MPs: • uphold the law; • act in the interests of the nation as a whole, with a special duty to their constituents; and • act in accordance with the public trust placed in them with probity and integrity ([5–7]).	Under the *Code of Conduct for Members of the House of Lords* (adopted 2009, amended 2010–2017; available at parliament.uk), members are required to: • comply with the Code of Conduct; • always act on their personal honour; • never accept any financial inducement as an incentive for exercising parliamentary influence; • not accept payment for providing parliamentary advice or services (para 8); • base their actions on consideration of the public interest (para 7); • observe the seven general principles of conduct set out by the Committee on Standards in Public Life (para 9).

Continued

Table 10.8 Standards of conduct *(Cont.)*

Standards of conduct in the House of Commons	Standards of conduct in the House of Lords
MPs can do paid work outside Parliament as long as it does not interfere with their parliamentary role, but they must register on the Register of Members' Interests any financial interest or benefit they receive (eg directorships, paid employment, income from property) which others might reasonably consider to influence their conduct or words as MPs. Failure to register is a contempt of Parliament. See parliament.uk.	Members must: • not act as a paid advocate in any proceeding of the House (para 14); • disclose all relevant interests in the Register of Lords' Interests; • declare any relevant interests when speaking in the House, when communicating with ministers or public servants, or when in committees.
Misconduct issues can be investigated by political parties in respect of backbenchers, or by the Cabinet Office in relation to ministers; this happened in 2017 in respect of a number of sexual harassment claims made against MPs. In 2018, a new Behaviour Code and independent complaints procedure was adopted to deal with bullying and harassment in Parliament (HC Hansard 8 February 2018, Vol 635 col 1668–1670).	In 2019, a House of Lords Conduct Committee was created, replacing the conduct functions of the Committee for Privileges and Conduct and the Sub-Committee on Lords' Conduct; it also reviews the code of conduct. Alleged breaches of the Code are investigated by the House of Lords Commissioner for Standards, an independent officer appointed by the House.

The Committee on Standards in Public Life, an independent advisory body, has conducted inquiries and reported on standards of conduct of public office-holders since 1994.

10.6.4 **Suspension and expulsion**

Until recently, it was uncertain whether the House of Lords could expel its members. In May 2009, the Privileges Committee concluded that members were subject to implied conditions on conduct and that the House had an inherent power to discipline its members and suspend them for a specific period not longer than the remainder of the current Parliament, but it had no power to expel a member permanently (*The Powers of the House of Lords in Respect of Its Members*, 1st Report of Session 2008–09, HL Paper 87).

The House of Lords' system for disciplining peers was criticised after a number of cases of misconduct. Lord Archer remained a member after being jailed for perjury in 2001. In 2010, following allegations concerning claims for allowances, Lord Bhatia, Baroness Uddin, and Lord Paul were suspended, but could then return to the House. In 2011, Lord Taylor of Warwick and Lord Hanningfield were imprisoned after fraudulently claiming parliamentary expenses but, although suspended from the House, they could not be permanently expelled. In 2009, the Prime Minister criticised the House of Lords' discipline procedures and procedures for dealing with its finances as not good enough (HC Hansard 10 Jun 2009, Vol 493 col 802). The Constitutional Reform and Governance Bill 2008–09 initially included provisions to allow peers to resign, be suspended, and be expelled from the House of Lords, but the clauses were later removed from the Bill.

The position was resolved by:

- The House of Lords Reform Act 2014: members can be expelled from the House of Lords if the Lord Speaker certifies that a member of the House of Lords has been convicted of a criminal offence, and sentenced or imprisoned for more than one year, regardless of whether or not they were a member of the House of Lords when they committed the offence (section 3);
- The House of Lords (Expulsion and Suspension) Act 2015 gives the House of Lords power to expel members, and extends the power to suspend members beyond the end of a Parliament, for breaching the code of conduct.

However, this does not apply to personal misconduct which does not breach the code, although members may resign voluntarily.

SUMMARY

- Electoral law is important in ensuring free and fair conduct in elections to the House of Commons.
- The MPs' expenses scandal was a catalyst in bringing about important reforms.
- As a counterbalance to the privileges and immunities of Parliament, both Houses have their own standards of conduct and the power to suspend or expel members.

? Questions

Self-test questions

1. What is a backbench MP?

2. Summarise the main functions of Parliament.

3. Why is the House of Commons the pre-eminent chamber?

4. What is the importance of representative democracy?

5. How do individuals become members of the House of Lords?

6. What was the effect of the Parliament Acts of 1911 and 1949?

7. What was the effect of the House of Lords Act 1999?

8. What are the arguments in favour of an elected second chamber? What are the arguments against?

9. What is parliamentary privilege and why is it important?

10. What is exclusive cognisance?

Exam question

'[T]he Lords are an archaic anomaly which fuels disillusionment with British politics. It exists purely on a democratic deficit which has been allowed to evolve unchecked for centuries.' (Peter Hain, <https://peterhain.uk/tag/house-of-lords/>)

Examine this statement and discuss whether the UK Parliament needs the House of Lords.

Further reading

Books

Bogdanor, V. *The New British Constitution* (Oxford and Portland, Oregon: Hart Publishing 2009).
See chapter 6 for discussion on Lords reform

Norton, P. *Parliament in British Politics* (2nd edn, Basingstoke: Palgrave Macmillan 2013).
See chapters 10–13

Norton, P. *Reform of the House of Lords* (Manchester: Manchester University Press 2017).
Analyses previous Lords reforms and considers options for future change

Besly, N., Goldsmith, T., Rogers, R. and Walters R. *How Parliament Works* (8th edn, Abingdon: Routledge 2019).
An excellent source of information on the operation of Parliament

Russell, M. *The Contemporary House of Lords: Westminster Bicameralism Revisited* (Oxford: Oxford University Press 2013).
Analyses the Lords since the House of Lords Act 1999

Journal articles

For in-depth discussion of the Parliament Acts in light of the *Jackson case* (also useful for parliamentary sovereignty), see:

Cooke, R. 'A Constitutional Retreat' (2006) 122 LQR 224

Ekins, R. 'Acts of Parliament and the Parliament Acts' (2007) 123 LQR 91
Forsyth, C. 'The Definition of Parliament after Jackson: Can the Life of Parliament Be Extended under the Parliament Acts 1911 and 1949?' (2011) 9(1) International Journal of Constitutional Law 132

On House of Lords reform, see:

Barber, N.W. 'House of Lords Reform: A Look in the Long Grass' UK Const L Blog (12 July 2012, available at http://ukconstitutionallaw.org).
Discusses House of Lords Reform Bill 2012 and whether an elected Lords is needed

Lord Bingham, 'The House of Lords: Its Future?' (2010) (April) Public Law 261.
Considers possible solutions to the elected Lords debate, notably a Council of the Realm

Mirfield, P. 'Can the House of Lords Lawfully Be Abolished?' (1979) 95 LQR 36.
Argues that Parliament could not lawfully abolish the House of Lords and considers the issues of invoking the Parliament Acts to achieve this

Phillipson, G. '"The Greatest Quango of Them All", "a Rival Chamber" or "a Hybrid Nonsense"? Solving the Second Chamber Paradox' (2004) (Summer) Public Law 352.
Though older now on reform detail, contains useful discussion on the elected versus appointed debate

On Parliamentary privilege, see:

Bradley, A. 'The Damian Green Affair—All's Well that Ends Well?' (2012) (July) Public Law 396–407.
Commentary on the Green affair

Joseph, P.A. 'Parliament's Privilege of Freedom of Speech: Still More Confusion' (2015) 131 LQR 12–15.
Case comment on *Makudi v Triesman*

Lord Lisvane KCB DL 'The Courts and Parliament' (2016) (April) Public Law 272–284.
A clear commentary on the *sub judice* rule in Parliament

Saunders, Sir John, 'Parliamentary Privilege and the Criminal Law' (2017) 7 Crim LR 521–536.
Good background to the *Chaytor* and *Hanningfield (2)* cases

Other sources

Gordon, R QC and Jack, Sir Malcolm, *Parliamentary Privilege: Evolution or Codification?* The Constitution Society 2013, at https://consoc.org.uk/wp-content/uploads/2013/05/Parliamentary-Privilege.pdf.
An in-depth report on parliamentary privilege and prospects for reform

Green Paper, *Parliamentary Privilege* (Cm 8318) 2012.
Clear background on parliamentary privilege

House of Commons Briefing Paper, *The Parliament Acts* No 00675, Richard Kelly and Lucinda Maer (25 February 2016) at http://researchbriefings.files.parliament.uk/documents/SN00675/SN00675.pdf.
A detailed explanation of the Parliament Acts

House of Commons Library, Oonagh Gay, *Parliamentary Privilege: Current Issues*, Standard Note: SN/PC/06390, 16 July 2013.
Good detail on the operation of parliamentary privilege

Lakin, S. 'Parliamentary Privilege, Parliamentary Sovereignty, and Constitutional Principle' UK Const L Blog (11 February 2013) (available at http://ukconstitutionallaw.org).
Considers the relationship between parliamentary sovereignty and parliamentary privilege

Phillipson, G. 'Lords Reform: Why Opponents of the Government Bill Were Wrong', UK Const L Blog (26 September 2012) (available at http://ukconstitutionallaw.org).
Good critique of reasons for and against Lords reform

Lord Burnett, 'Parliamentary Privilege – Liberty and Due Limitation', 21st Commonwealth Law Conference 2019 (available at https://www.judiciary.uk/wp-content/uploads/2019/04/20190405-Parliamentary-Privilege-for-publication-2.pdf).

Useful websites

The Parliament website: https://www.parliament.uk/.

An online edition of Erskine May: https://erskinemay.parliament.uk/section/4570/what-constitutes-privilege/

؛ Online resources

www.oup.com/he/dennett2e

This chapter is accompanied by a selection of online resources to help you with this topic, including:

- Multiple-choice questions
- Answers to the self-test questions
- Guidance on answering the exam question

11 The key functions of Parliament

LEARNING OBJECTIVES

By the end of this chapter, you should be able to:

- Discuss why Parliament needs to scrutinise the government and the procedures it uses to achieve this
- Evaluate the strengths and weaknesses of those procedures
- Assess whether there is sufficient scrutiny of legislation
- Appreciate the nature of secondary legislation and analyse rule of law issues that it can raise

Introduction

Just after 7.15pm on 13 December 2017, a packed House of Commons sat in a moment's stunned silence as the result of a hotly contested vote became clear: the government had just been defeated by four votes on a proposed amendment to the EU (Withdrawal) Bill (now the EU (Withdrawal) Act 2018). The Commons had voted by 309 to 305 to give Parliament a vote on the final Brexit deal. Eleven Conservative MPs had rebelled and voted against the government, resulting in the first government defeat on amendments to the Bill (though this was only one step on the 'meaningful vote' journey; in the end, section 13(2) of the EU (Withdrawal) Act provided for a debate and vote by the Commons 'so far as practicable', and was repealed by the EU (Withdrawal Agreement) Act 2020). A tweet by Guy Verhofstadt, then the European Parliament's lead Brexit co-ordinator, echoed the views of some UK politicians: 'British Parliament takes back control . . . A good day for democracy' (www.bbc.co.uk/news/uk-politics-42346192). It encapsulates the underlying theme of this chapter—Parliament's control over the government—as we focus on how the UK Parliament performs its key activities of making law and scrutinising central government. It is important to appreciate the strong link between both activities: government bills need Parliament's assent to become law and Parliament's effective scrutiny of government-driven legislation acts as a check or influence on executive action.

This chapter discusses how Parliament carries out scrutiny of government through ministerial questions, debates, and select committees, then examines the legislative process, particularly legislative scrutiny. It is also important to consider how the principles of the separation of powers and rule of law apply here.

11.1 Scrutiny of the executive

One of Parliament's main functions is to examine and challenge the work of the government, or in John Stuart Mill's words, 'to watch and control the government: to throw the light of publicity on its acts' (*Considerations on Representative Government* (1861) chapter 5). Parliament's scrutiny of government has been defined as:

> the process of examining expenditure, administration and policy in detail, on the public record, requiring the government of the day to explain itself to parliamentarians as representatives of the citizen and the taxpayer, and to justify its actions. (Robert Rogers and Rhodri Walters, *How Parliament Works*, (7th edn, Abingdon: Routledge 2015) p 331)

In the absence of a codified constitution and entrenched limits on executive power, the requirement for the government to answer to Parliament for its actions is an essential check and control, and the Supreme Court has recognised parliamentary accountability (government accountability to Parliament) as a fundamental principle of the constitution (*R (Miller) v The Prime Minister; Cherry and others v Advocate General for Scotland* [2019] UKSC 41 [46]).

Scrutiny serves a number of purposes:

- It prevents the government from exceeding its powers.
- It allows MPs to question, investigate, and challenge government policy and actions.
- It encourages the government to refine, review, and reconsider policy, and enables Parliament to contribute to policy-making.
- It requires the government to be answerable for its public expenditure, policies and errors, ensuring accountability.
- Parliamentary questions and debates, and the fact that government responses are normally a matter of public record, ensure that government is open and transparent.
- It encourages dialogue between Parliament and the government, and allows Parliament to be informed.
- It helps to promote more efficient and effective government.

Scrutiny of the executive can involve Parliament putting the brakes on when the government accelerates, and because Parliament is an elected body, it conveys the voice of electors to the government between elections (see The Report of the Commission to Strengthen Parliament, *Strengthening Parliament*, July 2000, p 4). However, it is important that the government engages with Parliament and its select committees to support their scrutiny, and it is vital that Parliament's scrutiny is effective and has impact:

> Government needs an effective Parliament . . . because its authority derives from Parliament. Government is elected through Parliament and its political authority derives from that very fact. Undermine the authority of Parliament and ultimately you undermine the authority of government . . . Parliamentary scrutiny should be seen by government as a benefit, not a threat (*Strengthening Parliament*, p 5).

Parliament's capacity to check governmental power does not work as effectively where a strong government dominates Parliament, which can result in executive control of the legislature rather than executive accountability to Parliament. This can be an inherent weakness in the Westminster system and is explored further in relation to the legislative process in section 11.2.

11.1.1 **Scrutiny in practice**

Dr Hannah White has analysed what the practice of scrutiny involves:

- identifying which aspects of government activity to scrutinise;
- examining whether the government is acting under its democratic mandate from the electorate and requiring explanation from the government;
- analysing whether the government is 'spending taxpayers' money wisely, administering itself efficiently and developing and implementing policies that achieve desirable outcome';
- influencing government directly or indirectly on the basis of conclusions reached through scrutiny.

(Dr Hannah White, *Parliamentary Scrutiny of Government*, Institute for Government, 22 January 2015, available at www.instituteforgovernment.org.uk)

While the government is primarily accountable to the House of Commons, the Commons and the Lords use similar methods to scrutinise, challenge and question the government, although procedures vary. By questioning government ministers, and investigating and criticising government policy and decisions, MPs and members of the Lords can shine a spotlight on how government policy is being applied, highlighting flaws, errors, or inconsistencies. A significant proportion of parliamentary activities revolve around the scrutiny process, which takes place through:

- Ministerial questions
- Debates
- Select committees

Together, they provide opportunities for critical enquiry. We now deal with each mechanism of scrutiny in turn.

11.1.2 **Questions**

There are two main opportunities in the parliamentary timetable to put questions to government ministers: Question Time and Prime Minister's Questions.

11.1.2.1 **Question Time**

In the Commons, MPs can put oral questions to government ministers during Question Time as a direct way of holding ministers to account; this informs the government of public concerns and enforces ministerial responsibility, which is a fundamental principle that ministers are responsible, and accountable to Parliament, for their department's actions. The Ministerial Code requires ministers to give accurate and truthful information to Parliament; without it, scrutiny cannot be effective, and ministers who knowingly mislead Parliament are expected to resign. Normally, Question Time takes place for one hour a day from Monday to Thursday and ministers

> **CROSS REFERENCE**
> For more about ministerial responsibility, see section 12.4.1

attend to answer questions on a rota basis (agreed by the government and Opposition parties). MPs must table oral questions at least three days ahead of the relevant Question Time; they may ask a supplementary question on the day on the same topic as their first question. In the House of Lords, questions may be put to government ministers in the first 30 minutes of business on Mondays to Thursdays. MPs and members of the Lords may also put written questions to ministers. Since 2014–2015, written answers from ministers have been published online in the Daily Report and are publicly accessible on the Parliament website. (See https://questions-statements.parliament.uk/ and for further details about parliamentary questions, see www.parliament.uk/about/how/business/questions/.)

Question Time, however, is not always an effective means of scrutiny, for the following reasons:

- The rota system in the Commons means waiting four or five weeks for a particular minister to appear.
- Only four hours a week are allocated in the Commons.
- Questions must fall within the responsibility of the relevant government department.
- There is a lack of sufficient time for thorough questioning on an issue. With an average of only seven and a half minutes available for the question, answer, and supplementary questions and answers in the House of Lords, the Leader's Group on Working Practices has observed that 'there is, instead of self-regulation, regulation by clock' [29]. It suggests that this discourages many members from participating in Question Time. As a result, 'The unique contribution of the Lords—the breadth of knowledge and experience of its Members—is wasted, and the Government is less effectively held to account' (House of Lords Leader's Group on Working Practices, *Report of the Leader's Group on Working Practices*, Session 2010–12, chapter 2 [30]). This applies equally to the Commons.

Backbenchers in the Commons are also increasingly applying for Urgent Questions to require a minister to come before the House on the same day to explain matters considered 'urgent and important'.

 EXAMPLE

On 28 November 2017, the government had to respond to an Urgent Question by Sir Keir Starmer, then Shadow Secretary of State for Exiting the European Union, about its failure to disclose assessments of the economic impact of Brexit on 58 sectors; they related to 'the most important set of decisions this country has taken for decades and they need to be subjected to proper scrutiny' (Sir Keir Starmer, HC Hansard 28 November 2017, Vol 632 col 163). The Speaker warned of the prospect that the government could be found in contempt of Parliament if it did not produce them. The Secretary of State for Exiting the European Union appeared before the Brexit Select Committee, where he had to explain that no impact assessments had been undertaken. The matter was also raised at Prime Minister's Questions. These processes press government to justify and clarify its actions.

11.1.2.2 Prime Minister's Questions

Prime Minister's Questions (PMQs) presents an opportunity for MPs in the Commons to question the Prime Minister directly on current issues and government policy every Wednesday from 12.00 to 12.30pm when the House is sitting. (For a lively overview of its recent history, see www.theguardian.com/politics/2011/oct/27/history-pmqs-prime-ministers-commons.) The leader of the Opposition has six questions but backbenchers wishing to ask a question enter a ballot; they often table a standard question about the Prime Minister's official engagements which enables them to ask one supplementary question in the chamber, on which the PM will not have advance notice. Although it is televised and carries a high media and publicity profile, PMQs is not always an effective scrutiny mechanism. It is party political, adversarial, often noisy, and can depend more on showmanship, soundbites, and quick-witted responses than on substantive detail.

 THINKING POINT

You might disagree. Watch PMQs (available online). How effective does it seem to you as a method of scrutiny?

11.1.3 Debates

Debates are a critical function of Parliament, providing an opportunity for government scrutiny by elected representatives (see Table 11.1). In the Commons, the topic for debate may be chosen by the government, Opposition, or backbenchers, and government ministers will attend and be required to present, explain, and defend government policy. Westminster Hall debates also give MPs an opportunity to raise specific issues and receive a response from a government minister, which broadens the scope for scrutiny.

Table 11.1 Opportunities for debates in the House of Commons

At second reading stage of Bills (see section 11.2.3)
Adjournment debates—this allows MPs to apply for a general debate on a matter of concern as the last business of the day and to receive a response from a minister. The House does not vote and the debate is not binding on the government
Opposition days—20 Opposition days in each parliamentary session are allocated for debates on topics chosen by Opposition parties, but Opposition day motions are not binding and the government is not required to make any policy changes as a result. An example is the non-binding vote in favour of pausing the roll-out of Universal Credit in October 2017
Backbench debates—35 days are available for backbench debate in the Commons Chamber or Westminster Hall. MPs put forward suggestions for debates to the Backbench Business Committee, but backbench motions are not binding on the government
Early day motions (EDMs) are submitted for debate in the House of Commons without a set date. Their aim is mainly to encourage support and show strength of interest in a particular topic, as there is little chance of it being debated

 THINKING POINT

Do any aspects of the debates in Table 11.1 suggest they might not always allow effective scrutiny? Should the public be able to participate in debates? See www.digitaldemocracy. parliament.uk/.

However, debates are a less efficient vehicle for scrutiny where:

- they are low-profile in terms of attendance and publicity;
- well-attended, important debates are dominated by the frontbenches, with less opportunity for backbenchers to be called on to speak;
- there is a lack of time for in-depth questioning or more detailed responses from government;
- the government can cut short debates;
- a debate is non-binding on the government.

11.1.4 Select committees

Select committees are an extremely important part of parliamentary business. They embody Parliament's 'grip' on the executive over a wide range of activities and, over the past decade or so, have become a highly effective method of public scrutiny (especially House of Lords committees), attracting increasing media coverage. Their overall aim is to hold ministers and government departments to account, requiring ministers to explain and justify their policy and decision-making (for select committees' core tasks, see Liaison Committee, *Select Committee Effectiveness, Resources and Powers*, Second Report of Session 2012–13, HC 697 November 2012 [11–20]).

Both Houses of Parliament have select committees (see Table 11.2). Many Commons select committees scrutinise government departments, investigating policy issues, administration, and relevant legislation in detail, although their remit can extend to broader concerns such as the Work and Pensions Committee's investigation into the BHS sale and pension fund in 2016. Committees' findings are evidence-based; they can call witnesses, call for production of documents, and have the power to take evidence on oath, though this is not often done. Their reports are intended to influence government policy—around 40 per cent of recommendations are accepted by the government (Meg Russell and Meghan Benton, *Selective Influence: The Policy Impact of House of Commons Select Committees*, Constitution Unit, June 2011, pp 47, 49); the government issues responses as a Command Paper or memorandum to the committee. Committee reports can also be discussed in Parliament. The select committee system was revitalised in 2010 following the reforms recommended by the Select Committee on the Reform of the House of Commons, known as the Wright reforms. One of the chief innovations was to introduce elected committee Chairs; previously, they were decided by a selection committee controlled by party whips, which meant that the government, through its whips, could influence who scrutinised it. Most select committee Chairs are elected by all MPs by secret ballot, while committee member elections take place within each party. This has made select committees more independent scrutineers.

11.1.4.1 Critique of select committees

Select committees are successful in influencing government (see House of Commons Liaison Committee, *Select Committee Effectiveness, Resources and Powers*, 2nd Report of Session 2012–13, HC 697 [61], though note the criticisms in [62]). They also enable the Commons to contribute to detailed policy-making (www.democraticaudit.com/2017/08/31/audit-2017-how-effective-is-the-westminster-parliament-in-scrutinising-central-government-policy-making/), but while the select committee system can provide effective and in-depth scrutiny, there are some deficiencies:

- Commons committees have cross-party membership of around 11 members reflecting party balance, so that the government always has a majority.
- There are limits on the power of select committees. They cannot compel ministers, MPs, or peers to give evidence, nor can they compel witnesses who are overseas to attend, though other witnesses within the UK can be formally summoned if they refuse to appear

Table 11.2 Select committees

House of Commons departmental select committees Created in 1979, the Commons' departmental select committee system has been called 'the most developed vehicle through which MPs can carry out detailed scrutiny of government policy and Ministerial conduct' (Select Committee on Modernisation of the House of Commons, Memorandum submitted by the Leader of the House of Commons, 12 December 2001, HC 440, para 5). Each government department has a corresponding select committee which scrutinises its spending, administration and policy, such as the Defence Committee, Foreign Affairs Committee, and Home Affairs Committee.

Other House of Commons select committees include:

- the Liaison Committee, which consists of the Chairs of each of the select committees, considers general matters relating to the work of select committees, and hears evidence from the Prime Minister on public policy;
- the Public Accounts Committee, which scrutinises public spending;
- the Public Administration and Constitutional Affairs Committee, set up in 2015, which examines reports of the Parliamentary and Health Service Ombudsman, the quality of civil service administration, and constitutional affairs.

Joint select committee members are drawn from both the House of Commons and House of Lords. Permanent Joint Committees include the Joint Committee on Human Rights, the Joint Committee on the National Security Strategy, and the Joint Committee on Statutory Instruments. Temporary Joint Committees can be set up to consider draft Bills and other matters.

House of Lords Select Committees include:

- European Union Committee
- Science and Technology Committee
- Constitution Committee
- Covid-19 Committee

Ad hoc committees may be set up for a specific purpose and then cease to exist after reporting back; an example is the Political and Constitutional Reform Committee, set up by the House of Commons in 2010 to consider political and constitutional reform and scrutinise constitutional bills in the 2010–2015 Parliament.

Committees' titles and areas of remit change from time to time. For current details, see: www.parliament.uk/about/how/committees/.

(if they still refuse, or if they refuse to answer questions, they can be reported to the House for contempt). Ministers decide who will appear on behalf of their department, and civil servants giving evidence do so under their minister's instruction.

- There can be over-scrutiny or a lack of co-ordination between different inquiries; for example, by October 2016, there were 18 separate inquiries on Brexit by Commons committees and another 13 in the Lords (www.instituteforgovernment.org.uk).
- When Parliament is dissolved before a general election, all select committees cease until they are reconstituted, leaving an operational gap.

Given that select committees face both inwards to Parliament and outwards to the public, the Liaison Committee has recommended promoting further public engagement work, more joint working between committees, better connections between committees and the House of Commons, and widening the scope of who select committees should hold to account (House of Commons Liaison Committee *The Effectiveness and Influence of the Select Committee System* Fourth Report of Session 2017–19, HC 1860).

SUMMARY

Parliament scrutinises government through ministerial and Prime Minister's questions, debates, and select committees. In his retirement letter in 2014, Sir Robert Rogers, the clerk of the House of Commons, recognised that the House was 'a more effective scrutineer of the executive . . . than I have ever known it' (old.parliament.uk/documents/commons-chief-executive/2014-04-29-RJR-to-Mr-Speaker-(signed).pdf).

11.2 The legislative process

Parliament's laws touch our everyday lives. Making law is a social and political process in which competing claims, interests, and needs of specific sections of society and the public interest of the wider community are considered and debated; interests such as justice, equality, or public finances may be taken into account. New law can be a reaction to events or to social, economic, or political issues, or can be proactive and innovative. The deliberation and approval of laws by an elected body means democratic endorsement, which legitimises the end product; it is, as Laws J has described, 'the consequence of the democratic political process' (*R v Lord Chancellor, ex parte Witham* [1997] EWHC Admin 237, [1998] QB 575, 581). The law-making process therefore weaves together accountability, representation, and legitimation.

Q CLOSE-UP FOCUS: LAW AND POLICY

Law evolves from policy, which Parliament is uniquely equipped to decide. Laws LJ has distinguished issues of 'macro-policy', which affect the general public and are issues for policy-makers, from cases involving the application of policy to individuals, which can be resolved by judges with 'no offence to the claims of democratic power' (*R v Secretary of State for Education and Employment, ex parte Begbie* [1999] EWCA Civ 2100 [81]; see also Jonathan Sumption QC, 'Judicial and Political Decision-Making: The Uncertain Boundary', F.A. Mann Lecture, 2011). This centres on the separation of powers.

Lord Sumption has observed that 'politics is quite simply a better way of resolving questions of social policy than judge-made law' ('The Limits of Law', 27th Sultan Azlan Shah Lecture, Kuala Lumpur, 20 November 2013). Politics in a democracy is about reconciling 'inconsistent interests and opinions' (pp 12–13) and he argues that political parties are effective at striking a balance 'between those in power and the public from which they derive their legitimacy' (p 14; see also the Reith lectures 2019 at https://www.bbc.co.uk/radio4). This process lies at the heart of law-making.

⯈ CROSS REFERENCE

See also the discussion on this point in section 7.4.1.1

11.2.1 Primary legislation

Primary legislation refers to the laws made directly by Parliament. A proposed statute is known as a Bill when it is introduced into Parliament, and it needs to be agreed by both Houses and assented to by the monarch to become an Act of Parliament and so become law. Bills fall into four broad categories: see Table 11.3.

Table 11.3 Categories of Bills

Private Members' Bills are Public Bills introduced in the House of Commons by backbench MPs or in the House of Lords by members who are not ministers

Public Bills have general application when they become law. Most bills introduced into Parliament are Public Bills and many are government-sponsored (ie put before Parliament by the government and piloted through the legislative process by the responsible minister)

Private Bills (not to be confused with Private Members' Bills) apply only to a particular area, body, or group of individuals, such as a local authority. They do not change the law for the general public. For further details, see http://researchbriefings.parliament.uk/ResearchBriefing/Summary/SN06508

Hybrid Bills have features of both public and private Bills; they are public Bills which specifically affect certain individuals or groups. They are used, for example, with major infrastructure projects such as High Speed Rail (HS2). Hybrid Bills follow both public Bill and private Bill procedures in Parliament. See http://researchbriefings.files.parliament.uk/documents/SN06736/SN06736.pdf

11.2.2 **Private Members' Bills**

Private Members' Bills have a significantly lower chance of becoming law than do public Bills. In 2015–2016, 23 out of 26 government Bills became law, but only six out of 118 Private Members' Bills were given royal assent. However, attracting cross-party or government support helps some succeed, as was the case with, for example, the Murder (Abolition of the Death Penalty) Act 1965 and the Abortion Act 1967. Two Private Members' Bills on Brexit were successful in 2019, both requiring the Prime Minister to request extensions to prevent a no-deal exit: Yvette Cooper MP introduced a Bill which came into force as the European Union (Withdrawal) Act 2019 and Hilary Benn MP introduced what became the European Union (Withdrawal) (No 2) Act 2019 (see Chapter 5).

In the Commons, Private Members' Bills can be introduced in one of three ways (with decreasing prospects of success for each one):

- Ballot Bills: 20 backbench MPs' names are drawn from a ballot giving them the opportunity to introduce a Bill.
- Ten minute rule Bills: a ten-minute time slot is allotted each week for backbench MPs to introduce a Bill; if the House decides it should be introduced, the Bill is taken to have had its first reading.
- Presentation Bills: under Standing Order No 57, MPs can introduce a Bill for first reading if they give notice; they do not speak in support of it and there is no debate.

11.2.3 **Public Bills**

Public Bills are the vehicle for transforming government policy into law—with Parliament's approval. The government normally introduces 35–50 Bills (known as government Bills) in a parliamentary session. It draws up a legislative programme for each session containing the year's major proposals for new law, which are announced in the Queen's Speech at the State Opening of Parliament. The government must then persuade Parliament to pass its legislation.

CLOSE-UP FOCUS: GOVERNMENT DOMINANCE IN THE LEGISLATIVE PROCESS

It is important to be aware of how government Bills can dominate the legislative programme in the House of Commons as shown in Figure 11.1. They normally stand a good chance of becoming law by virtue of the government's inbuilt support as the party with the largest number of seats within the Commons. A large majority gives the government much greater control in both the Commons and committees, and this is the elective dictatorship that concerned Lord Hailsham (see Chapter 12).

Figure 11.1 Parliament controls the executive but the executive controls law-making?

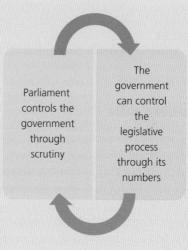

As most Bills are introduced by the government, Lord Norton has described the normal legislative process as Parliament adopting or assenting to laws rather than making laws (see Jeffrey Jowell, Dawn Oliver, and Colm O'Cinneide (eds), *The Changing Constitution*, 8th edn (Oxford: Oxford University Press 2015), p 172). Parliament has more of a policy-influencing role than a policy-making one; it can change or reject government policy but cannot substitute its own ('Parliament and Policy in Britain: The House of Commons as a Policy Influencer' (1984) 13(2) Teaching Politics 198), though it imposed Commons sentiment over a no-deal Brexit (see Chapter 5). Meg Russell and Philip Cowley have found that Parliament's influence over policy behind the scenes of decision-making is significant and increasing ('The Policy Power of the Westminster Parliament: The "Parliamentary State" and the Empirical Evidence' (2016) 29(1) Governance, 121–137).

Meg Russell and Daniel Gover expand on this and argue that Parliament has greater influence on government legislation than may be thought, identifying 'six faces of Parliamentary power' as legislator:

1. visibly amending bills;

2. the government anticipates reactions within Parliament and takes action to avoid conflict, particularly with its backbenchers;

3. the government is aware in advance of what Parliament will accept and knows what not to attempt;

4. Parliament decides what gets discussed;

5. amendments can be tabled in Parliament, as a public arena, to require government to explain itself ('accountability and exposure');

6. Parliament can support the government.

(Meg Russell and Daniel Gover, *Legislation at Westminster: Parliamentary Actors and Influence in the Making of British Law* (Oxford: Oxford University Press 2017)

A government Bill begins with policy. Before Bills are introduced to Parliament, government proposals for new laws are often shaped and refined by consultation, particularly by inviting public and informed responses, allowing early scrutiny by means of:

- **A Green Paper:** a consultation document setting out the government's policy or legislative proposals and inviting feedback and discussion from interested parties.

- **A White Paper:** a policy document setting out government proposals for a new law when policy and legislative proposals have been firmed up, often including a draft Bill and inviting further comments and discussion.

Within government departments, Bill teams, including policy specialists and departmental lawyers, prepare instructions to the Office of Parliamentary Counsel, who will draft the Bill. Before the Bill can be formally introduced into Parliament, it must be approved by the Parliamentary Business and Legislation Committee of the Cabinet, which considers bids for Bills in the legislative programme and is—or should be—a gatekeeper for quality. Table 11.4 shows the legislative procedure for a public Bill introduced by the government into the House of Commons. Although many public Bills begin life in the House of Commons, a third of government Bills are introduced in the Lords (with the chief exceptions of constitutional Bills and money Bills) and follow a broadly similar process. Variations for procedure in the Lords are shown below in blue.

> See the online resources to follow the Modern Slavery Act 2015 from proposal to Act of Parliament

Table 11.4 Legislative procedure for Public Bills

Pre-legislative scrutiny Some Bills may be published in draft for pre-legislative scrutiny by parliamentary committee before they are introduced into Parliament, though not all Bills are subject to this (see section 11.3.2.1).

First reading This stage is a formality with no debate. The title of the Bill is read out in Parliament and the minister responsible for the Bill names a date for the second reading. The Bill is then ordered to be printed and published.

Second reading This is an important stage. The minister responsible for the Bill outlines its policy and content, the Opposition reply, and a debate usually follows. Amendments to the Bill can be suggested and procedural amendments made. A vote then takes place on whether the Bill should be given its second reading (if the vote goes against it, the Bill will be lost). Under the Salisbury convention, government Bills containing a manifesto commitment and passed by the Commons should not be rejected by the House of Lords at second reading. At second reading in the Lords, a Bill is debated but passes to the next stage without a vote.

Committee stage Bills are usually referred to a Public Bill Committee which considers the Bill line by line, makes amendments, and reports back to the Commons. At Committee stage, the government can propose its own amendments in response to backbench or other views. Bills of major constitutional importance can be referred to a Committee of the whole House (considered in the chamber of the House of Commons); for example, the EU (Withdrawal) Bill was considered over eight days in November and December 2017. In the House of Lords, Bills are usually referred to the Committee of the Whole House. As there is no time limit on how long Bills spend at Committee stage in the Lords, all amendments may be debated.

Report stage The Bill goes from the Committee back to the House of Commons for debate on any amendments made; the House can accept or reject those amendments. MPs may put forward new amendments.

Continued

Table 11.4 Legislative procedure for Public Bills *(Cont.)*

Third reading This is usually a short formal stage unless a Bill is controversial. There can be further debate but no amendments can be made to the Bill. At third reading in the Lords, further amendments may still be introduced.

The House of Lords The Bill then goes to the House of Lords for consideration. A clerk carries a copy of the Bill from the Commons to the Lords and similar procedures follow. Any amendments by the Lords return to the House of Commons to be accepted or rejected. The Commons will return any disputed amendments to the Lords and the Bill goes back and forth in a process known as 'ping pong' until both Houses agree. If the Lords do not agree, a Bill may be lost if it runs out of time in the parliamentary session, or the Parliament Act may be invoked (see section 11.2.4).

Royal assent Once a Bill has been agreed by both Houses, it must be given royal assent by the monarch to become an Act of Parliament and have the force of law. Under the Parliament Acts 1911 and 1949, a Bill rejected by the House of Lords can be given royal assent after one year (see section 10.4). A public Bill must normally receive royal assent in the same session in which it is put before Parliament. The Speakers in both Houses announce when royal assent has been given to specific Acts; in the Commons, the Speaker states: 'I have to notify the House, in accordance with the Royal Assent Act 1967, that the Queen has signified her Royal Assent to the following Acts'.

The new Act of Parliament is then promulgated (published) and brought into force either immediately or at a later date.

Before the dissolution of Parliament, there is a period known as 'wash-up'. Bills cannot be carried over into a new Parliament and will fall if not agreed; the government will try to get uncompleted legislation through, arriving at agreement with the Opposition to pass some bills at the expense of others.

11.2.3.1 The legislative role of the House of Lords

The Lords primarily revises and improves legislation originating in the Commons, carrying out detailed analysis of Bills (both overall principles and textual detail), identifying issues, and amending, questioning, and occasionally rejecting legislation; Bills can also be introduced in the Lords. Its scrutiny of legislation has been described as 'an exercise in "quality control"' (House of Lords Leader's Group on Working Practices, *Report of the Leader's Group on Working Practices*, Session 2010–12, HL Paper 136 [73]). This is especially important where passages in Bills may not have had full scrutiny in the Commons. There is also more time to consider legislation in the House of Lords Chamber than there is in the more frenetic House of Commons. In the 2016–2017 parliamentary session, for example, the Lords made 2,270 changes to Bills (www.parliament.uk/business/lords/work-of-the-house-of-lords/work-of-the-house-of-lords-2016-17/). The Lords spends around 50 per cent of its time considering primary legislation (mainly government Bills) (*Report of the Leader's Group on Working Practices* [71]); by contrast, in the 2017–2019 parliamentary session, the Commons spent 18.6 per cent of its sitting hours considering government Bills (House of Commons, Sessional Returns 2017–19, HC (2019) 1).

Defeats by the House of Lords

The Lords is generally mindful of the supremacy of the House of Commons in the legislative process, although in 1976 James Callaghan, then Prime Minister, felt the need to remind the Lords 'that its role is not that of a wrecking chamber, but of a revising chamber' (HC Deb 09 November 1976, Vol 919 col 211). Certainly, amendments to Bills proposed by the House of Lords (often referred to as 'defeats' on Bills) can persuade the Commons and the government to think again, make concessions and adjust proposed legislation, and many amendments proposed by the Lords are accepted by the Commons. In the 2017–2019 parliamentary session, there were 62 defeats by the House of Lords on government bills, and 39 between January and October 2020 (www.ucl.ac.uk/constitution-unit/research/parliament/house-of-lords/lords-defeats); even the prospect of a defeat in the Lords can concentrate minds in the House of Commons. In November 2017, for example, Sir Oliver Letwin MP expressed his concern that clause 6 of the EU (Withdrawal) Bill was 'a frightful mess', containing contradictory provisions on the interpretation of retained EU law, and warned the government to reconsider it or 'it will, rightly, be massacred in the House of Lords' (HC Hansard 14 November 2017, Vol 631 col 311).

Q CLOSE-UP FOCUS: DEFEATS BY THE HOUSE OF LORDS

The Anti-Terrorism, Crime and Security Act 2001

The government introduced the Anti-Terrorism, Crime and Security Bill 2001 to implement measures to fight international terrorism after the September 11 terrorist attacks on the United States. The government imposed a tight time limit for its passage. However, the House of Lords imposed ten defeats on the Bill in eight days (with five defeats in one session), resulting in brinkmanship between the two Houses.

The Lords were objecting to powers that in their view went beyond the purpose of the Act. This included the indefinite detention without trial of terrorist suspects, wide new Police powers, unacceptable narrowing down of judicial review provisions, and making incitement to religious hatred a criminal offence (this proved to be one of the most controversial aspects of the bill and was defeated twice by the Lords). 'All we are doing', said Lady Williams, 'is removing those parts of the bill that are disproportionate, threaten civil liberties and go beyond the fight against terrorism' (www.theguardian.com/politics/2001/dec/07/uk.conservatives). Lord Wallace of Saltaire spoke of the need for 'reasoned debate on Bills of this complexity in which we ask the government to justify their proposals and we do our job in holding up their proposals to careful scrutiny' (HL Deb 10 December 2001, Vol 629 col 1147). However, the Home Secretary, David Blunkett, saw this not as scrutiny but as 'a deliberate sabotage' (www.theguardian.com/politics/2001/dec/08/uk.september11).

Nevertheless, between 7 and 12 December 2001, the government made a number of significant concessions, including abandoning the religious hatred offence provisions and agreeing to a clause requiring the legislation to be reviewed within two years.

The amended Bill received royal assent on 14 December, having taken only one month to become law.

For further details on the legislative process, see: www.parliament.uk/about/how/laws/passage-bill/; www.gov.uk/guidance/legislative-process-taking-a-bill-through-parliament.

Cabinet Office, 'Guide to Making Legislation': www.gov.uk/government/publications/guide-to-making-legislation.

11.2.3.2 The role of committees

Public Bill Committees play an important role in the legislative process. They are temporary committees (formerly known as Standing Committees) established to examine a specific public Bill in detail in the House of Commons during its committee stage (Private Bill Committees are appointed for Private Bills). Select committees can also have a significant impact on proposed legislation. For example, even after the EU (Withdrawal) Bill had passed through the Commons, the House of Lords Constitution Committee concluded that it was 'fundamentally flawed from a constitutional perspective in multiple ways' and was constitutionally unacceptable as drafted *(European Union (Withdrawal) Bill*, 9th Report of Session 2017–19, HL Paper 69, [4–5]).

11.2.4 **Invoking the Parliament Act**

> The Parliament Act can be invoked where:
>
> - a public Bill originating in the House of Commons has been passed by the Commons and rejected by the House of Lords in two successive sessions of Parliament (as long as it was sent to the Lords at least one month before the end of the session); and
> - one year has elapsed between the second reading of the Bill in the Commons in the first session, and the date when it passes the Commons in the second session.

The Speaker of the House of Commons certifies that the conditions set out in the Parliament Acts 1911 have been complied with, and the Bill can then be given royal assent. A money bill (whose only purpose is to authorise expenditure or taxation or related matters) can be presented for royal assent where the House of Lords has not passed it unamended within one month.

11.2.5 **English votes for English laws**

The English votes for English laws (EVEL) procedure changed the legislative process for some Bills. This was a response to the West Lothian question, which asks why MPs representing constituencies in Scotland, Wales, and Northern Ireland can vote in the UK Parliament on legislation that only applies to England, while MPs representing constituencies in England cannot vote on legislation in the devolved parliaments. Over the years, a number of proposals have been made to address this imbalance, including:

❱ CROSS REFERENCE

See section 4.5

- Kenneth Clarke's proposal for a Democracy Task Force in 2008 to give only English MPs the right to amend Bills applying only to England, though the whole Bill would require final approval from all MPs across the UK.
- Sir Malcolm Rifkind's proposal in 2009 for a Grand Committee of English MPs in the House of Commons to decide 'purely English business'.
- The 2013 McKay Commission recommendation to change Commons procedures to allow MPs for English or English and Welsh constituencies to support decisions only affecting England or England and Wales, with the whole House still voting on legislation.

The Conservative party's 2015 election manifesto pledged to introduce English votes for English laws but instead of legislating to introduce this significant change, the House of Commons agreed to changes to its Standing Orders (written rules of the House which can be changed by majority vote in the Commons) to give effect to the new EVEL procedure in October 2015. This allows MPs from England or England and Wales the opportunity to consent to entire bills, or clauses of bills, relating exclusively to England/England and Wales (see Table 11.5). (See on this Daniel Gover and Michael Kenny, '"English Votes for English Laws: A Viable Answer to the English Question?' The Constitution Unit, https://constitution-unit.com/2015/07/07/english-votes-for-english-laws-a-viable-answer-to-the-english-question/)

Table 11.5 The English votes for English laws procedure

The new procedures apply to public bills and to statutory instruments.

New certification stage For Bills, the Speaker of the House of Commons decides whether the whole Bill, or clauses in it, relate exclusively to England/England and Wales. If so, the Speaker certifies this.

Certification can happen at various stages: before Second Reading, after Report stage, after a new stage called Reconsideration, and on Commons consideration of Lords Amendments.

First Reading and Second Reading take place as normal.

Committee stage Where a *whole* Bill is certified as England/England and Wales-only, only MPs representing English/English–Welsh constituencies sit on the Public Bill Committee.

After Committee stage, the Bill continues to the Report stage as normal.

After Report stage, the Speaker decides whether any amendments to Bills are England/England and Wales only.

The Legislative Grand Committee is a new stage for England/England and Wales-only bills. This allows MPs representing those constituencies to vote on whether to consent to any England/England and Wales-only parts. This is known as a consent motion.

- They cannot make amendments, but can consent to or veto the whole bill.
- If they veto clauses of a bill, there is a reconsideration stage when further amendments can be made. All MPs can participate in this.
- It is followed by a second Legislative Grand Committee at which all MPs representing constituencies in England/England and Wales are asked to consent to the amendments made by the whole House. If no agreement is reached at this point, the disputed parts of the bill fall.

After the Legislative Grand Committee, Bills continue to third reading at which *all* MPs from across the UK can participate.

Bills starting in the Commons then go to the House of Lords, where the legislative process has not changed.

When the Bill returns to the Commons, the Speaker must decide whether to certify any Lords amendments as England/England and Wales only. If so, they are subject to a double majority vote and require support from a majority of MPs representing constituencies in England/England and Wales *and* a majority of all UK MPs before they can become law.

Secondary legislation EVEL only applies to secondary legislation related *entirely* to England or England and Wales and it is only certified once by the Speaker. Votes on statutory instruments are subject to double majorities.

For a helpful diagram of the EVEL process, see: www.parliament.uk/about/how/laws/bills/public/english-votes-for-english-laws/.

THINKING POINT

What are your impressions of the EVEL procedure?

It is important not to overlook the fact that despite EVEL, *all* legislation still requires the consent of *all* MPs in the House of Commons. MPs from across the UK still have opportunities to debate, amend, and vote on legislation for England or England and Wales.

By 2019, the Speaker had certified that 35 bills had England or England and Wales-only provisions, and the EVEL procedure has been kept under close review. There had been concerns that:

- The Speaker might be 'politicised', because s/he receives advice on specific bills from the government when making the certification decision but by 2017, the Speaker had disagreed with the government's advice on nine occasions, reinforcing his independence.
- The Speaker's certification decisions cannot be subject to legal challenge as they are protected by Article 9 of the Bill of Rights (see House of Lords Select Committee on the Constitution, *English Votes for English Laws*, 6th Report of Session 2016–17, HL Paper 61 [81]).

The government's 2017 Review on the impact and operation of EVEL concluded that the new procedures were working well and the government did not propose any substantive changes to the current procedure (*Technical Review of the Standing Orders Related to English Votes for English Laws and the Procedures they Introduced*, CM9430 March 2017), but it affects few Bills and has had relatively light impact.

For details and critique of EVEL, see Daniel Gover and Michael Kenny, 'Answering the West Lothian Question?' in Further reading; House of Commons Procedure Committee, *English Votes for English Laws Standing Orders: Report of the Committee's Technical Evaluation*, 3rd Report of Session 2016–17, HC 189.

11.3 Issues arising from the legislative process

Badly made law can be overly complex, ineffective, or in need of early amendment, and a number of issues can arise from the law-making process that affect the quality of parliamentary scrutiny or have rule of law implications:

- the volume and complexity of legislation;
- lack of scrutiny;
- the speed of legislating;
- drafting errors.

11.3.1 **The volume and complexity of legislation**

Complex, inadequately scrutinised legislation raises rule of law issues if it is not intelligible and clear (see Tom Bingham, *The Rule of Law* (London: Penguin 2011) pp 40–42) but it is not always possible to scrutinise legislation adequately in the Commons and although the number of Acts passed each year has decreased, there has been a significant increase in the average *length* of Bills introduced to Parliament (see Table 11.6).

The Office of the Parliamentary Counsel has identified:

- The difficulty of estimating how much legislation is in force at any one time.
- The increase in 'Christmas Tree' Bills (also known as portmanteau bills): these are multi-purpose Bills containing various unconnected provisions, for example, the Deregulation Act 2015. It is easier for such provisions to escape scrutiny in the Commons.

Table 11.6 The annual volume of legislation

Decade	Number of public Acts passed annually	Number of pages of public Acts annually
1960s	52–98	771–1879
1970s	53–86	636–1949
1980s	46–76	671–2290
1990s	35–69	2060–3150
2000–2009	24–55	1594–4911
Since 2010	29–49	2167–2761

(Source: House of Commons Library, Briefing Paper CBP 7438, 21 April 2017)

- The increase in new criminal law: from 1983 to 2009, Parliament approved more than 100 criminal justice Bills and created more than 4,000 new criminal offences. The Ministry of Justice has now established a procedure to limit the creation of new criminal offences.

See *When Laws Become Too Complex*, Office of the Parliamentary Counsel, published 16 April 2013 (www.gov.uk/government/publications/when-laws-become-too-complex/when-laws-become-too-complex).

11.3.2 **Scrutiny of Bills**

In 1997–1998, 42.3 per cent of sitting time in the House of Commons was spent debating legislation; this fell to only 29.8 per cent in 2015–16 (Briefing Paper CBP 7438, 21 April 2017). Decreasing scrutiny of legislation by Parliament has implications for parliamentary control of the executive. Lord Judge describes the legislative process as 'a torrent', and foresaw 'a legislative tsunami' with the Brexit process:

> How much of this lawmaking, whether by primary or delegated legislation, has actually been read, just read, let alone scrutinised, by how many of us in Parliament in advance of the enactment coming into force? Yet . . . legislative scrutiny is an essential ingredient of our Parliamentary democracy. The government should be held to account for its actions, and its policies, and consequentially for the laws it seeks to enact to implement its policies and legitimise its actions. (The Right Hon Lord Judge PC, 'A Judge's View on the Rule of Law', Bingham Lecture, 3 May 2017 pp 2–3)

See also Daniel Greenberg, *Dangerous Trends in Modern Legislation . . . And How to Reverse Them*, Centre for Policy Studies Report, April 2016. To improve the scrutiny of legislation, the Constitution Committee made a number of recommendations in 2004 including pre-legislative scrutiny of draft bills by a Departmental Select Committee or a joint or temporary committee; every Bill to be scrutinised by a committee of the House of Commons or House of Lords or both, taking evidence to allow outside views; and post-legislative scrutiny for most Acts within three years of coming into force or six years of enactment, whichever was sooner. (House of Lords Select Committee on the Constitution, *Parliament and the Legislative Process*, 14th Report of Session 2003–04, HL Paper 173-I; see the critique and recommendations in Select Committee on Modernisation of the House of Commons, *The Legislative Process: Preparing Legislation for Parliament*, 4th Report of Session 2017–19, HL Paper 27 [108–183]).

11.3.2.1 Pre-legislative scrutiny

Draft Bills can undergo pre-legislative scrutiny by select committees in the Commons or the Lords, or a joint committee, before being formally introduced into Parliament; for example, in 2015 the draft Investigatory Powers Bill was scrutinised by three committees. Pre-legislative scrutiny by parliamentary committees was introduced after a recommendation of the Modernisation Committee in 1997 (Select Committee on Modernisation of the House of Commons, *The Legislative Process*, 23 July 1997, HC 190 1997–98, [20]). Better pre-legislative scrutiny decreases the need for post-legislative scrutiny. Judges can be asked to take part in the process though they do not comment on government policy (see section 13.5.1). For Bills of constitutional significance, the House of Lords Constitution Committee publishes a report once a Bill arrives in the House.

However, many Bills are not subject to pre-legislative scrutiny and the initial take-up was low in the first decade or so (often six draft Bills or fewer; see comments on this in Modernisation Committee, *The Legislative Process*, 1st Report of Session 2005–06, HC 1097 [30]). Recommendations for reform have included:

- a presumption that 'all bills embodying important changes of policy (particularly constitutional bills) should be subject to pre-legislative scrutiny' (*Report of the Leader's Group on Working Practices*, 26 April 2011 [84]);

- departmental select committees should be given legislative scrutiny functions and become dual-purpose committees (Camilla Hagelund and Jonathan Goddard, *How to Run a Country: A Parliament of Lawmakers*, Reform Report, March 2015, Section 2).

THINKING POINT

The Coalition government piloted a Public Reading Stage on the Protection of Freedoms Bill in 2011 and the Small Charitable Donations Bill in 2012 (www.gov.uk/government/publications/when-laws-become-too-complex/when-laws-become-too-complex). Do you think that members of the public should be able to participate formally in the law-making process?

11.3.2.2 Post-legislative scrutiny

The aim of post-legislative scrutiny is to see whether legislation is working in practice as intended, whether policies are being delivered, to identify good practice, and to enable government, Parliament, and others to learn how to avoid negative and unintended consequences from legislation (see House of Lords Select Committee on the Constitution *Parliament and the Legislative Process*, 14th Report of Session 2003–04 HL Paper 173-I, chapter 5). In 2006, the Law Commission found overwhelming support for more systematic post-legislative scrutiny, though its recommendation for a Joint Committee for Post-Legislative Scrutiny was not implemented (The Law Commission, *Post-Legislative Scrutiny* (Law Com No 302) October 2006, Cm 6945).

11.3.2.3 Sunset clauses

Acts, especially controversial ones, can contain a 'sunset clause'—effectively an expiry date after which the Act, or a provision in it, will no longer have effect unless it is renewed. This enables the Act to be revisited and debated again by Parliament at a later date. Sunset clauses effectively say:

'Right, we will give you—the Government—the power you need to do X, Y and Z, but, at the end of a certain period of time, that will come to an end and you will have to produce something fresh'. Then it could be considered in the more measured way that I would hope would be in the best interests of the country. (Baroness Fookes, Select Committee on the Constitution, *The Great Repeal Bill and Delegated Powers*, 9th Report of Session 2016–17, HL Paper 123 [71])

 EXAMPLES

Part 4 of the Anti-terrorism, Crime and Security Act 2001 (see section 11.2.3.1 above) allowed the indefinite detention without charge or trial of terrorist suspects who were not UK nationals and could not be removed from the UK. A 'sunset' clause was inserted into the Bill (later section 29(1) of the Act) providing that Part 4 of the Act would cease to operate at the end of 10 November 2006. Before that, it could be renewed for no more than one year by statutory instrument made by the Secretary of State. The Act was also subject to post-legislative review after two years by a committee of Privy Councillors appointed by the Secretary of State.

The Coronavirus Act 2020, which gave temporary exceptional powers to public authorities to enable them to respond to the outbreak, has a two year expiry date for most provisions (section 89) though the expiry of any provision can be earlier or later (section 90). Parliament also reviews the Act's operation every six months (see section 98); on 30 September 2020, the Commons voted to renew the Act. See also https://ukconstitutionallaw. org/2020/04/08/sean-molloy-covid-19-emergency-legislation-and-sunset-clauses/.

11.3.3 **Speed of legislating**

Legislating in haste can mean repealing at leisure. While legislation can be fast-tracked through Parliament, usually for reasons of urgency—the Coronavirus Act 2020 was passed in four days— it reduces the time for parliamentary scrutiny and debate. It is important to maintain effective scrutiny and transparency and the 'qualities of good law', allowing outside bodies the opportunity to influence the legislative process, ensuring a 'proportionate, justified and appropriate response to the matter in hand' and not jeopardising fundamental constitutional rights and principles (House of Lords Select Committee on the Constitution, *Fast-track Legislation: Constitutional Implications and Safeguards*, 15th Report of Session 2008–09, HL Paper 116–I [16]).

 EXAMPLE

The Data Retention and Investigatory Powers Act 2014 passed through its House of Commons stages in one day. It was emergency or 'sticking plaster' legislation to preserve the law after the Court of Justice of the European Union declared that the EU Data Retention Directive was invalid (UK law requiring telecoms companies to retain data was based on the Directive; this data can be required in police and security service investigations, which could have been jeopardised had Parliament not acted). Even though the Act contained a sunset clause and expired on 31 December 2016, it was successfully challenged by David Davis MP and Tom Watson MP, who argued that it had been passed without adequate parliamentary scrutiny and was drafted too widely (see *Davis & Others v Secretary of State for the Home Department* [2015] EWCA Civ 1185, [2016] HRLR 1; *Tele2 Sverige AB v Post- och telestyrelsen and Secretary of State for the Home Department v Tom Watson and others*, C203/15 and C698/15 of 21 December 2016).

11.3.4 **Drafting errors**

Unidentified drafting errors can create legislative loopholes which can affect individuals. For example, the Pensions Act 2008 introduced automatic enrolment of employees into workplace pensions to help people save more for retirement. In October 2012, a five-year transitional process of automatic enrolment began, but a drafting error which had slipped through in the complex Act meant that some employers did not have to enrol their staff until 2017 because of the types of pension scheme they were offering, resulting in some employees missing several thousand pounds of employer pension contributions. The 2008 Act was amended by the Pensions Act 2014.

11.4 Secondary legislation

The power to make secondary legislation (also known as delegated or subordinate legislation) is granted by an Act of Parliament called an enabling Act or a 'parent Act'. Parliament often confers powers on government ministers to make secondary legislation. The enabling Act usually sets out a broad framework of principles and policy and allows secondary legislation to set out the detail. This enables complex or technical provisions to be made outside the primary legislative process, and prevents the parliamentary timetable from becoming unworkable and primary legislation unduly complex.

Secondary legislation

- **Orders in Council** are made by the Privy Council.
- **Statutory instruments** are made by government ministers.
- **Byelaws** are made by local authorities.

11.4.1 **Orders in Council**

The Privy Council has an important law-making power to issue Orders in Council. There are two categories of Orders in Council: statutory and Prerogative Orders. Statutory Orders in Council are made under powers given to the Queen in Acts of Parliament, are formally approved by the Queen on the advice of her ministers, and have the status of secondary legislation (statutory Orders made after 1948 have the status of Statutory Instruments under section 1 of the Statutory Instruments Act 1946). Statutory Orders may be required to be laid before Parliament before or after being made, or to be approved by Parliament before coming into force. The rarer Prerogative Orders are made under the Royal Prerogative and are regarded as *primary* legislation made not by Parliament, but by the executive. Both types of Order can be judicially reviewed by the courts because they are an exercise of executive power (*R (Bancoult) v Secretary of State for Foreign and Commonwealth Affairs (No 2)* [2008] UKHL 61, [2009] 1 AC 453 [35] (Lord Hoffmann)).

 EXAMPLES OF ORDERS IN COUNCIL

Statutory Orders in Council can be used to transfer ministerial functions; for example, the Scotland Act 1998 (Transfer of Functions to the Scottish Ministers etc) Order 1999 transferred relevant powers from UK government ministers to the newly devolved government in Scotland. An Order in Council was also required under section 30 Scotland Act 1998 to give the Scottish Parliament temporary power to legislate to allow the 2014 Scottish independence referendum.

Prerogative Orders can be exemplified by the British Indian Ocean Territory Order 1965, which removed the whole population of the Chagos Islands to Mauritius (see *R (Bancoult) v Secretary of State for Foreign and Commonwealth Affairs (No 2)*).

THINKING POINT

Pause and consider Prerogative Orders: read paragraphs 34 and 35 of the *Bancoult case* (see previous citation). Do Prerogative Orders have *exactly* the same characteristics as Acts of Parliament? Is the government making law without parliamentary scrutiny?

11.4.2 **Statutory Instruments**

Statutory Instruments (SIs) are secondary legislation made by government ministers. Introduced in the 1940s, they can be made in the form of Regulations, Orders, or Rules, as required by the parent Act, and can be used to:

- 'bulk out' the provisions of an Act of Parliament;
- make emergency provisions; for example, the Civil Contingencies Act 2004 section 20;
- bring provisions of an Act of Parliament into force (known as a commencement order);
- make technical changes or updates to an Act without the need to pass a new statute.

The process of making SIs allows for flexibility and consultation; for example, before banning the sale and manufacture of plastic microbeads in cosmetics and personal care products to protect marine life under the Environmental Protection (Microbeads) (England) Regulations 2017, the Department for Environment, Food and Rural Affairs held a public consultation on the proposals.

However, a number of critical issues arise that again have an impact on parliamentary scrutiny and rule of law requirements:

- the increased use of delegated legislation;
- the effectiveness of scrutiny;
- the use of skeleton Bills;
- Henry VIII powers.

11.4.2.1 **Increased use of delegated legislation**

The volume of delegated legislation has increased markedly even in the past decade. In 1950, 2,144 SIs were made, but this has risen to more than 3,000 per year, reaching a total of 4,150 in 2001. In 1911, there were 330 pages of SIs; by 2009, there were 11,888. Between January and October 2020, 266 SIs relating to coronavirus were laid before Parliament made under a number of enabling Acts including the Coronavirus Act 2020 and the Public Health (Control of Diseases) Act 1984 (https://www.hansardsociety.org.uk/publications/data/coronavirus-statutory-instruments-dashboard#total-coronavirus-sis).Daniel Greenberg also notes a growing trend of government-made 'quasi-legislation' such as guidance-making powers and codes:

So the first bite of the cherry is the Act; the second bite of the cherry is the Regulations; and the third bite of the cherry, which amounts to a continuous attempt to direct the meaning and application of the primary and secondary legislation, is the stream of guidance which emerges from the Executive . . . quasi-legislation has become a powerful tool for the Executive to control legislation after its enactment. (Daniel Greenberg, 'Dangerous Trends in Modern Legislation' (2015) (January) Public Law 96, 99–100)

This indicates a legislation cascade, starting with primary legislation, then secondary legislation, then tertiary legislation made under powers conferred by secondary legislation, allowing government rule-making beyond Parliament's control although policy and guidance documents can be judicially reviewed in the courts (see, eg, *R (Letts) v Lord Chancellor* [2015] EWHC 402 (Admin)).

11.4.2.2 Scrutiny of secondary legislation

Delegated legislation can be scrutinised:

- by both Houses of Parliament;
- by parliamentary committee;
- by the courts.

Scrutiny by Parliament This provides democratic legitimacy and effective parliamentary oversight of ministerial decision-making, ensuring a check on executive action, but secondary legislation made by the government can often be subject to much less scrutiny and debate than primary legislation, and sometimes none at all. These scrutiny gaps increase the risk of arbitrary law-making and 'governing from the shadows', raising rule of law concerns.

The **Statutory Instruments Act 1946** sets out the procedures by which SIs are laid before Parliament and which Parliament has the opportunity to scrutinise:

- **Affirmative instruments** allow more parliamentary scrutiny. They are laid before Parliament in draft, always debated, and must be approved by both Houses of Parliament before they can become law (the affirmative procedure).

- **Negative instruments** are laid before both Houses, usually *after* being made, but are only debated if a Member specifically requests a debate; they may be annulled (rejected) by a resolution of either House within 40 days. Negative instruments can therefore become law without a debate or vote in Parliament. Around 75 per cent of SIs are negative instruments.

Super-affirmative instruments are much less frequently used and undergo additional scrutiny by each House of Parliament, including a statutory 60-day consultation period; the minister must respond to any representations made.

Hybrid instruments are affirmative SIs that affect specific individuals or bodies who have the opportunity to challenge them.

The 'made affirmative' or 'urgent' procedure is a fast-track route that allows for retrospective parliamentary scrutiny and approval.

In 2020, secondary legislation was used to implement coronavirus restrictions using the 'urgent' procedure where Parliament retrospectively approved regulations; for example, the lockdown regulations (the Health Protection (Coronavirus, Restrictions) (England) Regulations 2020) did not receive parliamentary approval before coming into force as a matter of urgency on 26 March—three days after the Prime Minister's televised address; they were only approved by

Parliament on 4 May, although they were subject to regular review by the government. The use of secondary legislation to implement coronavirus restrictions has led to concerns about 'rule by decree' and Parliament being sidelined, and prompted the House of Commons Speaker, Sir Lindsay Hoyle, to state:

> The way in which the Government have exercised their powers to make secondary legislation during this crisis has been totally unsatisfactory. All too often, important statutory instruments have been published a matter of hours before they come into force, and some explanations why important measures have come into effect before they can be laid before this House have been unconvincing; this shows a total disregard for the House . . . The use of made affirmative statutory instruments under the urgency procedure gives rise to particular concern. (HC Hansard 30 September 2020, Vol 681 col 331)

In September 2020, the government agreed to give MPs a vote in parliament on any new significant UK or England-wide coronavirus restrictions. For critique on scrutiny of secondary legislation relating to coronavirus, see Joint Committee on Human Rights, *The Government's response to COVID-19: human rights implications* 7th Report of Session 2019–21, HC 265/HL Paper 125 67–69.

For more detail on coronavirus law, see the online resources

Parliament cannot amend secondary legislation unless allowed by the parent Act. The SI as a whole falls or stands. Even more importantly, some SIs are required to be laid before Parliament without any subsequent scrutiny procedure, and some are not subject to any parliamentary procedure at all. (See Constitution Committee, *Delegated Legislation and Parliament: A Response to the Strathclyde Review*, 9th Report of Session 2015–16, HL Paper 116, chapter 2.) The House of Lords rarely votes down SIs. A regret motion can be used in the Lords to express criticism of an aspect of a statutory instrument (such as the Lords vote on 27 March 2017 to regret the government's draft regulations on disability benefits known as Personal Independence Payments), but it does not require the government to act and does not challenge the instrument.

Q CLOSE-UP FOCUS: TAX CREDIT CUTS DEFEAT 2015

On 26 October 2015, the House of Lords considered a statutory instrument implementing the government's policy on cutting tax credits (the Tax Credits (Income Thresholds and Determination of Rates) (Amendment) Regulations 2015). The Lords rejected a 'fatal motion' (which would have vetoed the instrument) but voted in favour of delaying the cuts and compensating low-paid workers. The Prime Minister, David Cameron, accused the Lords of breaching the constitutional convention of respecting financial proposals from the House of Commons although it was uncertain whether the convention only applied to financial measures in Bills, not statutory instruments. Lord Butler's view was that it 'was established 100 years ago that the House of Lords doesn't oppose the House of Commons on tax and financial matters. The government would have a quite legitimate grievance if it did. It would be really an example of the House of Lords getting too big for its non-elected boots' (Today programme, BBC R4, 23 October 2015). The Chancellor, George Osborne, subsequently agreed to introduce a transitional compensation scheme.

The Prime Minister responded to the tax credit defeat by commissioning a rapid review by Lord Strathclyde on how statutory instruments could pass through Parliament with more certainty and clarity, and to ensure the House of Commons' authority over secondary legislation. The Strathclyde Review recommended a new statutory procedure for the Lords to 'invite the Commons to think again' where both Houses disagreed on a statutory instrument. The Commons could vote again and still decide to assert its primacy, thus guaranteeing that statutory instruments could not be overturned by the Lords against the Commons' wishes (Strathclyde Review: *Secondary Legislation and the Primacy of the House of Commons*, December 2015, Cm 9177). The Public Administration and Constitutional Affairs Committee rejected the Review's recommendation.

Watch Lord Lisvane at https://www.youtube.com/watch?v=Wo52KebLPkM; see also http://researchbriefings.files.parliament.uk/documents/SN05996/SN05996.pdf.

Scrutiny by Parliamentary Committee The scrutiny of SIs by a number of committees helps to reinforce the gaps outlined above, though there is more scrutiny of SIs in the Lords than the Commons:

- **The Joint Committee on Statutory Instruments** informs Parliament about any issues of legality of a statutory instrument, for example, if it imposes a tax; if its parent Act says that it cannot be challenged in the courts; if it has unauthorised retrospective effect; if there may not be power to make it; or if there is defective drafting or other technical issues (see Joint Committee on Statutory Instruments, Fourth Report of Session 2017–19, HL 44, HC 542-iv).

- **Delegated Legislation Committees** in the Commons consider the merits of affirmative and negative SIs.

- The **House of Lords Secondary Legislation Scrutiny Committee** considers flaws, inadequacies, and the political or legal significance of secondary legislation laid before Parliament; for example, statutory instruments concerning coronavirus measures.

- **The Regulatory Reform Committee** in the Commons examines and reports on Draft Legislative Reform Orders, a specific type of statutory instrument which can amend primary legislation under the Legislative and Regulatory Reform Act 2006.

- In the House of Lords, the **Delegated Powers and Regulatory Reform Committee** reports on whether the provisions of a bill introduced into the Lords inappropriately delegate legislative power, or subject the exercise of legislative power to an inappropriate degree of parliamentary scrutiny. For example, on 1 February 2018, the Committee published a report criticising the EU (Withdrawal) Bill (now the EU (Withdrawal) Act 2018) for giving excessively wide law-making powers to ministers and failing to provide sufficient parliamentary scrutiny of those law-making powers (*European Union (Withdrawal) Bill*, 12th Report of Session 2017–19, HL Paper 73).

- **The Joint Committee on Human Rights** reports to Parliament on delegated legislation called remedial orders. These orders are made by a minister under the Human Rights Act 1998 to correct primary legislation that a UK court or the ECtHR has declared incompatible with the ECHR.

 THINKING POINT

How do the Committees above help protect the rule of law? See Chapter 8.

Scrutiny by the courts A minister's power to make a statutory instrument can be challenged in the courts through judicial review. This ensures executive accountability. See Chapters 15 and 16 for details.

11.4.2.3 The use of skeleton bills

'Skeleton bills' set out overall plans or policy targets but leave detailed policy questions for delegated legislation. Government reliance on delegated powers where policy decisions have not yet been taken has been criticised as 'constitutionally objectionable', with 'a significant and unwelcome increase in this phenomenon' (Constitution Committee, *The Legislative Process: The Delegation of Powers* 16th Report of Session 2017-19, HL Paper 225 [26]). Lord Lisvane, a former clerk of the Commons, has observed that the threshold between primary and secondary legislation is moving upwards, with secondary legislation being used 'increasingly for matters of policy and principle which should be the subject of primary legislation' (HL Hansard 3 Dec 2015, Vol 767 col 1199). This highlights not only a blurring of the distinction between primary and secondary legislation, but also a lowering of the parliamentary scrutiny bar. Lord Judge has expressed concern that by the end of the Brexit process, 'we shall have irremediably cemented lawmaking by un-scrutinised legislation into our constitutional arrangement' ('A Judge's View on the Rule of Law').

11.4.2.4 Henry VIII powers

The most trenchant criticisms are reserved for Henry VIII powers which have been called 'a departure from constitutional principle' (Constitution Committee, *The Legislative Process: The Delegation of Powers* [67]). A Henry VIII clause in a statute allows government ministers to make secondary legislation to repeal or amend *primary* legislation. The concern is that this has the potential to deliver wide law-making power to the executive and can enable the government to rewrite primary law without further parliamentary scrutiny. It is therefore important that Henry VIII clauses are used sparingly, are carefully drafted, and allow for legal certainty (Bingham Centre Briefing Note, *The Rule of Law in Parliament in 2015–16*, January 2017).

Q   CLOSE-UP FOCUS: THE EUROPEAN UNION (WITHDRAWAL) ACT 2018

The European Union (Withdrawal) Act 2018 contains Henry VIII powers, including a 'correcting power' to allow retained EU law to be amended as and when needed after Brexit (section 8). This was included because of the short-term need for continuity of the law given the Brexit timetable, and the complex long-term need to amend and domesticate EU law.

However, its use of Henry VIII powers has proved very controversial and was sharply criticised by select committees during its passage through Parliament as the EU (Withdrawal) Bill:

- The Constitution Committee concluded that 'the Bill weaves a tapestry of delegated powers that are breath-taking in terms of both their scope and potency' (Select Committee on the Constitution, *European Union (Withdrawal) Bill: Interim Report*, 3rd Report of Session 2017–19, HL Paper 19, Summary). It was concerned about the Bill's potential to disrupt the constitutional balance of power between the legislature and executive by transferring legislative competence from Parliament to government, and avoiding meaningful parliamentary scrutiny and control of the executive.

- The Committee stated that the broad delegated powers in the Bill would create 'an unprecedented and extraordinary portmanteau of effectively unlimited powers upon which the government could draw. They would fundamentally challenge the constitutional balance of powers between Parliament and government and would represent a significant—and unacceptable—transfer of legal competence' (*European Union (Withdrawal) Bill: Interim Report* [44]); see also Select Committee on the Constitution, *The 'Great Repeal Bill' and Delegated Powers*, 9th Report of Session 2016–17, HL Paper 123 [47]).

- The Bill even allowed ministers to make regulations that amended or repealed the European Union (Withdrawal) Act itself (see DPRRC, *European Union (Withdrawal) Bill*, 12th Report of Session 2017–19, HL Paper 73 [22]).

Safeguards were included in section 8(7) of the EU (Withdrawal) Act and the Bill was amended at committee stage to create a new scrutiny mechanism to rein in the broadest Henry VIII powers. A parliamentary sifting committee, the European Statutory Instruments Committee, considers proposed negative SIs made under the Act and recommends greater scrutiny of those about which they have most concern. The Hansard Society has recommended going further with a new Delegated Legislation Scrutiny Committee in the House of Commons to sift and scrutinise all delegated legislation (*Taking Back Control for Brexit and Beyond: Delegated Legislation, Parliamentary Scrutiny and the EU (Withdrawal) Bill*, September 2017).

The Coronavirus Act 2020 also gives wide delegated powers to ministers, including Henry VIII powers, with limited or no parliamentary scrutiny. While the government needed powers to ensure a swift, effective response to the COVID-19 pandemic, the Constitution Committee criticised the Act at the Bill stage as complex and lengthy, stating that the very broad delegated powers would not be acceptable outside the exceptional circumstances. Parliamentary scrutiny and the availability of adequate legal accountability were key limitations on the broad powers (Select Committee on the Constitution *Coronavirus Bill*, 4th Report of Session 2019–21, HL Paper 44 [3, 11, 15].

In a House of Lords debate on the legislative process, Lord Beith said: 'Excessive and inappropriate use of the delegation of powers undermines the quality of legislation, leading to legislation that is unclear, incoherent, inaccessible or badly scrutinised . . . The policy has not been worked through and properly consulted on, so the Bill leaves gaps to be filled by regulations' (HL Hansard 12 June 2019, Vol 798 col 438).

 SUMMARY

The constitutional balance of powers between Parliament and government is crucial, especially the requirement for parliamentary scrutiny and control of the executive. Parliament's scrutiny of Bills is a critical part of the legislative process, particularly with government Bills, but it can be affected by the volume of modern legislation. Parliament can delegate law-making powers to ministers but does not always have the opportunity to scrutinise statutory instruments. This can enable government-made secondary legislation to avoid parliamentary scrutiny. It is important for secondary legislation to comply with rule of law requirements.

? Questions

Self-test questions

1. Explain why parliamentary scrutiny of the government is important.

2. Outline the three main ways in which scrutiny takes place. Are they effective?

3. What is a public Bill?

4. Outline the stages of the legislative process for a public Bill.

5. How can the government dominate the law-making process?

6. What is secondary legislation?

7. Explain the issues that can arise in relation to scrutiny of statutory instruments.

8. What are Henry VIII powers and what potential issue do they raise?

Exam question

Leo Amery MP described Parliament as 'an overworked legislation factory' (L.S. Amery, *Thoughts on the Constitution*, Oxford: Oxford University Press 1964, p 41).

Discuss the extent to which this is an accurate description, and assess whether there are adequate opportunities for parliamentary scrutiny of Bills in the legislative process.

Further reading

Books

Horne, A. and Le Sueur, A. (eds), *Parliament: Legislation and Accountability* (Oxford and Portland, Oregon: Hart Publishing 2016).
Analyses Parliament's two key functions

Besly, N., Goldsmith, T., Rogers, R., and Walters, R. *How Parliament Works* (8th edn, Abingdon: Routledge 2019).
See chapters 6 and 8–10

Norton, P. *Parliament in British Politics* (2nd edn, Basingstoke: Palgrave Macmillan 2013).
See chapters 4 and 5

Russell, M. and Gover, D. *Legislation at Westminster: Parliamentary Actors and Influence in the Making of British Law* (Oxford: Oxford University Press 2017).
Challenges current views about the UK Parliament's influence on legislation

Journal articles

Gover, D. and Kenny, M. 'Answering the West Lothian Question? A Critical Assessment of "English Votes for English Laws" in the UK Parliament' (2018) 71(4) Parliamentary Affairs 760.
Analyses whether EVEL has successfully answered the West Lothian question

Kennon, A. 'Pre-legislative Scrutiny of Draft Bills' (2004) (Autumn) Public Law 477.
Analysis of pre-legislative scrutiny

Other sources

For detailed critique of the legislative process, see:

House of Commons Library, Briefing Paper Number 06509, *Statutory Instruments*, Richard Kelly, 15 December 2016.
A helpful guide to Statutory Instruments

House of Lords Select Committee on the Constitution, *The Legislative Process: Preparing Legislation for Parliament*, 4th Report of Session 2017–19, HL Paper 27, especially chapter 4.

House of Lords Select Committee on the Constitution, *The Legislative Process: The Passage of Bills Through Parliament*, 24th Report of Session 2017–19, HL Paper 393.
Critical focus on the scrutiny of Bills

White, H. *Parliamentary Scrutiny of Government*, Institute for Government, 22 January 2015 (available at https://www.instituteforgovernment.org.uk).
Detailed study of scrutiny; note in particular the helpful scrutiny summary grids at the end

Useful websites

www.parliament.uk

www.instituteforgovernment.org.uk/publication/parliamentary-monitor-2020/time
On select committees, see:

www.democraticaudit.com/2018/09/24/audit2018-how-effective-are-the-commons-two-committee-systems-at-scrutinising-government-policy-making/

https://www.instituteforgovernment.org.uk/explainers/select-committees

; Online resources

www.oup.com/he/dennett2e

This chapter is accompanied by a selection of online resources to help you with this topic, including:

- Multiple-choice questions
- Answers to the self-test questions
- Guidance on answering the exam question

12 The executive

☐ **LEARNING OBJECTIVES**

By the end of this chapter, you should be able to:

● Explain the overall organisation of central government in the UK

● Discuss the significance of accountability

● Explain the sources of government power

● Evaluate the nature and operation of prerogative executive powers

● Analyse issues raised by ministerial responsibility

● Assess the effectiveness of legal and political controls on the executive

Introduction

In this chapter we examine the executive, the administrative branch of government which creates and implements (or executes) policy, and implements laws. We specifically focus on central government in the UK, and the chapter is arranged into three sections:

- Organisation of central government

- Executive power (including the royal prerogative)

- Control of the executive

An accountable executive is a key facet of adherence to the rule of law and we examine how effective legal and political controls on the executive are in reality.

In the UK, members of central government are drawn from Parliament: the political party with the largest number of seats in the House of Commons after a general election normally forms the new government. The executive is therefore embedded in the heart of the legislature (the Westminster system). The government is accountable to Parliament for its activities (this is the principle of responsible government) and it must command the confidence of the House of Commons in order to function. Each government needs parliamentary approval to turn its policies into law and relies on it for finance (see Table 12.1). However, Lord Irvine, a former Lord Chancellor, has observed: 'In our country, the legislative, the Executive and the judicial branches

Table 12.1 The relationship between Parliament and the government

Parliament	Central government
Parliament makes laws	Government governs the country by carrying out administration, formulating and implementing policy, and implementing laws. It introduces laws into Parliament but needs parliamentary support and approval to turn its policies into law and secure its legislative programme
Parliament holds government to account by subjecting it to critical enquiry to discover wrongdoing, incompetence, and mistakes, and make them known to the electorate	Government is accountable to Parliament for its policies and actions (particularly to elected representatives in the Commons), and is ultimately accountable to voters
The House of Commons controls the supply and expenditure of public money, authorising around £500 billion of government spending each year	Government allocates public spending and relies on the Commons for public money. The Treasury needs parliamentary approval of Consolidated Fund Bills for spending on public services
The House of Commons has power to dismiss an incompetent government which has lost Parliament's confidence	Government dominates the House of Commons because it is usually the majority party

CROSS REFERENCE

See section 7.3 on the separation of powers

are not equal and co-ordinate as in the United States of America. Parliament is the senior partner in principle and the Executive is very powerful in practice' (HL Hansard 17 Feb 1999, Vol 597 col 734). In reality, therefore, the executive often has the capacity to exert its power over Parliament, with the potential to diminish the effectiveness of parliamentary control (see also Chapter 10).

The 'elective dictatorship' The government can dominate the UK Parliament because of the first past the post electoral system and the lack of separation of powers between the executive and the legislature. Where a government has a large majority in the House of Commons (such as the Conservative majority of 144 in 1983 and Labour's majority of 177 in 1997), its power is, as Lord Steyn pointed out in *Jackson v AG* [2005] UKHL 56, 'redoubtable' ([71]). This means that the government will carry votes in the House of Commons with little likelihood of losing them. About one sixth of MPs are members of the government (rising to 20 per cent of MPs if parliamentary aides are included) so their support is guaranteed; this is known as the 'payroll vote'. This is Lord Hailsham's 'elective dictatorship': dominant government at the heart of a sovereign Parliament where the elected party of government can exert control over law-making and decision-making in the Commons (Lord Hailsham, *The Dilemma of Democracy: Diagnosis and Prescription* (London: Collins 1978)).

Constitutional reforms such as devolution and the Constitutional Reform Act 2005 have put limits on government, and the government's dominance decreased with the hung Parliaments in 2010 and 2017; as Andrew Mitchell MP pointed out, 'in a hung Parliament . . . power passes from the Cabinet room to the Floor of the House of Commons' (HC Deb 1 May 2018, Vol 640 col 191). See the Governance of Britain Green Paper's proposals for strengthening the role of Parliament in calling government to account (Cm 7170, July 2007).

12.1 How central government is organised

Central government in the UK carries out day-to-day administration in relation to England and the whole of the UK on non-devolved matters. Its functions include the conduct of foreign affairs, defence, national security, and oversight of the Civil Service and government agencies. Central government essentially consists of the government and civil service but modern government is extensive, multi-layered, and complex, as shown in Figure 12.1.

The number of bodies carrying out executive functions in the UK changes, but in September 2020 there were:

23 government departments

20 non-ministerial departments

412 agencies and other public bodies

98 high-profile groups; 12 public corporations

3 devolved administrations (the Scottish Government, Welsh Government, and Northern Ireland Executive)

(Source: www.gov.uk/government/organisations)

The broader executive also includes the National Health Service and the Armed Forces. Below, we discuss:

- The Crown
- The Prime Minister
- Ministers

Figure 12.1 The organisation of central government

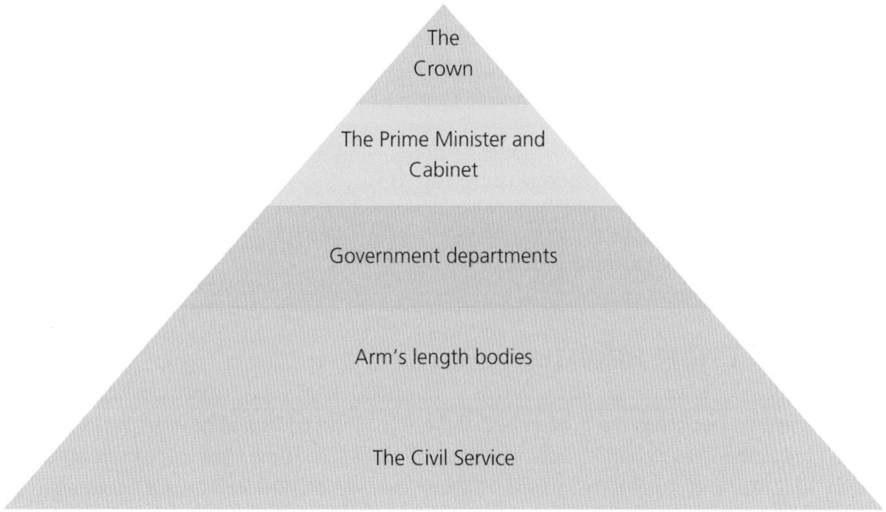

- The Cabinet
- Government departments and arm's length bodies
- The Civil Service

12.1.1 **The Crown**

> 'The Crown' can refer to the Crown as monarch in her public or personal capacity, or the
> Crown as executive (*M v Home Office* [1994] 1 AC 377, 395 (Lord Templeman); and see
> Chapter 4). Thus the Crown in its executive sense refers to a corporate, collective idea which
> includes government ministers and the wider administration.

The Crown is at the apex of government. The monarch is no longer the active head of the
executive and must be politically neutral, but government is carried out in the name of the
Crown (Sedley cites 1714 as the year in which the Crown stopped governing through its ministers and ministers started governing through the Crown (Stephen Sedley, *Lions under the
Throne* (Cambridge: Cambridge University Press 2015), p 70)). The Crown's administrative
powers are exercised by Her Majesty's government through government ministers (ministers
of the Crown) who are answerable to the UK Parliament (see *R (Bapio) v SSHD* [2008] 1 AC
1003 [33] (Lord Rodger)).

 THE BIGGER PICTURE: THE KING'S 'TWO BODIES'

As early as the thirteenth century, the idea was emerging that the Crown included 'more
than the King—the King in Council, the King in Parliament, the King, Lords and Commons—a corporation somehow separate from his natural body' (Allison, *The English
Historical Constitution*, p 51). This means that the king has two 'bodies': (a) the physical
person and (b) the more abstract, artificial idea of the king embodying a separate, continuing power that lives on when he dies and passes to all who succeed him. This is what
is meant by 'the king is dead; long live the king'. The idea in (b) above is known as the
'body politic', as opposed to the physical body, and represents the idea of the Crown as
a corporation sole with a separate existence. The 'two bodies' idea has been ridiculed
and Maitland, for example, criticises the 'subterfuge . . . of slowly substituting "the
Crown" for King or Queen'.

See:

J.W.F. Allison, *The English Historical Constitution: Continuity, Change and European Effects* (2007) Cambridge: Cambridge University Press

Frederic Maitland, 'The Crown as Corporation' (1901) 17 Law Quarterly Review 131
R (Bapio) v SSHD [27–28] (Lord Scott)

12.1.2 **The Prime Minister**

> The Prime Minister heads the government and exercises the powers of government. S/he is
> First Lord of the Treasury and Minister for the Civil Service. The Prime Minister bears responsi-
> bility for policy and is supported by their Cabinet (see section 12.1.4). There is no separate

Prime Minister's department but support is provided by the Cabinet Office and the Prime Minister's private office. (The Cabinet Office, described as 'the corporate headquarters for government', is a ministerial department supported by the Cabinet Secretary, the UK's most senior civil servant.)

The office of Prime Minister was created, and is regulated, by constitutional convention. The Prime Minister is traditionally *primus inter pares* or first among equals; this means that the Prime Minister has the same rank as other ministers but is the leading minister, although the role is now recognised as more than this. He or she is appointed by the monarch under the royal prerogative, and by convention the monarch must appoint as Prime Minister the leader of the party with a majority of seats in the House of Commons. The monarch has the right to dismiss the Prime Minister but has not done so since 1783. After the Second World War a constitutional convention was established that the Prime Minister is a member of the House of Commons; before that, the Prime Minister could be a member of the House of Lords (the last Prime Minister to sit in the Lords was Lord Salisbury). The Prime Minister's powers, summarised in Figure 12.2, are fluid and flexible because they are, largely, not contained in statute and are therefore exercised with a significant level of discretion.

The Prime Minister used to exercise the power of dissolution, deciding when to hold an election. This was a powerful tool of control which, timed well, could ensure successful re-election and could also be used as a weapon for leverage: the Prime Minister could threaten the dissolution of Parliament to secure Cabinet and backbench support, as John Major did in 1994 on a Bill concerning increased EC budget contributions by the UK. The power of dissolution is now governed by the Fixed-term Parliaments Act 2011, which removed the Prime Minister's discretion and provides for general elections every five years. However, the 2017 and 2019 elections

Figure 12.2 Powers of the Prime Minister

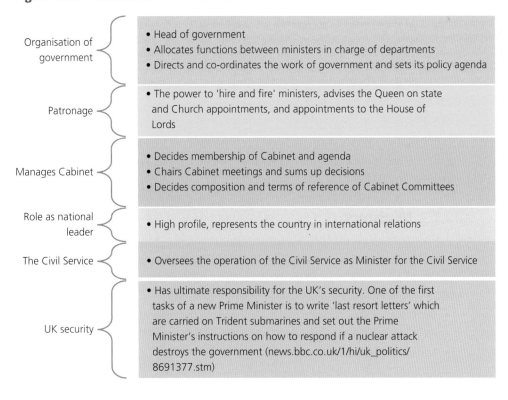

Organisation of government	• Head of government • Allocates functions between ministers in charge of departments • Directs and co-ordinates the work of government and sets its policy agenda
Patronage	• The power to 'hire and fire' ministers, advises the Queen on state and Church appointments, and appointments to the House of Lords
Manages Cabinet	• Decides membership of Cabinet and agenda • Chairs Cabinet meetings and sums up decisions • Decides composition and terms of reference of Cabinet Committees
Role as national leader	• High profile, represents the country in international relations
The Civil Service	• Oversees the operation of the Civil Service as Minister for the Civil Service
UK security	• Has ultimate responsibility for the UK's security. One of the first tasks of a new Prime Minister is to write 'last resort letters' which are carried on Trident submarines and set out the Prime Minister's instructions on how to respond if a nuclear attack destroys the government (news.bbc.co.uk/1/hi/uk_politics/8691377.stm)

showed that the Prime Minister can still exert some control over their timing. In April 2017, Theresa May, then Prime Minister, announced that she planned to call a snap election on 8 June. Under section 2(1) of the Act, an early general election can take place if it is agreed by at least two-thirds of all MPs in the House of Commons, and on 19 April, the House of Commons agreed a motion for an early election. In 2019, unable to achieve the two-thirds majority agreement under the Act, Boris Johnson's government succeeded in circumventing it by getting the Early Parliamentary General Election Act 2019 passed to allow an election on 12 December 2019.

The Prime Minister's powers can be limited in practice by:

- the available 'talent pool' of potential ministers;
- political differences with members of Cabinet (eg Margaret Thatcher and the resignations of Geoffrey Howe (Foreign Secretary) and Nigel Lawson (Chancellor); see also the Westland affair discussed presently);
- leaks of information from Cabinet meetings;
- government defeats in votes or withdrawing proposed Bills;
- backbench dissent and rebellions, eg on Europe in John Major's government;
- public opinion and media criticism;
- by-election defeats, eg during John Major's term in office;
- leadership challenges, eg the challenge to Margaret Thatcher in 1990.

Andrew Lansley MP recalls Margaret Thatcher's view that:

> [T]he closer she got to where people regarded the 'centre of power' as being, in 10 Downing Street, the more she realised that there wasn't such a 'centre of power' . . . the only time she actually felt that she had the power that people imagined she had, was . . . during the period of the Falklands War, when Prime Ministers make decisions and the armed forces go and do what the Prime Minister says. Almost all the rest of time, people have a debate before you make a decision, then the PM makes a decision, then they try to have another debate after the decision: power is more distributed. ('The Legislature and the Executive', Parliament Open Lecture, 24 April 2013)

See also Peter Hennessy, 'What Are Prime Ministers For?' (2014) (2) Journal of the British Academy 213–230 (www.thebritishacademy.ac.uk/).

For the Prime Minister's functions, see House of Commons Political and Constitutional Reform Committee, *Role and Powers of the Prime Minister*, Written evidence, 17 May 2011, Lord Hennessy, Ev 3.

For critique, see Political and Constitutional Reform Committee, *The Role and Powers of the Prime Minister*, 1st Report of Session 2014–15, HC 351.

12.1.3 **Ministers**

Ministers represent the Crown in Parliament, speaking on behalf of the government from the frontbenches, and their key role is to drive forward and deliver government policy. The *Cabinet Manual* categorises government ministers as: senior ministers; junior ministers; the Law Officers; and whips ([3.7]). Senior and junior ministers comprise:

- Secretaries of State (senior ministers appointed by the Prime Minister to take responsibility for a specific government department and who sit in Cabinet);
- Ministers of State (junior ministers);
- Parliamentary Under-Secretaries of State (junior ministers).

In September 2020, including the Prime Minister, there were 119 ministers in the UK government, with 20 Cabinet ministers and 98 other ministers drawn by convention from the legislature (see www.gov.uk/government/how-government-works). However, the Ministerial and other Salaries Act 1975 restricts the number of paid ministers to a maximum of 109 (additional ministers can be unpaid), while the House of Commons Disqualification Act 1975 limits the maximum number of ministers sitting and voting in the House of Commons at any one time to 95 (the remainder are drawn from the House of Lords). Very occasionally, ministers have been appointed from outside Parliament.

 THINKING POINT

What is the significance of imposing limits on the number of ministers in the House of Commons?

Ministers are constrained by their accountability to Parliament and can only spend public money for the purposes that Parliament authorises. They rely on the support of the Commons for their policies, and on the confidence of the Prime Minister to stay in office. Their conduct is governed by the Ministerial Code, which requires ministers to protect the integrity of public life (see *Ministerial Code*, August 2019 [1.3]; see also *The Cabinet Manual*, October 2011, chapter 3).

For more information on what ministers do, see:

- Public Administration Committee, *Smaller Government: What Do Ministers Do?* 7th Report of Session 2010–11, HC 530 [7–48]; Table 1 is particularly helpful.
- Nicola Hughes, *How to Be an Effective Minister: What Ministers Do and How to Do It Well*, Institute for Government, March 2017.
- Peter Riddell, Zoe Gruhn, and Liz Carolan, *The Challenge of Being a Minister: Defining and Developing Ministerial Effectiveness*, 2011; note the identikit of an ideal minister on p 9 and roles of a government minister on p 11.

 CLOSE-UP FOCUS: THE GOVERNMENT LAW OFFICERS

The Law Officers of the Crown are government ministers and senior lawyers. In central government, they are the Attorney General for England and Wales, and the Solicitor General for England and Wales. The Advocate General for Scotland advises the UK government on Scottish law, and the Attorney General also holds the office of Advocate General for Northern Ireland. (The Lord Advocate in Scotland is the devolved Scottish government's Law Officer, the Counsel General in Wales is the Welsh Government's Law Officer, and there is a separate Attorney General for Northern Ireland.)

Attorney General

The Attorney General (an office created in the thirteenth century) is Chief Legal Advisor to the Crown and Government, and superintends the Crown Prosecution Service, the Serious Fraud Office, the Government Legal Department, and HM Crown Prosecution Service Inspectorate.

S/he is a member of the House of Commons or the Lords, but, although a minister, is not a full member of the Cabinet. However, s/he attends Cabinet meetings at the Prime Minister's invitation, and is also a member of some Cabinet Committees, notably the Parliamentary Business and Legislation Committee, which considers issues concerning the government's legislative programme and scrutinises government bills. The Attorney also has independent public interest functions which include referring unduly lenient sentences to the Court of Appeal, bringing proceedings for contempt of court, and giving consent to certain prosecutions.

The Solicitor General of England and Wales is the Attorney's deputy, and any function of the Attorney General may be exercised by the Solicitor General (section 1 Law Officers Act 1997). The Attorney General and Solicitor General are supported by the Attorney General's Office, a ministerial department.

The Law Officers give legal advice to government and help ministers 'to act lawfully and in accordance with the rule of law' (*Cabinet Manual* [6.4, 6.7]). They support the Lord Chancellor in his duty to oversee the rule of law, and can be consulted by Parliamentary Counsel and government departmental lawyers (see Constitution Committee, *The Office of Lord Chancellor*, 6th Report of Session 2014–15, HL Paper 75 [69–81]).

The Law Officers have an inward and outward-facing role: they are MPs and in government, advising the government on legal issues, but at the same time act as 'guardians of the public interest'. (The AG for Northern Ireland is not in government.) A former Solicitor General has described the Law Officers' unique position as 'the point at which politics and law meet' (Robert Buckland QC MP, Solicitor General, 'Role of Law Officers on Devolution and Bills', Speech, Public Law Wales, 9 November 2016); Sir Francis Bacon called it 'the painfullest task in the realm'.

See:

- *Cabinet Manual*, chapter 6
- Sir Elwyn Jones, 'The Office of Attorney-General' (1969) 27(1) CLJ 43–53
- Constitutional Affairs Committee, *Constitutional Role of the Attorney General*, 5th Report of Session 2006–07, HC 306
- House of Commons Library Standard Note: SN/PC/04485 *The Law Officers*, 1 August 2014, Alexander Horne
- The Attorney General on who should decide what the public interest is (speech delivered at University College London, Law Faculty, 8 February 2016) (www.gov.uk/government/speeches/the-attorney-general-on-who-should-decide-what-the-public-interest-is)
- Robert Buckland QC MP, 'The Model of a Modern Solicitor General: Thoughts on the Constitution in the Time of Brexit', 13 October 2017 (www.robertbuckland.co.uk/news/model-modern-solicitor-general-thoughts-constitution-time-brexit)
- *The Governance of Britain*, Cm 7170, July 2007, p 24

12.1.4 The Cabinet

The Cabinet is the heart of government, and is governed by constitutional convention, not statute. Chaired by the Prime Minister, it meets every week during Parliament in the Cabinet room in 10 Downing Street to debate and make collective decisions on policy and strategy, government business, its legislative programme, public expenditure, and national affairs. The Cabinet's collective decision-making gives the stamp of legitimacy to its decisions, which are binding on the government. It consists of:

- the Prime Minister;
- between 19 and 24 Secretaries of State;
- the Chancellor of the Duchy of Lancaster, Minister for the Cabinet Office;
- the Leader of the House of Lords.

Attending Cabinet but not full members are:

- the Leader of the House of Commons and Lord President of the Council;
- the Parliamentary Secretary to the Treasury and Chief Whip;
- the Chief Secretary to the Treasury;
- the Attorney General;
- others at the PM's discretion.

For current members of the Cabinet, see www.gov.uk/government/ministers.

12.1.4.1 How effective is the Cabinet system?

In the absence of a statutory framework, the effectiveness of the Cabinet depends in large part on the personality and leadership style of the Prime Minister. A strong, presidential-style Prime Minister can weaken the collective Cabinet process and reduce its role to updating on, and rubberstamping, decisions already made. The Duke of Wellington is alleged to have said about his first Cabinet meeting as Prime Minister: 'An extraordinary affair. I gave them their orders and they wanted to stay and discuss them.' A more collegiate Prime Minister encourages collective discussion and decision-making. (For interesting comment, see Select Committee on the Constitution, *The Cabinet Office and the Centre of Government*, 4th Report of Session 2009–10, HL Paper 30 [122–128]); see also Colin Turpin and Adam Tomkins, *British Government and the Constitution: Text and Materials*, 7th edn (Cambridge: Cambridge University Press 2011) pp 418–419.)

However, collective decisions can be made outside the full Cabinet:

- Cabinet committees steer business away from the busy main Cabinet; chaired by a Cabinet minister, a smaller group of Cabinet ministers makes collective decisions on policy and recommendations in specific areas. Their meetings are technically meetings of the Cabinet; their decisions have the same status as full Cabinet decisions and are binding across government. The Prime Minister can create or abolish them as and when needed, often reflecting current government concerns; for example, the National Security Council, established in 2010 by David Cameron to co-ordinate national security strategy, is now firmly embedded as a Cabinet Committee.
- Some Cabinet Committees have sub-committees: for example, the National Security Council sub-committee on Nuclear Deterrence and Security. Ministers can also be members of Implementation Taskforces or implementation committees which drive delivery of government priority policies, such as the Covid-19 response. For the increasingly interwoven layers of the Committee system, see www.instituteforgovernment.org.uk/explainers/cabinet-committees.
- Partial Cabinets consist of selected Cabinet members to deal rapidly and directly with a particular issue and make decisions without reference to full Cabinet, such as a War Cabinet.

> The media often refers to meetings of the intriguingly named COBRA (or COBR) committee. This is an emergency response committee of ministers and others which has met, for example, after terrorist attacks at home or abroad, flooding, the collapse of Carillion, and the nerve agent attack in Salisbury (if you were wondering, COBRA stands for Cabinet Office briefing room A).

The phrase 'inner Cabinet' can be used to describe small, informal meetings of the Prime Minister, selected advisors, and ministers (often the Prime Minister's inner circle) to discuss policy or specific issues, but they are normally not part of the Cabinet structure and have no formal status. Margaret Thatcher used inner Cabinets partly to combat leaks from full Cabinet meetings, and an inner Cabinet called 'the Quad' was used under the Coalition government of 2010–2015 for regular meetings between the Prime Minister, Deputy Prime Minister, Chancellor of the Exchequer, and Chief Secretary to the Treasury. However, the scope for informal governmental decision-making outside full Cabinet was considered in the Butler Inquiry, which investigated the accuracy of intelligence on Iraqi weapons of mass destruction leading up to the Iraq conflict. The Butler Report 2004 concluded that Tony Blair's 'sofa style' of decision-making on the Iraq conflict with selected ministers, officials, and advisors was too informal. Briefing documents were not discussed in Cabinet meetings, which tended to be briefing sessions rather than allowing for collective decision-making (Lord Butler of Brockwell, *Review of Intelligence on Weapons of Mass Destruction*, 14 July 2004, HC 898 [606–611]).

12.1.4.2 The core executive

Rather than simply Prime Minister and Cabinet, Dunleavy and Rhodes have suggested the idea of a core executive to describe the reality of the distribution of power within modern central government 'Core Executive Studies in Britain' ((1990) 68 Political Administration 3). This requires negotiation-based political decision-making which more closely reflects Margaret Thatcher's perception of prime ministerial power referred to in section 12.1.2 (see Figure 12.3).

Figure 12.3 The core executive

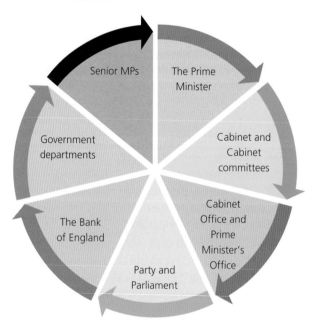

12.1.5 Government departments and agencies

We turn now to the operation of government departments and their agencies which put government policy into practice. They are divided into:

- Ministerial departments
- Arm's length bodies

12.1.5.1 Ministerial departments

Each Secretary of State heads a specific ministerial department for which s/he is directly accountable to Parliament. Government policies and priorities for each department are decided by the Cabinet, and the Treasury allocates their funding. The Prime Minister can create, merge, or abolish ministerial departments. In 2003, for example, the Lord Chancellor's Department briefly became the Department of Constitutional Affairs as a transitional arrangement before the Ministry of Justice was created in 2007. When Theresa May became Prime Minister in 2016, she created a new Department for International Trade and a Department for Exiting the European Union (with responsibility for Brexit); the latter closed on exit day. In 2020, Boris Johnson merged the Department for International Development into the Foreign and Commonwealth Office to create a new department: the Foreign, Commonwealth and Development Office. For current government departments, see www.gov.uk/government/organisations.

12.1.5.2 Arm's length bodies

The complexity of modern government can be seen through 'arm's length bodies' (ALBs), which are part of central government but are separate public bodies subject to less ministerial control, and so operate at a distance (arm's length) from government.

> An arm's-length body is an organisation that delivers a public service, is not a ministerial government department, and which operates to a greater or lesser extent at a distance from ministers. The term can include non-departmental public bodies (NDPBs), executive agencies, non-ministerial departments, public corporations, NHS bodies, and inspectorates. (Public Administration Select Committee, *Who's Accountable? Relationships between Government and Arm's-length Bodies*, 1st Report of Session 2014–15, HC 110 [1])

To be designated as an arm's length body, they must perform a technical function, require political impartiality, or act independently to establish facts (www.gov.uk/guidance/public-bodies-reform). The last two categories *need* to be independent from ministerial control. ALBs can be set up by government or, more often, by statute, but they radiate from the centre, with differing levels of independence from government (see Figure 12.4).

Accountability for arm's length bodies has been described as 'confused, overlapping and neglected, with blurred boundaries and responsibilities' (House of Commons Public Administration Select Committee, *Who's Accountable?* [13]; see also www.instituteforgovernment.org.uk/blog/what's-non-ministerial-about-new-national-crime-agency). Some ALBs are accountable to Parliament and some to ministers. Generally, the further a body is from the centre, the weaker the accountability link between minister and Parliament. Ministers are accountable to Parliament for all ALBs under the umbrella of their department but where they are the 'sponsoring' minister their department simply keeps a watch over ALBs, as opposed to hands-on control, so that the minister can account to Parliament for its performance or continued existence. To see examples of how government departments work with ALBs, go to www.gov.uk/government/organisations.

CROSS REFERENCE

Decisions of public bodies can be subject to judicial review. See Chapters 15 and 16

See the online resources for more details of ALBs

Figure 12.4 Arm's length bodies

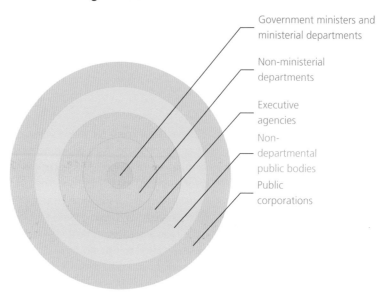

Government ministers and ministerial departments

Non-ministerial departments

Executive agencies

Non-departmental public bodies

Public corporations

Modern government could not function without supporting public bodies but the National Audit Office has criticised the public body landscape as 'confused and incoherent', with no single list of all ALBs and different definitions of ALBs between departments (National Audit Office, *Departments' Oversight of Arm's-Length Bodies: A Comparative Study*, Report by the Comptroller and Auditor General, Session 2016–17, HC 507, 5 July 2016). In March 2017, there were 305 public bodies: 38 Executive Agencies, 245 non-departmental public bodies, and 22 non-ministerial departments (Cabinet Office, *Public Bodies 2017*, p 6). Some bodies can fall into more than one category or change status: Ordnance Survey, for example, was a non-ministerial department with executive agency status but since 2015 has been a public corporation. So complex had the network of public bodies become that the Public Bodies Reform programme reduced their number by a third between 2010 and 2015, and the Public Bodies Act 2011 empowers ministers to modify or transfer functions of public bodies through secondary legislation to streamline and reduce their number. The public bodies transformation programme is underway to review public bodies and improve scrutiny, and current government policy requires new bodies to be set up only as a last resort. For further details, see:

- Constitution Committee, *The Accountability of Civil Servants*, 6th Report of Session 2012–13, HL Paper 61, chapter 5

- Public Administration Select Committee, *Who's Accountable? Relationships between Government and Arm's-Length Bodies*, 1st Report of Session 2014–15, HC 110, Annex p 40

12.1.6 The Civil Service

The Civil Service consists of around 400,000 civil servants in the UK who are employed by the Crown in government departments and many arm's length bodies. They carry out the administrative work of government; give objective, impartial advice and support to ministers; and help the government develop and implement its policies. The most senior civil servant in a government department is the permanent secretary who is responsible for the day-to-day running of the department; together with the Secretary of State, s/he is directly accountable to Parliament for the department's performance and spending. Recruitment to the Civil Service is on merit after fair and open competition.

Civil servants are independent of government and owe a duty to serve the government of the day, no matter which political party is in power. They are permanent in the sense that they do not change with each election. The *Civil Service Code*, introduced in 1996, sets out standards of conduct for civil servants and the core Civil Service values, established in 1854 in the Northcote–Trevelyan Report:

- integrity (putting the obligations of public service above personal interest)
- honesty (being truthful and open)
- objectivity (basing advice and decisions on rigorous analysis of the evidence)
- impartiality (acting solely according to the merits of the case and serving equally well governments of different political persuasions) (*The Civil Service Code*, 30 November 2010, updated 16 March 2015)

Civil servants must also comply with the law and uphold the administration of justice (thus upholding the rule of law). Breaches of the Code are investigated by the independent Civil Service Commission.

The Prime Minister is responsible for the civil service, and until 2010 management of the Civil Service was based on prerogative powers (see section 12.3), but this was put on a statutory footing by the Constitutional Reform and Governance Act 2010 Part 1.

12.2 Executive power

We turn now to the sources of ministerial power and it is important to remember that 'in a democratic society, the exercise of state power requires legal authority' (Constitution Committee, *The Pre-emption of Parliament*, 13th Report of Session 2012–13, HL Paper 165 [4]). Ministers' legal authority can derive from:

- Statute
- Common law
- Royal prerogative

Their use of power may be challenged in the courts (*Cabinet Manual* [3.24]).

The Carltona principle recognises that, for practical reasons, ministers' powers are usually exercised by responsible officials in their department; therefore an official's decision made on behalf of a minister is regarded as a decision of the minister, who is constitutionally responsible to Parliament (see *Cabinet Manual* [3.40–3.45]; *Carltona Ltd v Commissioners of Works* [1943] 2 All ER 560, 563; *R (Bourgass) v Secretary of State for Justice* [2015] UKSC 54 [48–52]). This ensures constitutional unity. Where a statute places a duty on a minister, it may generally be exercised by a member of their department for whom they accept responsibility. However, in *Buick, Re Judicial Review* [2018] NICA 26, where no minister was in place after the collapse of devolved government in Northern Ireland, decisions which would normally have gone before a minister for approval were beyond the competence of a senior civil servant. See also section 12.4.1.1.

12.2.1 **Statutory power**

Most government power is conferred by statute, including the power to make secondary legislation (for details, see section 11.4). Here we see the dominance of parliamentary sovereignty: by granting powers to ministers through primary legislation, Parliament expressly authorises ministerial action. Where a statutory power exists, ministers cannot operate under their prerogative powers or common law powers in the same area (Constitution Committee, *The Pre-emption of Parliament* [54] (Attorney General)). The superiority of statute was also emphasised in *R (Miller) v Secretary of State for Exiting the European Union* [2017] UKSC 5, [2018] AC 61 [50] ('*Miller I*'): the exercise of prerogative powers by ministers must be compatible with legislation, otherwise ministers would be changing (or infringing) the law, which they cannot do (see section 12.3.1.1).

12.2.2 **Common law powers**

Common law powers may authorise government action where there is no statutory or prerogative power, but the extent and nature of these powers has been a matter of debate.

CLOSE-UP FOCUS: MINISTERS' COMMON LAW POWERS

- The 1945 Ram memorandum (an advisory opinion drafted by Sir Granville Ram, First Parliamentary Counsel) stated that ministers' common law powers cover any powers which the Crown has power to exercise, except as precluded by statute.

- The Ram doctrine (applied by government): ministers can do anything a natural person can do, unless limited by legislation; this helps government carry out its administrative business, for example, employing people and conveying property (see HL Deb 25 February 2003, Vol 645 cols 2-3WA (Baroness Scotland)). The *Cabinet Manual* applies the Ram doctrine: a minister may exercise any of the legal powers of an individual ([3.31–3.32]).

- The view that the Crown (ministers) can do what a natural person can do, for example make contracts, was echoed in *R v Secretary of State for Health, ex parte C* [2000] 1 FLR 627, but in *Shrewsbury and Atcham BC v Secretary of State for Communities and Local Government* [2008] EWCA Civ 148, Carnwath LJ, *obiter*, preferred the view that ministers can only exercise their powers for 'governmental' purposes.

- Lord Sumption queried *obiter* whether the analogy with a natural person was apt in the case of public or governmental action, as opposed to managerial acts (*R (New London College Ltd) v Secretary of State for the Home Department* [2013] UKSC 51 [28]).

However, the Constitution Committee concluded that the Ram memorandum is not an accurate reflection of the law today. Ministers' ability to exercise common law powers is limited by public law principles enforced through judicial review (eg the requirement to exercise their powers in a rational way (see Chapter 16)), under the Human Rights Act 1998, and through constitutional principle such as parliamentary scrutiny (see *The Pre-emption of Parliament* [50–60]).

See further Matthew Weait and Anthony Lester, 'The Use of Ministerial Powers Without Parliamentary Authority: The Ram Doctrine' (2003) (Autumn) Public Law, 415–428; ukconstitution-allaw.org/2014/10/25/adam-perry-the-source-of-the-crowns-general-administrative-powers/.

12.2.3 **Royal prerogative**

Despite its royal roots, the royal prerogative is now closely aligned with the executive. Prerogative powers enable government to function efficiently and at speed, particularly in peacetime emergencies or time of war. The Supreme Court in *Miller I* recognised that some important areas of governmental activity which are essential to the effective operation of the state are still reserved to ministers and are not covered by statute ([49]), but two key issues arise with the exercise of unwritten prerogative powers: (1) where their limits lie, and (2) their potential to slip through the accountability net. For example, making and unmaking treaties can be carried out by ministers without legislative authority and is not reviewable by the courts (*Miller I* [55]). These issues are examined next in section 12.3.

▶ CROSS REFERENCE

For an introduction to royal prerogative, see section 3.2.3

> **THINKING POINT**
>
> If Parliament does not approve the use of most prerogative powers, where is the accountability?

12.3 Royal Prerogative: prerogative executive powers

> The royal prerogative 'encompasses the residue of powers which remain vested in the Crown, and they are exercisable by ministers, provided that the exercise is consistent with Parliamentary legislation' (*Miller I* [2017] UKSC 5 [47]; see generally [40–53]).

We focus here on prerogative executive powers which are discretionary, not derived from statute and are exercised on behalf of the Crown by government ministers without needing Parliamentary approval. They include:

- foreign affairs—making treaties, recognising foreign governments, appointing diplomats;
- declaring war, deployment of armed forces abroad;
- command of the armed forces (the Queen is Commander-in-Chief);
- defence of the realm (protecting the UK);
- maintaining the Queen's peace (keeping public order);
- PM's powers of appointment;
- recommending honours;
- granting and revoking passports;
- granting pardons;
- administration of justice.

The exercise of ministers' prerogative power can have a very broad reach, even affecting the rights of individuals outside the UK; for example, the governance of British overseas territories is a prerogative power and the Crown can make legislation for its territories under the prerogative in the form of Orders in Council which are approved by the Queen at meetings of the Privy Council and are not made by Parliament (see Chapter 11). This was an issue in the *Bancoult case*.

🔍 CASE CLOSE-UP: *R (BANCOULT) v SECRETARY OF STATE FOR FOREIGN AND COMMONWEALTH AFFAIRS (NO 2)* [2008] UKHL 61, [2009] AC 453

The Chagos Islands are part of the British Indian Ocean Territories (BIOT); the largest island is Diego Garcia, which, in 1966, the UK agreed to lease to the United States as a military base. As a result, between 1968 and 1973, the inhabitants of Diego Garcia were removed. The Immigration Ordinance 1971 prohibited anyone from entering or being present in BIOT without a permit. After a successful judicial review challenge by Mr Bancoult to the Immigration Ordinance 1971, the government progressed with a feasibility study on resettlement, which concluded in 2002 that resettlement would be uneconomic and problematic, especially given rising sea levels. In 2004, the BIOT (Constitution) Order 2004 was made by prerogative Order in Council banning residence or entry in the BIOT (an Immigration Order was also made about immigration control). Mr Bancoult brought judicial review proceedings to challenge the 2004 Order.

The House of Lords held that (1) prerogative Orders in Council are judicially reviewable and (2) by 3 to 2, the prerogative Orders in Council preventing the return of Chagos Islanders to their homes were lawful. Their right of abode was 'purely symbolic' ([53] (Lord Hoffmann)), and not a fundamental right, and had to be weighed against the UK's security and diplomatic interests.

See Thomas Poole, 'United Kingdom: The Royal Prerogative' (2010) 8(1) International Journal of Constitutional Law 146–155. Note *R (Bancoult) v Secretary of State for Foreign and Commonwealth Affairs (No. 2)* [2016] UKSC 35, where Mr Bancoult unsuccessfully sought to set aside the 2008 judgment on the basis that new evidence had come to light on the feasibility study's findings.

12.3.1 Restricting prerogative power

> 'A prerogative power is . . . limited by statute and the common law, including . . . the constitutional principles with which it would otherwise conflict' (*R (Miller) v The Prime Minister; Cherry and others v Advocate General for Scotland* [2019] UKSC 41 [49]).

There are significant constraints on prerogative power, particularly since the *Miller/Cherry* decision. Prerogative power is limited by: (1) constitutional principles, especially parliamentary sovereignty; and (2) common law principles developed in case law by the courts eg the government cannot exercise prerogative powers depriving people of their property without paying compensation (*Burmah Oil Co Ltd v Lord Advocate* [1965] AC 75).

12.3.1.1 Prerogative power and parliamentary sovereignty

As the Supreme Court pointed out in *Miller/Cherry*, the courts have been keen to protect parliamentary sovereignty from encroachment by the royal prerogative and maintain the limits that parliamentary sovereignty places on it ([41]). It is a fundamental principle that the royal prerogative is inferior to statute and it is a source of power which is 'only available for a case not covered by statute' (*Burmah Oil Co Ltd v Lord Advocate* [1965] AC 75, 101 (Lord Reid)). Two points flow from this:

- As a sovereign body, Parliament can abolish, change, or limit a prerogative power by express words in a statute, and
- ministers cannot alter UK domestic law unless Parliament allows it.

Parliament can abolish, change, or limit a prerogative power

In the Bill of Rights 1689, Parliament restricted royal power, prohibiting the monarch from raising taxes, making law, or maintaining a standing army in peacetime without Parliament's consent. The Crown (government) is subject 'to the overriding powers of the democratically elected legislature as the sovereign body' (*R v Home Sec ex p Fire Brigades Union* [1995] 2 AC 513, 552 (Lord Browne-Wilkinson)). Where a statute and prerogative power cover the same subject matter, and the statute has not expressly abolished the prerogative, the statute takes priority and the prerogative goes into abeyance (is suspended). The Crown must apply the statutory power while the statute is in force and must not use prerogative powers incompatibly with it.

 EXAMPLES

This principle was applied in *AG v De Keyser's Royal Hotel* [1920] AC 508, where the Crown requisitioned the plaintiff's hotel in the First World War under the Defence of the Realm Act 1914, which gave the right to compensation where property was requisitioned. After the war, the plaintiff sued for payment. The Crown argued that it had in fact been using its prerogative power of defence of the realm, by which the government could requisition property *without compensation* if necessary for the conduct of war.

The House of Lords held that the Crown could not choose which power to rely on, depending on advantage. The statutory powers were so wide that they made exercise of the prerogative unnecessary, and while the Defence of Realm Act 1914 was in force, the common law prerogative power was in abeyance. The Crown was bound by the statute so had to pay compensation. See also *Laker Airways Ltd v Department of Trade* [1977] QB 643.

The House of Lords in *R v Home Sec ex p Fire Brigades Union* [1995] 2 AC 513 also made it clear that government cannot rely on prerogative power to avoid Parliament's wishes. Where an Act of Parliament gave a minister discretion about when to bring a criminal injuries compensation scheme into operation, he did not have power to decide that it should not take effect at all and continue to use the scheme set up under prerogative which gave lower compensation.

Key point: In both cases, the court was preventing the government from using the prerogative to bypass a statute.

However, before a statute applies over prerogative power, the statute needs to be clear that it is abridging (limiting) or displacing a prerogative power, either by express words or by necessary implication:

- In *R v Secretary of State for Home Department ex parte Northumbria Police Authority* [1989] QB 26, the Home Secretary decided to supply the police from a central store with CS gas and plastic bullets for use in serious public disorder. The Police Authority, concerned that UK police had never used plastic bullets, asked for judicial review of the decision, arguing that the Home Secretary had no legal power to issue them without their consent except in an emergency, and that it was not consistent with the Police Authority's powers to maintain equipment under the Police Act 1964. The Court of Appeal held that the Act did not give the Police Authority a monopoly of power over equipment and the Home Secretary had been entitled to act under the prerogative power to keep the Queen's peace. As Lord Pearce stated in *Burmah Oil v Lord Advocate*, 'The Crown must have power to act before the ultimate crisis arises' (p 144).

- In *R (XH and AI) v Secretary of State for the Home Department* [2017] EWCA Civ 41, the claimants argued that the royal prerogative to cancel passports had been impliedly abrogated (abolished) by the Terrorism Prevention and Investigation Measures Act 2011. The Act allowed the cancellation of passports of individuals suspected of planning to travel abroad to engage in terrorism-related activity. The Court of Appeal held that the prerogative power to issue and cancel passports was broader than the statutory power and still existed (see [89–101]).

 SUMMARY

The courts interpret the relevant statute. Does the statute occupy the same ground as a prerogative power? If it does not fully cover, or extend beyond, the same area as the prerogative power, the prerogative may still be exercisable. The courts apply a strict test for whether a statute impliedly displaces a prerogative power.

A statute can also replace a prerogative power, for example, the Fixed-term Parliaments Act 2011 replaced the Crown's prerogative power to dissolve Parliament (a power exercised formally by the monarch acting on the advice of the Prime Minister). The Conservative 2019 election manifesto promised to repeal the Act, but if the FTPA is repealed does the prerogative power revive or has it been extinguished by the Act? The point is unclear. The court in *Miller I* suggested that prerogative powers might be reinstated on repeal of a statute that 'curtailed' them [112], and Lord Browne-Wilkinson agreed that they remain in existence where Parliament has not expressly or implicitly extinguished them (*Fire Brigades Union case*, 552). However, the Constitution Committee concluded that the dissolution power would not revive if the FTPA was repealed; once put into statute, it was permanently extinguished (see Constitution Committee, *A Question of Confidence? The Fixed-term Parliaments Act 2011*, 12th Report of Session 2019–21, HL Paper 121 [32–39]; Robert Craig, 'Restoring Confidence: Replacing the Fixed-Term Parliaments Act 2011' (2018) 81(3) MLR 480).

Ministers cannot alter UK domestic law unless Parliament allows it

The royal prerogative does not enable ministers to change statute law or common law unless an Act of Parliament allows it (Bill of Rights 1689; see *The Zamora* [1916] 2 AC 77; *R (Bancoult) v Secretary of State for Foreign and Commonwealth Affairs (No 2)* [2009] AC 453 [44] (Lord Hoffmann); *Miller I* ([50]).

 THINKING POINT

How is the separation of powers being applied here?

For example, while ministers have the prerogative power to enter into and withdraw from treaties, the prerogative does not allow them to alter the rights of individuals in domestic law without the intervention of Parliament (see *JH Rayner (Mincing Lane) Ltd v Department of Trade and Industry* [1990] 2 AC 418, 500 (Lord Oliver)). This was clearly applied by the Supreme Court in *Miller I* where the Court saw ministers as 'constitutionally the junior partner' and Parliament as the 'constitutionally senior partner' ([90]). The Court emphasised that:

- The exercise of ministers' prerogative powers must be consistent with the common law and statutes ([50, 56]).
- Nothing in the European Communities Act 1972 allowed withdrawal from the EU Treaties by prerogative act without Parliament's prior authorisation ([77]).
- Ministers do not have the right to use a treaty-making power to remove an important source of domestic law and rights ([87]; but see [177, 217] (Lord Reed)).
- Ministers alone could not bring about such a far-reaching change as Brexit to the UK's constitutional arrangements; it had to be done by parliamentary legislation ([81–82]).
- Ministers therefore could not use the prerogative to give notice to withdraw from the EU without the prior authority of an Act of Parliament ([101]).

However, David Feldman argues that the Crown may, by legislation under the prerogative, alter domestic law in the UK legal systems when it is not inconsistent with an Act of Parliament in the same field (see ukconstitutionallaw.org/2016/11/08/david-feldman-brexit-the-royal-prerogative-and-parliamentary-sovereignty/).

12.3.1.2 The courts' control of prerogative power

Coke CJ pronounced in the early seventeenth century that the king's prerogative powers were limited. In *Prohibitions del Roy* (1607), he held that the king could not dispense justice personally, only through judges. In the *Case of Proclamations* (1611), he held that the king could no longer change common law, statute, or custom by royal proclamation, declaring 'The King hath no prerogative but what the law of the land allows'.

> CROSS REFERENCE
For more details, see section 2.4

Until 1984, the courts could determine whether a prerogative power existed and what its extent was, but could not question *how* a minister had exercised a *prerogative* power (though they could review how a minister had exercised a *statutory* power); see *Chandler v DPP* [1964] AC 763; *Burmah Oil v Lord Advocate* [1965] AC 75. This changed with the landmark *GCHQ case* (*CCSU v Minister for the Civil Service* [1985] AC 374).

CASE CLOSE-UP: *COUNCIL OF CIVIL SERVICE UNIONS v MINISTER FOR THE CIVIL SERVICE* [1985] AC 374

Here, Mrs Thatcher, then Prime Minister, exercised the prerogative power of management of the Civil Service. Acting under the Civil Service Order in Council 1982, made under the royal prerogative, which authorised her to give instructions about the conduct and conditions of service of civil servants who are employed at the Crown's pleasure, she decided that civil servants employed at GCHQ at Cheltenham (one of the intelligence services) should end their membership of trade unions. The decision was challenged on the basis that the terms and conditions of service at GCHQ could not be changed without consultation with the workers and their unions.

The House of Lords held that:

- the Prime Minister had been justified in not holding a consultation before the instruction had been given because of the risk to national security from industrial action;

- the courts *could* review the way in which ministers had exercised prerogative power as long as it did not involve politically sensitive policy. This was an important step forward.

Lord Roskill saw no logical reason why the fact that the source of the power was the prerogative, and not statute, could deprive citizens of the right to challenge it. 'In either case the act in question is the act of the executive. To talk of that act as the act of the sovereign savours of the archaism of past centuries' (p 417).

Justiciability

> Justiciability means raising a legal question on which the courts can properly adjudicate

However, Lord Roskill went on to state that the right of challenge is not unqualified and must depend on the subject matter of the prerogative power being exercised. He referred to certain prerogative powers that the courts could not judicially review ('excluded categories'), including 'the making of treaties, the defence of the realm, the prerogative of mercy, the grant of honours, the dissolution of Parliament and the appointment of ministers' (p 418). Thus '[t]he issue of justiciability depends, not on general principle, but on subject matter and suitability in the particular case' (*R (Abbasi) v Secretary of State for Foreign and Commonwealth Affairs* [2002] EWCA Civ 1598 [85] (Lord Phillips MR)).

High policy matters, particularly international affairs, are 'non-justiciable' (not suitable for decision by a court); more precisely, the courts will be 'slow to review' them unless there is a domestic foothold (see *R (Al-Haq) v Secretary of State for Foreign and Commonwealth Affairs* [2009] EWHC 1910 (Admin) [53–59] (Cranston J)); but the courts can review how a prerogative power has been exercised where it has minimal political or policy content (see *R v Secretary of State for Foreign & Commonwealth Affairs ex p Everett* [1989] QB 811; see also *R v Secretary of State for the Home Department ex p Bentley* [1994] QB 349). The Supreme Court in *Miller/Cherry* summarised the position on justiciability. The courts can determine:

- whether a prerogative power exists, and if it does exist, its extent/legal limits (this is justiciable and open to the courts to decide)
- whether the lawfulness of the exercise of a prerogative power within its legal limits can be challenged in the courts on another basis. It is this issue that raises questions of justiciability depending on the nature and subject matter of the prerogative power being exercised [35–36].

Justiciability is therefore the key to the door for the courts to determine an issue, and this was central in *Miller/Cherry*.

Q CASE CLOSE-UP: *R (MILLER) v THE PRIME MINISTER; CHERRY AND OTHERS v ADVOCATE GENERAL FOR SCOTLAND* [2019] UKSC 41, [2020] AC 373

Background

In this constitutionally significant case, the issue was whether the Prime Minister's decision to prorogue Parliament was lawful. Prorogation ends the current session of Parliament, normally for a few days before a Queen's speech starts a new session; Parliament cannot perform its essential functions of scrutinising government action or making law until a new session begins (see *Miller/Cherry* [2] for a clear explanation of prorogation). The power to prorogue Parliament is a prerogative power exercised by the Crown, that is, the monarch acting on the advice of her ministers. The monarch then makes a proclamation by Order in Council to order prorogation. Parliament has no say in the exercise of this prerogative power. As Lord Drummond Young put it, 'The proroguing of Parliament suspends the operation of the body that is responsible for subjecting the executive to critical scrutiny' (*Cherry v Advocate General for Scotland* [2019] CSIH 49 [106]).

In August 2019, the Prime Minister, Boris Johnson, decided to prorogue Parliament and the Queen was advised accordingly. On 28 August 2019, an Order in Council proclaimed that Parliament would be prorogued for five weeks from a date between 9 and 12 September until 14 October when a Queen's Speech would take place. Parliament would not sit, except in a very limited way, during that period. At this point, the UK was due to leave the EU on 31 October.

Two legal actions were launched challenging the lawfulness of the Prime Minister's advice to the Queen that Parliament should be prorogued: one in the Scottish courts by a group of MPs and members of the House of Lords, led by Joanna Cherry QC MP, and the second in the English High Court by Gina Miller. At first instance, both the High Court and the Outer House dismissed the claims on the ground of being non-justiciable because the Prime Minister's decision and advice to Her Majesty were political, and there were no legal standards against which to judge their legitimacy (*R (Miller) v The Prime Minister* [2019] EWHC 2381 (QB); *Cherry v Advocate General for Scotland* [2019] CSOH 70). The Scottish Inner Court of Session, however, held that the advice to prorogue was justiciable and unlawful because the purpose was to prevent parliamentary scrutiny of the government (*Cherry* [2019] CSIH 49; see in particular [52, 116–117, 123–124]). Both cases went on appeal to the Supreme Court.

Giving the unanimous judgment of the court, Lady Hale and Lord Reed described the case as of 'grave constitutional importance' [26].

The legal issues

(1) Is the question of whether the Prime Minister's advice to the Queen was lawful justiciable?

The Supreme Court was firmly of the opinion that it was justiciable. Although the courts cannot decide political questions, they can consider a legal dispute even if it concerns a political matter [31] and '[t]he fact that the minister is politically accountable to Parliament does not mean that he is therefore immune from legal accountability to the courts' [33]. The Court was ensuring that the government did not use the power unlawfully so as to prevent Parliament from carrying out its proper functions [34]. The Court decided that this case involved the *extent* of the prerogative power and what its lawful limits are, which was a justiciable issue [52] (this sidestepped trickier justiciability issues).

(2) If so, by what standard is its lawfulness to be judged?

The legal limits of the power to prorogue were the point where it conflicted with the fundamental constitutional principles of parliamentary sovereignty and parliamentary accountability [38]. They provided the standard by which to judge its lawfulness. An unlimited power to prorogue Parliament for as long as the government wished would undermine the sovereignty of Parliament ([41–42, 44]) and a legal limit was needed on the power to make it compatible with Parliament's ability to carry out its constitutional functions of law-making and supervising the executive ([46, 48]).

(3) By that standard, was it lawful?

Did the Prime Minister's action have the effect of frustrating or preventing Parliament's constitutional role of holding the government to account [55]? The Court's view was: 'of course it did' [56]. This was not a normal prorogation; it prevented Parliament from carrying out its constitutional role for five weeks [56] and no reason was given for closing it down [58]. The decision was therefore unlawful [61] because it was outside the powers of the Prime Minister to give the advice.

(4) If not lawful, what remedy should the court grant?

The Court declared that the Order in Council was unlawful and should be quashed because it was based on unlawful advice, which meant the prorogation was unlawful and had no effect [69–70].

Consequently, as Parliament was not prorogued, it resumed sitting the next day.

Key points

- Constitutional principles can limit a prerogative power where they would otherwise conflict [49]
- A decision to prorogue Parliament will be unlawful if the prorogation frustrates or prevents, without reasonable justification, Parliament's ability to carry out its constitutional functions of law-making and supervising the executive [50, 52]
- And if the consequences are sufficiently serious to call for the court's intervention [51]

Thinking point: Do you think that the *Miller/Cherry* judgment is upholding constitutional principles or that the court intervened in a political matter?

See: https://commonslibrary.parliament.uk/research-briefings/cbp-9006/.

Paul Craig, 'The Supreme Court, Prorogation and Constitutional Principle' (2020) (April) Public Law 248.

12.3.1.3 Reform of the royal prerogative

The prerogative has been criticised and 'the idea of the prerogative as the black sheep of the constitutional fold . . . has been hardwired into British constitutional thinking' (Thomas Poole, 'United Kingdom: The Royal Prerogative' (2010) 8(1) ICON 146, 147). It is an ancient, unwritten, discretionary, secretive source of power. Table 12.2 below sets out proposals for reforming the prerogative.

Some reforms have subsequently taken place. The Constitutional Reform and Governance Act 2010 put on a statutory footing:

- the management of the Civil Service;
- the ratification of treaties (formal confirmation of a treaty): although the government makes treaties, from the late nineteenth century a practice developed of laying a treaty before both Houses of Parliament 21 days before ratification to allow Parliament to object. In 1924, after a previous government did not follow the practice, Arthur Ponsonby, the Parliamentary Under-Secretary of State for Foreign Affairs, assured the Commons that ministers would follow it in future, and the Ponsonby rule emerged as a constitutional convention. It was put on a statutory basis by section 20 of the Constitutional Reform and Governance Act 2010;
- the Fixed-term Parliaments Act 2011 put the dissolution of Parliament on a statutory basis.

Table 12.2 Reform proposals

In 2004, the Public Administration Select Committee suggested reforming the prerogative (*Taming the Prerogative*)	Parliament should have the right to know what powers are being exercised by ministers, otherwise there is no effective accountability
	Proposals to ensure parliamentary scrutiny on armed conflict, ratifying treaties, issuing and revoking passports
	Legislation to give Parliament greater control over ministers' powers and allow scrutiny over prerogative action
Governance of Britain Green Paper, Cm 7170, July 2007. See also *Governance of Britain: Review of the Executive Royal Prerogative Powers: Final Report*, Ministry of Justice (2009)	More parliamentary involvement in the exercise of government powers and a rebalancing of power
	Place prerogative powers on a statutory footing to bring them under parliamentary control and scrutiny
	Reform: deploying Armed Forces abroad, ratifying treaties, dissolving Parliament, and placing the Civil Service on a statutory footing

However, Anne Twomey argues that experience in other countries shows that codifying prerogatives in statute can sometimes create problems about their interpretation and the courts' involvement in enforcing them: ('Should we codify the royal prerogative?' 1 November 2019 at https://constitution-unit.com/.)

We turn next to how executive power is controlled.

12.4 Control of the executive

Tom Paine asserted that an elected government is 'a despotism, if the persons so elected, possess afterwards, as a parliament, unlimited powers'. We examine below who exerts control over government power, decision-making, and implementation of policy (see Figure 12.5).

Figure 12.5 Oversight of government

12.4.1 Control by Parliament: ministerial responsibility

'The road to tyranny is paved by Executives ignoring Parliament.' (Sir Edward Leigh MP, HC Hansard 19 October 2017, Vol 629 col 1009)

'The first function of Parliament is to hold the Government to account' (Robin Cook MP, HC Deb 26 February 1996, Vol 272 col 617)

Ministerial responsibility is about government accountability to Parliament under the principle of responsible government. It is a constitutional convention which provides a crucial mechanism for Parliament to call ministers to account through answering questions and appearing before committees. Parliament 'holds the government's feet to the fire' by subjecting it to critical scrutiny as shown in Figure 12.6, though this only works effectively with an assertive Parliament. The two facets of ministerial responsibility are:

- individual ministerial responsibility;
- collective responsibility.

Figure 12.6 Parliamentary scrutiny of government

| Parliament holds the government to account | Effective scrutiny of the executive by Parliament | constrains government power | publicises government mistakes to inform the electorate |

12.4.1.1 Individual ministerial responsibility

> Ministers 'are constitutionally responsible to Parliament for the discharge of all their functions and the exercise of all their powers' (Constitution Committee, *The Pre-emption of Parliament* [4]). Ministers have a duty to Parliament to account, and be held to account, for the policies, decisions, and actions of their departments and agencies (*Ministerial Code* [1.3]).

Each minister is politically accountable to Parliament for their department's conduct, and civil servants should not be blamed. If something goes wrong, the responses available to a minister are to:

- give an explanation to the House of Commons (the usual response);
- apologise;
- take remedial action;
- resign.

≫ CROSS REFERENCE

See section 11.1 for more details of how Parliament holds the government to account generally

Opportunities to require ministers to account and explain to Parliament include: making oral statements to the House, written ministerial statements, responding to parliamentary questions, giving evidence before select committees, and annual reports to Parliament.

In 1997 the House of Commons agreed a resolution on ministerial accountability, making it clear that ministers who knowingly mislead Parliament are expected to resign (HC Deb 19 March 1997, Vol 292 col 1047). This is now contained in the *Ministerial Code* ([1.3(c)]). Even inadvertently misleading Parliament can lead to resignation. For example, Amber Rudd resigned as Home Secretary in 2018 after mistakenly telling a select committee that she was unaware of targets for removing illegal immigrants. Ministers are also expected to resign where they are personally to blame for a serious departmental error, but for all other issues, resignation is not automatic. For more examples, see researchbriefings.files.parliament.uk/documents/RP96-27/RP96-27.pdf; Diana Woodhouse, 'Ministerial Responsibility in the 1990s: When Do Ministers Resign?' (1993) 46(3) Parliamentary Affairs 277–292; Diana Woodhouse, 'UK Ministerial Responsibility in 2002: The Tale of Two Resignations' (2004) 82(1) Public Administration 1–19.

Ministers and civil servants

By constitutional convention known as the Haldane convention (after the Haldane Review 1918), civil servants are accountable to ministers (not Parliament), and ministers are accountable to Parliament for their departments' actions—and ultimately to the public.

The relationship between minister and civil servant should be indivisible, and the act of every civil servant is regarded as the act of his or her minister.

The golden example of a minister falling on his sword for civil servants' mistakes is often cited as the Crichel Down affair. This involved the resignation of Sir Thomas Dugdale, the Minister of Agriculture, in 1954, after an inquiry criticised his department. In 1938, the Air Ministry had compulsorily purchased land for a bombing range. The government promised the landowners that the land would be returned to them after the Second World War when it was no longer needed, but instead of offering it back to the former owners, the Ministry of Agriculture leased it out. In the Commons debate on the inquiry's report, the minister accepted full responsibility to Parliament for any mistakes and inefficiency of officials in his department, in order to avoid bringing the civil service into the political arena (even though the inquiry report named five of them).

THE BIGGER PICTURE

Crichel Down prompted Sir David Maxwell Fyfe, the Home Secretary, to set out four categories of accountability of ministers for their civil servants. You can find them in Constitution Committee, *The Accountability of Civil Servants* [4] Box 1; and HC Deb 20 July 1954, Vol 530 cols 1285–1287. See also Richard A. Chapman, 'Crichel Down Revisited' (1987) 65(3) Public Administration 339–347.

After civil servant Clive Ponting was acquitted of charges under the Official Secrets Act after passing confidential information to Tam Dalyell MP, Sir Robert Armstrong, the Head of the Home Civil Service, drafted the Armstrong Memorandum in 1985, setting out the duties and responsibilities of civil servants in relation to ministers (amended 1996). The Armstrong memorandum was replaced by the *Civil Service Code* also in 1996.

The Osmotherly rules are guidelines for civil servants when appearing before parliamentary select committees. They emphasise that civil servants give evidence on behalf of their ministers in accordance with ministerial accountability, but now allow civil servants running key projects (Senior Responsible Owners) to be directly accountable to select committees. See *Giving Evidence to Select Committees—Guidance for Civil Servants*, October 2014 at www.gov.uk/government/publications/departmental-evidence-and-response-to-select-committees-guidance; note also para 1.3(e) *Ministerial Code*.

Table 12.3 The accountability/responsibility division

Accountability	Responsibility
• Ministers are always accountable to Parliament for the work of their department • They have a duty to explain to Parliament what happens	• Ministers are not necessarily responsible for everything that happens in their department • They are responsible where their acts and omissions have contributed to a policy or operational failure

The accountability/responsibility debate

Accountability means providing information and explaining; responsibility means taking the blame. The distinction between ministerial accountability and responsibility came to prominence in the 1990s. In evidence to the Scott Inquiry, Sir Robin Butler (then the most senior civil servant) distinguished between accountability and responsibility as shown in Table 12.3.

This opened up a dividing line between departmental policy—for which ministers accepted responsibility—and day-to-day operational matters carried out by civil servants—for which they did not.

EXAMPLE

In 1995, following the escape of three prisoners from Parkhurst, a high-security prison, the Prisons Service (an executive agency) was heavily criticised in the Learmont Report. Michael Howard, then Home Secretary, dismissed the Director General of the Prisons Service, Derek Lewis, as the operational side had been found at fault. Derek Lewis claimed that the Home Secretary had intervened in the day-to-day running of the Service. The Home Secretary was criticised in the Commons for not accepting responsibility for serious operational failures (HC Deb 19 October 1995, Vol 264 cc 502–551). He stated that he was personally accountable to Parliament for all matters concerning the Prison Service; he was accountable and responsible for all policy decisions relating to the service, and the Director General was responsible for day-to-day operations (col 517).

See the online resources for more on the background to the Scott Report

In the 1990s, Lord Justice Scott chaired the 'arms to Iraq' inquiry into the export of defence equipment to Iraq. Three ministers had reformulated government policy on non-lethal arms sales to Iraq without disclosing it to Parliament, and this had come to light in a high-profile prosecution. The Scott Report was published in 1996 (*Report of the Inquiry into the Export of Defence Equipment and Dual-Use Goods to Iraq and Related Prosecutions* (1995–1996) HC 115) and stated:

- 'The obligation of Ministers to give information about the activities of their departments and to give information and explanations for the actions and omissions of their civil servants, lies at the heart of Ministerial accountability' (K8.2).
- Failing to meet the obligations of ministerial accountability undermines the democratic process (K8.3).
- Ministerial accountability does not necessarily require blame to be accepted by a minister 'unless he has some personal responsibility for or some personal involvement in what has occurred' (K8.15–16).

However, while the Scott Report favoured Sir Robin Butler's accountability/responsibility distinction, the Public Service Committee rejected it. Its chair, Giles Radice, said in the Commons: 'Ministers have an obligation to Parliament which consists in ensuring that government explains its actions. Ministers also have an obligation to respond to criticism made in Parliament in a way that seems likely to satisfy it—which may include, if necessary, resignation' (HC Deb 12 February 1997, Vol 290 cc 273–274).

 SUMMARY

The accountability/responsibility divide is not clear-cut:

- 'it is not possible absolutely to distinguish an area in which a minister is personally responsible, and liable to take blame, from one in which he is constitutionally accountable. Ministerial responsibility is not composed of two elements which have a clear break between the two.' (Public Service Committee, *Ministerial Accountability and Responsibility*, 2nd Report of Session 1995–96, HC 313 [21])

- 'under our current constitutional arrangements there will never be precise clarity about the boundaries of ministerial accountability.' (Select Committee on Public Administration, *Politics and Administration: Ministers and Civil Servants*, 3rd Report of Session 2006–07, HC 122 [29])

- 'We maintain our view that there is no constitutional difference between the terms responsibility and accountability.' (Constitution Committee, *The Accountability of Civil Servants* [17]).

Ministerial responsibility and the prerogative

According to the Public Administration Select Committee, ministers are accountable to Parliament for the use of prerogative powers just as they are for exercising statutory or common law powers, but only *after* the event (*Taming the Prerogative* [13]). However, MPs are prevented from raising certain matters in the House of Commons because of confidentiality, national security, sensitive foreign policy matters, or a royal connection, which are often areas covered by the prerogative.

Ministerial responsibility in the twenty-first century

In the nineteenth and early twentieth centuries, government was organised along much simpler lines and ministers were more aware of what was happening in their departments, but the issue now is whether the complexity and fragmented nature of the modern state has made the convention unrealistic. In evidence to the Constitution Committee, Margaret Hodge MP pointed out that:

> When Haldane established the constitutional convention that Ministers are accountable to Parliament and civil servants are accountable to Ministers, there were 28 civil servants in the Home Office. Now . . . there are 34,000. The idea that one Cabinet Minister can be accountable for the actions of some 34,000 people is, I think, mistaken. (*The Accountability of Civil Servants* [7])

The Committee concluded that it was hard to see how any alternative system could work in practice in the Westminster model and that ministerial responsibility is essential for Parliament to perform its function of holding the government to account ([11–12]) although Richards and Smith argue that a principal and agent relationship between civil servants and ministers has replaced the traditional Haldane convention (see David Richards and Martin J. Smith, 'The Westminster Model and the "Indivisibility of the Political and Administrative Elite": A Convenient Myth Whose Time Is Up?' (2016) 29(4) Governance 499–516).

Responsibility for personal conduct

Ministers are responsible for individual mistakes and personal conduct. They are personally responsible for deciding how to act and conduct themselves, and for justifying their actions and conduct to Parliament and the public (*Ministerial Code* [1.6]). A minister is unlikely to resign if s/he has the support of the Prime Minister, government, and party, but media criticism can ratchet up pressure to resign.

 EXAMPLES

Use of parliamentary expenses: David Laws, 2010.

Breach of the Ministerial Code: Damian Green, First Secretary of State, 2017.

Personal conduct: Andrew Mitchell, Chief Whip, 2012; Sir Michael Fallon, Defence Secretary 2017.

12.4.1.2 Collective responsibility

The principle of collective responsibility applies to all government ministers (*Ministerial Code* [1.3]): 'Ministers should be able to express their views frankly in the expectation that they can argue freely in private while maintaining a united front when decisions have been reached. This in turn requires that the privacy of opinions expressed in Cabinet and Ministerial Committees, including in correspondence, should be maintained' ([2.1]).

Collective ministerial responsibility (also known as Cabinet collective responsibility) is based on the idea that a government stands or falls together. This consists of a number of strands:

- Maintaining unity: all ministers and their parliamentary aides must vote with the government and support government policy in Parliament and in public; if they are unable to do so, they should resign their ministerial post (eg Robin Cook resigned from the Cabinet over the Iraq war in 2003; in July 2018, Boris Johnson resigned as Foreign Secretary and David Davis resigned as Secretary of State for Exiting the European Union over the Prime Minister's Brexit plans; and four ministers resigned on 15 November 2018, unable to support the withdrawal agreement).

- Cabinet ministers and Cabinet committees are bound by collective responsibility. All ministers are bound by Cabinet decisions and must support them publicly. Ministers should not disclose what has been discussed in Cabinet to preserve unity (though this has not prevented ministers from leaking details of Cabinet discussions to the press where they thought it necessary). In 1986, Michael Heseltine, the Defence Secretary, resigned from the Cabinet in protest at the lack of Cabinet discussion allowed on the takeover of Westland Helicopters, leading to newspaper headlines about open war between ministers and government disunity.

- The government must command the confidence of the House of Commons. Once it loses that confidence, the government must resign; but only three governments have resigned after a vote of no confidence in the last century: twice in 1924, and once in 1979.

A government with a strong majority is unlikely to lose office because it will win a vote of confidence. Under the Fixed-term Parliaments Act 2011 (section 2(4) and 2(5)), an election must be held if a motion of no confidence in the government is passed by a simple majority and the Commons has not passed a confidence motion in a new government within 14 days.

In 2018, Bernard Jenkin MP maintained that 'ministerial collective responsibility really matters' when he criticised the Chancellor's stance on advocating a softer Brexit than the Prime Minister, and pointed out the difficulties for civil servants if ministers are divided: who do they follow? (*Sunday Telegraph*, 4 February).

12.4.2 **Control by the law and the courts**

> Ministers' powers derive from legislation passed by Parliament, the royal prerogative and common law. They are subject to an overarching duty to act in accordance with the law. The courts rule on whether ministerial action is carried out lawfully (*Cabinet Manual*, p 3 [12]; see also chapter 3 of the Manual, and the *Ministerial Code* 2019 [1.3])

Ministers are accountable to Parliament for their decisions but they are also accountable to the law. The legality of decision-making by ministers can be reviewed by the courts through the process of judicial review, and Lord Diplock has stated:

> It is not, in my view, a sufficient answer to say that judicial review of the actions of officers or departments of central government is unnecessary because they are accountable to Parliament for the way in which they carry out their functions. They are accountable to Parliament for what they do so far as regards efficiency and policy, and of that Parliament is the only judge; they are responsible to a court of justice for the lawfulness of what they do, and of that the court is the only judge. (*R v Inland Revenue Comrs, ex p National Federation of Self-Employed and Small Businesses Ltd* [1982] AC 617, 644)

❯ CROSS REFERENCE
See Chapters 15 and 16

While the monarch cannot be sued in her personal capacity in her own courts, ministers of the Crown can also be sued for breaching the law. As Lord Templeman has explained:

> The judges cannot enforce the law against the Crown as monarch because the Crown as monarch can do no wrong but judges enforce the law against the Crown as executive and against the individuals who from time to time represent the Crown. A litigant complaining of a breach of the law by the executive can sue the Crown as executive bringing his action against the minister who is responsible for the department of state involved. (*M v Home Office* [1994] 1 AC 377, 395)

In order to enforce the law, the courts have power to grant remedies including injunctions against a minister in their official capacity. If the minister has personally broken the law, the litigant can sue the minister in their personal capacity.

The Crown Proceedings Act 1947 was introduced to enable legal proceedings to be brought against government *departments* for the first time, removing many immunities of the Crown in civil cases (though some are preserved, notably the Queen's personal immunity from being sued).

12.4.3 **The monarch**

The Queen has the right 'to be consulted, to encourage, and to warn' her ministers in private; this includes the right to advise (Walter Bagehot, *The English Constitution*, London: Chapman and Hall, p 103). The Queen may retain the right to dismiss a Prime Minister who is acting unconstitutionally, but she would need to be advised that it was in the national interest.

12.4.4 **Self-regulation**

The conduct of government ministers is regulated by the *Ministerial Code*. Ministers of the Crown are required 'to maintain high standards of behaviour and to behave in a way that upholds the highest standards of propriety' (*Ministerial Code*, Cabinet Office, August 2019 [1.1]). The Seven Principles of Public Life in Annex A require ministers to act with selflessness, integrity, objectivity, accountability, openness, honesty, and leadership. The Code includes a provision that 'harassing, bullying or other inappropriate or discriminating behaviour wherever it takes place is not consistent with the *Ministerial Code* and will not be tolerated' ([1.2]).

The Prime Minister is the ultimate judge of the standards of behaviour expected of a minister. When there are allegations of a breach of the Code, the Prime Minister may, if s/he feels that it warrants further investigation after consulting the Cabinet Secretary, (a) ask the Cabinet Office to investigate the facts and/or (b) refer the allegations to the independent advisor on ministers' interests ([1.4]). The Director-General of the Propriety and Ethics Team will investigate the matter.

12.4.5 **External scrutiny**

 CROSS REFERENCE

See section 14.2 on public inquiries

Public inquiries set up by government to examine matters of public concern act as an independent scrutiny mechanism and can hold government or other public bodies to account (for example, the Scott, Hutton, and Butler Inquiries). However, the government is not bound to accept the inquiry's recommendations and may terminate an inquiry midway through, as happened with the Gibson Inquiry.

 EXAMPLE

The Gibson Inquiry was a judicial inquiry into whether UK security and intelligence agencies were involved in the improper treatment or rendition of detainees held by other countries after the terrorist attacks of 9/11 (the 'detainee inquiry'). It was set up by the Prime Minister in 2010 but in 2012 the Justice Secretary, Kenneth Clarke, announced that the Inquiry would not proceed as the police and MI5 were investigating allegations of improper treatment. In 2013, the Inquiry published its report (*The Report of the Detainee Inquiry*, December 2013), which highlighted 27 areas of concern that it would like to have investigated further, raising important questions about the intelligence agencies' and government's policies, procedures, and conduct in relation to detainees.

A range of independent audit, regulation, and inspection bodies monitor and scrutinise government policy and delivery of services and may be required to report formally to Parliament, enabling it to hold government to account. More broadly, campaign groups and think-tanks publish reports scrutinising aspects of government; their findings can influence public opinion and government itself. Not least, media scrutiny of government policy and decisions is at the forefront of influence and public attention.

SUMMARY

- Government is subject to constant scrutiny and inquiry from a range of sources
- Prerogative powers are exercised by, or on the advice of, ministers in the absence of a statute, and cover important areas of governmental activity which are often essential to the effective operation of the state, including emergency powers

- Ministers are politically accountable to Parliament for their decisions but they are also answerable to the law
- Collective responsibility promotes collective decision-making and enables Parliament to hold the whole government to account

? Questions

Self-test questions

1. What are the main roles of central government?
2. Outline the organisation of central government.
3. What are the Prime Minister's powers and what is the role of the Cabinet?
4. What is an arm's length body?
5. What is the accountability issue with arm's length bodies?
6. What is the royal prerogative? Give three examples of prerogative executive powers.
7. How can a statute affect a prerogative power?
8. What was the significance of the *GCHQ case*?
9. Explain (a) individual ministerial responsibility and (b) collective responsibility.
10. What is the Haldane convention?

Exam question

Sir Robin Butler has described 'the accountability paradox', where Parliament has more control over ministers through ministerial responsibility than it has over arm's length bodies. Discuss the extent to which this is an accurate description.

☰ Further reading

Books

Hennessy, P. *The Prime Minister: The Office and Its Holders since 1945* (London: Penguin 2001).
A readable account of the role of Prime Minister

King, A. *Who Governs Britain?* (London: Pelican 2015).
A concise overview of UK central government

Journal articles

Finer, S.E. 'The Individual Responsibility of Ministers' (1956) 34(4) Public Administration 377–396.
Examines when ministerial resignation is required

Foster, Sir C. 'Cabinet Government in the Twentieth Century' (2004) 67(5) MLR 753.
Examines the development of, and changes to, Cabinet, with interesting insights

Howell, J. 'What the Crown May Do' (2010) 15(1) Judicial Review 36.
Analyses the Crown's common law powers debate

Markesinis, B.S. 'The Royal Prerogative Re-Visited' (1973) 32(2) CLJ 287–309.
A classic account of the prerogative and its historical control (though pre-*GCHQ case*)

Norton, P. (Lord Norton of Louth), 'Governing Alone' (2003) 56(4) Parliamentary Affairs 543.
Commentary on the fragmentation of the Westminster model of government

Riddell, P. 'Prime Ministers and Parliament' (2004) 57(4) Parliamentary Affairs 814–829.
Interesting observations on changes in the role of Prime Minister, particularly the presidential Prime Minister issue

Scott, Sir R. 'Ministerial Accountability' (1996) (Autumn) Public Law 410–26.
A post-inquiry analysis of the nature of ministerial responsibility

Other sources

Bartlett, G. and Everett, M. *The Royal Prerogative*, House of Commons Library Briefing Paper Number 03861, 17 August 2017.
A very helpful source

Cabinet Manual 2011 (at www.gov.uk/government/publications/cabinet-manual).
An essential point of reference

Endicott, T. *Parliament and the Prerogative: From the Case of Proclamations to Miller*, Judicial Power Project, 1 December 2016 (at judicialpowerproject.org.uk/wp-content/uploads/2016/12/Endicott-2016-Parliament-and-the-Prerogative.pdf).
Tracks views on executive power through the centuries; interesting to see the evolution

Winetrobe, B. *The Accountability Debate: Ministerial Responsibility*, House of Commons Library, Research Paper 97/6, 28 January 1997.
An excellent source on the accountability/responsibility debate

Useful websites

www.gov.uk/government/history/past-prime-ministers

www.gov.uk/government/how-government-works

Online resources

www.oup.com/he/dennett2e

This chapter is accompanied by a selection of online resources to help you with this topic, including:

- Multiple-choice questions
- Answers to the self-test questions
- Guidance on answering the exam question

13 The judiciary

LEARNING OBJECTIVES

By the end of this chapter, you should be able to:

- Evaluate the importance and operation of judicial independence and judicial neutrality
- Appraise the application of the rule of law and separation of powers
- Evaluate the impact of the Constitutional Reform Act 2005
- Appreciate issues arising from the judiciary's relationship with Parliament and the government
- Be aware of debate on limitations on judicial power

Introduction

On 21 March 2018, Baroness Hale, former President of the Supreme Court, warned a parliamentary select committee that the EU (Withdrawal) Bill, as then drafted, might lead judges into making political decisions after Brexit. Can judges do that? Does it breach separation of powers? We find out later how this works.

In this chapter, we examine the role of the judiciary in the UK constitution, the critically important concepts of judicial independence and neutrality (including the impact of the Constitutional Reform Act 2005 on the judiciary's relationship with the executive), accountability of judges, and judicial power. This prepares you for the next section of the book, on administrative law. The chapter also builds on separation of powers principles by examining in more depth the subtleties of the interaction between the judiciary and the other branches of state.

Recap on the separation of powers

The judiciary acts as a check on government power by enforcing the rule of law against the executive through judicial review. The courts co-exist and avoid conflict with Parliament, respect its sovereignty, and have no power to question the validity of Acts of the UK Parliament. Equally, Parliament respects the courts' independence and neutrality, although it can change the common law by statute. Figure 13.1 summarises key points.

>> CROSS REFERENCE

See Chapters 6, 7, and 8

Figure 13.1 The judiciary's constitutional position

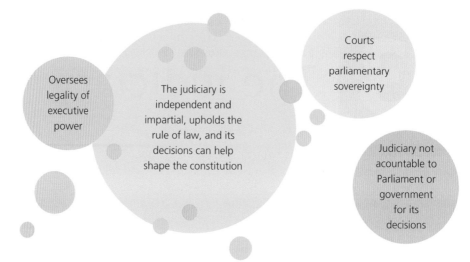

13.1 The role of the judiciary in the constitution

The Latimer House Principles state: 'An independent, impartial, honest and competent judiciary is integral to upholding the rule of law, engendering public confidence and dispensing justice' (Commonwealth (Latimer House) Principles on the Three Branches of Government 2004 (adopted by the Commonwealth in 2003), Principle IV Independence of the Judiciary). The UK courts:

- administer justice;
- uphold the rule of law;
- act as a check on executive power.

 THINKING POINT

Note how the concepts in what follows interlink, especially through the recurrent theme of judicial independence.

13.1.1 The administration of justice

The administration of justice is 'the constitutional responsibility of the courts' (*R (Privacy International) v Investigatory Powers Tribunal* [2017] EWHC 114 (Admin) [50] (Leggatt J)). It is a fundamental value, safeguarded by a judiciary that is independent of the government and Parliament to avoid undue influence over its decision-making. It is essential that there is unhindered access to the courts, a guaranteed fair hearing by judges who are impartial and politically neutral in their decision-making, and that justice is administered openly, with trials conducted, and judgments given, in public (see *Bank Mellat v HM Treasury (No 1)* [2013] UKSC 38 [2-3] (Lord Neuberger); [81] (Lord Hope)).

Justice is administered every day in the courts by judges determining legal disputes through interpreting and applying the law made by Parliament, creating and applying common law, and assessing the compatibility of Parliament's statutes with the Human Rights Act 1998 (as instructed by Parliament). Furthermore, in resolving legal constitutional questions, judges also help to shape the constitution; see, for example, *R (Miller) v Secretary of State for Exiting the European Union* [2017] UKSC 5 ('*Miller I*') and (*R (Miller) v The Prime Minister; Cherry v Advocate General for Scotland* [2019] UKSC 41).

13.1.2 Upholding the rule of law

The judiciary plays a critical role in upholding the rule of law on behalf of the people (see *Miller I* [42]). When he became Lord Chancellor in 2017, David Lidington referred to the rule of law and the independence of the judiciary as 'the very bedrock of a free and democratic society' (David Lidington MP, Speech at his Lord Chancellor swearing-in ceremony, 19 June 2017). His successor, David Gauke, said in 2018: 'You, the judiciary, are at the heart of the Rule of Law. You uphold and exercise that every day in the judgments and decisions you make' (Speech given by the Rt Hon David Gauke at his Lord Chancellor swearing-in ceremony, 18 January 2018). Impartial, independent judges, accessible justice, and determination of cases according to the law are visible features of the rule of law, and promote public confidence in the judiciary and the justice system.

❯ CROSS REFERENCE

For details on the rule of law, see Chapter 8

13.1.3 Calling the executive to account

Lord Neuberger has commented that '[w]ith the ever-increasing power of Government . . . this function of calling the executive to account could not be more important' ('Justice in an Age of Austerity', Justice–Tom Sargant Memorial Lecture 2013), and the judiciary acts as a strong check on the arbitrary or unlawful exercise of government power through the mechanism of judicial review:

> The rule of law requires that the courts have jurisdiction to scrutinise the actions of government to ensure that they are lawful . . . it is from executive pressure or influence that judges require particularly to be protected. (Lord Phillips, 'Judicial Independence and Accountability: A View from the Supreme Court', Constitution Unit Lecture, 8 February 2011)

Given that public law cases form more than half the Supreme Court's workload (Lord Phillips, 'Judicial Independence and Accountability', p 19) it is essential that the judiciary is independent of the executive, and it is to the key concept of judicial independence that we turn next.

13.2 Judicial independence

> 'Judicial independence describes the position of a judge upon whom no outside influences are brought to bear, direct or indirect, in relation to the performance of his judicial duties.' (Lord Phillips of Worth Matravers, Ev. Q16 House of Lords Select Committee on the Constitution, *The Office of Lord Chancellor*, 6th Report of Session 2014–15, HL Paper 75 [27])

Judicial independence requires that judges should be free from external influences in their decision-making, and make decisions without political interference or fear of reprisal. This is upheld in the judicial oath, which provides: 'I will do right to all manner of people after the laws and usages of this Realm, without fear or favour, affection or ill-will.' There are various factors which could potentially influence judges' decisions: fear of losing office, or being punished or sued for the outcome of a case; government or parliamentary pressure on how they decide a case; being criticised or attacked for their decisions; being subject to abuse in court; or being influenced by the media, public opinion, parties to a case, or even other judges not involved in the case.

Chris Grayling, a former Lord Chancellor and Minister for Justice, captured the elements of judicial independence when he defined the rule of law as:

> [A]n independent justice system, free from interference from outside, free from corruption, free from influence, that is respected and treated as independent by those in Government and those in Parliament, and . . . we respect the ability of the courts and the responsibility of the courts to take decisions according to their best judgment about what the law of the land requires. (Constitution Committee, *The Office of Lord Chancellor* Ev. Q49 [18])

The features of an independent judiciary are:

- security of tenure;
- a judiciary that is separate from the executive and legislature;
- judicial immunity from civil liability for what judges say and do in exercising their judicial function;
- protection from criticism by ministers or in Parliament;
- protection of the administration of justice.

Each feature is explained in what follows, before we examine the practical application of some in more depth (see also Lord Hodge's ten pillars to ensure judicial independence in 'Upholding the Rule of Law: How We Preserve Judicial Independence in the United Kingdom', Lincoln's Inn Denning Society, 7 November 2016).

13.2.1 Security of tenure

This means that holding judicial office is protected by statute. Until 1701, judges were often appointed—and dismissed—at the King's pleasure, which meant that their appointment was dependent on the wishes of the monarch. In 1701, the Act of Settlement established judicial independence by providing for security of tenure 'during good behaviour'; consequently, judges, once appointed, are guaranteed to stay in office as long as they conduct themselves well. This applies to judges of the High Court, Court of Appeal, and Supreme Court, who hold office during good behaviour and can only be removed from office through an address to the Queen agreed by both Houses of Parliament (for more on this, see section 13.4.2). The importance of security of tenure is that judges cannot be arbitrarily dismissed by the monarch, government, or Parliament for their decisions in court or for political reasons. This ensures the judiciary's independence, safeguards its freedom from political interference, and removes fear of punishment or loss of office for judicial decision-making.

 THINKING POINT

How would appointment at the government's pleasure be likely to affect membership of the judiciary and judicial decision-making?

13.2.2 Judicial separation from the executive and the legislature

❱ CROSS REFERENCE
See further section 13.5.2

Judicial separation from the executive and the legislature prevents political interference in judicial decisions. Lord Irvine, a former Lord Chancellor, expressed it in this way: 'The Executive cannot tell the judges how to decide cases, civil or criminal, nor what sentences in criminal cases to impose within the discretion conferred by Parliament. Any Executive is capable of being tempted, but Executive interference with judicial independence must never be allowed' (HL Hansard 17 February 1999, Vol 597 col 734).

Before 2005, there were strong links between the judiciary and the executive through the Lord Chancellor, who was a Cabinet minister, presided over the House of Lords, and was a senior judge, which raised at least theoretical issues of (a) executive influence on the judiciary and (b) deciding cases on the basis of legislation that he had helped to create. The latter point also applied to the Law Lords who sat in the House of Lords until 2009. Before the creation of the Supreme Court, the Law Lords trod a delicate line between bringing judicial expertise to debates in the House of Lords' chamber in Parliament, and engaging in controversial debate which risked undermining their political impartiality. If they criticised government decisions in the chamber, they were not able to sit as a judge in any subsequent case involving that decision.

 EXAMPLE

Law Lords who opposed the Home Secretary's introduction of a cheaper criminal injuries compensation scheme, using prerogative power instead of bringing into force a fairer statutory scheme, were unable to be members of the House of Lords Appellate Committee in *R v Secretary of State for the Home Department ex parte Fire Brigades Union* [1995] 2 AC 513, which subsequently decided that the Home Secretary had acted unlawfully.

For an example of a judge (Lord Hoffmann) proposing a legislative amendment in Parliament, see House of Commons Library Research Paper 96/61, 16 May 1996.

Q CASE CLOSE-UP: *McGONNELL v UK* (2000) 30 EHRR 289

The case of *McGonnell v UK* (2000) 30 EHRR 289 made it clear that where a judge also has connections with legislative or executive bodies, there is a contravention of Article 6 ECHR. Article 6(1) provides that 'everyone is entitled to a fair and public hearing within a reasonable time by an independent and impartial tribunal established by law'. The European Court of Human Rights stated that there needed to be the appearance of independence, and that independence and objective impartiality were closely linked.

As a result of this decision, the Lord Chancellor undertook not to sit as a judge in cases involving legislation with which he had been involved. (See also *Procola v Luxembourg* [1995] ECHR 33 and *Davidson v The Scottish Ministers* [2004] UKHL 34.)

In 2005, the Constitutional Reform Act (CRA) radically strengthened the separation between the judiciary and the executive and brought a re-organisation of responsibility, increasing the judiciary's independence and accountability (see *Cabinet Manual* p 4 [16] and [6.37–6.41]).

❱ CROSS REFERENCE
See also section 7.5

STATUTE: THE CONSTITUTIONAL REFORM ACT 2005 AND JUDICIAL INDEPENDENCE

Section 1 upholds the rule of law. Judicial independence is now guaranteed by section 3, the first time it has been protected by statute (this provision was added as a result of the 2004 concordat (agreement) between Lord Woolf and Lord Falconer).

Under section 3(1), the Lord Chancellor and other government ministers have a duty to uphold the continued independence of the judiciary, although there are no prescribed sanctions if they do not do so.

Section 3(5) provides that the Lord Chancellor and other ministers must not try to influence judicial decisions through special access to the judiciary. This ensures that the judiciary can act without undue pressure from the executive.

By section 3(6), the Lord Chancellor must consider:

(a) the need to defend judicial independence;

(b) the need for the judiciary to have the necessary support to exercise their functions;

(c) the need for the public interest in matters relating to the judiciary or the administration of justice to be properly represented in decisions affecting those matters.

In other words, (b) and (c) require the Lord Chancellor to ensure that the justice system is adequately resourced and that public funds are used efficiently in doing so.

On taking office, the Lord Chancellor takes an oath to respect the rule of law, defend judicial independence, and ensure the provision of resources for the efficient and effective support of the courts (section 17(2)).

The 2005 Act also removed many judiciary/executive overlaps by passing the Lord Chancellor's responsibilities for judicial leadership and management to the judiciary itself, and removed the judiciary/Parliament overlap by creating the Supreme Court (see Figure 13.2).

13.2.2.1 The appointment of judges

UK judges are appointed to office, not elected. Senior judges are formally appointed by the Queen on the advice of her ministers, but before the CRA 2005 the executive was actively involved in selecting judges, who were appointed on the Lord Chancellor's recommendation.

THINKING POINT

What are the potential issues where judges are appointed by the executive?

Lord Hodge has pointed out that the pre-2005 system of appointment 'worked rather well' because the Lord Chancellor selected candidates on merit after taking informal soundings and consulting with the judiciary ('Upholding the Rule of Law' [16]). This 'tap on the shoulder' approach was based on ascertaining judicial ability, following the principle established by Lord Haldane in the early twentieth century of appointments based on legal qualification and not political views. Nevertheless, the Lord Chancellor had become strongly embedded within the executive and political sphere (see Diana Woodhouse, 'The Office of Lord Chancellor: Time to Abandon the Judicial Role—The Rest Will Follow' (2002) 22 Legal Studies 128).

Figure 13.2 How the CRA strengthened judicial separation

| The Lord Chief Justice replaced the Lord Chancellor as the head of the judiciary. The LCJ is also President of the Courts of England and Wales. The head of the judiciary in Scotland is the Lord President of the Court of Session and in Northern Ireland, the Lord Chief Justice of Northern Ireland | • The Lord Chief Justice is responsible for representing judicial concerns and views to Parliament and government ministers, for judicial welfare, training and guidance, and allocation of work in the courts (s 7 CRA) |

| The Supreme Court replaced the judicial function of the House of Lords as the final court of appeal for all UK civil cases and all criminal cases in England, Wales and Northern Ireland (s 23 CRA) | • Justices of the Supreme Court are no longer members of the legislature, although former Law Lords still take part in debates
• New Justices of the Supreme Court do not automatically receive life peerages |

The CRA 2005 limited executive involvement in judicial appointments. Since April 2006, judges have been appointed by the independent Judicial Appointments Commission to ensure openness and transparency (sections 61–107 CRA). The Commission selects candidates for judicial appointment on merit through fair and open competition; for judicial appointments to the High Court and above, it makes recommendations for appointment to the Lord Chancellor, who has only a limited power to accept, reject, or ask for reconsideration of recommended candidates. For judicial appointments below the High Court, the Lord Chief Justice accepts, rejects, or asks for reconsideration of recommendations.

🔍 CLOSE-UP FOCUS: JUDICIAL DIVERSITY

A judiciary that reflects society is important for legitimacy, but the lack of diversity in the judiciary has been an issue and remains a priority. In October 2005, 26 per cent of judges were women and 5 per cent were BAME (black, Asian, and minority ethnic). In recent years, there have been moves to broaden the judicial profile.

- Under section 64 of the CRA, the Judicial Appointments Commission has a duty to 'encourage diversity in the range of persons available for selection for appointments' (see also section 63).
- In 2013, a Judicial Diversity Committee was created to speed up progress.
- The Crime and Courts Act 2013 (Schedule 13 Part 2) introduced provisions to further improve the transparency and diversity of judicial appointments, including:
  - An 'equal merit provision': where two individuals are of equal merit, a candidate can be selected on the basis of improving diversity.

- A requirement for the Lord Chancellor and Lord Chief Justice to take appropriate steps to encourage judicial diversity.

As of 1 April 2020, 21 per cent of Court of Appeal judges, 28 per cent of judges in the High Court, and 32 per cent of all court judges were female. Of BAME judges, 8 per cent were court judges and 12 per cent were tribunal judges. Four High Court judges and one Court of Appeal judge were BAME as at 1 April 2020 (www.gov.uk/government/statistics/diversity-of-the-judiciary-2020-statistics; justice.org.uk/wp-content/uploads/2020/01/Judicial-Diversity-Update-Report.pdf). Broader diversity has been slow to reach the senior courts, although as at September 2020, there were two female Justices of the Supreme Court: Lady Black and Lady Arden (Lady Hale, who became the first female President of the Supreme Court in 2017, retired in 2020). However, there has been criticism of the slow progress made on diversity, with the warning that 'a senior judiciary that so markedly does not reflect the ethnic, gender or social composition of the nation is a serious constitutional issue' *(Increasing Judicial Diversity*, A Report by Justice, April 2017). See also Constitution Committee, *Judicial Appointments*, 25th Report of Session 2010–12, HL Paper 272; Professor Alan Paterson OBE and Chris Paterson, *Guarding the Guardians? Towards an Independent, Accountable and Diverse Senior Judiciary*, CentreForum 2012.

13.2.3 **Judicial immunity**

Judges have immunity from suit; this means that they are protected from being sued in relation to acts carried out in performance of their judicial function within their jurisdiction, including actions for defamation for what they say while hearing cases, even if malicious. This allows judges to make decisions freely and independently without fear of being sued (see *Sirros v Moore* [1974] 3 AER 776 at 781J –782D; *Re McC (A minor)* [1985] AC 528; *Mazhar v Lord Chancellor* [2017] EWHC 2536 (Fam)).

13.2.4 **Protection from ministerial criticism**

By convention, judges should not be subject to personal criticism or attack by ministers or by Parliament, unless Parliament is debating their dismissal. This preserves respect for the dignity and authority of judges when exercising their judicial functions. In 1999, however, there was 'unprecedented antagonism between the judiciary and the Government' over judicial review of ministerial decisions (Lord Irvine of Lairg, HL Hansard 17 Feb 1999, Vol 597 col 734). David Blunkett, Home Secretary in the Blair government from 2001 to 2004, was openly critical of judges, particularly on judicial review and human rights decisions against ministers, as well as on sentencing powers (see Anthony Bradley, 'Judicial Independence under Attack' (2003) (Autumn) Public Law 397). Shortly before the *Miller/Cherry* case in 2019, Kwasi Kwarteng, Minister for Business, Energy and Clean Growth, was criticised for alleging that many people were questioning the partiality of judges (www.bbc.co.uk/news/uk-politics-49670901). In 2012, David Cameron, who had criticised decisions on occasion, took the *quid pro quo* view that 'judges make critical remarks about politicians; and . . . politicians make critical remarks about judges. To me, that is part of life in a modern democracy' (HC Deb 18 Apr 2012, Vol 543 col 317). For an example of criticism flowing the other way, see 'Lord Chief Justice Attacks Ministers' Quango Plans' at www.theguardian.com/politics/2010/dec/17/lord-judge-attacks-quango-plans.

Lord Dyson has observed extrajudicially that the convention against criticism of judges' decisions has been eroded, although judges' motives should not be criticised (see 'Criticising Judges: Fair Game or Off-Limits?' The Third Annual Bailii Lecture, 27 November 2014; see also judicial-powerproject.org.uk/wp-content/uploads/2018/02/JPP-submission-to-JCHR-inquiry.pdf [4–8]).

13.2.5 Protecting the administration of justice

The contempt laws protect the dignity of judicial office and the administration of justice. The Contempt of Court Act 1981 prevents conduct that prejudices the course of justice in active court proceedings, such as newspapers printing material that might affect the outcome of an ongoing criminal or civil case. Criminal contempt calculated to interfere with the administration of justice includes alleging that a judge is not impartial or abusing a judge in court. Civil contempt involves disobeying judgments and court orders.

 SUMMARY

The principle of judicial independence:

- Is a significant element of the rule of law
- Requires judges to be free from external influences and political interference by the government and Parliament
- Ensures fair hearings
- Protects the justice system and fosters public confidence in the judiciary
- The judiciary's independence from the executive enables individuals to challenge the legality of the actions of the executive in the courts through judicial review

13.3 Judicial neutrality

> Judicial neutrality means that judges should determine legal disputes impartially, objectively, and solely by applying the law.

Judicial neutrality is important because:

- Judges should be politically neutral and should only decide cases objectively in accordance with the law.
- They must not take part in political activities or give political views in public.
- They must be impartial and unbiased when making judicial decisions.

13.3.1 Political neutrality in decision-making

Judicial decisions must be free from politics: judges must not be swayed by party politics or allow their political beliefs or opinions to influence their judgments. The courts, however, operate in a largely political constitution. Judicial review in particular requires judges to determine the lawfulness of government action, and the issue is whether judges are making politically neutral judgments.

CASE CLOSE-UP: *BROMLEY LONDON BOROUGH COUNCIL v GREATER LONDON COUNCIL* [1983] 1 AC 768

At first sight, *Bromley* gives the appearance of unelected judges intervening in an elected body's policies.

The Greater London Council (GLC) introduced a scheme of reduced public transport fares in London to help people socially (Labour members had promised it in their election manifesto), but it would have to be subsidised by increased rates in London boroughs. The GLC had a duty under the Transport (London) Act 1969 to develop and encourage measures to promote integrated, efficient, and economic transport for Greater London. The House of Lords Appellate Committee interpreted the statute as meaning that services should be run in accordance with ordinary business principles and be cost-effective, and the GLC's financial duty to ratepayers not to run the system at a loss took precedence over the manifesto promise, therefore the transport subsidy was illegal.

THINKING POINT

What was guiding the court's decision in *Bromley*—politics or interpretation of a statute?

THE BIGGER PICTURE

Griffith analysed the judiciary's relationship with politics and argued that judicial neutrality is a myth because the way in which judges decide cases can be influenced by their upbringing, education, social class, and political beliefs. If judges are from similar backgrounds (white, male, middle class, educated at public school and Oxbridge, coming to the Bench from the Bar), it can influence and define their view of what the public interest is. Griffith found common themes in judicial decisions in the 1970s and 1980s, where judges supported the police, property rights, and the interests of the state, and were anti-trade unions. See J.A.G. Griffith, *The Politics of the Judiciary* (5th edn, London: Fontana Press, 1997).

For the view that 'there is no such thing as the relationship between law and politics. Law and politics collide and combine in a dazzling variety of (not always compatible) ways', see Adam Tomkins, 'In Defence of the Political Constitution' (2002) 22(1) Oxford Journal of Legal Studies 157, 169. See also Jonathan Sumption, The Reith Lectures 2019: Law and the Decline of Politics, available at www.bbc.co.uk/radio4; and www.lawgazette.co.uk/news/new-attorney-general-criticised-unelected-unaccountable-judges/5103089.article.

13.3.2 Speaking out in public

In 1955, Lord Kilmuir, the Lord Chancellor, wrote to the Director General of the BBC to prevent serving judges from taking part in interviews on the basis that silence preserved their reputation for wisdom, and 'every utterance made in public', except in court, exposed judges to criticism.

The Kilmuir Rules, as they became known, were revoked in 1987 by Lord Mackay of Clashfern, a subsequent Lord Chancellor; this enabled judges to express their views publicly, often in extrajudicial speeches, though they must exercise caution on controversial subjects and when commenting publicly on decisions in individual cases (see *Supreme Court Guide to Judicial Conduct* (2019) [2.5]).

 EXAMPLE

Extrajudicial comment has the potential to affect decisions. In a newspaper interview in 2009, Lord Phillips, then a Law Lord, admitted supporting assisted suicide as a personal view after he had been a member of the House of Lords Appellate Committee in *R (Purdy) v DPP* [2009] UKHL 45, which involved issues of assisted suicide. Campaigners subsequently brought an application to have the *Purdy* decision set aside on the grounds of apparent bias (giving the appearance of bias), although this was unsuccessful. (See Lord Hope, 'What Happens When the Judge Speaks Out?' Holdsworth Club Presidential Address, 19 February 2010, p 7; www.telegraph.co.uk/news/uknews/law-and-order/6170706/Lord-Phillips-new-era-as-Law-Lords-face-supreme-challenge.html.)

See also Lord Neuberger of Abbotsbury MR, 'Where Angels Fear to Tread', Holdsworth Club 2012 Presidential Address, 2 March 2012; Constitution Committee, *Relations between the Executive, the Judiciary and Parliament,* 6th Report of Session 2006–07, HL Paper 151, chapter 4: Judiciary, Media and Public.

Judges now exercise an important outreach role, promoting public understanding and awareness of the work and role of the judiciary. Lord Thomas, a former Lord Chief Justice, makes the point that judicial independence does not mean judicial isolation and that it is necessary in the 'changing constitutional landscape' to engage with the public to protect justice and an independent judiciary ('Judicial Independence in a Changing Constitutional Landscape', Speech to the Commonwealth Magistrates' and Judges' Association, 15 September 2015 [28, 31, 39]). See also The Lord Chief Justice's Report 2017, p 6 (www.judiciary.uk/wp-content/uploads/2017/09/lcj-report-2017-final.pdf).

However, the Constitution Committee has noted that since the Kilmuir Rules were revoked and judges have spoken more openly, they are seen as 'fair game' by the tabloid press and have correspondingly been subject to greater public criticism by some ministers (*Relations between the Executive, the Judiciary and Parliament* [146]). A prime example of this is the reaction to the High Court decision in *Miller 1* (*R (Miller) v Secretary of State for Exiting the European Union* [2016] EWHC 2768 (Admin)), which unleashed a barrage of media criticism, where the judges were called 'enemies of the people' by a national newspaper (*Daily Mail*, 4 November 2016). Lord Burnett CJ has expressed the view that while judges should not be immune from criticism for their decisions, they are increasingly facing personal abuse online and on social media for their decisions, which could undermine the rule of law (Press Conference, The Lord Chief Justice of England and Wales, 5 December 2017 at The Royal Courts of Justice, London; see also www.theguardian.com/law/2017/dec/05/lord-chief-justice-judges-face-increasing-torrent-of-threats-and-abuse). Giving evidence to the Constitution Committee in 2019, Baroness Hale discussed the issue of media pressure, stating that, ultimately, the judiciary had to uphold the law and adjudicate on the arguments in front of them no matter what the media thought of it. It was also important that judges acted according to their oaths without fear or favour, affection or ill will, which social media could affect if they paid too much attention to it (Select Committee on the Constitution, Uncorrected oral evidence: President and Deputy President of the Supreme Court, 20 March 2019, Qs 5 and 6). Fear of personal abuse could compromise judicial independence, and if judges are publicly criticised they do not have a corresponding platform from which to respond; it can damage their independence to be drawn into a public debate, although as we see in section 13.5.2.1, there *are* outlets for judicial response to criticism.

13.3.3 Impartial decision-making

The rule of law requires that judges should be impartial, deciding issues on the law and facts of the case. Judicial decisions should not be influenced by any external interest or pressure and should be free from bias and prejudice or any appearance of it, so that justice is seen to be done. Bias means 'a prejudice against one party or its case for reasons unconnected with the legal or factual merits of the case' (*Bubbles & Wine Ltd v Lusha* [2018] EWCA Civ 468, [17] (Leggatt LJ)).

The Supreme Court *Guide to Judicial Conduct* (2019) sets out political and extra-judicial activities that Justices should avoid because of the risk of the appearance of bias, conflict of interest, or not being detached from the political process; even political activity by a close family member might raise concerns about impartiality. Justices should also be aware of situations suggesting favouritism in relation to members of the legal profession, and must not sit in a case where they have close family relationships or friendships with a party, advocate, or a judge in a court below, or a significant financial interest in the outcome of the case (see [3.2–3.6 and 3.9–3.12]).

Where a judge has a relevant interest in the subject matter of a case, s/he is disqualified from sitting. 'What disqualifies the judge is the presence of some factor which could prevent the bringing of an objective judgment to bear, which could distort the judge's judgment' (*Davidson v Scottish Ministers* [2004] UKHL 34 [6] (Lord Bingham)).

CASE CLOSE-UP: *R v BOW STREET METROPOLITAN STIPENDIARY MAGISTRATE EX P PINOCHET UGARTE (NO 1)* [2000] 1 AC 61

The House of Lords' decision in *R v Bow Street Metropolitan Stipendiary Magistrate, ex p Pinochet Ugarte* (No 1) [2000] 1 AC 61 was set aside and heard again by a different panel of Law Lords because one of the judges, Lord Hoffmann, had links with a party to the case, Amnesty International (AI), a human rights organisation. The case involved whether General Pinochet, the former president of Chile, was entitled to immunity in respect of charges of torture. Lord Hoffmann had been a director and chair of a subsidiary of AI, Amnesty International Charity Limited, and his wife had worked for them for many years in administrative roles. Even though there was no allegation of actual bias, this gave the *appearance* of not being impartial (*R v Bow Street Metropolitan Stipendiary Magistrate, ex p Pinochet Ugarte (No 2)* [2000] 1 AC 119).

SUMMARY

- The rule of law requires judges to be impartial
- Judicial decisions must be free from politics and made in accordance with the law

- They must be free from bias or the appearance of bias, and not influenced by external factors
- Judges may speak out publicly but must exercise caution

13.4 Accountability of the judiciary

Quis custodiet ipsos custodes is a Latin maxim which means 'who watches over those who guard?' It is often referred to in the context of 'who judges the judges'.

At first sight, judicial accountability seems inconsistent with being independent, but it is essential that the judiciary adheres to the highest standards in carrying out its functions. The Bangalore Principles of Judicial Conduct 2002, adopted by the United Nations Human Rights Commission on Human Rights in 2003, set out a framework of standards for regulating and guiding judicial conduct based on six principles:

(i) Judicial independence

(ii) Impartiality

(iii) Integrity

(iv) Propriety and the appearance of propriety

(v) Ensuring equality of treatment to all before the courts

(vi) Competence and diligence

These principles have been distilled into UK judicial guidance. A *Guide to Judicial Conduct* was first published by the Judges' Council in 2004 and the current version sets out guidance to judges based on judicial independence, impartiality and integrity (*Guide to Judicial Conduct*, March 2020; see www.judiciary.uk). The Supreme Court has issued its own *Guide to Judicial Conduct* (2019) setting out guidance and standards of ethical conduct to be expected of the Court (available at www.supremecourt.uk/docs/guide-to-judicial-conduct.pdf).

With increased post-2005 independence and responsibilities came more accountability (see Lord Thomas, 'Judicial Leadership', Conference on the Paradox of Judicial Independence, UCL Constitution Unit, 22 June 2015 [38–47]). Judicial accountability can be individual (applying to individual judges) or institutional (applying to the judiciary as a whole), and the Judicial Executive Board and the Judges' Council recognised two specific types of judicial accountability in 2007:

- explanatory;
- sacrificial.

13.4.1 **Explanatory accountability**

This means explaining judicial actions or decisions, and can apply on an individual or institutional basis. Judicial accountability can take place through:

- giving the reasons for judicial decisions in judgments;
- the appeal process;
- hearings in open court with public access where justice can be seen to be done;

- annual reports to Parliament by judges in leadership positions such as the Lord Chief Justice;
- judicial appearances before parliamentary select committees;
- speeches and lectures promoting public understanding of the role of the judiciary;
- publishing guides setting out expectations for judicial conduct.

See Lord Hodge, 'Upholding the Rule of Law' ([26]).

Even public criticism of judicial performance can be a means of ensuring accountability if it is *legitimate* (Latimer House Guidelines for the Commonwealth, 19 June 1998, Principle VI). There is also institutional accountability through the Lord Chancellor's consideration of the public interest in funding and resourcing the judicial system, which requires the Lord Chief Justice to justify the efficient spending of public money.

13.4.2 **Sacrificial accountability**

This refers to being disciplined or dismissed because of misconduct (see Lord Justice Beatson, 'Judicial Independence: Internal and External Challenges and Opportunities', Atkin Lecture, The Reform Club, London, 14 November 2017 [11]).

 THINKING POINT: THE ISSUE OF JUDICIAL PERFORMANCE

A system of regular appraisals for judges has been discussed in recent years (see Constitution Committee, *Judicial Appointments* [181–187]), and a head of division may speak to a judge whose judgments are regularly being overturned on appeal. What issues arise if a judge could be dismissed for having judgments frequently overturned on appeal?

Before the CRA 2005, disciplinary matters were decided by the Lord Chancellor. Since the Act, the Lord Chancellor and the Lord Chief Justice have been jointly responsible for judicial discipline, and there are now formal complaints procedures in place. Judges who are subject to disciplinary proceedings for misconduct will not necessarily be removed from office; they may be given a formal warning or reprimand by the Lord Chief Justice, or suspended from office, but any disciplinary sanctions need the agreement of the Lord Chief Justice and the Lord Chancellor. Judges may voluntarily resign after a finding of misconduct, but the process for removing a judge from office is set out in Table 13.1.

We turn now to examine the boundaries between the judiciary and the other branches of state (see also Chapter 7).

Table 13.1 Procedure for removal from office

Justices of the Supreme Court	Are removable only by an address to the Queen by both Houses of Parliament (Constitutional Reform Act 2005 section 33); this means that Parliament makes the decision
Judges of the Court of Appeal and High Court	Are removable only by an address to the Queen by both Houses of Parliament under s 11(3) Senior Courts Act 1981. The Lord Chancellor then recommends removal to the Queen (section 11(3A)). No English High Court or Court of Appeal judge has been removed under this power. (It has only been used to remove Sir Jonah Barrington as a judge of the Irish Courts for misappropriating funds in 1830.) Section 11(8) provides for compulsory retirement if a judge is incapacitated for medical reasons
Circuit and District Judges	Can be removed from office for professional misconduct by the Lord Chancellor with the agreement of the Lord Chief Justice after disciplinary proceedings

13.5 The judiciary's relationship with the government and Parliament

Since the CRA 2005, the senior judiciary have had a more interactive relationship with both government and Parliament, which blends 'independence and interdependence, with due respect afforded to the roles and functions of each branch of the State' (The Lord Chief Justice's Report 2017, p 31; see also Lord Thomas of Cwmgiedd, 'The Judiciary within the State—The Relationship between the Branches of the State', Michael Ryle Memorial Lecture, 15 June 2017; Lord Thomas, 'The Judiciary, the Executive and Parliament: Relationships and the Rule of Law', Institute for Government, 1 December 2014). However, judicial dialogue and engagement with the other two branches of state must *always* operate within the overriding requirement not to compromise judicial independence.

13.5.1 **The judiciary and Parliament**

In the post-2005 landscape, serving judges are no longer members of the House of Lords legislative chamber. Although this removed a channel of communication between the judiciary and Parliament, other channels of interaction have strengthened:

- The Lord Chief Justice has a duty to represent the views of the judiciary to Parliament and ministers (section 7(2)(a) CRA 2005).

- The Lord Chief Justice can make written representations to Parliament on matters of importance relating to the judiciary or the administration of justice (section 5(1) CRA 2005; *Cabinet Manual* [6.40]).

- Senior judges give evidence to parliamentary select committees; for example, once a year, the Lord Chief Justice and the President and Deputy President of the Supreme Court appear before the House of Lords Constitution Committee, and the Lord Chief Justice also appears before the House of Commons Justice Committee.

> **Q CLOSE-UP FOCUS: JUDICIAL APPEARANCES BEFORE SELECT COMMITTEES**
>
> Judges appeared before parliamentary select committees even before the CRA but the practice has increased markedly since 2004, corresponding with the constitutional changes being made at that time; there were 296 appearances by serving judges before parliamentary committees between 1979 and 2014 (The Politics of Judicial Independence Project Conference note, *Conference on the Paradox of Judicial Independence*, Institute of Government, 22 June 2015, p 3).
>
> This process facilitates a productive dialogue between the judiciary and Parliament, informing Parliament about 'front line' issues and the broader impact of its laws. However, it must be carefully managed. The Judicial Executive Board has produced guidance for judges on appearing before select committees and makes it clear that such appearances are

exceptional (*Guidance to Judges on Appearances before Select Committees*, October 2012, available at www.judiciary.uk). To maintain judicial independence, they should not comment on individual cases, or the meaning or likely effect of provisions in a Bill with limited exceptions, and the *Cabinet Manual* makes it clear that judges must not comment on government policy or on matters that might disqualify them from sitting in a subsequent case (*Cabinet Manual* [6.40]).

While appearing before select committees enables judges to comment on proposed legislation, it *only* applies to how those proposals might affect the operation of the courts or the administration of justice.

The interactive dialogue can be seen in this example. Between November 2017 and March 2018, senior judges (Baroness Hale and Lord Mance) and former judges (including Lord Hope, Lord Neuberger, and Lord Thomas) gave evidence to select committees on Clause 6(2) of the European Union (Withdrawal) Bill. The clause set out how judges would interpret retained EU law after Britain left the EU and provided that it was a matter for a judge whether to take into account a decision of the Court of Justice of the EU on a particular point. They drew attention to the lack of guidance in the clause as drafted, which gave too wide a discretion to judges—leaving open the possibility of taking into account political or economic factors, which are matters for the legislature, not judges, and raising the risk of politicising the judiciary. However, Baroness Hale made it clear that it was not the judges' job to tell government what they would like to see in proposed legislation: 'We think that is inappropriate from a separation of powers point of view . . . What we can do is point out the problems with any existing draft' (Select Committee on the Constitution, Uncorrected oral evidence: President and Deputy President of the Supreme Court, 21 March 2018). Joanna Cherry MP QC repeated, and further reinforced, the judiciary's concerns in a Commons debate on the Bill (HC Hansard 20 December 2017, Vol 633 col 1103).

The clause (now section 6(2) European Union (Withdrawal) Act 2018) was subsequently amended by Parliament.

See:

Constitution Committee, *European Union (Withdrawal) Bill,* 9th Report of Session 2017–19, HL Paper 69

Constitution Committee, *The Office of Lord Chancellor,* 6th Report of Session 2014–15, HL Paper 75 [83]

P. O'Brien, 'Judges and Select Committees: A Developing Accountability Culture', UK Const L Blog (7 Sept 2015) (ukconstitutionallaw.org/)

Robert Hazell and Patrick O'Brien, 'Meaningful Dialogue: Judicial Engagement with Parliamentary Committees at Westminster' (2016) (January) Public Law, 54–73

Robert Hazell and Juliet Wells, 'Judicial Input into Parliamentary Legislation' (2018) (January) Public Law, 106–127

13.5.2 The judiciary and government

Paradoxically, greater judicial independence and the wider constitutional divide between the judiciary and government have led to more contact between them (see Gee et al, *The Politics of Judicial Independence in the UK's Changing Constitution*, p 262, in 'Further reading'; see also Constitution Committee, *The Office of Lord Chancellor* [84–86]). The dialogue between the judiciary and government ministers takes place through consultation and regular meetings (*Cabinet Manual*, [6.40]) but again must operate within the strict framework of constitutional principles and conventions. Constitutional conventions do not allow judicial comment on the merits of legal cases or decisions, or on policy or the meaning or likely effect of prospective legislation unless it affects judicial independence or the rule of law (see www.judiciary.uk/about-the-judiciary/the-judiciary-the-government-and-the-constitution/jud-acc-ind/judges-and-parliament/). In particular, interaction between the executive and the judiciary should not compromise judicial independence (Latimer House Principles, p 10); so a Home Secretary's proposal to meet Law Lords to discuss the lawfulness of counter-terrorism measures was declined by judges (see the Select Committee on the Constitution, *Relations between the Executive, the Judiciary and Parliament*, 6th Report of Session 2006–07, HL Paper 151 [93–97]).

THINKING POINT

What would the issue have been if judges had given legal advice to the government? To help, consider *Davidson v Scottish Ministers*.

In 2016, the Judicial Executive Board published its *Guidance to the Judiciary on Engagement with the Executive* to assist the judiciary on where the 'red lines' are when engaging with the executive on policy and legislation (see www.judiciary.uk). Engagement can be in the public interest and it may be appropriate for the judiciary to comment on technical and procedural aspects of policy or legislation, policy formulation, drafting of legislation, and consultation; a Judicial Working Group, for example, assisted the government on Brexit issues affecting the judiciary and justice system (The Lord Chief Justice's Report 2017, p 32).

13.5.2.1 The judiciary's relationship with the Lord Chancellor

The member of government with whom the judiciary is most closely connected is, of course, the Lord Chancellor. Traditionally, the Lord Chancellor was a key link between the judiciary and the executive, representing the judiciary in the Cabinet, and the Cabinet in the judiciary. It was a subtly balanced role based on unwritten, informal, principled understandings between the judiciary and executive. Lord Chancellors were lawyers who understood the importance of the rule of law and judicial independence, and knew the Lord Chancellor was 'a buffer between the judiciary and the Executive which protects judicial independence' (Lord Irvine, HL Hansard 17 February 1999, Vol 597 col 734). Lord Woolf also defended the Lord Chancellor's pre-2005 position as an advocate for the courts and the justice system, ensuring proper resourcing for the courts and explaining the law to the Cabinet, and political constraints on resources to the judiciary: 'The justice system is better served by having the head of the judiciary at the centre of government than it would be by having its interests represented by a Minister of Justice who would lack these other roles' (H. Woolf, 'Judicial Review—The Tensions between the Executive and the Judiciary' (1998) 114 LQR 579, 582).

Since the Constitutional Reform Act 2005, the Lord Chancellor *is* now the Minister of Justice and sits squarely within government; though no longer in a position to empathise so closely with judicial concerns as a senior judge, s/he remains an important intermediary between the two branches. The dialogue between the Lord Chancellor and the judiciary has moved from taking internal soundings about judicial issues, to hearing external representations directly from senior judges who bring judicial concerns to the government's attention. There is a system of

⟫ CROSS REFERENCE

See also section 7.5

'concurrence and consultation' between the Lord Chancellor and the Lord Chief Justice (see *Cabinet Manual*, p 54 [6.37]). The Lord Chancellor has monthly meetings with the Lord Chief Justice and regular meetings with the President of the Supreme Court, and the Lord Chief Justice meets the Prime Minister twice a year (Constitution Committee, *The Office of Lord Chancellor*, chapter 2: The Rule of Law and Judicial Independence [82–86]).

However, in 2013, Lord Judge, then Lord Chief Justice, told the Constitution Committee that since the CRA, the judiciary had lost someone in government who could speak for them (www.theguardian.com/law/2013/jan/30/lord-chief-justice-changes-judiciary). The Constitution Committee anticipated that the post-reform Lord Chancellor's 'more political position' as a minister and member of the Commons might mean that they were less willing or able to act independently and 'stand up to Cabinet colleagues or the Prime Minister when necessary', and were likely to be more 'reactive' guardians than their predecessors (Constitution Committee, *The Office of Lord Chancellor* [61–63]). The Lord Chancellor's duty to defend the judiciary proved to be an issue after the *Miller I case*.

🔍 CLOSE-UP FOCUS: DEFENDING THE JUDICIARY

The Lord Chancellor's duty to 'defend' judicial independence is more active than 'upholding' it. The Counsel General for Wales has expressed it as defending judicial institutions from 'political interference, unwarranted and unsubstantiated attacks and criticism in the exercise of their public responsibilities' (Mick Antoniw, Counsel General, *Written Statement—Independence of the Welsh Tribunals*, 21 March 2017).

This duty was tested with the Lord Chancellor's refusal to condemn media criticism of the High Court judges in the *Miller I case* (see section 13.3.2). On 1 March 2017, Liz Truss, then Lord Chancellor, told the Constitution Committee that it was 'dangerous' for a government minister to say what was and was not an acceptable headline: 'I am a huge believer in the independence of the judiciary; I am also a very strong believer in a free press and the value it has in our society' (House of Lords Select Committee on the Constitution, Corrected oral evidence: Oral evidence session with the Lord Chancellor and Secretary of State for Justice, 1 March 2017).

On 22 March, in a very unusual step, Lord Thomas, then Lord Chief Justice and one of the High Court judges in *Miller*, publicly criticised the Lord Chancellor for failing to support the judges. In evidence to the Constitution Committee, he said that the Lord Chancellor had taken a position that was 'constitutionally absolutely wrong' and that she had a duty to defend the judiciary (Select Committee on the Constitution, Oral evidence session with the Lord Chief Justice, 22 March 2017). Lord Thomas took care to preserve the principles of independence and impartiality, telling the Committee it had seemed inappropriate to say anything during the time of the decision or until the relevant legislation had been passed, and that he did not want to be drawn into the politics or compromise the judiciary's position on Brexit, 'which is to get on with the legal problems and leave the politics to the politicians'. He also believed that people ought to criticise the judiciary:

Criticism is very healthy . . . but there is a difference between criticism and abuse, which I do not think is understood. It is not understood either how absolutely essential it is that we are protected, because we have to act, as our oath requires us, without fear or favour, affection or ill will. (https://old.parliament.uk/documents/lords-committees/constitution/Annual-evidence-2016-17/CC220317LCJ.pdf)

In a radio interview *after* the Supreme Court decision in *Miller*, Lord Neuberger, then President of the Supreme Court, stated that politicians could have defended the judiciary more quickly and clearly after the High Court hearing, and commented that attacks on the judiciary without good reason undermined the rule of law (see www.bbc.co.uk/news/uk-38986228).

The Constitution Committee subsequently concluded that there is a difference between challenging a judgment and attacking the character and integrity of a judge, and the Lord Chancellor's constitutional duty is clear: to defend the independence of the judiciary. The Committee added a stern warning that if members of the judiciary should suffer such personal attacks again, it would expect 'any person holding the office of Lord Chancellor to take a proactive stance in defending them publicly, as they are unable to defend themselves' (House of Lords Select Committee on the Constitution, *Judicial Appointments: Follow-up*, 7th Report of Session 2017–19, HL Paper 32 [57]).

Further reading

Patrick O'Brien, '"Enemies of the People": Judges, the Media, and the Mythic Lord Chancellor' (2017) (Nov Supp) PL 135

The Rt Hon The Lord Thomas Of Cwmgiedd *The Judiciary within the State—The Relationship between the Branches of the State*, Michael Ryle Memorial Lecture, Palace Of Westminster, 15 June 2017

13.6 Judicial power

This discussion focuses on locating the unwritten limits of judicial power.

Recap

Judicial deference means respecting and not interfering in certain areas of activity of the other two branches of state, such as Parliament's law-making power, or the government's politically sensitive powers such as deploying armed forces. Judicial activism means 'an intention to develop the law rather than just apply it, to provide guidance for the future rather than just supply reassurance concerning the *status quo*' (Brice Dickson, 'Activism and Restraint within the UK Supreme Court' (2015) 21(1) EJoCLI).

> **CROSS REFERENCE**
> See section 7.4.2.1

The tension between judicial deference and activism can be seen in two statements. Lord Scarman expressed the traditional, restrained view of the judges' role:

in the field of statute law the judge must be obedient to the will of the Parliament as expressed in its enactments . . . the judge's duty is to interpret and to apply the law, not to change it to meet the judge's idea of what justice requires. (*Duport Steel v Sirs* [1980] 1 All ER 529 at 551)

By contrast, Sir John Laws has said: 'An Act of Parliament is words on a page. Only the common law gives it life' ('The Common Law Constitution', Hamlyn Lectures, 2013). This is supported

> **CROSS REFERENCE**
> See Chapters 6 and 9 for the scope of statutory interpretation

by Sedley LJ's description of the interpretative function: 'what an Act of Parliament means is what the courts decide it means' (London Review of Books, 2 April 1998).

THINKING POINT

Lord Neuberger refers to three baseball umpires who were asked how they rule on a ball. 'The first said "I call it like it is"; the second said "I call it like I see it"; and the third said "It ain't nothin' till I call it"' (www.supremecourt.uk/docs/speech-150129.pdf [8]). Which one reflects the Laws–Sedley approach?

Lord Sumption has identified two sources of deference when the courts are assessing how much weight to give to a decision-maker's judgment:

- constitutional deference: based on the separation of powers and a body's special constitutional function;
- institutional deference: assessing judgments of the other body based on its specialist competence and knowledge (*R (Lord Carlile of Berriew QC) v Secretary of State for the Home Department* [2014] UKSC 60 [22–26]).

Lord Hodge prefers the term 'role recognition' over 'deference' or 'restraint'. It is for judges to see the clear limits of the judicial role and, beyond that boundary, the primary policy decisions which fall within 'the domain of the elected branches of government' who are politically accountable for them and have the resources to formulate policy and assess the consequences ('Judicial Law-making in a Changing Constitution' (2015) 26(3) Stellenbosch Law Review 471, 482).

CASE CLOSE-UP: *R (CAMPAIGN AGAINST THE ARMS TRADE) v SECRETARY OF STATE FOR INTERNATIONAL TRADE [2019] EWCA CIV 1020; [2017] EWHC 1726 (QB)*

This case involved whether the Secretary of State for International Trade had a legal duty to suspend existing licences to export arms to Saudi Arabia and to stop new licences where there was a clear risk that they might be used to commit a serious violation of international humanitarian law (IHL). The government argued that it was in a unique position to judge whether Saudi Arabia was genuinely committed to compliance with IHL because of its specialised knowledge of the situation. The High Court accepted that the Secretary of State had been entitled to conclude, on the evidence before him, that there was no such risk. '[I]n an area where the Court is not possessed of the institutional expertise to make the judgments in question, it should be especially cautious before interfering with a finely balanced decision reached after careful and anxious consideration by those who do have the relevant expertise to make the necessary judgments' ([209]).

However, the Court of Appeal found that the Secretary of State had acted irrationally and unlawfully by not considering whether there had been past breaches of IHL, though the court emphasised that it had borne in mind that this was an area 'particularly far within the responsibility and expertise of the executive branch' [145], and agreed with the Divisional Court that in a case like this, the courts must give considerable respect to the decision-maker.

The role recognition issue picks up momentum in judicial review cases where judges need to locate the boundary between the lawfulness of a government policy, which they *can* decide, and its merits, which they cannot. However, the boundary is not always clear and judges can be drawn into considering policy and political matters which are the preserve of Parliament and government. Restraint by judges is therefore needed when determining the lawfulness of a policy; ministers are decision-makers, not judges (but see John Laws, 'Law and Democracy' (1995) Public Law 72).

THE BIGGER PICTURE: JUDICIAL POWER

Judicial power has expanded in recent years, particularly with the Human Rights Act 1998, and there is a divide between supporters of the expansion of judicial power and those against. It is an argument between traditionalists and expansionists.

Sir John Laws has argued that judicial activism means either law-making by judges or judicial decision-making in areas of policy. He sees judicial interpretation as 'an autonomous creative process' where the common law supplies the omission of the legislature ([7]). Judges are 'guardians of constitutional principle' ([34]), and they make law in cases where they interpret a statute in a way that protects a fundamental constitutional principle, rather than giving effect to legislative intention ([24]) (Sir John Laws, 'Judicial Activism', 12 December 2016 (judicialpowerproject.org.uk/wp-content/uploads/2016/12/Laws-text-final.pdf)).

Against this, Jeffrey Goldsworthy warns that if judges interpret legislation according to common law rights, regardless of Parliament's intentions, they subordinate Parliament's will to their preferred criteria. Parliament is no longer the 'sole author' of its statutes (judicialpowerproject.org.uk/jeffrey-goldsworthy-losing-faith-in-democracy-why-judicial-supremacy-is-rising-and-what-to-do-about-it/). Professor Forsyth argues that 'the ultimate guardians of constitutional principle are the elected representatives of the people' and emphasises the importance of judicial obedience to parliamentary supremacy [7] (Professor Christopher Forsyth, 'Who Is the Ultimate Guardian of the Constitution? In Reply to Sir John Laws' (judicialpowerproject.org.uk/wp-content/uploads/2016/12/Forsyth-reply-to-Laws2.pdf)). See also H.W.R. Wade and C.F. Forsyth, *Administrative Law*, 11th edn (Oxford: Oxford University Press 2014), pp 22–23.

Professor Finnis states, 'Just as the Rule of Law is not the rule of judges . . . so too judicial power is not a power to remake the constitution' (judicialpowerproject.org.uk/john-finnis-judicial-power-past-present-and-future/).

Further reading

See:
The Rt Hon Lord Dyson, Master of the Rolls, 'Are the Judges Too Powerful?' 12 March 2014 (www.judiciary.uk/wp-content/uploads/JCO/Documents/Speeches/mor-speech-have-judges-become-too-powerful.pdf)

Mark Elliott's response to Professor Finnis, at judicialpowerproject.org.uk/mark-elliott-judicial-power-in-normative-institutional-and-doctrinal-perspective-a-response-to-professor-finnis/

Richard Ekins, 'Judicial Supremacy and the Rule of Law' (2003) 119 LQR 127

▶ CROSS REFERENCE

See also the discussion in Chapter 9

SUMMARY

- Since the CRA 2005, the judiciary has greater independence but the senior judiciary has a more interactive relationship with both government and Parliament
- In the absence of a codified constitution, the boundaries of judicial power operate within a framework of constitutional principles and conventions, but there is debate over the limits of that power

? Questions

Self-test questions

1. What is the role of the judiciary?

2. Why is judicial independence important?

3. What are its features?

4. Why is judicial neutrality important?

5. Who appoints judges?

6. How are senior judges removed from office?

7. When giving evidence to select committees, on what aspects of proposed legislation may judges comment?

8. What is the Lord Chancellor's duty in respect of the judiciary?

Exam question

'Lord Howard, the former Tory leader, stated in a Radio 4 programme: "The power of the judges, as opposed to the power of elected politicians, has increased, is increasing and ought to be diminished. More and more decisions are being made by unelected, unaccountable judges, instead of accountable, elected Members of Parliament who have to answer to the electorate for what has happened". These statements evidence a failure to understand the role of the judiciary.' (Lord Phillips, 'Judicial Independence and Accountability: A View from the Supreme Court', Constitution Unit Lecture, 8 February 2011, p 16).

In the light of this statement, critically assess the constitutional role of the judiciary.

Further reading

Books

Gee, G., Malleson, K., O'Brien, P., and Hazell, R. *The Politics of Judicial Independence in the UK's Changing Constitution* (Cambridge: Cambridge University Press 2015).

Analyses the modern judiciary's accountability and relationships with government and Parliament as well as independence

Shetreet, S. and Turenne, S. *Judges on Trial: The Independence and Accountability of the English Judiciary* (2nd edn, Cambridge: Cambridge University Press 2013).
Discusses the elements of judicial independence

Journal articles

Barak, A. 'A Judge on Judging: The Role of a Supreme Court in a Democracy' (2002) 116 Harvard Law Review 19.
Very long but worth dipping into for insight into the judicial decision-making process from a former president of Israel's Supreme Court

Brooke, Sir H. 'The History of Judicial Independence in England and Wales' (2015) (5) European Human Rights Law Review 446.
Written before the CRA 2005, sets out the foundations of judicial independence

Ekins, R. and Gee, G. 'Putting Judicial Power in Its Place' (2017) 36(2) University of Queensland Law Journal 375–398.
Reflections on the judicial power debate

Gee, G. 'What Are Lord Chancellors For?' (2014) (January) PL 11.
Helpfully compares the 'old' and 'new' Lord Chancellors

Jowell, J. 'Judicial Deference: Servility, Civility or Institutional Capacity?' (2003) (Winter) PL 592.
Considers issues of delineating the judiciary/Parliament boundary

Stevens, R. 'A Loss of Innocence? Judicial Independence and the Separation of Powers' (1999) 19 (3) Oxford J Legal Studies 365.
Good background for the judiciary pre-CRA

Other sources

For the structure of the court system in England and Wales, see www.judiciary.uk/wp-content/uploads/2012/08/courts-structure-0715.pdf.

Judicial Office, 'The Judicial System of England and Wales: A Visitor's Guide'. (Available at www.judiciary.uk/wp-content/uploads/2016/05/international-visitors-guide-10a.pdf).
A very clear guide to the court system in England and Wales

Extrajudicial lectures provide detailed, topical insight into the work and experience of serving judges (www.judiciary.uk or www.supremecourt.uk for speeches by Justices of the Supreme Court). Below is a selection (see also the online resources and references throughout the chapter):

Lady Hale, 'Judges, Power and Accountability', Constitutional Law Summer School, Belfast, 11 August 2017.
Topical discussion of judicial selection

Lady Hale, 'Should the Law Lords have left the House of Lords?' Michael Ryle Lecture 2018, 14 November 2018.
Discusses the transition to the Supreme Court

Lord Mance, 'The Role of Judges in a Representative Democracy', lecture given during the Judicial Committee of the Privy Council's Fourth Sitting in The Bahamas, 24 February 2017.

Good discussion of the three pillars of the state

Lord Neuberger, '"Judge not, that ye be not judged": Judging Judicial Decision-making', FA Mann Lecture, 2015.
Fascinating insight into how judges decide cases

Lord Thomas of Cwmgiedd, 'Judicial Leadership', Conference on the Paradox of Judicial Independence, UCL Constitution Unit, 22 June 2015.
Very detailed discussion on the relationship between the judiciary and the other branches of state

Useful websites

The Supreme Court: www.supremecourt.uk

The judiciary: www.judiciary.uk

The JAC: https://judicialappointments.digital/

⁏ Online resources

www.oup.com/he/dennett2e
This chapter is accompanied by a selection of online resources to help you with this topic, including:

- Multiple-choice questions
- Answers to the self-test questions
- Guidance on answering the exam question

PART 4

THE RELATIONSHIP BETWEEN THE INDIVIDUAL AND THE STATE

Our focus in this part of the book moves to the arena of administrative justice, administrative law, and human rights, and the relationship between the citizen and the state. Administrative law regulates the exercise of power by the executive, protecting the citizen against abuses or excesses of state power. The Human Rights Act requires public bodies to strike a balance between the rights of the individual and the interests of society.

14 Challenging government action

LEARNING OBJECTIVES

By the end of this chapter, you should be able to:

- Explain the role of administrative law and administrative justice
- Evaluate the importance of grievance mechanisms
- Assess issues raised by the operation of public inquiries
- Discuss the role and purpose of the Parliamentary and Health Service Ombudsman
- Evaluate reforms to the tribunal system

Introduction

This chapter focuses on the administrative justice system, which 'is crucial to how the state treats its citizens' (House of Commons Public Administration Select Committee, *Oversight of Administrative Justice*, Written Evidence submitted by the Administrative Justice and Tribunals Council (OAJ 01) [2]). Administrative justice refers to the systems that enable individuals to resolve complaints, grievances, and disputes about administrative or executive decisions of public bodies, and to obtain redress. It also covers the procedures and law that regulate decision-making by public bodies. We will explore:

- Public inquiries
- Ombudsmen
- Tribunals

The administrative justice system:

'is generally understood as including the mechanisms by which individuals can challenge, question and seek to change decisions which central and local public bodies have made about them, in cases where there have been errors, misunderstandings or unacceptable standards of service. It includes complaint schemes operated by government departments and other public bodies, ombudsmen, tribunals . . . and the administrative court'. (Public Administration Committee, *Future Oversight of Administrative Justice: The Proposed Abolition of the Administrative Justice and Tribunals Council*, 21st Report of Session 2010–12, HC 1621 [5])

14.1 Background

Administrative justice is more of a shifting landscape than a well-defined system. Sir Ernest Ryder, the Senior President of Tribunals, has observed that it 'is not yet a coherent or organised system' ('Driving Improvements: Collaboration And Peer Learning', speech delivered at Ombudsman Association Conference, Belfast, 21 May 2019), but its reach should not be underestimated: it 'directly affects a much larger section of the population in their day-to-day lives than do the civil, family or criminal justice systems' (ukaji.org/2017/03/14/administrative-justice-oversight-must-continue/). It helps uphold the rule of law by securing accountability of public bodies but its dominant theme is ensuring justice and fairness for citizens when public bodies make decisions about, for instance, their healthcare, benefits, or pensions. Unfairness or injustice can be caused through various abuses or failures by public bodies, including:

- decisions that are unlawful or unreasonable;
- failing to follow correct procedures;
- not treating people fairly, consistently, or equally;
- making biased decisions or discriminating against individuals;
- contravening human rights;
- providing a poor service.

On a larger scale, individuals may be affected by systemic or catastrophic failings by a public body, or a disaster such as the Grenfell Tower fire in June 2017.

> Redress means obtaining a remedy for a wrong or grievance

Grievance mechanisms exist to achieve redress (see Figure 14.1), and to ensure accountability and improved public administration. They include formal court action through judicial review (see Chapters 15 and 16) but range well beyond the courts to informal, non-legal mechanisms.

The Law Commission identified four pillars of administrative justice for aggrieved citizens to seek redress:

1. internal mechanisms for redress, such as formal complaint procedures (this refers to administrative review by public bodies of their own decisions);
2. external non-court avenues of redress, such as public inquiries and tribunals;
3. the public sector ombudsmen;
4. the remedies available in public and private law by way of a court action.

Figure 14.1 Grievance mechanisms

Complaints and grievances with public bodies → Investigation and complaints mechanisms → Dispute resolution - tribunals → Judicial review → Redress

(The Law Commission, Consultation Paper No 187, *Administrative Redress: Public Bodies And The Citizen* [2.3])

Administrative justice is underpinned by administrative law; they overlap considerably, but administrative justice (a) extends beyond legal grounds for complaint to rudeness or poor service and (b) focuses on obtaining redress at an individual level, while administrative law has a broader reach.

> Administrative law controls the actions and decision-making of the executive in its broadest sense, and is strongly centred on judicial review. It focuses on legality and accountability. There is a strong link between administrative law and the state but traditionally there is no concept of 'the State' in Britain; instead, there has been a kingdom and its subjects. With the emergence of local government in the nineteenth century and the growth of the welfare state in the mid-twentieth century, the number of public bodies increased significantly, with a consequent increase in the need to regulate them. Lord Phillips observes: 'the increased complexity of modern society . . . brings with it an increasing amount of executive control over the activities of the citizen. This has been coupled with a growing recognition by the citizen and by public interest bodies of the possibilities of challenging such action' ('Judicial Independence and Accountability: A View from the Supreme Court', Constitution Unit Lecture, 8 February 2011).

For further details of the administrative justice system, see Robert Thomas and Joe Tomlinson, 'Mapping Current Issues in Administrative Justice: Austerity and the "More Bureaucratic Rationality" Approach' (2017) 39(3) Journal of Social Welfare and Family Law 380; Gordon Anthony, 'Administrative Justice in the United Kingdom' (2015) 7(1) Italian Journal of Public Law 9.

 SUMMARY

> 'Administrative justice has at its core the administrative decisions by public authorities that affect individual citizens and the mechanisms available for the provision of redress.' (ukaji. org/what-is-administrative-justice/)

We look next at how the state responds to issues of public concern through public inquiries.

14.2 Public inquiries

'The tradition of the public inquiry has become a pivotal part of public life in Britain, and a major instrument of accountability' (Public Administration Select Committee, *Government by Inquiry*, 1st Report of Session 2004–05 HC 51-I, para 2).

Public inquiries:

- are set up by government (either the UK government or the devolved administrations) to investigate issues of serious public concern on the public's behalf;
- are an important way of holding people or organisations to account;

- are not permanent but are established to objectively investigate a major failure or high-profile disaster and set out 'lessons learned' for the future;
- make findings of fact on what happened, what went wrong, and why;
- publish a report of their findings and any recommendations.

Liberty, a civil liberties and human rights organisation, has referred to public inquiries as:

a key component of the constitutional and administrative justice system in the UK. Inquiries provide a means for the truth about an event or series of events to be reached by an independent and authoritative body, but in a manner which is more inclusive and restorative than litigation . . . Frequently, the acts or events that have given rise to concern will be the acts or alleged acts of state authorities. Public inquiries therefore play an essential role in holding state power to account. (House of Lords Select Committee on the Inquiries Act 2005, Liberty—Written evidence 'The Purpose and Importance of Inquiries', p 267; see also Professor Adam Tomkins, Ev Q.23 and Q.31)

Public inquiries are one of the UK's accountability and investigatory mechanisms. Lord Butler has called them 'a lightning rod for the anger of the public and particularly of those who have been bereaved or suffered personally' (Peter Riddell, www.instituteforgovernment.org.uk/blog/public-inquiries-be-careful-what-you-wish). There have been calls for a public inquiry into the government's response to the Covid-19 pandemic. In July 2020, the Parliamentary and Health Service Ombudsman urged the government to establish 'a robust and independent lessons-learned exercise' into the handling of the pandemic with a fully independent, open and transparent inquiry (PACAC Inquiry, 'Written submission from the Parliamentary and Health Service Ombudsman', 13 July 2020 at www.ombudsman.org.uk/; see also www.prospectmagazine.co.uk/politics/public-inquiry-coronavirus-covid-government; www.democraticaudit.com/2020/05/12/if-there-is-a-public-inquiry-into-covid-19-what-will-it-look-like/). On 15 July 2020, the Prime Minister confirmed that the government would hold an independent inquiry after combatting the pandemic (HC Hansard 15 July 2020, Vol 678 col 1514). However, setting up an inquiry depends on a minister's initiative.

In a Commons debate on the Chilcot Inquiry, David Cameron identified an inquiry's important tasks: 'to make clear recommendations, to go wherever the evidence leads, to establish the full truth and to ensure that the right lessons are learned, and it has to do so in a way that builds public confidence' (HC Deb 15 June 2009, Vol 494 col 25). The main purposes of a public inquiry are therefore to:

- establish the facts and get to the truth;
- learn from events and prevent mistakes from happening again;
- provide an opportunity for healing and reconciliation;
- provide reassurance and rebuild public trust and confidence;
- hold people and organisations to account;
- serve the government's political interests to show that 'something is being done' or to bring about change.

(See Public Administration Select Committee, *Government by Inquiry*, 1st Report of Session 2004–05 HC 51-1, [12]; Geoffrey Howe, 'The Management of Public Inquiries' (1999) 70 Political Quarterly 294.)

Public inquiries:

- are not courts;
- are not initiated by citizens and do not determine individual rights;
- do not impose criminal or civil liability on a person (though their findings might be used to bring criminal or civil proceedings);
- do not make formally binding decisions, so the government is not bound to follow their recommendations.

Public inquiries are often chaired by a serving or retired judge (these are known as judicial inquiries), although there is no legal requirement for this. The inquiry's terms of reference set out its purpose and remit, any limitations on what it should examine, or whether it should produce a written report with recommendations. Terms of reference are drafted by government but can be changed by consultation with the chair, and can be debated in the House of Commons (this happened before the Franks Inquiry in 1982: see HC Deb 8 July 1982, Vol 27 cols 469–508). The inquiry will take oral and documents-based evidence about the events in question, and many inquiries appoint counsel to the inquiry to carry out the questioning.

THE BIGGER PICTURE

Various other investigatory mechanisms can be used at state level, including:

- Parliamentary Inquiry (inquiries by select committees—from fake news to fracking— or by other parliamentary committees; in 2020, for example, both the Public Administration and Constitutional Affairs Committee and the Constitution Committee carried out inquiries into the government's response to the Covid-19 pandemic);

- independent reviews (eg the Kerslake Review on the emergency response to the Manchester Arena attack in 2017, commissioned by the Mayor of Greater Manchester);

- the Hillsborough Independent Panel, chaired by the Bishop of Liverpool (this was not a public inquiry but was set up by the government to oversee the public release of documents relating to the 1989 Hillsborough football disaster);

- inquests (inquisitorial, fact-finding proceedings by a coroner to investigate how a person died but not to decide blame, or criminal or civil liability; a public inquiry can replace or supplement an inquest).

14.2.1 Statutory and non-statutory inquiries

Public inquiries can be either statutory or non-statutory. Statutory inquiries (known as statutory commissions of inquiry) are set up under statute, chiefly the Inquiries Act 2005; non-statutory inquiries are set up mainly under prerogative power. (For a table of differences, see section 1.1 www.sibf.org.uk/appg/.)

14.2.2 **Non-statutory inquiries**

Ad hoc means set up for a particular purpose

A government minister can initiate a non-statutory inquiry where it relates to matters of public concern. It can be:

- a non-statutory ad hoc inquiry set up under prerogative power;
- a Committee of Privy Counsellors;
- a Royal Commission (a formal, ad hoc advisory committee set up by the government to investigate and advise on broader issues of public importance; it takes evidence and produces a report making recommendations for change).

Non-statutory inquiries are still regularly used by the government because of their flexibility:

- They can hold hearings in public or in private (a private hearing may be appropriate where sensitive material will be examined, eg concerning national security, whereas there is a presumption that statutory inquiries will be held in public).
- They are not bound by the same procedural rules as an inquiry under the Inquiries Act 2005, so can be less prescribed, less adversarial, and less formal.
- But they do not have the power to compel witnesses to attend or documents to be produced, or to take evidence on oath, so the government needs to be confident that participants will attend and co-operate.
- Without the power to compel the attendance of witnesses, non-statutory inquiries may not comply with the obligation for an effective and independent investigation into deaths caused by state authorities (eg deaths in police custody) required by Article 2 ECHR (the right to life; see *Edwards v UK* (2002) 35 EHRR 19; and Chapter 18).

 EXAMPLES OF NON-STATUTORY INQUIRIES

Non-statutory ad hoc inquiries

- **The Hutton Inquiry**, a judicial inquiry by Lord Hutton into the circumstances surrounding the death of Dr David Kelly, who had been a weapons inspector in Iraq on behalf of the United Nations (see Sir Louis Blom-Cooper and Colin Munro, 'The Hutton Inquiry' (2004) (Autumn) Public Law 472).

- **The Deepcut Barracks Review**, an independent review into the deaths of four soldiers at Deepcut Barracks between 1995 and 2002.

- **The Zahid Mubarek Inquiry** into the murder of a prisoner in a young offender institution in 2000 (see also *R v Secretary of State for the Home Department ex parte Amin* [2003] UKHL 51).

- **The Morecambe Bay Investigation** into maternity and neonatal services in Morecambe Bay NHS Trust hospitals.

Inquiries by a Committee of Privy Counsellors

These tend to be used for the 'big ticket', high-profile inquiries investigating decisions at government or state agency level (Privy Counsellors can have access to security and intelligence material). Examples include:

- **The Butler Inquiry**, which investigated the accuracy of intelligence on Iraqi weapons of mass destruction leading up to the Iraq conflict. See Richard J. Aldrich, 'Whitehall and the Iraq War: The UK's Four Intelligence Enquiries' (2005) 16 *Irish Studies in International Affairs* 73.

- **The Chilcot Inquiry** on the Iraq war. In 2009, Gordon Brown, then Prime Minister, announced an inquiry to identify lessons that could be learned from the controversial 2003 Iraq conflict. It would be fully independent of government, have access to all information, and receive the government's full co-operation (HC Deb 15 June 2009, Vol 494 col 23). It examined the way decisions were made and actions were taken from the run-up to the conflict to post-conflict but did not have power to determine whether the invasion was illegal, or to allocate blame. (For the key issues considered by the Inquiry, see Executive Summary [7] at www.iraqinquiry.org.uk.) After oral and written evidence from more than 150 witnesses and 150,000 documents, it published its report in 2016 (*The Report of the Iraq Inquiry*, 6 July 2016, HC 264).

- **The Gibson Inquiry** into whether Britain was implicated in the improper treatment of detainees held by other countries after 9/11 (see section 12.4.5).

For further details, see Commons Library Briefing Paper Number 02599, *Public Inquiries: Non-statutory Commissions of Inquiry*, 30 November 2016.

14.2.3 Statutory inquiries under the Inquiries Act 2005

The Inquiries Act 2005 was introduced to make the public inquiry process faster, more effective, and less costly, and sets out the statutory framework for public inquiries established by ministers into matters of public concern. The Act consolidated previous legislation and repealed the Tribunals of Inquiry (Evidence) Act 1921 which had allowed parliamentary involvement in establishing a tribunal of inquiry into a matter of urgent public importance. The 2005 Act was partly a response to the Bloody Sunday Inquiry chaired by Lord Saville, which took 12 years and cost £192 million (it investigated events surrounding the shooting of civilians in 1972 by the British Army in Londonderry, and was the last inquiry held under the 1921 Act).

 EXAMPLES

More than 20 public inquiries have been set up under the Inquiries Act since 2005, investigating, for example:

- phone hacking by the press (the Leveson Inquiry);
- deaths in custody in prison (the Bernard Lodge Inquiry) and in army custody (the Baha Mousa Inquiry);
- a death after a police shooting (the Azelle Rodney Inquiry);
- child sexual abuse (the Independent Inquiry into Child Sexual Abuse);
- significant loss of life in a disaster (the Grenfell Tower Inquiry; the Manchester Arena Inquiry).

14.2.3.1 How independent from government are statutory inquiries?

Statutory inquiries under the 2005 Act are set up by the government but, once established, are conducted independently. As Lord Heseltine told the Public Administration Committee, 'No government wants inquiries; they are usually in circumstances where the government is in trouble . . . and so governments will do their best to avoid inquiries' (Public Administration Select Committee, *Government by Inquiry,* HC 51-1 2004-05 para 217 Q.615).

However, there is still the potential for government control over public inquiries under the Act:

- The government decides whether to hold an inquiry.
- Ministers decide who should chair it and appoint panel members.
- Ministers frame the inquiry's terms of reference.
- Governments do not have to accept the inquiry's recommendations.
- The 2005 Act strengthened ministerial powers over inquiries, as shown below.

 STATUTE: KEY PROVISIONS OF THE INQUIRIES ACT 2005

Inquiries do not have power to determine criminal liability (section 2). They can be conducted by a chairman alone or with a panel (section 3).

Powers of ministers under the Act

Only a minister from the UK government or devolved administrations can establish an inquiry under the Act where it appears to him/her that events have caused public concern, or there is public concern that certain events might have happened (section 1). This gives the minister wide discretion.

When proposing an inquiry, a minister must inform Parliament (or the devolved legislature), detailing the chair, panel members, and terms of reference (section 6).

Ministers have the power to:

- appoint panel members (section 4), though they must ensure they have the necessary expertise (section 8) and are impartial (section 9), and, when appointing a judge, must consult with the Lord Chief Justice or other senior member of the judiciary (section 10);
- set out the terms of reference of the inquiry (section 5), though they must consult the proposed chair before setting out or amending them;
- terminate the appointment of a panel member (section 12(3));
- suspend an inquiry (section 13) or bring it to an end before publication of the report (section 14) though in both cases they must consult the chair;
- convert a non-statutory inquiry into an inquiry under the Act (section 15);
- restrict attendance, or disclosure or publication of evidence, at an inquiry (section 19), and they may in some circumstances withhold material in the report from publication (section 25).

The chair has the power to:

- direct the procedure and conduct of an inquiry (section 17(1)), but must act with fairness and avoid unnecessary cost (section 17(3));

- take evidence on oath (section 17(2));

- compel a person to attend to give evidence or produce documents (section 21); it is an offence to intentionally suppress or conceal a relevant document, or prevent it from being given to the inquiry panel (section 35);

- restrict attendance or access to documents in certain circumstances (section 19), though the chair is required to do what s/he considers reasonable to ensure that members of the public can attend the inquiry or see evidence; at the chair's discretion, proceedings can be broadcast (section 18);

- withhold material in the report from publication in certain circumstances (section 25).

14.2.3.2 **Procedure**

A Royal Commission chaired by Lord Salmon in 1966 formulated six principles governing fair procedure for public inquiries. The 'Salmon principles' include informing potential witnesses of any allegations made against them, giving them an adequate opportunity to prepare their case and of being assisted by legal advisors, and having the opportunity of being examined by their own solicitor or counsel and of stating their case in public at the inquiry (see *Royal Commission on Tribunals of Inquiry*, Cmnd 3121 (1966); for criticism of the principles, see *Select Committee on the Inquiries Act 2005*, HL Paper 143 [27–31, 229–235]). Statutory inquiries are governed by the Inquiry Rules 2006 (procedural rules which apply to England and Wales) or the Inquiries (Scotland) Rules 2007.

Under Rule 5 of the Inquiry Rules 2006, the chair can designate a person as a 'core participant', with their consent, where they have played a direct and significant role in the matters being investigated, have a significant interest in them, or might be criticised during the inquiry or in the report. They are entitled to special status with recognised legal representation; their lawyers may be permitted to question witnesses, and they may be given advance disclosure of witness statements.

14.2.4 **Challenging inquiry decisions**

Judicial review can be used to challenge a minister's decision in relation to an inquiry, or a decision by a member of an inquiry panel, but the time limit is only 14 days (section 38 Inquiries Act 2005; *R (EA) v Chairman of the Manchester Arena Inquiry* [2020] EWHC 2053 (Admin)).

EXAMPLE: *R (LITVINENKO) v SECRETARY OF STATE FOR THE HOME DEPARTMENT* [2014] EWHC 194 (ADMIN)

Alexander Litvinenko, a former Russian spy, died in London in 2006 as a result of being poisoned by polonium, a radioactive substance. His widow brought a judicial review claim to challenge the Home Secretary's refusal to set up a statutory inquiry into his death. The High Court held that the Home Secretary's reasons for not setting up an inquiry did not provide a rational basis for her decision. An inquiry was subsequently set up in 2014 under the Inquiries Act, reporting in 2016 (an inquiry rather than an inquest was held as some evidence was too sensitive to be heard in open court).

14.2.5 **Critique**

Public inquiries can be controversial. Peter Riddell points out that they 'rarely satisfy everyone', mainly because of differences of expectation about their aims (Institute for Government, 'The Role of Public Inquiries', 26 July 2016, at www.instituteforgovernment.org.uk/blog/role-public-inquiries). Controversy may be caused by:

- the choice of inquiry chair;

- the terms of reference (too wide or too narrow—eg the Hutton Inquiry terms were criticised as too narrow but Lord Hutton decided not to ask for them to be extended as it would prolong the inquiry);

- examining events stretching too far back (eg 40 years in the Saville Inquiry), so the lessons learned may have less immediacy;

- an inquiry not resolving an issue, which might result in greater sense of injustice (eg the Widgery Inquiry on Bloody Sunday; and, after the Hillsborough disaster, there was an inquiry, an inquest, an investigation, an independent panel, and another inquest).

The appointment of judges as inquiry chairs may lead to more adversarial proceedings, while political subject matter and the investigatory inquiry process can take judges beyond their traditional role of deciding cases. Lord Woolf has commented that 'Judges are very experienced with determining facts. But they're not necessarily experts in making recommendations' (BBC Radio 4, Today Programme, 23 May 2012; www.bbc.co.uk/news/uk-politics-18171819). See also Tim Buley, 'Judges Chairing Public Inquiries: Observations on DCA "Effective Inquiries"', (2004) 9(4) Judicial Review 293; ukhumanrightsblog.com/2017/11/09/inquiries-into-historical-events-have-a-troubled-past-will-history-repeat-itself/.

The potential for government control over inquiries is an issue:

- Government has discretion to decide whether to establish a non-statutory or 2005 Act inquiry.

- The Inquiries Act 2005 has been criticised for strengthening ministerial control and reducing Parliament's involvement in inquiries (see PASC, *Government by Inquiry* [175]), although Parliament can call for an inquiry, and holds ministers accountable to Parliament (House of Lords Select Committee on the Inquiries Act 2005, *The Inquiries Act 2005: Post-legislative Scrutiny,* Report of Session 2013–14, HL 143, [106]).

- The potential for ministerial influence on an inquiry set up under the Act could risk compromising the independent investigation required by Article 2 ECHR when the right to life is engaged (Joint Committee on Human Rights, *Scrutiny: First Progress Report* 4th Report of Session 2004–05, HL Paper 26, HC 224 [2.6, 2.12–2.16]).

For the Scott Inquiry see section 12.4.1.1 and the online resources.

 THINKING POINT

Do you think that Parliament, not government, should set up inquiries?

Public inquiries can be long and costly. From 1990 to 2017, 68 inquiries made 2,625 recommendations for change, and cost a total of around £639 million (Institute for Government, *How Public Inquiries Can Lead to Change*, p 3). Inquiry reports may take several years to produce, are often long (ten volumes for Saville), may make an excessive number of recommendations (290 for the Mid-Staffordshire Inquiry), or may make legal rather than practical recommendations. The recommendations may not be implemented, so errors may recur. The process of 'Maxwellisation' (which requires the chairman to send a warning letter to people criticised in an inquiry's report to allow them to respond before its publication (Inquiry Rules 2006 13–15)) can prolong the inquiry process considerably and delay its report.

On the other hand, inquiries can:

- be 'a safety valve when feelings are running high' (see www.bbc.co.uk/news/uk-40950945);

- provide a cathartic 'truth and reconciliation' process, allowing victims or their families to be heard, and anger to be expressed (see The Truth Project used in the Child Abuse Inquiry);

- allow facts to be investigated thoroughly and bring a sense of closure;

- draw public attention to issues such as 'institutional racism', as done by the Macpherson Inquiry into the murder of Stephen Lawrence;

- enhance ministerial accountability, because ministers need to respond to an inquiry's findings with a full explanation or by taking action; Parliament can hold the minister accountable for the inquiry's findings and for implementing any recommendations made (House of Commons Public Administration Select Committee, *Government by Inquiry,* 1st Report of Session 2004–05, HC 51-1 [168–170]);

- result in changes in practice or public apologies; after publication of the Saville Inquiry report in 2010, David Cameron apologised in the House of Commons on behalf of the government and the country, adding that the report and the inquiry 'demonstrate how a state should hold itself to account' (HC Deb 15 Jun 2010, Vol 511 col 741).

Nevertheless, reforms have been suggested (see Table 14.1).

THE BIGGER PICTURE

See *Government Response to the Report of the House of Lords Select Committee on the Inquiries Act 2005*, Cm 8903, June 2014, where the government accepted some recommendations (including a full Lessons Learned paper) but rejected others, including normally holding inquiries under the 2005 Act (it wished to retain current flexibility and control) and a central inquiries unit ('not appropriate or necessary').

For further comment, see:

- https://ukaji.org/2015/03/18/reforming-public-inquiries-time-to-review/

- The Institute for Government Report, *How Public Inquiries Can Lead to Change,* December 2017, available at www.instituteforgovernment.org.uk

- Peter Watkin Jones and Nicholas Griffin QC, 'Public Inquiries: Getting at the Truth', Law Society Gazette, 22 June 2015

Table 14.1 Proposals for reform

In 2005, the Public Administration Committee observed that 'inquiries matter greatly to the public' ([10]). Their recommendations included:	Regular reporting by government departments on how they have implemented inquiry recommendations (para 147)
	Parliament should be able to decide that an inquiry should be established where the events causing public concern involve ministers' conduct (178)
	Clear criteria for calling inquiries (193); ministers should justify their decisions whether or not to hold an inquiry (184)
	Inquiries into the conduct and actions of government should be via a Parliamentary Commission of Inquiry, rather than an inquiry set up under the Executive's prerogative power (215)

(Public Administration Select Committee, *Government by Inquiry*, pp 82–85)

The 2014 post-legislative scrutiny report concluded that the Inquiries Act provided 'the right procedural framework . . . to conduct an inquiry efficiently, effectively and above all fairly' (para 215), but made 33 recommendations, including:	Ministers should set up inquiries under the 2005 Act unless there are overriding reasons of security or sensitivity for doing otherwise
	Ministers should give reasons for a decision not to hold an inquiry under the Act
	The Inquiries Act should be amended to reduce the powers of ministers
	A central inquiries unit in HM Courts and Tribunals Service should be created to deal with setting up inquiries and ensuring delivery of a full Lessons Learned paper after an inquiry
	A ministerial statement should be made to Parliament when every government response to an inquiry report is published to enable Parliament to hold ministers to account on their response and implementation plans

(Select Committee on the Inquiries Act, *The Inquiries Act 2005: Post Legislative Scrutiny*, pp 89–95)

 SUMMARY

- Inquiries are held in the public interest and are a government response to public concern when something goes wrong
- Inquiries can be statutory (usually under the Inquiries Act 2005) or non-statutory
- There are issues with the potential for government control over the inquiry process
- There are insufficient procedures for holding government to account for how it responds to inquiry reports, implements findings, and makes changes
- Recommendations for reform have called for regular progress updates to select committees to enable Parliament to hold government to account

We turn now to complaints procedures at an individual level.

14.3 Ombudsmen

> Ombudsmen (or Ombuds):
>
> - provide a complaints procedure for individuals against public (and some private) bodies;
> - provide a flexible, informal means of resolving a complaint outside the court system;
> - investigate and resolve complaints in a fair, independent, and impartial way;
> - provide a free service;
> - produce a report outlining their findings and make recommendations about the appropriate action that a public body should take in order to remedy the injustice.

Whereas an inquiry may concern a grievance of a larger section of the public and can raise political issues, an inquiry by an Ombudsman concerns a grievance of an individual or small group, with a different fact-finding process (see Cecil Clothier, 'Fact-finding in Inquiries—The PCA's Perspective' (1996) (Autumn) Public Law 384, 389). An Ombudsman is a Scandinavian concept, meaning 'a representative', someone to whom an individual takes a grievance or complaint against a more powerful organisation. Since the first Ombudsman in Sweden in the early nineteenth century, an increasing number of Ombudsmen (sometimes referred to as 'Ombuds'), in the UK and globally, have enabled citizens to bring complaints about public and other bodies. Ombudsmen will not normally commence an investigation before an individual has complained to the organisation first and given it an opportunity to resolve the complaint; they should complain to an Ombudsman if still dissatisfied at the end of the complaints process. Although some Ombudsmen deal with complaints about private sector companies and organisations, we are concerned with public services Ombudsmen, in particular, the Parliamentary and Health Service Ombudsman.

14.3.1 Public services Ombudsmen

Lord Sumption has commented that 'ombudsmen have come to fulfil an increasingly important role in mediating between the state and the public service on the one hand and the citizen on the other' (*In the matter of an application by JR55 for Judicial Review (Northern Ireland)* [2016] UKSC 22 [1]). Public services Ombudsmen investigate administrative injustice suffered by citizens and help them obtain redress against public bodies that are directly or indirectly subject to democratic accountability:

- government departments and agencies;
- local authorities;
- the NHS.

(See www.ombudsmanassociation.org/.)

The Law Commission identified three functions of a public services Ombudsman:

1. to address individual complaints ([2.49]);
2. to 'address systemic failures that occur across the administrative landscape' by addressing issues in their recommendations and reports ([2.50]);

3. to 'disseminate knowledge across governance networks' which means spreading good practice through reporting on performance, setting out codes of practice or creating principles to aid and inform administrative behaviour ([2.51]).

(The Law Commission, *Public Services Ombudsmen,* Consultation Paper No 196)

14.3.2 **The Parliamentary and Health Service Ombudsman**

The Parliamentary and Health Service Ombudsman:

- is part of the administrative justice system;

- impartially investigates complaints of maladministration (unfair treatment or poor service) by government departments and other public organisations and agencies across the UK—unless they are devolved—and the NHS in England;

- does not decide questions of law or whether the law has been breached;

- is independent of government and helps holds the executive to account;

- is accountable to Parliament as 'an officer of the House of Commons' and is scrutinised by the Public Administration and Constitutional Affairs Committee (PACAC), including monitoring complaints about the Ombudsman;

- submits an annual report to Parliament which is scrutinised by PACAC;

- can submit a special report to Parliament if injustice caused by maladministration has not been or will not be remedied.

The Parliamentary and Health Service Ombudsman (PHSO) combines two roles:

1. The Parliamentary Commissioner for Administration, known as the Parliamentary Ombudsman (created by the Parliamentary Commissioner Act 1967);

2. The Health Service Commissioner for England, known as the Health Service Ombudsman (set up under the NHS Reorganisation Act 1973 and now regulated by the Health Service Commissioners Act 1993).

The 1967 Act and the 1993 Act (as amended) form the legislative framework of the Ombudsman's powers.

 CLOSE-UP FOCUS: WHY WAS THE PARLIAMENTARY OMBUDSMAN CREATED?

The Parliamentary Ombudsman was created by the Parliamentary Commissioner Act 1967 (PCA) to provide independent scrutiny of the executive and 'to humanise relationships between the politician, the civil servant and the individual citizen' (Richard Crossman, HC Deb 18 October 1966, Vol 734 col 47).

Traditionally, citizens' grievances are aired in Parliament, where MPs can raise constituents' concerns in parliamentary questions and debates or through correspondence with government ministers. In 1961, the Whyatt Report recommended a Parliamentary Ombudsman for the UK (Sir John Whyatt QC, *The Citizen and the Administration: The Redress of*

Grievances, Report on behalf of JUSTICE). The subsequent 1965 White Paper envisaged the Ombudsman as sitting alongside and supporting Parliament's traditional function of receiving the grievances of citizens and holding ministers to account (*The Parliamentary Commissioner for Administration*, Cmnd 2767, 1965 [4]; see *In the matter of an application by JR55 for Judicial Review (Northern Ireland)*, [26] (Lord Sumption)).

The White Paper also envisaged that the Act would increase confidence in the executive by allowing administrative action to be fully and impartially investigated, and enabling the improvement of administrative standards and efficiency ([15]).

The Parliamentary Ombudsman was therefore intended to be an additional mechanism for MPs to call on to protect the citizen and call the executive to account.

14.3.2.1 **The MP filter**

Only MPs can refer a complaint about UK government departments and other public bodies to the PHSO; complaints cannot come directly from the public (section 5(1) PCA 1967). Citizens must therefore first make a complaint in writing to an MP (usually their constituency MP) within 12 months of becoming aware of an issue, although individuals can complain direct to the PHSO about Health Service complaints, which creates a disparity. While it retains the parliamentary link envisaged by the PCA 1967 and was designed to prevent a flood of claims to the Ombudsman, the MP filter denies citizens direct access to the Ombudsman, places the onus for action on MPs, and can lead to delay. It also means that when Parliament is dissolved before a general election, there are no MPs to whom the public can refer complaints (see Public Administration Committee, *Parliament and the Ombudsman*, 4th Report of Session 2009–10, HC 107).

Under the PCA 1967:

- The PHSO may investigate any administrative action taken by or on behalf of a government department or other public body where a member of the public claims to have sustained injustice as a result of maladministration (for a full list of bodies which can be investigated, see Schedule 2).
- Not all actions are subject to the PHSO's jurisdiction (see the exclusions in Schedule 3).

However, government departments cannot veto an investigation by the PHSO.

14.3.2.2 **Maladministration**

Maladministration covers a wide range of issues but was left undefined by the PCA 1967; the government believed that its meaning would be filled out as cases developed. When asking the House of Commons to give a Second Reading to the Parliamentary Commissioner Bill in 1967, Richard Crossman, the Leader of the House, listed what might constitute maladministration (this is known as the Crossman catalogue): 'bias, neglect, inattention, delay, incompetence, inaptitude, perversity, turpitude, arbitrariness and so on', adding, 'It would be a long and interesting list' (HC Deb 18 October 1966, Vol 734 col 51).

Subsequent judicial interpretations have emphasised that maladministration:

- is 'open-ended, covering the *manner* in which a decision is reached or discretion is exercised' (*R v Local Commissioner for Administration for the North and East Area of England ex parte Bradford Metropolitan City Council* [1979] 1 QB 287, 311H (Lord Denning));

- is not concerned with 'the nature, quality or reasonableness of the decision itself' (*R v Local Commissioner for Administration ex parte Eastleigh Borough Council* [1988] QB 855, 863E (Lord Donaldson MR));
- is not the same as unlawfulness (*R v Parliamentary Commissioner for Administration ex parte Balchin* [1996] EWHC Admin 152, [15] (Sedley J)).

> The Crossman catalogue of maladministration was expanded by Sir William Reid, then Parliamentary Ombudsman, in 1993 (Parliamentary Commissioner for Administration, *Annual Report for 1993*, HC 290, 1993–94, [7]). The list essentially included: rudeness, refusal to answer questions, not informing people of their rights or entitlements (including the right to appeal), giving incorrect or misleading advice, offering no redress or manifestly disproportionate redress, bias, faulty procedures, unfair treatment, and failure to follow correct procedures or guidance.
>
> For the full list, see John Halford, 'It's Public Law, But Not As We Know It: Understanding and Making Effective Use of Ombudsman Schemes' (2009) 14(1) Judicial Review 81 [16].
>
> See also the Ombudsman's principles for good administration by public bodies, which endorse legality, flexibility, transparency, fairness, and accountability (www.ombudsman.org.uk/about-us/our-principles).

When investigating health service complaints, the PHSO examines whether there has been maladministration or service failure in the case of health bodies and practitioners.

14.3.2.3 Injustice

The maladministration must have caused injustice, hardship, or financial loss to the complainant. Injustice refers to 'the sense of outrage aroused by unfair or incompetent administration, even where the complainant has suffered no actual loss' (Richard Crossman, HC Deb Vol 734 col 51).

14.3.2.4 Process

Most cases involve individual complaints, though the PHSO occasionally carries out large-scale investigations (eg *Equitable Life: A Decade of Regulatory Failure*, Report of the Parliamentary and Health Service Ombudsman (2007–08) HC 815).

A case will not be investigated if the complainant had, or has, an alternative remedy available in the courts, unless it was not reasonable to pursue it (section 5(2)(b) PCA 1967; see *Miller v Health Service Commissioner* [2018] EWCA Civ 144 [87–88]). Many cases of maladministration may also fall within the grounds for judicial review but the Ombudsman process has the advantage of:

- being low-cost;
- being investigatory, not adversarial, so representation by lawyers is not necessary;
- using investigatory powers to get to the bottom of a case, whereas judicial review requires evidence (see *R v Local Commissioner for Local Government for North and North East England ex parte Liverpool City Council* [2000] EWCA Civ 54 [21–28]).

The PHSO has the same powers as a High Court judge to require the attendance of witnesses and provision of information and documents (section 8 PCA 1967), and applies a test of fairness and reasonableness to reach a resolution, taking into account the circumstances of each case, the law, and relevant guidance, codes of practice, and good practice. If the Ombudsman finds the complaint is justified, s/he can *recommend* ways in which the public body can remedy the injustice, such as issuing an apology or paying compensation, and can identify failings or areas for future improvement (going beyond what a court can do), but does not have the power to change a public body's decision or award compensation, or to enforce their recommendations.

The PHSO's reports are covered by absolute privilege and there is no right of appeal against their decisions, but a report can be judicially reviewed (for a summary of relevant principles, see *R (Rapp) v The Parliamentary and Health Service Ombudsman* [2015] EWHC 1344 [38]). However, there is limited scope for interference by the courts (*R v Parliamentary Commissioner, ex parte Dyer* [1994] 1 WLR 621). The recommendations are only challengeable in the courts on grounds of irrationality (unreasonableness) or a failure to give reasons for findings on a principal controversial issue (*R v Parliamentary Commissioner for Administration ex p Balchin No 2* [1999] EWHC Admin 484; and see P. Giddings, 'Ex p. Balchin: Findings of Maladministration and Injustice' (2000) Public Law 201). In *Miller v Health Service Commissioner* [2018], for example, the Court of Appeal found the Health Service Ombudsman's standard for determining maladministration was irrational and unlawful.

However, the Ombudsman's recommendations are non-binding and a public body cannot be forced to accept them. The minister or other decision-maker can exercise their discretion about whether to accept the Ombudsman's findings of fact, but a minister's decision to reject them can be challenged by judicial review on the grounds of being irrational—that is, did the minister have cogent reasons for rejecting them? If not, the rejection can be quashed (*R (Bradley) v Secretary of State for Work and Pensions* [2008] EWCA Civ 36; *R (Equitable Life Members Action Group) v HM Treasury* [2009] EWHC 2495 (Admin)). A minister who does not accept a finding of maladministration must therefore have cogent reasons for doing so.

If a government department does not remedy an injustice after the Ombudsman's findings of maladministration, the Ombudsman can submit a special report to Parliament and Parliament can decide whether to call the minister to account, but only seven special reports have been presented since 1967.

Other public services Ombudsmen include:

The Local Government and Social Care Ombudsman investigates complaints by members of the public about maladministration by local authorities, various other bodies providing local public services, and adult social care providers. The Local Government Ombudsman for England and Wales was created by the Local Government Act 1974, and was renamed the Local Government and Social Care Ombudsman in 2017. (Its sponsoring and main funding department is the Ministry of Housing, Communities and Local Government.)

The Parliamentary and Health Service Ombudsman and Local Government and Social Care Ombudsman can carry out joint investigations of complaints covering both jurisdictions, for example, social care and health issues (Regulatory Reform (Collaboration Between Ombudsmen) Order 2007).

The Local Government and Social Care Ombudsman can also conduct joint investigations with the Housing Ombudsman.

The Housing Ombudsman investigates complaints about providers of social housing. This includes housing associations and, from April 2013, local authorities as landlords of social housing in England (see Localism Act 2011 section 180).

Continued

Public Services Ombudsmen in devolved administrations Scotland, Wales, and Northern Ireland each have separate Public Services Ombudsmen who are independent of government and investigate complaints about the public services devolved in their respective countries (for example, the NHS and local authorities):

- The Scottish Public Services Ombudsman
- The Public Services Ombudsman for Wales
- The Northern Ireland Public Services Ombudsman

Other Ombudsmen within the public sphere include the Prisons and Probation Ombudsman and the Judicial Appointments and Conduct Ombudsman. There are also complaint handlers outside the Ombudsman system such as the Office of the Independent Adjudicator for Higher Education, which investigates complaints from students about universities in England and Wales, and the Independent Office for Police Conduct (formerly the Independent Police Complaints Commission), which investigates complaints about the police in England and Wales and staff at other bodies including the National Crime Agency and Her Majesty's Revenue and Customs.

14.3.3 **Critique**

The Ombudsman system relies on citizens bringing complaints and on public awareness that the system is available. Complaints about government departments make up only a small percentage of the PHSO's casework because of the MP filter which is regarded as an unnecessary restriction on access to justice when complaining to the Ombudsman (*The Ombudsman's Casework Report 2019*, 3 March 2020, HC 63, p 11). The Public Administration Committee was concerned at a 'toxic cocktail' in respect of complaints handling generally where citizens were reluctant to voice complaints and services were defensive about hearing and addressing them (*More Complaints Please!* 12th Report of Session 2013–14 HC 229 [25]). The Committee also highlighted that the administrative justice system lacked an integrated approach and presented different avenues for redress of grievances about public services which could be confusing and complex ([69]; see the complaints maze at https://publications.parliament.uk/pa/cm201314/cmselect/cmpubadm/writev/229/m06.pdf). This is particularly true of the current system of disparate Ombudsmen, requiring complainants to decide which one is appropriate. The Public Administration Committee recommended a single minister for government policy on complaints ([20, 34]) and a single point of contact for citizens to make complaints about government departments and agencies to help complainants navigate the systems ([81]). A single public sector Ombudsman was also proposed by the Colcutt Review in 2000 (*Review of the Public Sector Ombudsmen in England: A Report by the Cabinet Office*, April 2000).

14.3.4 **Reform**

There has been piecemeal, fragmented development of the Ombudsman system and various suggestions for reform have been made, as outlined in Table 14.2.

Following a review in 2014 by Robert Gordon (*Better to Serve the Public: Proposals to Restructure, Reform, Renew and Reinvigorate Public Services Ombudsmen*, Report to The Rt Hon Oliver Letwin MP, Minister for Government Policy and Chancellor of the Duchy of Lancaster, October 2014), the government published a draft Public Service Ombudsman Bill in December 2016. Its aim was to modernise public service Ombudsmen by abolishing the PHSO and Local Government Ombudsman and creating a single Public Service Ombudsman as a clear point of contact for complainants, but it did not make legislative progress. The PHSO has argued that the draft Bill 'no longer represents international best practice in the Ombudsman sector' (House of Commons Public Administration and Constitutional Affairs Committee, *Parliamentary and Health Service Ombudsman Scrutiny 2018–19*, Second Report of Session 2019–21, HC 117 [50]), and PACAC has called for an updated draft Bill to create a single Public Service Ombudsman ([51]). New legislation would need to take account of the 2019 Venice Principles, an international set of standards for Ombudsmen (Principles on the Protection and Promotion of the Ombudsman Institution, adopted by the Venice Commission (Venice, 15–16 March 2019) at www.venice.coe. int). The Principles recognise the important role of Ombudsmen in 'strengthening democracy, the rule of law, good administration and the protection and promotion of human rights and fundamental freedoms' ([1]), and include giving Ombudsmen discretionary power to investigate cases on their initiative or as a result of a complaint ([16]). In relation to the MP filter, PACAC took the view that new legislation should retain a role for MPs to support their constituents ([52]).

Table 14.2 Proposals for reform

The Law Commission's provisional proposals for reform included:	Allowing appropriate cases to be transferred from the courts to the public services Ombudsmen under a 'stay and transfer power' ([4.66–4.76])
	Allowing public services Ombudsmen to: refer a case to a court on a point of law ([5.85]); open a complaint themselves ([4.42]); deal with complaints other than by an investigation ([4.85])
	Reforming the MP filter with a dual-track approach where complaints could be made either through an MP or directly by a citizen ([4.106])
	None of the proposals were implemented
(Law Commission, *Public Services Ombudsmen*, Consultation Paper No 196)	
In 2014, the Public Administration Select Committee concluded that the Ombudsman should be seen as 'a People's Ombudsman service' as well as Parliament's Ombudsman ([45]) and recommended:	New legislation for a simpler, more straightforward Ombudsman service
	Abolishing the MP filter to allow citizens direct access ([56])
	Allowing the Ombudsman to receive complaints not just in writing but also in person, by telephone, or online ([60]), and to investigate areas of concern under their own initiative without having to receive a complaint first ([72])
	Parliament should strengthen the accountability of the Ombudsman. Departmental Select Committees should use Ombudsman's reports to hold government to account ([88])
	A consultation on creating a single public services Ombudsman for England ([99])
	A minister for government policy in respect of the Parliamentary and Health Service Ombudsman ([46])
(House of Commons Public Administration Select Committee, *Time for a People's Ombudsman Service*, 14th Report of Session 2013–14, HC 655 pp 43–46)	

Sir Ernest Ryder has suggested that administrative courts and tribunals should be able to refer maladministration matters to an Ombudsman for consideration; Ombudsmen could refer issues to the Administrative Appeals Chamber of the Upper Tribunal for judicial review or individual redress beyond their powers; and judges should be able to work as Ombuds and vice-versa (Sir Ernest Ryder, 'Driving Improvements: Collaboration And Peer Learning' available at https://www.judiciary.uk).

 SUMMARY

Public services Ombudsmen:

- promote the interests of citizens;
- protect against maladministration and injustice;
- help to hold the executive to account and uphold the rule of law.

We turn next to resolution of citizen and state disputes in tribunals.

14.4 Tribunals

Tribunals:

- are permanent, specialised judicial bodies within the justice system;
- determine rights and entitlements in disputes between citizens and state in specific areas of law, for example, social security, immigration and asylum, tax;
- have a less adversarial, more inquisitorial procedure than the court system; hearings often take place without lawyers so can be less formal and less expensive than courts;
- make binding decisions based on fact and law;
- are created by statute and operate within a statutory framework.

14.4.1 Background

'Tribunals are an essential component of the rule of law. They enable citizens to hold the state and employers to account for decisions that have a significant impact on people's lives. The hallmark of the tribunals system is the delivery of fair, specialist and innovative justice.' (*Transforming Our Justice System*, The Lord Chancellor, the Lord Chief Justice and the Senior President of Tribunals, September 2016, p 15).

Lord Justice Gross observes that 'the Justice system must provide a framework for dealing with disputes between the citizen and the State, concerning rights, entitlements and liabilities. Much of this work is undertaken by Tribunals' ('The Judicial System in a Modern Democracy', RCDS Lecture, 8 May 2015 [24]). Tribunals are part of the administrative justice system and many resolve 'citizen and state' disputes (the Employment Tribunal and Property Chamber deal with 'citizen and citizen' disputes). Cases often involve appeals against administrative decisions by government departments or public bodies, for example, on:

- entitlement to a benefit such as social security or child support;

- mental health;

- immigration and asylum decisions by the Home Office.

There are differences between a court and a tribunal:

- Courts usually hear a broader, more general range of disputes; each tribunal operates within a limited, specific area of law (or 'jurisdiction') with expertise within their area of jurisdiction.

- Rules of evidence are applied less strictly in tribunals, which have their own procedures.

Tribunals developed in a piecemeal, haphazard way without overall co-ordination or structure. They were set up as needed and were initially regarded as administrative bodies, often closely linked to, and administered by, government departments, multiplying rapidly as social legislation increased through the twentieth century.

 THINKING POINT

Note the administrative origins of tribunals and their close links to the executive. Now note the transformation that happens.

Both the Donoughmore Committee (1932) and the Franks Committee (1957) recognised tribunals as part of the *justice system* (this is referred to as the 'judicialisation' of tribunals). The Franks Report stated:

> [T]ribunals are not ordinary courts, but neither are they appendages of government departments . . . We consider that tribunals should properly be regarded as machinery provided by Parliament for adjudication rather than as part of the machinery of administration. (Report of the Committee on Administrative Tribunals and Enquiries (Cmnd 218) 15 July 1957 [40])

The Report recommended that tribunal proceedings should have the underpinning values of 'openness, fairness and impartiality', which meant public hearings, giving reasons for decisions, allowing parties a fair hearing, and not being influenced by other bodies ([23–24]).

However, by 2001, there were 70 or more different tribunals, and a review of the tribunal system was carried out by Sir Andrew Leggatt. The Leggatt Report acknowledged that tribunals were the largest part of the civil justice system in England and Wales (*Tribunals for Users, One System, One Service*, Report of the Review of Tribunals by Sir Andrew Leggatt, March 2001 [1.1]), but found:

- A 'collection of tribunals, mostly administered by departments, with wide variations of practice and approach, and almost no coherence' which had developed to meet the needs of departments, not the user ([1.3]).

- Tribunals were isolated from each other ([1.18]) and not co-ordinated in their operations, with delays and lack of efficiency.

- They used old-fashioned methods ([1.23]).

- There needed to be separation between ministers and tribunals.

The Report therefore recommended a system that was accessible and user-friendly, independent from ministers, modernised, co-ordinated, and on a par with the court system. It proposed:

- bringing tribunals together in a single tribunals system with a two-tier structure
- managed by a new independent Tribunals Service.

For helpful detail on the development of tribunals, see Lord Thomas of Cwmgiedd, Lord Chief Justice of England And Wales, 'Building the Best Court Forum for Commercial Dispute Resolution', Wales Commercial Law Association, Cardiff, 21 October 2016.

14.4.2 Organisation

In order to implement the Leggatt reforms:

- A 2004 White Paper set out proposals for an improved system of dispute resolution and a new Tribunals Service (*Transforming Public Services: Complaints, Redress and Tribunals* Cm 6243, July 2004).

- In 2006, the Tribunals Service was created to administer tribunals. It was governed by, but operationally independent from, the Ministry of Justice, ensuring a clearer separation of powers between the executive and tribunals.

- The Tribunals, Courts and Enforcement Act 2007 created the current independent two-tier tribunal system: a First-tier Tribunal and an Upper Tribunal (see Table 14.3). This streamlined most tribunals into a single unified tribunal system. The changes were phased in during 2008 and 2009.

- In 2011, Her Majesty's Courts and Tribunals Service (HMCTS), an executive agency of the Ministry of Justice, took over administration of the two-tier tribunal system in England and non-devolved tribunals.

For a timeline of tribunal development, see The Senior President of Tribunals' Annual Report, *Tribunals Transformed*, February 2010, pp 8–9; available at www.judiciary.uk. For a tribunal organisation chart, see www.judiciary.uk/wp-content/uploads/2020/08/tribunals-chart-updated-May-2020.pdf.

However, there is still some variation in the system. Some tribunals are outside the two-tier structure but are administered by HMCTS (eg the Employment Tribunals and the Employment Appeals Tribunal, Gender Recognition Panel, Proscribed Organisations Appeals Committee, and Special Immigration Appeals Commission). A small number outside the unified structure are not administered by HMCTS and are still accountable to ministers.

Table 14.3 The two-tier tribunal system

The First-tier Tribunal and Upper Tribunal are both divided into chambers, organised by subject matter or expertise	**The First-tier Tribunal** has seven chambers, mainly hearing appeals from individuals against decisions made by government departments or agencies, for example on war pensions, benefits and tax credits, health, education and social care, tax
	The Upper Tribunal decides appeals on points of law from the First-tier Tribunal and has judicial review powers over certain First-tier Tribunal decisions. It has equivalent status to the High Court and is divided into four chambers: Administrative Appeals, Tax and Chancery, Immigration and Asylum, and the Lands Chamber

Figure 14.2 Tribunals judiciary

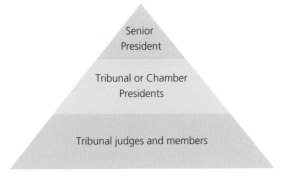

Some tribunals have UK-wide jurisdiction, such as the tribunals on immigration and asylum and tax, while some parts of the tribunals system are devolved to Scotland, Wales, and Northern Ireland. The Mental Health Tribunal, for example, covers England only. The Tribunals (Scotland) Act 2014 created the First-tier Tribunal for Scotland and the Upper Tribunal for Scotland. The Welsh Tribunals are defined in the Wales Act 2017, which created a President of Welsh Tribunals.

The Tribunals, Courts and Enforcement Act 2007 (section 2 and Schedule 1) created a new, independent judicial office of Senior President of Tribunals to head the tribunals judiciary (see Figure 14.2) and represent their views to Parliament and the government. The Senior President is selected from among Court of Appeal judges (or equivalent in Scotland and Northern Ireland) or through the Judicial Appointments Commission.

Tribunal or Chamber Presidents, who are selected from among High Court judges or through the Judicial Appointments Commission, are responsible for their tribunal or chamber (Schedule 3). Tribunal judges are legally qualified, while non-legal tribunal members have specific areas of expertise and are often professionally qualified, such as doctors or accountants. Most tribunal appointments are made through the Judicial Appointments Commission.

14.4.3 Procedure

Access to justice in tribunals is important (see *R (UNISON) v Lord Chancellor* [2017] UKSC 51). Tribunals often sit as a panel, consisting of a tribunal judge and non-legal panel members. Hearings are normally in public and in many cases individuals represent themselves without lawyers, so the emphasis is on accessibility, guidance, and less formality than a court. Tribunal decisions are legally binding on the parties and, depending on the nature of the case, some tribunals may reverse a public body's decision, for example allowing a benefit that has been refused; some may award compensation or impose fines and penalties.

14.4.4 Appeals and judicial review

The Upper Tribunal may hear some cases at first instance but it provides a dedicated appeal route within the tribunal system. There is a right of appeal to the Upper Tribunal from First-tier Tribunals on a point of law (permission to appeal must be granted). It may also judicially review decisions of First-tier Tribunals in specified circumstances (see section 31A Senior Courts Act 1981). See Figures 14.3 and 14.4 for key points on appeals from the Upper Tribunal and judicial review of Upper Tribunal decisions.

⏩ CROSS REFERENCE

For judicial review in the courts, see Chapters 15 and 16

14.4.5 **Critique**

The reformed tribunal structure has been described by Sir Jeremy Sullivan, a former Senior President, as 'robust and flexible' and 'fit for purpose' (Senior President of Tribunals' Annual Report, February 2015, p 4). However, further reform is ongoing. A wider reform pro-gramme of the justice system was launched in 2016 (see *Transforming Our Justice System*, The Lord Chancellor, the Lord Chief Justice and the Senior President of Tribunals, Septem-ber 2016, p 15) under which tribunal procedures are being simplified with online routes to access services.

There was controversy over the abolition in 2013 of the Administrative and Justice Tribunals Council, which was an important independent overseer of the tribunal system and the admin-istrative justice landscape (it had replaced the Council on Tribunals, which had been created

Figure 14.3 Appeals from the Upper Tribunal

Decisions of the Upper Tribunal may be appealed to the Court of Appeal

But permission will only be granted if the appeal raises **an important point of principle or practice or some other compelling reason**

This is because they are second appeals, having already been appealed once to the Upper Tribunal (Access to Justice Act 1999 section 55)

There needs to be 'a compelling reason why the issue on which the claimant has failed twice should be subjected to a third judicial process', as Parliament has created a two-tier tribunal system which is competent to determine matters (*R (PR (Sri Lanka)) v Secretary of State for the Home Department* [2011] EWCA Civ 988 [41])

Figure 14.4 Judicial review of Upper Tribunal decisions

A refusal of leave to appeal to the Upper Tribunal may be subject to judicial review by the High Court

But only where there is **an important point of principle or practice or some other compelling reason for the case to be reviewed** (*R (Cart) v Upper Tribunal* [2011] UKSC 28)

The Supreme Court stated that this was because of the new tribunal structure, and it applied the appeal criteria above (see *Cart* [37–38, 51–58])

While no system of decision-making is infallible, judicial review should be no more than necessary and proportionate for maintaining the rule of law to keep errors of law to a minimum ([37,56])

following the Franks Report). The government believed that a standing body to oversee tribunals was not needed because administration by HMCTS sufficiently ensured the tribunals system's independence from decision-makers, and policy development and oversight of the wider administrative justice system would be led from within the Ministry of Justice. However, in 2018, a new, independent Administrative Justice Council was set up to oversee the UK administrative justice system, promote fairness, accessibility, and efficiency in administrative justice, and advise central and devolved governments and the judiciary.

 SUMMARY

- Tribunals began as administrative bodies but now are an integral part of the independent judicial system
- Specialist expertise underpins the tribunal system
- The major structural reforms after the Leggatt Report have been successful in producing a streamlined, unified, coherent tribunals system, though some tribunals still lie outside

14.5 Judicial review

The most formal component of the administrative justice system is judicial review. Here, citizens challenge decision-making by government departments or other public bodies and pursue remedies in the courts. We examine in Chapter 15 the bigger picture of judicial review in terms of its development, context, and key procedural elements as a pathway to analysing the grounds of judicial review in Chapter 16.

? Questions

Self-test questions

1. What is the main purpose of the administrative justice system?
2. Explain what is meant by (a) redress; (b) grievance mechanisms.
3. When will a public inquiry be set up?
4. Are public inquiries fully independent from government?
5. What is the role of the PHSO?
6. How does the Ombudsman process differ from the court process?
7. What is the function of tribunals?
8. What key reform was introduced after the Leggatt Report?

Exam question

'The administrative justice system is currently constructed in such a way that someone with a grievance could be directed down a number of different paths, for example an internal complaints process or an appeal process. An integrated approach to administrative justice is lacking.' (Public Administration Select Committee, *More Complaints Please!* 12th Report of Session 2013–14, HC 229 [69]).

Evaluate the extent to which the administrative justice system provides a coherent, integrated mechanism for providing redress for citizens.

Further reading

Books

Kirkham, R. and Gill, C. (eds) *A Manifesto for Ombudsman Reform* (Basingstoke: Palgrave Macmillan 2020).
Explains the need for Ombudsman reform and the powers a modern public Ombudsman should have

Journal articles

Beatson, J. 'Should Judges Conduct Public Inquiries?' (2005) 121 Law Quarterly Review 221.
Assesses the benefits of judicial inquiries but also good background on inquiries generally, especially Hutton

Clothier, C. 'The Value of an Ombudsman' (1986) (Summer) Public Law 204.
Helpful insight into the nature of the Parliamentary Ombudsman's work

Elias, S. 'Administrative Law for "Living People"' 2009 68(1) CLJ 47.
Written from a New Zealand perspective, a readable overview of the development and scope of Administrative Law

Elliott, M. and Thomas, R. 'Tribunal Justice and Proportionate Dispute Resolution' (2012) 71(2) Cambridge Law Journal 297.
Examines the *Cart case* and more broadly the issues of judicial review of tribunal decisions

Seneviratne, M. '"Joining Up" the Ombudsmen—The Review of the Public Sector Ombudsmen in England' (2000) (Winter) Public Law 582.
Assesses the Colcutt proposals

Other sources

Abraham, A. 'The Parliamentary Ombudsman and Administrative Justice, Shaping the Next 50 Years', Justice–Tom Sargant memorial annual lecture, 2011. Available at https://files.justice.org.uk/wp-content/uploads/2015/02/06172428/Parliamentary-Ombudsman-and-Administrative-Justice.pdf.
Oversight of the Ombudsman scheme and the administrative justice system by a former Parliamentary Ombudsman

Carnwath, Sir R. *Tribunals Transformed*, Senior President of Tribunals' Annual Report, February 2010. Available at www.judiciary.uk/wp-content/uploads/JCO/Documents/Reports/senior-president-tribunals-report-2010.pdf.
A detailed account of the development and operation of the tribunals system

Harlow, C. 'What Price Inquiries?' UK Const L Blog (28 February 2013).
Available at ukconstitutionallaw.org. Good critical comment on inquiries

House of Commons Library Briefing Paper Number 02599, 30 November 2016, *Public Inquiries: Non-statutory Commissions of Inquiry*, Jack Simson Caird.
For more detail on non-statutory inquiries

House of Commons Library Briefing Paper Number 06410, 8 September 2020, *Statutory Commissions of Inquiry: The Inquiries Act 2005*, Graeme Cowie and Mark Sandford.
For more detail on statutory inquiries

House of Commons Library Briefing Paper Number 07587, 12 August 2016, *A Public Service Ombudsman for the UK*, Michael Everett.
Background to the Public Service Ombudsman Bill 2016

Kirkham, R. 'The Parliamentary Ombudsman: Withstanding the Test of Time', 4th Report Session 2006–2007, HC421.
A critique of the Parliamentary Ombudsman

Law Commission, Consultation Paper No 187, Administrative Redress: Public Bodies and the Citizen.
See part 3 for an in-depth overview of the administrative justice system

Public Law Project, *An Introduction to Public Law* at https://publiclawproject.org.uk/what-is-public-law/guides-public-law-2/.
A short guide to complaint mechanisms, including judicial review

Useful websites

www.ombudsman.org.uk/

www.judiciary.uk/about-the-judiciary/who-are-the-judiciary/judicial-roles/tribunals/tribunals/

; Online resources

www.oup.com/he/dennett2e

This chapter is accompanied by a selection of online resources to help you with this topic, including:

- Multiple-choice questions
- Answers to the self-test questions
- Guidance on answering the exam question

15 Introduction to judicial review

LEARNING OBJECTIVES

By the end of this chapter, you should be able to:

- Evaluate the constitutional significance of judicial review
- Be aware of the significance of the preliminary issues for judicial review claims
- Appraise the need for the public/private law dividing line
- Explain how the source of power and *Datafin* tests are used by the courts
- Appreciate why the rules on standing exist and how they operate
- Evaluate key steps in the judicial review process

Introduction

Imagine that the Health Minister has just announced the closure of the Accident and Emergency unit at your local hospital without allowing public consultation as required by statute. What action could you take? As an aggrieved local resident, you could consider bringing a judicial review claim in the High Court, asking that the decision be quashed (declared void). Judicial review is the process by which individuals can challenge decision-making by government departments or other public bodies in court; the claimant must show that the public body has exercised its power unlawfully, unreasonably, unfairly, or, in some cases, disproportionately under the grounds set out by Lord Diplock in *Council of Civil Service Unions v Minister for the Civil Service* [1985] AC 374 (see Table 15.1).

In this chapter, we examine the purpose and constitutional significance of judicial review and the important procedural 'hurdles' that claimants must satisfy in order to bring a claim.

CROSS REFERENCE

For details of the grounds of judicial review, see Chapter 16

Table 15.1 The grounds of judicial review

Ground	Meaning
Illegality (unlawfulness)	Has the public body acted lawfully within the legal powers given to it by statute, or under the royal prerogative?
Irrationality (unreasonableness)	Has it acted rationally when making decisions?
Procedural impropriety (procedural unfairness)	Has it followed fair procedures?
Proportionality	Not a standalone ground for judicial review but it is used in cases involving human rights (see Chapter 17). The court assesses whether the public body used its power in a disproportionate way.

15.1 Why is judicial review important?

Judicial review is increasingly essential as we have an increasingly powerful executive. It is an irritant to the executive, but it is a very important, fundamental control on the executive, and the fact that members of the executive at all levels know that they are subject to judicial review helps ensure that they carry out their job properly. (Lord Neuberger, oral evidence to the House of Lords Constitution Committee, 13 February 2013, Q.14)

Powers are given to public bodies 'to be exercised in the public interest, and the public has an interest in ensuring that the powers are not abused' (*R (Molinaro) v RB of Kensington & Chelsea* [2001] EWHC Admin 896 [67] (Elias J)). Public bodies include: government departments and agencies; local authorities; coroners' courts, the police, prisons, the NHS; and administrative, regulatory, and supervisory bodies. Where public bodies overreach themselves by acting unlawfully, the judicial review process allows individuals to hold them to account in the courts, ensuring that governmental and public powers are lawfully exercised. This maintains the rule of law by helping to protect the public from the arbitrary or unreasonable exercise of government power, reinforcing the fundamental idea of government according to law embodied in *Entick v Carrington*. Judicial review is therefore a powerful check and control by the courts on executive action, but it also raises issues of whether the process gives the judiciary too much power over the elected government.

15.1.1 Background

'. . . judicial review is an important mechanism for the maintenance of the rule of law. It serves to correct unlawful conduct on the part of public authorities. However, judicial review is not an appeal against governmental decisions on their merits. The wisdom of governmental policy is not a matter for the courts and, in a democratic society, must be a matter for the elected government alone. . . . Judicial review is not, and should not be regarded as, politics by another means.' (*R (Hoareau and Bancoult) v Secretary of State for Foreign and Commonwealth Affairs* [2019] EWHC 221 (Admin) [326])

Judicial review derives from common law as a supervisory process. Judicial review claims are brought in the Administrative Court, a specialist court within the High Court which has an inherent supervisory jurisdiction over lower courts, tribunals, and administrative bodies; this allows it to correct their legal errors, and thereby maintain the rule of law. The High Court is therefore regarded as the 'constitutional guardian of the rule of law' (*R (Privacy International) v Investigatory Powers Tribunal* [2019] UKSC 22 [139]). The term 'judicial review' was first used in 1977 in Order 53, Rules of the Supreme Court, and the right to judicial review is now enshrined in sections 29 and 31 of the Senior Courts Act 1981. Technically, reflecting its supervisory nature, a judicial review claim is brought by the Crown on the application of the claimant (denoted by the use of R or The Queen in the case name eg *R (Miller) v The Prime Minister*), although the Crown is not actually involved in the case. The claim is brought against the public body making the decision, not a named individual within it, though the relevant Secretary of State is the defendant where the decision is made by their department.

The modern law on judicial review was developed by the courts in the 1960s, and the number of cases increased dramatically over the next 40 years. Lord Neuberger attributes this to the fact that there has simply been more for the courts to review:

(i) the enormous increase in the powers of the executive

(ii) the expansion of executive bodies

(iii) a plethora of new laws, most of them secondary legislation, which were themselves judicially reviewable

(iv) a more questioning and litigation-inclined society

(v) the growth of legal aid

(vi) the weakness of the legislature, which for most of the time enjoyed comfortable government majorities, and

(vii) a general public awareness of rights, prompted partly by the [European Convention on Human Rights].

('The Role of Judges in Human Rights Jurisprudence: A Comparison of the Australian and UK Experience', speech delivered at the Supreme Court of Victoria, Melbourne, 8 August 2014 [20])

However, although the number of judicial review applications peaked at more than 15,000 in 2013, this was mainly due to immigration and asylum cases, which, since 2013, are heard by the Upper Tribunal (Immigration and Asylum Chamber); by 2019, the total had fallen to 3,400 applications (www.gov.uk/government/statistics/civil-justice-statistics-quarterly-january-to-march-2020).

It is important to note the following:

- Judicial review is not an appeal process; the court does not substitute its own decision for that of the public body, or make findings of fact.

- The court is examining the *decision-making process* rather than the merits of the decision itself (though be prepared for a few inroads on this idea in Chapter 16).

- **Judges cannot judicially review Acts of the UK Parliament**; while they have been expressly empowered by Parliament to measure legislation for human rights-compatibility under the Human Rights Act 1998, the courts cannot otherwise review, and cannot strike down, primary legislation, thus respecting parliamentary sovereignty (but see argument on the 'nuclear option' in section 8.3.3).

Secondary legislation *is* judicially reviewable: so is legislation from the devolved administrations. However, when judicially reviewing legislation from devolved legislatures, the courts give greater weight to their decisions as democratically elected bodies (*AXA General Insurance Ltd v HM Advocate* [2011] UKSC 46, [2012] 1 AC 868 [49] (Lord Hope)).

15.1.2 The constitutional significance of judicial review

> To understand the points made in this chapter, you need to know that *ultra vires* means that a public body has acted outside its powers, and *Wednesbury* unreasonableness refers to the test developed in *Associated Provincial Picture Houses Ltd v Wednesbury Corporation* (1948) 1 KB 223 and means that an executive or administrative decision by a public body will be set aside if no reasonable decisionmaker could have made it.

Different constitutional justifications for judicial review have been advanced:

1. It upholds parliamentary sovereignty. To ensure that public bodies act within their lawful authority, the courts interpret and apply Parliament's intention as expressed in the statutes conferring legal powers on those bodies. Lord Browne-Wilkinson has observed that Parliament gives those powers on the assumption that they will be exercised only within the jurisdiction conferred, in accordance with fair procedures and reasonably, in the *Wednesbury* sense; if public decision-makers fail to do so, they are acting *ultra vires* and therefore unlawfully (*R v Hull University Visitor, ex parte Page* [1993] AC 682, 701). (See further Christopher Forsyth, 'Of Fig Leaves and Fairy Tales: The Ultra Vires Doctrine, the Sovereignty of Parliament and Judicial Review' (1996) 55(1) CLJ 122; Lord Steyn, 'The Constitutionalisation of Public Law', The Constitution Unit, May 1999; Mark Elliott, 'The Ultra Vires Doctrine in a Constitutional Setting: Still the Central Principle of Administrative Law' (1999) 58(1) Cambridge Law Journal 129.)

2. It upholds common law constitutional principles which are protected by the rule of law, such as fairness and equality. Executive action that breaches those principles can be overturned. (See Paul Craig, 'Ultra Vires and the Foundations of Judicial Review' (1998) 57(1) Cambridge Law Journal 63; R.M.W. Masterman and J.E.K. Murkens (2013) 'Skirting Supremacy and Subordination: The Constitutional Authority of the United Kingdom Supreme Court' (2013) Public Law 800; for a shared sovereignty view, see T.R.S. Allan, 'Constitutional Dialogue and the Justification of Judicial Review' (2003) 23(4) OJLS 563.)

15.1.2.1 Judicial review and the rule of law

There is strong judicial support for the idea that judicial review goes beyond redressing individual grievances and has a constitutional function of upholding the rule of law (see *Walton v The Scottish Ministers* [2012] UKSC 44 [90] (Lord Reed)). Lord Dyson has stated that 'there is no principle more basic to our system of law than the maintenance of rule of law itself and the constitutional protection afforded by judicial review' (*R (Cart) v Upper Tribunal* [2011] UKSC 28 [122]; see also Lord Hoffmann in *R (Alconbury Developments Ltd) v Secretary of State for the Environment, Transport and the Regions* [2003] 2 AC 295 [73]). The rule of law depends on the availability of judicial review (*R (Privacy International) v Investigatory Powers Tribunal* [2019] UKSC 22 [199]). There are two key strands to this: (1) an independent judiciary; (2) calling the executive to account.

> **CROSS REFERENCE**
>
> For the rule of law, see Chapter 8

An independent judiciary is essential for effective judicial review, requiring:

- the independence of the judiciary from any executive interference;

- the duty of the court to stand between citizen and state;
- the duty of the court to order the executive to comply with the law and not overreach itself.

(See Lord Irvine, HL Hansard 17 February 1999, Vol 597 col 734.)

 THINKING POINT

Consider the significance of the separation of powers here (see Chapter 7).

In the UK constitution, the courts' function of calling the executive to account is essential. Jonathan Sumption argues that judicial review has increased because of Parliament's declining power to hold the government to account ('Judicial and Political Decision-Making: The Uncertain Boundary', The F.A. Mann Lecture, 2011). Lord Neuberger's view is that:

> The courts have no more important function than that of protecting citizens from the abuses and excesses of the executive—central government, local government, or other public bodies . . . the more power that a government has, the more likely it is that there will be abuses and excesses which result in injustice to citizens, and the more important it is for the rule of law that such abuses and excesses can be brought before an impartial and experienced judge who can deal with them openly, dispassionately and fairly. ('Justice in an Age of Austerity', Justice– Tom Sargant Memorial Lecture 2013 [37])

15.1.3 **Theories: red, green, and amber light theory**

Red and green light theories were put forward by Harlow and Rawlings in the 1980s to explain the role of Administrative Law (C. Harlow and R. Rawlings, *Law and Administration* (London: Weidenfeld & Nicolson 1984)). They highlight the tension between the government powering

Table 15.2 Red, green, and amber light theory

Red light theory	Green light theory	Amber light theory
Law is superior to politics. Government is subject to the law (the rule of law) and there must be limits on its power.	The role of the law and the courts in controlling government power should be minimised to allow the state to function and expand. Courts are seen as an external control and obstacles to progress within the state.	Combines judicial control with accountable, effective public bodies.
Administrative law should subject public bodies to legal and judicial control to stop excesses of state power.		Law is separate from, and superior to, politics, and public bodies can be limited by law, especially where constitutional and human rights are affected.
Parliament controls the executive through limits in statutes.	Administrative law is part of the machinery of government to encourage good practice. Policy-making is a political function, and control of government power comes through the political process and internal regulation by public bodies.	Judicial rules are the best way to control the state but the law should allow public bodies some discretionary power.
Independent judges can review administrative decisions by applying the law.		

ahead with policy decisions and the practical realities of running the state, and the judges who restrain them by upholding the rule of law (see the summary in Table 15.2). The key to the red/green light debate is how far judges and Parliament should control executive power, and whether we perceive the state/government as a force to be strictly limited by law and kept within its bounds (red theory) or a progressive force for good, with legal checks merely contributing to better administration (green theory).

For an overview, see Adam Tomkins, 'In Defence of the Political Constitution' (2002) 22(1) Oxford Journal of Legal Studies 157, 157–161.

15.2 Ouster clauses

> A statute may contain a provision that decisions of a tribunal or other body shall be final, or shall not be reviewed or questioned by the courts. This is known as an 'ouster clause' because it ousts or excludes the jurisdiction of the courts and the judicial review process. (For an explanation of different forms of ouster clauses, and generally, see Anna Eliasson, Robert Chiarella, and Shameem Ahmad, 'Ousting the Ouster Clause?' (2017) 22(3) Judicial Review 263.)

Ouster clauses are controversial because they exclude (a) the right to go to court for redress and (b) the power of the courts to correct legal errors. For this reason, Laws LJ has called attempts to oust the High Court's supervisory jurisdiction over public authorities 'repugnant to the constitution' (*A v B* [2009] EWCA Civ 24 [22]). The issue is that tribunals might make errors of law which need to be reviewed by the courts through judicial review (see *Cart* [2012] 1 AC 663 [42–43] (Baroness Hale)). The rule of law requires that questions of law should be consistently interpreted and applied through the courts; the 'integrity of the legal system would be undermined if a statutory tribunal operated as a legal island' where its decisions on questions of law could not reach the courts for review (*R (Privacy International) v Investigatory Powers Tribunal* [2017] EWHC 114 (Admin) [48–50] (Leggatt J)).

> ### 🔍 CASE CLOSE-UP: *ANISMINIC LTD v FOREIGN COMPENSATION COMMISSION* [1969] 2 AC 147
>
> The leading case on ouster clauses is *Anisminic Ltd v Foreign Compensation Commission* [1969] 2 AC 147, where a clause in the Foreign Compensation Act 1950 provided that determinations by the Foreign Compensation Commission of any application made to them under the Act shall not be called in question in any court of law. The House of Lords interpreted the clause as not intended to oust the courts' jurisdiction entirely, but only applying to determinations that were not null and void; the courts had jurisdiction where the Commission acted beyond its powers, such as in making an error of law.

Anisminic exemplified the courts' restrictive approach to interpreting ouster clauses in a way that protects the jurisdiction of the court. Lord Justice Sales has stated that it defeats the rule of law if individuals 'cannot get before a court or tribunal to determine a complaint that a public authority has engaged in unlawful conduct' (*R (Privacy International) v Investigatory Powers Tribunal* [2017] EWCA Civ 1868 [19]). He took the view that the restrictive approach to interpreting ouster clauses is an application of the principle of legality which presumes that

>> CROSS REFERENCE

For an explanation of the principle of legality, see section 9.2.2

'Parliament intends to legislate for a liberal democracy subject to the rule of law, respecting human rights and other fundamental principles of the constitution', including the right to have access to a court or tribunal ([21]).

THINKING POINT

Does the *Anisminic* approach mean that the courts are telling Parliament 'you didn't mean what you said' in this Act?

CLOSE-UP FOCUS: CLAUSE 11 (LATER CLAUSE 14) OF THE ASYLUM AND IMMIGRATION (TREATMENT OF CLAIMANTS, ETC) BILL 2004

This clause attempted to prevent the courts from reviewing the lawfulness of tribunal decisions on asylum and immigration; the government's aim was to reduce delays and costs.

The clause caused judicial and constitutional outrage and was widely condemned. Judges and lawyers made it clear that it was legally unacceptable; it was not consistent with the rule of law to allow a tribunal to make decisions that were immune from review by the higher courts. Those speaking against it included Lord Woolf, Lord Steyn, and David Pannick QC; Lord Irvine, the former Lord Chancellor, advised the government that Clause 11 was unlikely to be effective (see HL Deb 15 March 2004, Vol 659 col 50–90; see also Immigration Law Practitioners' Association, 'A Briefing for Peers on the Asylum and Immigration (Treatment of Claimants, etc) Bill', Second Reading in the House of Lords, 15 March 2004; and Lord Steyn, Speech at Inner Temple Hall, 3 March 2004).

The clause was removed from the Bill, but Lord Donaldson later speculated about the constitutional crisis that would have arisen had it remained in the Act: 'we would simply have to say: "We [the judges] are an independent estate of the realm and it's not open to the legislature to put us out of business. And so we shall simply ignore your ouster clause"' (www.theguardian.com/politics/2005/apr/26/constitution.election2005).

Can an ouster clause ever be effective? Section 67(8) of the Regulation of Investigatory Powers Act 2000 excluded decisions of the Investigatory Powers Tribunal (IPT) from appeal or challenge in any court ('shall not be subject to appeal or be liable to be questioned in any court'). The IPT is a court, with High Court judges, that exclusively hears complaints against UK intelligence and security services. Although the Court of Appeal decided the clause was effective in rendering decisions of the IPT immune from judicial review (*R (Privacy International) v Investigatory Powers Tribunal* [2017] EWCA Civ 1868)—the first time a 'shall not be questioned' ouster clause was judged effective—the Supreme Court disagreed (*R (Privacy International) v Investigatory Powers Tribunal* [2019] UKSC 22). The Court of Appeal had found that the clause was drafted differently from the ouster clause in *Anisminic* and, given the nature and function of the IPT, its judicial expertise, and the fact that it had been created with power to examine confidential evidence in private, Parliament had trusted the IPT to make sensible decisions on questions of law.

Lord Brown had also referred *obiter* in *A v B* to the clause as 'an unambiguous ouster' ([2009] UKSC 12 [23]) and Laws LJ had stated that 'Statutory measures which confide the jurisdiction to a judicial body of like standing and authority to that of the High Court, but which operates subject to special procedures apt for the subject-matter in hand, may well be constitutionally inoffensive' (*A v B* [2009] EWCA Civ 24 [22]). However, a 4 to 3 majority of the Supreme Court in *Privacy International* held that the wording of the clause was not explicit enough to exclude judicial review challenges based on an error of law, so the exclusion only applied to decisions that were not wrong in law ([107]). The court applied the common law presumption that judicial review can only be excluded by 'the most clear and explicit words' ([37, 111]). Lord Carnwath, for the majority, stated that it is for the courts to determine the extent to which an ouster clause should be upheld, 'having regard to its purpose and statutory context, and the nature and importance of the legal issue in question; and to determine the level of scrutiny required by the rule of law' ([144]). An ouster clause will not protect a nullity ([107]) and there are certain fundamental requirements of the rule of law which no ouster clause could exclude from the supervision of the courts ([122]). To deny the effectiveness of an ouster clause is an application of principles of the rule of law ([123]) and 'the ultimate safeguard of judicial review remains essential if the rule of law is to be maintained' ([126]). Lords Sumption and Reed, on the other hand, held that the clause clearly ousted the High Court's jurisdiction in this case. Lord Sumption took the view that the presumption against ouster clauses was about protecting the rule of law, not the jurisdiction of the High Court 'in some putative turf war with other judicial bodies on whom Parliament has conferred an equivalent review jurisdiction' ([199]). Lord Wilson considered the words to be totally clear in excluding judicial review of all the IPT's decisions, and an exclusion of judicial review in relation only to legally valid determinations made no sense ([229]).For commentary on the *Privacy International case*, see H. Wilberg, 'The Limits of the Rule of Law's Demands: Where Privacy International Abandons Anisminic', UK Const Law Blog (11 September 2019 at https://ukconstitutionallaw.org/).

SUMMARY

Judicial review:

- is a constitutionally significant process;
- ensures that public bodies are subject to the rule of law, protecting individuals against excessive state power;
- enables the courts to assess the lawfulness, fairness, and reasonableness of public body decision-making (not whether the decision itself is right or wrong);
- cannot normally be excluded by ouster clauses.

15.3 Beginning the judicial review process

We turn now to the procedural requirements of the judicial review process and the three preliminary or threshold issues that a claimant needs to satisfy when bringing a judicial review claim. To be amenable to judicial review:

- The claim must raise a public law matter and involve a public body.
- It must be justiciable.
- The claimant must have standing (*locus standi*).

> 'Amenable' means suitable to be heard

It is worth noting here that standing is not only a preliminary issue but is also considered at the full hearing of a claim.

There is no automatic right to a judicial review remedy, and the three 'hurdles' for a claim above act as a filter mechanism to ensure that a claim is appropriate for the judicial review process. It is also seen as a remedy of last resort so if the claimant has an adequate remedy through another avenue, permission for judicial review will not be granted (*R (Sivasubramaniam) v Wandsworth County Court* [2003] 1 WLR 475). Strict time limits apply to judicial review claims. They must be brought promptly and normally within three months of the decision or action being taken. This is because decisions by public bodies usually affect other people and the public needs to be sure that the decision is valid (*Hardy v Pembrokeshire County Council* [2006] EWCA Civ 240; see also *O'Reilly v Mackman* [1983] 2 AC 237, 280–281 (Lord Diplock)). There are different time limits for judicial review of:

- planning decisions: a six-week time limit was introduced in 2013;
- decisions of the Upper Tribunal: no later than 16 days after the date of sending notice of the Upper Tribunal's decision to the applicant;
- decisions of a minister in relation to a public inquiry, or a member of an inquiry panel: 14 days.

15.3.1 A public law matter

There is a boundary between public law and private law; judicial review applies exclusively to public law cases involving public bodies or bodies exercising public functions. This is known as the exclusivity principle.

> Private law relates to legal rights and obligations between individuals, for instance, in contract and tort. Where a public body such as a local council enters, for example, into a contract to sell or lease land, the question arises whether any dispute is about breach of contract (raising private law issues) or an unlawful use of public power. Judicial review would only be available if its actions related to its public powers and duties. See *Dudley Muslim Association v Dudley MBC* (2015) ECWA Civ 1123 [22].

15.3.1.1 The exclusivity principle

This means that a claim must fall within the court's judicial review jurisdiction over public bodies.

> The rule in *O'Reilly v Mackman* [1983] 2 AC 237 strictly required that the judicial review procedure must be used *exclusively* to challenge the abuse of public law powers. In this case, prisoners attempted to challenge decisions of the prison board of visitors through the ordinary court procedure as they were out of time for judicial review, but the court held that it was an abuse of the court process to use the ordinary procedure when alleging that a public body's decision had infringed their rights.

However, this rule was moderated in *Roy v Kensington and Chelsea and Westminster Family Practitioner Committee* [1992] 1 AC 624, where the court held that, while judicial review should still be used for purely public law issues, an *incidental* public law issue can be questioned in ordinary court proceedings that are *primarily* intended to enforce a private law right.

Maintaining flexibility on the use of public law and private law procedures was emphasised in *Mercury Communications Ltd v Director General of Telecommunications* [1996] 1 WLR 48, though the proceedings must not be an abuse of the court process. The Court of Appeal gave further guidance on the public/private divide in *Hampshire County Council v Supportway Community Services Limited* [2006] EWCA Civ 1035:

- The fact that a public body is in breach of contract does not necessarily transform a private law claim into a public law claim (though in some circumstances public law remedies may be appropriate). Where a claim is fundamentally contractual in nature, in principle, the claimant is limited to private law remedies ([38] (Neuberger LJ)).

- Claimants cannot base their claim in public law simply because private law does not give them 'a sufficiently attractive remedy', as this would place parties contracting with public bodies in an unjustifiably more privileged position [42–43] (Neuberger LJ).

- There needs to be a link between the public body's activity and its public law powers ([59] (Mummery LJ)).

15.3.1.2 Is a public body involved?

Public law powers are exercised by public bodies, and public bodies are subject to judicial review. Two tests have evolved to ascertain whether a decision-maker is a public body or a body exercising public functions: the source of power test, and the source and nature of power (or *Datafin*) test.

The source of power test

Look at where the body's power comes from:

- Statute: if it derives its powers from a statute (ie Parliament has conferred powers on it directly) or through secondary legislation, it will be a public body.

- Prerogative power: a government minister may be exercising a power under the royal prerogative which is also judicially reviewable (see section 12.3.1.2).

'[T]he source of the power will often, perhaps usually, be decisive. If the source of power is a statute, or subordinate legislation under a statute, then clearly the body in question will be subject to judicial review' (*R v Panel on Take-Overs and Mergers, ex parte Datafin* [1987] QB 815, 847 (Lloyd LJ)). If the source of power is contractual, judicial review is not available. However, this test does not always provide a clear answer because (a) some private bodies may exercise public functions eg housing associations and (b) the government has increasingly outsourced delivery of public services to private sector companies and third sector organisations (independent, not-for-profit groups such as charities and voluntary and community groups, which are neither public nor private sector; see www.theguardian.com/voluntary-sector-network/2016/may/20/10-public-services-run-charities). A second test has therefore evolved.

The source and nature of power test

This is the *Datafin* test, where the Court of Appeal held that not only the *source* of the power should be looked at, but the *nature* of the power: 'If the body in question is exercising public law functions, or if the exercise of its functions have public law consequences, then that may . . . be sufficient to bring the body within the reach of judicial review.' (*R v Panel on Take-Overs and Mergers, ex parte Datafin,* 847 (Lloyd LJ))

This broader test extends the reach of judicial review to private bodies exercising functions that are public in nature (eg administrative, regulatory, or supervisory functions, such as the Take-Over Panel's regulatory function in the financial services market in *Datafin*). Here, the body's powers do not need to derive from statute or prerogative power; it is the public nature of what they do that is important. However, in *R v Disciplinary Committee of the Jockey Club ex p Aga Khan* [1993] 1 WLR 909, the Jockey Club's powers and duties were not of a public nature because they were not 'woven into any system of governmental control of horseracing'; it was a private organisation with a contractual relationship with its members, and private law remedies, not judicial review, were appropriate. Moreover, a body exercising private functions cannot assume public functions by its own action alone; some governmental intervention is required (*R (Mullins) v Jockey Club Appeal Board (No 1)* [2005] EWHC 2197 (Admin), [30] (Stanley Burnton J)).

Human rights cases can give further guidance on the public element needed for judicial review. In *Poplar Housing and Regeneration Community Association Ltd v Donoghue* [2002] QB 48, 69–70, Lord Woolf CJ identified features imposing 'a public character or stamp' on an act or decision:

- Statutory authority for what is done.
- How much control is exercised by a public authority over the functions in question? Are the acts 'enmeshed in the activities of a public body'?
- How close is the relationship between the private body and a public body, for example, was it created by the public body or is it guided by it?
- Does the private body stand in the place of a public body?

In *R (Heather) v Leonard Cheshire Foundation* [2002] 2 All ER 936 [35], Lord Woolf pinpointed the following issues:

- The degree of public funding of the body is relevant but not a single determining factor of a public flavour to the body's functions.
- Is the body standing in the shoes of a public body?

The 'public flavour' aspect has subsequently been emphasised.

 CROSS REFERENCE

See also discussion on public authorities for Human Rights Act purposes in Chapter 17, especially *YL v Birmingham City Council*

Q CASE CLOSE-UP: *R (BEER) v HAMPSHIRE FARMERS MARKETS LTD* [2004] 1 WLR 233

Here, a local council set up a private company to operate a programme of farmers' markets. Its decision about the right of access to markets could be judicially reviewed because it involved 'a public element or flavour':

- It was controlling the right of access to markets held on land owned by local authorities to which the public had access.
- The company had a close relationship with the council: it owed its existence to it, stepped into the council's shoes, and was assisted by it.

Dyson LJ expressed the *Datafin* test in 'public flavour' terms:

unless the source of power clearly provides the answer, the question whether the decision of a body is amenable to judicial review requires a careful consideration of the nature of the power and function that has been exercised to see whether the decision has a sufficient public element, flavour or character to bring it within the purview of public law. ([16])

See Dyson LJ's judgment generally for a helpful guide to the authorities.

See also *R (Holmcroft Properties Ltd) v KPMG* [2018] EWCA Civ 2093 where it was held that all the circumstances should be considered and there must be a 'sufficient public law flavour' to them. Here, KPMG, appointed as an independent reviewer in a bank's past business review exercise, was not amenable to judicial review because the scheme was set up to pursue private rights, the engagement of the independent reviewer was contractual, and the dispute was fundamentally a private law matter.

Whether a function is public is a question of fact and degree in each case. In *R (Weaver) v London and Quadrant Housing Trust* [2010] 1 WLR 363, there was sufficient public flavour to a housing trust's termination of a tenancy because it was so bound up with the provision of social housing. On the other hand, in *R (Macleod) v The Governors of the Peabody Trust* [2016] EWHC 737 (Admin), there was insufficient public flavour to a housing association's refusal to approve an exchange of flats because the properties were not pure social housing and the Trust was not working closely with a local council (see [20–21]).

To further determine whether a function is public, the courts may also apply:

- The 'statutory underpinning' test: are the body's functions regulated by statute? Is the body discharging a statutory power? (In *R (A) v Partnerships in Care Ltd* [2002] EWHC 529 (Admin), decisions by managers of a private psychiatric hospital about its facilities were of a public nature with statutory underpinning ([24–25]).)

- The 'but for' test: but for this body (ie if this body did not exist), would the state have to intervene to carry out the same function? (See *R v Servite Houses, ex p Goldsmith* [2000] EWHC Admin 338.)

- The monopoly power test: where one person or body has a (near) monopoly in a particular sector, it should be amenable to judicial review (see *Datafin*), but this test does not find much judicial favour as it stretches judicial review too widely: see Alexander Williams, 'Judicial Review and Monopoly Power: Some Sceptical Thoughts' (2017) 133 LQR 656.

THINKING POINT

Under this test, would Tesco plc's activities be amenable to judicial review? See *R (Mullins) v Jockey Club Appeal Board* [31].

SUMMARY

Judicial review claims must raise a public law issue. The decision-maker must be a public body whose *source* of power is statute or prerogative, or a body carrying out a function with a public flavour under the *Datafin* test (look at the *nature* of power being exercised).

15.3.2 Justiciability

The claim must be one that a court can properly hear. This is not normally an issue where only an individual is affected, but the courts will decline to determine politically sensitive matters which are for the executive to decide as a matter of political judgment; in *McClean v First Secretary of State* [2017] EWHC 3174 (Admin), for example, a claim challenging the confidence and supply agreement between the government and the Democratic Unionist Party was non-justiciable ([20–22]). Justiciablity can arise particularly where exercise of a prerogative power is being questioned and it falls into one of the non-justiciable high policy categories (see *Council of Civil Service Unions v Minister for the Civil Service* [1985] AC 374). As Lord Hodge observes, policy-making is the province of democratic politics; the lawfulness of policy is the province of the courts ('Upholding the Rule of Law: How We Preserve Judicial Independence in the United Kingdom', Lincoln's Inn Denning Society, 7 November 2016 [42]).

❯ CROSS REFERENCE
See section 12.3.1.2

❱ CROSS REFERENCE

Note the narrower 'victim' test for standing under the Human Rights Act 1998. See Chapter 17

15.3.3 Standing (*locus standi*)

The claimant can be an individual, a company, an unincorporated association, or even another public body, but they must have legal status or capacity to bring a judicial review claim. The court considers standing at permission stage and more fully at the hearing stage (see section 15.5) and the extent of the claimant's interest in the claim can also affect the remedy.

> The test for standing is that the applicant must have 'a sufficient interest' in the matter to which the application relates (section 31(3) Senior Courts Act 1981); in other words, some right or interest has been adversely affected. This is 'discretionary and not hard-edged' (*R (DSD and NBV) v Parole Board of England and Wales* [2018] EWHC 694 (Admin) [111]).
>
> See the helpful discussion of relevant case law in *R (Wylde) v Waverley Borough Council* [2017] EWHC 466 (Admin) at paras 19–28.

Where an alleged abuse of power is more wide-reaching and affects more people, it raises the issue of who can bring a claim before the courts as a matter of public interest. Lord Fraser suggested that the correct approach to ascertain standing is 'to look at the statute under which the duty arises, and to see whether it gives any express or implied right to persons in the position of the applicant to complain of the alleged unlawful act or omission' (*R v IRC, ex parte National Federation of Self-Employed and Small Businesses Ltd* [1982] AC 617, 646). Lord Reed saw it as depending on 'the context, and in particular upon what will best serve the purposes of judicial review in that context' (*AXA General Insurance Ltd v Lord Advocate* [2011] UKSC 46, [2012] 1 AC 868 [170]).

The courts may recognise the standing of public-spirited citizens without any direct interest where the public body's breach affects the public generally. An interest or pressure group can have standing if it has national and international recognition, and is a responsible and respected body with a genuine interest in the actions of a public body (*R v HM Inspectorate of Pollution, ex parte Greenpeace (No 2)* [1994] 4 All ER 329 [79–81]). In *R v Secretary of State for Foreign and Commonwealth Affairs, ex parte World Development Movement Ltd* [1995] 1 WLR 386, Rose LJ identified a number of significant factors giving a pressure group standing to challenge the Foreign Secretary's decision to grant £316 million of development aid to an uneconomic Malaysian dam project: the importance of vindicating the rule of law; the importance of the issue raised; the absence of another responsible challenger; the nature of the breach of duty; and the prominent role of the particular applicants (p 395). We examine this further below.

Q CLOSE-UP FOCUS: BRINGING CLAIMS IN THE PUBLIC INTEREST

Normally, a person must show some particular interest in order to demonstrate that s/he is not a mere busybody, but sometimes any individual 'simply as a citizen' has sufficient interest without having to show they have been more affected than other members of the public (*Walton v The Scottish Ministers* [2012] UKSC 44 [94]). The courts consider various issues in this broader approach. Note how they often interlink.

- **Protecting the rule of law:** Lord Reed stated in the *AXA case* that insisting that an individual had a particular interest could prevent a matter being brought before the court. This 'might disable the court from performing its function to protect the rule of law' ([170]). 'The rule of law would not be maintained if, because everyone was equally affected by an unlawful act, no-one was able to bring proceedings to challenge it' (*Walton* [94] (Lord Reed); and see [152–153] (Lord Hope's 'osprey test')). See also *R v IRC, ex parte National Federation of Self-Employed and Small Businesses Ltd* at 644 (Lord Diplock).

- **The public importance of the issue raised:** The standing of Lord Rees-Mogg, then the editor of the *Times*, to challenge the Foreign Secretary's decision to ratify the Maastricht Treaty on the EU was accepted 'because of his sincere concern for constitutional issues' (*R v Secretary of State for Foreign and Commonwealth Affairs ex parte Rees Mogg* [1994] QB 552, 562). See also *R v Secretary of State for Social Services ex p Child Poverty Action Group* [1990] 2 QB 540, 556; *R v HM Treasury ex p Smedley* [1985] QB 657.

- **Who else would challenge?** If this claimant is unable to proceed, who else would bring a claim? See *R v HM Inspectorate of Pollution, ex parte Greenpeace (No 2)* [82].

- **The legal and factual context of the case:** The question of sufficient interest will not be considered as an isolated point but as part of the legal and factual context of the case, such as the nature of the breach (see *ex parte National Federation of the Self Employed and Small Businesses Ltd* at 630 (Lord Wilberforce)). Where justified by the circumstances, the court may recognise standing where individuals or organisations are not directly affected by an administrative act (*R (O) v Secretary of State for International Development* [2014] EWHC 2371 [12]).

- **Directly affecting a section of the public:** 'A personal interest need not be shown if the individual is acting in the public interest and can genuinely say that the issue directly affects the section of the public that he seeks to represent' (*AXA* [63] (Lord Hope)). Compare this with the narrow approach in *R v Secretary of State for Environment ex parte Rose Theatre Trust Co* [1990] 1 QB 504, where a group of individuals formed a company to preserve the remains of the historic Rose Theatre as a national monument, but did not have standing to challenge the minister's refusal to schedule them for preservation. The court held that no individual members of the public had sufficient interest to apply for judicial review, and therefore the company that individuals had created had no standing. Contrast this with *ex parte Greenpeace (No 2)*, where a pressure group could claim on behalf of its local members in relation to a decision to allow the discharging of radioactive waste to test a new reprocessing plant at Sellafield in Cumbria.

However, the court may look at the claimant's motives and the real reason why they are bringing a claim. If the claimant is acting out of ill will, a lack of genuine concern, or other improper purpose, s/he should not be permitted to bring a claim, even though there is a public interest (*R (Feakins) v Secretary of State for the Environment, Food and Rural Affairs* [2003] EWCA Civ 1546 [23] (Dyson LJ)).

Standing proved an issue for the Mayor of London in the *Worboys case*.

CASE CLOSE-UP: *R (DSD AND NBV) v PAROLE BOARD OF ENGLAND AND WALES* [2018] EWHC 694 (ADMIN)

The Parole Board directed that John Worboys (now known as John Radford) should be released from prison. Worboys had been convicted of 19 serious sexual offences while working as a black-cab driver. Judicial review claims were brought by the Mayor of London, two of Worboys' victims (DSD and NBV), and News Group Newspapers Ltd (this was the first Parole Board judicial review by anyone other than a party to the proceedings).

The court decided that the Mayor did not have standing as his legal responsibilities for tackling crime in London did not relate to decisions of the Parole Board ([109]), but denying him standing would not disable the court from performing its function to protect the rule of law ([111]). The court also limited NBV's right to make representations to the proposed licence conditions, and not whether Worboys should be released at all.

The court commented that the Secretary of State for Justice would have been a natural claimant. However, the Secretary of State had announced to the House of Commons in January 2018 that it would not be appropriate for the government to seek a judicial review of the Parole Board's decision (HC Deb 19 January 2018, Vol 634 col 1193).

SUMMARY

- Standing requires the claimant to have 'a sufficient interest' in the matter complained of

- Often a public body's decision directly affects an individual but the courts may recognise the standing of individuals or groups without a direct interest where the public body's breach affects the public generally

- The broader the tests for 'a public law matter' and for standing, the more the scope of judicial review is extended

15.4 Government reforms to judicial review

By 2012, the government had become concerned by the way in which judicial review was being used as a delaying tactic to major projects or to challenge policies, and felt that it had developed far beyond its original intentions. In evidence to a select committee, Kenneth Clarke, then Lord Chancellor, said that judicial review lay behind half of the discussions he had in government or in his department, and he warned of the risk of politicised interventions by judges (House of Lords Select Committee on the Constitution, *Annual Meeting with the Lord Chancellor*, 19 January 2011, Qs 9, 21).

In 2012, David Cameron announced plans to restrict judicial review applications to speed up decision-making (Prime Minister's speech to CBI, 19 November 2012) and a consultation was launched on proposals that included increased court fees for judicial review and a reduced time limit in planning cases (Ministry of Justice, *Judicial Review Proposals for Reform*, December 2012, Consultation Paper CP25/2012). Despite criticisms of the proposals, particularly their potential to affect the rule of law or change the constitutional balance of power (see Amy Street, *Judicial Review and the Rule of Law: Who Is in Control?* The Constitution Society, 2013 at www.consoc.org.uk), they were implemented.

THINKING POINT

How would restricting judicial review affect the rule of law?

In 2013, the government proposed further reforms. It took the view that the courts' 'increasingly expansive' approach to the test for standing was allowing judicial review to be used for publicity purposes or to hinder the proper decision-making process. The government therefore proposed narrowing the definition of 'sufficient interest' to require a *direct* interest (Ministry of Justice, *Judicial Review Proposals for Further Reform*, Cm 8703, September 2013 [74, 79]) and see generally [67–90]). The government's view contrasted with the opposite direction of travel in the *AXA case*, which broadened the test for standing in Scots law to 'sufficient' interest: see *Walton v The Scottish Ministers* [2012] UKSC 44 [90–94]. The standing proposal was not implemented but other changes were introduced by the Criminal Justice and Courts Act 2015 (Part 4) to restrict judicial review claims (eg on financing claims and costs).

On 31 July 2020, following the Conservative party's 2019 election manifesto commitment to examine judicial review, the government created an Independent Review of Administrative Law. A review panel will advise the government on potential reform of judicial review to ensure balance between protecting the rights of individuals against 'an overbearing state' and the work of the government. Its remit includes consideration of:

1. whether amenability to judicial review and the grounds of public law illegality should be codified in statute;

2. whether the principle of non-justiciability needs clarifying and whether some executive decisions should be non-justiciable;

3. which grounds and remedies should be available in justiciable claims; and

4. whether procedural reforms to streamline judicial review are necessary (including time limits and standing). See www.parliament.uk/business/publications/written-questions-answers-statements/written-statement/Commons/2020-09-01/HCWS427/; https://publiclawforeveryone.com/2020/08/10/the-judicial-review-review-ii-codifying-judicial-review-clarification-or-evisceration/.

15.5 Judicial review procedure

In court, judicial review involves a two-stage process: the court must grant permission to bring a claim before the full hearing takes place (see Table 15.3). The specific judicial review procedure is set out in section 31 Senior Courts Act 1981 and the details are contained in Part 54 of the

Civil Procedure Rules 1999 (CPR). This procedure *must* be used where the claimant is seeking specific judicial review remedies (see Chapter 16) and *may* be used where the claimant is seeking a declaration or an injunction (CPR 54.3(1)).

Table 15.3 The judicial review process

The pre-action protocol sets out the steps that parties should follow before making a judicial review claim, unless the claim is urgent. The claim must be brought in the Administrative Court, and a two-stage process follows.

Permission stage: the claimant must apply for the court's permission to bring the claim. This filters out inappropriate actions and usually takes place on the papers without a hearing, though there can be reconsideration at an oral hearing (oral renewal stage).

- The court can refuse permission if the applicant lacks standing or is a vexatious litigant. This enables the court to prevent abuse of the legal process by mere 'busybodies' and 'other mischief-makers' (*R v IRC, ex parte National Federation of Self-Employed and Small Businesses Ltd* [1982] AC 617, 646 (Lord Fraser); 653 (Lord Scarman)).

- Permission can be refused if the claimant has another adequate remedy.

- The claimant must show an arguable ground for judicial review having a realistic prospect of success (*Sharma v Brown-Antoine* [2007] 1 WLR 780).

- The court will take into account any undue delay in bringing the application when considering permission or remedies (section 31(6) Senior Courts Act 1981).

- As of April 2015, the court must apply the 'no substantial difference' test at permission stage. Permission must be refused if it appears highly likely that the outcome for the claimant would not have been substantially different if the conduct complained of had not happened. This should normally be based on material existing at the time of the decision, not 'post-decision speculation by an individual decision maker' (*R (Logan) v London Borough of Havering* [2015] EWHC 3193 (Admin) [55]). There is a heavy onus on public bodies to show that judicial review should be refused because the decision inevitably would have been the same (*R (BM) v London Borough of Hackney* [2016] EWHC 3338 (Admin) [85]). The court may still grant permission if there are exceptional public interest reasons (section 84 Criminal Justice and Courts Act 2015; section 31(3C)–(3F) Senior Courts Act 1981; for comment, see *Judicial Review and the Rule of Law: An Introduction to the Criminal Justice and Courts Act 2015,* Part 4, Bingham Centre for the Rule of Law, JUSTICE and the Public Law Project, London, October 2015).

- At this stage, a claim can be rejected as totally without merit, which means that it is bound to fail (*R (Grace) v SSHD* [2014] EWCA Civ 1091).

- Following the decision in *Cart*, there is a restrictive test for permission for judicial review of an Upper Tribunal decision; an application for permission is determined on the papers only, with no reconsideration at an oral hearing (CPR 54.7A).

In 2019, 2,100 claims reached permission stage; 430 cases were granted permission to proceed; 12 per cent were found to be totally without merit (Ministry of Justice, Civil Justice Statistics Quarterly, England and Wales, October to December 2019).

Hearing stage: If permission is granted, the application proceeds to the substantive hearing stage. The hearing is usually in public, although the court may decide the claim on the papers without a hearing where all the parties agree (CPR 54.18). The claimant's standing may be fully considered at this stage. The public body is under a duty of candour and co-operation to assist the court with full and accurate explanations of all the facts (*R (Hoareau) v Secretary of State for Foreign and Commonwealth Affairs* [2018] EWHC 1508 (Admin) [20]).

? Questions

Self-test questions

1. What is the constitutional role of judicial review?

2. What is an ouster clause? Can the courts be prevented from judicially reviewing decisions of other bodies?

3. What is the exclusivity principle?

4. What is the *Datafin* test?

5. What is the test for standing? Why is the claimant's standing important in judicial review cases?

6. Why did the government propose narrowing the test for standing? Was the proposal adopted?

7. Why is permission stage needed? What test does the claimant need to satisfy?

Exam question

'[T]he test for standing should require a more direct and tangible interest in the matter to which the application for judicial review relates. That would exclude persons who had only a political or theoretical interest, such as campaigning groups.' (Ministry of Justice, *Judicial Review Proposals for Further Reform*, Cm 8703, September 2013, para 80).

Critically assess the arguments for and against narrowing the test for standing for judicial review claims.

≡ Further reading

Books

Allan, T.R.S. *The Sovereignty of Law: Freedom, Constitution, and Common Law* (Oxford: Oxford University Press 2013).
See chapter 6 for detail on the constitutional foundations of judicial review

Leyland, P. and Anthony, G. *Textbook on Administrative Law* (8th edn, Oxford: Oxford University Press 2016).
Comprehensive text on judicial review and other areas of the administrative justice system

Journal articles

Ahmed, F. and Perry, A. 'Standing and Civic Virtue' (2018) 134 (Apr) LQR 239–256.
Analyses the 'sufficient interest' test for standing in public interest cases from the interesting point of view of civic virtue

Arvind, T.T. and Stirton, L. 'The Curious Origins of Judicial Review' (2017) 133 LQR 91–117.
Analyses the transformative development of judicial review and argues that it has reached an unsatisfactory destination

Campbell, C. 'The Nature of Power as Public in English Judicial Review' (2009) 68(1) Cambridge Law Journal 90–117.
Critically examines the practical application of the nature of power test for determining whether power is public

Duxbury, N. 'The Outer Limits of English Judicial Review' (2017) (April) Public Law 235–248.
Helpful for the public–private distinction and explaining why judicial review is confined to public law

Mills, A. 'Reforms to Judicial Review in the Criminal Justice and Courts Act 2015: Promoting Efficiency or Weakening the Rule of Law?' (2015) (October) Public Law 583–595.
Argues that reforms have weakened judicial review

Morgan, J. 'A Mare's Nest? The Jockey Club and Judicial Review of Sports Governing Bodies' (2012) 12(2) LIM 102–109.
Examines the use of judicial review to challenge decisions of sports governing bodies; helpful for application of *Datafin*

Williams, A. 'Public Functions and Amenability: Recent Trends' (2017) 22(1) Judicial Review 15.
Discusses public functions and recent amenability cases

Other sources

For a short, readable guide to the judicial review process, see:

publiclawproject.org.uk/wp-content/uploads/data/resources/6/PLP_Short_Guide_3_1305.pdf.

For clear, detailed information on the judicial review process, see:

The Administrative Court Judicial Review Guide, July 2020 at www.gov.uk/government/publications/administrative-court-judicial-review-guide.

Bondy, V. and Sunkin, M. 'Judicial Review Reform: Who Is Afraid of Judicial Review? Debunking the Myths of Growth and Abuse' UK Const L Blog (10 January 2013, available at ukconstitutionallaw.org).
Addresses claims of an increase in, and abuse of, judicial review challenges

Online resources

www.oup.com/he/dennett2e

This chapter is accompanied by a selection of online resources to help you with this topic, including:

- Multiple-choice questions
- Answers to the self-test questions
- Guidance on answering the exam question

16 Judicial review: grounds and remedies

LEARNING OBJECTIVES

By the end of this chapter, you should be able to:

- Explain the significance of judicial review
- Evaluate and apply judicial review principles
- Appreciate the open-ended nature of some rules
- Evaluate the impact of context on the application of judicial review principles
- Assess the relationship between irrationality and proportionality
- Discuss emerging trends in judicial review cases

Introduction

Judicial review is a dynamic, judge-made area of law with an extensive seam of case law, and the courts control its principles, boundaries, and development. This chapter examines judicial review and the rule of law, the three traditional grounds of judicial review, proportionality, the modern approach to judicial review, and remedies.

> 'Judicial review is the means of ensuring that public bodies act within the limits of their legal powers and in accordance with the legal principles governing the exercise of their decision-making functions.' (*Dolan v Secretary of State for Health and Social Care* [2020] EWHC 1786 (Admin) [6])

Lord Bingham describes judges as 'auditors of legality' in the judicial review process because they are reviewing the lawfulness of executive and administrative action by public bodies (Tom Bingham, *The Rule of Law*, London: Penguin 2011, p 61). More specifically, the courts review the lawfulness of 'an enactment or a decision, action or failure to act in relation to the exercise of a public function' (Civil Procedure Rules 54.1). 'Enactment' refers to secondary legislation and Acts of the devolved administrations; decisions may include proposals, policies, and guidelines drafted by public bodies. The ultimate aim of judicial review is to foster good administration and a successful claim often invalidates an executive decision.

Generally in judicial review cases, claimants challenge how a public body has applied law or policy specifically to them; or they challenge the lawfulness of a public body's procedure or policy generally; or pressure groups or others bring a public interest claim where a public body's decision affects the community as a whole (see Bondy et al, https://publiclawproject.org.uk/resources/the-value-and-effects-of-judicial-review/).

> **Key principle** In judicial review cases, the courts act in a supervisory rather than an appellate role (see Chapter 15). This means that they review the way in which public bodies have made a decision and whether it was arrived at lawfully, but they do not question whether the decision itself was right or wrong (a 'merits review'), or substitute their own decision in its place; this would be an appeal process. The purpose of judicial review is for the courts to act as a check on the executive, not to step into the shoes of the executive and make what they regard as the correct decision. This is what makes 'review' distinct from 'appeal'.

This point was made by Lord Browne-Wilkinson:

> [T]he legality of the Home Secretary's policy (which is the only proper concern of the courts) does not depend on the preferences and perceptions of individual judges. There is no general principle yet established that the courts have any right to quash administrative decisions on the simple ground that the decision is unfair. (*R v Secretary of State for the Home Department, ex parte Pierson* [1998] AC 539, 575)

Otherwise, where Parliament gives powers to a *minister* in a statute, the court would be overriding Parliament's intention if it substituted its own idea of a fair decision. Instead, the courts 'police' the legal boundaries of executive decision-making.

THINKING POINT

How does this relate to parliamentary sovereignty and the separation of powers?

The question for the court is therefore: was this a decision that the public body was lawfully entitled to make? (See *R (Corner House Research) v Director of the Serious Fraud Office* [2008] UKHL 60 [41–42].)

16.1 Judicial review and the rule of law

Before we examine the grounds, this section helps you to get an overall sense of judicial review through its strong link to the rule of law. Judicial review is the rule of law in action, and Lord Bingham's fourth principle of the rule of law is that 'ministers and public officers at all levels must exercise the powers conferred on them in good faith, fairly, for the purpose for which the powers were conferred, without exceeding the limits of such powers and not unreasonably' (*The Rule of Law*, chapter 6). This is also the basis for judicial review. It is fundamentally important that individuals can challenge the lawfulness of decisions or actions of public bodies, and they can be reviewed by judges to ensure that they conform to rule of law requirements. It ensures that 'administrative decisions will be taken rationally, in accordance with a fair procedure and within the powers conferred by Parliament' (*R (Alconbury Developments Ltd) v Secretary of State for the Environment, Transport and the Regions* [2001] UKHL 23, [2003] 2 AC 295 [73] (Lord Hoffmann)).

Through judicial review, the courts place constraints on executive power by upholding and projecting rule of law principles on to executive actions:

- Government power needs legal limits: it should not be arbitrary or based on wide discretion, it should be clearly specified and predictable, and it must be authorised and controlled by law.
- Public decision-making should be procedurally fair and rational.
- The law should protect fundamental rights and values, such as human rights, equality, and access to justice.

In modern judicial review, the courts have moved from applying a thin version of the rule of law to a thick version, upholding the underlying 'pool' of constitutional rights and principles protected by the rule of law. Lord Steyn observes that 'As the scope of judicial review came to be broadened, the rule of law has played an ever larger role. Initially, its role was largely restricted to ensuring procedural fairness. Gradually, the rule of law acquired substantive content' ('Democracy, the Rule of Law and the Role of Judges' (2006) EHRLR 243, 248; see also *R v Secretary of State for the Home Department, ex parte Pierson* [1998] AC 539, 591F (Lord Steyn)). The rule of law thus enforces substantive and procedural standards, and through judicial review the courts place a template of procedural and substantive legal limits over executive actions to determine whether they fall outside those limits.

The procedural and substantive limits include 'legality, procedural propriety, participation, fundamental rights, openness, rationality, relevancy, propriety of purpose, reasonableness, equality, legitimate expectations, legal certainty and proportionality' (Professor Paul Craig, 'The Rule of Law', Paper, Appendix 5 to House of Lords Select Committee on the Constitution, *Relations between the Executive, the Judiciary and Parliament*, 6th Report of Session 2006–07, HL 151).

CROSS REFERENCE

You will find it useful to read Chapters 8 and 9 to help with background for this chapter

THINKING POINT

Identify which of the limits or principles in the preceding paragraph are being applied as you work through the grounds of judicial review in what follows.

SUMMARY

- The rule of law enforces minimum standards of fairness, substantive and procedural (*Pierson* (Lord Steyn))
- Judicial review upholds the rule of law
- Judicial review ensures that administrative decisions are taken rationally, in accordance with a fair procedure, and within the powers conferred by Parliament

16.2 The grounds for judicial review claims

Until the 1960s, the courts controlled executive power with a fairly rigid adherence to the express limits imposed on public bodies by statute. They would mainly intervene where a public body had acted outside its lawful powers (*ultra vires*), not followed correct procedures, made an error of law on the face of the record (a decision), or exceeded its jurisdiction. In 1948, the Court of Appeal in the *Wednesbury case* (*Associated Provincial Picture Houses v Wednesbury Corporation* [1948] 1 KB 223) required a public body's powers to be exercised reasonably, though to cross the *Wednesbury* unreasonableness threshold a public body's decision must be deemed extremely unreasonable by the courts, so the *Wednesbury* test still accorded public bodies very wide latitude. Three landmark cases in the 1960s were the springboard for judicial review's modern development: *Ridge v Baldwin* [1964] AC 40 (the rules of natural justice can apply to administrative bodies' decisions), *Padfield v Minister of Agriculture, Fisheries and Food* [1968] AC 997 (the courts can review how a public body uses its discretionary power), and *Anisminic v Foreign Compensation Commission* [1969] 2 AC 147 (any error of law by a public body can be judicially reviewed). Collectively, they allowed judges greater scope for intervention. See J.F. Garner, 'Notes on Cases' (1968) 31 MLR 446–449.

> **THINKING POINT**
>
> Look at section 8.2.1. Can you see elements of the 'thin' or formal view of rule of law being applied here?

The classic statement of the grounds for modern judicial review was made by Lord Diplock in the *GCHQ case* in the 1980s:

> Judicial review has I think developed to a stage today when . . . one can conveniently classify under three heads the grounds upon which administrative action is subject to control by judicial review. The first ground I would call 'illegality', the second 'irrationality' and the third 'procedural impropriety', That is not to say that further development on a case by case basis may not in course of time add further grounds. I have in mind particularly the possible adoption in the future of the principle of 'proportionality'. (*CCSU v Minister for the Civil Service* [1985] AC 374, p 410; see also p 414 (Lord Roskill))

In other words, has the public body exercised its decision-making power lawfully, rationally, and with procedural fairness (see Figure 16.1)?

> **THINKING POINT**
>
> Note that the list was open-ended and further grounds could be added. Note particularly the reference to proportionality as a possible future ground (the disproportionate use of power); this is explored further in section 16.6.

Figure 16.1 The grounds of judicial review

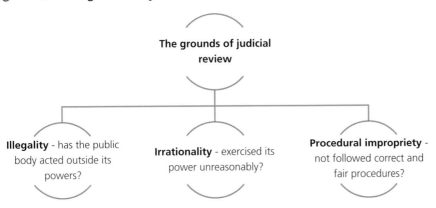

You need to be aware that the grounds for judicial review are not mutually exclusive boxes that judges dip into but 'a rich tapestry of many strands, which cross, re-cross and blend to produce justice' (*R v SSHD, ex parte Oladehinde* [1991] 1 AC 254 (Lord Donaldson MR)) so a claim can be brought on more than one ground. But we begin by breaking down the principles into step-by-step rules.

16.3 Illegality: the unlawful use of power

> Has the public body acted beyond the legal powers given to it?

The principle is that all executive and administrative actions should be lawful. Public bodies are given legal powers by statute (an enabling Act), and ministers may also exercise prerogative power under common law. The court must ensure that they act lawfully within the limits of those powers; if a public body's decision is *ultra vires* (outside its powers), it will be unlawful and void. Any action must therefore be justified by positive law and follow the purpose for which the power was conferred (*R v Somerset County Council ex parte Fewings* [1995] 1 All ER 513, p 524 (Laws J)). This is fundamentally about promoting 'congruence', ensuring that the actions of decision-makers correspond with the law which governs their actions (*Osborn v Parole Board* [2013] UKSC 61, [2014] AC 1115 [71] (Lord Reed)).

A public body can act unlawfully by:

1. Doing something which it has no legal power to do (simple lack of power).
2. Making an error of law.
3. Improperly using a discretionary power.

16.3.1 Simple lack of power (or *ultra vires*)

The question here is: does the public body have express or implied legal powers to do what it has done? Has it exercised its power in accordance with the law? Look at Parliament's requirements in the framework legislation.

EXAMPLES

***AG v Fulham Corporation* [1921] 1 Ch 440**

The local authority had a statutory power to provide wash-houses where people could wash their own clothes, but it introduced a new laundry system where people paid to have their clothes washed. Did the council have power to do that? The new scheme was held to be *ultra vires*; the legislation was aimed at providing facilities for people unable to pay for them.

***Wheeler v Leicester City Council* [1985] UKHL 6, [1985] AC 1054**

Leicester City Council suspended a rugby club from using a recreation ground for one year after the club did not prevent three members from joining a tour of South Africa (at that time, South Africa operated a system of apartheid or racial segregation). The club condemned apartheid but left the final decision to the players. The House of Lords held that the club had done nothing wrong; the council should not have used its statutory powers to manage the ground in order to penalise the club on the basis of political opinion and it was an improper exercise of its power.

Errors of jurisdictional fact (or precedent fact) Some statutes require a particular fact to exist before a public body may lawfully take action, and here, there is a right or wrong answer—the court decides whether the required fact exists, as Lady Hale explains in *R (A) v Croydon LBC* [2009] UKSC 8 [26]–[27]. For example, in *White and Collins v Minister of Health* [1939] 2 KB 838, a local authority had power under the Housing Act 1936 to compulsorily purchase land unless it was part of a park, garden, or pleasure ground; its order to purchase part of a park was therefore *ultra vires*. Similarly, the Immigration Act 1971 requires a person to be an 'illegal entrant' before an immigration officer has power to order their detention (see *Khawaja v Home Secretary* [1984] 1 AC 74, p 104 (Lord Wilberforce); p 108 (Lord Scarman)). If that fact does not exist, the public body is giving itself jurisdiction to act that it does not have and will be acting unlawfully.

16.3.2 **Errors of law**

From tribunal decisions to guidance issued by government departments, a public body may 'get the law wrong'. There used to be a difficult distinction between errors of law where inferior courts and tribunals exceeded their jurisdiction and errors of law made within their jurisdiction, but this disappeared with the *Anisminic case* (see *O'Reilly v Mackman* [1983] 2 AC 237, 278 (Lord Diplock)). *Anisminic* made it clear that by making *any* error of law, a public body acts outside its jurisdiction. Parliament has given the public body a decision-making power to be exercised on the correct legal basis; by misdirecting itself on the law (ie misunderstanding the scope of its statutory or common law powers), it acts outside its power and its decision will be *ultra vires* and void (see *R v Lord President of the Privy Council, ex p. Page* [1993] AC 682, 701–702 (Lord Browne-Wilkinson)). In short, it has asked itself the wrong question. In *R (Letts) v Lord Chancellor* [2015] EWHC 402 (Admin), for example, the Lord Chancellor's guidance to the Legal Aid Agency was found to contain an error of law in its interpretation of the scope of Article 2 European Convention on Human Rights (see Chapter 18) which could lead a caseworker to refuse legal aid where it should be granted. It was therefore unlawful, and as a result of the decision new guidance was published.

16.3.3 **Improper use of a discretionary power**

Statutes often give public bodies a power to be exercised within their discretion, such as the power to give funding. Words in a statute indicating a discretionary power include, for example, 'as the minister thinks fit'. This is known as a statutory discretion, but while the statute does not specify the limits of that power, what appears to be a wide discretion can be fenced in by judges *implying* limits.

It was *Padfield v Minister of Agriculture* that strengthened the courts' review of discretionary powers on the basis that:

> Parliament must have conferred the discretion with the intention that it should be used to promote the policy and objects of the Act: the policy and objects of the Act must be determined by construing the Act as a whole, and construction is always a matter of law for the court. (p 1030 (Lord Reid))

This is the *Padfield* principle: a discretionary power relies on 'the Minister to use his discretion to promote Parliament's intention' by acting in accordance with the statute's policy and objectives (p 1054 (Lord Pearce)). No statute gives any minister an unfettered discretion; discretion must not be exercised to defeat or frustrate the object of the relevant legislation (*R v Secretary of State for the Environment, Transport and the Regions, ex p Spath Holme Ltd* [2001] 2 AC 349, 381 (Lord Bingham)). Thus the courts ensure that the executive is following Parliament's (perceived) intention. A public body can improperly use a discretionary power in a number of ways, as shown in Figure 16.2.

Figure 16.2 Improper use of discretionary power

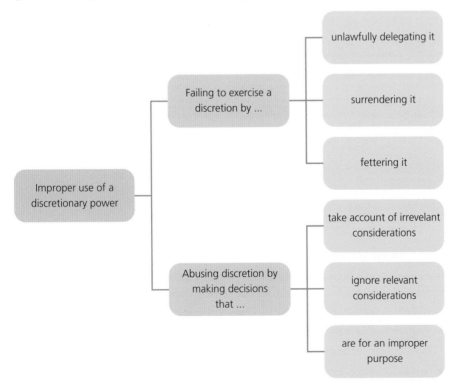

16.3.3.1 **Failing to exercise its discretion**

Here, a public body has not used the discretionary power conferred on it by Parliament. A discretion given to a decision-maker needs to be exercised and they should not sidestep Parliament's intentions by imposing their own arbitrary rules on whether or not to use it (see *R (Sandiford) v Secretary of State for Foreign and Commonwealth Affairs* [2014] UKSC 44, [2014] 1 WLR 2697 [81] (Lord Sumption)). A public body must not:

- delegate decision-making to an unauthorised person (in *Barnard v National Dock Labour Board* [1953] 2 QB 18 the Dock Labour Board had power to suspend workers but it allowed the port manager to exercise the power, which was unlawful);

- surrender (give up) its decision-making power to another body (see *Lavender v Minister of Housing and Local Government* [1970] 1 WLR 1231 where the Minister of Housing refused applications for planning permission if the Minister of Agriculture objected to them, so was not making the decision for which Parliament made him responsible);

- fetter (restrict) its discretion by rigidly applying a blanket policy. It is free to formulate a policy for exercising the discretionary power but must not apply it inflexibly with no exceptions so that it does not consider each case; 'anyone who has to exercise a statutory discretion must not "shut his ears to an application"' (*British Oxygen Co. Ltd v Minister of Technology* [1971] AC 610, 625 (Lord Reid)) or, as Lord Pearce said, do not throw applications 'unread into the waste paper basket' (*Padfield* p 1053). The applicant has a statutory right to be considered by the person exercising the discretion (*R (Elias) v Secretary of State for Defence* [2006] EWCA Civ 1293, [2006] 1 WLR 3213 [191] (Mummery LJ); *R v Secretary of State for the Home Department, ex p Venables* [1998] AC 407, 496 (Lord Browne-Wilkinson)). However, this only applies to policies for exercising a statutory power; ministers are free to decide whether or not to exercise a prerogative power because it has not been conferred by Parliament (*Sandiford* [55, 61–65, 82–83]).

EXAMPLE: *ADATH YISROEL BURIAL SOCIETY v HM SENIOR CORONER FOR INNER NORTH LONDON* [2018] EWHC 969 (ADMIN)

The claimants challenged the lawfulness of the Senior Coroner's policy not to prioritise burials because of the deceased's religion. For members of the Jewish and Muslim faiths, a funeral must take place as soon as possible, and one of the grounds of challenge was that the policy fettered discretion. The court held that the policy, by imposing a blanket rule and not taking account of individual circumstances, was an unlawful restriction on the Coroner's decision-making powers [87].

For a review of the principles, see [78–85].

16.3.3.2 **Abusing discretion**

This involves a public body exercising its discretion but not properly. When exercising a discretionary power, a public body will take various considerations into account, but will be acting unlawfully in its decision-making if it:

- is influenced by matters that are irrelevant;

- does not take account of relevant considerations;

- makes a decision for an improper purpose, that is, a purpose which does not coincide with the purpose of the statute giving it power to act.

These are factors that lead the public body to ask itself the wrong question and they are a fruitful basis for judicial review claims. They are also factors that can contribute to a decision being irrational, and you will see similarities between improper use of discretionary power as a sub-ground of illegality and unreasonableness (see section 16.4) though they are separate concepts.

Being influenced by irrelevant matters and not taking relevant considerations into account

Sedley L.J. stated in *R (National Association of Health Stores) v Department of Health* [2005] EWCA Civ 154 that the decision-maker 'must know or be told enough to ensure that nothing that it is necessary, because legally relevant, for him to know is left out of account' [62]. Ministers in particular, who rely on advice from civil servants, are not required to know everything that is relevant but the key question is whether they have taken into account a consideration which is not only relevant but which they are legally obliged to take into account.

 EXAMPLES

Roberts v Hopwood [1925] AC 578

Local authorities have a fiduciary duty to their ratepayers. Here, ratepayers objected to the high level of pay for men and women fixed by a council which ignored the fall in the cost of living. The court held that the council had not acted for the authorised purpose of protecting the ratepayers but had been influenced by 'philanthropic' considerations of being a model employer. This was not a reasonable exercise of its discretion.

R (Palestine Solidarity Campaign Ltd) v Secretary of State for Housing, Communities and Local Government [2020] UKSC 16

The Secretary of State had published guidance for local authorities who administer the local government pension scheme which included a provision that they should not make investment decisions that were contrary to UK foreign or defence policy. The claimants argued that the minister was acting outside the statutory purposes authorised by the Public Services Pensions Act 2013. Although the Act conferred a very wide discretion on the minister, the Supreme Court held by 3 to 2 that the Secretary of State's guidance was unlawful as it went beyond the powers conferred by Parliament. The minister was attempting to enforce the government's foreign and defence policies [27] and did not have power to direct what investments should not be made [31].

R (Plan B Earth) v Secretary of State for Transport [2020] EWCA Civ 214

The Court of Appeal held that the government's policy statement in favour of developing a third runway at Heathrow was unlawful and had no legal effect because the Secretary of State had not fully complied with the statutory requirements imposed by Parliament. He had a duty under section 5(8) Planning Act 2008 to take government policy into account when preparing the policy statement, but did not take into account the government's commitment to the Paris Agreement on climate change; in fact he had been advised not to take it into account which the court said was a material misdirection of law. The court therefore remitted the policy statement to the Secretary of State for reconsideration. Permission to appeal to the Supreme Court was granted in May 2020.

> **CROSS REFERENCE**
>
> See Late News section for the Supreme Court's decision

Key point: did the reasons for the decision fall within the policy and objects of the relevant Act?

Similar considerations come into play with the exercise of prerogative powers. In *Elgizouli v Secretary of State for the Home Department* [2020] UKSC 10, the Home Secretary was exercising prerogative powers in the conduct of foreign affairs. The appellant's son was suspected of being a member of a terrorist group called 'the Beatles', thought to be responsible for killing US and British citizens in Syria. His prosecution in the US depended on evidence obtained by the UK police which the Home Secretary agreed to provide despite the US refusing to give a full assurance that the death penalty would not be imposed or at least not carried out. The issue was whether it was lawful for the Home Secretary to provide evidence to the US that could facilitate the death penalty being imposed. The Supreme Court held that the Home Secretary's decision to supply the information was unlawful because he had failed to consider his duties under the Data Protection Act 2018 (Lord Reed also took the view that irrationality might have been an appropriate ground [181–187]).

Making a decision for an improper purpose

Again, the courts construe the framework legislation and must first ascertain the relevant statutory purpose. In accordance with the Padfield principle, any discretion conferred on a minister by a statute with the intention that it should be used to promote the policy and objects of the Act must promote the purpose for which the power was conferred and not frustrate the Act's objectives (*R (GC) v Commissioner of Police of the Metropolis* [2011] UKSC 21, [2011] 1 WLR 1230 [83] (Lord Kerr)).

 EXAMPLES

R v Lewisham London Borough Council, ex parte Shell UK Ltd [1988] 1 ALL ER 938

A council decided to boycott Shell products and to campaign to encourage other councils to do the same; it was held to be an improper purpose and therefore unlawful because it was not simply in pursuit of good race relations but to put pressure on Shell to end its interests in apartheid South Africa.

Porter v Magill [2002] 2 AC 357

A Conservative council's policy to target council house sales at tenants in marginal wards to encourage the Conservative vote was held to be unlawful because it promoted electoral advantage, which was not the purpose for which the power to dispose of its property had been conferred by the Housing Act 1985.

R (Rights of Women) v Lord Chancellor [2016] EWCA Civ 91, [2016] 1 WLR 2543

The court found that the purpose of the Legal Aid, Sentencing and Punishment of Offenders Act 2012 (LASPO) was to save money by limiting the scope of legal aid for some types of case but also to make it available for most victims of domestic violence. Secondary legislation passed under LASPO provided that legal aid would not be available unless supporting evidence of domestic violence was provided in the 24-month period before the application was made. The claimants argued that many victims of domestic violence would not be able to satisfy this rule. The court held that the 24-month rule, by excluding so many and operating in a completely arbitrary manner, frustrated the purposes of the legislation.

See also *Wheeler, Bromley v GLC* [1983] 1 AC 768 (discussed in section 13.3.1), and *R (Core Issues Trust) v Transport for London* [2014] EWCA Civ 34.

SUMMARY

Having been given a discretionary power, a public body must exercise it lawfully as intended by Parliament, and in accordance with the policy and objectives of the relevant statute.

16.4 Irrationality

Public bodies' decision-making must be rational and they must exercise their discretionary powers reasonably. Here, the courts apply the test of *Wednesbury* unreasonableness or irrationality.

CASE CLOSE-UP: *ASSOCIATED PROVINCIAL PICTURE HOUSES LTD v WEDNESBURY CORPORATION* [1948] 1 KB 223

Wednesbury unreasonableness emerged as a ground for judicial review in this leading case where a local council, Wednesbury Corporation, exercised its discretionary power under the Sunday Entertainments Act 1932 to impose conditions on cinema licences by requiring that children below the age of 15 should not be allowed to attend the local cinema on Sundays, whether accompanied by an adult or not. The court found that the Corporation had acted lawfully within its discretion. Lord Greene MR stated that the discretion must be exercised reasonably; 'if a decision on a competent matter is so unreasonable that no reasonable authority could ever have come to it, then the courts can interfere' (p 230). This is the *Wednesbury* test.

Note that the question is not 'would *a reasonable person* have reached this decision' but 'would *no reasonable person* have reached this decision'. This sets a high bar.

Lord Greene explained that something 'overwhelming' is needed, 'something so absurd that no sensible person could ever dream that it lay within the powers of the authority' (*Wednesbury* p 229), and gave the example of a red-haired teacher dismissed because she has red hair. In the *GCHQ case*, Lord Diplock rebadged unreasonableness as irrationality.

Lord Diplock's irrationality test: 'A decision which is so outrageous in its defiance of logic or of accepted moral standards that no sensible person who had applied his mind to the question to be decided would have arrived at it.' (*CCSU v Minister for the Civil Service* [1985] AC 374, 410)

In other words, the decision would not have been reached by any reasonable person. It is perverse, absurd; in *R v NE Devon HA ex p Coughlan* [2001] QB 213, it was described as a decision which defies comprehension and is reached by flawed logic. While discretion involves choosing between courses of action, the tipping point is where the decision-maker departs from what any reasonable person would do. The above tests will apply where:

- A decision or action is in itself not rational: Lord Greene in *Wednesbury* stated that a decision-maker might remain within the 'four corners of the matters which they ought to consider', but has come to a conclusion 'so unreasonable that no reasonable authority could ever have come to it' (p 234). This means that they have considered the right factors but the decision itself is beyond the range of reasonable responses open to the decision-maker.

- There is a flaw in the decision-making process such as relevant factors being ignored or irrelevant ones taken into account, no evidence to support an important step in the reasoning, or the reasoning involves 'a serious logical or methodological error' (*R (Law Society) v Lord Chancellor* [2018] EWHC 2094 (Admin), [2019] 1 WLR 1649 [98]). A wide statutory discretion must be exercised reasonably and there must be a real exercise of the discretion:

    a person entrusted with a discretion must . . . direct himself properly in law. He must call his own attention to the matters which he is bound to consider. He must exclude from his consideration matters which are irrelevant to what he has to consider. If he does not obey those rules, he may truly be said . . . to be acting 'unreasonably'. (*Wednesbury* p 229 (Lord Greene))

Overall, a reasonable balance must be struck and the courts have jurisdiction to overrule or quash the exercise of that discretion if it is unreasonable. Lord Diplock summarised the question for the court as: did the decision-maker 'ask himself the right question and take reasonable steps to acquaint himself with the relevant information to enable him to answer it correctly?' (*Secretary of State for Education and Science v Tameside Metropolitan BC* [1977] AC 1014, 1065.) This is known as the *Tameside* duty (see further *R (Plantagenet Alliance Ltd) v Secretary of State for Justice* [2014] EWHC 1662 (Admin) (QB) [99–100]). The decision-maker must inform themselves so as to arrive at a rational conclusion, and the wider the discretion, the more important it is that they have all the relevant material to enable them to exercise it properly.

Points to note

- With irrationality, the court looks more intensely at the decision itself (rather than the decision-making process) and can consider whether the public body asked itself the right question.

- But the court is not substituting its *own* idea of what is reasonable—it is not an appeal.

- The primary decision-maker is the public body which decides on the merits of a matter (usually under a statutory power); the secondary decision-maker is the court which assesses the decision for irrationality.

16.4.1 The irrationality threshold

Wednesbury unreasonableness and irrationality are tough tests to satisfy; for this reason, claimants often plead other grounds as well. You may wonder why the tests were devised, but there is a high threshold because judicial review is a supervisory, not appellate, process (*R v Home Secretary ex p Brind* [1991] 1 AC 696, 757 (Lord Ackner)). The high bar prevents judges from abusing their supervisory power by interfering too easily in decisions that they think are unreasonable, otherwise it crosses over into an appeal procedure where the courts examine the merits of a decision itself and substitute their own decision in its place.

EXAMPLES OF IRRATIONALITY

Decisions or policies which discriminate against individuals and infringe fundamental principles such as equality

In *R (Gurung) v Ministry of Defence* [2002] EWHC 2463 (Admin), G, a national of Nepal, had served in the Gurkha regiment in the Second World War, and was captured by the Japanese and held as a prisoner of war. In 1955 and again in 2000, the Ministry of Defence decided to exclude Gurkhas from a scheme awarding compensation to former prisoners of war of the Japanese. G and other Nepalese nationals asked for judicial review, arguing that the MoD's decision was irrational. They were successful; it was held that the decision to exclude Nepalese nationals from the scheme was based on racial grounds, and was irrational and inconsistent with the principle of equality in UK law.

In *Adath Yisroel Burial Society v HM Senior Coroner for Inner North London*, discussed previously, was the Coroner's policy capable of rational justification? The answer was no; it was held to be irrational because it singled out and excluded religious beliefs from consideration for no good reason. It was therefore discriminatory, and could still not be rationally justified even if it meant taking *no* individual circumstances into account, whether religious or not ([91–92, 160]).

Policies that do not 'make sense' or stand up to scrutiny

In *R (Rogers) v Swindon NHS Primary Care Trust* [2006] EWCA Civ 392, Ann Rogers was diagnosed with breast cancer but her local NHS Primary Care Trust (PCT) would only fund treatment with the drug Herceptin if there were exceptional clinical or personal circumstances. PCTs have a discretion whether to provide particular drugs but here, the trust had not defined what constituted exceptional circumstances and what justified funding one patient rather than another. Ms Rogers argued that this policy was arbitrary and irrational.

It was held that the policy was irrational, therefore unlawful, and should be quashed because there was no rational basis for preferring one patient to another ([81–82] (Sir Anthony Clarke MR)). It was for the PCT to formulate a lawful policy for future decisions.

Contrast this decision with *R (AC) v Berkshire West Primary Care Trust* [2011] EWCA Civ 247 where the claimant began gender reassignment treatment but the PCT reasonably concluded, when refusing funding for breast augmentation surgery, that there was an absence of evidence that it was likely to be clinically effective to improve the claimant's health; the decision was therefore not irrational.

Decisions that ignore relevant matters

In *R (DSD and NBV) v Parole Board of England and Wales and John Radford* [2018] EWHC 694 (Admin), John Worboys (now Radford) had been convicted of 19 serious sexual offences. The court held that the Parole Board's decision in December 2017 to release him on licence from prison was irrational, not because it was surprising (the Parole Board had given clear, detailed reasons why they considered he could be safely released on licence ([130])) but because the Board should have followed up on references to other victims and carried out further inquiries about other offences which would have provided relevant additional material. The release direction was quashed and the case remitted to the Parole Board for rehearing before a different panel ([156–164]).

See also *R v Immigration Appeal Tribunal ex p Manshoora Begum* [1986] Imm AR 385.

16.4.2 The irrationality thought process

With irrationality, the courts consider the weight and balance given to different interests by the primary decision-maker. The court looked in detail at how a minister had struck a balance in *Secretary of State for Work and Pensions v Johnson* [2020] EWCA Civ 778 where the way the new universal credit rules applied to claimants who were employed and paid monthly was 'odd in the extreme' ([46] (Rose LJ)). The system did not make allowance for individuals being paid on a different day if their usual payment date fell on a weekend or bank holiday, especially around the last working day of the month. As a result, they could receive two salary payments in one universal credit assessment period so received much less universal credit, then no salary in the next assessment period, so the rule had an arbitrary effect of sudden drops in income. The court found that the Secretary of State acted irrationally by failing to change the assessment rules to resolve this problem and include an exception to the general rule. No reasonable minister would have struck the balance in that way ([107] (Rose LJ)). The change in salary payment date was common and predictable, and the rule had a harmful impact on large numbers of claimants. There was nothing to justify concluding that no solution could be devised without unacceptable cost or problems elsewhere in the system [114] (Underhill LJ); see also [92]. The fundamental question was 'whether Parliament can have intended the rule-making power to be exercised in a way which produces so arbitrary and harmful an impact on the Respondents and the very many other claimants who are in the same position' [115]; the court did not believe that it could.

Where a public body has given serious consideration to a matter with coherent and relevant reasons, its decision will generally not be unreasonable or irrational; see, for example, *Keyu v Secretary of State for Foreign and Commonwealth Affairs* [2015] UKSC 69, where ministers' refusal to hold an inquiry into events from 70 years ago was not irrational, especially as they had expressed 'a justifiable concern' that the truth may not be ascertainable and 'a justifiable belief' that little useful for current actions and policies could be learned from an inquiry ([129, 136]). This focuses an irrationality review on the decision-maker's fact-finding processes; for a clear example of this balancing exercise and irrationality reasoning, see *Keyu* [308–311] (Lady Hale).

▶ CROSS REFERENCE

See discussion on *Keyu* in Chapter 18

However, Lady Hale, dissenting in *Keyu*, concluded that the ministers' decision was one which no reasonable authority could reach because it did not take into account all the possible purposes and benefits of an inquiry and the value of establishing the truth was overwhelming [313]. The ministers had not considered the wider public interest of an inquiry into such an event, or the private interests of the families and survivors in knowing the truth, or the importance of setting the record straight [312].

 THINKING POINT

Pausing there, consider how, for some members of the court in *Keyu*, the relevant matters had been considered; the matters that Lady Hale thought relevant had not been considered, therefore she reached a different conclusion.

16.4.3 The sliding scale of review

The courts have developed a sliding scale of how hard they look at decisions for irrationality; this is known as the intensity of review and depends on the context of the case (*R (Mahmood) v Secretary of State for the Home Department* [2001] 1 WLR 840 [18] (Laws LJ); see Figure 16.3). The result is a flexible approach in which the courts can turn the level of scrutiny up or down, so that what is reasonable or rational depends on the context.

Figure 16.3 Irrationality: the sliding scale

Low intensity review - a higher
unreasonableness bar and less
scrutiny where issues are about
political judgment

Anxious scrutiny - lower
unreasonableness bar and more
scrutiny where fundamental
rights are involved

'Low intensity review' is applied in cases involving ministers' political and economic judgment where the courts are less willing to intervene. For decisions involving the formulation and implementation of national economic policy, the courts apply a 'super-*Wednesbury* test'; this is a *high* level of unreasonableness, where they require 'bad faith, improper motive or manifest absurdity' before intervening (*R v Secretary of State, ex p Hammersmith and Fulham London Borough Council* [1991] 1 AC 521, 597 (Lord Bridge); see also *R v Secretary of State, ex p Nottinghamshire County Council* [1986] AC 240).

 EXAMPLES

R (Packham) v Secretary of State for Transport **[2020] EWCA Civ 1004**

Chris Packham challenged the lawfulness of the government's decision to continue with the HS2 project in February 2020, arguing that the government had failed to take account of the project's environmental effects. The court said that this was a macro-political decision, taken at the very highest level of government and largely a matter of political judgment [52]; it therefore required a low intensity of review or a 'light touch' approach [51]: was it irrational for the Secretary of State not to take into account something that was 'obviously material'? The government was entitled to a wide margin of discretion and had to balance significant—and potentially conflicting—political, economic, social and environmental considerations, and a decision either way might be perfectly reasonable [52]. The court saw no basis for concluding that ministers had disregarded any obviously material consideration. As there was no viable argument that the government's decision was irrational, the court refused permission to apply for judicial review [103].

R (Campaign Against Arms Trade) v Secretary of State for International Trade **[2019] EWCA Civ 1020**

This case involved a challenge to the lawfulness of the government's grant of licences for the export of arms or military equipment to Saudi Arabia, which could possibly be used in the conflict in Yemen. The court emphasised that it was not concerned with the merits of the Secretary of State's decision [56] and emphasised the complex and difficult nature of the decisions in question, which were 'particularly far within the responsibility and expertise of the executive branch' [145]. Consequently, the court had to give considerable respect to the decision-maker and could only interfere if the decision was irrational: was the process adopted by the Secretary of State one which was not reasonably open to him [57]? The court concluded that it *was* irrational for the Secretary of State, in making his decision, not to have regard to whether or not there had been past breaches of International Humanitarian Law by Saudi Arabia.

At the other end of the scale is 'anxious scrutiny', a term first used by Lord Bridge in *R v Secretary of State for the Home Department, ex parte Bugdaycay* [1987] AC 514; it is also known as 'heightened' scrutiny. Lord Bridge stated:

> the court must . . . subject an administrative decision to the more rigorous examination, to ensure that it is in no way flawed, according to the gravity of the issue which the decision determines. The most fundamental of all human rights is the individual's right to life and when an administrative decision . . . may put the applicant's life at risk, the basis of the decision must surely call for the most anxious scrutiny. (*Bugdaycay* p 531)

Where a decision infringes fundamental rights (eg an asylum seeker's life is at risk if their asylum application is refused), a *lower* level of unreasonableness than the absurdity/perversity level is applied. The test is 'whether a reasonable Secretary of State, on the material before him, could reasonably make that primary judgment' (*ex p Brind* [1991] 1 AC 696, 749 (Lord Bridge)). This allows the court's scrutiny to be stricter and more intense where the courts look more closely at the decision (see *IBA Health Ltd v Office of Fair Trading* [2004] EWCA Civ 142, [2004] ICR 1364 [90–92] (Carnwath LJ); *Elgizouli* [234]).

 THINKING POINT

Compare this with the *Wednesbury* test in section 16.4.

 EXAMPLE: *R v MINISTRY OF DEFENCE EX PARTE SMITH* [1996] QB 517

Here, the Court of Appeal held that the Ministry of Defence policy not to allow homosexuals to serve in the armed forces was not irrational. The court applied anxious scrutiny because human rights were involved.

Sir Thomas Bingham (as he then was) endorsed the requirement that the courts will not interfere with the exercise of an administrative decision unless satisfied 'that it is beyond the range of responses open to a reasonable decision-maker', but the 'more substantial the interference with human rights, the more the court will require by way of justification before it is satisfied that the decision is reasonable'. This means that the decision-maker has a narrower range of rational responses open to them (p 554).

The greater the impact of a public body's decision on an individual, the more substantially it needs to be justified by the public body, and review by the courts is stricter; however, the threshold of irrationality was not crossed here. The policy was supported by Parliament and by professional advice given to the MoD.

However, in the ensuing Strasbourg case of *Smith and Grady v UK* (2000) 29 EHRR 493, the ECtHR found that the threshold for irrationality was so high that it was not sufficient to protect human rights ([137–138]).

For a critical examination of anxious scrutiny, see Lord Sumption, 'Anxious Scrutiny', Speech delivered at the Administrative Law Bar Association Annual Lecture, 4 November 2014. See also Michael Fordham, 'What Is "Anxious Scrutiny"?' (1996) 1(2) Judicial Review 81.

For varied meanings of rationality, see Y. Nehushtan, 'The Unreasonable Perception of Rationality and Reasonableness in UK Public Law', UK Const L Blog (available at https://ukconstitutionallaw.org/ (1 July 2019)).

SUMMARY

The more policy a decision contains, the less the courts will intervene to find irrationality. The more serious the impact of a decision on an individual, the more substantially the public body will need to justify it.

16.5 Procedural impropriety

This ground of judicial review promotes procedural fairness in decision-making by public bodies. Procedural impropriety applies where the decision-maker has acted unfairly, and therefore unlawfully, by not following the correct procedures, and its decision will be void *ab initio* (as if it had never happened). It is not about unfairness plain and simple, but rather unfairness that crosses the threshold of being an excess or abuse of power. This is because judicial review is traditionally only available for public bodies' acts which are *ultra vires* or unlawful, not for acts done lawfully which a claimant complains of as unfair (*R v Inland Revenue Commissioners, ex p National Federation of Self-Employed and Small Businesses Ltd* [1982] AC 617, 637 (Lord Diplock)). For example, in the *HS2 case*, the High Court held that the consultation process for compensating some of the property owners affected by the high speed train route was 'so unfair as to be unlawful', and the government had to hold another consultation on compensation arrangements (*R (Buckinghamshire County Council and others) v Secretary of State for Transport* [2013] EWHC 481 (Admin) [761, 843]).The key question is whether the decision-maker has failed to follow procedural requirements in a statute, or the common law requirements of procedural fairness as summarised in Figure 16.4. As an extension of the duty to

Figure 16.4 Procedural impropriety

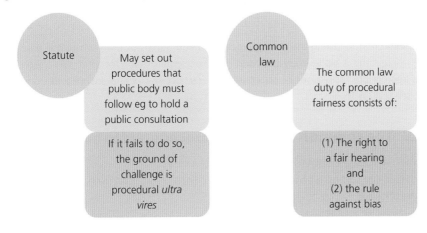

act fairly, the courts have also developed rules on legitimate expectations and the duty to consult which are examined in section 16.5.2.3.

16.5.1 Statutory requirements: procedural *ultra vires*

Procedural *ultra vires* applies where the public body acts outside its powers by not following the procedure specified in a statute before making a decision, but whether this is so unfair as to be unlawful depends on the court's interpretation of the statute.

A procedural requirement in a statute may be mandatory or directory: a mandatory requirement must be complied with, so failure to comply invalidates the action or decision; a directory requirement is less imperative, so an action or decision will not be invalidated if there was substantial compliance (*R v Soneji* [2005] UKHL 49 [14] (Lord Steyn)).

> **➡ EXAMPLES**
>
> - Mandatory requirement: In *R v Camden LBC ex p Cran* (1996) 94 LGR 8, the relevant statute required a consultation with local residents before the local authority implemented a controlled traffic zone; it failed to consult, therefore the traffic scheme was *ultra vires* and invalid. (See section 16.5.2.3 for more on the duty to consult.)
> - Directory requirement: In *Coney v Choyce* [1975] 1 All ER 979, a local authority was required to put up notices outside schools about changes to the school system but failed to do so. The court interpreted it as a directory requirement; the council had given adequate publicity by advertising changes in newspapers and elsewhere, so had validly achieved the desired result in a different way.

For some judges the mandatory/directory distinction has outlived its usefulness, and the emphasis should be on the consequences of non-compliance and interpreting Parliament's intentions about invalidity (*R v Soneji* [23] (Lord Steyn)). In *R v Immigration Appeal Tribunal ex p Jeyeanthan* [1999] EWCA Civ 3010 ([16]), Lord Woolf stated that whether a requirement is mandatory or directory is only a first step; the court should also look at the consequences of not complying with a procedural requirement. Has there been substantial compliance, even if not strict? Can the non-compliance be waived? If not, what is the consequence of the non-compliance? However, Lord Carswell acknowledged that, while the distinction had gone out of fashion, it could still be useful (*Soneji* [61]).

Bear in mind that following the correct procedure might have made no substantial difference to the result; if this is highly likely, the court must refuse permission for a judicial review claim, unless appropriate for reasons of public interest (section 84 Criminal Justice and Courts Act 2015; see section 15.5).

16.5.2 The common law duty of procedural fairness

 The right to a fair hearing is also reflected in Article 6 ECHR

This was traditionally known as the rules of natural justice, which are common law procedural rules that ensure fairness when public bodies make decisions affecting individuals. The rules of natural justice are:

- the right to a fair hearing (*audi alteram partem*, or 'hear the other side');
- the rule against bias (*nemo judex in causa sua*: no one should be a judge in their own cause).

The rules of natural justice are now referred to as the common law duty of procedural fairness. This can be applied as a self-contained requirement or an additional safeguard to ensure that a statutory procedure is followed fairly: in the well-known dictum of Byles J, 'although there are no positive words in a statute requiring that the party shall be heard, yet the justice of the common law will supply the omission of the legislature' (*Cooper v Wandsworth Board of Works* (1863) 14 CB (NS) 180, 194). This means that the duty to act fairly will be implied into a statutory framework even 'when the legislation is silent and does not expressly require any particular procedure to be followed' (*R (Citizens UK) v Secretary of State for the Home Department* [2018] EWCA Civ 1812, [2018] 4 WLR 123 [68]). There is a presumption that Parliament, in granting powers to a public body, implicitly requires their decision to be made in accordance with the duty to act fairly (*Plantagenet Alliance* [90]). The test for whether there has been procedural fairness is an objective question for the *court* to decide, not whether the *decision-maker's* judgment of what fairness required was reasonable (*R (Osborn) v Parole Board* [2013] UKSC 61, [2014] AC 1115 [65] (Lord Reed)). The significance of following a fair procedure is that it results in better decisions by ensuring that the decision-maker receives all relevant information which is properly tested, avoids a sense of injustice, allows the person affected to participate in the procedure by which the decision is made, and promotes the rule of law (*Osborn v Parole Board* [67–71] (Lord Reed)). Until 1964, it was thought that the requirements of natural justice or procedural fairness only applied to judicial decisions, not administrative decision-making by public bodies. In the landmark case of *Ridge v Baldwin* [1964] AC 40, the House of Lords removed that distinction and required all public decision-makers to follow fair procedures. The determining factor is the effect on a person's rights: the more an individual is affected by a public body's decision, the more they are entitled to procedural justice, even where the public body is acting administratively.

> ## 🔍 CASE CLOSE-UP: *RIDGE v BALDWIN* [1964] AC 40
>
> Following two trials at which he was acquitted, the Chief Constable of Brighton was dismissed by the police authority without being given notice of their grounds or the opportunity to defend himself. The dismissal was not just an executive or administrative act; it was serious enough to be decided in a judicial way, as a court would do. Lord Reid stated that the decision-maker cannot lawfully go on to make a decision until it has given the person affected a proper opportunity to state their case, otherwise the decision will be void (p 80). The rationale is that the person affected must have a chance of dealing with matters which may have influenced the decision-maker.

The sliding scale of fairness Over the next decade or so, the courts began to emphasise the variability of the rules according to the context when a public body makes a decision affecting the rights of individuals. The court in *McInnes v Onslow-Fane* [1978] 3 All ER 211 developed a sliding scale of the duty to act fairly where the requirements of fairness are lowest for application cases and highest for forfeiture cases (as shown in Figure 16.5).

An application case is where an individual applies for a job or a licence, for example, with no prior expectations or promises. An expectation case is where a public body's promise or usual practice leads an individual to expect a benefit (see section 16.5.2.3). A forfeiture case is where an individual is deprived of a benefit. Simon Brown LJ summarised this more concisely: 'the demands of fairness are likely to be somewhat higher when an authority contemplates depriving someone of an existing benefit or advantage than when the claimant is a bare applicant for a future benefit' (*R v Devon County Council, ex p Baker* [1992] EWCA Civ 16, [1995] 1 All ER 73, 90).

Figure 16.5 The sliding scale of fairness

application cases	expectation cases	forfeiture cases

For Lord Bridge in *Lloyd v McMahon* [1987] AC 625, the requirements of fairness were 'not engraved on tablets of stone'; they vary depending on the character of the decision-making body, the kind of decision it has to make, and the statutory or other framework in which it operates. The crucial question is: was a fair procedure followed by the public body? In *Doody*, Lord Mustill set out the requirements of fairness, including:

- the presumption that an administrative power will be exercised fairly;
- the standards of fairness may change over time;
- what fairness demands depends on the context of the decision;
- fairness often requires that the person adversely affected has an opportunity to make representations before or after the decision or both, and needs to know the gist of the case which s/he has to answer.

(See *R v Secretary of State for the Home Department, ex parte Doody* [1994] 1 AC 531, 560.)

16.5.2.1 The right to a fair hearing

In this context, a 'hearing' refers to proper consideration of the case by the decision-maker, so consideration of relevant paperwork can suffice instead of an oral hearing. A person is entitled to be treated fairly at all relevant decision-making stages (*Citizens UK* [94]). Procedural fairness ensures that the decision-maker is fully informed when a decision is still at a formative stage and enables the individual concerned to know that they have had the opportunity to influence a decision before it is made (*Balajigari v Secretary of State for the Home Department* [2019] EWCA Civ 673 [60]).Where an individual might be prejudicially affected by a public body's decision, the crucial elements are those shown in green in Table 16.1. The application of the elements shaded in yellow can vary case by case depending on the consequences of the decision, nature of the public body, or any relevant statute. The important question is: would it lead to a just decision?

Table 16.1 Rights that may be included in a fair hearing

To be informed of the case against you in advance	The duty to give advance notice allows representations to be made by a person who foreseeably would be significantly detrimentally affected before a decision is taken unless a relevant statute provides otherwise or it would be 'impossible, impractical or pointless' to give that opportunity (*Bank Mellat v HM Treasury (No 2)* [2013] UKSC 39, [2014] AC 700 [179] (Lord Neuberger)).
A reasonable time to prepare a response	This is an integral part of sufficient advance notice to allow representations to be made.

Table 16.1 Rights that may be included in a fair hearing *(Cont.)*

To be heard, either orally or in writing	An oral hearing is appropriate whenever fairness requires it, eg where a decision has important consequences or there are likely to be disputed facts. See *Osborn v Parole Board* [80–86]; *R (West) v Parole Board* [2005] UKHL 1 [31, 35]. Where a decision-maker is inclined to make an adverse decision affecting an individual's rights, eg in a housing or immigration case, because they disbelieve what they say and it is critical to their application, they must give the applicant an opportunity to deal with it eg an interview (*R v London Borough of Hackney, ex p. Decordova* (1994) 27 HLR 108, 113 (Laws J); see also *Balajigari* [55–56]). Only being able to make representations *after* a decision has been taken will not usually satisfy the demands of common law procedural fairness unless it is impracticable (*Balajigari* [60])
To cross-examine people who give evidence to the decision-maker	This depends on the circumstances of the case; it can apply where there is a right to an oral hearing (see *Bushell v Secretary of State for Environment* [1981] AC 75)
Legal representation	This applies where an oral hearing would not be fair without representation, eg if complex law is involved (see *R v Home Sec ex p Tarrant* [1985] 1 QB 251)
To be given reasons for the decision	There is no general common law duty to give reasons (*R (Hasan) v Secretary of State for Trade and Industry* [2008] EWCA Civ 1311) but the courts are increasingly willing to find that reasons should be given, particularly where liberty is at stake (*R v Secretary of State for Home Department ex p Doody* [1994]). In *Oakley v South Cambridgeshire District Council* [2017] EWCA Civ 71, Elias LJ stated that generally reasons should be given unless there is proper justification for not doing so. It improves the quality of decisions, instils public confidence into the decision-making system, assists the courts in performing their supervisory function over decision-makers, and enables an individual or court to understand why a decision has been made and assess whether it has been made lawfully (see *Citizens UK* [184] (Hickinbottom LJ))

EXAMPLE: *R (SHOESMITH) v OFSTED* [2011] EWCA CIV 642

Sharon Shoesmith was Director of Children's Services at Haringey LBC. Following an Ofsted report on the death of Baby P, a high-profile child abuse case, the Secretary of State announced in a press conference that he would be directing Haringey LBC to appoint a new Director of Children's Services. Ms Shoesmith was then summarily dismissed by Haringey without payment in lieu of notice and her internal appeal was unsuccessful. The Court of Appeal decided that her dismissal was procedurally unfair and unlawful; 'she was entitled to be treated lawfully and fairly and not simply and summarily scapegoated' ([135] (Maurice Kay LJ)).

16.5.2.2 The rule against bias

It is also fundamental to procedural fairness that a decision-maker whose decision could detrimentally affect others is independent, impartial, and free from bias (which means being prejudiced or predisposed against a party and not deciding a case on its merits). They must consider the facts fully, objectively, and in good faith. A decision-maker must not be a judge in their own cause, that is, a party to the case or having a personal or financial interest in its outcome, and where there is a conflict of interest s/he must disclose it or will automatically be disqualified from making a decision, regardless of any likelihood of bias (*R v Bow Street Metropolitan Stipendiary Magistrate, ex parte Pinochet Ugarte (No 2)* [2001] 1 AC 119, 132G–133C (Lord Browne-Wilkinson)). This enables justice to be seen to be done. Bias can be:

▶ CROSS REFERENCE
For details of the *Pinochet case*, see section 13.3.3

- actual (this requires clear evidence of bias and can be difficult to prove);
- financial (or pecuniary), for example *Dimes v Grand Junction Canal Proprietors* (1852) 3 HL Cas 759 (where the Lord Chancellor had shares in one of the parties);
- other personal interest;
- apparent; here, the test in *Porter v Magill* applies: would the fair-minded and informed observer, having considered the facts, conclude that there was a real possibility that the tribunal was biased? See, for example, *R v Abdroikov* [2007] UKHL 37.

In the last three categories, actual bias does not need to be shown; the appearance or real possibility of bias is enough to render a decision unlawful.

16.5.2.3 Legitimate expectations

> Where a clear and unambiguous undertaking is made, the authority giving the undertaking will not be allowed to depart from it unless it is shown that it is fair to do so (*In the matter of an application by Geraldine Finucane for Judicial Review (Northern Ireland)* [2019] UKSC 7 [62]).

The law on legitimate expectation and consultation is growing rapidly, extending the category of procedural unfairness and increasingly forming the basis for many judicial review cases.

An expectation is less than a right or entitlement, but this is about ensuring fairness through holding public bodies to their promises. Public bodies have wide discretion to change their policies but have a legal duty to act fairly where their promise, publicly declared policy, or usual practice leads an individual to expect a benefit or advantage (see *R (Bhatt Murphy) v Independent Assessor* [2008] EWCA Civ 755 [41–42, 50] (Laws LJ); *GCHQ case* [1985] AC 374, 408–409 (Lord Diplock)).

> Where a public authority has issued a promise or adopted a practice which represents how it proposes to act in a given area, the law will require the promise or practice to be honoured unless there is good reason not to do so (*R (Nadarajah) v* Secretary *of State for the Home Department* [2005] EWCA Civ 1363 [68] (Laws LJ)).

The court will enforce the legitimate expectation where, because of its earlier conduct, the decision-maker's proposed action would be so unfair that it would be an abuse of power (*Bhatt Murphy* [42] (Laws LJ)).

 THINKING POINT

Consider this scenario. Miss Coughlan was a severely disabled patient who agreed to be moved to a purpose-built NHS care home, relying on a promise by the local health authority that she and other patients would have a home for life there. The health authority later decided to close the home and transfer the patients' nursing care to the local authority.

By failing to honour its promise, did the public body act unfairly? What would your answer be?

The public body's promise or representation must be 'clear, unambiguous and devoid of relevant qualification' (*R (Bancoult) v Secretary of State for Foreign and Commonwealth Affairs (No 2)* [2008] UKHL 61, [2009] AC 453 [60] (Lord Hoffmann); *R (Association of British Civilian Internees v Secretary of State for Defence* [2003] EWCA Civ 473, [2003] QB 1397). The public body must identify a sufficient public interest to justify overriding the legitimate expectation, and the court weighs the requirements of fairness against that interest (see *Paponette v Attorney-General of Trinidad and Tobago* [2010] UKPC 32 [36–37, 49]).

Legitimate expectations fall broadly into two categories:

- substantive expectations;
- procedural expectations.

Substantive expectations may arise where a public body deprives an individual or limited group of people of a substantive benefit or advantage which they have enjoyed and legitimately expect to continue to enjoy (such as a place in a nursing home) because of the public body's promise or undertaking. While it is not essential for the individual to rely on it to their detriment, it is relevant in deciding whether there has been an abuse of power (*Bancoult (No 2)* [60] (Lord Hoffmann)).

 EXAMPLE

Returning to Miss Coughlan's case above (*R v North and East Devon HA, ex p Coughlan* [2001] QB 213), the failure to honour the promise was held to be so unfair as to amount to an abuse of power. Where a promise or practice has induced a legitimate expectation of a substantive benefit, the court asks: is frustrating that expectation 'so unfair that to take a new and different course will amount to an abuse of power'? The court weighs 'the requirements of fairness against any overriding interest relied upon for the change of policy' (Lord Woolf MR [57]; and see generally [55–82]).

See also *R v Devon County Council, ex p Baker.*

Procedural expectations can arise in the following cases:

1. Where a public body's promise or usual practice leads individuals to expect a specific *procedure* to be followed; for example, fairness requires that a public body is held to an assurance not to withdraw a public service without consultation before making a decision. Laws LJ referred to this as 'the paradigm case of procedural expectation' (*Bhatt Murphy* [29–30]). See *R (Luton Borough Council) v Secretary of State for Education* [2011] LGR 553 [83] (Holman J); *R v Liverpool Corporation, ex parte Liverpool Taxi Fleet Operators' Association* [1972] 2 QB 299; *Council of Civil Service Unions v Minister for Civil Service* [1985] AC 374.

2. Where a public body has not made any assurances but its policy clearly affects an individual or identifiable group who rely on it continuing, it must consult them before making any proposed changes. Procedural fairness protects their interest in it; for example, it should not be withdrawn without the opportunity to comment on the reasons for withdrawal (see *R v Devon County Council, ex p Baker* [88–89] (Simon Brown LJ)). This is Laws LJ's secondary case of procedural expectation (*Bhatt Murphy* [39, 47–49]).

EXAMPLES

In the matter of an application by Geraldine Finucane for Judicial Review (Northern Ireland) [2019] UKSC 7

This case involved a policy statement about procedure. Patrick Finucane was a Belfast solicitor who was killed by gunmen in his home and it later emerged that there was collusion between Mr Finucane's murderers and members of the security forces. The Supreme Court held that Mrs Finucane had a legitimate expectation that there would be a public inquiry into her husband's death based on various undertakings given by ministers which together amounted to an unequivocal undertaking to hold a public inquiry. The government had failed to show valid grounds for not adhering to the promise made to Mrs Finucane.

RF v Secretary of State for Work and Pensions [2017] EWHC 3375 (Admin)

Regulations made in 2017 excluded people with psychological distress from claiming benefits called Personal Independence Payments for help with travel. Mostyn J held that a measure introducing such a change should have been consulted on, and the failure to consult was unlawful. The regulations also discriminated against people with certain disabilities, and were *ultra vires*. They were therefore quashed.

On the other hand, after the remains of King Richard III were found in a Leicester car park, there was no legitimate expectation of public consultation about where they should be buried because there were only two possible options (see *R (Plantagenet Alliance) v Secretary of State for Justice* [2014] EWHC 1662 (QB) [98, 150–153]).

The duty to consult

The duty to consult lets 'those who have a potential interest in the subject matter know in clear terms what the proposal is and exactly why it is under positive consideration, telling them enough (which may be a good deal) to enable them to make an intelligent response. The obligation, although it may be quite onerous, goes no further than this' (*ex p Coughlan* [2001] QB 213 [112] (Lord Woolf MR)). A duty to consult can arise from statute or the common law duty to act fairly so arises where:

1. there is a statutory duty to consult;
2. there has been a promise to consult;
3. there has been an established practice of consultation;
4. in exceptional cases, a failure to consult would lead to conspicuous unfairness (*Plantagenet Alliance* [98]).

Otherwise, there is no obligation on a public body to consult.

Statutory duty to consult A statute may create a duty to consult and will normally set out the requirements eg specifying the subject matter, who should be consulted and when, and how views should be canvassed. Statutory duties of consultation vary depending on the terms of the statute, context, and purpose of the consultation (*R (Moseley) v London Borough of Haringey* [2014] UKSC 56, [2014] 1 WLR 3947 [36] (Lord Reed)). If its purpose is to ensure effective public participation in a local authority's decision-making process, there may be a requirement that consultees should be provided with clear, understandable consultation documents, an outline of realistic alternatives, and the reasons for the local authority's preferred choice (*Moseley* [41] (Lord Reed)).

The common law duty to consult There is no general common law duty to consult people who may be affected by a decision but the duty to consult arises when a person has an interest which the law decides is one to be protected by procedural fairness (*R (LH) v Shropshire Council* [2014] EWCA Civ 404 [28] (Longmore LJ)); for example, the parents' interest in a decision to close a school. This can be where there is a legitimate expectation of consultation, a promise or established practice of consultation (*Moseley* [35] (Lord Reed)), or conspicuous unfairness (*Plantagenet Alliance* [150]).

Consultations must satisfy the 'Gunning' or 'Sedley' criteria set out in *R v Brent London Borough Council, ex p Gunning* (1985) 84 LGR 168, 189:

1. Consultation must be at a time when proposals are still at a formative stage.

2. The proposer must give sufficient reasons for any proposal to permit of intelligent consideration and response (ie by the public).

3. Adequate time must be given for consideration and response.

4. The product of consultation must be conscientiously taken into account in finalising any statutory proposals.

The criteria, which promote fairness, were expressly endorsed by Lord Wilson in *Moseley* [25]; see [23–28, 35–42] for the Supreme Court's guidance on conducting fair consultations, both at common law and under statute.

For very helpful reviews of the principles and authorities on the common law requirement of consultation, see *Plantagenet Alliance* [98]; *R (Dudley Metropolitan Borough Council) v Secretary of State for Communities and Local Government* [2012] EWHC 1729 (Admin); *R (The Law Society) v Lord Chancellor* [2018] EWHC 2094 (Admin) [67–74].

For further reading, see:

Paul Craig, 'Legitimate Expectations: A Conceptual Analysis' (1992) 108 LQR 79
Rebecca Williams, 'The Multiple Doctrines of Legitimate Expectations' (2016) 132 LQR 639

 SUMMARY

Public bodies have a duty to act according to procedural fairness. The standards of fairness are fact-sensitive and may change according to the context of the decision.

16.6 Proportionality

Proportionality is a standard of review, rather than a free-standing ground, and affects the intensity of review being carried out by the courts. The courts use proportionality when applying EU law and in cases involving ECHR rights, though the approaches are different for each (see *R (Lumsdon) v Legal Services Board* [2015] UKSC 41 [26, 33–39, 108]; *Bank Mellat (No 2)* [2013] UKSC 39), and it is increasingly applied when a claimant can identify interference with a common law right. It was referred to in the *GCHQ case* as a possible future ground for judicial review but is not yet recognised as a self-contained ground (see section 16.6.3).

> **CROSS REFERENCE**
>
> For proportionality in human rights cases, see Chapter 17

It requires that the use of discretionary power by a public body should not disproportionately interfere with the rights of individuals. It is a European concept which balances the public body's objectives against any adverse effects on the rights of individuals so that the public body only does what is proportionate to the result to be achieved.

16.6.1 **The proportionality thought process**

There is greater intensity of review with proportionality than with traditional judicial review grounds because the court judges for itself whether the decision or policy was proportionate by reviewing the public body's reasons and how it weighed up competing interests (*R v Secretary of State for Home Department ex p Daly* [2001] 2 AC 532). The four questions for the court to consider with proportionality are:

1. Is the legislative objective sufficiently important to justify limiting a fundamental right?

2. Are the measures which have been designed to meet it rationally connected to it?

3. Are they no more than are necessary to accomplish it?

4. Do they strike a fair balance between the rights of the individual and the interests of the community? (See *R (Quila) v SSHD* [2011] UKSC 45 [45].)

Proportionality therefore draws the courts into assessing the decision, what was in the primary decision-maker's mind, and the balance struck between competing interests.

But where ministers' decisions are concerned, the court can fine-tune the level of intensity and apply a less searching review where there are politically sensitive issues such as national security, foreign affairs, and economic policy, and the weight to be given to respecting the judgment of the executive decision-maker. And the court can never substitute its own decision: 'while judicial bravery and independence are essential, the rule of law is not served by judges failing to accord appropriate respect to the primary policy-making and decision-making powers of the executive' (*R (Rotherham Metropolitan Borough Council) v Secretary of State for Business, Innovation and Skills* [2015] UKSC 6 [65] (Lord Neuberger); see also *Keyu* [272]; *Bank Mellat* [71] (Lord Reed)).

🔍 **CASE CLOSE-UP: *PHAM v SECRETARY OF STATE FOR THE HOME DEPARTMENT* [2015] UKSC 19, [2015] 1 WLR 1591**

Pham's British citizenship was removed under section 40(2) British Nationality Act 1981. He was believed to have undergone terrorist training in Yemen and was ordered to be deported to Vietnam, but its government did not recognise him as a Vietnamese national. He argued that he would be made stateless and because he would also lose European citizenship, EU law applied; therefore the court should adopt a proportionality approach. The court was not persuaded that EU law applied and held that the UK government did not make him stateless as he had Vietnamese citizenship at the time of removal. Nevertheless, the Justices engaged in an important discussion of proportionality.

Lord Sumption described the balancing exercise at paragraph 108. The court had to weigh his right to British nationality, which was 'manifestly at the weightiest end of the sliding scale', against the security of the UK against terrorist attack, which was 'a countervailing public interest which is potentially at the weightiest end of the scale', depending on how much of a threat he represented. The court must also have regard to the fact that the Home

Secretary is the statutory decision-maker, and to the executive's special institutional competence in the area of national security.

Where do you think is the fair balance? The individual's right to British nationality or UK security?

Lord Mance took the view that, as removal of British citizenship was 'a radical step', a strict standard of judicial review should be applied, and proportionality would be an 'available and valuable' tool for such a review [98]. In considering whether the withdrawal was proportionate, the court could also take into account whether withdrawing British nationality also meant losing European citizenship. Lord Sumption noted that if a person was deprived of European citizenship, a test of proportionality would be applied; if it only concerned British nationality, the three traditional grounds of judicial review would be applied, and not proportionality [104].

16.6.2 Comparing proportionality and irrationality

Proportionality overlaps with irrationality—though not exactly. A reasonable decision-maker would not make a disproportionate decision (*R v Home Sec ex p Brind*); if a decision is disproportionate, it is irrational. The classic comparison between proportionality and irrationality was made by Lord Steyn in the *Daly* case.

CASE CLOSE-UP: *R v SECRETARY OF STATE FOR THE HOME DEPARTMENT EX P DALY [2001] 2 AC 532*

A prisoner challenged the Home Secretary's policy that prisoners were not allowed to be present during searches of their cells when prison officers were looking at legally privileged letters between prisoners and their lawyers. He argued that it was not authorised by section 47(1) Prison Act 1952, and breached his common law right to confidential communication with lawyers and Article 8 ECHR.

The House of Lords held that the policy was unlawful and void because the intrusion on the prisoner's right to confidentiality of privileged legal correspondence was *greater than* the objectives of preventing crime and maintaining order and discipline in prisons.

Note the court's reasoning here, using a balance to find that the policy was disproportionate.

Lord Bingham stated that it was a blanket policy and there was no justification for routinely excluding all prisoners. Other prisons had minimised the interference. The result was the same whether applying common law principles or Article 8 ECHR (note that the Human Rights Act was not yet in force) ([18–23]).

Lord Steyn made some important observations ([27–28]). Most cases would be decided the same way whether using traditional judicial review or proportionality but there were differences between them:

1. Proportionality may require the court itself to assess the *balance* struck by the decision-maker between competing interests, not merely whether it is within the range of reasonable decisions.

2. The proportionality test may go further than the traditional judicial review grounds because it may require assessment of the relative weight given to interests and considerations.

3. Even the heightened scrutiny test in *R v Ministry of Defence, ex p Smith* [1996] is not necessarily appropriate to protect human rights.

There is a more intense review with proportionality because the court is looking at whether the limitation of a person's right is necessary in a democratic society and whether the interference is proportionate to the aim being pursued.

In *Pham*, Lord Sumption pointed out that the differences just set out may vary depending on the significance of the right interfered with, the degree of interference involved, and the extent to which the court is competent to reassess the balance which the decision-maker had to make given the subject matter (*Pham* [107]).

There is, however, considerable overlap between irrationality and proportionality, as Figure 16.6 suggests (*Keyu* [273] (Lord Kerr)). For both, the courts consider the weight and balance given to different interests by the primary decision-maker, especially where fundamental rights are involved. This balance can be seen in *Smith* and *Pham*. The intensity and weight vary depending on the context and the nature of the rights involved. Many reviews will have the same result whether conducted under irrationality or proportionality (*Pham* ([98]; *Keyu* [139, 143, 283]), and the court is assessing the range of possible rational decisions in each case. Supporters of proportionality, notably Lord Mance, favour its structured, forensic nature and 'innate superiority' as a tool to review decisions (*Kennedy v Charity Commission* [2014] UKSC 20, [2014] 2 WLR 808 [54]; *Keyu* [274]; *Pham* [96]). Dyson LJ has also observed that the 'criteria of proportionality are more precise and sophisticated' (*R (Association of British Civilian Internees) v Secretary of State for Defence* [34]).

> Ultimately, at the end of the balancing exercise in irrationality, the court asks whether a rational decision-maker would think that the decision was proportionate; with proportionality, the court judges for itself whether the decision was proportionate.

However, there are differences. Lord Sumption has noted that 'rationality is a minimum condition of proportionality, but is not the whole test' (*R (Lord Carlile of Berriew) v Secretary of State for the Home Department* [2014] UKSC 60, [2014] 3 WLR 1404 [32]). Lord Reed did not regard the tests of proportionality and irrationality as identical even with 'anxious' scrutiny (*Pham* [115]). In *Daly*, Lord Steyn noted a material difference between the *Wednesbury* and *Smith* grounds of review and the approach of proportionality in cases where Convention rights were at stake ([26]).

Figure 16.6 Irrationality and proportionality

Low intensity review - less scrutiny where issues are about political judgment

Proportionality - was interference proportionate - assess the relative weight given to interests and considerations

Anxious scrutiny - more scrutiny of weight and balance where fundamental rights are involved

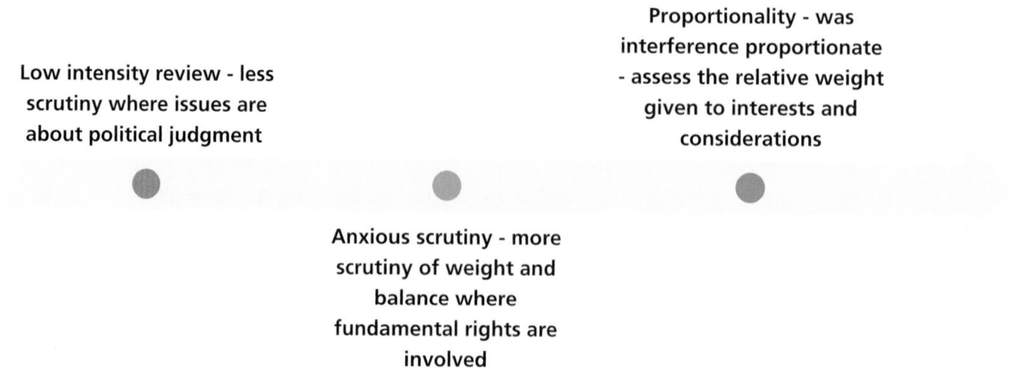

16.6.3 Is proportionality part of English domestic law yet?

This is very much on the courts' radar; there is a sense of a blending of irrationality and proportionality at the weighty end of the scale, but the gap has not fully closed.

> **CLOSE-UP FOCUS: IS PROPORTIONALITY PART OF ENGLISH LAW?**
>
> **The case in favour**
>
> - Lord Sumption recognised that 'although English law has not adopted the principle of proportionality generally, it has for many years stumbled towards a concept which is in significant respects similar' (*Pham* [105]). The courts, 'sometimes without acknowledgment', have expanded their approach on irrationality to incorporate significant aspects of the proportionality approach by differentiating between rights and interference with them and considering weight and balance (*Pham* [105]). An example of this is *R v Barnsley MBC ex p Hook* [1976] 1 WLR 1052, where, without referring to proportionality, it was held that revoking a market traders' licence was excessive and out of proportion as a response to a 'trifling incident' of urinating in a side street.
>
> - Lord Slynn considered that the time has come to recognise that proportionality is part of English administrative law, and 'trying to keep the *Wednesbury* principle and proportionality in separate compartments seems . . . unnecessary and confusing' (*Alconbury* [51]).
>
> - Lord Cooke called *Wednesbury* 'an unfortunately retrogressive decision in English administrative law' where only 'a very extreme degree' of unreasonableness can allow the courts to intervene (*Daly* [32]).
>
> - Extrajudicially, Lord Sumption has argued that anxious scrutiny in irrationality reviews imports some aspects of proportionality (www.supremecourt.uk/docs/speech-141104.pdf).
>
> - Lord Mance thought there was no reason why the proportionality approach should not be relevant in judicial review outside the ECHR and EU law (*Kennedy* [54]), while Lord Sumption agreed that at common law, the court could assess the balance drawn by the decision-maker between rights and relevant public interests (*Pham* [108]).
>
> **The case against**
>
> - In *Brind*, the House of Lords did not accept that proportionality had become a self-contained ground of judicial review in domestic law.
>
> - This is supported by Dyson LJ, who acknowledges:
>
> The Wednesbury test is moving closer to proportionality, and in some cases it is not possible to see any daylight between the two tests . . . we have difficulty in seeing what justification there now is for retaining the Wednesbury test . . . But we consider that it is not for this court to perform its burial rites. The continuing existence of the Wednesbury test has been acknowledged by the House of Lords on more than one occasion. (*R (Association of British Civilian Internees (Far East Region)) v Secretary of State for Defence* [34–35])

- After reviewing the authorities, Coulson LJ concluded that proportionality was not part of English domestic law in cases not involving EU law or Convention rights and, for now, the common law test for judicial review is based on the principle of rationality (*Browne v Parole Board of England and Wales* [2018] EWCA Civ 2024 [54–58])

In *Keyu*, the appellants grasped the nettle and asked the court to consider replacing the *Wednesbury* rationality ground of judicial review with a more structured approach based on proportionality ([131]). The court declined. Lord Neuberger thought it would not be appropriate for a five-Justice panel of the court to decide that argument, which has profound constitutional implications ([132]), and moving from rationality to proportionality would involve the court considering the merits of a public body's decision, although he also highlighted dicta suggesting that domestic law might be moving away from the irrationality test in some cases ([133]). However, Lord Kerr suspected that it was a question that would have to be addressed by the Supreme Court sooner rather than later and seemed to suggest that it was not a stark binary choice between proportionality and irrationality (*Keyu* [271]).

For the time being, *Wednesbury* unreasonableness/irrationality remains the common law test for domestic cases with no human rights, EU law, or common law constitutional rights element following the *Pham* approach.

Further reading

Paul Craig, 'Proportionality, Rationality and Review' (2010) 2 New Zealand Law Review 265

James Goodwin, 'The Last Defence of Wednesbury' (2012) (July) Public Law 445

Andrew Le Sueur, 'The Rise and Ruin of Unreasonableness?' (2005) 10 Judicial Review 32

Dr Yossi Nehushtan, 'UK Public Law Non-Identical Twins: Reasonableness and Proportionality' (2017) 50(1) Israel Law Review 69

Sir Philip Sales, 'Rationality, Proportionality and the Development of the Law' (2013) 129 LQR 223

16.7 The modern approach to judicial review

The common law of judicial review is not static and has continued to evolve since Lord Diplock formulated the three grounds in the *GCHQ case*. There is now much more of the blending that Lord Donaldson referred to in *Oladehinde*. The courts have developed what Lord Phillips has called 'an issue-sensitive scale of intervention' to carry out their judicial review function in an increasingly complex state (*R (Q) v Secretary of State for the Home Department* [2003] EWCA Civ 364, [2004] QB 36, [112]; and see *Kennedy v Charity Commission* [52]). This is particularly seen with the sliding scales used in fairness and rationality reviews, and anxious scrutiny where fundamental human rights or constitutional principles are at stake. The nature of judicial review is now very dependent on the context (see *Kennedy* [51–55] (Lord Mance); *Pham* [60]). The sliding-scale, context-based approach allows the courts more flexibility, especially where important rights are involved, and the courts are firmly in control of its development. While the courts 'continue to abstain from merits review . . . in appropriate classes of case they will today look very closely at the process by which facts have been ascertained and at the logic of the inferences drawn from them' (*R (Q) v Secretary of State for the Home Department* [2004] QB 36 [112] (Lord Phillips MR)).

16.7.1 The *Kennedy* approach: judicial review upholding constitutional rights and values

We saw in Chapter 9 that there is an underlying 'pool' of principles, values, and fundamental rights which are upheld through the rule of law. The Supreme Court suggested a value or principle-based approach in judicial review in the *Kennedy* case, advocating that rather than treating 'all cases of judicial review together under a general but vague principle of reasonableness', it is better to locate the underlying principle to be protected in the case and the importance of the value threatened to indicate the basis of the court's approach ([55]). For example, in *Kennedy*, the Supreme Court interpreted the Charity Commission's duties under the Charities Act in light of the principles of accountability and openness, and in the *UNISON case*, the court protected the principle of unimpeded access to the courts (*R (UNISON) v Lord Chancellor* [2017] UKSC 51 [68]). In *Miller/Cherry*, the Supreme Court protected the principles of parliamentary sovereignty and government accountability to Parliament from infringement by the prerogative power to prorogue Parliament. See Gordon Anthony, 'Public Interest and the Three Dimensions of Judicial Review' (2013) 64(2) Northern Ireland Legal Quarterly, 125, 128–130.

In this way, the courts are extending judicial review to protect fundamental principles. However, for this approach to work, there must be consensus on what constitutes a free-standing principle for the courts' protection. The Supreme Court in *R (Gallaher Group Ltd) v Competition and Markets Authority* [2018] UKSC 25 held that equal treatment by public bodies is not recognised as a distinct principle of English administrative law; there is no general principle of substantive unfairness (as opposed to the recognised judicial review ground of procedural unfairness).

Sedley J has noted: 'Public law is not at base about rights, even though abuses of power may and often do invade private rights; it is about wrongs—that is to say misuses of public power' (*R v Somerset County Council and ARC Southern Limited, ex parte Dixon* [1997] EWHC Admin 393, [1998] Env LR 111, 121). Nevertheless, a rights-based approach is becoming embedded, particularly with irrationality and Human Rights Act challenges (see Chapter 17), which raises the issue of whether traditional judicial review is losing touch with its constitutional roots as a supervisory mechanism.

16.8 Public law remedies

Finally, judicial review has unique remedies known as prerogative orders which comprise:

- mandatory orders: to compel a public body to perform a public law duty imposed on it by statute or prerogative.
- prohibiting orders: to prevent a public body from taking *ultra vires* actions or decisions.
- quashing orders: to quash a decision which was *ultra vires* or in breach of natural justice.

They were formerly prerogative writs called mandamus, prohibition, and certiorari, which, along with *habeas corpus* (which was used to challenge the lawfulness of detention), were used for centuries.

The judicial review procedure *must* be used where the claimant is seeking any of the three remedies above (CPR 54.2). The judicial review procedure *may* be used where the claimant is seeking a declaration or an injunction (CPR 54.3(1)). A claim for judicial review may include a claim for damages, restitution, or the recovery of money, but cannot request one of those remedies alone (CPR 54.3(2)).

 EXAMPLE: A QUASHING ORDER

Here, a judicial review claim had been brought on the grounds of irrationality to challenge the Home Secretary's refusal to set up a statutory inquiry into the death of a former Russian spy.

> I am satisfied that the reasons given by the Secretary of State do not provide a rational basis for the decision not to set up a statutory inquiry at this time but to adopt a 'wait and see' approach. The deficiencies in the reasons are so substantial that the decision cannot stand. The appropriate relief is a quashing order. (*R (Litvinenko) v Secretary of State for the Home Department* [2014] EWHC 194 (Admin) [74] (Richards LJ))

However, Richards LJ also emphasised that while the Home Secretary would need to give fresh consideration to the exercise of her discretion and take into account the points made in the court's judgment, the court's judgment did not dictate a particular outcome ([76]).

Remedies are at the court's discretion and are not awarded automatically. The court will take into account the claimant's conduct, any delay in bringing proceedings, or the effect of granting a remedy on the public body. The claimant also has a duty of candour in judicial review proceedings and must ensure that the judge 'has the full picture' (*R (Khan) v Secretary of State for the Home Department* [2016] EWCA Civ 416 [45]). One final thought: ultimately the cost of bringing judicial review claims—which Tom Hickman describes as 'a Rolls Royce form of litigating disputes with public bodies'—is a practical but powerful factor in determining whether a claimant pursues a claim (ukconstitutionallaw.org/2017/02/09/tom-hickman-public-laws-disgrace/).

 SUMMARY

- Judicial review is a vital control on executive power in the UK enabling individuals to challenge decisions of public bodies in the courts, ensuring accountability
- The traditional judicial review grounds of illegality, irrationality, and procedural impropriety are applied flexibly to protect individuals against the unreasonable, arbitrary, procedurally unfair, or unlawful use of power
- Judicial review is not concerned with the merits of decisions but with the decision-making process by public bodies
- The nature of judicial review in every case depends on the context
- The courts continue to expand the boundaries of judicial review

? Questions

Self-test questions

1. Summarise the purpose of judicial review.

2. What are the grounds of judicial review?

3. In what ways can a public body act unlawfully?

4. Explain the significance of the *Padfield* case.

5. What does a claimant have to demonstrate for irrationality?

6. How does the context of the case affect the courts' approach to reviewing irrationality claims?

7. What does the common law duty of procedural fairness require?

8. What is a legitimate expectation?

9. How do the courts apply proportionality?

10. What are the three specific remedies for judicial review?

Exam question

In a speech to the CBI in 2012, David Cameron described judicial review as a 'massive growth industry'. Basing your argument on case law, critically discuss whether judicial review has expanded too far in its development.

≡ Further reading

Books

Endicott, T. *Administrative Law* (4th edn, Oxford: Oxford University Press 2018).
A thematic approach to judicial review

Loveland, I. *Constitutional Law, Administrative Law, and Human Rights: A Critical Introduction* (8th edn, Oxford: Oxford University Press 2018).
See Part IV for an in-depth discussion of judicial review

Wade, H.W.R. and Forsyth, C.F. *Administrative Law* (11th edn, Oxford: Oxford University Press 2014).
A comprehensive analysis of judicial review

Journal articles

Bell, J. 'The Doctrine of Legitimate Expectations: Power-constraining or Right-conferring Legal Standard?' (2016) (July) Public Law 437.
For more detail on legitimate expectations but also the question of whether judicial review is about constraining power or protecting rights

Craig, P. 'The Nature of Reasonableness Review' (2013) 66(1) Current Legal Problems 131.

Detailed analysis of unreasonableness and the proportionality debate

Jowell, J. and Lester, A, 'Beyond Wednesbury: Substantive Principles of Administrative Law' (1987) (Autumn) Public Law 368.
Analyses the development of principle-based review of discretionary powers

Turner, I. 'Judicial Review, Irrationality, and the Limits of Intervention by the Courts' (2010) 21(2) King's Law Journal 311.
Analysis of how closely the courts approach merits review of executive decision-making

Other sources

Lord Carnwath, 'From Judicial Outrage to Sliding Scales—Where Next for Wednesbury?' ALBA Annual Lecture 12 November 2013 at www.supremecourt.uk/docs/speech-131112-lord-carnwath.pdf.
Helpful discussion of the sliding scale in irrationality reviews, particularly anxious scrutiny

Government Legal Department, 'The Judge over Your Shoulder: A Guide to Good Decision Making'. Available at www.gov.uk/government/publications/judge-over-your-shoulder.
A guide for civil servants, first issued in 1987 and known as JOYS, focusing on judicial review principles of good administration and fairness

Singh, J. 'Judicial Review and the Rule of Law', South West Administrative Lawyers Association Lecture, Bristol, 15 June 2017 at www.judiciary.gov.uk/wp-content/uploads/2017/06/mr-justice-singh-swala-lecture-20170616.pdf.
Clear discussion and overview of judicial review principles

⁏ Online resources

www.oup.com/he/dennett2e
This chapter is accompanied by a selection of online resources to help you with this topic, including:

- Multiple-choice questions
- Answers to the self-test questions
- Guidance on answering the exam question

17 The Human Rights Act 1998

LEARNING OBJECTIVES

By the end of this chapter, you should be able to:

- Explain the connection between the European Convention on Human Rights and the Human Rights Act 1998
- Analyse the key provisions of the Act and their operation
- Appraise issues arising from identifying 'victims' and 'public authorities'
- Evaluate the constitutional impact of the Act
- Discuss the British Bill of Rights debate

Introduction

This chapter examines the Human Rights Act 1998, detailing its development, its key provisions, and some of the issues that it raises. We will examine:

- The European Convention on Human Rights 1950
- Before the Human Rights Act in the UK
- The Human Rights Act 1998
- The role of the courts under the Act
- A British Bill of Rights
- Human rights post-Brexit

The European Convention on Human Rights 1950 (ECHR) is an international treaty setting out a code of guaranteed rights known as Convention rights; under the Convention, the *state* is answerable for any violation of an individual's rights. The Human Rights Act (HRA) came into force on 2 October 2000, and it incorporates the rights in the Convention into UK law. Before the Act was passed, individuals had to take an action against the UK for breach of their Convention rights to the European Court of Human Rights (ECtHR) in Strasbourg. The Human Rights Act allows individuals to bring proceedings in the UK courts where a public authority has acted incompatibly with their rights. The Act therefore provides an additional avenue of review of executive action by the courts, and many judicial review claims now include claims under the Human Rights Act.

CLOSE-UP FOCUS: FREEDOMS IN ENGLISH LAW

English law has traditionally recognised freedoms and civil liberties, rather than rights. In the UK, freedoms and civil liberties derive from the common law, as Dicey recognised. In the Petition of Right (1628), for example, Parliament referred to existing ancient liberties of the people including freedom from arbitrary arrest and punishment (see Chapter 2). The courts have protected common law rights such as the freedom of an individual's home and property and the freedom of the press (*Wilkes v Wood* (1763), *Leach v Money* (1765); *Entick v Carrington* [1765]), the right to liberty (*Wilkes v Halifax* (1769)), and freedom from slavery (*Somersett's Case* (1772)). Parliament has also enshrined rights in statute, for example, the Bill of Rights 1689 providing for freedom from 'cruel or unusual punishment', and the Habeas Corpus Act 1679 guaranteeing the right of individuals to challenge the lawfulness of their detention in court, thus protecting against arbitrary imprisonment without legal authority. Note how these issues also link to the rule of law.

See Lord Wright, 'Liberty and the Common Law' (1945) 9(1) CLJ 2.

What is the difference between a right and a freedom?

- A right gives rise to a corresponding duty; rights are often guaranteed in a written constitution or code.
- A liberty is a basic freedom with which the state may not interfere.
- A residual freedom is what individuals are free to do after legal restrictions by the state, that is, they can do what is not banned.

 EXAMPLE

With freedom of speech, Lord Goff explained that Article 10 of the ECHR states the fundamental right and then qualifies it, but the traditional approach was to 'proceed on an assumption of freedom of speech, and turn to our law to discover the established exceptions to it' (*Attorney-General v Guardian Newspapers Ltd (No 2)* [1990] 1 AC 109 p 283F).

17.1 The European Convention on Human Rights 1950

The atrocities of the Second World War—such as forced labour, torture, persecution, imprisonment, or being killed because of race, religion, or political beliefs—turned post-war international attention to the human rights of individuals. Led by individuals such as Eleanor Roosevelt, Raphael Lemkin, and René Cassin, the aim was to develop overarching codes protecting human rights and fundamental freedoms. In 1948, in his speech at the Congress of Europe in The Hague, Churchill advocated European unity for common causes such as the protection of common values, and referred to 'the idea of a Charter of Human Rights, guarded by freedom and sustained by law'; the Congress proposed establishing a Charter of Human Rights and a court to ensure compliance. In the same year, the Universal Declaration of Human Rights (UDHR) was adopted by the General Assembly of the United Nations, although it was not legally binding.

THINKING POINT

Read the Preamble (the introductory paragraphs) to the UDHR to see the significance of human rights protection.

In May 1949, the Council of Europe was created as a regional body to protect human rights and the rule of law and to promote democracy across Europe. It authorised the drafting of a code of legally enforceable rights, drawing on those set out in the UDHR, and a team of international lawyers began work on drafting; chief among them was David Maxwell-Fyfe, a British barrister and MP who had prosecuted at the Nuremberg Trials and helped draft the UDHR. The final version was adopted by the Council of Europe as the Convention for the Protection of Human Rights and Fundamental Freedoms (the European Convention on Human Rights). It was signed by ten states on 4 November 1950 (including the UK), was ratified by the UK in 1951, and came into force on 3 September 1953. For background, see Geoffrey Marston, 'The United Kingdom's Part in the Preparation of the European Convention on Human Rights, 1950' (1993) 42(4) ICLQ 796. For differences between the UDHR and ECHR, see *R (Pretty) v DPP* [2001] UKHL 61 [56] (Lord Steyn).

Important points

Do not confuse the European Convention on Human Rights with the European Union

The European Convention on Human Rights is an international treaty adopted by the Council of Europe which is completely separate from, and pre-dates, the European Union.

Do not confuse the European Convention (a treaty) with constitutional conventions (rules of political practice)

The ECHR created a code of guaranteed rights protecting individuals (see Table 17.1). As an international treaty, the Convention applies to, and is legally binding on, states; by signing the ECHR, states (known as High Contracting Parties) accept a legal obligation to apply those rights to everyone within their jurisdiction (Article 1).

▶ CROSS REFERENCE

For the difference between domestic law and international law, see section 3.2.6

There are three types of rights under the Convention: absolute, limited, and qualified rights.

Absolute rights The rights in Articles 2, 3, 4(1), and 7 are absolute, which means that the state cannot restrict them at all (except that Article 2 sets out the strict circumstances in which the right can lawfully be departed from).

Limited rights The right in Article 5 can be restricted by the state in the specific situations listed in the Article, for example, a person can be deprived of the right to liberty by lawful detention after conviction by a competent court.

Table 17.1 Convention rights

Article	Right
2	The right to life
3	Freedom from torture and inhuman or degrading treatment or punishment
4	Freedom from slavery and forced labour
5	The right to liberty and security of the person
6	The right to a fair trial
7	No punishment without law (the right not to be punished for a criminal offence that was not illegal at the time)
8	The right to respect for private and family life
9	Freedom of thought, conscience, and religion
10	Freedom of expression
11	Freedom of assembly and association
12	The right to marry and start a family
13	The right to an effective remedy
14	The right not to be discriminated against in respect of these rights
	ECHR rights have been further supplemented by a series of Protocols, eg: • the right to education (Protocol 1, Article 2) • the right to participate in free elections (Protocol 1, Article 3) • the abolition of the death penalty (Protocol 13)

Article 6 is more difficult to categorise; the right to a fair trial is an absolute right, setting a minimum standard for a fair trial which cannot lawfully be deviated from, but what is fair can vary in each case so the subsidiary rights in Article 6 are not absolute (see *R v Forbes* [2001] 1 AC 473 [24]; *Brown v Stott* [2001] 2 WLR 817; see also L Hoyano, 'What Is Balanced on the Scales of Justice? In Search of the Essence of the Right to a Fair Trial?' (2014) 1 Criminal Law Review 4).

Qualified rights The freedoms in Articles 8, 9, 10, and 11 are qualified rights which can be restricted by the state. For example, Article 10(1) provides for freedom of expression, but it can be restricted for the reasons listed in Article 10(2), including national security, public safety, preventing disorder or crime, protecting the reputation of other people, safeguarding confidential information, or maintaining the impartiality of judges. Any restriction must:

- be in accordance with the law or prescribed by law (it must have a basis in the state's domestic law which conforms to the Convention standards of legality);

- pursue one of the legitimate aims set out in each article, for example, the protection of health;

- be necessary in a democratic society (be proportionate and no more than necessary to achieve that legitimate aim).

With Articles 8–11, public authorities have to strike a balance between the rights of the individual and protecting the rights of others or the interests of the wider community to achieve a fair result. See Chapter 18 for more details.

Key terms

The margin of appreciation The ECtHR recognises that state authorities and national courts may be better placed to judge pressing social needs at national level when deciding whether the state has struck an appropriate balance in restricting a right, so it allows them a measure of flexibility, as long as they meet a minimum standard. This is known as the 'margin of appreciation' (from the idea of administrative discretion in civil law in Europe) and it was applied in *Handyside v UK* [1976] ECHR 5 [48–49]. Handyside had claimed that his conviction for possessing obscene publications breached his right to freedom of expression but the ECtHR recognised that there was no consensus across Europe on protecting public morals so states should have discretion in deciding whether a measure was necessary; see also *Belfast City Council v Miss Behavin'* [2007] UKHL 19 [16, 46]. However, the margin of appreciation is not always consistently applied by the ECtHR.

The ECtHR regards the Convention as a '**living instrument**', which means interpreting its provisions flexibly in the light of changing modern standards (for examples, see section 17.3).

Positive and negative obligations Some Convention rights impose a positive obligation on the state requiring it to do a specific act to secure the right, for example, to protect individuals; some impose a negative obligation, which means the state must *not* take an action. Article 2 contains both a positive and a negative obligation: to protect everyone's right to life by law, and not to deprive anyone of their life intentionally.

First generation rights are civil and political. **Second generation rights** are social and economic (such as access to food and healthcare, and workplace rights). The ECHR primarily protects civil and political rights which, in 1950, were regarded as more important, promoting freedom *from* the state rather than freedom *through* the state as with second generation rights, but the distinction is not now regarded as productive (see Sandra Fredman, *Human Rights Transformed*, Oxford: Oxford University Press 2008).

17.2 The European Court of Human Rights

The European Court of Human Rights is based in Strasbourg (not to be confused with the Court of Justice of the European Union). Set up in 1959 to hear complaints about violations of the Convention by states, it is now accessible by 800 million people in 47 states across Europe.

- Under Article 34 ECHR, 'any person, non-governmental organisation or group of individuals claiming to be the victim of a violation' by a state can petition the court alleging a breach of their Convention rights. The UK recognised the right of individuals to petition the ECtHR in 1966 (recognition at that time was optional).

- It is a court 'of last resort' so individuals can only bring a petition when they have exhausted all remedies in their domestic (home) courts.

- Under Article 33, states may also bring applications to the court for violations of human rights by other states (eg the inter-state case brought by Georgia against Russia in relation to the 2008 armed conflict), though this is more unusual.

Cases are assigned to one of the Court's five administrative Sections and applications may be heard by a single judge, a three-judge Committee, a seven-judge Chamber, or a 17-judge Grand Chamber. Under Article 46 of the Convention, states are required to give effect to judgments of the court; this is a binding international law obligation, although they can decide exactly how to implement them. The Council of Europe's committee of ministers monitors implementation and is responsible for enforcement of judgments. Domestically, the UK Parliament and government are not obliged to give effect to a Strasbourg judgment, but despite the issues with *Hirst v UK (No 2)*, the UK has one of the strongest compliance records.

▶ CROSS REFERENCE
See section 10.2.3.2

From 1 August 2018, the ECtHR has had advisory jurisdiction, allowing the highest courts of states that have ratified Protocol 16 to request advisory opinions from the court on questions of interpretation of the Convention and its protocols.

For helpful guides to the court, see www.echr.coe.int.

17.3 Before the Human Rights Act in the UK

At the time of ratifying the ECHR, the UK took the view that its domestic law already protected most rights contained in the Convention, and nearly 50 years elapsed before the ECHR was incorporated into UK law. During that time, individuals who wished to enforce Convention rights against the UK had to take their case to the ECtHR in Strasbourg, and an infringement of a Convention right which was not already reflected in English law would not be enforced by the UK courts because there was no breach of UK domestic law. In *Malone v Metropolitan Police Commissioner* [1979] Ch 344, for example, the police had tapped Malone's phone but he was unable to obtain a remedy for breach of privacy because there was no right to privacy in English law (even though it was protected by Article 8 ECHR).

However, the UK did not operate in a vacuum. As a party to the ECHR, the UK has always been bound in international law to observe it and be answerable for any violations. Parliament was mindful of the UK's international legal responsibilities under the Convention when passing laws—though if there was a conflict between the Convention and a UK statute, the UK statute would prevail if it was clear and unambiguous. The Convention also influenced UK law and social attitudes and some ECtHR decisions had a liberalising effect: attitudes to corporal punishment in the UK were changed by the judgments in *Tyrer v UK* [1978] ECHR 2 and *A v UK* (1999) 27 EHRR 611 (where the judicial punishment of birching on the Isle of Man and hitting a child with a garden cane, respectively, were found to be inhuman treatment), while *Dudgeon v UK* (1982) 4 EHRR 149 led to a change in the law on homosexuality in Northern Ireland. The UK courts also used the Convention as an aid to interpreting statutes (R *(Brind) v SSHD* [1991] 1 AC 696) or reconciling conflicting case law (*Derbyshire CC v The Times Newspapers* [1993] AC 534), while the decision in *Sunday Times v UK* [1979] ECHR 1 prompted a change in English contempt law, resulting in the Contempt of Court Act 1981.

17.4 The Human Rights Act 1998

The government made the case for the new Bill in its White Paper, *Rights Brought Home: The Human Rights Bill* (1997, Cm 3782), citing the delay and cost of going to Strasbourg ([1.14–1.17]) and the fact that public authorities were not required by UK law to comply with the ECHR ([2.2–2.4]). The subsequent Human Rights Act 'brought rights home' by incorporating the ECHR into domestic (UK) law so that almost all Convention rights became domestic rights which could be directly enforced in UK courts (though proceedings may still be brought in Strasbourg), and required public bodies to act compatibly with Convention rights. Its effect is summarised in Figure 17.1. Lord Bingham explained the purpose of the Act: 'to enable those subject to the jurisdiction of the United Kingdom and able to establish violations by United Kingdom public authorities to present their claims in the domestic courts of this country and not only in Strasbourg' (*R (Quark Fishing Ltd) v Secretary of State for Foreign and Commonwealth Affairs (No 2)* [2005] UKHL 57 [25]). Table 17.2 sets out an overview of the Act.

We turn now to how the Act operates, examining:

- Who can bring a claim
- The role of the courts
- Claiming against public authorities

Figure 17.1 The effect of the Human Rights Act

| Under the ECHR, there is an *international law* obligation on the UK to comply | The Human Rights Act introduced a *domestic law* obligation on public authorities not to act incompatibly with Convention rights | This means that the UK courts can provide a remedy |

17.4.1 Who can bring a claim under the Human Rights Act?

The claimant must have 'victim status':

- Under section 7(1), a victim of an unlawful act by a public authority can bring proceedings under the Act (compare this with the sufficient interest test for standing in traditional judicial review cases; see section 15.3.3).

- Section 7(7) adopts the same victim test as under Article 34 ECHR (see section 17.2 above) though 'victim' is not defined. The ECtHR has subsequently amplified it as: a 'direct victim or victims of the alleged violation [and] any indirect victims to whom the violation would cause harm or who would have a valid and personal interest in seeing it brought to an end' ('Practical Guide on Admissibility Criteria' (2015) 60 EHRR SE8 [15]).

- The 'general rule is that a victim must show that he is affected in some way by the matter complained of' (*Daniel v St George's Healthcare NHS Trust and London Ambulance Service* [2016] EWHC 23 [148] (Lang J)). This means that a victim must be the person directly affected by a public authority's decision, or, where the alleged victim has died or

Table 17.2 At a glance: the overall scheme of the Human Rights Act

Section	
1	Defines Convention rights (see also Schedule 1)
2	UK courts must take into account judgments and decisions of the ECtHR
3	Primary and subordinate legislation must be read and given effect in a way which is compatible with Convention rights
3(2)(b)	But any incompatible primary legislation remains valid and continues in operation; the courts cannot declare the Act void, which preserves parliamentary supremacy
4	Where an Act is incompatible with a Convention right, the High Court and above can make a declaration of incompatibility
4(6)	This does not affect the validity of the Act
6	It is unlawful for a public authority to act incompatibly with a Convention right (this includes courts)
7	A victim of an unlawful act by a public authority may bring proceedings. Under section 7(5), there is a one-year time limit in which to bring a claim
8	The court has power to grant remedies as it considers just and appropriate
10	Remedial orders allow government ministers to change part of an Act declared incompatible
19	When a Bill reaches second reading, the relevant minister must make a statement of compatibility that it is (or is not) compatible with Convention rights
Schedule 1	Sets out relevant Convention rights. It omits Article 13, the right to an effective remedy, because the Act itself provides the remedy in sections 6 to 9, and only includes Protocols 1 and 6 to the Convention

disappeared, their next of kin or close family members as indirect victims (see *Daniel* [17–19]; see also *Rabone v Pennine Care NHS Trust* [2012] UKSC 2 [44–48] (Lord Dyson)).

- Indirect victims can include unmarried partners or fiancé(e)s (a 'blood tie or marriage is not essential' (*Daniel* [151])); the test for indirect victim status includes considering all the circumstances of the case to assess the nature of the legal/family relationship and personal ties between the indirect and direct victims, the extent to which the alleged violations of the Convention affected them personally and caused them to suffer, and involvement in the proceedings arising out of the direct victim's death ([150–154]; see also *Morgan v Ministry of Justice* [2010] EWHC 2248 (QB) [63] (Supperstone J)).

However, the ECtHR (and therefore the UK courts) will not hear public interest claims, so pressure groups, for example, cannot bring a challenge where they are not themselves a victim, though public interest groups may support victims' claims or intervene in proceedings. The 'victim test' is therefore narrower than the 'sufficient interest' test in judicial review claims. Thus, a majority of the Supreme Court held that the Northern Ireland Human Rights Commission did not have standing to challenge the compatibility of Northern Ireland's abortion law with the ECHR because there was no identified victim of an unlawful act (*In the matter of an application by the Northern Ireland Human Rights Commission for Judicial Review (Northern Ireland)* [2018] UKSC 27). However, Lady Hale, Lord Kerr, and Lord Wilson thought the Commission *did* have standing to challenge compatibility of legislation—as opposed to an unlawful act by a public authority—according to its powers under the Northern Ireland Act 1998 ([17]).

🔍 CLOSE-UP FOCUS: VERTICAL AND HORIZONTAL EFFECT

The Human Rights Act was intended to have vertical effect, that is, allowing individuals to bring actions against the state in the form of public authorities, not against other individuals or private bodies who breach Convention rights.

However, Wade argues that the Human Rights Act also has horizontal effect, that is, individuals can enforce Convention rights against each other, not just the state ('Horizons of Horizontality' (2000) 116 LQR 217).

This is because, under section 6(3)(a), the courts are public authorities and must act consistently with Convention rights when deciding any case. However, this argument was not successful in relation to a private landlord (see *McDonald v McDonald* [2016] UKSC 28 [41]; *Southward Housing Co-Operative Limited v Walker* [2015] EWHC 1615 (Ch) [227–231]).

See also Murray Hunt, 'The "Horizontal Effect" of the Human Rights Act' (1998) (Autumn) Public Law 423, 435–443; Jane Wright, 'A Damp Squib? The Impact of Section 6 HRA on the Common Law: Horizontal Effect and Beyond' (2014) (April) Public Law 289.

The HRA can apply to individuals outside the UK (extraterritorially). *Bankovic v Belgium* [2001] ECHR 890 held that in exceptional cases, state activities carried out abroad could be an exercise of jurisdiction under Article 1 ECHR. In *R (Al Skeini) v Secretary of State for Defence* [2007] UKHL 26, the House of Lords held that the Act applied, outside UK territory, to a military prison in Iraq where a UK public authority (the British Army) had effective control through its exercise of public powers. The ECtHR subsequently extended 'jurisdiction' in *Al Skeini v UK* [2011] ECHR 1093 beyond military prisons or bases to where the UK exercises authority or control over individuals in another state, thus extending the reach of Convention rights.

17.5 The role of the courts under the Human Rights Act 1998

The Human Rights Act provides two ways for the courts to ensure compliance with Convention rights:

- where legislation is not human rights-compliant (sections 3–5 and 10);
- where a public authority has acted incompatibly with an individual's rights (sections 6–9).

See *Wilson v First County Trust Ltd (No 2)* [2004] 1 AC 816 [205] (Lord Rodger).

Table 17.3 breaks this down by following Lord Carnwath's analysis of how the courts give effect to Convention rights (*Kennedy v Charity Commission* [2014] UKSC 20 [210]).

Table 17.3 How the courts give effect to Convention rights

Legislation	Interpretation	Interpreting UK legislation as far as possible in a way compatible with Convention rights (section 3(1))
	Incompatibility	Making a declaration of incompatibility if a provision of primary legislation is incompatible with a Convention right (section 4); secondary legislation which is incompatible with the HRA can be quashed, whereas primary legislation cannot
Acts of public authorities		Determining whether a public authority has acted unlawfully by acting incompatibly with a Convention right (section 6(1)). If so, the court has power to provide a remedy (section 8)

17.5.1 Interpreting legislation

> Under section 2 of the Act, whenever interpretation of a Convention right arises, the courts must *take into account* decisions of the ECtHR (often referred to as 'Strasbourg jurisprudence').

The UK courts are not *bound* to follow decisions of the ECtHR, although they usually do (however, exceptionally, the Supreme Court did not in *R v Horncastle* [2009] UKSC 14). The UK courts have interpreted 'taking into account' as meaning that the courts should follow a 'clear and constant' line of ECtHR case law (*R (Alconbury Developments Ltd) v Secretary of State for the Environment, Transport and the Regions* [2003] 2 AC 295 [26] (Lord Slynn)). Lord Bingham developed the 'Ullah principle' that the courts must 'keep pace with the Strasbourg jurisprudence as it evolves over time: no more, but certainly no less' (see *R (Ullah) v Special Adjudicator* [2004] UKHL 26, [2004] 2 AC 323 [20]; see also *Al Skeini* [2007] [105–107] (Lord Brown)). Lord Carnwath, however, took the view that there is no single working rule (*Kennedy v Charity Commission* [211–213]). In practice, the courts have applied the 'mirror principle' where their decisions on Convention rights match exactly those of the ECtHR.

 THE BIGGER PICTURE

Lord Irvine has argued that the UK courts should not be subservient or 'hamstrung' by ECtHR decisions and must decide cases for themselves (Lord Irvine of Lairg, 'A British Interpretation of Convention Rights' (2012) (April) Public Law 237) and signs of greater judicial assertiveness are emerging:

- Lord Neuberger hinted at the possibility of not following ECtHR authority if it was inconsistent with a fundamental aspect of UK law, or its reasoning overlooked or misunderstood an argument or point of principle (*Manchester City Council v Pinnock* [2010] UKSC 45, [2011] 2 AC 104 [48]).

- Lord Wilson referred to a modified *Ullah* principle: where there is no directly relevant decision of the ECtHR, the UK courts must determine for themselves whether an alleged Convention right exists (*Moohan v Lord Advocate* [2014] UKSC 67 [104–105]).

- Lady Hale has stated that the courts do not have to follow ECtHR authority slavishly; in cases where there is 'no clear and constant line of Strasbourg jurisprudence', the

UK courts can work out for themselves where the answer lies, taking into account not only Strasbourg principles but also the UK's legal, social, and cultural traditions (*Keyu v Secretary of State for Foreign and Commonwealth Affairs* [2015] UKSC 69 [291]).

- Lord Kerr also identifies a departure from the mirror principle (see *Commissioner of Police of the Metropolis v DSD* [2018] UKSC 11 [77–78]).

See R Masterman, 'The Mirror Crack'd', UK Const L Blog (13 February 2013, available at http://ukconstitutionallaw.org); Nuno Ferreira, 'The Supreme Court in a Final Push to Go beyond Strasbourg' (2015) (July) Public Law 367.

The next step is important. By section 3, Parliament has essentially directed the courts to review its legislation for human rights compatibility:

Section 3 requires that so far as possible, all legislation (primary and secondary) passed before and after the Human Rights Act is to be read and given effect (ie interpreted) in a way that is compatible with Convention rights. This is called 'reading down'.

This provides a new rule of statutory interpretation and gives judges significant discretion in how they interpret statutes. In 2001, Lord Woolf noted that judges needed to change the traditional role of interpreting legislation; before the HRA, they interpreted statutes in accordance with Parliament's intention but now, where a statute could breach a Convention right, they must interpret the words to keep it compatible with the ECHR (*Poplar Housing and Regeneration Community Association Ltd v Donoghue* [2001] EWCA Civ 595 [75]).

Lord Steyn has further defined the courts' interpreting exercise under section 3:

- the interpretative obligation under section 3 is strong and applies even where the language of a statute is not ambiguous and capable of two different meanings;
- it goes much further than ordinary methods of interpretation by requiring a court to find an interpretation compatible with Convention rights if possible to do so;
- the courts must try their best to interpret the words of an Act so that they are compatible with Convention rights even if it means 'linguistically strained' language;
- this applies not only to interpreting 'express language in a statute but also the implication of provisions' (see *R v A* [2001] UKHL 25 [44]).

Lord Neuberger agrees that judges 'can give provisions meanings which they could not possibly bear if the normal rules of statutory interpretation applied' ('The Role of Judges in Human Rights Jurisprudence: A Comparison of the Australian and UK Experience', Melbourne, 8 August 2014 [12]). By doing this, judges are not stepping on Parliament's toes but are following its directions in section 3.

But section 3 does *not* allow judges to step into Parliament's shoes and legislate (see *R v A* [108] (Lord Hope); *Bellinger v Bellinger* [2003] UKHL 21 [67] (Lord Hope); *Poplar Housing v Donoghue* [75] (Lord Woolf CJ). Their role is still to interpret statutes, as Lord Rodger has explained:

If the court implies words that are consistent with the scheme of the legislation but necessary to make it compatible with Convention rights, it is simply performing the duty which Parliament has imposed on it and on others. It is reading the legislation in a way that draws out the full implications of its terms and of the Convention rights. And, by its very nature, an implication will go with the grain of the legislation. By contrast, using a Convention right to read in words that are inconsistent with the scheme of the legislation or with its essential principles as disclosed by its provisions does not involve any form of interpretation, by implication or otherwise. It falls on the wrong side of the boundary between interpretation and amendment of the statute. (*Ghaidan v Godin-Mendoza* [2004] UKHL 30 [121])

There is therefore a fine dividing line between liberal interpretation, which is permitted, and crossing into Parliament's territory and legislating, which is not; going with, not against, the grain (the scheme) of the legislation is of key importance.

EXAMPLES OF JUDICIAL INTERPRETATION UNDER SECTION 3

R v Offen [2000] EWCA Crim 96

Section 2 of the Crime (Sentences) Act 1997 required an automatic life sentence for a defendant convicted of two serious offences unless there were exceptional circumstances. The Court of Appeal interpreted 'exceptional' in a less arbitrary, more proportionate way to keep it compatible with Articles 3 and 5 ECHR—and with Parliament's intention—and held that a life sentence should be imposed unless an offender was not a significant risk to the public ([109–112] (Lord Woolf CJ)).

Ghaidan v Godin-Mendoza [2004] UKHL 30, [2004] 2 AC 557

The House of Lords interpreted 'spouse' and 'living together as husband and wife' in the Rent Act 1977 to include a same sex partner to avoid difference in treatment and ensure compatibility with Article 14, which requires that Convention rights must be applied without discrimination.

Principal Reporter v K (Scotland) [2010] UKSC 56

Scottish law did not give unmarried fathers the right to take part in hearings relating to children with whom they had established family ties, but the Supreme Court held that was incompatible with Article 8 ECHR and, going with the grain of the legislation, read into section 93(2)(b)(c) Pt II Children (Scotland) Act 1995 the words 'or who appears to have established family life with the child with which the decision of a children's hearing may interfere'. K was then a 'relevant person' (see [60–69] (Lord Hope and Lady Hale)).

However, if a statute is incompatible with Convention rights, it remains valid and in force (section 3(2)(b)); the courts have no power to declare the Act void, thus preserving parliamentary supremacy.

17.5.2 **Incompatibility**

Where legislation is incompatible with a Convention right, but the words are clear, and there is no room for interpretation, the High Court, Court of Appeal, or Supreme Court may make a declaration of incompatibility under section 4. A declaration of incompatibility is a statement that the statute is not compatible with a right, but it does *not* affect the validity of the Act, which continues in force (section 4(6)(a)).

The courts cannot strike down an Act of Parliament under the HRA but a declaration of incompatibility alerts Parliament about the incompatibility issue. For this reason, declarations of incompatibility have been referred to as a 'democratic dialogue' between the courts and Parliament (Clayton, 'Judicial Deference and "Democratic Dialogue": The Legitimacy of Judicial Intervention under the Human Rights Act 1998', in 'Further reading').

However, the courts cannot grant a declaration of incompatibility unless they have first carried out their interpreting duty under section 3 (*Wilson v First County Trust Ltd* [2003]). As Lord Steyn has explained, interpretation under section 3(1) is the primary remedy and making a declaration of incompatibility is a 'measure of last resort' which must be avoided unless plainly impossible (*Ghaidan v Godin Mendoza* [50]; *R v A* [44]). In fact, only two declarations of incompatibility were made in the Act's first year of operation, and a total of 42 by 2019.

 EXAMPLE OF A DECLARATION OF INCOMPATIBILITY

Bellinger v Bellinger **[2003] UKHL 21**

Mrs Bellinger, a male to female transsexual, asked the court for a declaration that her marriage was lawful under the Matrimonial Causes Act 1973. Section 11(c) of the Act provided that a marriage was void unless the parties were male and female:

- The House of Lords noted that the ECtHR had become critical that the UK's laws had failed to keep up with developments on the human rights of transsexual people (see [20–24] and see [25–27] for the UK's response; see also *Goodwin v UK* (2002) 35 EHRR 447).

- The court was unable to grant a declaration that Mrs Bellinger's marriage was lawful, which would require giving 'male' and 'female' in the Act an extended meaning and would entail a major change in the law, which was a matter for Parliament (see [39–49] (Lord Nicholls); [68–69] (Lord Hope)). Lord Hobhouse stated that reading in words such as 'or two people of the same sex one of whom has changed his/her sex to that of the opposite sex' would go beyond interpretation to a legislating exercise ([78]).

- However, the House of Lords held that non-recognition of gender reassignment for the purposes of marriage, and section 11(c) of the Act, were incompatible with Articles 8 and 12 ECHR, and made a declaration that the Act was incompatible with Convention rights.

- The Gender Recognition Act was subsequently enacted by Parliament in 2004, providing for full legal recognition to be given to gender reassignment.

 SUMMARY

- The court must first carry out the interpretative duty under section 3. They are required to interpret legislation 'so far as possible' in a way that ensures compatibility with Convention rights—including reading words in if consistent with the scheme of an Act—but must not step into Parliament's territory as legislator.

- If it is not possible to interpret legislation to ensure compatibility with Convention rights, the court can issue a declaration of incompatibility under section 4.

- 'It is crystal clear that the carefully and subtly drafted Human Rights Act 1998 pre-serves the principle of parliamentary sovereignty. In a case of incompatibility, which cannot be avoided by interpretation under section 3(1), the courts may not disapply the legislation. The court may merely issue a declaration of incompatibility which then gives rise to a power to take remedial action' (*R v DPP, ex p Kebilene* [2000] 2 AC 326, 367 (Lord Steyn)).

17.5.2.1 What happens after a court makes a declaration of incompatibility?

One of three things can happen:

- Under section 10, a minister may fast-track changes to the incompatible Act by a remedial order, which is a form of delegated legislation approved by each House of Parliament.
- Parliament can amend the statute or pass another Act if it sees fit, but there is nothing in the Act to require this; it is Parliament's decision whether to change the law.
- Alternatively, Parliament can choose to do nothing.

THINKING POINT

How is parliamentary supremacy being preserved here?

The Ministry of Justice is the 'light-touch coordinator' for how adverse judgments from both the ECtHR and domestic courts are implemented. It issues reports to the Joint Committee on Human Rights on implementation of adverse judgments, and government departments update the Joint Committee on new declarations of incompatibility by the UK courts and their plans for response. See Ministry of Justice, *Responding to Human Rights Judgments*, Report to the Joint Committee on Human Rights on the Government Response to Human Rights Judgments 2016, December 2017, Cm 9535, pp 8–9.

17.5.3 Reviewing acts of public authorities

Under section 6, it is unlawful for public authorities to act incompatibly with Convention rights, unless they are obeying an Act of Parliament. This provides an additional form of judicial review by the UK courts, protecting the rights of individuals against the state.

Section 6(1) does not define 'public authority', but there are two categories:

- Core (also known as pure) public authorities under section 6(1).
- Functional (or hybrid) public authorities under section 6(3); this applies to bodies which are not public authorities but carry out functions of a public nature.

Both categories must act compatibly with the Convention rights of individuals.

> **CROSS REFERENCE**
>
> Compare with the definition of public body for judicial review in section 15.3.1.2

Under section 6(3)(a), 'public authority' also includes courts and tribunals. The courts must therefore act compatibly with Convention rights in deciding cases before them (*Venables v News Group Newspapers* [2001] Fam 430, 446 (Butler-Sloss P); *Soering v UK* [1989] ECHR 14).

Note that Parliament is not a public authority for the purposes of the Human Rights Act (section 6(3)).

17.5.3.1 **Core (pure) public authorities**

In *Parochial Church Council of the Parish of Aston Cantlow and Wilmcote v Wallbank* [2003] UKHL 37, Lord Nicholls defined a public authority as 'a body whose nature is governmental in a broad sense of that expression', such as government departments, local authorities, and the police and armed forces; their public nature is characterised by 'possession of special powers, democratic accountability, public funding in whole or in part, an obligation to act only in the public interest, and a statutory constitution' ([7]). Identifying a core public authority is based on the *nature* of the body, rather than the functions it performs (*Aston Cantlow* [41] (Lord Hope)). A core public authority does not have Convention rights of its own so cannot be a victim of an infringement of a Convention right (*Aston Cantlow* [8]).

17.5.3.2 **Functional (or hybrid) public authorities**

These public authorities are not core public authorities but are bodies which exercise both public and private functions. They only fall within section 6(3)(b) as public authorities when they are exercising a function of a public nature. They then have an obligation under the Human Rights Act to comply with individuals' Convention rights. Where a hybrid authority is carrying out acts of a private nature, it is not a public authority under section 6(3)(b) and will not have any liability under the Act (section 6(5)). If a body does not carry out *any* public functions—Facebook or Google, for example—it is not a hybrid public authority (see *Richardson v Facebook* [2015] EWHC 3154 (QB) [60–63]).

Section 6(3)(b) reflects the increased number of private bodies exercising functions previously exercised by public authorities. Similar issues therefore arise in separating out public and private functions as in judicial review (see Chapter 15). Lord Mance has taken the view that 'while authorities on judicial review can be helpful, section 6 has a different rationale, linked to the scope of State responsibility in Strasbourg' (*YL v Birmingham City Council* [2007] UKHL 27 [87]), but Dyson LJ suggested that the tests for judicial review and functional public authorities under the Human Rights Act are practically the same (*R (Beer) v Hampshire Farmers' Markets Ltd* [2003] EWCA Civ 1056 [14–15]).

Parliament left the interpretation of section 6(3)(b) to the judiciary but in 2004 the Joint Committee on Human Rights was concerned at how narrowly the courts were interpreting 'public authority'. This meant that private providers of public services were falling outside the Act with no obligation to comply with it, leaving a gap in human rights protection (Joint Committee on Human Rights, *The Meaning of Public Authority under the Human Rights Act*, 7th Report of Session 2003–04, HL Paper 39, HC 382 [41]; see also [43, 138]). The Committee took the view that:

- the test of whether a function is public should not be limited to functions which only the state can carry out, but includes ones for which the government has taken responsibility in the public interest ([140, 142, 148, 157]), for example, a body providing housing because it has contracted with a local authority.

(See also 'Conclusions and Recommendations' pp 52–56; Joint Committee on Human Rights, *The Meaning of Public Authority under the Human Rights Act*, 9th Report of Session 2006–07, HL Paper 77, HC 410; and *The Human Rights Act 1998: The Definition of 'Public Authority'*, Government Response to the Joint Committee on Human Rights, 9th Report of Session 2006–07, October 2009, Cm 7726.)

The key question is whether the body is exercising functions of a public nature not involving acts of a private nature, and the courts set out guidelines on determining the dividing line in two important cases: *YL v Birmingham City Council* and *Aston Cantlow*. Lord Bingham thought that a generous interpretation of 'public function' was appropriate (*YL* [4]) and it is the *function* that the body is performing that determines whether it is a hybrid public authority, not the nature of the body (*Aston Cantlow* [41] (Lord Hope); *YL* [6] (Lord Bingham)). According to Lady Hale, 'While there cannot be a single litmus test of what is a function of a public nature, the underlying rationale must be that it is a task for which the public, in the shape of the state, have assumed responsibility, at public expense if need be, and in the public interest' (*YL* [65]). Factors to be taken into account include:

- whether the body is publicly funded for carrying out the relevant function, exercising statutory powers, taking the place of central government or local authorities, or providing a public service (*Aston Cantlow* [12] (Lord Nicholls); see generally [9–12]);

- whether the state has assumed responsibility for seeing that the particular task is performed, the public interest in having that task undertaken, whether the function 'involves . . . the use of statutory coercive powers' (*YL* [63, 66–69]) (Lady Hale); see also [7–11] (Lord Bingham)).

Lord Bingham points out that it is irrelevant whether the body is amenable to judicial review (*YL* [12]) and 'no summary of factors likely to be relevant or irrelevant can be comprehensive or exhaustive' (*YL* [13]).

See also: the tests and their application in *TH v Chapter of Worcester Cathedral* [2016] EWHC 1117 (Admin) [64, 67] (Coulson J); Alexander Williams, 'Public Authorities and the HRA 1998: Recent Trends' (2017) 22(3) Judicial Review 247–262.

 EXAMPLES

The following have been held to be hybrid public authorities:

- A housing association effectively doing the same job as a local council (*Poplar Housing and Regeneration Community Association Ltd v Donoghue* [2001]).

- A social housing organisation when terminating a tenancy (*R (Weaver) v London Quadrant Housing Trust* [2009] EWCA Civ 587, [2010] 1 WLR 363).

- A private psychiatric hospital: its managers' decisions about its facilities were of a public nature and there was statutory underpinning (*R (A) v Partnerships in Care Ltd* [2002] EWHC 529 (Admin)).

The following were not hybrid public authorities:

- A Parochial Church Council (*Aston Cantlow*).

- A private care home looking after local authority-funded residents: in *R (Heather) v Leonard Cheshire Foundation* [2002] EWCA Civ 366, the Court of Appeal held that provision of care to state-funded patients in a privately operated care home was not a 'public function' (but Lady Hale in *YL* regarded this as wrongly decided ([73])). The majority in *YL v Birmingham City Council* reached a similar conclusion, but Lord Bingham and Lady Hale in the minority decided that it *was* performing a function of a public nature pursuant to statutory arrangements, at public expense and in the public interest. Lord Bingham took the view that this was precisely the sort of case to which Parliament had intended section 6(3)(b) to apply ([19–20]). Lady Hale was persuaded by the fact that the individual's care was paid for by the local authority. Parliament subsequently passed the Health and Social Care Act 2008, which provided that care homes *do* act as public authorities in these circumstances (section 145).

SUMMARY

To determine whether a body is a public authority under section 6, the court has to ask:

1. Is it a 'core' public authority?

2. Is it a 'hybrid' public authority?

3. Is the act in question private in nature? (See *TH v Chapter of Worcester Cathedral* [59] (Coulson J).)

'[A] core public authority is bound by section 6(1) in relation to every one of its acts whatever the nature of the act concerned; there is therefore no need to distinguish between private and public acts or functions of a core public authority. On the other hand, a hybrid public authority is only bound by section 6(1) in relation to an act which (a) is not private in nature and (b) is pursuant to or in connection with a function which is public in nature.' (*YL* [131] (Lord Neuberger)).

17.5.4 **Applying proportionality**

Where a public authority's use of discretionary power causes disproportionate interference with a Convention right, it is unlawful. The courts apply a proportionality exercise here which Lord Reed has described as the 'search for a fair balance between the demands of the general interest of the community and the requirements of the protection of the individual's fundamental rights' (*Bank Mellat v HM Treasury (No 2)* [2013] UKSC 39, [2014] AC 700 [70]) (see Figure 17.2).

In assessing proportionality under the HRA, the court drills down into the basis for the decision, making its own 'value judgment' about what is a fair balance between the public authority's reasons and aims, and the extent of interference with the individual's rights (see *Bank Mellat* [71] (Lord Reed); Lord Neuberger, 'The Role of Judges in Human Rights Jurisprudence' [23]). This is more intense and intrusive than traditional judicial review—some judges refer to it as a 'merits review'—though the court can never substitute its own decision for that of the decision-maker.

Lord Sumption has summarised the current proportionality test applied by the UK courts to determine whether a public authority's decision strikes a fair balance between the competing interests in human rights cases:

Figure 17.2 Assessing a fair balance

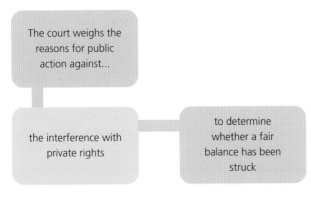

(i) whether its objective is sufficiently important to justify the limitation of a fundamental right;

(ii) whether it is rationally connected to the objective;

(iii) whether a less intrusive measure could have been used; and

(iv) whether, having regard to these matters and to the severity of the consequences, a fair balance has been struck between the rights of the individual and the interests of the community. (*Bank Mellat (No 2)* [20] (Lord Sumption); see also [74] (Lord Reed)).

However, Laws LJ has expressed concern about requirement (iv) because:

> It appears to require the court . . . to decide whether the measure, though it has a justified purpose and is no more intrusive than necessary, is nevertheless offensive because it fails to strike the right balance between private right and public interest; and the court is the judge of where the balance should lie. (*R (Miranda) v Secretary of State for the Home Department* [2014] 1 WLR 3140 [40])

Laws LJ thought it was very close to 'a political question to be decided by the elected arm of government', and had to be plainly within the judicial sphere for such a decision to be made.

In applying proportionality, therefore, the court will need to be sensitive to when to recognise the elected body's discretionary area of judgment and defer to its opinion of where the balance is to be struck between individual rights and the needs of society where a difficult choice has to be made (*R v DPP ex parte Kebilene*, p 381 (Lord Hope); see also *Bank Mellat* [71] (Lord Reed); *R (Al Rawi) v Secretary of State for Foreign and Commonwealth Affairs* [2006] EWCA Civ 1279 [146]). Where a decision is about sensitive or political issues such as national security, foreign affairs, or economic matters, the court will normally give greater weight to the views of the elected decision-maker. See T.R.S. Allan, 'Human Rights and Judicial Review: A Critique of "Due Deference"' (2006) 65(3) CLJ 671.

Q | CLOSE-UP FOCUS

Lord Sumption laid down some key markers on this in *R (Lord Carlile of Berriew QC) v Secretary of State for the Home Department* [2014] UKSC 60, [2015] AC 945, which also have relevance to the HRA's constitutional significance in section 17.6:

- 'traditional notions of the constitutional distribution of powers have unquestionably been modified by the Human Rights Act 1998': the courts are reviewing the substance of public authorities' decisions more than is the case in traditional judicial review [29];

- in human rights cases, there are no forbidden areas and 'no absolute constitutional bar' to relevant and necessary inquiry by the court [30];

- the Human Rights Act has not transferred decision-making powers to the courts but 'the traditional reticence of the courts about examining the basis for executive decisions in certain areas of policy can no longer be justified on constitutional grounds' [31];

- 'the Human Rights Act requires the courts to treat as relevant many questions which would previously have been immune from scrutiny' [32];

- the court will give greater weight to the judgment of a decision-maker with special institutional competence [32];

- the court is the judge of the appropriate balance, but will not remake the decision [34].

These markers have the potential to make inroads on the separation of powers and blur the divisions in decision-making but Lord Sumption is careful to pull back to recognising institutional competence and emphasising that it is not for the courts to remake decisions.

See also Lord Neuberger [56–58, 67–68], Lady Hale [105], Lord Kerr (dissenting) [150–152]. Note Lord Neuberger's spectrum of types of decision at [68]. At one end, judges have the evidence, experience, knowledge, and institutional legitimacy to confidently form their own view; at the other, judges cannot claim any such competence; only exceptional circumstances would justify judicial interference.

For case comment, see Hayley J Hooper, 'The Future Is a Foreign Country' (2015) 74(1) Cambridge Law Journal 23.

 THINKING POINT

What argument is Lord Sumption making about the effect of the HRA on separation of powers?

17.6 The constitutional impact of the Human Rights Act 1998

There is no specialist human rights court in the UK but the Act transformed the mainstream judiciary into 'the guardians of human rights' (see *International Transport Roth GmbH v Secretary of State for Home Department* [2002] EWCA Civ 158 [27] (Simon Brown LJ)). By providing a new benchmark for measuring UK legislation for compatibility with Convention rights, the Act gives judges a powerful interpreting role which effectively allows them to review Acts of Parliament—but within carefully prescribed limits. At the same time, the Act was carefully drafted to respect and preserve parliamentary sovereignty and does not give the UK courts power to invalidate, overrule, or strike down an Act of Parliament that is incompatible with a Convention right; and while the Human Rights Act has special status as a constitutional statute, it is not entrenched and cannot override other statutes.

Lord Reed has pointed out that the HRA 'entails some adjustment of the respective constitutional roles of the courts, the executive and the legislature' (*R (Nicklinson) v Ministry of Justice* [2014] UKSC 38 [296]; see the close-up focus box in section 17.5.4), but a 2006 review concluded that generally its impact on UK law had been beneficial, and had not significantly altered the constitutional balance (Department for Constitutional Affairs, *Review of the Implementation of the Human Rights Act*, July 2006, p 1). However, Vernon Bogdanor's view is that the Act required a compromise between parliamentary sovereignty and the rule of law, where both judges and Parliament operate under 'a sense of restraint', and he warns of the dangers of

Figure 17.3 The constitutional balance

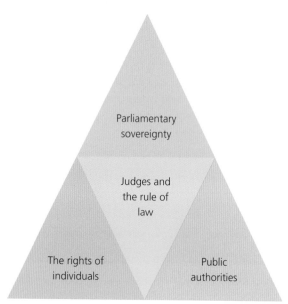

conflict and erosion of parliamentary sovereignty if that restraint is not observed ('Human Rights and the New British Constitution', Justice–Tom Sargant Memorial Annual Lecture, 2009, pp 3, 4–6). This can be seen in Figure 17.3, where, if the parliamentary sovereignty and judicial sectors flipped over, the constitutional balance would be significantly altered.

Crucially, the Act provides an additional mechanism for the judiciary to hold the executive to account, but there have been concerns about the extent to which the Act politicises the judiciary by taking them into the arena of government policy, particularly on terrorism and asylum seekers. For example, *A & Others v Secretary of State for Home Department* [2004] UKHL 56 could be seen as a robust decision against government counter-terrorism policy, where Lord Hoffmann said that the 'real threat to the life of the nation' was laws like the Anti-Terrorism, Crime and Security Act 2001 ([97]), but Lord Bingham in *R (Limbuela) v Secretary of State for Home Department* [2005] UKHL 66 was careful to point out that government policy on asylum seekers was not in issue and represented a legislative choice ([2]). He also pointed out that the '1998 Act gives the courts a very specific, wholly democratic, mandate' (*A v Secretary of State for the Home Department* [42]). However, policy-related decisions go with the territory of human rights review of state activities, and Lord Irvine reminds us that 'the law is no stranger' to politically controversial cases such as *Liversidge v Anderson* and *Brind* (Lord Irvine of Lairg, *Human Rights, Constitutional Law and the Development of the English Legal System* (Oxford: Hart Publishing 2003, p 116)). For insight on these issues, see evidence given by Lord Thomas, Lord Hope, and Lord Neuberger to the Joint Committee on Human Rights, Oral evidence: 'Human Rights: Attitudes to Enforcement', HC 669, 18 April 2018.

Ministerial statements of compatibility The Act introduced a new addition to the legislative process by requiring a ministerial statement of compatibility when a Bill reaches second reading (section 19). This means that the responsible minister must make a statement in Parliament either that the Bill is compatible with Convention rights or that s/he cannot make such a statement but the government nevertheless wishes to proceed with the Bill. The Bill can go ahead but with clear awareness of incompatibility.

17.7 Derogation from the ECHR

Article 15 ECHR allows states to temporarily suspend their obligations to secure certain rights in a national emergency, such as during the Troubles in Northern Ireland (see *Lawless v Ireland (No 3) (1961)* 1 EHRR 15 and *Ireland v UK (1978)* 2 EHRR 25). This is called derogating from the Convention:

- Derogation is only allowed in time of war or other public emergency threatening the life of the nation (Article 15(1)).

- The derogation measures must only be what are 'strictly required by the exigencies of the situation' (Article 15(1)).

- They must not be inconsistent with the state's other obligations under international law (Article 15(1)).

- The rights in Articles 2 (except for lawful acts of war), 3, 4(1), and 7, and certain protocol rights, are non-derogable (cannot be derogated from) (see Article 15(2)).

- The state must keep the Secretary General of the Council of Europe fully informed of the measures taken, the reasons for them, and when the derogation measures no longer apply and their Convention obligations are operative again (Article 15(3)).

> **EXAMPLE: *A & OTHERS v SECRETARY OF STATE FOR HOME DEPARTMENT* [2004] UKHL 56**
>
> In 2001, after the attacks on America of 11 September, the UK government made a designation order (the Human Rights Act 1998 (Designated Derogation) Order 2001 (SI 2001/3644)) proposing a derogation from Article 5 ECHR on the grounds of a public emergency. Section 14 of the Human Rights Act allows for this. This enabled the Anti-Terrorism Crime and Security Act 2001 to be passed, allowing detention of foreign terrorist suspects in prison without trial. The House of Lords held that the government was entitled to conclude that there was a public emergency, which is a political question, but the derogation measures were not proportionate; they discriminated against foreign nationals, which was a violation of Article 14 and the order was quashed. The court also declared section 23 of the 2001 Act incompatible with Articles 5 and 14 ECHR.

See www.echr.coe.int/Documents/FS_Derogation_ENG.pdf.

17.8 A British Bill of Rights

The issue of a Bill of Rights was much discussed before the advent of the Human Rights Act, but with the Act, new issues arose: does the Act place too much emphasis on the rights of individuals and not enough on responsibilities? Does it give judges too much power? Should the HRA be repealed? Does the ECtHR exert too much power over the UK's sovereignty? Should the UK

CROSS REFERENCE

See discussion on *Hirst* in section 10.2.3.2

withdraw from the ECHR? The British Bill of Rights debate soon gathered new momentum, primarily driven by the following considerations:

- breaking away from the Strasbourg jurisprudence;
- reasserting parliamentary sovereignty;
- perceptions of an over-assertive judiciary in upholding human rights.

A Bill of Rights and Duties to redress the rights/responsibilities balance was discussed in the 2007 Governance of Britain Green Paper (July 2007, CM 7170, pp 60–63) but did not materialise; then in 2010, David Cameron announced, 'we will abolish the Human Rights Act and introduce a new Bill of Rights, so that Britain's laws can no longer be decided by unaccountable judges' ('Rebuilding Trust in Politics', speech delivered at the University of East London, 8 February 2010). In 2012, a Commission considered whether the Human Rights Act should be replaced by a UK Bill of Rights but failed to agree (Commission on a UK Bill of Rights, *A UK Bill of Rights? The Choice before Us*, December 2012). Two years later, a government policy paper ('Protecting Human Rights in the UK') proposed repealing the Human Rights Act 1998 and replacing it with a British Bill of Rights and Responsibilities. The 2015 Conservative party manifesto promised to 'scrap' the HRA and in 2016 proposals for a British Bill of Rights were promised in the Queen's Speech. In evidence to the EU Committee, the Secretary of State for Justice claimed that human rights were seen by the public as 'foreign intervention', so a British Bill of Rights would affirm all Convention rights (with possible changes in interpretation and weighting) but would identify them as fundamental British rights, and repealing the Human Rights Act would affirm parliamentary sovereignty (House of Lords European Union Committee, *The UK, the EU and a British Bill of Rights*, 12th Report of Session 2015–16, HL Paper 139, chapter 3). However, the Committee concluded: 'Doubts about the wisdom of introducing a British Bill of Rights grew with each evidence session we held' (p 3). See also Joint Committee on the Draft Voting Eligibility (Prisoners) Bill *Draft Voting Eligibility (Prisoners) Bill*, Report, Session 2013–14, HL Paper 103, HC 924 (see especially Section 4); House of Commons Library Briefing Paper Number 7193, 'A British Bill of Rights?' 19 May 2015.

There are concerns that repealing the Human Rights Act would leave human rights protection markedly weaker, and opponents of withdrawing from the ECHR have argued that the ECHR prevents national sovereignty from shielding human rights abuses, and withdrawal would adversely affect the UK's reputation (see Anthony Lester, 'Human Rights Must Be Protected against the Abuse of Power', *The Guardian*, 16 May 2016; for a balance of views, see Lord Dyson, 'What Is Wrong with Human Rights?' (lecture delivered at Hertfordshire University, 3 November 2011); Professor Conor Gearty, 'The Human Rights Act Should Not Be Repealed', LSE Law: Policy Briefing Papers, LSE Law, 16/2016; Dominic Grieve QC MP, 'Can a Bill of Rights Do Better than the Human Rights Act?' (2016) (April) Public Law 223). Those changes would also need the consent of the devolved administrations. On the other hand, a British Bill of Rights could provide an opportunity to craft a more wide-ranging set of rights beyond those in the ECHR, especially social and workplace rights.

If a more specifically 'British' human rights law developed under the HRA, would a British Bill of Rights be needed? Several serving and former judges have advocated less subservience to the ECtHR by the UK courts and the creation of a more home-grown British human rights law. Lord Hoffmann has questioned the ECtHR's constitutional legitimacy to lay down uniform rules on Convention rights for all member states (Lord Hoffmann, 'The Universality of Human Rights' (2009) 125 LQR 416; Lord Justice Laws, Lecture III: 'The Common Law and Europe', Hamlyn Lectures, 2013; Lord Judge, 'Constitutional Change: Unfinished Business', Constitution Unit, 2013 [40–48]).

In December 2016, proposals to replace the Act were suspended due to Brexit; the government's plans were that the UK would remain party to the ECHR for the duration of Parliament and it would consider the human rights legal framework when the process of leaving the EU concluded. In the Conservative party manifesto for the 2019 general election, the government committed to 'updating' the Human Rights Act.

17.9 Human rights in a post-Brexit world

'The UK has a long tradition of commitment to human rights which will not change after withdrawal from the European Union' (*Charter of Fundamental Rights of the EU: Right by Right Analysis*, 5 December 2017 [25]).

Britain's withdrawal from the EU does not in itself affect its position as a signatory to the ECHR, or the continuing operation of the Human Rights Act. The 2018 Brexit White paper stated that the UK is committed to membership of the ECHR (*The Future Relationship between the United Kingdom and the European Union*, Cm 9593, July 2018, p 52) and the European Union made it clear during Brexit negotiations that European security co-operation depended on this, so any prospect of withdrawal from the ECHR has receded.

However, there is another facet to post-Brexit human rights protection: while the UK was a member of the EU, it was bound by the EU's Charter of Fundamental Rights which was separate from the ECHR but, as EU law, it could override inconsistent UK legislation. In January 2018, MPs voted not to retain it in UK law after Brexit (see EU (Withdrawal) Act 2018 section 5(4)). A number of human rights organisations expressed concern that this would create gaps in UK human rights law as the Charter included some rights not included in the ECHR, such as the right to dignity and a general right to non-discrimination (open letter, *The Observer*, 14 January 2018). The government's position was that it did not intend substantive rights protected in the EU Charter to be weakened and they would be protected as retained EU law, corresponding rights in the ECHR and in the common law or UK statutes (see *Charter of Fundamental Rights of the EU: Right by Right Analysis*, 5 December 2017), though this underlines a return to traditional scattered sources rather than a code. Important UK statutes such as the Equality Act 2010 will remain in force unless repealed by a future Parliament.

In the new constitutional landscape, Brexit may drive fresh impetus for a codified constitution containing guaranteed rights to remove lingering uncertainty. The EU Charter gap will require assertive human rights scrutiny within Parliament and may well strengthen the role of the judiciary; the anxious scrutiny by the courts of public authorities' infringements of rights will be more critical, and the protection of common law rights may become more significant. See https://publiclawforeveryone.com/2018/02/08/human-rights-post-brexit-the-need-for-legislation/.

17.10 Common law rights

Extrajudicially, Lady Hale has identified the emergence of 'renewed emphasis on the common law and distinctively UK constitutional principles as a source of legal inspiration' ('UK Constitutionalism on the March?' Keynote address to the Constitutional and Administrative Law Bar Association Conference, 12 July 2014; see also Chapter 9). Is the common law reasserting itself in the sphere of human rights? There are certainly intriguing references in some Supreme Court decisions to a common law way of applying Convention rights, and reminders that common law rights exist alongside Convention rights. For example:

- Human rights law has developed through the common law, and the common law should not be overlooked after the HRA (see *Kennedy v Charity Commission* [133] (Lord Toulson); *Osborn v Parole Board* [2013] UKSC 61 [57–62] (Lord Reed)).

- Lord Mance refers to the 'modelling' of Convention rights through the common law (*Kennedy* [38]) and points out that 'the natural starting point in any dispute is to start with domestic law, and it is certainly not to focus exclusively on the Convention rights without surveying the wider common law scene' ([46]; *A v BBC* [2014] UKSC 25 [56–57] Lord Reed).

See also Lord Neuberger, 'The Role of the Supreme Court Seven Years On—Lessons Learnt', Bar Council Law Reform Lecture, 21 November 2016 [38–39]; Mark Elliott, 'Beyond the European Convention: Human Rights and the Common Law' (2015) 68(1) Current Legal Problems 85; Richard Clayton, 'The Empire Strikes Back: Common Law Rights and the Human Rights Act' (2015) (January) Public Law 3; *Elgizouli v Secretary of State for the Home Department* [2020] UKSC 10 [107].

 SUMMARY

The Human Rights Act has had far-reaching impact, turning Convention rights into rights in UK law, giving the UK courts a new constitutional role and influencing the interpretation of domestic law but it is not entrenched and has faced the threat of repeal. The common law is still relevant, continuing to develop alongside, and often influenced by, Convention rights.

? Questions

Self-test questions

1. What is the ECHR? How is it linked to the Human Rights Act?

2. Why was the Human Rights Act introduced?

3. What are the two types of case that the UK courts consider under the HRA?

4. Which key principle is carefully preserved by the Act?

5. What is the difference between a declaration of incompatibility and a ministerial statement of compatibility?

6. Explain the judges' function under section 3 HRA.

7. Do judges have power to overturn Acts of Parliament under the HRA?

8. Who is a 'victim' under the Act?

9. What is a hybrid public authority?

10. What is 'derogation'?

Exam question

Under section 3 of the Human Rights Act, 'Judges must perform a quasi-statute-writing function'. (Lord Neuberger, '"Judge not, that ye be not judged": Judging Judicial Decision-making', FA Mann Lecture 2015 [47]).

Discuss.

Further reading

Books

Gearty, Conor *On Fantasy Island: Britain, Europe and Human Rights* (Oxford: Oxford University Press 2016).
Analyses arguments for repealing the HRA

Loveland, I. *Constitutional Law, Administrative Law, and Human Rights: A Critical Introduction* (8th edn, Oxford: Oxford University Press 2018).
See Part V for an in-depth discussion of human rights

Journal articles

Amos, M. 'The Value of the European Court of Human Rights to the United Kingdom' (2017) 28(3) European Journal of International Law 763.
Examines the UK's relationship with the ECtHR through the impact of its decisions

Bellamy, R. 'Political Constitutionalism and the Human Rights Act' (2011) 9(1) International Journal of Constitutional Law 86.
Challenging but examines review by the courts under the Act in constitutional terms

Clayton, R. 'Judicial Deference and "Democratic Dialogue": The Legitimacy of Judicial Intervention under the Human Rights Act 1998' (2004) (Spring) Public Law 33.
A frequently cited analysis of the judicial dialogue in the early years of the HRA's operation

Duxbury, N. 'Judicial Disapproval as a Constitutional Technique' (2017) 15(3) International Journal of Constitutional Law 649.
A different way of looking at declarations of incompatibility

Fenwick, H. and Masterman, R. 'The Conservative Project to "Break the Link between British Courts and Strasbourg": Rhetoric or Reality?' (2017) 80(6) MLR 1111.
A thorough analysis of the mirror principle and how rights would be protected under a Bill of Rights

Irvine, D. 'The Human Rights Act: Principle and Practice' (2004) 57(4) Parliamentary Affairs 744.
Very helpful background and insight on the Human Rights Act and its operation

Jay, Z. 'Keeping Rights at Home: British Conceptions of Rights and Compliance with the European Court of Human Rights' (2017) 19(4) The British Journal of Politics and International Relations 842.
Argues that there is a British approach to human rights

Klug, F. 'Judicial Deference under the Human Rights Act 1998' (2003) 2 EHRLR 125.
Analyses the application of sections 3 and 4 of the Act

Oliver, D. 'The Frontiers of the State: Public Authorities and Public Functions under the Human Rights Act' (2000) (Autumn) Public Law 476.
A respected early article on the meaning of public authority (though pre-*YL* and *Aston Cantlow*)

Vick, D.W. 'The Human Rights Act and the British Constitution' (2002) 37 Texas International Law Journal 329.
See pp 340–372 for detail on the pre-HRA position and the Act's operation

Other sources

Elias, LJ. 'The Rise of the Strasbourgeoisie: Judicial Activism and the ECHR', Annual Lord Renton Lecture, Statute Law Society, 24 November 2009, Institute for Advanced Legal Studies.
Examines the effect of the Human Rights Act on the relationship between the courts and Parliament.

Masterman, R. 'Supreme, Submissive or Symbiotic? United Kingdom Courts and the European Court of Human Rights', The Constitution Unit, October 2015.
A good all-round source on HRA issues

Neuberger, Lord. '"Judge not, that ye be not judged": Judging Judicial Decision-Making', F.A. Mann Lecture 2015.
See [46–53] for a pertinent summary of key points on the HRA

O'Cinneide, C. *Human Rights and the UK Constitution*, The British Academy, September 2012.
Helpful on the Bill of Rights debate

Useful websites

ECHR: www.echr.coe.int/Documents/Convention_ENG.pdf

ECtHR: www.echr.coe.int. A wide range of factsheets are available

Online resources

www.oup.com/he/dennett2e

This chapter is accompanied by a selection of online resources to help you with this topic, including:

- Multiple-choice questions
- Answers to the self-test questions
- Guidance on answering the exam question

18 Human rights in action

LEARNING OBJECTIVES

By the end of this chapter, you should be able to:

● Explain the significance and operation of specific Convention rights

● Evaluate the substantive and procedural duties under Article 2

● Evaluate the impact of Article 8 on the development of specific areas of UK law

● Discuss issues arising from the application of Article 9

● Compare competing rights and analyse how they are balanced by the courts

Introduction

What legal action could you take if you had a family member who died in police custody, or photographs of you in the street were published in a newspaper without your consent, or your employer refused to allow you to wear religious symbols at work? We explore these issues as we examine below how three Convention rights operate in practice: the right to life (Article 2), the right to a private and family life (Article 8), and freedom of religious belief (Article 9). We also discuss the interaction between Article 8 and Article 10 (freedom of expression). The defining feature of Articles 2 and 8 in action is the wide judicial interpretation which has led to their dynamic development and impact; Article 9, on the other hand, has been given much narrower application because of its impact on other rights.

⊅ CROSS REFERENCE

See Chapter 19 for discussion of Article 11 (freedom of assembly)

To ascertain whether the claimant is a victim of an unlawful act by a public authority, the court must first determine whether a specific Convention right has been 'engaged'. This means that a person has relevant rights which have been affected. The court must then determine whether the interference with those rights was justified; this varies according to the right in issue. See *R (Lord Carlile of Berriew QC) v Secretary of State for the Home Department* [2014] UKSC 60 [34] (Lord Sumption).

18.1 Article 2: the right to life

Article 2

1. Everyone's right to life shall be protected by law. No one shall be deprived of his life intentionally save in the execution of a sentence of a court following his conviction of a crime for which this penalty is provided by law.

2. Deprivation of life shall not be regarded as inflicted in contravention of this Article when it results from the use of force which is no more than absolutely necessary: (a) in defence of any person from unlawful violence; (b) in order to effect a lawful arrest or to prevent the escape of a person lawfully detained; (c) in action lawfully taken for the purpose of quelling a riot or insurrection.

Lord Bingham has stated that complying with the substantive obligations in Article 2 'must rank among the highest priorities of a modern democratic state governed by the rule of law' and any breach 'must be treated with great seriousness' (*R (Middleton) v West Somerset Coroner* [2004] UKHL 10 [5]). However, there is more to Article 2 than appears from its wording. The ECtHR and, increasingly, the UK courts have developed multi-layered duties under Article 2(1).

Article 2 imposes three obligations on a state, as set out in Table 18.1.

However, the state does not breach Article 2 where a death results from the use of force which is no more than absolutely necessary to defend someone from unlawful violence, make a lawful arrest, or prevent a prisoner escaping, or to put down a riot or rebellion lawfully. Although Article 2(1) also refers to a lawful death penalty as an exception, all but two member states of the Council of Europe have signed Protocol 13, which abolishes the death penalty and,

Table 18.1 Article 2 obligations

Obligation	Comment
1. A duty not to take life intentionally apart from the exceptions in the Article	This is a substantive obligation, and also a negative obligation, ie the duty *not* to do something
2. The duty to protect life by setting up 'a framework of laws, precautions, procedures and means of enforcement which will, to the greatest extent reasonably practicable, protect life' (*Middleton* [2] (Lord Bingham); see also *R (Letts) v Lord Chancellor* [2015] EWHC 402 (Admin) [66] (Green J))	This is also a substantive obligation and a positive obligation, ie a duty to take an action. It is sometimes referred to as a 'systemic duty' to set up a system designed to protect life, eg to prohibit homicide in national law
3. A duty to carry out an effective investigation into any death where it appears that one of the substantive obligations has been violated and agents of the state might be responsible (see *Middleton* [3] (Lord Bingham))	This is a procedural or investigative obligation which has been implied by the ECtHR (see *McCann v UK*, discussed presently)

according to the ECtHR, strongly indicates that Article 2 has been amended so as to prohibit the death penalty (*Al-Saadoon and Mufdhi v UK* [2010] ECHR 282 [120]).

18.1.1 **What engages the right in Article 2?**

On its face, Article 2 mainly covers intentional killing and killing by state agents, but in recent years it has been interpreted increasingly broadly to cover any death in suspicious circumstances even where the state is not at fault. Lord Mance has listed:

- deaths caused by agents of the state (such as the police, and intelligence and security services);
- deaths in custody;
- military conscripts and mental health detainees taking their own life;
- 'other situations where the State has a positive substantive obligation to take steps to safeguard life' (see *R (Smith) v Secretary of State for Defence* [2010] UKSC 29 [210]).

That last category has expanded to include:

- An implied obligation on authorities, especially the police, to take preventive operational steps in some circumstances to protect the lives of people at risk from the criminal acts of another individual (*Osman v UK* (2000) 29 EHRR 245 [115–116]). This is known as the 'Osman duty'.
- An obligation on health authorities to protect the lives of patients in their hospitals, with an additional operational obligation where a patient presents a 'real and immediate' risk of suicide (see *Powell v UK* (2000) 30 EHRR CD 362; *Savage v South Essex Partnership NHS Foundation Trust* [2008] UKHL 74, [2009] AC 681 [68–72]). In *Rabone v Pennine Care NHS Foundation Trust* [2012] UKSC 2, [2012] 2 AC 72, the Supreme Court extended the obligation to protecting the life of a mentally ill woman who had been admitted to hospital informally (ie not detained under the Mental Health Act 1983) because of her attempts to take her own life. However, the UK's regulatory framework governing withdrawal of medical treatment is Article 2-compliant (*NHS Trust v Y* [2018] UKSC 46).
- The ECtHR has further broadened the obligations on the state to 'any activity, whether public or not, in which the right to life may be at stake' (*Watts v United Kingdom* (2010) 51 EHRR 66 [82]), requiring the state to react reasonably wherever the state knows or ought to know of a real and immediate threat to human life (*Rabone* [96–99] (Lady Hale)). See Figure 18.1.

Figure 18.1 Article 2 has expanded to cover these matters

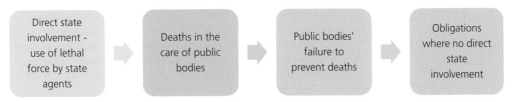

Direct state involvement - use of lethal force by state agents → Deaths in the care of public bodies → Public bodies' failure to prevent deaths → Obligations where no direct state involvement

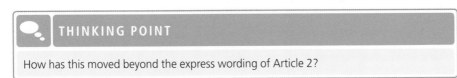

THINKING POINT

How has this moved beyond the express wording of Article 2?

18.1.2 **The substantive obligations**

The substantive obligations in Article 2 are the duty not to take life and the duty to protect life; they apply to the state and state agents. One of the leading cases on this is *McCann v UK* [1995], which involved the issue of what constitutes absolutely necessary force, and the proportionality of the broader response.

🔍 CASE CLOSE-UP: *MCCANN v UK* [1995] ECHR 31

This case involved the shooting of three Irish Republican Army (IRA) suspects by members of the SAS (Special Air Service) in Gibraltar in 1988. The authorities were aware from intelligence that the Provisional IRA were planning a terrorist attack on Gibraltar; the likely targets were members of the Royal Anglian Regiment at a changing of the guard ceremony, and indications were that a car bomb might be used. A group of SAS soldiers arrived in Gibraltar to assist police in arresting the IRA active service unit if needed. The operation (Operation Flavius) aimed to arrest the suspects using minimum force, take them into custody, and enable evidence to be gathered for trial.

The IRA unit arrived in Gibraltar and surveillance was carried out. One suspect was observed to park a car, 'fiddle' with something between the car seats, and leave the vehicle; as a result, it was reported as a suspected car bomb. Two soldiers followed McCann and another suspect, Farrell, and opened fire, believing that McCann was going to detonate the car bomb after he looked back and moved his hand suddenly across the front of his body. Farrell moved and grabbed for her handbag and was also shot and killed; the third suspect, Savage, was shot dead by another soldier. The intention had been to kill to stop them becoming a threat and detonating a bomb. It was subsequently discovered that the suspects were unarmed, that they did not have a detonator, and that there was no bomb in the car. However, Farrell was carrying keys to a car that did contain explosives.

The parties' arguments The government argued that the deprivation of life was justified under Article 2(2)(a), as the use of force was no more than absolutely necessary to defend the people of Gibraltar from unlawful violence. The applicants argued that the planning and execution of the operation was not in accordance with Article 2(2) so the killings were not absolutely necessary.

The court's decision The court rejected the applicants' allegations that the killings were premeditated ([180–184]). On the facts, the belief that the car contained a bomb was not implausible. But the court found by ten votes to nine that there had been a breach of Article 2. The use of force went beyond what was absolutely necessary to defend people from unlawful violence and breached Article 2(2)(a) because of:

- the decision not to prevent the suspects from travelling into Gibraltar;
- the failure of the authorities to make sufficient allowances for the possibility of error in their intelligence assessments;
- the automatic recourse to lethal force when the soldiers opened fire ([213]).

The operation was therefore not proportionate.

Reasoning

- **Proportionality of the state's response** The court had to consider not only the use of deliberate lethal force by the agents of the state, but all the surrounding circumstances, including the planning and control of their actions [150]. The training and instruction of the agents and the operational control raised issues under Article 2(2) about the proportionality of the state's response to the perceived threat of a terrorist attack ([156]).

- **Use of lethal force must be strictly proportionate** The court accepted that the soldiers honestly believed that their actions were absolutely necessary to prevent a bomb being detonated and to protect lives ([200]). The use of force by agents of the state may be justified under Article 2(2) where it is based on an honest but mistaken belief, held for good reasons, otherwise there would be an unrealistic burden on the state and its law enforcement personnel.

- **Planning and control of the operation (the operational duty)** Key questions were: was the operation as a whole controlled and organised in a way that respected the requirements of Article 2? Did the information and instructions given to the soldiers take adequately into consideration the right to life of the three suspects [201]? Were other courses of action available (eg arresting the suspects at the border or preventing them from entering Gibraltar [203])? The operational planning failed to make sufficient allowances for a margin of error or other possibilities, eg that the three suspects were on a reconnaissance mission, or might have been unlikely to explode the bomb on that particular occasion ([208]; see also [209–210]). The soldiers were trained to continue firing until certain that a suspect was no longer a threat, in contrast to the more cautious use of firearms by law enforcement personnel ([211–212]).

 SUMMARY

Article 2 required that the force used by the soldiers was strictly proportionate to the aim of protecting people against unlawful violence, and that the anti-terrorist operation was planned and controlled by the authorities so as to minimise, to the greatest extent possible, recourse to lethal force ([194]).

 THINKING POINT

How, if at all, do you think the operation in *McCann* could have been planned proportionately? See *McCann* [33–37]. Would taking action earlier have been feasible?

18.1.3 **The procedural obligation: effective investigation**

We stay with *McCann* here because, crucially, the ECtHR also made it clear that Article 2(1) *implies* a duty on states to carry out an effective investigation into any death occurring in suspicious circumstances (see also *Keyu v Secretary of State for Foreign and Commonwealth Affairs* [2015] UKSC 69 [66, 69]).

> The state's duty to protect the right to life under Article 2 'requires by implication' some form of effective official investigation when individuals have been killed as a result of the use of force by agents of the state (*McCann* [161]).

This means there needs to be a procedure for reviewing the lawfulness of the use of lethal force by state authorities. In *McCann* there had been a 'thorough, impartial and careful examination' of the circumstances surrounding the killings ([163]) with a public inquest lasting 19 days (see [162]), so there was no breach of the procedural obligation in Article 2(1) on this ground.

The state's duty to investigate (referred to as the procedural or investigative obligation) is important (*R (Amin) v Home Secretary* [2003] UKHL 51, [2004] 1 AC 653 [31] (Lord Bingham)), and Smith LJ has identified two layers of investigative obligation:

1. A broader obligation to provide a legal system which gives access to open, independent investigation of deaths (the system in England and Wales always satisfies this obligation);

2. A narrower obligation to initiate a thorough investigation into a death where there is an arguable breach by the state of its substantive duty to protect life (*R (Humberstone) v Legal Services Commission* [2010] EWCA Civ 1479 [67]; for key principles, see [21–24]).

18.1.3.1 What triggers the duty to investigate?

Any of the categories of death in section 18.1.1 can trigger the obligation to investigate where there are grounds for suspecting that the state may have breached a substantive obligation imposed by Article 2 (*R (Smith) v Secretary of State for Defence* [2010] UKSC 29, [2011] 1 AC 1 [70, 84] (Lord Phillips)) or where the state bears some potential responsibility for a death (*Letts* [71]). In the case of suicide by individuals under state care and control, such as prisoners, the fact that someone has died *automatically* triggers the duty to investigate because the state's system for preventing suicide has failed, and the burden is on the state 'to provide a satisfactory and plausible explanation' (*Jordan v UK* (2003) 37 EHRR 2 [113]; and see *Letts* [71–74]).

Where an individual is compulsorily detained by a public authority and dies in state detention, the death must be reported to the coroner, who must undertake an investigation (section 1(2)(c) Coroners and Justice Act 2009). An obvious example is a death in custody; in *Edwards v UK* (2002) 35 EHRR 487 a man was killed by his prison cellmate, who had suffered from schizophrenia and was known to be violent; this information had not been passed on to the prison authorities, and there was a breach of the state's obligation to protect Edwards' life. However, state detention no longer includes individuals deprived of their liberty under the Mental Capacity Act 2005 (section 178 of the Policing and Crime Act 2017), so there is no automatic requirement to hold an inquest into their deaths unless there are concerns about the cause of death. For a thorough examination of the authorities, see *Letts* [58–91].

The UK's framework for carrying out investigations into suspicious deaths consists of (a) inquests and (b) inquiries under the Inquiries Act 2005 (*Keyu* [117]; see Chapter 14). Both have a fact-finding function, and the ECtHR is satisfied that the inquest procedure in England and Wales is capable of fulfilling the requirements of Article 2 (*Bubbins v UK* (2005) 41 EHRR 458 [153]).

> Traditional inquests only look at the cause of death. A more rigorous inquest that complies with Article 2 also considers any system failures leading to a death and steps taken to prevent it; this is known as a '*Middleton* inquest' (after *R (Middleton) v HM Coroner for Western Somerset* (2004) 2 AC 182). '*Middleton* inquest' is often used as shorthand for an Article 2-compliant inquest, and is required for all deaths in custody and killings by state agents.

18.1.3.2 The importance of effective investigation

The primary aim of an investigation is to ensure accountability for deaths involving state agents or bodies, or occurring under their responsibility. The purposes of the duty to investigate are:

> to ensure so far as possible that the full facts are brought to light; that culpable and discreditable conduct is exposed and brought to public notice; that suspicion of deliberate wrongdoing (if unjustified) is allayed; that dangerous practices and procedures are rectified; and that those who have lost their relative may at least have the satisfaction of knowing that lessons learned from his death may save the lives of others. (*R (Amin) v Home Secretary* [31] (Lord Bingham)).

These are reflected in the ECtHR's requirements in *Jordan v UK* ([105–109]). An effective investigation must be:

- initiated by the state (not left to the next of kin to take action) and independent from people involved in the events;
- capable of establishing the cause of death, whether the force used was justified, and leading to the identification and, if appropriate, punishment of those responsible;
- carried out promptly and with reasonable expedition; this is essential to maintain public confidence in the state's adherence to the rule of law and prevent any appearance of collusion in or tolerance of unlawful acts ([108]);
- subject to sufficient public scrutiny to ensure accountability;
- accessible to the victim's next of kin to safeguard their legitimate interests.

See also *Armani Da Silva v UK* [2016] ECHR 314 [232–239, 257]; *Edwards v United Kingdom* [72–73]; *R (L (a patient)) v Secretary of State for Justice* [2008] UKHL 68, [2009] 1 AC 588 (Lord Philips); *Letts* [59]; *R (Birks) v Commissioner of Police of the Metropolis* [2014] EWHC 3041 (Admin) [52]; *R (Birks) v Commissioner of Police of the Metropolis* [2018] EWHC 807 (Admin); *In the matter of an application by Geraldine Finucane for Judicial Review (Northern Ireland)* [2019] UKSC 7 [134, 138].

 THINKING POINT

Note the importance here of:

- investigation;
- accountability;
- public confidence that the state respects the rule of law.

EXAMPLES

Jordan v UK concerned the shooting of an unarmed man by police in Belfast in 1992. The inquest into his death was significantly delayed, and the Director of Public Prosecutions (DPP) decided not to prosecute any police officers. The ECtHR held that there had been a violation of Article 2 because of failings in the investigative procedures into his death ([145]): the police officers investigating the incident were not independent from the officers involved in it; there was a lack of public scrutiny, and of information to the victim's family on the reasons for the DPP's decision not to prosecute; the police officer who shot him could not be required to attend the inquest as a witness; the inquest procedure could not effectively identify or lead to the prosecution of any criminal offences ([130–131]); the applicant's ability to participate in the proceedings as next of kin was prejudiced by legal aid not being available for inquests in Northern Ireland and witness statements not being disclosed in advance; the inquest proceedings did not commence promptly and were not pursued with reasonable expedition ([142]). See also *Jordan v Lord Chancellor* [2007] UKHL 14.

By contrast, in *Armani Da Silva v UK* [2016] ECHR 314, Jean Charles de Menezes, a Brazilian national, was shot and killed by the police in 2005 after being mistakenly identified as a suicide bomber. His cousin complained that the decision not to prosecute any police officer breached the state's duty to ensure accountability for his death. The court held that the UK had complied with its procedural obligations to conduct an effective investigation under Article 2. The decision not to prosecute any officer was the result of a thorough, in-depth investigation of the responsibility of individual police officers and the police authority by the Independent Police Complaints Commission and Crown Prosecution Service. There had also been a criminal trial, a judicial review of the prosecutor's decision, and an inquest.

See also *Bubbins v UK* (2005) 41 EHRR 458.

 SUMMARY

Article 2 implies a procedural obligation on the state to initiate an effective public investigation into any death in suspicious circumstances where there is an arguable breach by the state of its substantive obligations. The ECtHR has significantly broadened the range of deaths covered by Article 2.

18.1.4 **Deaths before the Human Rights Act**

Initially, the UK courts took the view that, as the Human Rights Act was not retrospective, there was no right to an investigation of a death before the Act came into force on 2 October 2000 (*In re McKerr* [2004] UKHL 12, [2004] 1 WLR 807). However, the Supreme Court later held that there was a duty to investigate a death *before* 2 October 2000 if the main investigations would take place after that date (*Re McCaughey's Application for Judicial Review* [2011] UKSC 20, [2012] 1 AC 725 [61–63] (Lord Phillips); [110, 135] (Lord Kerr); *Keyu* [206, 208]; *Šilih v Slovenia* (2009) 49 EHRR 996; *In the matter of an application by Geraldine Finucane for Judicial Review (Northern Ireland)* [2019] UKSC 7 [83–109]).

CLOSE-UP FOCUS: *KEYU v SECRETARY OF STATE FOR FOREIGN AND COMMONWEALTH AFFAIRS* [2015] UKSC 69

In 1948, British soldiers killed 23 unarmed men while on patrol in a village called Batang Kali in Malaya (now Malaysia and then a British colony). The UK government referred to it as killing of bandits who had attempted to escape, but in 1969, one of the patrol members alleged that the victims had not been escaping when they were killed. The allegations were investigated by the Metropolitan Police between 1969 and 1970, and by the Royal Malaysian Police in 1993, but the investigations were closed down. From 2008 onwards, relatives of the victims campaigned for a public inquiry into the deaths, but government ministers refused to hold one. The campaign group argued that an inquiry was required under Article 2 ECHR (see section 16.4.2).

If the ECHR been in force in 1948, the killings would have occurred within the UK's jurisdiction under Article 1 ECHR [189–90], but the issue here was that events had taken place before the ECHR was even created. The Supreme Court had to decide exactly when the ECHR entered into force; they called this 'the critical date'. The majority held that it was the date when the UK recognised the right of individuals to petition the ECtHR in 1966 [81, 87] but Lady Hale thought it was the date when the ECHR came into force [290–291, 299].

The court held that the ECHR is not retrospective, but a state can have Article 2 obligations to investigate a death occurring before the ECHR entered into force where there are:

1. relevant acts or omissions after that date (here, there had been no full investigation of the killings and no publicly available evidence suggesting that the killings had been unlawful before 1969 [75]);

2. a genuine connection between the death and the critical date, which means there has to be a reasonably short time—no more than ten years—between the death and the critical date [76]. Therefore, as the killings occurred more than ten years before 1966, there was no genuine connection and the Article 2 claim failed [88–89] (though see the *Finucane* case [108]).

Lady Hale, dissenting, would have dismissed the Article 2 claim because the inquiry was to establish historical truth rather than legal liability [300] and it was difficult to find a genuine connection between killings before the coming into effect of the ECHR and obligations imposed by the ECHR [301].

See Harriet Moynihan, 'Regulating the Past: The European Court of Human Rights' Approach to the Investigation of Historical Deaths under Article 2 ECHR' (2016) 86(1) British Yearbook of International Law 68.

18.1.5 **UK soldiers and Article 2**

The deaths of British soldiers in Iraq did not give rise to an Article 2 obligation to hold a public inquiry into the lawfulness of the Iraq invasion; that was made clear by the House of Lords in *R (Gentle) v Prime Minister* [2008] 1 AC 1356. But does Article 2 apply to protect British soldiers serving abroad? In *R (Smith) v Secretary of State for Defence* [2010] UKSC 29, the Supreme Court's answer was: only if they were on premises under the army's effective control such as a military hospital; otherwise, British soldiers on active service abroad were not within the UK's jurisdiction under Article 1 ECHR and were outside the protection of the Human Rights Act. Private

Jason Smith had died from heatstroke while on active service in Iraq, and his mother brought a claim for judicial review of the inquest into his death. Lord Phillips stated that the death of a soldier on active service did not trigger an automatic presumption that the state has breached its substantive Article 2 obligations; there had to be grounds for suspicion of a breach by the state ([84]).

In 2011, the ECtHR expanded the meaning of 'jurisdiction' to where British officials exercise 'control and authority' over foreign nationals overseas, even outside UK military bases (*Al-Skeini v UK* [2011] ECHR 1093). This meant that foreign civilians could fall within UK human rights protection when British soldiers did not. Consequently, in the landmark decision of *Smith v MoD* [2013] UKSC 41, the Supreme Court departed from the *Smith* [2010] case and held that UK human rights jurisdiction extended to members of the armed forces serving overseas, so the UK had to secure their protection under Article 2, even outside military premises. This means that Article 2 now applies to British soldiers in combat situations, but the court must only give effect to those obligations where it would be reasonable to expect protection of the individual and must not impose 'unrealistic or disproportionate' obligations on the state relating to the planning and conduct of military operations in armed conflict ([55, 76] (Lord Hope)).

18.1.6 **The right to die?**

Diane Pretty, who had motor neurone disease, argued before the UK courts and the ECtHR that the right to life in Article 2 also meant the right to choose when to die. She was challenging the DPP's refusal to give an assurance that her husband would not be prosecuted if he assisted her to commit suicide (assisting suicide is a crime under section 2(1) Suicide Act 1961). The courts held that Article 2 is about protecting the sanctity of life and does not confer a right to die (see *R (Pretty) v Director of Public Prosecutions* [2001] UKHL 61, [2002] 1 AC 800; *Pretty v UK* [2002] ECHR 427; see also *R (Purdy) v Director of Public Prosecutions* [2009] UKHL 45, [2010] 1 AC 345). Claimants in 'right to die' cases therefore rely on Article 8 as the basis for challenge; it is to this article that we now turn.

> **CROSS REFERENCE**
>
> See discussion on *Pretty* in Chapter 7

18.2 Article 8: the right to respect for private and family life

> **Article 8**
>
> 1. Everyone has the right to respect for his private and family life, his home and his correspondence.
> 2. There shall be no interference by a public authority with the exercise of this right except such as is in accordance with the law and is necessary in a democratic society in the interests of national security, public safety or the economic well-being of the country, for the prevention of disorder or crime, for the protection of health or morals, or for the protection of the rights and freedoms of others.

Article 8 is remarkably versatile and elastic, and has been relied on to enforce rights in a wide range of cases, from surveillance by the state to challenging the law on assisted suicide, as shown in the examples that will be given. The object of Article 8 is to protect individuals against arbitrary interference by public authorities. It is a qualified right so interference with it may be justified under Article 8(2), but any interference must be in accordance with the law, pursue a legitimate aim and be necessary in a democratic society, so a fair balance must be struck between the competing interests of the individual and the community. Being 'in accordance with the law' requires safeguards which are 'essential to the rule of law because they protect against the abuse of imprecise rules or unfettered discretionary powers' (*R (P) v Secretary of State for the Home Department* [2019] UKSC 3, [2019] 2 WLR 509 [41] (Lord Sumption)).

Article 8(1) comprises four main areas of protection:

- private life, which includes privacy;
- family life;
- home;
- correspondence.

THINKING POINT

What is being protected in the different examples below—for example, personal information, family life?

Surveillance The state can interfere with Article 8 rights on the grounds of national security, but interception of communications, such as phone tapping, must be in accordance with the law (*Malone v UK* [1984] ECHR 10). This requires the law to be compatible with the rule of law, that is, it must be sufficiently accessible and foreseeable for individuals to regulate their behaviour. In *Liberty v UK* [2009] 48 EHRR 1, the ECtHR found a violation of Article 8 because UK domestic law did not indicate clearly enough the extent of the state's discretion to intercept communications, particularly on examining, sharing, and storing intercepted material, so the interference was not in accordance with the law. In *Liberty v GCHQ* [2014] UKIPTrib 13_77-H, the Investigatory Powers Tribunal set out key requirements for Article 8 compliance: there must be controls on the state's discretion, rules must be clear, and their scope must be publicly available where possible so that people can foresee any interference with their privacy ([37]). See also *Privacy International v Secretary of State for Foreign and Commonwealth Affairs* [2018] (IPT/15/110/CH); *R (Liberty) v Secretary of State for the Home Department* [2018] EWHC 975 (Admin); *R (Liberty) v Secretary of State for the Home Department* [2019] EWHC 2057 (Admin).

Obtaining personal information In *Roche v UK* [2008] ECHR 926, the applicant was suffering health problems after being exposed to mustard gas and nerve gas during tests at Porton Down in 1962/3, and he had been given inadequate access to information about the tests when he had requested his medical and test reports. The ECtHR held that there was a violation of Article 8 because the UK had not provided an effective, accessible procedure giving access to relevant and appropriate information to enable him to assess any risk to which he had been exposed during the tests ([168]).

Deportation Foreign nationals may be deported from the UK on various grounds; for example, their leave to remain in the UK may have been refused, or they may have been convicted of a crime and may be deported if it is conducive to the public good (deportation is the Home Secretary's decision). However, they may also have married and had a family in the UK, which engages their Article 8 rights, which need to be balanced against the public interest in removal—although only 'very compelling' human rights grounds will successfully resist deportation (*Ali v Secretary of State for the Home Department* [2016] UKSC 60). The effect of deportation on all family members must be considered, particularly children (see *Beoku-Betts v Secretary of State for the*

Home Department [2008] UKHL 39; *ZH (Tanzania) v Secretary of State for the Home Department* [2011] UKSC 4; *Makhlouf v Secretary of State for the Home Department (Northern Ireland)* [2016] UKSC 59). In *R (Kiarie and Byndloss) v Secretary of State for the Home Department* [2017] UKSC 42, the Supreme Court held that the 'deport first, appeal later' scheme (see section 8.3.2) was incompatible with the claimants' right to respect for private and family life; they needed the opportunity to bring their appeals and give live evidence from within the UK.

Challenging the law on assisted suicide In *Pretty v UK* [2002] ECHR 427, Diane Pretty asked for a declaration that section 2(1) of the Suicide Act was incompatible with her rights under Article 8. The court held that Article 8 included a 'right to self-determination' but the ban on assisted suicide was not disproportionate so Article 8 was not breached. In *R (Nicklinson) v Ministry of Justice* [2014] UKSC 38, two judges took the view that the ban on assisted suicide did breach Article 8 but the majority thought it was for Parliament to decide. Four years later, Noel Conway unsuccessfully sought a declaration that section 2(1) was incompatible with his rights under Article 8, which he argued required the law to be adjusted to allow others to assist to enable *him* to commit suicide; the Court of Appeal held that section 2(1) achieves a fair balance between the interests of the wider community and the interests of people in his position (*R (Conway) v Secretary of State for Justice* [2018] EWCA Civ 1431).

▶ **CROSS REFERENCE**

See discussion on *Nicklinson* in section 7.4.1.1

Private life In this category, changing social concerns can significantly shape the law. In *R (Elan-Cane) v Secretary of State for the Home Department* [2020] EWCA Civ 363, although it was held that HM Passport Office's policy of not issuing non-gendered passports was not an unlawful breach of the claimant's Article 8 rights, the court recognised that Article 8 rights include gender identification ([47]). In *R (Steinfeld and Keidan) v Secretary of State for International Development* [2018] UKSC 32, [2020] AC 1, the Supreme Court declared that sections 1 and 3 of the Civil Partnership Act 2004 were incompatible with Articles 8 and 14 by not allowing heterosexual couples to enter into a civil partnership; the Civil Partnerships, Marriages and Deaths (Registration Etc.) Act 2019 and Civil Partnership (Opposite-sex Couples) Regulations 2019 changed the law to extend civil partnerships to heterosexual couples. While the human rights compatibility of Northern Ireland's abortion legislation was unsuccessfully challenged in *In the matter of an application by the Northern Ireland Human Rights Commission for Judicial Review (Northern Ireland)* [2018] UKSC 27—no declaration of incompatibility was made because of issues on standing—five Justices would have made a declaration, and dicta urging the need for the law to be reviewed sent a powerful message to legislative and executive bodies. The law was subsequently changed by The Abortion (Northern Ireland) (No 2) Regulations 2020 made pursuant to the Northern Ireland (Executive Formation) Act 2019.

Article 8 has also significantly developed protection of privacy against press intrusion, which we examine next.

18.2.1 **Privacy against press intrusion**

The driving force of Article 8 on UK law's development can be seen here, and this category of case raises two important issues.

> 1. It involves enforcement of Article 8 rights against other individuals or private bodies, not against the *state*; Article 8 protects privacy only against public authorities.

The courts, as public authorities, must act compatibly with the parties' Convention rights (section 6 HRA 1998), so the question is whether an individual is entitled to have their privacy protected by the court (see Dame Elizabeth Butler-Sloss P in *Venables v News Group Newspapers*

Ltd [2001] Fam 430, 446). The ECtHR has also recognised that states are obliged to protect one individual from an unjustified invasion of private life by another individual, and its courts are obliged to achieve that result (*Douglas v Hello! (No 3)* [2005] EWCA Civ 595 [49] (Lord Phillips)).

> 2. For the courts to do this, domestic law needs to provide a cause of action (see *Campbell v MGN* [49] (Lord Hoffmann)), but there is no privacy statute and no free-standing tort of invasion of privacy in English law (*Kaye v Robertson* [1990] EWCA Civ 21; *Wainwright v Home Office* [2004] 2 AC 406). So how can the UK courts protect privacy rights?

The solution is that, while there has never been a common law tort of privacy in the UK, there was—and still is—an equitable action for breach of confidence. This required a relationship between the parties that gave rise to a legal duty not to disclose confidential information, such as solicitor and client, or employer and employee (see *Coco v Clark* [1969] RPC 41; *Seager v Copydex* [1967] 2 All ER 415; *AG v Jonathan Cape* [1976] 1 QB 752; *AG v Guardian Newspapers Ltd (No 2)* [1990] 1 AC 109). This is what the courts have used as the basis for protection of privacy.

 THINKING POINT

Track the way in which the UK courts extend privacy rights in what follows.

The first post-HRA 'privacy' case against the media was *Douglas v Hello! Limited* [2001] EMLR 9, where Michael Douglas and Catherine Zeta-Jones successfully obtained an injunction to prevent *Hello!* magazine from publishing unauthorised photographs of their wedding. Their argument was based on breach of confidence and Article 8, and the Court of Appeal held that they had a legal right to respect for their privacy. The law no longer needed an artificial relationship of confidentiality between the parties and could recognise privacy as a legal principle based on personal autonomy ([126] (Sedley LJ)); this relates to an individual's control over facts about their identity, such as 'name, health, sexuality, ethnicity . . . image' (*R (Wood) v Commissioner of Police of the Metropolis* [2009] EWCA Civ 414, [2010] 1 WLR 123 [21] (Laws LJ)).

> In *Douglas v Hello!* Sedley LJ observed that the 'common law develops reactively' ([109]) and has a 'perennial need . . . to appear not to be doing anything for the first time' ([111]). However, he concluded that the common law had reached a position 'to respond to an increasingly invasive social environment by affirming that everybody has a right to some private space' and that the Human Rights Act required the courts to give effect to the right in Article 8 ([111]; see also [61, 64–74] (Brooke LJ); [113–127] (Sedley LJ)).

 THINKING POINT

What is driving the expansion of the law here?

Stirring Article 8 into the mix breathed new life into the law on privacy. As Lord Woolf CJ has explained, the courts were developing the law so as to give effect to Convention rights and were acting compatibly with the ECHR by 'absorbing the rights which Articles 8 and 10 protect into the long-established action for breach of confidence . . . giving a new strength and breadth to the action so that it accommodates the requirements of those articles' (*A v B* [2002] EWCA Civ 337, [2003] QB 195 [4]; see also *Theakston v MGN* [2002] EWHC 137 (QB)). At first it was uncertain whether, by extending breach of confidence in this way, the courts had created a new right of privacy in English law, but the law took a firm step forward in *Campbell v MGN*.

🔍 CASE CLOSE-UP: *CAMPBELL v MGN LIMITED* [2004] UKHL 22

In this case, the House of Lords held by 3 to 2 that C's privacy had been invaded by publication of an article detailing her treatment for drug addiction, accompanied by photographs of her leaving a Narcotics Anonymous meeting. The House of Lords confirmed the law's direction of travel, that is, breach of confidence protected against infringement of privacy.

Lord Nicholls took the view that:

- Breach of confidence no longer needed a confidential relationship and had changed its nature even before the Human Rights Act (citing *Attorney-General v Guardian Newspapers Ltd (No 2)* [1990] 1 AC 109, 281). The law now imposed a duty of confidence whenever a person receives information they know or ought to know is 'fairly and reasonably to be regarded as confidential'. But it was better encapsulated as 'private information' ([14]).

- 'The time has come to recognise that the values enshrined in articles 8 and 10 are now part of the cause of action for breach of confidence.' Those values applied as much in disputes between individuals or non-governmental bodies as between individuals and public authorities ([17–18]).

- The touchstone is whether the person in question had a reasonable expectation of privacy in respect of the disclosed facts [21].

See generally [11–22].

Lord Hoffmann reasoned that:

- The right to privacy was an underlying value of breach of confidence [43].

- There had been two developments of the law of confidence: (a) acknowledging the artificial distinction between confidential information obtained through a confidential relationship or in another way; and (b) accepting that the privacy of personal information is worth protecting in its own right ([46]).

- This had led to 'a shift in the centre of gravity' of breach of confidence when used as a remedy for the unjustified publication of personal information ([51]) (though Lord Hope doubted this [86]).

- 'The cause of action focuses upon the protection of human autonomy and dignity— the right to control the dissemination of information about one's private life and the right to the esteem and respect of other people' [51].

Baroness Hale was careful to point out that:

- '[T]he courts will not invent a new cause of action to cover types of activity which were not previously covered . . . our law cannot, even if it wanted to, develop a general tort of invasion of privacy' ([133]).

- Reasonable expectation of privacy 'is a threshold test which brings the balancing exercise into play'. Once the information is identified as private, the court must balance the claimant's interest in keeping the information private against the interest of the recipient in publishing it ([137]).

SUMMARY

This decision shaped breach of confidence into an action based on misuse of private information by identifying a change of focus in the law. Did the claimant have a reasonable expectation of privacy in relation to the information in question?

The law marched on, despite Lord Phillips MR's dissatisfaction at having to 'shoe-horn' claims for publication of unauthorised photographs of a private occasion into breach of confidence (*Douglas v Hello! (No 3)* [2005] EWCA Civ 595, [2006] QB 125 ([53]). *McKennitt v Ash* [2006] EWCA Civ 1714, [2008] QB 73) emphasised the misuse of private information, considering two questions: (a) is the information private? (b) If so, does the claimant's interest under Article 8 yield to the right to freedom of expression and publication? In *Mosley v News Group Newspapers* [2008] EWHC 1777 (QB) [10], Eady J framed the test as:

1.   The claimant must show a reasonable expectation of privacy.

2.   The court must weigh competing Convention rights with 'an intense focus' on the facts of the case. Is there a public interest consideration to justify intrusion, such as to expose a crime or hypocrisy?

The balancing of competing interests became more pronounced here. Eady J highlighted the modern perception that there is a public interest in respecting personal privacy and the court must take account of conflicting public interest considerations and evaluate them according to increasingly well recognised criteria ([130]). In *Mosley*, there was no public interest in publishing images of private sexual activities between consenting adults. See also Eady J's statement of the principles in *CTB v News Group Newspapers Ltd* [2011] EWHC 1232 (QB) [19–28, 31].

18.2.1.1 **A reasonable expectation of privacy**

If the claimant can show a reasonable expectation of privacy, this engages Article 8 (the 'touchstone' for engagement). In 2004, the ECtHR decided in *Von Hannover v Germany* (2005) 40 EHRR 1 that photographs of Princess Caroline of Monaco shopping and playing tennis breached her right to privacy, which broadened expectations of protection of private life, even in public places. So in *Murray v Big Pictures (UK) Ltd* [2008] EWCA Civ 446, where photographs of JK Rowling's son were taken in the street without consent, the Court of Appeal held that the child had a reasonable expectation of privacy; factors to take into account included:

> the attributes of the claimant, the nature of the activity in which the claimant was engaged, the place at which it was happening, the nature and purpose of the intrusion, the absence of consent and whether it was known or could be inferred, the effect on the claimant and the circumstances in which and the purposes for which the information came into the hands of the publisher ([36] (Sir Anthony Clarke MR)).

Similarly, in *Weller v Associated Newspapers* [2015] EWCA Civ 1176, Paul Weller's children had a reasonable expectation of privacy in relation to photographs taken of them while they were shopping and sitting at a café in Santa Monica, California, and which were published on the MailOnline website. The court observed that the approach for deciding whether there is a reasonable expectation of privacy is the same for children and adults, but in some cases a child has a reasonable expectation of privacy where an adult does not ([29–30]).

However, a 14-year-old boy who was involved in rioting in Derry, Northern Ireland complained that the publication of CCTV images of him in two newspapers breached his Article 8 rights (*In the matter of an application by JR38 for Judicial Review (Northern Ireland)* [2015] UKSC 42). The Supreme Court disagreed. The images were published at the request of the police to identify those involved and discourage sectarian violence. Three members of the court concluded that Article 8 was not engaged as he did not have a reasonable expectation of privacy; Lord Kerr and Lord Wilson thought Article 8 was engaged because of his age and the effect which publication of the photographs may have on him, but the interference was justified because publication struck a fair balance between the boy's interests and the community's interests in preventing and detecting crime.

The courts have recognised a reasonable expectation of privacy in areas of people's lives such as personal and sexual relationships, and health or addiction issues, so in *CC v AB* [2006] EWHC 3083 (QB), it was recognised that a public figure engaging in an extramarital affair had a right to privacy. However, in *Campbell v MGN*, Lord Nicholls said that if a public figure chooses to present a false image and make untrue statements about their life, the press will normally be entitled to put the record straight ([24]). So if they had lied about not taking drugs, for example, they could no longer have a reasonable expectation that this aspect of their life should be private.

18.2.1.2 Balancing privacy and freedom of expression

Article 8 (the right to privacy) or Article 10 (freedom of expression and the right to publish): which one gives way? Articles 8 and 10 protect conflicting interests but are of equal value; there is no hierarchy of rights, so neither has automatic precedence. The ECtHR was balancing Article 10 against other interests long before the Human Rights Act came into force (as in *Handyside v UK* [1976] and *Goodwin v UK* [1996]), regarding it not as choosing between conflicting principles, but acknowledging that freedom of expression is subject to certain exceptions (*Sunday Times v United Kingdom* (1979) 2 EHRR 245 [65]).

Article 10 ECHR

(1) Everyone has the right to freedom of expression. This right shall include freedom to hold opinions and to receive and impart information and ideas without interference by public authority and regardless of frontiers . . .

(2) The exercise of these freedoms, since it carries with it duties and responsibilities, may be subject to such . . . restrictions . . . as are prescribed by law and are necessary in a democratic society . . . for the protection of the reputation or rights of others, for preventing the disclosure of information received in confidence, or for maintaining the authority and impartiality of the judiciary.

Article 10(1) recognises the importance of an individual's right to freedom of expression and the public's right to receive information, but it is a qualified right. Both Article 8(2) and Article 10(2) recognise that interference may be justified to protect the rights of others (see *Campbell* [20] (Lord Nicholls) and [55] (Lord Hoffmann)). As Lord Hope put it, the right to privacy has to be balanced against the right of the media to impart information to the public, and the right of the media to impart information to the public has to be balanced against the respect to be given to private life (*Campbell* [105]).

Lord Woolf CJ in *A v B* set out balancing guidelines for the courts including:

- The existence of a free press is desirable and any interference with it has to be justified. ([11(iv)])
- A public figure is entitled to a private life but should accept that their actions will be more closely scrutinised by the media; if they have sought publicity, they have less ground to object to any intrusion. ([11(xii)])

The public interest According to Lord Bridge, 'any restriction of the right to freedom of expression requires to be justified and . . . nothing less than an important competing public interest will be sufficient to justify it' (*R v Secretary of State for the Home Department, ex p Brind* [1991] 1 AC 696, 748–749). One of the key questions for the courts in the balancing exercise is therefore whether publication is in the public interest: does the general public have a legitimate interest in knowing, as opposed to merely satisfying curiosity (see *Mosley v UK* (2011) ECHR 774 [114]).

In *Von Hannover v Germany* (2005) 40 EHRR 1, the ECtHR held that the decisive factor in balancing Articles 8 and 10 is the contribution that published photographs or articles make to a debate of general interest. However, in *Von Hannover v Germany (No 2)* (2012) 55 EHRR 15, the court expanded this to five criteria for balancing Article 8 and 10 rights:

- The contribution made by photos or articles in the press to a debate of general interest in a democratic society.
- How well known is the person concerned and what is the subject of the report? (Public figures may not be able to claim the same protection for their private life as ordinary individuals.)
- Prior conduct of the person concerned.
- Content, form, and consequences of the publication.
- The circumstance in which the photos were taken. ([107–113])

The court in *Weller* made it clear that where children are involved, a child's right is not 'a trump card' in the balancing exercise, but where a child's interests would be adversely affected by publication, their best interests have primacy. This means that they must be given considerable weight, so very powerful Article 10 rights would be needed to outweigh a child's Article 8 rights ([40]). In the case, the children's Article 8 rights outweighed the defendant's Article 10 right to publish.

The Supreme Court thought that there was no public interest (at least in a legal sense) in 'kiss and tell' stories about private sexual encounters which constitute the tort of invasion of privacy (see *PJS v News Group Newspapers Ltd* [2016] UKSC 26 [21–22, 32]). Reporting a public figure's extramarital activities with a view to criticising them was 'at the bottom end of the spectrum of importance' and might not even fall within Article 10's protection at all ([24] (Lord Mance)). However, in *Ferdinand v MGN* [2011] EWHC 2454 (QB), publication of a 'kiss and tell' story about a footballer's affair was held to be in the public interest because it corrected a public image which he had presented and the information was relevant to his suitability to be the captain of the England football team.

 STATUTE

Section 12 of the Human Rights Act 1998 applies where a court is considering whether to grant any relief which might affect the exercise of the right to freedom of expression.

Note: Do not mistake section 12 for Article 10 of the ECHR. It is Article 10 that protects the right to freedom of expression, not section 12

Under section 12(4), the court must have particular regard to the importance of the right to freedom of expression. Where the proceedings relate to journalistic, literary, or artistic material, the court must have regard to (a) the extent to which the material has, or is about to, become available to the public or it is, or would be, in the public interest for the material to be published; (b) any relevant privacy code.

Sedley LJ interpreted this as meaning that the qualifications in Article 10(2)—the reputations and rights of others—are as relevant as the right of free expression in Article 10(1) (*Douglas v Hello!* [2000] EWCA Civ 353 [136]).

18.2.1.3 Development of the law

The law in this area continues to evolve as the common law adapts itself to the needs of contemporary life, to borrow Lord Hoffmann's phrase (*Campbell* [46]). In *CTB v News Group Newspapers Ltd* [2011] EWHC 1326 (QB), Eady J stressed that 'the modern law of privacy is not concerned solely with information or "secrets": it is also concerned importantly with intrusion' [23]. This view was endorsed by Lord Neuberger in *PJS Claims* ([61–62]).

THINKING POINT

How has the focus moved on from *Douglas v Hello!*?

Has the application of Article 8 produced a fully fledged cause of action in English law? In 2015, the Court of Appeal's state-of-progress review in *Google v Vidal-Hall* [2015] EWCA Civ 311 concluded that misuse of private information should now be recognised as a tort. It was not creating a new cause of action but giving 'the correct legal label to one that already exists' ([21, 43, 51]; see [17–43] for a helpful review of authorities). Although the court in *Google v Vidal-Hall* cited authorities stating that there is no English domestic law tort of invasion of privacy, it is worth noting that in 2016, Lord Mance in the Supreme Court referred to the tort of invasion of privacy (see *PJS* [21–22, 32]). This journey was driven by Article 8.

Privacy and criminal investigations A significant case in 2018 highlighted the impact of the right to privacy on police investigations and how the media report them. In *Richard v BBC* [2018] EWHC 1837 (Ch), Sir Cliff Richard brought an action against the BBC and South Yorkshire Police claiming a breach of his right to privacy and his rights under the Data Protection Act 1998 after a police raid on his home was filmed by the BBC in 2014. The BBC broadcast details of the investigation and footage of the search, identifying Sir Cliff as a suspect in an alleged historical sexual assault of which he was then unaware; no charges were subsequently brought against him. Sir Cliff claimed that he had a legitimate expectation of privacy in relation to the investigation and search. Mann J carried out a balancing exercise between the claimant's Article 8 rights and the BBC's competing rights under Article 10, and held that as a general principle, a suspect has a reasonable expectation of privacy in relation to a police investigation ([248]); Sir Cliff had a legitimate expectation of privacy under Article 8 against the police in relation to the investigation and the search ([257]) and against the BBC ([261]), and his privacy rights were not outweighed by the BBC's rights to freedom of expression. Although there was a significant public interest in police investigations into historical sex abuse, there was no public interest in identifying individuals in this case ([317]). Mann J also found that the sensationalist style of reporting, including use of a helicopter, increased the impact of the invasion of privacy.

The decision has raised concerns about press freedom and restricting media reporting about people under investigation by the police before they are charged. The BBC had argued that if the claim was successful it would undermine long-standing press freedom to report the truth about police investigations and it should be a matter for Parliament, not the courts, to undermine that freedom ([321–322]), but Mann J's response was that if the position of the press is now different, it is because of the Human Rights Act. On the other side of the balance is the individual's right to privacy, and protection of a suspect's pre-charge anonymity.

SUMMARY

Driven by the impetus of Article 8, case law has evolved rapidly to protect individuals' privacy rights through misuse of private information. The test is:

1. Establish that an individual has a reasonable expectation of privacy in this area of their life; this engages their Article 8 rights.

2. Apply an intense focus to the balance between the individual's right to privacy, and the other party's right to freedom of expression, taking into account public interest.

18.3 Article 9: freedom of thought, conscience, and religion

Article 9

1. Everyone has the right to freedom of thought, conscience and religion; this right includes freedom to change his religion or belief and freedom, either alone or in community with others and in public or private, to manifest his religion or belief, in worship, teaching, practice and observance.

2. Freedom to manifest one's religion or beliefs shall be subject only to such limitations as are prescribed by law and are necessary in a democratic society in the interests of public safety, for the protection of public order, health or morals, or for the protection of the rights and freedoms of others.

The central issue that arises under Article 9 is the tension between religious belief and discrimination either against, or by, believers, and the fact that social attitudes can change more quickly than deeply held religious beliefs. The ECtHR has stated that freedom of thought, conscience, and religion is one of the foundations of a democratic society (*Eweida v UK* [2013] ECHR 37 [79]). It encompasses:

- private thought and conscience, including non-religious beliefs such as veganism (*W v UK* Application No 18187/91 (1993)) and pacifism (*Arrowsmith v UK* (1978) 3 EHRR 218);

- the freedom to manifest (express) one's religion either in private or in public (see *Eweida* [80]);

- the freedom not to manifest one's religion or belief (*Isik v Turkey* App no 21924/05 (ECtHR, 2 February 2010) [37]);

- the freedom to have no religion.

Look at Article 9(2): only the individual's right to manifest their religion or beliefs can be limited; thought and conscience, and freedom to change religion or belief, cannot. As Lord Nicholls observes, under Article 9, freedom to *hold* a belief is absolute, and freedom to *manifest* a belief is qualified (*R (Williamson) v Secretary of State for Education and Employment* [2005] UKHL 15, [2005] 2 AC 246, [15–19]).

 THINKING POINT

What do you think the reason is for this?

To be justified under Article 9(2), a limitation (or interference) must be prescribed by law and necessary in a democratic society to pursue one of the legitimate purposes in paragraph 2. It must be proportionate; there should be a fair balance struck between the rights and interests of different people in society (see *R (Adath Yisroel Burial Society) v HM Senior Coroner for Inner North London* [2018] EWHC 969 (Admin) [99, 107]). So, for example, in *SAS v France* [2014] ECHR 695, a French law banning the wearing of face veils in public places was upheld because France's aim of 'living together' was linked to the legitimate aim of protecting the rights and freedoms of others; but in *Adath Yisroel*, refusing priority to expedited burials for religious reasons rendered the balance unfair.

The courts' approach under Article 9 is:

- Does an individual hold a genuine belief of perceived obligation, that is, that their religion requires an act (*Williamson* [22–23, 32])? If so, their rights are engaged.

- Has there been interference with that right?

- If so, is the interference justified?

 EXAMPLE

In *R (Begum) v Governors of Denbigh High School* [2006] UKHL 15, [2007] 1 AC 100, a teenage Muslim girl was not allowed by her school to wear a jilbab (a long coat) instead of the prescribed school uniform. She held a sincere religious belief that she was required to wear it, therefore Article 9(1) was engaged, but the majority of the House of Lords held that there was no interference with her right; she could have gone to another school where she would have been allowed to wear it (see [50] (Lord Hoffmann)). Lord Nicholls and Lady Hale held that it *was* an interference, but was justified.

> Any adequate alternatives available to individuals to practise their religion will be taken into account when weighing proportionality (*Eweida* [83]).

In *R (Harrison) v Secretary of State for Justice* [2020] EWHC 2096 (Admin), the claimants were humanists who argued that English law did not recognise humanist weddings which was discriminatory and breached their rights under Article 14, taken together with Articles 8 and 9. The court held that the facts of the case fell within Article 9 but given the government's on-going review of the law of marriage, a fair balance had been struck between the individual rights of the claimants and those of the broader community ([129]).

18.3.1 **The right to manifest one's religion**

The ECtHR has observed that not every act 'inspired, motivated or influenced by a belief' is necessarily a manifestation of that belief and there needs to be 'a sufficiently close and direct nexus between an act and the underlying belief' which depends on the facts of each case (*Eweida v UK* [82]).

In *Eweida*, four practising Christians complained that each of their employers had violated their rights to manifest their religion under Article 9. They had already brought unsuccessful actions in the UK courts or employment tribunal for discrimination:

- Nadia Eweida, a member of check-in staff at British Airways, began openly wearing a cross on a chain, contrary to BA's uniform guide; as a result, she was suspended from work until BA changed its policy to allow visible religious symbols to be worn where authorised, but BA refused to compensate her for lost earnings. The ECtHR upheld Ms Eweida's claim because BA's refusal to allow her to remain in her post while visibly wearing a cross was an interference with her Article 9 right ([91]). The ECtHR considered whether the state had protected her right and decided that the Court of Appeal had given too much weight to BA's protection of its corporate image and not enough to Ms Eweida's right to manifest her religion with a discreet cross ([93–95]): see *Eweida v British Airways plc* [2010] EWCA Civ 80. BA's amendment of its uniform policy also diminished the importance of the earlier ban (see [94]).

- Shirley Chaplin, a nurse, refused on religious grounds to stop wearing a cross on a chain, contrary to the NHS Trust's uniform policy, but she was unsuccessful before the ECtHR because the policy was based on health and safety grounds to reduce the risk of injury when handling patients in hospital. It had been applied to other workers of differing religions and Ms Chaplin had been offered alternative ways of wearing a cross which she had refused. The interference was therefore not disproportionate and her claim was dismissed ([98–100]).

18.3.2 **Differences in treatment based on sexual orientation**

The cases here involve the effect of manifestation of religious beliefs on the rights of others, raising issues of discrimination; under Article 14 ECHR, differences in treatment based on sexual orientation require particularly serious justification (*Eweida* [105]). The other two complainants in *Eweida* were:

- Lillian Ladele, a registrar, who refused to officiate at civil partnerships because of her religious beliefs and lost her job;

- Gary McFarlane, a Relate counsellor, who was dismissed for refusing to agree to give counselling to same sex couples on sexual issues.

The ECtHR decided that in Ms Ladele's case, the local authority's aim of promoting equal opportunities was legitimate to protect the rights of others ([105–106]). In Mr McFarlane's case, the domestic courts' refusal to uphold his complaints did not violate Article 9; his employer aimed to deliver a service without discrimination ([109–110]). In both cases, the proper balance had been struck between the right to manifest their religion and securing the rights of others, so the claimants were unsuccessful.

Article 9 can therefore conflict with equality law. The Equality Act (Sexual Orientation) Regulations 2007 (now replaced by the Equality Act 2010) prohibited discrimination on the ground of sexual orientation. In *London Borough of Islington v Ladele* [2009] EWCA Civ 1357, the Court of Appeal held that the Regulations did not entitle Ms Ladele to refuse to carry out civil partnership duties. Similarly, in *Bull v Hall* [2013] UKSC 73, Christian hotel owners refused a double room to a homosexual couple in a civil partnership on the ground that they only let double rooms to heterosexual married couples because of their religious belief in the sanctity of marriage between a man and a woman. The hotel owners argued that the requirement not to discriminate on grounds of sexual orientation in the 2007 Regulations was incompatible with Article 9. The Supreme Court held that the Regulations engaged Article 9 and did limit their right to manifest their religious belief, but it was necessary in a democratic society to protect the rights of others and ensure equal treatment, and the Regulations were a justified and proportionate protection of the rights of others. See also *Black v Wilkinson* [2013] EWCA Civ 820.

Competing rights and beliefs can also be seen in what is popularly known as the 'gay cake case'.

> ### Q CASE CLOSE-UP: *LEE v ASHER BAKING COMPANY LTD* [2018] UKSC 49
>
> Ashers Bakery in Belfast refused to decorate a cake with the logo 'Support Gay Marriage' because of the owners' Christian beliefs (there was then no provision for same sex marriage in Northern Ireland; this has subsequently been introduced by the Marriage (Same-sex Couples) and Civil Partnership (Opposite-sex Couples) (Northern Ireland) Regulations 2019 made under section 8 Northern Ireland (Executive Formation etc) Act 2019). The McArthurs (the bakery owners) argued that their religious beliefs and political opinions about same sex marriage were being penalised. Upholding a decision that the company had discriminated on the grounds of sexual orientation, the Court of Appeal in Northern Ireland stated that a balance had to be struck between prohibiting discrimination on the grounds of sexual orientation in providing goods and services, and protecting religion, belief, and conscience. The legislation was not treating their religious belief or political opinion less favourably but the McArthurs were distinguishing unlawfully between those who may or may not receive their service.
>
> However, the Supreme Court held that the appellants had objected to the *message* on the cake, not to Mr Lee's sexual orientation, and anyone else promoting the same message would have been treated in the same way ([47]). Articles 9 and 10 protect an individual's right not to be obliged to manifest beliefs they do not hold ([50, 52]). While the bakery could not refuse to provide a cake to Mr Lee because he was a gay man or because he supported gay marriage, the McArthurs could not be obliged to supply a cake iced with a message with which they profoundly disagreed, and they were entitled to refuse to do that [55].

This decision adds an additional element to be weighed and assessed by the courts: whether the objection was to a person's sexual orientation or the message being promoted, and whether anyone promoting it would have been treated in the same way. In underscoring the right *not* to express an opinion which an individual does not hold, the judgment also places emphasis on the protection that Articles 9 and 10 can give where there are competing rights and interests.

The cases above raise the issue of how far secular law takes precedence over any right to manifest religious belief. Are religious beliefs sufficiently protected? Where manifestation takes the form of discrimination on the ground of sexual orientation, it is prohibited by the law and 'very weighty' reasons are required to justify it (*Bull v Hall* [51–54] (Lady Hale)). Laws LJ attempted to rationalise this, arguing that a law giving protection to a position held purely on religious grounds could not be justified because it would be irrational, preferring 'the subjective over the objective', and would be 'divisive, capricious and arbitrary', as not everyone shares the same religious beliefs; one religion could not have preference over another (*McFarlane v Relate Avon Ltd* [2010] EWCA Civ 880 [22–24]).

 SUMMARY

Human rights evolve at different speeds. The judiciary has expanded Articles 2 and 8 well beyond their original reach into rapidly growing areas of law, but the rights under Article 9 have been interpreted and applied more narrowly without the same creative drive because of their potential impact on the rights of others.

? Questions

Self-test questions

1. What obligations does Article 2 impose on a state?

2. Summarise the key principles from the *McCann case*.

3. What is the 'investigative duty' under Article 2?

4. Does Article 2 apply to UK soldiers serving abroad?

5. What rights are protected by Article 8?

6. How can Article 8 be used by individuals challenging deportation?

7. Briefly outline how the courts balance competing rights under Articles 8 and 10.

8. What happens where Article 9 rights conflict with laws on equality?

Exam question

Freedom of speech 'is a trump card which always wins' (*R v Central Television plc* [1994] Fam 192, 203 (Hoffmann J)). Consider this statement in the light of Article 8 ECHR rights.

Further reading

Books

Costigan, R. and Stone, R. *Civil Liberties and Human Rights* (11th edn, Oxford: Oxford University Press 2017).
See chapters 6 and 7 on privacy and freedom of expression

Fenwick, H. *Fenwick on Civil Liberties and Human Rights* (5th edn, Abingdon: Routledge 2016).
See in particular chapter 10 on the right to privacy

Journal articles

Barendt, E. 'Problems with the "Reasonable Expectation of Privacy" Test' (2016) 8(2) Journal of Media Law 129–137.
Analyses reasonable expectation of privacy in the *JR38* and *Weller* cases

Chevalier-Watts, J. 'Effective Investigations under Article 2 of the European Convention on Human Rights: Securing the Right to Life or an Onerous Burden on a State?' (2010) 21(3) European Journal of International Law 701–721.
Interesting analysis of the duty to investigate

Leigh, I. and Hambler, A. 'Religious Symbols, Conscience, and the Rights of Others' (2014) 3(1) Oxford Journal of Law and Religion 2–24.
Analysis of the *Eweida* case

Morgan, J. 'Privacy, Confidence and Horizontal Effect: "Hello" Trouble' (2003) 62(2) CLJ 444.
Interesting to see how the law has developed since this post-*Douglas* analysis

Phillipson, G. 'Transforming Breach of Confidence? Towards a Common Law Right of Privacy under the Human Rights Act' (2003) 66 MLR 726.
A respected analysis, often judicially cited

Roberts, C.K. 'Is There a Right to Be "Free from" Religion or Belief at Strasbourg?' (2017) 19(1) Ecclesiastical Law Journal 35–41.
Evaluates whether there is a freedom from religion

Other sources

Joint Committee on Privacy and Injunctions, *Privacy and Injunctions*, Session 2010–12, HL Paper 273, HC 1443.
Contains helpful discussion on the balance between freedom of expression and privacy.

For extrajudicial discussion of cases and issues surrounding Article 9, see:

Lady Hale, 'Freedom of Religion and Belief', Annual Human Rights Lecture for the Law Society of Ireland, 13 June 2014 (www.supremecourt.uk/docs/speech-140613.pdf).

Lady Hale, 'Religious Dress', Sultan Azlan Shah Lecture, Oxford, 25 January 2018 (www.supremecourt.uk/docs/speech-180125.pdf).

Useful websites

For guides to Articles 8 and 9, see:

www.echr.coe.int/Documents/Guide_Art_8_ENG.pdf

www.echr.coe.int/Documents/Guide_Art_9_ENG.pdf

Online resources

www.oup.com/he/dennett2e

This chapter is accompanied by a selection of online resources to help you with this topic, including:

- Multiple-choice questions
- Answers to the self-test questions
- Guidance on answering the exam question

19 Police powers

LEARNING OBJECTIVES

By the end of this chapter, you should be able to:

- Explain the significance and application of PACE
- Evaluate the application of the Human Rights Act to police powers
- Analyse issues arising from stop and search powers
- Appraise the approach of the courts in determining breaches of specific Convention rights
- Evaluate competing interests relating to the freedom of assembly
- Summarise avenues of police accountability

Introduction

From road policing to organised crime and counter-terrorism, it is the function of the police to keep the public secure by preventing and detecting crime, and maintaining public order. This involves the exercise of public power and engages the relationship between the citizen and the state. There are clear links between police powers and the rule of law: it is imperative that police powers are not used in a random, arbitrary way; are clear, foreseeable, and accessible; are not unlimited; and are in accordance with the law. Preventing arbitrary application of powers by police officers is particularly important: 'The public must not be vulnerable to interference by public officials acting on any personal whim, caprice, malice, predilection or purpose other than that for which the power was conferred' (*R (Gillan) v Commissioner of Police of the Metropolis* [2006] UKHL 12, [2006] 2 AC 307 [34]) (Lord Bingham)).

In this chapter, we will look at:

- The impact of the Human Rights Act
- Specific police powers
- Public order and freedom of assembly
- Police powers and the coronavirus emergency
- Accountability

19.1 Organisation

In England and Wales, the Home Secretary and Home Office are responsible for policing (although the 2019 Commission on Justice in Wales report recommended that responsibility for policing should be devolved to Wales (*Justice in Wales for the People of Wales*, Commission on Justice in Wales, October 2019)). Apart from reserved matters such as national security, counter-terrorism, and firearms, for which the Home Secretary retains responsibility, policing is devolved to Scotland and Northern Ireland. For an overview, see Figure 19.1.

Figure 19.1 Police organisation

> There are 43 police forces in England and Wales, one in Scotland (Police Scotland) and one in Northern Ireland (Police Service of Northern Ireland)

> Under the Police Act 1996 section 1, police forces in England and Wales are organised into police areas which are often county-based (see Schedule 1) and also include the Metropolitan Police district, and the City of London police area

> Each police force is led by a Chief Constable (or a Commissioner in the Metropolitan Police district and the City of London) who controls, and has responsibility for, the delivery of policing services in their area

> In addition, there are four national specialist forces: the British Transport Police, Civil Nuclear Police, Ministry of Defence Police, and National Police Air Service

> The National Crime Agency (NCA) was created in 2013 by the Crime and Courts Act 2013 to combat serious and organised crime; it can work in partnership with the police and other law enforcement organisations

19.2 Police powers

There is a tension between the powers of the police and the rights and freedoms of the citizen, particularly the right to liberty, which has been recognised for centuries in English law and is now protected by Article 5 European Convention on Human Rights (ECHR). However, there are overriding constraints on all police powers, as pointed out by Lady Hale and Lord Reed in *R (Roberts) v MPC* [2015] UKSC 79 [42]:

- All powers must be operated in a lawful manner.
- As police forces are public authorities under section 6(1) Human Rights Act 1998, it is unlawful for police officers to act incompatibly with the Convention rights of members of the public.

- The Equality Act 2010 makes it unlawful for a police officer to discriminate in the exercise of his/her powers on racial or other grounds. The public sector equality duty in section 149 requires public authorities (such as police forces), when carrying out their functions, to have due regard to the need to eliminate discrimination, harassment and victimisation, and to advance equality of opportunity and foster good relations between people who share a 'relevant protected characteristic' and people who do not share it.

Breaching either Act will be unlawful and result in legal liability. There are some important principles which cut across many areas of modern police powers and three key benchmarks measure police actions: reasonableness, necessity, and proportionality which we will see applied in statutes and cases in this chapter.

19.2.1 The impact of the Human Rights Act

Through the lens of the Human Rights Act, police powers come under very close scrutiny by the courts. Where a public authority—here, the police—interferes with an individual's Convention rights under Article 8, for example, it must be in accordance with the law (sometimes referred to as 'legality'). This means it must be compatible with the rule of law in the sense used in the Convention (see the preamble to the ECHR):

- there must be a **lawful domestic basis** for it eg a UK statute although the rules need not be statutory, as long as they operate within a framework of law and set out principles which are 'capable of being predictably applied to any situation' (*R (Catt and T) v Commissioner of Police of the Metropolis* [2015] UKSC 9 [11] (Lord Sumption));
- that law must be adequately **accessible** to the public;
- its operation must be sufficiently **precise and foreseeable** to enable people to regulate their conduct (see *Malone v UK* (1984) 7 EHRR 14 [66–68], where police powers to intercept communications were not contained in an identifiable statute and were largely within the discretion of the executive);
- the law must contain **sufficient safeguards** to protect against the arbitrary exercise of power which would be an unjustified interference with a fundamental right; this ensures necessity and proportionality;
- domestic law must clearly indicate **how much discretion** is given to the public authority and how it is exercised; this ensures that discretion is not too wide.

See *Beghal v Director of Public Prosecutions* [2015] UKSC 49 [29–30]; *S and Marper v UK* (2008) 48 EHRR 1169 [95].

The exercise of police powers must also be proportionate. In relation to Article 8, for example, this means considering whether:

- the police were pursuing a legitimate aim in Article 8(2) such as the prevention of disorder or crime;
- any interference with a person's rights was strictly necessary in a democratic society by answering to a pressing social need;
- it is proportionate to the legitimate aim pursued (this means looking at whether a fair balance has been struck between the interference with a person's rights and the interests of the community); and
- if 'the reasons adduced by the national authorities to justify it are relevant and sufficient' (*Catt v UK* [2019] ECHR 76 [109]).

19.2.2 **PACE**

Police powers are mostly statute-based, the most significant of which is the Police and Criminal Evidence Act 1984 (PACE) which was enacted to achieve a balance between protecting citizens' rights and effective police powers. Under section 66, the Home Secretary issues detailed Codes of Practice regulating the exercise of police powers and providing clear guidelines for the police and safeguards for the public (see Table 19.1).

Table 19.1 Codes of Practice

Code A	Powers of stop and search
Code B	Searches of premises and seizure of property
Code C and H	Detention, treatment, and questioning of suspects
Code D	Identification and keeping criminal records
Code E and F	Recording of interviews of suspects
Code G	Arrest

Available at www.gov.uk/guidance/police-and-criminal-evidence-act-1984-pace-codes-of-practice

We examine below the following powers:

- Stop and search
- Searches of property
- Arrest
- Detention and questioning
- Retention of data

19.3 Stop and search

'It is an old and cherished tradition of our country that everyone should be free to go about their business in the streets of the land, confident that they will not be stopped and searched by the police unless reasonably suspected of having committed a criminal offence.' (*Gillan* [1] (Lord Bingham))

With the stop and search powers discussed here, a person is detained without being arrested, and this power intrudes on the public's right to move freely in public places. At common law, the police do not have the right to stop a person unless they are going to arrest them; there is no legal duty to answer their questions (*Rice v Connolly* [1966] 2 QB 414), and it is unlawful to search individuals to establish whether there are grounds for an arrest (*Jackson v Stevenson* (1897) 2 Adam 255).

Parliament therefore authorised general stop and search powers in PACE sections 1–7 (see also PACE Code A):

- The search must be in a public place or place to which the public has ready access (section 1(1)).
- A constable may search any person or vehicle or anything in or on it for stolen or prohibited articles (section 1(2)); a prohibited article includes an offensive weapon or an article that has been or could be used to commit a crime.

- A constable can only search if s/he has reasonable grounds for suspecting those articles will be found (section 1(3)).

'Reasonable grounds' means that there must be a genuine suspicion that they will find the article *and* that suspicion must be reasonable with an objective basis on facts or information (Code A 2.2).

Before beginning the search, the constable, if not in uniform, must provide documentary evidence that they are a police officer (section 2(2)). Under section 2(3), the officer must take reasonable steps to tell the person being searched their name and police station, the object of the search, and the grounds for making it. The person can only be detained for the time reasonably required to permit a search (section 2(8)). Breach of section 2 requirements will make the search unlawful (*Osman v DPP* [1999] All ER (D) 716; *R v Bristol* [2007] EWCA Crim 3214). Under section 3, the constable must make a written record of the search unless this is not practicable, and the person searched can have a copy of the record if s/he asks for one within three months.

Other statutes may also allow specific stop and search powers based on reasonable suspicion, for example, the Firearms Act 1968 section 47, Misuse of Drugs Act 1971 section 23, Terrorism Act 2000 section 43 (as amended), and Psychoactive Substances Act 2016 section 36. But they all require the PACE information to be given before a search.

It is important that stop and search powers are used fairly, effectively, and in a non-discriminatory way, but in 2011–2012 only 9 per cent of stop and searches led to arrests (www.justiceinspectorates.gov.uk) and there are concerns about their disproportionate use on racial or other grounds. In 2013, a report by HM Inspectorate of Constabulary highlighted issues in the use of stop and search powers, particularly that they seldom led to an arrest and that officers were failing to use them lawfully by stopping people only when they had reasonable grounds for suspicion (HMIC, *Stop and Search Powers: Are the Police Using Them Effectively and Fairly?* 2013; www.justiceinspectorates.gov.uk). In 2014, the Home Secretary introduced the non-mandatory Best Use of Stop and Search Scheme which aims to achieve greater transparency (requiring, for example, recording of the outcome of a stop and search and whether an arrest is made) and more positive outcomes, such as increasing the arrest ratio.

19.3.1 Suspicionless stop and search powers

An officer can stop and search a person *without* reasonable grounds for suspicion if authorised under a specific statute, chiefly to prevent terrorism or serious violence. As Lady Hale and Lord Reed observe, a 'random "suspicionless" power of stop and search carries with it the risk that it will be used in an arbitrary or discriminatory manner in individual cases', but there are also benefits in its deterrent effect precisely because of its randomness and unpredictability (*Roberts* [41]).

19.3.1.1 Counter-terrorism powers

As originally enacted, the Terrorism Act 2000 contained enhanced police powers in sections 44–47. Under section 44, if it was considered 'expedient' for preventing acts of terrorism, an assistant chief constable (or higher) could designate an area where police officers were authorised to stop and search any vehicles, drivers, passengers, and pedestrians. Under section 45, the power could only be exercised for the purpose of searching for articles that could be used in connection with terrorism, but it could be exercised without any grounds for suspecting such articles were present. Under section 45(4), the person or vehicle could be detained for as long as reasonably required for the search to be carried out. The authorisation had to be confirmed by the Home Secretary, could last up to 28 days, and could be renewed (section 46).

In *R (Gillan) v Commissioner of Police of the Metropolis*, senior police officers had given a section 44 authorisation for the Metropolitan Police to carry out random stop and searches for terrorist materials during an arms fair at Docklands in London. Mr Gillan, a student, and Ms Quinton, a journalist, were each stopped and searched; nothing was found and they applied for judicial review. The House of Lords held that the stop and search authorisations were lawful: the power to give authorisations was closely controlled, there was no deprivation of liberty under Article 5 because the claimants had only been temporarily stopped in the street, and Article 8 was not breached by a superficial search of that kind (see [14, 34–35] (Lord Bingham)). For Lord Brown, while the stop-and-search power in section 44 was a radical departure from traditional limits of police power, it was not a 'substantial invasion of our fundamental civil liberties' ([74]). For Lord Bingham, the power did not allow officers to act arbitrarily; while they did not need suspicion before acting, this was not 'a warrant to stop and search people who are obviously not terrorist suspects', but ensured that officers were not put off stopping and searching a person they suspected as a potential terrorist because they could not show reasonable grounds for their suspicion ([35]). The statute aimed to deter potential terrorists and disrupt proposed terrorist attacks, and the police needed to be able to search people acting on a hunch ([77] (Lord Brown)). In the light of this decision, Gillan and Quinton took their case to the European Court of Human Rights (ECtHR).

CASE CLOSE-UP: *GILLAN AND QUINTON v UK* [2010] ECHR 28

Here, the ECtHR found that the stop and search powers breached Article 8 ECHR because they were too wide and open to abuse, and the safeguards were not enough to protect against arbitrary interference. The court's concerns were:

- the lack of a necessity requirement for making an authorisation; 'expedient' only meant advantageous or helpful ([80]);
- the 28-day time period and geographical restrictions were not a sufficient limit because the specified area could be the whole of a police area, for example, Greater London, and the power was renewable indefinitely ([81]);
- the broad discretion given to individual police officers; although they had to comply with the PACE Code, it governed how the stop and search was carried out, rather than the decision to stop and search ([83]);
- the aim of the search—to look for articles which could be used in connection with terrorism—was very wide and could cover many articles commonly carried by people in the streets; police officers did not even need grounds for suspecting the presence of such items ([83]);
- the lack of requirement for reasonable suspicion or even subjective suspicion; the decision could be made on intuition ([83]);
- with no obligation on the officer to show a reasonable suspicion, it was difficult, if not impossible, to prove that the power was improperly exercised ([86]);
- the risks of discriminatory use and misuse against demonstrators and protesters, breaching Articles 10 and 11 ECHR ([85]).

As a result of this decision, the Terrorism Act 2000 (Remedial Order) 2011 was brought into force in March 2011 as a temporary measure, providing that the stop and search powers in sections 44–47 were no longer in effect as if they had been repealed. The Protection of Freedoms Act 2012 (sections 59 and 61) repealed and replaced sections 44–47, inserting a new section 47A into the Terrorism Act for stop and search powers in specified places. Under section 47A, there is a more demanding test for authorisation, changing from 'expedient' to 'necessary', though it still allows suspicionless stop and searches.

Another provision in the Terrorism Act 2000 which has led to legal challenges is Schedule 7 (subsequently amended by the Anti-social Behaviour, Crime and Policing Act 2014). Schedule 7 paragraph 2 allows a police or immigration officer to stop and question people passing through ports and borders as they enter or leave the UK by air or ship to determine whether they appear to fall within section 40(1)(b) (ie whether they are or have been concerned in the commission, preparation, or instigation of acts of terrorism). The officer does not need reasonable grounds for suspicion for this. There are additional powers to search and detain the person for a short time.

CASE CLOSE-UP: *BEGHAL v DIRECTOR OF PUBLIC PROSECUTIONS* [2015] UKSC 49

Under the Schedule 7 powers, Mrs Beghal was stopped and questioned for an hour and three quarters on returning to the UK from visiting her husband in France, who was in custody in relation to terrorist offences. She was prosecuted for refusing to answer certain questions.

The Supreme Court held by a majority that the prosecution did not unjustifiably interfere with her Convention rights under Article 8. In order for the questioning and search to be justified, it had to be:

- in accordance with the law (which the court referred to as 'legality');
- 'a proportionate means to a legitimate end' ([28]).

Legality

The court distinguished the Schedule 7 powers from the section 44 powers in *Gillan* and found that there were adequate safeguards against arbitrary use of the Schedule 7 powers and effective controls, including judicial review, to prevent or correct any arbitrary use of the power; legality was satisfied ([43, 45]).

- The Schedule 7 powers were more foreseeable and less arbitrary than those in *Gillan* and justified their lawfulness ([87] (Lord Neuberger and Lord Dyson)); they could only be exercised at ports and airports against people passing through the UK's borders, and could only be used for a limited purpose ([88]), whereas the section 44 power could be exercised in relation to anyone in the street.

- There have always been border controls, including searches and questioning for security purposes; intercepting, detecting, and deterring terrorists at border points is important; and there is less intrusion in stop and search at border points ([38]).

- There were restrictions on the purpose of the search, the duration of questioning, and the type of search, and individuals could consult a solicitor; see Lord Hughes' full list of effective safeguards at [43].

- The Schedule 7 powers produced useful results ([20, 89]) and could not be used against demonstrators and protesters.

Proportionality

The questioning and search powers achieved a fair balance between the rights of the individual and the interests of the community and were not an unlawful breach of Article 8 ([51]).

- Any deprivation of liberty was for no longer than necessary to complete the process, there was no requirement to attend a police station, and there was no breach of Article 5 ([56]).
- Random and unpredictable searches had benefits in detecting and preventing terrorism, and in deterring potential terrorists ([49, 78, 91]); if not allowed, the power would have to be abandoned, or exercised more invasively and extensively by questioning everyone passing through ports and airports ([91]).

Conclusion To paraphrase Lady Hale's summary, the interference was slight, the independent justification convincing, and the supervision impressive. There were substantial safeguards, the benefits were potentially substantial, and 'no equally effective but less intrusive proposal has been forthcoming' ([79]).

Beghal v UK [2019] ECHR 181

However, in *Beghal v UK* [2019] ECHR 181, the European Court of Human Rights held that the Schedule 7 powers violated Mrs Beghal's Article 8 rights because they were not in accordance with the law. The law needed to give a measure of legal protection against arbitrary interference with Convention rights ([88]). Although a requirement of reasonable suspicion was not in itself necessary to avoid arbitrariness ([94]), the court considered that the absence of needing to show reasonable suspicion, coupled with the power to examine people for up to nine hours, meant that the Schedule 7 scheme did not contain adequate legal safeguards against arbitrary interference or abuse ([109]). This was because, while being examined, people would have to answer questions without the right to have a lawyer present, and judicial review of the exercise of the power was more difficult where it did not require reasonable suspicion.

In the *Miranda case*, different arguments were raised on the Schedule 7 powers (*R (Miranda) v Secretary of State for the Home Department* [2016] EWCA Civ 6). Mr Miranda had collected encrypted storage devices containing data stolen by Edward Snowden from the US National Security Agency and was bringing them back to the UK for his spouse, Glenn Greenwald, a journalist. Some devices contained UK intelligence material and MI5 briefed UK police about his arrival. The police exercised their Schedule 7 powers to detain and question him at Heathrow Airport, and the devices were seized. In judicial review proceedings, Mr Miranda argued that:

- The police had used the powers for an improper purpose: to seize the items rather than determine whether he appeared to be a terrorist; but the Court of Appeal held that Parliament had set a low bar for exercising the power and here it had been exercised for a lawful purpose ([58]).
- The stop power disproportionately interfered with press freedom under Article 10 ECHR; but the Master of the Rolls stated that determining proportionality was fact-sensitive and the court should give substantial deference to the expertise of the police when they assess risks to national security and weigh them against competing interests ([79, 82]). In the balancing exercise, the greater the potential harm to the community if the security risk materialises, the greater the weight to be given to the community interests; here, the

national security interests outweighed Mr Miranda's Article 10 rights ([83–84]). (On a narrow point, the power was declared incompatible with Article 10 because the restrictions on the power did not effectively protect journalists' Article 10 rights.)

Similar powers have been enacted in the Counter-Terrorism and Border Security Act 2019 (Schedule 3 Part 1) giving the power to stop, question, and detain people at ports and borders to determine whether they appear to be a person who is, or has been, engaged in hostile activity whether or not there are grounds for suspecting that they are or have been engaged in hostile activity.

19.3.1.2 Preventing serious violence

Section 60 Criminal Justice and Public Order Act 1994 gives powers to stop and search pedestrians or vehicles for offensive weapons to prevent the risk of violence in a particular area. Under section 60(1), an authorisation may be made by a senior police officer if they reasonably believe that: serious violence may take place; a person is carrying a dangerous instrument or offensive weapon used in an incident of serious violence; or offensive weapons are being carried without good reason. The authorisation then allows police officers to stop and search persons or vehicles for offensive weapons or dangerous instruments (section 60(4)) without grounds for suspecting that they are carrying them (section 60(5)).

CASE CLOSE-UP: *R (ROBERTS) v COMMISSIONER OF POLICE OF THE METROPOLIS* [2016] 1 WLR 210

There was a significant problem of gang-related violence in Haringey in London, with violent crime involving firearms, knives, and other offensive weapons. Following one attempted murder and two stabbings in two days, police intelligence indicated that firearms could be used or were being moved, suggesting a risk of further violence. A senior police officer therefore considered that a section 60 authorisation was 'Proportionate, Legal, Accountable and Necessary, in order to protect members of the public from being involved/ surrounded by serious unlawful violence between opposing gang members'. Note the useful acronym PLAN, encapsulating human rights requirements.

Mrs Roberts was 37 and of African-Caribbean background; she was stopped and searched by the police acting under the section 60 authorisation after she had failed to pay a bus fare and had given a false name. The officer considered that she was holding her bag in a suspicious manner and might have an offensive weapon inside it.

The Supreme Court decided that section 60 is in accordance with the law and compatible with Article 8 ECHR. The court reasoned that it was necessary in a democratic society because:

- while the power interfered with Article 8 rights, it pursued the legitimate aim of prevention of disorder or crime ([3]);

- there were much tighter constraints on the grounds for making a section 60 authorisation than in *Gillan*, including the need for reasonable belief that the grounds for making an authorisation exist and whether it is necessary and proportionate to the threat, and the limited time and geographical area for an authorisation ([44–47]);

- other safeguards included those in section 2 of PACE, Code A, and the Metropolitan Police Service's published Standard Operating Procedures [7, 33–39, 43];

- there is legal protection and a remedy for individuals if an officer acts unlawfully [29–32, 47].

The Best Use of Stop and Search Scheme aimed to reduce section 60 suspicionless stop and searches by imposing a number of conditions which went beyond the legislation, such as requiring a reasonable belief that an incident involving serious violence *will* (rather than *may*) take place, and limiting initial authorisations to a maximum of 15 hours (rather than 24 hours). However, in 2019, as a response to an increase in violent crime, the government removed the expectation that police forces would follow those conditions when authorising section 60 searches.

19.4 Searches of property

The police may enter and search property:

- with the owner's consent;
- with a search warrant;
- without a warrant in specified circumstances.

Sections 8–16 of PACE relate to police powers to enter and search premises where a search warrant is required. The police apply to a judge or magistrate for a warrant to search property and must make a full and frank disclosure of the facts (*R v Lewes Crown Court ex p Hill* (1991) 93 Cr App R 60; but see *R v Zinga and Pillai* [2012] EWCA Crim 2357 where a warrant was upheld despite a police officer's omission to tell the magistrates that a private prosecution by Virgin Media was expected, because the appellant had not shown that the magistrates would have refused the warrant had they known). However, misrepresentations and inaccurate information leading to a defective search warrant make the search and seizure unlawful (*R (Tchenguiz) v Director of SFO* [2012] EWHC 2254 (Admin)). A subsequent search of someone's home must be reasonable and proportionate because it interferes with home and private life under Article 8 ECHR (*Williams v Chief Constable of Dyfed Powys Police* [2010] EWCA 1627; *Keegan v UK* (2007) 44 EHRR 33).

Under section 17 of PACE, police have power to enter and search without a warrant:

- to make an arrest for specified offences if they reasonably believe the person is on the premises;
- to recapture a person;
- to save life or limb or prevent serious damage to property (see *Hobson v Chief Constable of Cheshire* [2003] EWHC 3011 (Admin)).

Section 18 allows entry and search after the occupier's arrest.

Entering without a warrant simply because of concern for a person's welfare is not a sufficient ground (*Syed v DPP* [2010] EWHC 81 (Admin), [2010] 1 Cr App R 34); nor is entering to investigate whether there might be a breach of the peace (*Friswell v Chief Constable of Essex* [2004] EWHC 3009 (QB)). Unlawful entry can result in claims for trespass, false imprisonment, and breach of Article 8 ECHR. See George Thomas and Aaron Rathmell, 'Can I Come In? The Perils of Summary Entry to a Home' (15 September 2014, at ukpolicelawblog.com/). Statutes continuously update specific search powers; for example, sections 37–39 of the Psychoactive Substances Act 2016 provide powers to enter and search vehicles, vessels, aircraft, and premises for relevant evidence, and the Policing and Crime Act 2017 section 163 provides the police with powers to enter premises to search for and seize cancelled UK passports and invalid foreign travel documents to disrupt travel for counter-terrorism purposes. Section 53 Offensive Weapons Act 2019 allows police officers to enter and search schools or further education premises and any person on them for a corrosive substance.

19.5 Arrest

Sections 24–33 of PACE (as amended by the Serious Organised Crime and Police Act 2005) concern powers of arrest. Under s 24, a constable may arrest without a warrant:

- anyone who is about to commit, or is in the act of committing, an offence; or
- where s/he has reasonable grounds for suspecting someone is about to commit, or is committing, an offence. Reasonable grounds for suspicion sets a low bar, which is much lower than the evidence required for a conviction and may even be based on 'assertions that turn out to be wrong' (*Parker v Chief Constable of Essex* [2018] EWCA 2788 (Civ) [115] (Sir Brian Leveson P)).

To exercise these powers of arrest, section 24(4) requires that the officer must also have reasonable grounds for believing that an arrest is necessary for any of the reasons in section 24(5); this was an amendment made in 2005 by the Serious Organised Crime and Police Act. So the constable must *subjectively* believe that arrest is necessary and, *objectively*, that belief must be reasonable. The necessity requirement 'imposes a comparatively high hurdle' (*Rashid v Chief Constable of West Yorkshire* [2020] EWHC 2522 (QB) [25] (Lavender J); *Commissioner of Police of the Metropolis v MR* [2019] EWHC 888 (QB) [47] (Thornton J)) and 'tightens up the accountability of police officers' (*Hayes v Chief Constable of Merseyside* [2011] EWCA Civ 911 [15] (Hughes LJ)). Furthermore, Code G requires arrest to be exercised in a 'non-discriminatory and proportionate manner'.

The officer must inform the person that they are under arrest and why, otherwise the arrest is not lawful (section 28 PACE; *R v Iqbal* [2011] EWCA Crim 273)—unless the person escapes. Under section 3 Criminal Law Act 1967, police officers may use reasonable force to prevent crime or assist in the lawful arrest of offenders, including where a suspect tries to escape or becomes violent when being arrested or taken into custody. Section 117 of PACE also allows the use of reasonable force in exercising any PACE power. However, police officers may be prosecuted for using excessive force. Under the Police Act 1996 section 89(2), it is an offence to resist or wilfully obstruct a police officer in the execution of their duty; a person commits an offence if they resist a lawful arrest, but no offence is committed if the arrest is not lawful. If an arrest is unlawful, and the person is taken into custody, they will have an action for false imprisonment (*Christie v Leachinsky* [1947] AC 573). The police have power to search the person when arrested and they are then normally taken to a police station for interview.

19.6 Detention and questioning

Part IV of PACE deals with detention, and Part V with questioning and treatment. Code C sets out the legal duties of the custody officer who is specifically responsible for the custody and protection of detainees, including undertaking risk assessments about them. The custody officer is responsible for the custody record's accuracy and completeness, and decides whether there is sufficient evidence to charge the person with an offence. Detainees must be dealt with expeditiously so if the custody officer decides there is not sufficient evidence, the person arrested must be released as soon as the need for detention no longer applies. The custody officer may authorise the person to be detained without being charged if there are reasonable grounds for believing that it is necessary to preserve or obtain evidence (section 37 PACE).

When in custody, a person can ask for someone to be informed of their arrest (section 56) and is allowed to ask for a solicitor (section 58), but both can be delayed if the suspect has been arrested in connection with an indictable offence and exercising the right may lead to interference with evidence, alerting other suspects, causing interference with or injury to witnesses, or interfering with recovering evidence (section 56(5) and (5A); section 58(8) and (8A)). The maximum period of detention without charge is usually 24 hours from the relevant time (normally the time of arrival) but may be extended for up to 36 hours (sections 41 and 42); a magistrate must authorise any extension beyond that. Under counter-terrorism legislation, the period for detention without charge can be crucial to allow questioning and enable evidence to be gathered, and it has changed over the years: after the 7/7 London bombings, under the Terrorism Act 2006, terrorist suspects could be detained without charge for 28 days (Tony Blair had wanted a 90-day limit but this was defeated during the legislative process), but the Protection of Freedoms Act 2012 section 57 reduced it to 14 days. Before being interviewed to assess whether there is sufficient evidence to charge them with an offence, the person must be cautioned (told that they have the right to legal representation and why they are being interviewed; see PACE Code C). Interviews are usually recorded. However, if a confession is obtained by oppression or is made unreliable by virtue of anything said or done, a court must not allow it to be given in evidence (section 76(2)), and the court *may* refuse to allow evidence if it would have an adverse effect on the fairness of the proceedings (section 78).

19.7 Retention of data

Storing data on a police database about individuals who have come to the attention of the police, even if not charged with or convicted of an offence, can be a valuable aid to policing and intelligence. However, it means that the state is retaining personal details without consent and which may sometimes be disclosed to others, such as potential employers. It can also include retention of very personal information in the form of DNA samples and fingerprints. The distinction between data which has been obtained by an intrusive method such as DNA sampling and information which has been obtained non-intrusively can be significant in determining whether there has been a violation of Article 8. Processing and retaining data for law enforcement purposes is also governed by the Data Protection Act 2018 (see sections 35 and 39) and data should be kept for no longer than necessary.

Retaining DNA samples and fingerprints Originally under section 64 of PACE, where a person was not convicted of an offence, retention of their fingerprints and DNA samples (biometric data) was unlawful and material had to be destroyed. PACE was then amended by section 82 Criminal Justice and Police Act 2001 to allow their retention for the prevention or detection of crime, criminal investigations, or the conduct of a prosecution, and they only had to be destroyed in exceptional circumstances. In *R (S) v Chief Constable of South Yorkshire* [2004] UKHL 39, the House of Lords held that this did not breach the claimant's rights under Article 8, but in *S and Marper v UK* (2009) 48 EHRR 50, the ECtHR disagreed: keeping fingerprints and DNA samples indefinitely from suspects who have not been convicted of a criminal offence is a breach of their rights under Article 8 because of:

- the unique personal information and how it might be used ([75]);

- the 'blanket and indiscriminate nature' of the retention powers ([119]);
- its failure to strike a fair balance between the competing interests; the retention was a disproportionate interference with their right to respect for private life and not necessary in a democratic society [125].

The court reinforced the requirement for clear, detailed rules on the scope and application of measures and minimum safeguards about duration of retention and so on, to sufficiently guarantee against the risk of abuse and arbitrariness ([99]).

S and Marper was followed in *R (GC) v Commissioner of Police of the Metropolis* [2011] UKSC 21, [2011] 1 WLR 1230 where the Supreme Court held that police guidelines on retention were unlawful. Similarly, retaining custody photographs of people who were not convicted of an offence was a breach of Article 8 (*R (RMC and FJ) v Commissioner of Police of the Metropolis* [2012] EWHC 1681 (Admin)).

PACE was subsequently amended by the Protection of Freedoms Act 2012 to reduce the periods for retention of biometric data, allowing only the indefinite retention of data of people convicted of a recordable offence (which is a crime for which an individual could be sentenced to imprisonment), and even then with some exceptions. These amendments applied to the DNA and fingerprints retention scheme in England and Wales. However, the law was not changed in Northern Ireland where photographs, fingerprints, a DNA sample and profile were taken from everyone arrested for a recordable offence and retained indefinitely. The European Court of Human Rights court held in *Gaughran v UK* [2020] ECHR 144 that this indefinite retention of data violated Article 8 because of its indiscriminate nature. The data could be retained even if an offence was spent (convictions can be removed from a person's criminal record after a certain length of time); there was no reference to the seriousness of the offence or the need for indefinite retention; there was no real possibility of review. This failed to strike a fair balance between the competing public and private interests, and retaining the data was a disproportionate interference with the applicant's Article 8 rights and not necessary in a democratic society ([96–97]).

On a related note, the use of live automated facial recognition technology (AFR) by South Wales Police for identification purposes was held to violate Article 8 in *R (Edward Bridges) v Chief Constable of South Wales* [2020] EWCA Civ 1058. They used a system where surveillance cameras capture images of members of the public which are then compared with digital images of people on a police watchlist, but the Court of Appeal held that too much discretion was left to individual police officers as to who could be placed on a watchlist and where AFR could be deployed [91], so the interference with the appellant's Article 8 rights was not in accordance with the law. By not sufficiently setting out when those discretionary powers could be exercised by the police, the current policies did not have 'the necessary quality of law' ([94]). Moreover, South Wales Police did not comply with the public sector equality duty in section 149 Equality Act 2010 to make sure that the software used did not have a racial or gender bias.

Retaining details of old cautions/convictions In *R (T) v Secretary of State for the Home Department* [2014] UKSC 35, [2015] AC 49, T was given police warnings after stealing two bicycles when he was 11 years old and JB received a police caution after stealing a pack of false fingernails from a store. The warnings and caution were disclosed on criminal record checks when T applied for a sport studies course and JB completed a training course for employment as a carer, which adversely affected their prospects. The Supreme Court held that the *automatic* retention of data about police cautions and old convictions, and their *compulsory* disclosure in criminal records checks to potential employers, meant there was no discretion about what to disclose. This was not 'in accordance with the law'. Flexibility was needed as a safeguard against automatic operation of the rule to avoid any unjustified (disproportionate) interference with Article 8 rights; for example, only what was relevant to a potential employer might be disclosed (see [114] (Lord Reed)). The Police Act 1997 Part V which regulated criminal record checks was declared incompatible with Article 8. See also *R (L) v Commissioner of Police of the Metropolis* [2009] UKSC 3; *MM v UK* [2012] ECHR 1906.

The Police Act was then amended by secondary legislation (the Police Act 1977 (Criminal Records Certificates: Relevant Matters) (Amendment) (England and Wales) Order 2013 (SI 2013/1200)), which introduced a filtering process. In 2019, the Supreme Court held by a majority that the schemes governing the disclosure of criminal records under the Rehabilitation of Offenders Act 1974 (as amended) and the Police Act 1997 (as amended) were in accordance with the law for the purposes of Article 8 ECHR (*In the matter of an application by Lorraine Gallagher for Judicial Review (Northern Ireland); R (P and others) v Secretary of State for the Home Department* [2019] UKSC 3, [2020] AC 185). This was because the legislation exactly defined the categories of disclosable convictions and cautions, and distinguished between different categories of conviction or caution, depending on the seriousness of the offence, the offender's age at the time, and the number of years which had passed [42, 44–45]. The legislation was also proportionate *except* for two provisions:

(1) the disclosure of multiple convictions rule, which required disclosing where a person has more than one conviction of *any* nature, whatever the similarity, number, or time between offences: 'A rule whose impact on individuals is as capricious as this cannot be regarded as a necessary or proportionate way of disclosing to potential employers criminal records indicating a propensity to offend' [63] (Lord Sumption).

(2) The provision on disclosure of warnings and reprimands for young offenders was wrongly included among offences which must be disclosed because warnings and reprimands were used as an alternative to prosecution and their purpose would be undermined by disclosure [64].

Lord Kerr, dissenting, held that the scheme did not satisfy the legality test because of insufficient safeguards [162] and the disclosure of the criminal records of the individuals concerned was disproportionate [188–190].

Retaining information about individuals' activities The police have a common law power to obtain and store information for policing purposes including the maintenance of public order and the prevention and detection of crime. The Article 8 implications of retaining information on a police database about individuals' activities where there was no criminal conviction were scrutinised by the Supreme Court in *Catt and T.*

> **Q** **CASE CLOSE-UP:** *R (CATT AND T) v COMMISSIONER OF POLICE OF THE METROPOLIS* **[2015] UKSC 9**
>
> Mr Catt, a 91-year-old seasoned protester, complained about the retention by police of information about his participation in political protests since 2005 (he had not been convicted of any offences). Ms T objected to the retention of a police harassment notice about a minor incident. They argued that, while it was lawful for the police to make a record of

the events when they happened, keeping the information on a searchable database interfered with their right to respect for their private life under Article 8 ECHR.

The Supreme Court held by a majority of 4 to 1 that:

- the state's systematic collection and retention of information about Mr Catt and Ms T interfered with their rights under Article 8 because it was personal information;

- but there were adequate safeguards in place, so collecting and retaining the information was in accordance with the law for the purpose of Article 8(2);

- and the interference with their Article 8 rights by retaining the information was proportionate to the objective of maintaining public order and preventing or detecting crime (see [17] (Lord Sumption)).

Important factors which justified the retention of information were:

- The information stored was not intimate or sensitive like DNA material or fingerprints, and had not been discovered by intrusive procedures. It was—in Mr Catt's case—information based on what uniformed police officers had observed about his activities in public places ([26]), and retaining it was justified by the legitimate requirements of police intelligence-gathering ([34–35]).

- Distinguishing this case from *R (T) v Secretary of State for the Home Department*, the information here was not available to potential employers and there were 'robust procedures' for ensuring that the restrictions were observed [27].

- Information about a person attending a demonstration did not suggest suspicion or guilt and was not used for political purposes.

- It was not retained for longer than needed for maintaining public order and preventing or detecting crime and was periodically reviewed for keeping or deleting 'according to rational and proportionate criteria' [27]; although the length of time before the police deleted Ms T's harassment notice was at the far end of the spectrum, it was not too long ([44]).

- There were adequate safeguards to protect against arbitrary behaviour by the police (such as the Data Protection Act 1998, the Code of Practice issued by the Home Secretary, and the Guidance on the Management of Police Information issued by the Association of Chief Police Officers).

Lord Toulson, dissenting, took the view that retention of the data was disproportionate.

CATT v UK [2019] ECHR 76

However, in *Catt v UK* [2019] ECHR 76, the European Court of Human Rights held that the collection and retention of data on Mr Catt was an unlawful interference with his Article 8 rights because:

- There was no clear and coherent legal basis for collecting and storing the data. Mr Catt's details were held on a 'domestic extremism database' but 'domestic extremism' was loosely defined. The criteria used by the police to govern the collection of the data were ambiguous so it was difficult to determine the exact scope and content of the data being collected for the database ([97, 105]).

- The Court accepted that there was a pressing need to collect the personal data about Mr Catt ([117]) but there was not a pressing need to keep it ([119]). There were no rules setting a definite maximum time limit on its retention. The only time limit was that the data would be held for at least six years, when it would be reviewed ([120]). So the data could potentially be retained indefinitely (though would not be disclosed to third parties). Although Mr Catt was able to apply for the deletion of his data, this was a limited safeguard because the request was refused and no explanation was given for its retention even though he was not considered a danger to anyone ([122]). There was also more personal data held on Mr Catt than revealed at the time of the UK court proceedings ([115]). Effective procedural safeguards were needed to allow data to be deleted when its retention became disproportionate ([119]).

- The decisions to retain Mr Catt's personal data did not take into account the heightened level of protection of personal data revealing political opinion ([112]). Engaging in peaceful protest is specifically protected under Article 11 ECHR ([123]).

- Retention of Mr Catt's data had not been shown to be absolutely necessary, nor for the purposes of a particular inquiry ([124]).

- Deleting the data would not be so burdensome as to render it unreasonable ([127]).

The court in *R (II) v Commissioner of Police of the Metropolis* [2020] EWHC 2528 (Admin) emphasised that the length of proportionate retention is fact-specific so will turn on the facts of each case. Here, the continued retention of a 16-year-old's personal data relating to an alleged risk of radicalisation when he was 11 was disproportionate and in breach of Article 8. The police had not shown a purpose for continuing to hold his personal data.

 SUMMARY

Where police powers interfere with Article 8 rights:

- The interference must be justified by being in accordance with the law and necessary in a democratic society: does it pursue a legitimate aim such as the prevention and detection of crime? Are there adequate safeguards against abuse or arbitrary, disproportionate application? Do rigid rules need more flexibility? Does a wide discretion need more safeguards?

- Is the interference proportionate? Weigh up the competing public and private interests.

19.8 Public order powers and freedom of assembly

Freedom of assembly is the right to attend meetings and join demonstrations and processions as long as they are peaceful (*Beatty v Gillbanks* (1882) 9 QBD 308). The common law right to peaceful protest has been described as 'a manifestation of the importance attached by the common law to both the right to protest and free speech' (*R v Roberts (Richard)* [2018] EWCA Crim 2739, [2019] 1 WLR 2577 [37] (Lord Burnett CJ, Phillips, and Cutts JJ)).

 THINKING POINT

Note the link between the right to peaceful protest and freedom of expression.

The law must balance the freedom of individuals to take part in public protests and demonstrations with restrictions to keep the peace and good public order. As Lord Sumption notes, 'Political protest is a basic right which the common law has always recognised, within broad limits directed to keeping the peace and protecting the rights and property of others' (*R (Catt) v Commissioner of Police of the Metropolis* [19]). Freedom of assembly and association, and the right of peaceful protest, is protected by Article 11 ECHR although the right may be restricted as set out in Article 11(2).

Article 11

1. Everyone has the right to freedom of peaceful assembly and to freedom of association with others . . .

2. No restrictions shall be placed on the exercise of these rights other than such as are prescribed by law and are necessary in a democratic society in the interests of national security or public safety, for the prevention of disorder or crime, for the protection of health or morals or for the protection of the rights and freedoms of others. This Article shall not prevent the imposition of lawful restrictions on the exercise of these rights by members of the armed forces, of the police or of the administration of the State.

The police have statutory and common law powers to enable them to keep good public order. The Public Order Act 1986 created public order offences including riot, violent disorder, affray (unlawful fighting), and using threatening, abusive, or insulting words or behaviour likely to cause or causing harassment, alarm, or distress (see sections 1–5). The Act also sets out police powers in relation to controlling demonstrations and public meetings which have the potential to conflict with Article 11 rights.

We now examine some of the restrictions imposed by UK law on the right to peaceful protest.

19.8.1 **Statutory powers**

The first Public Order Act was passed in 1936 to deal with disturbances resulting from marches by British Nazi movements in the East End of London in the 1930s, particularly Oswald Mosley's Blackshirts, while the Public Order Act 1986 was enacted after serious public disturbances in the 1980s such as the Brixton riots in 1981. The 1986 Act (as amended) is an important statutory restriction on freedom of assembly and gives the police wide powers in relation to public processions and assemblies in Part 2 of the Act (an assembly is a static meeting or gathering while a procession is moving).

Public processions

Section 11: Written notice must be given to the police for public processions intended to show support for or opposition to the views or actions of any person or body of persons, to publicise a cause or campaign, or mark or commemorate an event, unless it is not reasonably practicable.

Section 12: A senior police officer can set conditions on the conduct of an ongoing or intended procession where s/he reasonably believes it might result in serious public disorder, serious damage to property, or serious disruption to the life of the community, or the organisers aim to intimidate others. It is an offence to organise or take part in a public procession and knowingly fail to comply with a condition, unless the failure arose from circumstances beyond their control (section 12(4) and 12(5)).

Section 13: Allows the police to apply to the local council for all public processions or a particular type of procession to be banned for up to three months; in London, the order is made by the Commissioner with the Home Secretary's consent.

Public assemblies

Section 14: A senior police officer can impose certain conditions on a public assembly (such as maximum duration or number of people present) where s/he reasonably believes it might result in serious public disorder, serious damage to property, or serious disruption to the life of the community, or the organisers aim to intimidate others. Where an assembly is actually taking place, those conditions may be imposed by the most senior police officer present at the scene; for an assembly intended to be held, they may be imposed by the chief officer of police (section 14(2)). It is an offence to organise or take part in an assembly and knowingly fail to comply with a section 14 condition unless that failure arose from circumstances beyond a person's control (section 14(4) and 14(5)).

'Public assembly' was interpreted as meaning one public assembly, not separate gatherings, in *R (Jones & Others) v Metropolitan Police Commissioner* [2019] EWHC 2957 (Admin). Extinction Rebellion, an environmental pressure movement, intended to hold protests at multiple sites in London between 7 and 19 October 2019, known as the 'Autumn Uprising', with the aim of causing disruption and inconvenience to the public in order to bring their aims to the attention of politicians. Believing that this was an assembly that may result in serious disruption to the life of the community, a senior police officer imposed a condition that any assembly linked to Extinction Rebellion must end by 2100 hours on 14 October 2019. The claimants brought a claim for judicial review, arguing that the condition was not validly imposed because it treated the Extinction Rebellion protests as one public assembly. The High Court agreed that the decision to impose the condition was unlawful because the protests were not a public assembly at the scene of which the senior officer was present on 14 October 2019, so there was no power to impose a condition. Section 14(1) required a 'scene' and 'a public place', not a series of different scenes and separate locations across the police areas ([66]). A public assembly must be in a particular location and be a particular assembly ([67–68]). The condition also prohibited intended future assemblies but under section 14(1), there is no power to prohibit, only to impose conditions on, gatherings that have not yet begun ([70–71]).

Section 14A: Gives the police power to ban intended trespassory assemblies, that is, gatherings held on land to which the public has no access or restricted right of access. The chief officer of police may apply to the local council for an order prohibiting all trespassory assemblies in the area for a specified period.

Section 14C: Gives police officers power to stop people going to a trespassory assembly.

Section 16: A public assembly means two or more people in a public place wholly or partly in the open air (as amended by Anti-Social Behaviour Act 2003).

Public protests, by their nature, take place in public places, including the streets. It is an offence to wilfully obstruct free passage along the highway without lawful authority or excuse (Highways Act 1980 section 137), but the courts recognise the public right of peaceful assembly on the highway. *DPP v Jones* [1999] 2 AC 240 made it clear that the right to use the highway extends beyond passing and re-passing along it, and could include a peaceful protest on a roadside verge near Stonehenge which did not unreasonably interfere with or obstruct the highway. See also *Hirst v Chief Constable of West Yorkshire* (1987) 85 Cr App R 143, where animal rights campaigners giving out leaflets outside a furrier's shop was a reasonable use of the highway. However, the right of lawful assembly and protest on the highway did not protect the Occupy Movement's long-term protest camp in the churchyard of St Paul's Cathedral (*City of London v Samede* [2012] EWCA Civ 160); here, the protesters' Article 10 and 11 ECHR rights were outweighed by the freedoms and rights of others, the interests of public health and public safety, the prevention of disorder and crime, and the need to protect the environment, and the City was entitled to an order for possession.

For obvious reasons, Parliament Square is a popular place for protests. Police officers have the power to direct people to stop them engaging in prohibited activities in Parliament Square, such as protesting through using amplified noise equipment and pitching tents for long-term protests (section 143 Police Reform and Social Responsibility Act 2011). See *R (Haw) v Secretary of State for Home Department* [2006] EWCA Civ 532, a case brought under the now repealed section 132 of the Serious Organised Crime and Police Act 2005.

19.8.2 Common law powers: breach of the peace

It is the duty of every police officer to do all that is reasonably necessary to prevent a breach of the peace. A breach of the peace 'involves actual harm done either to a person or to a person's property in his presence or some other form of violent disorder or disturbance and itself necessarily involves a criminal offence' (*R (Laporte) v Chief Constable of Gloucestershire Constabulary* [2006] UKHL 55, [2007] 2 AC 105 [111] (Lord Brown); *R v Howell* [1982] QB 416, p 427). A police officer—and an ordinary citizen—has a common law power to arrest anyone who is committing, or whom they reasonably believe to be about to commit, a breach of the peace (*Albert v Lavin* [1982] AC 546). The requirements are:

- A breach of the peace must be occurring in the police officer's presence, or if it has occurred is likely to be renewed, or is about to occur (see *Laporte* [29] (Lord Bingham)).

- 'There must . . . be a sufficiently real and present threat to the peace to justify the extreme step of depriving of his liberty a citizen who is not at the time acting unlawfully' (*Foulkes v Chief Constable of Merseyside Police* [1998] EWCA Civ 938, [1998] 3 All ER 705, p 711 (Beldam LJ)). Lord Rodger has noted the exceptional nature of arrest to prevent a breach of the peace, which 'if not kept within proper bounds . . . could be a recipe for officious and unjustified intervention in other people's affairs'; this explains the requirement that a breach should be imminent (*Laporte* [62]).

- An officer's belief that a breach of the peace is imminent must be reasonable (*Redmond-Bate v DPP* [1999] EWHC Admin 733).

- The arrest or other preventive action is only lawful if it is a necessary and proportionate response. Are there other ways of preventing the breach than by an arrest?

CASE CLOSE-UP: *R (HICKS) v METROPOLITAN POLICE COMMISSIONER* [2017] UKSC 9, [2017] AC 256

Before the wedding of the Duke and Duchess of Cambridge in 2011, the police had intelligence that activities aimed at disrupting the celebrations were being planned through social websites. The appellants had been arrested to prevent an imminent breach of the peace and were detained, then released. The Supreme Court held that the preventative arrest and detention was lawful and in accordance with Article 5(1)(c) ECHR. The decisions to arrest and detain were taken in good faith, were proportionate to the situation, and were not arbitrary. If the police could not lawfully arrest and detain a person for a relatively short time where reasonably considered necessary to prevent imminent violence, it would severely hamper their ability to maintain public order and safety at mass public events ([31] (Lord Toulson)).

The individuals concerned took their case to the European Court of Human Rights (*Eiseman-Renyard and Others v UK* [2019] ECHR 237) but the court held that the UK courts had struck a fair balance between the importance of the right to liberty and the importance of preventing the applicants from disturbing public order and causing a danger to public safety.

The police can prevent people from going to a place to take part in a procession or assembly if they reasonably believe there is a real risk of a breach of the peace; this includes picket lines. In *Moss v MacLachlan* [1985] IRLR 76, police were trying to stop striking miners from joining pickets at collieries during the miners' strike in 1984. They lawfully stopped a group of 60 miners from proceeding to a colliery because there was a substantial risk of violence. Four miners disobeyed the police and continued their journey, and their convictions for obstructing the police in the execution of their duty were upheld (see also *Piddington v Bates* [1960] 3 All ER 660).

However, in the leading case of *R (Laporte) v Chief Constable of Gloucestershire Constabulary*, protesters were travelling to Fairford airbase to protest against the Iraq war. Police heard that three coaches were travelling to the base with hard-line protesters, known as the Wombles, on board. Laporte, a peaceful protestor, was travelling on one of them. The police stopped and searched the coaches and sent all three back to London with a police escort to prevent a future breach of the peace. The House of Lords held that a breach of the peace was not imminent when the coaches were stopped and searched therefore it was disproportionate for the police to restrict Laporte's right to protest. Lord Mance stated that the reasonable apprehension of an imminent breach of the peace was an important threshold requirement ([141]) and here, the action taken was not justified. Turning the coaches back to London was general and indiscriminate, and neither reasonable nor proportionate ([152–153]).

SUMMARY

The important test is whether a breach of the peace is at least imminent. The actions of the police must be reasonable and proportionate, balancing the rights of protesters with those affected by the protest and maintaining public order.

THINKING POINT

In *Duncan v Jones* [1936] 1 KB 218, Mrs Duncan was going to address a meeting in a street opposite a training centre for the unemployed. She had addressed a meeting there over a year earlier and a disturbance had resulted. Police believed that a breach of the peace might occur and ordered Mrs Duncan to hold the meeting in another street. She refused and was arrested and convicted for obstructing a police officer in the execution of his duty. The arrest was held to be lawful.

Applying the tests above, do you think this case would be decided in the same way today?

In *Austin v Metropolitan Police Commissioner* [2009] 1 AC 564, the House of Lords held that the police had the power to detain demonstrators and passers-by in a cordon for seven hours to maintain the peace during a violent 'May Day Monopoly' protest; this is known as 'kettling'. If crowd control measures by the police were in good faith, proportionate to the situation, and enforced for no longer than reasonably necessary, there was no breach of Article 5 ECHR ([33–34, 37] (Lord Hope)). Article 5 provides that no one shall be deprived of their liberty except in the cases specified in the Article—which do not include acting in the interests of public safety or protection of public order—but Lord Hope drew a distinction between the right to liberty under Article 5(1), which is absolute, and freedom of movement, which may be restricted in the interests of public safety or to maintain public order ([16]). While the appellant's freedom of movement was restricted by the police cordon, this did not amount to detention within Article 5 ([64] (Lord Neuberger)).

In *Austin v UK* [2012] ECHR 459, the ECtHR agreed that 'kettling' during the demonstration did not amount to deprivation of liberty; in dangerous and volatile conditions, this had been the least intrusive and most effective way of protecting the public from violence and the crowd could not safely have been dispersed any earlier. See, however, limitations on going beyond these containment powers in *Mengesha v Commissioner of Police of the Metropolis* [2013] EWHC 1695 (Admin); see also *Wright v MPC* [2013] EWHC 2739 (QB), which emphasised the three-point test of reasonableness, necessity, and proportionality.

19.9 Police powers and the coronavirus emergency

Emergency measures—such as restrictions on movement and gatherings, and the requirements to wear face coverings and self-isolate—have been introduced to protect public health during the coronavirus pandemic, and specific powers have been given to the police to enforce them. In doing so, the police have followed 'the 4 Es' approach: engaging with individuals, explaining how they think they are breaking the rules, encouraging them to change their behaviour to reduce the risk to public safety and health, and enforcing the rules where people still do not comply (www.police.uk/advice/advice-and-information/c19/coronavirus-covid-19/coronavirus-covid-19-police-powers/). Enforcement powers include telling people to disperse where the police suspect an illegal gathering (eg regulation 9(3) Health Protection (Coronavirus, Restrictions) (All Tiers) (England) Regulations 2020), or imposing a fine on people aged 18 or over by issuing

Fixed Penalty Notices. A person who continues to ignore police instructions can be arrested if it is proportionate and the officer has reasonable grounds for believing that it is necessary to maintain public health or public order (see regulation 10(5) Health Protection (Coronavirus, Restrictions) (All Tiers) (England) Regulations 2020). The police can use reasonable force if necessary, for example, to remove a person from a gathering that contravenes the restrictions (Health Protection (Coronavirus, Restrictions) (All Tiers) (England) Regulations 2020 regulation 9(4)). Under current lockdown regulations in England, police officers do not have power to enter private property where they suspect laws may be being broken unless they have consent.

See House of Commons Library Briefing Paper Number 9024, 17 December 2020, *Coronavirus: Enforcing restrictions*, Jennifer Brown.

19.10 Accountability

The mechanisms for ensuring the accountability of police officers include:

- Complaints about the misuse of police powers to the relevant chief constable or Commissioner (each police force has a professional standards department which deals with complaints).

- Elected Police and Crime Commissioners who are responsible for holding their local police force to account and reviewing the complaint handling of their forces (see section 4.8.1.5). In London, this is carried out by the Mayor's Office for Policing and Crime in relation to the Metropolitan Police; the City of London Corporation oversees the City of London Police; and policing in Greater Manchester is overseen by the mayor. In both London and Manchester, the Deputy Mayors for Policing and Crime are specifically responsible for ensuring oversight of the police.

- Her Majesty's Inspectorate of Constabulary and Fire and Rescue Services, an independent body which inspects and reports on police forces across England and Wales, the Police Service of Northern Ireland, and other bodies including the National Crime Agency. HM Chief Inspector reports to the Home Secretary annually on the efficiency and effectiveness of police forces in England and Wales; the Home Secretary lays the reports before Parliament, where issues can be scrutinised by the Home Affairs Select Committee (see section 54 Police Act 1996).

- The Independent Office for Police Conduct (IOPC) oversees the police complaints system in England and Wales. It replaced the Independent Police Complaints Commission in January 2018 and investigates incidents such as deaths or serious injury in police custody or through use of firearms by police, and allegations of misconduct. Its investigations may result in disciplinary proceedings against an officer. For more information, see www. policeconduct.gov.uk.

- The Policing and Crime Act 2017 introduced changes to the police complaints system to ensure speedier and more streamlined investigations; it increased the IOPC's powers and independence, including allowing it to start its own investigations without referral by a police force and to have the final decision as to whether an officer should face a misconduct hearing. Decisions of police complaints bodies can be judicially reviewed (see, eg, *R (Mackaill) v Independent Police Complaints Commission* [2014] EWHC 3170 (Admin); *R (Green) v Independent Police Complaints Commission* [2016] EWHC 2078 (Admin); *R (Birks) v Commissioner of Police of the Metropolis* [2018] EWHC 807 (Admin)).

For further details, see *R (Roberts) v MPC* [2015] UKSC 79 [30–32].

There is also accountability through the courts, and recent decisions have been resetting and cementing the boundaries of principles regarding police functions.

Public law duties In *Commissioner of Police of the Metropolis v DSD* [2018] UKSC 11, the Supreme Court held that serious failures by the police to investigate crimes effectively can give rise to liability under the Human Rights Act. Two of John Worboys' victims, DSD and NBV, successfully claimed that Scotland Yard had failed to conduct effective investigations into sexual attacks carried out by Worboys. The court held that there is an operational duty on state authorities to investigate ill treatment, such as sexual assault, amounting to a breach of Article 3 (freedom from inhuman or degrading treatment), but emphasised that the police are not under a general common law duty of care in relation to how they investigate crime.

▶ **CROSS REFERENCE**

For more detail on the *Worboys cases*, see section 15.3.3 and 16.4.1

Private law duties According to the *Hill* principle (from *Hill v Chief Constable of West Yorkshire Police* ([1989] AC 53)), the police do not have liability for negligent acts done in the course of investigating and suppressing crime. This was sometimes regarded as a principle of general immunity from negligence claims but this perception was overturned by *Robinson v Chief Constable of West Yorkshire* [2018] UKSC 4. An elderly lady was injured by police officers who were carrying out an arrest of another person, and sued for negligence. The Supreme Court held that there is no general rule that the police are not under *any* duty of care when preventing and investigating crime (see [55] (Lord Reed)). They can be sued for causing injury to a member of the public through lack of care. As Lord Mance expressed it: 'we should now recognise the direct physical interface between the police and the public, in the course of an arrest placing an innocent passer-by or bystander at risk, as falling within a now established area of general police liability for positive negligent conduct which foreseeably and directly inflicts physical injury on the public' ([97]). (See also *Michael v Chief Constable of South Wales Police* [2015] UKSC 2.)

? Questions

Self-test questions

1. What is the most significant statute in relation to police powers and why?

2. Most stop and search powers require reasonable suspicion; what does this require?

3. What issues are raised by 'suspicionless' stop and searches?

4. How did the court in *Roberts* test whether section 60 was in accordance with the law?

5. Why did the ECtHR in *S and Marper* decide that retention of DNA and fingerprints breached Article 8?

6. Is section 14 Public Order Act 1986 a lawful restriction on Article 11 ECHR?

7. Why was the police action in *Laporte* disproportionate?

8. What is the role of the IOPC?

Exam question

Selecting relevant examples of statute and case law, discuss how effectively UK law safeguards against arbitrary application of police powers.

Further reading

Books

Card, R. and English, J. *Police Law* (15th edn, Oxford: Oxford University Press 2017).
A practical text; see the chapters on police powers and PACE

Fenwick, H. *Fenwick on Civil Liberties and Human Rights* (5th edn, Abingdon: Routledge 2016).
See Part IV for police powers

Journal articles

Davenport, A. 'Apprehended Breach of the Peace: Lawfulness and Proportionality of Preventive Action' (2007) 71(3) JCL 211.
Case comment on *Laporte*

Glover, R. 'Keeping the Peace and Preventive Justice—A New Test for Breach of the Peace?' (2018) (July) Public Law 444.
Critical analysis of the law on breach of the peace

Hepple, B. 'The Right to Privacy and Crime Detection' (2009) 68 Cambridge Law Journal 253.
Case comment on *S and Marper*

Johnson, H. 'Data Retention—Scope of Police Powers' (2015) 20(2) Communications Law 56.
Analysis of the *Catt case*

Marshall, K.L. 'Reformed offenders, criminal record disclosures and employment' (Case Comment) (2019) 78(3) Cambridge Law Journal 503.
Case comment on the *P and Others case*

Martin, S. 'The Meaning of "Public Assembly": Policing Protest in the Twenty-First Century' (2020) 79(1) Cambridge Law Journal 1.
Case comment on *R (Jones & Others) v Metropolitan Police Commissioner*

Murray, CRG. 'Nudging or Fudging? The UK Courts' Counterterrorism Jurisprudence Since 9/11' (2016) 21(1) J Conflict Security Law 91.
See pages 103–105 for more detail on counter-terrorism powers

Parpworth, N. 'Section 60 and the Supreme Court' (2016) 89(2) Police Journal 174.
Analysis of the *Roberts case*

Parpworth, N. 'Stop and Search and Police Legitimacy: Part 1' (2016) 180 JPN 272.
Analyses issues arising from stop and search powers

Other sources

Equality and Human Rights Commission, Stop and Think: A Critical Review of the Use of Stop and Search Powers in England and Wales, 2010. Available at www.equalityhumanrights.com.
Critical analysis of discrimination issues with stop and search

Home Office, *User Guide to: Police Powers and Procedures, England and Wales*, October 2020. Available at www.gov.uk/government/publications/police-powers-and-procedures-in-england-and-wales-201112-user-guide.
Helpful background detail on PACE powers

House of Commons Library Briefing Paper Number CBP6441, 17 May 2019, *The Retention and Disclosure of Criminal Records*, Jacqueline Beard.
For more detail on retention and how law and practice are kept under review

House of Commons Library Debate Pack Number CDP-2018-0125, 22 May 2018, *Effect of Police Stop and Search Powers on BAME Communities*, Sarah Pepin.
Clear explanation of principles and contemporary issues

House of Commons Library Briefing Paper Number 3878, 4 November 2020, *Police powers: stop and search*, Jennifer Brown.
Good background information and statistics on stop and search powers

Useful websites

For recent statistics on the use of police powers, see www.gov.uk/government/collections/police-powers-and-procedures-england-and-wales

；Online resources

www.oup.com/he/dennett2e
This chapter is accompanied by a selection of online resources to help you with this topic, including:

- Multiple-choice questions
- Answers to the self-test questions
- Guidance on answering the exam question

Index

Note: Tables, Figures and Boxes are indicated by an italic *t*, *f* and *b* following the page number.